MW00607688

The Japanese Missionary Journals of
Elder Alma O. Taylor, 1901–10

Reid L. Neilson

BYU Studies

Joseph Fielding Smith Institute for Latter-day Saint History

Provo, Utah

Dissertations in Latter-day Saint History

Produced by the Joseph Fielding Smith Institute for Latter-day Saint History
and
BYU Studies

Also in the Series:

*A Study of the Origins of The Church of Jesus Christ of Latter-day Saints
in the States of New York and Pennsylvania*
by Larry C. Porter

A Call to Arms: The 1838 Mormon Defense of Northern Missouri
by Alexander L. Baugh

A History of the Latter-day Saints in Northern Missouri from 1836 to 1839
by Leland Homer Gentry

"To Make True Latter-day Saints": Mormon Recreation in the Progressive Era
by Richard Ian Kimball

The Historical Development of the Doctrine and Covenants
by Robert J. Woodford

Alexander Schreiner: Mormon Tabernacle Organist
by Daniel Frederick Berghout

© 2001 Reid L. Neilson. All rights reserved.
Contact the author at ReidNeilson@hotmail.com

Cover: Portrait courtesy of Carla Christensen, design by Nichole Klein.

This dissertation was approved in August 2001. No part of this book may be reproduced in any form or by any means without permission in writing from the author. To contact the Joseph Fielding Smith Institute for Latter-day Saint History, write to: 121 KMB, Brigham Young University, Provo, Utah 84602. To contact BYU Studies, write to 403 CB, Brigham Young University, PO Box 24098, Provo, Utah 84602.

ISBN 0-8425-2495-9

Printed in the United States of America
10 9 8 7 6 5 4 3 2

Dissertations in Latter-day Saint History

Over the years, graduate students have written many important dissertations on Latter-day Saint topics. Unfortunately, they have typically been unavailable or unknown to lay readers. All too often, good copies of dissertations reside only at the institution at which they were written or on a few researchers' book shelves. BYU Studies and the Joseph Fielding Smith Institute for Latter-day Saint History hope to fill this gap by producing and distributing selected dissertations of interest to Latter-day Saints, making them available to a larger audience.

The works in this series have been reformatted from the originals. Nevertheless, these dissertations have undergone only minimal editing. For example, some typographical errors have been corrected. Original page numbers are referenced in the text by superscripted italicized numerals in brackets (e.g., $^{[3]}$). Occasionally, the author has included additional information in the endnotes to update old material. Those additions have been placed in brackets and italicized to distinguish them from the original text. Otherwise, the text is identical to the work accepted by the dissertation committee.

To the Japanese Saints

Contents

Index available free online at http://byustudies.byu.edu. Click on dissertations, then follow the links to *The Japanese Missionary Journals of Elder Alma O. Taylor, 1901–10.*

Illustrations

Acknowledgments

This study of Alma O. Taylor's early life and mission to Japan is the result of countless hours and almost as many people. Finally done, I find myself already forgetting the work and appreciating more the help.

My graduate committee has been wonderful. Many thanks to Ronald W. Walker, my friend and graduate chair. Everyone deserves a Heber J. Grant figure in their life. Thank you for being mine. To R. Lanier Britsch, thank you for recording and laying the historical foundation of the Restoration in Asia. I hope that this contribution will be seen as an extension of your research. To John W. Welch, thank you for helping me understand the value of historical documents and how to make them accessible to readers. Your William E. McLellin publication has been a model of scholarship for my own work.

I express my gratitude to the members of the Brigham Young University, L. Tom Perry Special Collections staff—David J. Whittaker, Russell C. Taylor, Susan L. Corrigian, and Spenser W. Call—for their constant support of my project. Spenser, your fingerprints are all over this work. Many thanks to my transcription team: Florence Beal, Melissa Clark, Glenda Egbert, Katrina Millet, Joan Naumann, Marny Parkin, Janae Sharp, and Heather Stonely. Furthermore, the BYU Studies interns deserve praise for their copy-to-copy editing: Alisa Baxter, Elizabeth Beus, Erick B. Carlson, Julianne Clegg, Ester Clement, Eliza C. Corbett, Karen Esplin, Amber Lee Fawson, Camille Graham, Elisabeth Lamb, Alena E. Lauritsen, Melanie Moore, Kathryn R. Price, Katherine F. Rawson, Kelli Ann Skinner, Christina Skousen, Elise Smith, Laura Summerhays, Anastasia M. Sutherland, Lauren Watson, and Andrew Witt. Other friends and scholars who deserve my thanks include Jeremy Andrus, Susan Easton Black, Elder L. Edward Brown, Ned and Carla Christensen, the Lee Daniels Family, Van C. Gessel, Jennifer Hurlbut, Janiece L. Johnson, Montrue G. Larkin, Mauri Liljenquist, Heather Seferovich, Greg Tedrow, Morris A. Thurston, John Wadsworth, and Jed Woodworth.

To my parents Ralph and Katherine Neilson—thank you for encouraging me, funding me, and loving me. This is our book.

Alma O. Taylor. Courtesy Church Archives.

Chapter 1

Introduction

On the evening of 26 June 1901, Salt Lake City was bustling. South Temple Street was clogged with buggies and streetcars filled with men returning to their homes after a long day's work. The local merchants, too, were packing up their wares and buttoning up their street front shops. Streetlights began to flicker and the faint glow of manufactured lights worked their magic as the sun drooped into the Great Salt Lake. The Beehive House—the residence of the President of The Church of Jesus Christ of Latter-day Saints—buzzed with preparations.

This particular evening held much promise for eighteen-year-old Alma O. Taylor and his three missionary companions called to open the Japan Mission. Although several private and public receptions had been held, this night was different. Lorenzo Snow, then President of the Church and General Superintendent of the Young Men's Mutual Improvement Association (Y.M.M.I.A.), presided over the evening's festivities. Present were members of the sponsoring Y.M.M.I.A. General Board together with several of the Church's General Authorities. However, it was the missionaries—Elders Heber J. Grant, Louis A. Kelsch, Horace S. Ensign, and Alma O. Taylor—who commanded the crowd's attention and affection.

Like other Church functions, the reception at the Beehive House began with song and prayer. Alma and the other guests were then entertained by several musical numbers.[1] Next, the four missionaries delighted the group by singing, "Do What is Right." Following the musical medley, a series of donation speeches and "one minute sentiments" were made in honor of the missionaries who would soon be leaving for Japan. Finally, President Snow arose from his seat and stood before the gathering. With his long, flowing beard and rimmed spectacles, he looked every bit a prophet. After surveying the crowd, President Snow began his short yet poignant remarks on the future of missionary work in Japan.

> When the Lord first sent forth his elders in this generation very little was known as to what their labors would be and what they could accomplish. They failed in some respects, but they did not fail in one thing: they did their duty. Apostle Orson Pratt and others were sent to Austria to open a mission there, but by reason of the rejection of their testimony they did not succeed. Nevertheless, they did their duty and were blessed. Noah preached 120 years. He was a grand man and did his duty but failed, and this because the people rejected him. However, by doing his duty he secured to himself exaltation and glory. Moses, in leading the children of Israel to the promised land, failed to accomplish what the Lord wanted by reason of the disobedience of the Israelites. Moses himself, through faithfulness, has attained to the Godhead. . . . As to these brethren who will shortly leave for Japan, the Lord has not revealed to me that they will succeed, but He has shown me that it is their duty to go.[1]

The four missionaries and others gathered to celebrate the opening of the Japan Mission were likely sobered by President Snow's less than enthusiastic remarks. For Alma and his companions, this was to be their dramatic entrance into the Church's missionary tradition. Now their prophet was telling them that their much-anticipated proselyting success in Japan was questionable, but their duty was not. President Snow's comments beg the question: what do the Lord and his prophets expect from their[2] missionaries and the missionary program? In tempering the expectations of this Japanese quartet, President Snow makes a distinction between *duty* and *success,* while at the same time suggesting a correlation between the two concepts.

Duty and Success

Duty is defined as obligatory tasks, conduct, service, or functions that arise from one's position. Following his resurrection, the Savior taught his Apostles: "Go ye therefore, and teach all nations, baptizing them in the name of the Father, and of the Son, and of the Holy Ghost: Teaching them to observe all things whatsoever I have commanded you: and, lo, I am with you alway, even unto the end of the world."[2] Clearly the duty of missionaries is to teach and baptize. The proper discharge of missionary duty is best understood by the free-agent missionary bending his or her will to match Christ's. At best, performance of one's duty can be judged qualitatively. On the other hand, *success* can also be described as achieving a favorable or desired outcome. In the case of missionary work, the actual teaching of the gospel and the performance of baptisms are easily quantifiable results to mark success. Unlike the performance of one's duty, missionary success is contingent on both the missionary and the investigator simultaneously bending their agency heavenward. The results are both qualitative and quantitative. Therein lies the dilemma: can one be a successful missionary while serving an unsuccessful mission?

Many missionaries today feel tremendous internal and external pressure to judge their missionary success based on conversion rates. However, even baptisms are relative. Are the missionary's converts men or women; young or old; children or youth; single or[3] married? Further, how do the missionary's baptismal statistics compare with their peer group (i.e., apartment, district, zone, mission), historical mission averages, past mission presidencies, intra-country missions, and extra-country missions?

In countries like Japan where baptismal rates are lower than some other regions of the world, some missionaries often try to bolster their lack of baptismal success with other success factors. They pride themselves on the number of copies of the *Book of Mormon* distributed, lessons taught, homes visited, people approached, and tracts distributed. Some also compensate with their ability to memorize missionary scriptures, skill in "passing off" missionary discussions, linguistic ability, and leadership advancement. Others find security in their personal obedience, scriptural knowledge, success with reactivation efforts, and popularity within the mission. Unfortunately, these metrics can demoralize missionaries.

While President's Snow's 1901 comments may have been disconcerting to Alma and his companions, they actually provide hope and encouragement—an explanation or justification—for modern-day missionaries trying to evaluate their own missionary experience. President Snow couched his comments regarding the Japan Mission in the experiences of other notable missionaries: Orson Pratt, Noah, and Moses. While these men "failed in some respects," President Snow noted they "did their duty." For example, in April 1864, Elders Orson Pratt and William W. Riter attempted to open a mission in Austria. Due to religious persecution and "the rejection of their testimony," however, the two were unsuccessful. "Nevertheless, they did their duty and were blessed," President Snow clarified. Next, President Snow referred to the missionary labors of Noah. Although Noah preached faith, repentance, baptism, and the reception of the Holy Ghost[4] for 120 years, no one but his wife, three sons, and their wives— only eight souls—ultimately accepted his testimony. Although Noah "failed" because he was rejected by the people, President Snow expressed that he "was a grand man and did his duty" and "secured to himself exaltation and glory." Similarly, Moses was unable to lead the children of Israel to the Promised Land because of their disobedience. Therefore, he "failed to accomplish what the Lord wanted." Regardless, President Snow assured his listeners that Moses "through faithfulness" had attained his heavenly reward— the ultimate success.[3] President Snow made it clear that missionaries can "successfully" fulfill their "duty" while failing to "succeed." While the Lord desires success, he seemingly only expects missionaries to fulfill their duty.

Centennial of the Church in Japan

In fall 2001, a hundred years will have passed since Alma O. Taylor and his companions—elders Heber J. Grant, Horace S. Ensign, and Louis A. Kelsch—opened the original Japan Mission; ten years will have passed since I, Reid L. Neilson, was called to the Japan Sapporo Mission. Much has changed in the interval between Alma's mission and my own. Japan has become a world economic power, and The Church of Jesus Christ of Latter-day Saints has over 100,000 members of record and two temples in Japan. Yet, when I first discovered Alma's missionary journals I was surprised to learn of the similarities between our Japanese mission experiences. I, too, felt like a "stranger in a strange land."

Through the following introductory essays and Alma's journal entries, I hope to recapture early Mormonism in Japan through the eyes of a young missionary. To do so I[5] will outline early efforts to create the Japan Mission and highlight the first eighteen years of Alma's life and his call to Japan. Next, I will present selected annotated journal entries. Lastly, I will recount Alma's missionary release and return to Salt Lake City and discuss how he may have viewed his own missionary experience.[6]

Notes

1. Journal History of the Church, 26 June 1901, Library Division, Historical Department, The Church of Jesus Christ of Latter-day Saints, Salt Lake City (hereafter cited as Church Archives) and Rudger Clawson, *A Ministry of Meetings: The Apostolic Diaries of Rudger Clawson,* Stan Larson, ed. (Salt Lake City: Signature Books, 1993), 287–89.

2. Matthew 28:19–20.

3. Journal History of the Church, 26 June 1901 and Clawson, *A Ministry of Meetings,* 287–89.

The first four missionaries to Japan at a missionary benefit dinner in Salt Lake City in summer 1901. Standing (left to right): Horace S. Ensign, Alma O. Taylor. Seated (left to right): Heber J. Grant, Louis A. Kelsch. Courtesy Church Archives.

Louis A. Kelsch, Alma O. Taylor, and Heber J. Grant at the dedication site in Yokohama, 1901. Horace S. Ensign took the picture. Courtesy John W. Welch.

Chapter 2

The Japan Mission: First Efforts, 1854–1900

What was the cause and country that drew Alma O. Taylor to missionary service? What was the historical background of Mormon efforts to establish a mission in Japan? This chapter will discuss these issues and provide answers as to why the Church's Japan Mission was announced in February 1901.

Beginning in 1830, missionary work was the lifeblood of The Church of Jesus Christ of Latter-day Saints. "From its founding Mormonism was designed to be a world faith. Its religious message was intended not for the few, but for the many," observed historian Leonard J. Arrington.[1] Its first prophet, Joseph Smith, sent missionaries to spread the gospel throughout the United States and Canada and to parts of Europe. His successor, President Brigham Young, "motivated by a conviction that the Millennium was imminent," called 108 elders to proselyte throughout the world in 1852.[2] Thereafter, the elders traveled to Europe, Gibraltar, South Africa, the West Indies, British Guiana, Siam (Thailand), Hindustan (India), Australia, China, and parts of the United States.[7]

It was not remarkable that Japan was overlooked, as it was not open to the commercial, diplomatic, and religious overtures of the West until 1854.[3] However, from the late 1850s until 1901, there were a series of positive contacts. Twice in the nineteenth century, Church leaders attempted to send the gospel to Japan: first in 1860 with Walter Murray Gibson, and second in 1895 under the direction of Elder Abraham H. Cannon. Both attempts ended in failure—Gibson apostatized, and Cannon passed away. Despite the tardiness of placing missionaries in Japan, the Church was slowly getting into a better position to support missionary work in the Empire of the Rising Sun. During the late nineteenth century, Japan was maturing into a modern nation-state, more receptive to receiving the Church's missionaries. Finally, in 1901, the First Presidency announced the opening of the Japan Mission and called Elder Heber J. Grant, a member of the Quorum of the Twelve Apostles, to perform the task.

Japan Opens its Door to Western Nations

Two hundred years before the Restoration of the gospel in 1830, Japan closed itself to the broader world. Beginning in 1639, the Tokugawa shogunate (Japanese government) introduced a policy of national seclusion, which limited trade relations to China, Korea, and the Netherlands. This was done by the shogunate to gain absolute control over its foreign relations and establish the government's internal and external authority. By the early 1800s, this policy of *sakoku* (closed country) had deepened to the point where non-Japanese culture and trade was essentially closed to the Japanese populous.[8]

About this time, the Dutch were being challenged for their supremacy in the Far East as other Western nations began to act on their colonial ambitions. For example, Russia began sending its ships and men to Hokkaidō in the 1790s to try to engage in trade with the Japanese. Britain continued to expand its colonial influence into India, Malaysia, and China. These and other outside threats seemingly encouraged the isolationist Japanese government to close its borders even tighter. In 1825 the Tokugawa government issued its Expulsion Edict, which mandated that foreign ships coming close to its shores would henceforth be fired upon.

The Dutch, Russians, and British were not alone in their expansionist policies. By the middle of the nineteenth century, the United States, with citizens now in Oregon and California, also turned its attention to the Far East. In 1852 President Millard Fillmore decided to send Commodore Matthew Perry to Japan to hopefully open diplomatic and commercial relations. In

5

July 1853, Perry and his infamous "black ships" initiated the first U.S. direct contact with Japan by sailing into Edo Bay, now Tokyo Bay. His visit and demands for treaty relations were received with mixed reactions from the various Tokugawa factions. The following February, Perry returned with a larger naval fleet to coerce the Tokugawa government to sign a treaty to normalize relations. Made official 31 March 1854 at Kanagawa (now Yokohama), the treaty required Japan to open two of its ports, Shimoda, Shizuoka Prefecture and Hakodate, Hokkaidō, to American ships and trade and allow an American consular agent to live in Shimoda. In following[9] years, the Japanese shogunate entered into similar agreements with the British, Russians, and Dutch. Japan's era of national seclusion had ended.[4]

For the U.S. government and Navy, Perry's success in Japan was but another confirmation of the growing power of the emerging imperialistic country. To the Latter-day Saints, however, the diplomatic opening of Japan suggested something very different. In September 1854, the Church's British periodical, the *Millennial Star*, featured an article entitled "Opening of Japan." Part of it read: "To us, as Latter-day Saints, this treaty with Japan has more important interests connected with it than the mere interest of trade, or the temporary policy of nations. It takes hold of futurity, and has an important bearing on the salvation of the inhabitants of that country." Many believed the Lord was "at work in His own way, breaking down the barriers" between nations, "pleading with them by His judgments" and "preparing the way for His servants to go forth to declare the glad tidings of salvation."[5]

In 1857, President Brigham Young prophesied that Japan would soon be opened up to LDS missionaries. "We have got to send men to the Islands to liberate[6] those who are there," Young was reported to have said. "We would gather the saints from there but the laws are against it."[7] In addition to sending missionaries to Japan, Young hoped to extend the work of the Church even to Siberia.[10]

Within a year President Young's prophesied opening of Japan began to materialize. In 1858, American Consul Townsend Harris negotiated and expanded upon the provisions of the earlier Kanagawa Treaty. Known as the Harris Treaty, it stipulated the opening of Edo, Kobe, Nagasaki, Niigata, and Yokohama to foreign trade, placed Japanese tariffs under international control, fixed import duties at low levels, and established extraterritoriality for foreign residents living in Japan. Most importantly for the Church, the treaty allowed the reintroduction of Christianity into Japan. Soon other Western powers demanded similar treaties. These unequal treaties were called the Ansei commercial treaties and would plague the shogunate's domestic and international power as they had demoted Japan into a "semicolonial status."[8]

Writing in his journal, Apostle Wilford Woodruff saw opportunities to preach the gospel in these new treaties with Japan. "Europe & America have made liberal treaties with China & Jappan which have opened their ports to the trade, Commerce & intercourse with the whole world which have been heretofore entirely Closed up for thousands of Generations."[9] Elder Woodruff realized that proselyting possibilities might follow diplomatic and commercial agreements.

The first recorded contact between Mormons and Japanese occurred in 1858 when William Wood, a twenty-one-year-old Mormon and member of the British Navy sailed from Hong Kong to Japan. His ship, *H.M.S. Retribution*, had been ordered to escort a "beautiful yacht," specially built as a gift for the emperor of Japan to encourage better[11] relations between the two nations. Arriving at Yokohama, the British presented their maritime gift, and Wood had the opportunity to walk among the Japanese. "I discerned a remarkable spirit of reform in them; more so than in any people I had met," he said. "I felt a desire to preach the Gospel to them."[10]

Wood went back to Britain, never to return to Japan. Subsequently, he immigrated to Utah, served colonizing missions to Arizona and Canada, and later went on a proselyting mission to his native England. Yet despite these events and the passage of time, Japan still held a special place in Wood's heart. "I have thought it possible that I was the first Mormon to visit Japan, and this increased my desire to present the Gospel to them," he wrote. "Years after, when I had gathered to Zion and had been ordained a Seventy, this feeling increased in my mind so much that in my prayers I often mentioned it. However, it was some years before the door for the Gospel was opened by Apostle Grant to the Japanese people, and I had become an old man."[11] Although William Wood was the first Church member to come into contact with the Japanese, others would follow—some with similar proselyting ambitions and one with more personal ambitions.

Walter Murray Gibson in the South Pacific and Asia

Perhaps Mormonism's most colorful and bizarre contact with the Japanese came in 1860 when Walter Murray Gibson met with Church leaders in Salt Lake City. As a young boy, Gibson had heard enchanting tales of the Far East. Young Gibson was charmed. "The spirit of adventure, to see strange people and far-off countries, sprang up[12] in me. . . . I felt a longing to go to sea, and join my uncle." Growing into manhood, he "looked forth toward the Pacific, and thought of early plans of fortune and renown as [he] looked on the pathway to the East." A doer as well as a dreamer, Gibson traveled to the island of Sumatra in the Dutch-controlled East Indian Archipelago and impetuously offered to help its inhabitants overthrow their colonial masters. Dutch officials discovered his plan and charged him with treason.[12]

Escaping incarceration, Gibson fled to the safety of the United States and filed a claim against the Dutch government. While his legal petition was languishing in the halls of the U.S. Congress, Gibson met John M. Bernhisel, a Church member representing the Territory of Utah in its claim for statehood. When Bernhisel spoke passionately about the persecutions of the Saints and their recent conflict with the U.S. government, the so-called "Utah War," Gibson devised a new self-serving South Seas plan: perhaps he could help the Mormons find peace by relocating to the islands of New Guinea. His enthusiasm renewed, Gibson traveled to Salt Lake City to meet Brigham Young. While rejecting Gibson's entreaty, President Young did encourage him to begin an investigation of the Church. Gibson was baptized 15 January 1860 by Heber C. Kimball. Three months later, Church authorities called him to a mission to the eastern United States.[13]

While serving his new Church on the East Coast, Gibson met several members of the Japanese embassy assigned to the U.S.[14] Gibson falsely reported that he was able to converse in the Japanese tongue with the embassy and that they invited him to visit Japan[13] as a missionary. In a letter dated 1 July 1860, he shared his newly created vision of Church expansion in Japan and Oceania with President Young. "Japan with her 30 millions of souls opens a great field for the missionary labor of the Saints," he wrote. "I have faith that a wonderful work will be accomplished there, but I doubt not that the Spirit of God will enlighten you as to the right time, when it shall be commenced. . . . Dear brother, I long to be engaged in this work; but I will be obedient unto your dictation."[15]

In November 1860, Gibson returned to Utah and sought permission to carry the gospel to Japan, China, the East Indies (India), and the Malay Islands.[16] Later that month, he and President Young shared the "Old Tabernacle" pulpit in Salt Lake City. Gibson expressed his excitement of going "forth with a message of life and salvation to the dark and benighted people of the Eastern hemisphere," it was reported. In turn, President Young announced that he had given Gibson authority "to negotiate with all the nations of the world who would obey the gospel of Christ."[17] Afterward, Young and his counselors in the First Presidency issued Gibson an official missionary certificate to be presented as credentials to the "Illustrious and Renowned Potentate His Imperial Majesty the Tycoon[14] of Niphon." This document may be construed as the first official act toward the creation of the LDS Japan Mission.[18]

Armed with his ecclesiastical commission and filled with personal ambition, Gibson left Salt Lake City for California, where he boarded a ship bound for the Sandwich (Hawaiian) Islands. He arrived in the islands 30 June 1861. Seeing the advantages offered in Hawaii, Gibson aborted his wider ecclesiastical commission for life in the mid-Pacific. A series of Gibson's intrigues and misrepresentations convinced the untutored Hawaiian Saints—bereft of leadership due to the recalling of missionaries to Salt Lake City during the recent Utah War—to look to him as their spiritual shepherd. To accomplish his personal goals, he girded himself in a white robe, forced the Hawaiians to enter his presence on hands and knees, and declared the island of Lanai the true Zion and the future site of a great temple.[19] In

1864 elders from Utah returned to the Sandwich Islands to excommunicate Gibson. Clearly, Gibson was not the anticipated messenger of "life and salvation" to the Japanese or to the other "dark and benighted people of the Eastern hemisphere."[20] Thus the first attempt to preach the gospel in Japan died stillborn.

Japan Encounters the American West and the Mormons

Having been pressured to sign the unequal treaties with the United States and other foreign powers, the Tokugawa[15] government had seriously weakened its already tenuous authority in Japan and abroad. In time, the revolutionary Chōshū and Satsuma samurai domains grew in power and ultimately joined forces to overthrow the Tokugawa government in January 1868. They replaced the shogunate with the boy Emperor Mutsuhito, later known as the Meiji Emperor. After two and a half centuries, the Tokugawa regime was quickly supplanted by the restoration of imperial rule.[21]

This Meiji Restoration began Japan's increasing openness to the West. One of the bright stars of the new imperial government was a Chōshū samurai, Itō Hirobumi. In 1863 members of his faction sent Itō to England to study. His experiences there exposed him to the force of economic industrialization and to the technological superiority of the West. Upon returning to Japan, Itō favored a policy of Westernization. A junior councilor in the Meiji government, he was initially responsible for diplomacy.

In 1870 he was sent to the United States to study American currency, politics, and business practices.[22] Traveling on the transcontinental railroad to Washington, Itō changed trains in Ogden, Utah. Angus M. Cannon, President of the Salt Lake Stake, business manager of the *Deseret News*, and brother of Elder George Q. Cannon, happened to board the same train. A train conductor introduced the curious newspaperman to Itō.

Soon the two men were engaged in "interesting conversation, each interviewing and being interviewed." Years later, Cannon described Itō as a "bright, earnest and interesting character who absorbed information as a sponge does water." Cannon also noted that Itō seemed proud of his fellow countrymen and their recent advancements as a modern nation. According to Itō, the population of Japan was about thirty-five million, compared to China's three hundred and fifty million, a multiple of ten. Yet he declared that the Japanese were the "equals if not the superiors" of the Chinese as a society. When[16] the conversation turned to religion, Itō "exhibited a lively interest" in the history of the Church. Before separating in Omaha, Nebraska, Itō asked his Mormon companion for more information about his religion.[23] This chance meeting of Cannon and Itō would prove important in the formation of the Church leader's impression of Japan.

Back in Japan, Itō was selected to accompany another Meiji government delegation, this one to tour the United States, Europe—including Russia—Malaya, Indochina, and Hong Kong.[24] The resulting Iwakura Mission, with forty-nine official members and nearly sixty attendants, was the largest and most important Japanese delegation ever to leave Japan, and Itō was one of its most important members. Through these efforts, the Meiji government hoped to display its power to help renegotiate the earlier Ansei commercial treaties with Western powers. Moreover, the Meiji government wanted to know how to organize its military and political bodies and what steps it should take to educate its youth. As one historian asked, "did Japan need to alter its culture and its class system, or did these need to be discarded altogether in its quest for modernization?"[25]

The Iwakura Mission embarked from Yokohama on 23 December 1871. Arriving in San Francisco, members of the mission boarded a train for Washington, D.C. However, near Ogden, Utah, snowstorms temporarily blocked the mountain railway passes and stranded the delegation in Utah. The Japanese were given tours of Salt Lake City, where they were exposed to the Latter-day Saints and their culture. The group entered the[17] newly completed Mormon Tabernacle, toured a local museum, and viewed the foundation of the Salt Lake Temple. Visits were paid to members of the Utah Territorial Legislature, the Utah Supreme Court, and Brigham Young. The Japanese observed the territorial military and the local educational system. The delegation attended numerous receptions and banquets prepared by their Utah hosts. Several delegates even attended LDS religious services.

After nineteen days in Utah, the snows melted sufficiently to allow the Japanese delegation to continue their journey. Over nearly the next two years they visited the principle cities of America's East Coast and then traveled throughout the nations of Europe. The delegates were exposed to the world's most advanced nations and determined to likewise westernize Japan. While abroad, the group became aware of how their anti-Christian policies might thwart their entrance into the modern political world and sent messages back to Japan to remove the anti-Christian edicts. Thus, by February 1873, Christians and Christian missionaries were at least nominally accepted in Japan.[26]

Upon their return, the government read the delegation's massive report and conclusions and began implementing its suggestions. The country began adopting new technology and institutions by hiring over 3,000 foreign advisors during the Meiji Period. All things Western, including Christianity, became popular and were encouraged by the Meiji government. The years between 1873 and 1889 were the golden era of Christian progress in modern Japan. Unfortunately for the Church and its missionary program, the pioneer settlement of the Great Basin, federal prosecution of polygamy, and the Utah territory's quest for statehood took precedence over LDS missionary expansion into Japan during these years.[18]

Friends with Japan

The Japanese were not alone as observers in Salt Lake City. To the citizens of Utah, their Asian visitors were fascinating and they watched their activities closely. One year earlier, Utahns had gotten their first glimpse of Japanese popular culture when the Royal Satsuma Japanese Troupe performed acrobatics in Salt Lake City—the same year as Itō's first visit.[27] Of particular importance to the eventual Japan Mission were the opinions formed by Elder Lorenzo Snow, Angus M. Cannon, and President George Q. Cannon. Snow, then president of the Utah Territorial Legislature and later president of the Church, was particularly impressed by the Japanese delegation. Nearly three decades later he acknowledged that the Iwakura Mission had made a lasting impression on him and was a catalyst for sending elders to Japan. "This is how the thought [of the Japan Mission] originated with me," Snow recalled:

> When I was president of the Legislative council . . . a party of distinguished officials of the Japanese government [Iwakura Mission] visited Salt Lake enroute to Washington from their own country. . . . They expressed a great deal of interest in Utah and the manner in which it has been settled by the Mormons. Our talk was altogether very pleasant and they expressed considerable wonderment as to why we had not sent missionaries to Japan. That, together with the knowledge that they are a progressive people has remained with me until the present time, and while it may not be the actuating motive in attempting to open a mission there now, it probably had something to do with it.[28]

The visit of the Iwakura Mission gave Angus M. Cannon the opportunity to renew his friendship with Itō.[29] "I recognized him at once and his recognition of me was just as[19] prompt," Cannon recalled. Members of Itō's party "marveled at the familiarity that Itō showed concerning our faith and people, adding that his knowledge seemed much more extensive in this particular than that of most Americans."[30] Cannon's brother George—later a member of the First Presidency and editor of the *Juvenile Instructor*—also formed a positive opinion of the Japanese. The General Authority believed that the Iwakura Mission's visit to Utah was providential:

> However great the importance that others may attach to this movement, it possesses a deep significance to the members of the [Church] than it possibly can to any other class, for in it they are preparing the way for the accomplishment of His purposes and the spread of His gospel. . . . It is perhaps not hazarding too much to say that the visit of the Japanese Embassy to Salt Lake . . . is the fore-runner of measures which may, at some future day, be the cause of some of the youth who read this article being sent as missionaries to Japan.[31]

Over the next three decades, George Q. Cannon became a strong advocate for the establishment of a Japan Mission. His *Juvenile Instructor* magazine played a major role in preparing the way. For example, during the 1870s alone, Cannon's magazine featured nine articles on Japan,[32] and when describing Japan, Cannon often included encouraging words about possible missionary labor. "It is not too much to expect that Western customs and the Christian religion will in a few years gain such a foothold in Japan that[20] the folly of idol worship will be entirely unknown amongst its highly intelligent people," said one article.[33] Similarly, "A Country Scene in Japan" had these words:

> It is probable that the next few years will effect a still greater improvement in that country, as quite a number of young men from Japan are being educated in the United States, who, of course, will carry home with them American ideals of living. . . . It is possible they will modify their laws so as to admit of the gospel being preached there, as it will certainly be at some future time.[34]

Likewise, during the 1880s, the *Juvenile Instructor* featured an additional ten articles on the subject.[35] Convinced of the fruits of Mormonism, Cannon wrote, "We firmly believe that Japan will yet be successfully visited by the Elders of our Church, and that from that race thousands of obedient souls will yet be gathered to swell the multitudes of those who shall be called to Zion."[36]

Contemporary events in Japan seemed to bolster Cannon's sentiments. By the mid-1880s, the Asian balance of power was shifting, which warranted further comment.

> Of all the Asiatic nations perhaps Japan is making the greatest strides at the present time in the way of education and an adoption of the inventions and discoveries of modern[21] times. The people of this empire are unquestionably more progressive than their neighbors the Chinese, and the interest that is now being taken in that people by civilized nations is very great.[37]

While Japan continued to Westernize, Church leaders determined to rekindle missionary work in India, which had been abandoned in the 1850s.[38] In 1884, William Willes, George Booth, Henry F. McCune, and Milson Pratt traveled from Salt Lake City to San Francisco, where they boarded the *City of New York* bound for Japan en route to India. While onboard, Willes broke up an argument between a drunken crew member and an English-speaking Japanese Christian by the name of K. Ishiye. Grateful to Willes, Ishiye manifested the kindest of feelings to the Mormons. In response, Willes and his companions preached to Ishiye during their voyage. They read to him "Joseph Smith's History," shared with him passages from John Jaques' *Book of References*, and presented him with a copy of the works of Orson Pratt. Willes recorded his hopes for Ishiye: "He is very much at home with

us. Very much the gentlemen and speaks fluently in educated English: his complexion is quite fair, and has an Israelitish appearance." Willis continued, "I pray my Eternal Father that he will yield obedience to His commandments, and be the opening power for converting millions of his countrymen."[39]

Ishiye seemed receptive and offered to introduce the elders to the Japanese people if they were ever to return to Yokohama.[40] He also taught the elders about Japan and[22] informed them about proselyting prospects, disclosing that all religious teachers were under the protection of the Japanese government. Furthermore, Ishiye promised to "obtain light from heaven" regarding his own baptism. If convinced of the truthfulness of the gospel, he promised he would "not hesitate a moment" to join. He also offered to have "a favorable mention made" of Mormonism in Japanese newspapers,[41] and invited the elders to return to Japan as his guests the following year.[42]

When *The City of New York* arrived in Yokohama, the elders disembarked and visited with several expatriate Americans. They learned that while Japan was open to Christianity, it was still "very much hampered with restrictions that are galling to free Americans." For example, while Westerners were free to move about the coastal foreign settlement ports, they were forced to travel with Japanese guides throughout the interior of Japan. Undaunted, Willes penned a letter to George Q. Cannon and described his recent experiences and impressions of Japan. "All with whom I have conversed are agreed that the Japanese are a superior race to the Chinese, which fills me with hope that some day the Lord will call many of them to be Saints," he concluded.[43] After posting his letter, Willes and his companions continued their voyage to India, never to return to Japan. Willis' journals are silent on whether Ishiye later attempted to "obtain light from heaven."[23]

Japan—A Progressive Nation

As historian Kenneth B. Pyle has argued, "for the quarter of a century preceding 1890 Japan had passed through a time of unprecedented ferment, a time of experimentation and groping, as it sought to reorient its institutions to the realities of the international order into which it was so suddenly thrust."[44] Many Japanese intellectuals and leaders felt that Japan had gone too far in adopting Western ways at the expense of Japanese culture and tradition. The Meiji government sensed this growing discontent and sought to unify the nation by "building an imperial ideology."

To gain support for the modern Japanese state, government officials "resorted to the traditional language of loyalty and obligation and drew on a mythical past to yield a distinctive national ideology."[45] As a result, the government institutionalized State Shintō and issued the Imperial Rescript on Education in 1890. This document declared in Confucian terms that the Emperor was the father of Japan and his subjects were his children. As a result, wrote Joseph A. Kitagawa, "Christianity came under severe attack as an unpatriotic religion."[46] The golden era of Western Christianity was over in the minds of the Japanese.

Meanwhile, after issuing the Manifesto of 1890 that formally declared an end to the practice of plural marriage in the United States (and enjoying the subsequent decline in federal prosecution), Church leaders looked abroad for missionary opportunities. Thanks in part to seven additional articles published in editor George Q. Cannon's[24] *Juvenile Instructor* in the 1890s, Japan was still positioned in the forefront of the Saints' international consciousness, even though Christianity was falling rapidly out of favor in Japan.[47] In 1893, one author predicted the gospel would soon reach Japan:

> The day is not far distant when the gospel of the Lord Jesus Christ will be introduced among this intelligent and progressive people. The door is already open for admission, at least in a limited extent, and greater opportunities for the promulgation of truth will gradually be provided until the extreme limits of the empire shall be reached by the Elders who may be sent as representatives of the Church.[48]

During this same decade, Japan was increasingly viewed as a progressive nation and an emerging world power. This provided the Meiji government the leverage to renegotiate the inequalities of the earlier Harris and Ansei commercial treaties. Furthermore, Japan displayed its military might when it shocked the world by crushing China during the Sino-Japanese War of 1895.[49] Cannon's *Juvenile Instructor* editorialized:

> Among the many surprising events which have occurred of late there is nothing that has aroused the attention of the world equal to the success of the Japanese in their recent war with China. . . . many have entertained the opinion that they were inferior in many respects to the Chinese. . . . In this contest, however, they have [25] exhibited qualities that have called forth the respect and admiration of the nations of Europe.[50]

Elder Abraham H. Cannon's Role in the Japan Mission

Japanese and Mormon economic interests combined in 1895 to produce the second stillborn Japan Mission. During the economically trying 1890s, Church leaders attempted to improve the Utah economy.[51] In 1895, Elder Abraham H. Cannon[52] and his fellow leaders decided to exploit Utah coal and iron deposits, expand railroad infrastructure throughout Utah, and construct a regional railroad from Salt Lake City to Los Angeles.[53] They named their proposed route the "Utah and California Railroad."[54] Once the projected tracks were laid, it was hoped, the Saints would benefit by shipping[26] Cedar City and Coalville coal and coke to southern California at a fraction of its current cost.[55]

Elder Cannon's coal and railroad dream was partially shared by Robert Brewster Stanton, a California mining promoter. Years earlier, Stanton researched whether a "water-level railroad" could be built along the Colorado River from Grand Junction, Colorado, south to the Gulf of California or from Yuma, Arizona, west to San Diego, California. It could. However, lacking financing, Stanton began promoting a smaller railroad from the Virgin River down the Colorado to Yuma, Arizona, and then west to his hometown of San Diego.[56] In 1895, Stanton met Cannon and proposed a merger of their railroad dreams. He confided that the Japanese government was then selecting a Pacific seaport for its country's expanding trade and national shipping line. According to Stanton, the Japanese favored San Diego. Would the Latter-day Saints be interested in constructing a railroad linking San Diego and the lucrative coal deposits of Utah?

Stanton's proposal offered the Church temporal and spiritual opportunity. The new railroad might simultaneously improve Utah's depressed economy and open the door for Mormon preaching in Japan. On 8 August 1895, Cannon shared Stanton's proposal with the First Presidency and the Quorum of the Twelve Apostles. Elder Heber J. Grant, who as a member of the Twelve was present, reported that the business proposal was discussed and[27] that the Japan Mission question was postponed.[57] Elder Grant at the time appears to have believed he might lead the mission.[58]

Cannon later traveled to San Francisco to meet Stanton and his associate Walter Smith. Smith, the *San Francisco Chronicle's* war correspondent in the Sino-Japanese War, had been attached to the Japanese commander-in-chief. In this capacity he learned of the Japanese government's business plans.

> Mr. Smith feels sure that we could induce the great Japanese steamship company, Nippon Yusen Kisha [Kaisha] to make San Diego its American terminus, providing we can assure them that a railway will be built to that place which will have connection with the eastern part of the United States. If such a connection can be made it will be very successful in a financial way.[59]

Stanton and Smith next introduced Cannon to Koya Saburo, the Japanese consul. Cannon reported that "he received us cordially. . . . He seemed a little reserved at first but gradually warmed up, and spoke freely on railway and other matters." Koya was familiar with the Mormons and Utah, having previously traveled there and read the Iwakura Mission's positive account of their short stay in Salt Lake City. He was also aware that Itō Hirobumi, the current Japanese prime minister, was impressed with the Saints.[28]

Cannon took this opportunity to broach the subject of sending Latter-day Saint missionaries to Japan. "Mr. Koya thought it very probable that we might secure permission to preach the Gospel in Japan without any government interference; in fact his people are anxious to hear the Christian religion proclaimed, as they have an idea that the success of the English-speaking people is due to their language and their religion," Cannon reported. Koya suggested something else that seemed to offer a favorable prospect: because of the recently negotiated Anglo-Japanese Treaty, "all the ports as well as the interior of Japan [would] be thrown open to the commerce of the world" in 1899. Finally, Koya disclosed that the Japanese parliament was going to meet soon to allocate the Chinese war indemnity. The Japanese navy would be strengthened first, but the government also planned to expand the Nippon Yusen

Kaisha shipping line. To further this last goal, Koya suggested that his government was indeed interested in San Diego and invited Cannon to attend sessions of the Japanese parliament to be held the following month.[60]

Cannon returned to Utah optimistic about both missionary and business plans. Within a week, he dictated a report to Church leaders who expressed a "very strong" feeling that one of the Apostles should soon open up Japan to missionary labor "at no distant day."[61] Attending the Salt Lake Fifth Ward, Cannon spoke "for about an hour on the missionary work . . . and the opening which seems now to [the Church] offered by Japan."[62] Continuing his enthusiasm, Cannon wrote an article in the Church periodical *Contributor* that expressed the growing hope of Church leaders to open Japan to[29] proselyting: "The authorities of the Church have of late had their minds more or less exercised in regard to Japan as country in which the Gospel might be profitably preached." He shared Koya's sentiments that "Japan would warmly welcome our Elders to labor as missionaries among the people" and that "any reluctance on our part to send missionaries to Japan for fear of the disastrous consequences, could be easily removed by our application to the parliament and ministers for permission to preach the Gospel."[63]

Although Cannon did not travel to Japan to lobby the Utah-California Railroad with members of the Japanese parliament, he and his partners nevertheless moved forward with the project, which by the following summer "appeared ready for success."[64] The partners retained engineer Henry Maxwell McCartney to make a final survey and financial estimates. However, their plans were derailed by the intervention of James J. Hill, owner of the Great Northern Railroad. Hill, also seeking an Asian steamship partner to complement his railroad empire, proposed Seattle instead of San Diego to the Japanese government and Nippon Yusen Kaisha.[65] Unfortunately for the Cannon-Stanton proposal, Japanese leaders accepted Hill's proposal on 11 July 1896.[66] To compound the setback, eight days later Cannon passed away—the Utah-California Railroad and the Japan Mission also expired as President Wilford Woodruff and other Church leaders soon[30] focused their attention on more pressing political issues.[67] That same year, Utah finally achieved statehood. Perhaps Church leaders felt that the establishment of the Japan Mission should be postponed until 1899 when missionaries could move freely throughout Japan.

President Lorenzo Snow's Administration and the Japan Mission

President Woodruff died 2 September 1898. Days later the Quorum of the Twelve sustained eighty-four-year-old Lorenzo Snow as the fifth president of the Church. Snow selected George Q. Cannon and Joseph F. Smith as counselors.[68] President Snow's administration was marked by the Church's improving financial position and higher international profile.

At the time of President Snow's selection, the Church owed an almost overwhelming $2.3 million to creditors. This debt was the result of the U.S. government's seizure and mismanagement of Church property during the antipolygamy Edmunds-Tucker Act episode and due to debt-financed public works projects in the 1890s. In 1899, President Snow, seeking a solution to the difficulty, toured the settlements of southern Utah and was inspired to reemphasize the paying of tithes. By the time of his[31] death in 1901, the Church's financial position had improved dramatically and a mission to Japan was financially feasible.[69]

"After the financial difficulties of the church were put in the way of adjustment [President Snow's] mind seemed to revert to this world-wide extension idea of the gospel," wrote historian B. H. Roberts.[70] As the Church entered the twentieth century, it had 283,765 members, 967 wards and branches, 43 stakes, and 4 temples, and all these were almost entirely U.S. based.[71] Hundreds of missionaries served in thirteen missions, the majority of which were located in the United States.[72] In contrast, during the administration of President Snow, increasing attention was put on nations and regions such as Russia, Austria, and South America—and to Japan.[73] To Lorenzo Snow, the central responsibility of the members of the Quorum of the Twelve was "to warn the nations of the earth and prepare the world for the coming of the Savior," not to overly busy themselves with stake and ward duties, which were the responsibilities of the Church's stake presidents

and bishops.[74] [32]

By summer 1900, the ill and weakening Snow was increasingly dependent upon the administrative skills of George Q. Cannon, who believed that the Church should review and possibly reallocate its missionary resources. As historian Davis Bitton points out, "the golden days of the early mass conversions seemed to be over."[75] To combat this decline, Cannon drafted a resolution outlining a new missionary course:

> That our policy be to stop sending Elders to the Southern States and Great Britain, unless it be in cases where Elders are specifically needed; and that in those and other English-speaking countries where our Elders are in too great numbers, we reduce the number; and that the Elders, where they were laboring in places without results, be encouraged to push into new fields.[76]

This new policy had important consequences for LDS missionary work in the South Pacific and Pacific Rim region. During the years 1895 to 1899, the 220 missionaries assigned to this region accounted for little more than 5 percent of the Church's total missionary force. However, over the next five years, this number grew to 275, or almost 8 percent of the Church's missionary total, a 25 percent increase. While Mormon proselyting in the Pacific and Asia areas continued to represent only a small portion of the missionary force, it is nevertheless clear that more notice was being taken of the region.[77] Beginning in 1901, the Japan Mission would be partially responsible for increasing this number.[33]

Notes

1. Leonard J. Arrington, "Historical Development of International Mormonism," *Religious Studies and Theology* 7 (January 1987): 9.

2. Eugene E. Campbell, *Establishing Zion: The Mormon Church in the American West, 1847–1869* (Salt Lake City: Signature Books, 1988), 174.

3. For a history of early Latter-day Saint missionary efforts in Asia see R. Lanier Britsch, *From the East: The History of the Latter-day Saints in Asia, 1851–1996* (Salt Lake City: Deseret Book, 1998), 8–42.

4. Kenneth B. Pyle, *The Making of Modern Japan* (Lexington, MA: D. C. Heath and Company, 1996), 57–60.

5. "Opening of Japan," *Millennial Star* 16 (2 September 1854): 552.

6. The word "liberate" had to do with spiritual darkness, and he hoped the Japanese would receive gospel teachings and ordinances.

7. Wilford Woodruff, *Wilford Woodruff's Journals*, Scott G. Kenney, ed., 9 vols. (Midvale, UT: Signature Books, 1985), 22 March 1857.

8. Pyle, *The Making of Modern Japan*, 65.

9. *Wilford Woodruff's Journals*, 31 December 1858. Two years earlier, on 18 November 1856, Elder Woodruff recorded, "I spent the evening in reading Comodore Perrys visit to Jappan."

10. Kate B. Carter, comp., *Our Pioneer Heritage*, "William Wood—Pioneer," (Salt Lake City: Daughters of Utah Pioneers, 1970), 13:264. See also William G. Hartley, "Adventures of a Young British Seaman, 1852–1862," *New Era* 10 (March 1980): 38–47.

11. Carter, *Our Pioneer Heritage*, 13:264.

12. Jacob Adler and Gwynn Barrett, eds., *The Diaries of Walter Murray Gibson, 1886, 1887* (Honolulu: The University Press of Hawaii, 1973), ix–x.

13. Jacob Adler and Robert M. Kamins, *The Fantastic Life of Walter Murray Gibson: Hawaii's Minister of Everything* (Honolulu: University of Hawaii Press, 1986), 45–46.

14. *Wilford Woodruff's Journals*, 4 November 1860.

15. Adler, *Life of Walter Murray Gibson*, 48.

16. Brigham Young Office Journals—Excerpts, 1853–62, 13 November 1860, New Mormon Studies CD-ROM (Smith Research Associates, 1998).

17. Adler, *Life of Walter Murray Gibson*, 49. Wilford Woodruff also recorded the event: "In the afternoon Capt Walter M Gibson . . . spoke followed by President Brigham Young. Brother Gibson said that He was about to take another mission. Was going to Jappan, Siam, & the Malay Islands. He has had an invitation by the Historian of Jappan to visit that Land. Is intimately acquainted with the King of Siam & has been Strongly invited by the princes & Chiefs of the Malay Islands to visit them. He seems to have been raised up as an instrument in the Hands of God to open the way among those Nations for the receptions of the gospel." *Wilford Woodruff's Journals*, 18 November 1860.

18. Brigham Young Office Journals, 20 November 1860.

19. Carter, *Our Pioneer Heritage*, 5:368.

20. For further treatment of Gibson's activities and interaction with the Latter-day Saints, see R. Lanier Britsch, *Moramona: The Mormons in Hawaii* (Laie, HI: Institute for Polynesian Studies, 1989), 50–8 and Adler, *Life of Walter Murray Gibson*, 44–68.

21. Pyle, *The Making of Modern Japan*, 71.

22. "Itō Hirobumi," *Japan: An Illustrated Encyclopedia* (Tokyo: Kodansha, 1993), 1:637.

23. "Opening of a Mission in Japan," *Deseret News*, 6 April 1901.

24. For a treatment of the Iwakura Mission's stay in Salt Lake City, see Wendy Butler, "The Iwakura Mission and Its Stay in Salt Lake City," *Utah Historical Quarterly* 66 (Winter 1998): 26–47.

25. Butler, "The Iwakura Mission," 29.

26. Britsch, *From the East*, 47.

27. See "The Japanese Troupe," *Deseret News*, 25 and 27 April 1870. After one show, Elder Woodruff thought the Japanese accomplished "the most wonderful feats" he had ever seen. *Wilford Woodruff Journals*, 27 April 1870.

28. "Opening of a Mission in Japan," *Deseret News*, 6 April 1901.

29. When the Japan Mission was opened in 1901, Cannon provided letters of introduction for Heber J. Grant to meet Itō, who was then prime minister. However, the anticipated Grant-Itō meeting never happened due to anti-Mormon pressures from other Christian missionaries living in Tokyo. "Opening of a Mission in Japan," *Deseret News*, 6

April 1901 and Alma O. Taylor, Journal, 19 October 1909.

30. "Opening of a Mission in Japan," *Deseret News*, 6 April 1901.

31. George Q. Cannon, "Editorial Thoughts," *Juvenile Instructor* 8 (17 February 1872): 28.

32. "A Japanese Idol," *Juvenile Instructor* 8 (10 May 1872): 73–4; "A Country Scene in Japan," *Juvenile Instructor* 8 (25 October 1873): 169–70; "Festival of the Idol Tengou in Japan," *Juvenile Instructor* 9 (28 February 1874): 49; "Japanese Peasant in Winter Costume," *Juvenile Instructor* 9 (23 March 1874): 81; "Japanese Amusements," *Juvenile Instructor* 10 (21 August 1875): 193–94; "Japanese Customs," *Juvenile Instructor* 11 (15 January 1876): 18–20; "Japanese Temple," *Juvenile Instructor* 11 (1 June 1876): 127–28; "A Japan Shoe Store," *Juvenile Instructor* 13 (15 June 1878): 133–34; "Japanese Children," *Juvenile Instructor* 13 (1 November 1878): 245.

33. "A Japanese Idol," *Juvenile Instructor* 8 (10 May 1872): 74.

34. "A Country Scene in Japan," *Juvenile Instructor* 8 (25 October 1873): 170. In "Japanese Temple" we read of young Japanese noblemen who are being educated in the United States, and it closes, "Let us hope some of them may hear of the gospel that has been restored to the earth in our day, and carry the 'glad tidings' to the land of the rising sun." "Japanese Temple," *Juvenile Instructor* 11 (1 June 1876): 127–28.

35. "Japanese Soldiers," *Juvenile Instructor* 17 (1 May 1882): 138–39; George Q. Cannon, "Editorial Thoughts," *Juvenile Instructor* 18 (15 January 1883): 24; "A Japanese Tea-House," *Juvenile Instructor* 18 (15 March 1883): 81–82; George Q. Cannon, "Editorial Thoughts," *Juvenile Instructor* 18 (1 June 1883): 168; "A Japanese Meal," *Juvenile Instructor* 19 (15 March 1884): 81–82; "A Japanese Execution," *Juvenile Instructor* 19 (15 April 1884): 126–27; "Varieties: A Word for the Japanese," *Juvenile Instructor* 19 (15 May 1884): 149; "The City of Yokohama, Japan," *Juvenile Instructor* 20 (15 June 1885): 177–78; "The Metropolis of Japan," *Juvenile Instructor* 22 (15 November 1887): 337–38; and "A Japanese Traveling Equipage," *Juvenile Instructor* 23 (15 April 1888): 113.

36. George Q. Cannon, "Editorial Thoughts," *Juvenile Instructor* 18 (1 June 1883): 168.

37. "The Metropolis of Japan," *Juvenile Instructor* 22 (15 November 1887): 337.

38. See R. Lanier Britsch, *Nothing More Heroic: The Compelling Story of the First Latter-day Saint Missionaries in India* (Salt Lake City: Deseret Book, 1999).

39. Charleen Cutler, ed., *The Life of William Willes: From His Own Personal Journals and Writings* (Provo, UT: Family Footprints, 2000), William Willes Journal, 17 June 1884.

40. Cutler, *Life of William Willes*, 14 June 1884.

41. William Willes, "Tidings from Japan and China," *Juvenile Instructor* 19 (1 October 1884): 291–92.

42. Cutler, *Life of William Willes*, 1 July 1884.

43. Willes, "Tidings from Japan and China," 292.

44. Pyle, *The Making of Modern Japan*, 125.

45. Pyle, *The Making of Modern Japan*, 126–27.

46. Joseph M. Kitagawa, *Religion in Japanese History* (New York: Columbia University Press, 1990), 243.

47. Vidi, "A Progressive People," *Juvenile Instructor* 28 (1 October 1893): 595–97; "The Parliament of Religions," *Juvenile Instructor* 28 (1 October 1893): 605–8; "A Commercial City of Japan," *Juvenile Instructor* 30 (15

January 1895): 41–42; Editor, "Strength in Unity, Not in Numbers," *Juvenile Instructor* 30 (1 June 1895): 341–43; "Japan," *Juvenile Instructor* 31 (1 January 1896): 9–12; Editor, "Japanese Progress," *Juvenile Instructor* 32 (1 June 1897): 354–55; and "In the Land of the Mikado," *Juvenile Instructor* 33 (15 December 1898): 809–11.

48. Vidi, "A Progressive People," *Juvenile Instructor* 28 (1 October 1893): 597.

49. In April 1895, the victorious Japanese forced the humbled Chinese government to sign the Treaty of Shimonoseki. Negotiated by Itō Hirobumi, China was forced to recognize the sovereignty of Korea, give up Taiwan and the Pescadores Islands, pay an indemnity equal to 230 million taels, and sign a commercial treaty with Japan.

50. Editor, "Strength in Unity, Not in Numbers," *Juvenile Instructor* 30 (1 June 1895): 341–42.

51. Leonard J. Arrington, *Great Basin Kingdom: An Economic History of the Latter-day Saints, 1830–1900*, reprint (Salt Lake City: University of Utah Press and Tanner Trust Fund, 1993), 399–400.

52. Born in 1859, Abraham H. Cannon was ordained a member of the Twelve in 1889, thereby joining his father (by then a member of the First Presidency) in the highest councils of the Church. Blessed with familial relations, tremendous energy, and business acumen, Abraham became involved in the leadership of the Bullion-Beck mining company, State Bank of Utah, Utah Loan and Trust Co., Z.C.M.I., George Q. Cannon & Sons Co., Co-operative Furniture Co., Salt Lake Chamber of Commerce, *Deseret News*, *Contributor*, and various Utah railroads. See Andrew Jenson, *Latter-day Saint Biographical Encyclopedia: A Compilation of Biographical Sketches of Prominent Men and Women in The Church of Jesus Christ of Latter-day Saints*, 4 vols. (Salt Lake City: Andrew Jenson History Co. and Andrew Jenson Memorial Association, 1901–1936), 1:167–68.

53. The Church provided at least $100,000 in preliminary financing but received little return. Arrington, *Great Basin Kingdom*, 399–400.

54. See Edward Leo Lyman, "From the City of Angeles to the City of Saints: The Struggle to Build a Railroad from Los Angeles to Salt Lake City," *California History* (Spring 1991): 76–93.

55. See Brian D. Corcoran, "'My Father's Business': Thomas Taylor and Mormon Frontier Economic Enterprise," *Dialogue* 28 (Spring 1995): 105–41.

56. Dwight L. Smith, "The Engineer and the Canyon," *Utah Historical Quarterly* 28 (July 1960): 273 and "Robert B. Stanton's Plan for the Far Southwest," *Arizona and the West* 4 (Winter 1962): 369–72.

57. "There was some negotiations pending to try and arrange a connection with the proposed Railroad company which is to be built to the coast by the Utah company making connection with a Japan Steam Ship Co. to have a line of steamers from Japan to San Diego. As this matter was now before the First Presidency the matter of a mission being opened up in Japan was allowed to pass from the present." Diary Excerpts of Heber J. Grant, 1887–1899, Internally Dated, 8 August 1895, New Mormon Studies CD-ROM (Smith Research Associates, 1998).

58. Elder Grant seems to have been "delighted with such a mission" and was eager to "get freed of debt so he can labor more among the saints or go on a foreign mission." Diary Excerpts of Heber J. Grant, 8 August 1895.

59. Abraham H. Cannon, Journal, 19 August 1895, Abraham H. Cannon Collection, L. Tom Perry Special Collections, Brigham Young University, Provo, Utah.

60. Abraham H. Cannon, Journal, 19 August 1895.

61. Abraham H. Cannon, Journal, 3 October 1895.

62. Abraham H. Cannon, Journal, 1 September 1895. See also 5 and 8 September 1895.

63. Abraham H. Cannon, "A Future Mission Field," *The Contributor* 16 (October 1895): 764–65.

64. Lyman, "From the City of Angeles to the City of Saints," 85.

65. Michael P. Malone, *James J. Hill: Empire Builder of the Northwest* (Norman, Oklahoma: University of Oklahoma Press, 1996), 164. See also Albro Martin, *James J. Hill and the Opening of the Northwest* (New York: Oxford University Press, 1976), 471–74.

66. E. Mowbray Tate, *Transpacific Steam: The Story of Steam Navigation from the Pacific Coast of North America to the Far East and the Antipodes, 1867–1941* (New York: Cornwall Books, 1986), 121.

67. President Woodruff retained his interest in Japan. On 22 April 1896 he attended a lecture by Frank G. Carpenter on Japan in Salt Lake City. The following year, President Woodruff allowed Senator Frank J. Cannon to speak on his recent trip to Japan and China to a large crowd in the Church's Tabernacle. See *Wilford Woodruff Journals*, 22 April 1896 and "Some People of the Far East," *Deseret News*, 29 November 1897.

68. Davis Bitton, *George Q. Cannon: A Biography* (Salt Lake City: Deseret Book Company, 1999), 423.

69. Maureen Ursenbach Beecher and Paul Thomas Smith, "Lorenzo Snow," *Encyclopedia of Mormonism*, 3:1369–70.

70. B. H. Roberts, *A Comprehensive History of The Church of Jesus Christ of Latter-day Saints, Century One*, 6 vols. (Provo, Utah: Corporation of the President, The Church of Jesus Christ of Latter-day Saints, 1965), 6:375.

71. *Our Heritage: A Brief History of The Church of Jesus Christ of Latter-day Saints* (Salt Lake City: The Church of Jesus Christ of Latter-day Saints, 1996), 104.

72. *LDS Conference Report*, October 1901, p.10

73. Joseph F. Smith, "The Last Days of President Snow," *Juvenile Instructor* 36 (15 November 1901): 689–90. On 28 September 1901, Lorenzo Snow made the following statement, later quoted by Joseph F. Smith: "We have started in this direction by sending Brother Grant over to Japan, but this is only a start. Things seem to be going favorably with him; but whether he will accomplish much or not matters not in one sense; it is for the Apostles to show to the Lord that they are His witnesses to all the nations, and that they are doing the best they can."

74. Joseph F. Smith, "The Last Days of President Snow," *Juvenile Instructor* 36 (15 November 1901): 690. See also Richard O. Cowan, *The Church in the Twentieth Century* (Salt Lake City: Bookcraft, 1985), 20 and Francis M. Gibbons, *Lorenzo Snow: Spiritual Giant, Prophet of God* (Salt Lake City: Deseret Book Company, 1982), 230–1.

75. Bitton, *George Q. Cannon*, 436.

76. George Q. Cannon Journal, 6 September 1900, as quoted in Bitton, *George Q. Cannon*, 436–37.

77. Gordon Irving, "Numerical Strength and Geographical Distribution of the LDS Missionary Force, 1830–1974," *Task Papers in LDS History*, No. 1 (Salt Lake City: Historical Department of the Church of Jesus Christ of Latter-day Saints, 1975), 11. Irving defines "Pacific-Asia" as "Australasian, Australian, East Indies, Japanese, New Zealand, Samoan, Sandwich Islands/Hawaiian, and Society Islands."

Left to right: Heber J. Grant, Mary Grant (daughter), and Augusta Grant (plural wife) in Japan, c. 1902. Courtesy John W. Welch.

Horace S. Ensign at the mission home in Tokyo. Courtesy John W. Welch.

Chapter 3

Alma O. Taylor: Among the First in the Japan Mission

On 14 February 1901, during a weekly meeting of the First Presidency and the Quorum of the Twelve Apostles, George Q. Cannon, on behalf of President Lorenzo Snow, stated that it was the mind of the First Presidency to open the Japan Mission with Elder Heber J. Grant as its first president. Church leaders had learned that he was free from "financial embarrassments" and was hoping to fulfill a long-considered apostolic tour of the world. In light of his situation, they felt it appropriate that he preside over the new Japan Mission and fulfill his proper role as an Apostle to the nations.[1] Although the possibility of Elder Grant fulfilling the task of leading a mission to Japan had been discussed before, he was nevertheless surprised by the timing and suddenness of his call, which he accepted without hesitation. The wishes and heartfelt prayers of William Wood, Angus M. Cannon, Lorenzo Snow, George Q. Cannon, William Willes, Abraham H. Cannon, and many others were answered with the creation of the Japan Mission.

Elder Grant now faced the challenge of selecting competent missionary companions to bring the light of the gospel to the Land of the Rising Sun. Many of his fellow Apostles encouraged him to "take not more than two companions," while some "favored only one." Elder Grant immediately invited Thomas A. Clawson to accompany[35] him to Japan but withdrew his invitation when he learned Clawson was in debt.[2] Over the next several months, Elder Grant successfully called three missionary companions: Horace S. Ensign, Louis A. Kelsch, and Alma O. Taylor. With the exception of eighteen-year-old Taylor, his seasoned companions would provide the proselyting experience the Apostle lacked.

Elder Grant's former private secretary Horace S. Ensign was the first to accept.[3] Ensign, then twenty-nine years old, was a native of Salt Lake City, Utah, with a remarkable aptitude and love

for music. In time he became a distinguished Mormon Tabernacle Choir soloist. At twenty-five, he had accepted a thirty-three month mission in Colorado. After this experience, Ensign worked for Elder Grant until he was employed by the Deseret Sunday School Union and the Mormon Tabernacle Choir.[4]

Elder Grant also received permission to extend a call to Louis A. Kelsch, the acting president of the Northern States Mission. Upon learning of Kelsch's acceptance, Grant was pleased. "Tears of gratitude filled my eyes while expressing my gratitude to my Heavenly Father, that Brother Kelsch was to be my companion."[5] Forty-five-year-old Kelsch, one of the Church's most experienced missionaries, was born in Vinnengen,[36] Bavaria, after which he immigrated to America and converted to Mormonism. His previous missionary tours included two years in the Southern States Mission, one year in the Northern States Mission, twenty-nine months in the European Mission, and then nearly five more years in the Northern States Mission.[6]

By the beginning of April, Elder Grant had his two veteran companions but still felt inadequate due to his own lack of missionary experience. "Brother Heber," his friend Francis M. Lyman countered during a meeting of the Quorum of the Twelve,

> you need not worry because you are not very well posted regarding the Doctrines of the Church [and] never [have] had any missionary experience. You are honest and the Lord will be with you and the Lord will fill your heart and you will be strong in preaching the Gospel, as you have been strong in business affairs at home, and you shall have wisdom in your labors.[7]

Troubled by his inexperience, Elder Grant suggested that it "would be a nice thing and a strength to him" to be accompanied by another Apostle, an idea with which Elder Marriner W. Merrill agreed.[8] However, other Church leaders disagreed, and Elder Grant's companions for the moment remained at two. Elder Grant's trauma was deepened when Elder Reed Smoot encouraged Grant and his companions to first go to Japan and then send for their wives. The members of the Twelve agreed.

"Considering the transportation and means of communication of the time, the excitement in Utah during the early years of the Mormon mission in Japan was somewhat analogous to excitement over early space flights," writes historian Leonard J. Arrington[37] with some exaggeration.[9] During the 1901 April general conference weekend, the *Deseret Evening News* reported that the Japan Mission "has aroused no little interest among the Latter-day Saints." Under the banner headline "OPENING OF A MISSION IN JAPAN," the newspaper showcased the Japan Mission and featured pictures and biographical sketches of each of the three missionaries. Elder Grant was asked his plans, to which he responded:

> I only know that I have been called on a mission, and that that mission is in Japan. Three of us will go—perhaps four, but I can't say definitely just now. It was at first thought that we would take our wives with us but that plan has changed. We will go on ahead, look over the country, see what we can do, and if everything is all right and conditions are propitious we will then send for our wives and will probably need more Elders.[10]

He again hinted, during a conference address, that he might choose one more companion.[11]

A month later, Elder Grant recorded in his journal the following event: "Called on Alma O. Taylor and had a little chat with him and his father regarding my mission to Japan and wanted to know how Alma felt about going with me. . . . My impressions in chatting with Alma were that he would be pleased to go." Elder Grant later made this call formal, notifying Joseph Taylor and asking Joseph to notify his son. Elder Grant also wanted a biographical sketch of Alma for a coming issue of the *Deseret Evening News*.[12] When the newspaper announced Alma's selection, it had high praise for the young man.[38] "Elder Taylor is a very young man to receive such an important call," the newspaper said, though "those that know him best say that he is made of the right metal and that he will prove himself an efficient as well as a faithful missionary." The article concluded: "He is a young man of the most studious habits, and a thinker beyond his years, while his industry is most pronounced. He is also a forceful speaker. . . . His call to the Japanese mission was wholly unexpected, but promptly responded to nevertheless."[13]

Alma O. Taylor

"I was born in a casket and cradled in a morgue," joked Alma O. Taylor of his birth and infancy.[14] He was only partly kidding. Several years before Alma's birth, his father—a Salt Lake City pioneer undertaker and sexton—decided to demolish his family's twelve-room home and replace it with a spectacular twenty-two-room, multi-story mansion. The cellar and bottom floors held his mortuary business while the upper rooms housed his family. The occupants of both portions of the home were a reminder that life and death were real. Taylor's first mortal cries on 1 August 1882 were likely mingled with the sobs of grieving customers downstairs at his father's mortuary. Truly, the Taylor home acted as a window for both sides of the veil that day.

Despite the morbid surroundings, Alma O. Taylor was born into remarkable family circumstances. His father, Joseph Edward Taylor, was born on 11 December 1830, at Horsham, Sussex, England. Although missing the finer elements of British life, Joseph's family lived comfortably. He received a common education and learned the principles of Christianity both at home and at church. Joseph's mother, a devout Presbyterian,[39] believed in the doctrines of predestination and foreordination. His father, a liberal "Free Salvationist," established a local congregation and became its first minister. A free thinker, young Joseph read the scriptures regularly and at the age of twelve began to question his mother's Calvinistic teachings. Open to a variety of religious ideas, Joseph was introduced to Mormonism and baptized in 1848. For the next several years, he served as a local missionary and converted many in his hometown. At the age of twenty, he immigrated to New Orleans aboard the *Ellen* and then traveled to Salt Lake City by steamboat up the Mississippi and wagon team across the plains and Rocky Mountains. Joseph arrived in the valley on 6 September 1852 and made his home in the Salt Lake Eleventh Ward. For the next six years, he wore various occupational hats to survive. He settled on undertaking and also acted as the city's sexton from 1864 until 1890.[15] Joseph eventually became the father of four polygamist families.[16] [40]

Alma's mother (Joseph's third plural wife), Lisadore Williams, was born on 23 March 1840, near Pinckneyville, Illinois. After joining the Church at a young age, she and her family endured the mobs of Illinois. In 1847 she and her father, mother, brother Parley, and three sisters—Luacine, Leanore and Eliza—packed up and followed the Saints to Council Bluffs, Iowa, where they prepared for their journey to Utah. When they arrived, however, Lisadore's father learned of the doctrine of plural marriage and immediately led his family back to Illinois. Finally in 1862, her father's opposition softened and the family set out by ox team for Utah. They arrived in Salt Lake City on 29 August and made their home in the Salt Lake Thirteenth Ward. Now in her mid-twenties, Lisadore Williams taught in the Bennion schoolhouse and lived with her family. Eventually she moved in with her bachelor brother and a widowed sister.[17]

In 1876, Joseph and Lisadore met and began courting. They were married a few months later on 11 October, in the Salt Lake Endowment House by Elder Wilford Woodruff. Thereafter, Joseph made his official residence with Lisadore. Soon after their marriage, Lisadore became pregnant, giving birth to their first child—a stillborn boy. Thereafter, the grieving couple moved to a larger home (which served as both the family's residence and the undertaking facility) located at 253 East 100 South, Salt Lake City. In March 1880, Lisadore gave birth to their first healthy child, Samuel Moore. Two years later, Alma joined the family on 1 August 1882. At two-weeks-old, Alma was[41] blessed and given the middle name "Owen" in honor of family friend Abraham Owen Smoot.[18]

Alma seems to have been born with innate spirituality. Beginning at age four, he and his brother attended their weekly Primary meetings.[19] There they learned Church doctrine, good manners, punctuality, obedience, service, prayer, hymns, games, and handicrafts.[20] At age five, he began Sunday School. He was baptized at age eight, on 6 August 1890, by George Peterson and confirmed a member of the Church the following day by Erick J. Peterson.[21] Together with his family, Alma attended Sunday School, sacrament meeting, and sometimes an afternoon meeting on Sundays. On the first Thursday of each month, he dutifully went to fast and testimony meeting.[22] "From childhood I heard the story of Joseph Smith and the Book of Mormon,"[42] he recalled. "Numerous testimonies to the divinity of Mormonism fell upon my ears and remained in my heart during the period of youth."[23]

Alma's early spiritual experiences were enhanced by his inherited membership in the Salt Lake Thirteenth Ward.[24] Until he left for Japan, he enjoyed the comforts of "the ward of the churches."[25] His ward, one of the original Salt Lake City wards and located in the heart of Zion, consisted of nine 10-acre blocks and claimed about 1,850 members by 1880.[26] Prominent buildings such as the Salt Lake City Hall, St. Marks School, the Gardo House, thirteenth ward Co-op Store, and the Salt Lake Theatre fell within the ward's boundaries. Thanks to Commercial Street, there were more businesses within Alma's ward than in any other ward in the valley. Many "fine private residences" also graced the area, including the Joseph Taylor home. ward members enjoyed a large ward hall and three adjoining schoolhouses.[27] Millen Atwood served as Alma's bishop until Atwood's death in December 1890 and was succeeded by Nelson A. Empey.[28] As historian Ronald W. Walker concludes: "The Thirteenth Ward was not cut from ordinary cloth. By virtue of its large,[43] able, and flourishing membership, its proximity to church headquarters, and its early and close experiences with non-Mormons, its congregation practiced what might be described as an 'ideal' Mormonism."[29]

Alma also benefited from his father's ecclesiastical position.[30] Joseph Edward Taylor served in a number of church leadership positions. He was ordained a seventy in 1853 and later a high priest in 1855 when called to serve as a counselor to Bishop John Lytle. In fall 1875, he was selected by Brigham Young to proselyte the "Josephites" living in Iowa and Nebraska. In April 1876, President Brigham Young called Joseph Taylor to serve as counselor to Salt Lake Stake President Angus M. Cannon. Their stake presidency enjoyed personal and ecclesiastical intimacy with the Church's highest officials. For example, they often shared offices and carriages with the First Presidency.[31] As the son of President Taylor, Alma was regularly exposed to the Church's leadership. For example, when his parents held a house-warming party for their new home, the entire First Presidency and the majority of the Twelve Apostles gathered to witness George Q. Cannon dedicate the structure.[32] Alma also grew up in the ward of Elder Heber J. Grant, who was good friends with his father. Elder Grant knew of Alma's birth, blessing, baptism, and church activity. Alma counted three of Elder Grant's children—Lucy, Florence, and Edith—among his closest chums.[44]

Growing into adolescence, Alma received the Aaronic Priesthood[33] and was ordained a deacon by his father on 20 November 1893.[34] He "took an active part in the priesthood quorums and auxiliary associations" of his ward.[35] As a deacon, he helped collect fast offerings, cut firewood for the poor, deliver food to the needy, and assist with custodial work at the thirteenth ward meetinghouse. He may have also helped pass the sacrament.[36] On 24 October 1898, he was called as president of his priesthood quorum. He selected Clarence H. Patten and Charles J. Thomas Jr. as his counselors and William Falco as his secretary.[37] Alma was also active in the ward's Young Men's Mutual Improvement Association (Y.M.M.I.A.).

Alma remembered that he "became conscious of the fact that [he] was a Latter-day Saint, not only because [he] was born of Mormon parents and reared under Mormon influence, but because the study of Mormon doctrine had satisfied [his] mind regarding its rationality." "By birth or nature I was a Mormon. By conviction of mind I was a Mormon." He "counted several miracles wrought in the name of Jesus" as part of his[45] conversion and was "often thrilled with the eloquence and logic" of his ecclesiastical leaders.[38] From his youth, he "looked upon the Book of Mormon as a sacred scripture, and ardently believed the story of its origin."[39]

The son of a former-schoolteacher mother, Alma was also encouraged in his secular studies. At the age of seven, he began his formal schooling at the Eagle Gate schoolhouse (previously Brigham Young's private school).[40] He next attended the nearby eighteenth ward seminary. At

age twelve, he continued his studies at the Latter-day Saints College. Founded in 1886, the "college" was actually a Church-sponsored preparatory school aimed at combining secular and spiritual learning. Alma graduated from the school's theological course in 1899.[41] "I never knew what the inside of a public school building looked like," he remembered. "I was educated in schools where Mormonism was the guiding light and all instruction given in harmony with its principles. This training and environment gave me a fair knowledge of the religion of my parents."[42]

Alma's parents did not leave his spiritual learning to chance. Schools, seminaries, and church meetings served their purposes, but Taylor's most important learning occurred at home. While his father's time was primarily occupied with ecclesiastical, professional, and other familial responsibilities (he had twenty-one other children), his mother spent her time in the home. Nothing was more important than her family, as she herself often said. On one November day, she wrote in her journal: "Thanksgiving. Yes I am very thankful to my Heavenly Father for all that I have and enjoy. <u>My husband and[46] my boys</u>, my sisters, my brother, and my friends that the true gospel has found for me."[43] She also offered up petitions in behalf of her sons and for help in properly raising them.

> <u>Oh, Lord! Help us to do it!</u> Help us to show our children the right path. May they never turn to one side nor the other. May they never be found in dishonor. . . . Father, if they will only seek Thee, find Thee, love and serve Thee—this will embrace all which may be our happiness to witness (as parents) is my earnest and constant prayer.[44]

To raise her sons righteously, she tried to make her large home a refuge from the outside world. This was no easy task since the family home doubled as a mortuary. To her, the business was a constant intrusion that desecrated the sanctity of her home. "What is home without its rights," she privately questioned when Alma was a teen.

> Its sacred rights! I long—I yearn for a home in which more joy can be found for the family than anywhere else on earth. . . . I mean the <u>real ideal</u> HOME. Not where a public business is mixed up in my living room, and office made of the dining room, business messengers running through the kitchen and any room that comes first.[45]

However, the caskets and corpses passing through

her home fascinated both her sons, who later joined the family business.

The clash of home and business was not the only issue that occasionally divided Taylor's parents. From his youth, Taylor enjoyed riding Old Billy, the family pony, with his older brother to their fishing spot on the banks of the Jordan River. There they spent lazy afternoons casting hooks into the flowing current, hoping for a bite. To the young[47] brothers, these outings were pure pleasure; to their mother, however, the danger of drowning was terrifying.

> Today I have again passed through the horrors of knowing that I had a little boy (Alma) on the banks (or in the water) of Jordan fishing. I fancy I hear the reader say "Why in the world do you let them go?" "True, oh King!" but their father says let them go and they go. That is one subject we are not united on.[46]

Despite these disagreements, Alma was raised in a fine Mormon household. For example, he traveled by train, with his mother and brother, to Sanpete County to visit friends and enjoy "pure air." The Taylors lodged in the "pleasant home" of the Crawford family. Alma and his brother relished the opportunity to play in the outdoors and make new friends. "After spending two weeks visiting with friends, luxuriating on fresh air, walks in orchards and gardens, with privilege of eating all we wished, at last we spoke goodbye at the depot," recorded his mother.[47] Alma's mother also introduced him to temple worship. In spring 1896, the two entered the newly completed Salt Lake Temple to perform vicarious baptisms for Lisadore's deceased relatives.[48] Together they were baptized for 63 family members. That evening his mother recorded: "[Aunty Sayers] asked me before she died (even before she was taken down) that if she did not get to attend to her dead, would we, Joseph and I, attend to it for her. Alma was a baby then and[48] she loved him. Today he represented her dead ones in this beautiful work of redemption."[49]

Taylor seemed to respond to his parents' teachings and example. He later defended his faith by referring to his own upbringing:

> Step into any "Mormon" home where lives a faithful Latter-day Saint, and you will find a peaceful spirit there; a love existing between every member of the family; never will they pertake of a meal, without first thanking God for it and asking his blessing thereon. Always before retiring to rest for the night and before entering upon the labors of the day the family will be brought together in a circle and upon bended knees they will express there gratitude to the Lord for his blessings and solicit a continuation of his kindness and mercy; praying for power to be humble and true, virtuous and pure, walking in all holiness before their God. You will see the mother teaching her children from their infancy to their majority to be kind and gentle, loving all mankind and exhibiting charity to their companions. Chastity and virtue are the greatest lessons taught. How well do I remember my mother telling me when I was a little boy, to value my virtue more than my life. How often have I thanked God for such a mother and such a father for he is an exemplary man teaching his children by precept and example to be men, <u>true men</u>; refraining from the use of tobacco and all intoxicating liquors; dealing honestly with our fellows in all things. The "Mormon" children and people are taught to love God and remember the Sabboth Day; to put forth every effort and to use every talent with which they have been blessed in endevoring to do good to their fellow men and in assisting others to actions of righteousness.[50]

As a young man, Alma was also influenced by the achievements and successes of his older half siblings—particularly Joseph William Taylor, Alvin Verender Taylor, and Samuel Moore Taylor. Joseph graduated from the University of Utah and served a two-year mission to Great Britain. Upon returning home, Joseph worked for the Oregon Short Line Railroad, traveled east to attend an embalming school, and started his own mortuary.[51] Alvin, too,[49] graduated from the University of Utah. He began his career at Western Union Telegraph but was later hired by the Denver & Rio Grande Western Railway as an operator and agent. He eventually abandoned business and entered the Columbian Law College in Washington, D.C., passed the bar, and opened his own law practice in Salt Lake City. Alvin also became a member of the Salt Lake delegation in the lower house of the first state legislature.[52] Alma's only full brother, Samuel, graduated from the Latter-day Saints College and joined the family undertaking business.[53] From these examples, Alma learned to value higher education, specialized training, and hard work.

In keeping with his brothers' traditions, seventeen-year-old Taylor traveled with his mother to Chicago, where he attended three weeks of intensive summer classes at the Harvey Medical College's school of embalming. There he studied under Dr. Carl A. Barnes, Sanitary Physician of

Chicago.[54] Alma graduated first in his large class, with an average class mark of 98 percent.[55]

Alma returned to Salt Lake City to resume work at his family's mortician business. Back in Zion, he was able to showcase his intellect and growing ability. In June 1900, he participated in the Salt Lake Stake Y.M.M.I.A.'s Speakers' Contest. Occupying the pulpit of the Assembly Hall at Salt Lake City's historic Temple Square, Taylor impressed the crowd and judging panel—which included such local luminaries as James E. Talmage, N. L. Nelson, Edward H. Anderson, Orson F. Whitney, George H. Brimhall,[50] and B. H. Roberts—with a discourse entitled "The First Vision." Of Joseph Smith's theophany, he concluded:

> To the minister, it had the force of the cyclone. . . . It placed a stumbling block in the path to impede the progress of Satan, and so well did the evil one understand the strength of this new antagonist, that he tried his utmost to destroy Joseph Smith, whom God had called to build the fortress of righteousness, and to throw up the earth-works of love. But the window of the ark had been opened, and the dove sent forth where it found lodgment to the hearts of men.[56]

Despite Alma's eloquence, he received neither the first nor second prize, a judgment that surprised Elder Rudger Clawson of the Quorum of the Twelve. Clawson recorded: "The judges rendered their decision giving to W. J. Sloane the first prize and to Mark C. Brown the 2nd prize. It was truly a most interesting and instructive contest, though the audience did not seem to be altogether satisfied with the decision. There appeared to be a pretty general sentiment in favor of Alma Taylor."[57] Later that summer, as a further indication of his growing maturity and religious background, Alma was ordained an elder at the age of eighteen.[58]

Elder Grant had chosen wisely. Alma Taylor had the advantage of the best that Mormonism could offer. Alma's intelligent and devout parents had given him the advantage of education and position. His thirteenth ward neighborhood must have also been stimulating, exposing him to both Mormonism and the secular culture that was infiltrating Utah. To these forces, Alma brought his own character and natural intelligence. Elder Grant, as a close neighbor was of course privy to nearly every aspect of Alma's physical and spiritual development. But it was Alma himself who would[51] demonstrate his mettle. His devotion to the Japanese Mission for eight and a half years

would show that the confidence placed in him was well deserved.

Preparations for Departing to Japan

With the date of departure for the Japanese missionaries approaching, Elder Grant arranged with the First Presidency to hold a benefit concert for the Japan Mission in the Tabernacle.[59] Local merchants sold tickets and invited subscriptions. The 1 June 1901 "Japanese Mission Benefit" was well attended. The Mormon Tabernacle Choir and some of Salt Lake City's finest musicians celebrated Alma O. Taylor and his companions in song and verse.[60] This was to be but the first of many events celebrating the impending departure of the four missionaries to Japan.

One week after the Tabernacle concert, Alma found himself again on Temple Square, this time as a contestant in the Salt Lake Stake's Y.M.M.I.A. second annual speakers' contest. Competing with four other finalists, Alma delivered a speech titled, "My Spirit Shall Not Always Strive With Man." Alma eloquently concluded his remarks with these sentiments:

> To all young hearts who live within the greatest century that has ever passed over our earth, there comes the reflection, that victory and happiness hasten toward sorrow and defeat for him in whom the inner light hath failed. For the saddest sight on earth is not that of a youth stricken down and laid beneath the turf—earth's greatest tragedy is the tragedy of those who have fallen from integrity and virtue, as the stars fall out of the sky. Happy, indeed, is he who hath ears to hear and heart to obey the still small voice that whispers: "He who neglects his finer spiritual sentiments will find that the Spirit of God has ceased to strive within him," for the Lord hath said: "My Spirit shall not always strive with man."[52]

Unlike the previous year, there was no debate among the distinguished panel of judges. Alma was presented with the first place, fifty-dollar silver cup by his soon-to-be mission president, Heber J. Grant, who must have seen Alma's success as a ratification of his own judgment and inspiration.[61]

Yet another premission event was hosted by ten Salt Lake City citizens of Japanese descent. When the four missionaries arrived at the twenty-first ward meetinghouse, they were greeted by Japanese and American flags hung side by side. Other items of décor "showed the strong art idea that predominates in Japanese life," said a *Deseret Evening News* report. In attendance were

President Joseph F. Smith and other members of the Twelve, together with all three members of the Salt Lake Stake Presidency. The audience was captivated by the rendition of several Japanese songs: "Haru no Asaki" (Sowing in the Morning), "Amine Su Su Hi Yaku" (He Leadeth Me), and "Haruka ni Dogi Miru" (Sweet Bye and Bye). These musical numbers were interspersed with speeches by General Authorities and with expressions delivered by the four missionaries. For refreshment, there was cake and ice cream. "The evening's entertainment concluded with general hand shaking and expressions of good will on the part of the Japanese to the Mormon Elders who were about to leave for the Orient," reported a local newspaper.[62]

There was a series of other receptions and testimonials. On 20 June, President Joseph F. Smith hosted a more intimate reception for the Japanese missionaries. During this event, Church President Lorenzo Snow prophesied that "the brethren going to Japan will be greatly and abundantly blessed. The Lord will be with them."[63] Six days later,[53] Alma and his companions met at the Beehive House for another celebration. Finally, Bishop Millen Atwood hosted a party for the missionaries to Japan in July.[64]

In the midst of these celebratory sendoffs, Taylor prepared for his mission. Lacking the foreign language tutorials of today's Missionary Training Center and unable to find Japanese language textbooks in Utah, he contacted a former friend from Chicago, Dr. Paul Carus. Carus encouraged him to contact the Reverend Nishijima Kakuryo, leader of the recently created Buddhist Mission of North America. Two years earlier, Nishijima and Dr. Sonada Shuei had arrived in San Francisco, taught classes on Buddhism, and introduced traditional Jōdō Shinshu rites and practices to the Bay area.[65]

Writing to Nishijima, Alma explained his missionary call and admitted his lack of Japanese language. In reply, Nishijima answered that he was unable to provide the textbooks Alma desired on such short notice. And there were warnings— any attempt to teach polygamy in Japan would end in failure, Nishijima said. "If you really belong to this sect and intend to teach it to our people," he continued, "I wish you would be so kind as to tell me how you will benifit our people

who are in the state of dullness and ignorance, by your own way of living of which all other Christian sects are so much dispiseing?" The question did not suggest a warm future reception for the "Japanese Quartet."

Alma responded cheerfully to Nishijima's letter. He explained the basic tenets of his religion, including the sanctity of the home, the loving leadership of faithful parents, and the industrious pioneering nature of the Latter-day Saints. He then tried to defend plural marriage as "a sacred principle revealed from God" but conceded that it had ended with the 1890 Manifesto. "We are <u>not</u> going to[54] Japan to preach polygamy, for it is a dead issue," Alma declared. His testimony concluded his epistle. "I bare my testimony to you that it is the truth, and that it [Mormonism] will elevate man to the highest possible standard."[66]

Thus ended Alma's first Japanese proselyting experience. Even at this early date, Alma had proven himself a capable defender of the faith. Yet he was likely humbled by the exchange, which did not result in conversion but rather more questions. Nishijima's concerns over Mormonism and polygamy could not have prepared Alma for the firestorm of criticism that awaited him and his companions in Japan.[67] Converting the followers of Buddha into disciples of Christ would be a difficult labor of love.

As Taylor's departure loomed ever closer, he and his companions bought their rail and steamship tickets and made their final goodbyes. On 18 July, Elder Rudger Clawson invited the four missionaries and their families to his home for a sendoff dinner. Once the dinner table was cleared, several Church leaders addressed the group.[68] Then Taylor and his companions were set apart[69] for the Japan Mission. Sitting in a chair and circled by members of the First Presidency and several Apostles, Alma was blessed by President Anthon H. Lund, who ordained Alma to the office of seventy in the Melchizedek Priesthood and then set him apart for his missionary labors. This blessing promised Alma the spirit of his calling, the ability to preach the gospel, and the gift of tongues for the[55] Japanese language. Lastly, President Lund promised Alma joy in his missionary labor and divine protection in his travels.[70]

On 23 July, the family of Joseph and Lisadore

Taylor gathered to say goodbye. Joseph gave Alma another blessing. "I bless thee as thou passest from the threshold of thy father's and thy mother's home, that thou mayest be protected by the power of God and the administration of holy angels; that every influence or spirit of evil that seeks to afflict thee, or in any way annoy thee, may be rebuked by the power of God and the administration of holy angels." Joseph also blessed his son with physical and mental strength and promised Alma that he would "be able to speak and converse [in Japanese] and, if necessary, preach the Gospel in the open synagogue, in simplicity and plainness and in a manner that they cannot misunderstand" by the gift of tongues.

The blessing picked up on President Snow's earlier theme of duty and success.

> What shall be the result of thy labors the Spirit does not make manifest at this time. . . . Whether thou or thy brethren baptize one soul or not, or whether you baptize hundreds, it shall be equally acceptable to God, for the result of your labor is in His hands. Noah preached one hundred and twenty years seemingly without success, yet he was justified of the Lord and stands next to our father, Adam, in authority upon this earth.

He concluded:

> Now I say unto thee, let thy heart be comforted and be thou made strong in the strength of Israel's God. Thou shalt go in peace and safety, thou shalt remain in peace and safety, thou shalt return in peace and safety, and thy father and thy mother and thy sisters and thy brothers and thy friends and the Priesthood of the Almighty God shall greet thee upon thy return and shall say unto thee, "Welcome, well done," and they shall recognize that thou hast been faithful in the discharge of the duties of this mission.[71] [56]

On 24 July 1901, Alma and his three companions left Salt Lake City for Japan. In fact, Alma did travel to and from Japan in "peace and safety." However, he and his family and friends would have been more than surprised had they known his Japanese mission would last nearly nine years. Alma, the eighteen-year-old lad, would return a twenty-seven-year-old man, having served what may be the longest continuous mission in the Church's history.[72] What follows are selected journal entries of his historic mission.[57]

Notes

1. Heber J. Grant, *A Japanese Journal*, comp., Gordon A. Madsen, (n.p.: the compiler, 1970), 14 February 1901 and Rudger Clawson, *A Ministry of Meetings: The Apostolic Diaries of Rudger Clawson*, Stan Larson, ed. (Salt Lake City: Signature Books, 1993), 247.

2. Grant, *Japanese Journal*, 14 February 1901 and Clawson, *A Ministry of Meetings*, 247. The previous week, the First Presidency had called Elder Francis M. Lyman to preside over the Church's European Mission. Both Lyman and Grant asked Thomas A. Clawson to accompany them to their respective missions, but upon learning that Clawson was $1,900 in debt, they withdrew the call. Diary Excerpts of Thomas A. Clawson, internally dated/paginated, 1895–1904 Bk, p. 199, 7 February 1901, New Mormon Studies CD-ROM (Smith Research Associates, 1998).

3. Grant, *Japanese Journal*, 21 February 1901.

4. "Opening of a Mission in Japan," *Deseret News*, 6 April 1901 and Andrew Jenson, *Latter-day Saint Biographical Encyclopedia: A Compilation of Biographical Sketches of Prominent Men and Women in The Church of Jesus Christ of Latter-day Saints*, 4 vols. (Jenson Memorial Association, 1901–36), 4:236.

5. Grant, *Japanese Journal*, 18 March 1901.

6. "Opening of a Mission in Japan," *Deseret News*, 6 April 1901.

7. Grant, *Japanese Journal*, 2 April 1901.

8. Clawson, *A Ministry of Meetings*, 259–60.

9. Leonard J. Arrington, "Utah's Ambiguous Reception: The Relocated Japanese Americans," as found in *Japanese Americans: From Relocation to Redress*, Roger Daniels, Sandra C. Taylor, and Harry H. L. Kitano, eds. (Salt Lake City: University of Utah Press, 1986), 92.

10. "Opening of a Mission in Japan," *Deseret News*, 6 April 1901.

11. *LDS Conference Report*, April 1901, p.81.

12. Grant, *Japanese Journal*, 9 May 1901.

13. "Alma O. Taylor Going to Japan: Young Man Called to Accompany Apostle Heber J. Grant and Elders Louis A. Kelsch and Horace S. Ensign to the Orient," *Deseret News*, 11 May 1901.

14. "Alma Owen Taylor," typescript, 45, copy in possession of the author.

15. Orson F. Whitney, *History of Utah* (Salt Lake City: George Q. Cannon & Sons, 1892–1904), 4:448–49.

16. All together Joseph Edward Taylor fathered twenty-two children from his four wives. On 21 September 1853, he married his first wife, Louisa Rebecca Capener. Their union produced ten children: Joseph William (b. 16 January 1855), Louisa Marie (b. 23 January 1857), Edward Theodore (b. 31 December 1858), Eleanor Groves (b. 22 March 1861), Annie Rebecca (b. 2 March 1863), Alvin Verrinder (b. 25 February 1865), Elizabeth Margaret (b. 10 April 1867), Josephine Luella (b. 31 May 1869), Jennie Eliza (b. 3 January 1871), and Fannie Augusta (b. 1 December 1874). On 9 July 1875, Joseph married his second wife, Jane Maria Capener (his first wife's younger sister and divorcee of Ephraim Hanks). She brought with her seven children from her previous marriage: William Albert Capener Hanks (b. 17 February 1859), Alice Maria Hanks (b. 15 January 1861), Elizabeth Sarah Hanks (b. 10 March 1863), Ephraim Knowlton Hanks (b. 18 May 1865), George Augusta Hanks (b. 3 January 1868), David Capener Hanks (b. 5 March 1870), and Louisa Rebecca Hanks (b. 27 June 1872). Joseph and Jane's union produced two additional children: Jane

Ann (b. 23 December 1877) and Margaret Wicks (b. 10 February 1883). This marriage, however, ended in divorce. Alma's mother, Lisadore Williams, was Joseph's third wife. Their union produced two sons: Samuel Moore (b. 11 March 1880) and Alma Owen (b. 1 August 1882). Joseph married his fourth wife, Clara Ann Sudbury, on 1 April 1884. Their union produced eight children: Ruth Emily (b. 16 January 1885), Lisadore Amelia (b. 21 August 1886), Joseph Edward (b. 22 February 1888), Mahonri Moriancumer (b. 25 January 1890), Clara Ann (b. 6 June 1892), Ida Irene (b. 20 June 1894), George Albert (b. 20 December 1896), and Eugene Eustace (b. 4 March 1899). See *Ancestral File* and Frank Esshom, ed., *Pioneers and Prominent Men of Utah Comprising Photographs, Genealogies, Biographies* (Salt Lake City: Utah Pioneers Book Publishing Company, 1913), 913.

17. Lisadore Williams Taylor, Journal of Lisadore Williams Taylor, typescript, microfilm, Church Archives.

18. "When babies are just a few weeks old, they are usually given a priesthood blessing for the special purpose of conferring a name by which the baby will be known and bestowing promises based on spiritual impressions regarding the baby's future life. A quality of prophecy attends this process." Bruce B. Clark, "Blessings," in *Encyclopedia of Mormonism*, ed. Daniel H. Ludlow, 4 vols. (New York: Macmillan, 1992), 1:129.

19. "The Primary is an organized program of religious instruction and activity in The Church of Jesus Christ of Latter-day Saints for children from eighteen months of age until their twelfth birthdays. Its purpose is to teach children the gospel of Jesus Christ and help them learn to live it. . . . Under the direction of local Church leaders, the first Primary was organized on August 11, 1878, with Aurelia Rogers as president. On August 25, the first Primary meeting was held in Farmington, Utah, where 224 boys and girls met to be taught obedience, faith in God, prayer, punctuality, and good manners." Naomi M. Shumway, "Primary," *Encyclopedia of Mormonism*, 3:1146.

20. Andrew Jenson, *Encyclopedic History of The Church of Jesus Christ of Latter-day Saints* (Salt Lake City: Deseret News Publishing Company, 1941), 680.

21. "Alma Owen Taylor," typescript, 44, copy in possession of the author.

22. Ronald W. Walker, "'Going to Meeting' in Salt Lake City's Thirteenth Ward, 1849–1881: A Microanalysis," in *New Views of Mormon History: A Collection of Essays in Honor of Leonard J. Arrington*, Davis Bitton and Maureen Ursenbach Beecher, eds. (Salt Lake City: University of Utah Press, 1987), 154.

23. Alma O. Taylor, "Independent Faith," Alma O. Taylor Collection, Perry Special Collections.

24. "The ward is the basic ecclesiastical unit in The Church of Jesus Christ of Latter-day Saints. It is comparable to a Protestant congregation or a Roman Catholic parish. Normally, its membership ranges between 300 and 600 people. A ward is part of a larger unit called a stake, which usually includes between five and ten wards. When a ward or stake grows beyond the usual size in membership and in number of active Melchizedek Priesthood holders, it is divided, creating a new ward or a new stake, usually determined by geographical boundaries. The ward is presided over by a bishop and his two counselors." Douglas D. Alder, "Ward," *Encyclopedia of Mormonism*, 4:1541.

25. *The Story of Salt Lake Stake, The Church of Jesus Christ of Latter-day Saints: 150 Years of History, 1847–1997* (Salt Lake City: Salt Lake Stake, n.d.), 189.

26. The thirteenth ward was bordered by the eighteenth ward to the north by South Temple Street, by the twelfth ward to the east by 3rd East Avenue, by the eighth ward to the South by 3rd South Avenue, and by the fourteenth ward to the west by East Temple Street.

27. Andrew Jenson, *The Historical Record* (Salt Lake City: Andrew Jenson, 1887), 6:319.

28. Jenson, *Encyclopedic History*, 749.

29. Walker, "'Going to Meeting,'" 140.

30. Whitney, *History of Utah*, 4:450.

31. Donald Q. Cannon, "Angus M. Cannon: Pioneer, President, Patriarch," in *Supporting Saints: Life Stories of Nineteenth-Century Mormons*, Donald Q. Cannon and David J. Whittaker, eds., (Provo, UT: Religious Studies Center, Brigham Young University, 1985), 379–80, 385.

32. Lisadore Williams Taylor Journal, 23 March 1893. Eventually the casket manufacturing factory—The Salt Lake Casket Company—moved to 257 East 100 South, behind the Taylor home. Kate B. Carter, comp., *Heart Throbs of the West* (Salt Lake City: Daughters of Utah Pioneers, 1945), 6:317. See also Harry W. Nelson, "The Casket Industry in Utah," *The Utah Payroll Builder* 13 (January 1925): 6.

33. "The two divisions of priesthood in The Church of Jesus Christ of Latter-day Saints are the Aaronic and the Melchizedek. Young men twelve to eighteen years of age, and older men who are new converts, are ordained to offices in the Aaronic Priesthood. . . . It is the priesthood authority by which John the Baptist prepared the way for Jesus Christ, teaching faith, repentance, and baptism for the remission of sins (Matt. 3:1–17; Mark 1:1–11; Luke 1:5–80; John 1:15–34; Acts 8:14–17; D&C 84:25–28). The Aaronic Priesthood does not have the power to confer the Holy Ghost (Matt. 3:11; Mark 1:7–8; John 1:33–34; JS-H 1:70) or to administer totally the affairs of the kingdom of God. It is power and authority God has given to man to prepare him and those to whom he ministers to receive the greater power, authority, and blessings of the Melchizedek Priesthood." Verdon W. Ballantyne, "Aaronic Priesthood," *Encyclopedia of Mormonism*, 1:1–2.

34. "Alma O. Taylor Going to Japan," *Deseret News*, 11 May 1901.

35. Alma O. Taylor, "Independent Faith," Perry Special Collections.

36. William G. Hartley, "From Men to Boys: LDS Aaronic Priesthood Offices, 1829–1996," *Journal of Mormon History* 22 (Spring 1996): 109–10.

37. Salt Lake City Thirteenth Ward Manuscript History, Church Archives.

38. Alma O. Taylor, "Independent Faith," Perry Special Collections.

39. Alma O. Taylor, "Translating the Book of Mormon," Perry Special Collections.

40. "Alma O. Taylor Going to Japan," *Deseret News*, 11 May 1901.

41. "Alma O. Taylor Going to Japan," *Deseret News*, 11 May 1901.

42. Taylor, "Independent Faith," Perry Special Collections.

43. Lisadore Williams Taylor Journal, 28 November 1895.

44. Lisadore Williams Taylor Journal, 7 June 1896.

45. Lisadore Williams Taylor Journal, 29 February 1895.

46. Lisadore Williams Taylor Journal, 10 June 1893.

See also 3 June 1893.

47. Lisadore Williams Taylor Journal, 8 and 22 August 1893.

48. "Baptism for the dead is the proxy performance of the ordinance of baptism for one deceased. Joseph Smith taught, 'If we can baptize a man in the name of the Father [and] of the Son and of the Holy Ghost for the remission of sins it is just as much our privilege to act as an agent and be baptized for the remission of sins for and in behalf of our dead kindred who have not heard the gospel or fulness of it.' The first public affirmation of the ordinance of baptism for the dead in the Church was Joseph Smith's funeral sermon for Seymour Brunson in Nauvoo in August 1840. Addressing a widow who had lost a son who had not been baptized, he called the principle 'glad tidings of great joy,' in contrast to the prevailing tradition that all unbaptized are damned. The first baptisms for the dead in modern times were done in the Mississippi River near Nauvoo." David H. Burton, "Baptism for the Dead," *Encyclopedia of Mormonism*, 1:95.

49. Lisadore Williams Taylor, Journal, 19 May 1896.

50. Alma O. Taylor, Journal, 28 July 1901. Excerpts from a letter to Nishijima Kakuryo (I have retained Alma's original spelling).

51. *Utah Since Statehood: Historical and Biographical* (Chicago–Salt Lake: The S. J. Clarke Publishing Company, 1919), 2:816–9. For more biographical information on Joseph William Taylor see Manly & Litteral, eds. *Utah: Her Cities, Towns, and Resources* (Chicago: Manly & Litteral, 1891–2), 99–100.

52. Mark Drumm, *Drumm's Manual of Utah, and Souvenir of the First State Legislature, 1896* (Salt Lake City: Mark Drumm, 1896), 80.

53. *Utah Since Statehood*, 3:228–31. For more biographical information on Samuel Moore Taylor see *Men of Affairs in the State of Utah: A Newspaper Reference Work* (Salt Lake City: The Press Club of Salt Lake, 1914).

54. Alma O. Taylor, Journal, 28 July 1901.

55. "Alma Owen Taylor," typescript, 46, copy in possession of the author.

56. Alma O. Taylor, "The First Vision: An Address Delivered at the Speakers' Contest, Y.M.M.I.A., Salt Lake Stake of Zion," *Improvement Era* 3 (July 1900): 682–86.

57. Clawson, *A Ministry of Meetings*, 175–76.

58. "Alma O. Taylor Going to Japan," *Deseret News*, 11 May 1901.

59. Clawson, *A Ministry of Meetings*, 274.

60. "The Japanese Mission Benefit," *Deseret News*, 30 May 1901.

61. Alma O. Taylor, "Speakers' Contest—The Oration Which Won the First Place and the Silver Cup—'My Spirit Shall not Always Strive with Man,'" *Improvement Era* 9 (July 1901): 676–82.

62. "American and Japanese Flags," *Deseret News*, 19 June 1901.

63. Clawson, *A Ministry of Meetings*, 285–86.

64. Clawson, *A Ministry of Meetings*, 294.

65. Rick Fields, *How the Swans Came to the Lake: A Narrative History of Buddhism in America* (Boston & London: Shambhala, 1986), 143–45 and Donald R. Tuck, *Buddhist Churches of America: Jodo Shinshu* (Lewiston/Queenston: The Edwin Mellon Press, 1987), 2–3.

66. See Alma O. Taylor, Journal, 28 July 1901, for the complete set of letters.

67. See Shinji Takagi, "Mormons in the Press: Reactions to the 1901 Opening of the Japan Mission," *BYU Studies* 40, no. 1 (2000): 141–75.

68. Clawson, *A Ministry of Meetings*, 301–4.

69. "Customarily, whenever any person is called to serve as a teacher or officer in any of the Church organizations, and always when a person is called to be a missionary or temple worker, persons holding proper priesthood authority place their hands on the person's head and the individual is set apart to the assignment. One of the priesthood bearers pronounces the blessing and expresses whatever counsel or thoughts he is impressed to say." Bruce B. Clark, "Blessings," *Encyclopedia of Mormonism*, 1:129.

70. "Ordination and Blessing of Elder Alma Owen Taylor," Alma O. Taylor Collection, Perry Special Collections.

71. "Father's Blessing," Alma O. Taylor Collection, Perry Special Collections.

72. Perrigrine Sessions was called to serve a mission in Maine in spring 1868. After nine years and nine months of labor, he returned to Bountiful, Utah, in January 1878. However, unlike Alma O. Taylor who remained in Japan for the entire eight and a half years, Sessions returned home four times to take care of his families. William E. Hughes, "A Profile of the Missionaries of the Church of Jesus Christ of Latter-day Saints, 1849–1900" (Masters Thesis, Brigham Young University, 1986), 149.

Chapter 4

Journal Editorial Guidelines

Alma O. Taylor began his regular (generally daily) record of events and feelings with honesty and surprising maturity on 24 July 1901—the day he and his three missionary companions departed from Salt Lake City to open the Japan Mission. For the next eight years and eight months, Alma wrote regularly in his ever-expanding collection of missionary journals. He often recorded events that his companions failed to note. For instance, only Alma detailed Elder Heber J. Grant's dedicatory prayer of Japan. Thus, his thirteen Japanese mission journals are the foundational documents of the early history of The Church of Jesus Christ of Latter-day Saints in Japan. No other set of personal, mission, or Church records document the events of the Japan Mission between 1901 and 1910 with Alma's consistency, thoroughness, and insight.

Although Alma completed his mission to Japan in 1910, his journals were first made available to non-family members during the mid-1950s when Murray L. Nichols began working on his history master's thesis at Brigham Young University. As a returned missionary from Japan, Nichols attempted to write the first scholarly history of the Church in Japan. While researching the original Japanese missionaries in the Church Historian's Office, Nichols was informed by a librarian that Alma's widow, Angeline H. Taylor, was still living in Salt Lake City.[59]

Excited, Nichols contacted Mrs. Taylor and shared his thesis topic. She readily consented to let him have access to Alma's journals, personal papers, and photographs. According to Nichols, she seemed pleased that someone was interested in her husband's extensive journals and experiences in Japan. She had hoped someone would finally bring these documents out of obscurity. She entrusted Nichols with the holograph journals for over a year until he completed his thesis.

After quoting Alma's journals extensively in his thesis entitled, "History of the Japan Mission of the Church of Jesus Christ of Latter-day Saints, 1901–1924," Nichols returned the journals and a copy of his thesis to Mrs. Taylor.[1] Thrilled with the contribution of her late husband's experiences to the thesis, Mrs. Taylor mentioned to Nichols that she would like to donate the documents to a professional archive, where they would be preserved and available for further research. Nichols suggested presenting them to Brigham Young University's library and Mrs. Taylor agreed.[2]

Before making her donation, Mrs. Taylor inscribed the following message to future readers of her husband's journals on the first page of Alma's last journal (Book M):

> This journal is the last of my husband's diaries. It not only records the song of gratitude to god that he was spared to finish the arduous task of translating the Book of Mormon into the Japanese language; but also in a masterful way describes the trip he and Fred Caine made for the church through Korea,[60] Manchuria & China. Because I hope this inspiring journal along with the ten[3] other diaries will do good to the Japanese mission & otherwise, I am giving these to the B.Y. University. It's the best way I know how to honor my husband's unwavering loyalty & true devotion to his Church.

She concluded: "This journal has much to give, as do all of them."[4]

I heartily concur. This publication of Alma's journals provides scholars, returned missionaries from Japan, and Church members on both sides of the Pacific the opportunity to study a first-hand account of the introduction of the gospel to Japan. In fact, no scholarly treatment of the first decade of the Church in Japan is complete without extensive referencing of Alma's journals.

Physically, the journals appear as follows: Alma's thirteen journals vary in size. With the exception of Journal B (typescript), all the volumes are holographic journals. In fact, aside from his wife's previously noted inscription, only Alma's handwriting appears throughout the journals. Fortunately, Alma had excellent penmanship and wrote in beautiful cursive characters. Thanks to Mrs. Taylor and the staff at BYU's Harold B. Lee Library, all thirteen journals are in good condition.

Journal A (24 July 1901–31 August 1901) measures 6½ x 4½ inches. It is written in a blue-lined, cardboard-bound notebook, which opens vertically and numbers 186 red-edged pages. The cover is textured and light brown, with a navy blue border design and red corner protectors. The back cover continues the border design but is blank. On several occasions, Alma pasted small newspaper articles into the journal, which I have not included. The handwriting in Journal A is especially large and clear.[61]

Unlike all the others, Journal B (1 September 1901–15 September 1903) is a 215-page typescript. Apparently, Alma decided to use a typewriter in his private residence or the mission headquarters for his daily entries for this two-year period. The majority of its pages are standard 8½ x 11-inch typing on onionskin paper, while some are 8 x 10 inch or 8 x 10½ inch. For the most part, the loose-leaf typescript is very clear. Occasionally, Alma typed on both the front and back of thin onionskin paper, which obscured some of the type. In Journal B, Alma pasted several long newspaper articles onto the actual typescript. Again, I have decided not to include these lengthy articles to conserve space. Toward the end of Journal B (9 April 1903–22 April 1903), Alma inserted a copy of a speech he handwrote in Japanese katakana characters. This speech has not been included.

Journal C (1 October 1903–26 January 1904) and Journal D (27 January 1904–11 June 1904) are identical 3¾ x 5⅜ inch lined, 175-page black plastic-bound volumes. Alma wrote neatly on its white pages with red edges, hand-numbering each page on the top middle margin. In these volumes, he begins creating an "index" in red ink at the front of each journal. The index contains summary statements of important events with the accompanying page reference. These indexed sections are then underlined in red ink with an explanatory note at the top of the page. Alma did

not include any newspaper articles in these two journals.

The next eight volumes—Journal E (12 June 1904–14 November 1904), Journal F (15 November 1904–10 May 1905), Journal G (11 May 1905–30 October 1905), Journal H (31 October 1905–15 June 1906), Journal I (16 June 1905–30 September 1906), Journal J (1 September 1906–6 March 1907), Journal K (7 March 1907–23 August 1907), and Journal L (24 August 1907–10 February 1908)—are identical 4¼ x 6½ inch lined,[62] 188-page, leather-bound books. The book's flyleaves are yellow or have yellowed and were made by the same Japanese stationary manufacture. Each page is hand-numbered in the top middle margin. Alma continues his indexing methods throughout these volumes and writes very legibly.

The final volume, Journal M (11 February 1908–12 February 1911), is a larger leather-bound record, measuring 7⅜ x 4⅝ inches. Its black leather cover is cracking in several places, the front center is embossed with "Journal," and the front lower right corner reads "Alma O. Taylor." The book's flyleaves are covered with tan and cream paisley designs. Each of its 540 pages is machine numbered in blue on the top outside corner. For whatever reason, Alma did not index this journal.

Throughout the transcription and editing process, I made editorial decisions with the assistance of my graduate committee chair, Ronald W. Walker, and committee members, John W. Welch and R. Lanier Britsch. Due to practical limitations, I have abridged Alma's journals by only selecting and reproducing certain entries. Although something is always lost through abridgment, my goal has been to enhance the readability of Alma's record. Over the past two years, I have spent countless hours reviewing and judging the various journals to select those entries that will be of the most value to the serious scholar and of the most interest to the casual reader.

Although the vast majority of Alma's writings are very legible, occasionally the original ink has faded or he complicated the text by inserting later editorial corrections. To make the selected journal entries more accessible I've determined:

• To leave all spelling, punctuation, and capitalization as written by Alma as in the original;

- To standardize the various lengths of dashes "—";[63]
- To retain Alma's emphasis on certain words or letters (such as underlining) by the use of bold type;
- To begin each day as a separate paragraph;
- To standardize the placement of date and location headings. Alma generally provided full dates and locations on two lines: the first containing the city he was laboring in and the second listing the day of the week and date. I have combined all of this information on a single line using "day/date/month/year/location" format;
- To include only the original black ink text and omit Alma's later red ink notations and indexing except for underlining;
- To combine the first sentence, which is usually a short reference to weather, with the first paragraph of the journal entry. In some cases, to improve readability, I have silently combined or split paragraphs according to topics;
- To include any of Alma's insertions above the normal text by enclosing the insertion with forward slashes on both sides: for example, "Today we went to the church /which was very large/ and met with the minister";
- To place in brackets and cross out underlying words that Alma wrote over with other words, and follow them in plain text with the revisions: for example, "[~~Friday~~] Thursday." When the deletion is illegible, a note was made in brackets: "[illegible deletion]";
- To delineate illegible characters by typing as many characters as are legible and then inserting dashes "-" within brackets for each illegible character: for example, "Man[--]uria, Ch[-]na";
- To bring down all superscript text and figures: for example, "November 21st" to "November 21st" or "$5.^{44}" to "$5.44";
- To leave blank spaces where Alma did, presumably intending to fill in the missing names or data later by inserting [blank]: for example, "Went to the Japanese government and tried to meet with Mr. [blank] who was not in his office.";
- To maintain a constant font size regardless of whether Alma used larger letters in headings;
- To note all foreign language characters—a brief note in brackets will describe the section rather than having bracketed dashes for each symbol: for example, "[Chinese characters]";[64]
- To insert the ampersand symbol "&" for all handwritten symbol variations of "and" in the journals: for example, "We met with Kawamura & Takahashi at the church building and then answered their gospel questions";
- To silently correct all Alma's handwritten editorial comments and type spacing problems in the typescript of Book B without noting them in the text;
- To separate Alma's journals according to year for easy reference and reading.

One hundred years have passed since Alma and his companions departed for Japan. However, thanks to the diligence of Alma and the generosity of his widow, Angeline Taylor, we can relive the highs and lows of his historic missionary experience in Japan. Mrs. Taylor was correct in surmising that her husband's journals have "much to give."[5] [65]

Notes

1. Murray L. Nichols, "History of the Japan Mission of the Church of Jesus Christ of Latter-day Saints, 1901–1924" (Masters Thesis, Brigham Young University, 1957).

2. Murray L. Nichols of Salt Lake City, interview by author, 15 March 2000, Provo, UT, email query, copy in possession of the author. The Japanese missionary journals and personal papers of Alma O. Taylor are now cataloged as Alma O. Taylor, "Journals, 1901–1946," L. Tom Perry Special Collections, Harold B. Lee Library, Brigham Young University, Provo, Utah. Hereafter citations from Taylor's journal will be cited as Alma O. Taylor, Journal, date.

3. There are actually twelve other journals in the Alma O. Taylor collection.

4. Alma O. Taylor, Journal, Book M, flyleaf.

5. Alma O. Taylor, Journal, Book M, flyleaf.

Map of Japan

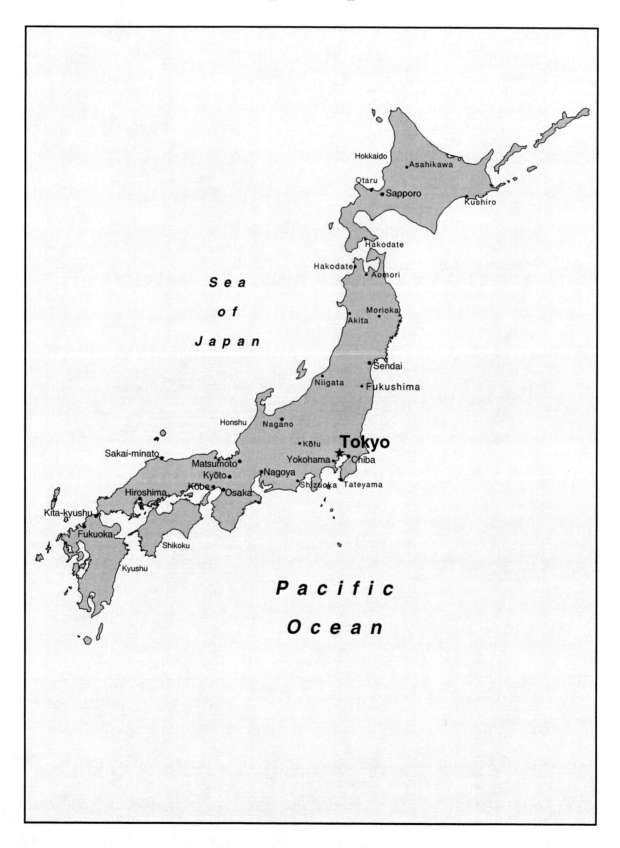

Chapter 5

Alma O. Taylor Journal, 1901

Wednesday, 24 July 1901, Salt Lake City, Utah

This being the day of starting on my mission to Japan, it is one of excitement and work. To prepare for such a journey as lies before me is by no means a small job, but one which keeps our heads & hands to work in packing and forgeting not to pack those things that are needful during the trip. With most people, the thoughts of leaving relatives and friends for so long a time as I may be gone on this mission, would be very sad but with me this contemplation of the labor lying before me is so pleasant that I say good-bye to all with joy.

This afternoon the following friends called to see me: Mrs Giles from Heber City, Helen Capener from Centreville, Geo Taylor, Joe Ostler, Mrs. Wm Hennefer Bp. Nelson A. Empey and wife, Bro. C. J. Thomas wife, and two children, Berenice Seidenfaden, & Lulu Ellis.

Aunt Clara, Ruth, Lisadore, and Mahonri came up and spent the evening.

Just before starting I went over to Mrs. Seidenfaden's to see her; she being too ill to get over to our house to say good-bye.

At 10:00 p.m. I left home and went up to Kolitz Candy Kitchen to say good-bye to my friend Mable Cunningham who had sent me, that afternoon, a six pound box of choice candy. After leaving with her my "Japanese" card and my "Article of Faith" card, I went on to the depot. Here I met with a large croud of people—all friends of the Japanese Missionaries—and the hearty handshakes and farewell greetings I received from them were, indeed, gratifying. To have the confidence and respect of our friends is, truly [a] desireable; and the realization of trust having been placed in us /by our friends/ is a stimulation, spurring us on to actions of honesty, virtue and industry, that we may continue worthy of their respect and confidence.

The train was detained 20 minutes so we did not start until 11:10 p.m. Among those who came to the depot to see us off were Father, Mother, Brother Sam, Aunt Hattie, Emma, Bessie Badger, Lutie, Florence, Edith Anna, Mary, Ray, and Sister Emily Grant's two oldest daughters, Sister Rachel Grant, Bp Empey and wife, Geo. E. Woolley and Sister Fanny, Lucile Badger, Josie Morris, Louise Badger, Ralph Badger, Minerva Smith, Edna Harker, Will Seidenfaden and cousin, Joseph F. Smith and wife, Apostles Lund and Cowley, Bro. Joseph McMurrin, Bro J. Golden Kimball, Bishop Millon Atwood and wife, Heber S. Goddard and wife Horaces Ensigns Mother and sister, his wife, Bro Kelsch's wife, Sister Lyrle, Miss Dougall, Arvilla Clark, Malcorn Butler and his mother, Aunt Louide Badger, John Taylor, Thos Hull and wife and daughter Susie, Lulu Sloan, Thomas Sloan and many others whose names I do not at present recall.

It was quite an auspicious day to make a start; it being the 54th Anniversary of the pioneers entering the Salt Lake Valley.[1] I felt that inasmuch as the Gospel had never been preached in Japan and that we were to be the first to sound the Gospel cry to that nation; that we were indeed going pioneering on pioneer day. Amid the waving of hankerchiefs, & and weaping of sweet maidens the last "farewells" were sounded as the train moved gentely off carrying the four Japanese Missionaries on their way to the Orient.[2]

Thursday, 25 July 1901, Ogden, Utah

One a.m. found us walking up and down the platform in Ogden. We had spent the time between 11:10 pm /the time of our leaving Salt Lake/ and the time of our arriving in Ogden, singing the songs of Zion and speaking of the departure we had just made with or loved ones. We left Ogden at 12:50. Soon after this starting we went to bed and enjoyed a good sleep until about 7 o'clock.

This day's travel was a pleasant one, so far as our thoughts a feelings were concerd, but the dust was very disagreeable and the car became extremely warm. We sang "Do What is Right," "Truth Reflects upon our senses," "God moves in a misterious way" and and other hymns found in the Hymn [~~Book~~] and S.S. song Books. Because of the lateness of an Eastern train we failed to make connections with a dining car, so that evening we ate supper about 9 pm at a little station known as [blank]. The resturant was in a two story Log house but the meal which they served that evening was fit for the table of a King. An old grey haired lady, I should judge of about 68 or 70 years, presided /over the supper/ and she seemed so whole souled and considerate of the tastes and appetites of her diners that everybody immediately [g] addressed her as grandma. Indeed, one could well imagine himself seated at his grandma's table, feasting on her dainty spread and enjoying the smiles of her pleasant face.

Friday, 26 July 1901, Portland, Oregon

Arrived in Portland, Ore. at 8:10 a.m. Took a room in the Beldevere Hotel and ate our meals at Watson's Resturant. After breakfast we went to the Canadian Pacific[3] Ticket Office and secured our tickets through to our destination—Yokohama. They cost us $100 each.

Leaving the Brethern I went to the Multnomah Block where some of my friends Mr. Charles Snelgrove an Mrs Geo Snelgrove had taken rooms; I went there to meet them according to appointment. They had come /from/ [~~to~~] Salt Lake to Portland for the purpose of taking home with them, my friend and neighbor Grace Frost, who had been in Dr. Coe's Nervous Sanitarium in Portland[4] for over one year undergoing a treatment for the benefit.

I went with Mr. and Mrs. Snelgrove out to the hospital to see Grace and bid her good-bye, and also to cheer her up if possible, that she might return home with joyous antisipations. To my great astonishment she was feeling very much cast down in spirit; practially without hope of ever recovering, for it seemed as though[t] her treatment had not benefitted her any, and the Doctor had told her that he was greately disappointed in her condition but could do nothing to better it. The fond antisipatitions of returning to her home a healthy and strong girl, had all been blighted and the feeling of disappointment and regret had simply overcome her faith and she saw nothing before her but the opened jaws of death.

She being a Latter-day Saint who at one time had great faith in the power of God and his servants, I reminded her of the fact that there was still hope and no matter if man with all his learning and skill had failed there still was a God who heard and answered prayer and recognized the faith of his children. I suggested to her that as there were four of us in the city who held the Priesthood of God (not knowing at the time that there were any Mormon Missionaries in Portland) that perhaps if she were anointed with oil and prayed for in faith, that she might receive a blessing /and be given strength to stand her homeward journey/. She grasped at the thought quickly and requested that we administer to her. Accordingly I went back to the room in the hotel, expecting to find the brethern there, but they were not. Thinking however that they would soon return I sat down and addressed a letter home. While writing Bro Grant came in and said that they had met 12 or 15 Elders who had just completed there conference and that they were going to have a group picture taken and desired us to appear in it. I told Bro Grant that I had come back to have him and the other two go /back/ to the hospital /with me/ for the purpose of administering to my friend. But as the Elders were already waiting for us, at the photographers, I went with Bro Grant and we were given the dignity of the central position in the picture.

Among the Elders whom I met was Bro A. H. Lundquist of Logan, Utah, Elder Elijah Hiatt, of Parker, Idaho, Elder W. T. Clark of Bingham Co, Idaho, and Bro Sims of Salt Lake City. The first three named gave me their photographs and in return I presented not only to them, but to all the Elders my Japanese Card. The Elders were very happily surprised in meeting with Apostle Grant and his companions and before leaving the photograph gallery, it was decided to hold a street meeting that evening so that an opper-tunity could be had of hearing Bro. Grant and of having the people who might stop and listen hear him.

Apostle Grant, having some letter writing to do, was unable to go out to the hospital but Bros Kelsch, Ensign & myself took the car and after a fifteen minute ride we arrived at the cottage where Sister Frost was staying. We administered to her in the name of the Lord and encouraged her to live in faith and hope so as to merit the fulfillment of the promises made.

According to arrangement we met the Elders on the street and opened our meeting on Adler between 3rd and 4th Streets. We sang two hymns, [and] had prayer, sang again, and succeeded in drawing a large crowd. This was a new and novel experience for me, one which was indeed funny, but I felt quite easy; thinking of course that Apostle Grant would be the speaker of the evening. When he called on Bro Kelsch to lead out I began to shake for fear that I would be captured next, (as I stood next to Elder Kelsch) and before Bro Kelsch had concluded his talk my knees were clashing to-gether and my mind was floundering around trying to settle on something to say but in vain. My impressions were correct and I became the next victim.

I took off my hat stepped into the middle of the ring and began to speak. What I said, I do not know; How I said it, was a mystery; and the **amen**, came as a relief, bringing me to a realization of the position I occupied, and giving me a consolation in the thought that it was over. Bro Ensign followed me speaking on the necessity of Faith and works. Following him, Bro Grant spoke with great force /for 20 minutes/ on the divinity of the mission of Joseph Smith. He created a great interest [and started] which resulted in considerable favorable comment on the part of the audience.

Leaving the Elders we went to the depot and took the 11 o'clock train for Seattle & Vancouver.

Saturday, 27 July 1901, Seattle, Washington

Arrived in Seattle in time for breakfast. Changed from the Northern Pacific[5] to the Seattle and International Ry. and continued on our way to Vancouver.

The movement of the train was very slow but the beautiful scenery of[h] the country through which we passed was so grand that a swiftly moving train would not /have/ been satisfactory. The gigantic pines towered up on either side of the track, waving gentley in the breeze they seemed to bid defiance to the keen edge of the woodmans ax many of whom were striking vigorusly at their base. As the lion is king of the jungle, so also are these mighty trees the monarchs of the Western Mountain ranges. But the hundreds of stumps which were seen along the way gave evidence, that as the parents of these massive monuments of wood had some time been forced to yield to the superior power of man, so also must they fall and become a means of promoting the wealth happiness and comfort of m-kind. Yet their memory shall not be lost, for silently, yet gracefully, were growing at their base thousands of their kind, that under the protecting hand of God, shall grow to reach the self same hights and kiss the clouds as they have done.

The ferns which grew luxuriantly with spontenous growth like grass covered the ground with a mantle of green which here & there was dotted with the delicate colors of wild flowers. Suddenly leaving the timbered hills [we] our train passed into the beautiful green and level valley of the Frazer River. Rolling slowly on its course this vast body of water (which I should judge was about one third of a mile wide) presented to the eye, of one who had been used to the gushing streams of the Wasatch Mountains, a picture of wonderment and awe. What mind can conceive the amount of water that daily flows along this river bed? much less imagine [ima] with its finite powers the volumes which roll on, eternally, toward the Western Sea? Yet nature with all her wonders is governed by one Creative hand and God oversees and measures all her deeds. For about two hours we followed the course of this river arriving in Vancouver at 4:50 p.m.

After visiting the ship ("The Empress of India")[6] in which we were to take our voyage across the sea, we went to the Commercial Hotel; (about 3/4 of a mile from the depot) and secured rooms.

Sunday, 28 July 1901, Vancouver, Washington

Most of the day was spent in writing letters to my friends. One or two days before leaving home, I received the following letter from the president of the Buddhist Mission in America. . . .[7]

In my search for text books on the Japanese /Language/ I was finally recommended by Dr. Paul Carus of Chicago to write to The Rev. K. Nishijima who then lived in San Francisco Cal. whom he thought would be able to find some for me, if there were any in the United States. I did so and after putting Mr.

Nishijima to considerable trouble, which ended in a failure to find the books I concluded to tell him why I was so anxious to secure them. I wrote him a letter on June 14th telling him that myself in company with three others were going to Japan as representatives of the Church of Jesus Christ of Latter-day Saints commonly called "Mormons" and that we were desireous of doeing what studying /of the language/ we could while on our journey. . . .

Together with the Brethern I took a stroll about the city for an hour or two. Although it was Sunday /and a large concorse of people were going to church/ yet we thought that our time could be more profitable spent singing the songs of Zion in our own room at the Hotel than in visiting any of the Sectarian Services. Accordingly we returned to our rooms and sang several hymns, some of which were, "We thank thee Oh God for a Prophet," "Come let us anew," "How Firm a Foundation" and "Do What is Right."

Monday, 29 July 1901, Vancouver, Washington

In the morning we checked our baggage onto the Steamer. Owing to the train from the east being late the departure of the vessel was delayed. The scheduled time for leaving was 1 p.m. but it was delayed until 5:30 am the following day. The passangers, however, were allowed to go on board so we left the hotel about 12 [pm] /N/ and occupied our cabins on the ship. At 1 pm we ate lunch which was the first meal I had ever had on board an ocean steamer. During the afternoon and Evening I wrote letters to the following friends and relatives: Father, Brother, Aunt Clara, Aunt Hattie, Emma Batt, Bp. N. A. Empey, Geo. E. Woolley, Chas. A. Johnson, Lutie Grant, Florence Grant, and Bessie Badger. These letters were sent as souvenirs of the steamer.

Leaving the steamer about 11 p.m. we went out to post our letters and also to telegraph to our folks at home that we were well and about to start on our voyage across the sea.

Tuesday, 30 July 1901, Pacific Ocean

As I did not go to bed until late last night, I /overslep myself and/ awoke to find that our ship was sailing beautifully out of the harbor. The motion of the vessel could not be felt in the least and the start had been so easy that most of the passengers including myself were not even aroused from our sleep. Our cabins were nos 209 and 211 on the port side considerably to the fore of the ship.

It was a most beautiful day and hundreds /of/ little /one sailed/ fishing crafts were dancing upon the glassy surface of the bay. As the wind filled their sails and they shot rapidly through the water, they looked like butterflies flitting restlestly over a pond.

At 11:30 we dropped anchor in the port at Victoria, Vancouver Island. During the half hour's stay which the ship made her I wrote and posted a letter to my mother.

We left Victoria at 12 [M] /N/ and were soon out upon the sea sailing swiftly toward the land of Japan. Standing upon the stern of the boat we watched with eager eyes, to catch the last glimpse of the land which we loved so well, and where lived those who were most dear to our hearts.

That evening as the sun was setting amidst the most beautiful display of colors I had ever seen, Bro. Ensign sang, "Out on the Deep when the sun is low." We also sang some of the songs of Zion. The Spirit of God was with us, and we had a peaceful and happy feeling burning in our hearts, because of which we looked upon the work laying before us with joy and satisfaction.

Wednesday, 31 July 1901, Pacific Ocean

This was another beautiful day. Not long after breakfast while standing upon the deck I saw four very large whales. I had the privilage of being introduced to Mr. and Mrs. Vanbuskirk who were on their way to Manila, P. I. Mr. Vanbuskirk was a Protestant Minister and his wife a very fine musician. I also met with many other passengers with whom I had some very pleasing talks on religious topics. There names, however, I did not learn, but on board ship names and formal introductions are not necessary to geniality.

On going to bed I noticed from the port hole of my room that dark clouds were rising in the Eastern Sky.

Thursday, 1 August 1901, Pacific Ocean

I awoke to find a miserable, foggy, windy, and rainy morning. The waves were rolling quite high and the ship was dipping considerably. About noon I felt a seasick sensation come over me but I succeeded, by exercising vigoriously, in overcoming it. During the evening Bro Grant had a slight attack of sickness and went to bed feeling very miserable.

Before leaving home the thought that I would soon be "rocked in the cradle of the deep" seemed too grand to be real, but to-day as I stood upon the deck of the ship and looked out into the distance; I could see, coming in ceaceless succession, the white capped waves which in their rapid roll spoke in terms plainer than words, "You are out upon the Sea." The day closed equally as dim and wet as it began, thus my nineteenth birthday (the first ever celebrated upon the ocean) passed under somewhat unpleasant conditions.

Friday, 2 August 1901, Pacific Ocean

To-day still continued storm and rough and a severe south east wind impeded the motion of the ship sufficiently to cause us to loose some ten or fifteen miles during the day. The distance traveled was 336 miles.

Saturday, 3 August 1901, Pacific Ocean

To my great joy and the joy of all the passengers this morning found us traveling upon a calm sea which presented a picture of serenity. The beautiful sight which the waters blue surface presented to the eye, brought to my memory a picture which I had once seen of a ship sailing in water, the movement of which could hardly be perceived; the picture was called "A Peaceful Sea" the beauty of which I can now appreciate.

This day I had a long walk, /upon the deck/ with the Captain of the ship, Mr. O. P. Marshall. I explained to him the organization of our church and the manner in which the Elders in the church are called and sent out to proclaim the Gospel. He seemed interested, but his comments and questions were few.

Sunday, 4 August 1901, Pacific Ocean

As is customary in all English ships to hold Sunday Devine Services, we entered the "saloon" at 10:45 a.m. and listened to the Captain who acts as chaplin of the ship read throught the customary ritual of the Morning Service in the Church of England. There was also the usual singing and reading of a chapter from the scriptures.

These services though sacred to those whose thoughts are in harmony with sectarian ideas, were /to us/ indeed hollow and absolutely devoid of anything characteristic of the Spirit of God. Such worship as this, where the spirit of man prevails, when compared to the humble gathering of two or three who drink in, with eagerness, the Word of the Lord, until their hearts burn within them establishes the truth of the revealed Word of God to Jos. Smith when he said concerning the churches upon the earth, "They draw near me with their lips, but their hearts are far from me" "Having a form of godliness but denying the power thereof."

After these services we retired to our cabins and sang the following songs: "Come Let us Anew," "We thank Thee Oh God for a prophet" "Oh My Father" and others. Following the singing we had prayer then read a chapter from the Doc. and Cov. (Sec 101)

The weather to-day was a renewall of the rough and foggy days we had previously had.

Monday, 5 August 1901, Pacific Ocean

Foggy, windy, & rough. The excessive /rolling/ of the ship has made it very uncomfortable during the entire day. Bro Grant, this evening, has been entirely overcome by the nauseation of seasickness. I also have been feeling bad, but am not yet numbered among the sick. At supper there were only 15 passengers out of the 45 who we at the table.

Wednesday, 7 August 1901, Pacific Ocean

Yesterday /(Monday)/ afternoon we crossed the 180th Meridian which devides the Eastern and Western Hemispheres—the East from the West, consequently on the east side of this line it is twenty four hours earlier than on the west side, so to make the difference we had to loose a whole day. There was, therefore, no Tuesday, but Wednesday morning followed Monday night.

To-day has been a continuation of yesterdays unpleasantness and Bro Grant has been unable to leave his bed. Just as I was going from my cabin to Lunch I was seized with a vomiting spill in which I lost my breakfast and missed my luncheon /for/ which I started out [for]. This evening I ate supper in my cabin not daring to venture to the dining room.

Thursday, 8 August 1901, Pacific Ocean

Still very disagreeable. To-day at noon Bro Grant got out on deck, but like me he did'nt feel the best in the world. In looking forth to my trip to Japan and comparing in my own mind, the relative pleasure of railroad and steamer travel, I had imagined that the voyage across the ocean would be by far, the more enjoyable, but now, after so much storm and wind and unpleasant weather, I [would] will be only to glad to see land, for the voyage has grown most monotonous.

Friday, 9 August 1901, Pacific Ocean

During the morning the sea was still rough, but by 3 pm it had grown calm and the sun shone occasionally through the fog, which still lingered on our course. We were all so glad to have it pleasant once more that we indulged in the games of cricket,[8] quoits,[9] croquet[10] and other exercises accessable on the ship.

In the evening there was an entertainment given in the saloon (dining room) consisting of a display of moving pictures and solo singing. Bro Ensign, having done some singing before, in which he attracted the attention of both officers and passangers, was requested to take part on the program which he readily concented to do.

When the man operating the machine attempted to start it to work he found that it was'nt focused right so he tried and tried to get it to go properly and after repeated failures at success, /in which the audience became tired and restless/ he gave up. So to save the reputation of the boat and to take off the disgrace of the occasion Horace was implored to continue in /giving/ his songs.

When we first got on the ship and we announced that we were Mormons the name spread like wildfire and in no time we became the "curios" of the ship. And the word "Mormon" being considerd in the world to mean everything that is low and debased we were shunned as much as possible and the feeling was generally indeed very cold toward us. But the Lord was with us to the extent that we were able to disprove, by our works, that we were as the world thaught us to be. We became the champion quoit players and it became a saying that "You cannot beat the Mormons when they are playing partners." In what few religious talks [which] we had, we succeeded in putting to naught the [religious] arguments of those with whom we conversed, until all on board, even the two Protestant ministers who were traveling with us, evaded religious topics. And now, to-night, [they] /the officers/ had to fall back on Bro Ensign ("that Mormon") to save them from disgrace. So by the time we left the ship we had demanded recognition because of the ability which God enabled us to display. After singing two hymns and thanking God for the blessings of the day, we retired with hearts overflowing with joy.

Saturday, 10 August 1901, Pacific Ocean

This has been another beautiful day and by putting on extra steam the ship has traveled 376 miles. Heretofore we have been muffeled up in overcoats and rugs to keep warm, but there was now a sudden change and the temperature /has/ jumped up remarkably.

Sunday, 11 August 1901, Pacific Ocean

After a very warm night we took a walk upon the deck to create an appetite for breakfast. At 10:45 we attended Devine Service in the Saloon.

During the afternoon we were occupied in packing our trunks preparatory to leaving the steamer the following day. The weather had become so warm and the atmosphere was so humid that our clothes /and books/ had become damp as though they had been put in water and my straw hat which had been hanging in the cabin was about twice its former weight because of being so badly water soaked by the moisture in the air.

The evening we spent in singing and I also wrote a number of letters to my friends.

Monday, 12 August 1901, Japan Coast/Yokohama

We arose this morning to find that we were sailing along the coast of Japan passing on our course hundreds of Japanese fishing crafts in which from 3 to 9 native fishermen (all neacked except, breach clouts) [who] were working enegerticlly at the nets.

At 10: am we dropped anchor about 2 miles out from the warf at Yokohama there being a law prohibiting any passenger of freight vessel from passing [a certain] this point until the quarentaine physicians had made an examination of all on board. We had been there but a few moments when a small tug boat came bringing the doctors, both of whom were native Japenese. The condition of the passengers was discovered to be healthful so we steamed into the port.

Here followed one of the novelties of Japan. After passing through the custom house we were directed to take a jinrikisha,[11] and by a motion of the finger [two] four men each pulling a small cart, (buggy top like rig) and came running toward us and making a low bow they dropped the schaffs [and] which was a signal for us to get in. We did so saying "Grand Hotel"[12] and like a shot they jumped into the schaafs and started on the trot like ponies. I however forgetting that it was human /nott horse/ flesh that was pulling me, unconsciously said "Get up" as I would to the dumb brutes.

The Hotel was about 3/8 of a mile from the depot, but they trotted at a good rate all the way and did not seem out of breath at all. The fact that humans are thus worked seems almost impossible but before night I saw hundreds and hundreds of these rikisha men and many others who were pulling freight carts on which there was as much as 1000 lbs. Also on the bay two men by the use of long poles which they stuck down to the bottom would move along through the water [as much] /enough/ coal and other freight to fill and ordinary, yes one of the late 100000 lbs capacity freight cars, which are run by American R. R. Companies.

After dinner I returned to the [custom house] /warf/ to see to the passage of our trunks and library books through the custom house. I took a rikisha and for the return trip paid the man 20 cens which equals 10 cents American money. And I should judge the distance to be nearly a mile. As I sat upon the veranda of the Hotel, which looks out over the bay and saw the Japanese men /almost stark neacked/ who were working on the shore and also those on their boats I could not help but admire their their large and powerful limbs which were developed almost beyond their limits. Seeing also the apparel and manners of the people, I indeed felt "A Stranger in a strange land."

Tuesday, 13 August 1901, Yokohama

In company with my companions I went with Apostle Grant to present the letter of introduction which we had to the agent of the Brandenstein Tea Co. and we also had the pleasure of meeting with Mr. Averall to whom Mr. Becker introduced us. These gentlemen extended to us much advice as to the manner of getting a place to live and also on the customs and manners of dealing with the people.

While reading the morning's paper know as the "Yokohama Advertizer"[13] we found the following statement of our arrival: "It is reported that four Mormon missionaries have arrived in Japan. They will find the native apparel better than their wares." This revealed to us the fact that the name "Mormon" was known to Japan and that the people had been made aware of our coming. This, however, is but a beginning of the ill feeling which we found had been created by the efforts of wicked men who claimed to be ministers of Christianity.[14]

During this afternoon we had been hunting for a place to board which would be cheaper than at the hotel and at one place to which Bro Kelsch Bro Grant & Bro Ensign were directed they found suitable rooms but when they were about to accept them, the landlord said: "We have been expecting some Mormon preachers from Utah" The Brethern said that they were the ones and had just arrived the day before on the steamer Empress of India "Oh!" said he, "I cannot take you under any consideration After talking with him a few moments during which they asked him if he would not like to hear the other side of Mormonism, [~~but~~] he said that he did not and would not have anything to do with them or their money, so they left him and saught elsewhere for acomodiations.[15] Thus the very first effort which we made to be received by the people was a fruitless one and it gave evidence that the Devil was on the alert to check the work of the Lord in the land of Japan. We felt to thank God for the prospect of persecution for we felt that it would be the means of bringing us to the front and attracting many who otherwise would not take enough interest in us to investigate the cause which we represented.

I have had the pleasure of meeting Mr. Wm R. Clarke who had visited Salt Lake City about two years ago and whose father [~~was~~] is now the President of the Crystal Salt Works there. He [~~was~~] /is/ now on his way home from the Phillipenes where he has been visiting Gen. Chaffee of the U.S. Army. Gen. Chaffee is his uncle. It was a great delight to me to meet one who was acquainted with many of my friends, which I found he was; knowing a number with whome I was quite intimate among whom is Maud Patrick, Prest Snow's daughter Mable, Young, Bp. O. F. Whitney and Bro Ensign one of our party.

Mr. Clark introduced me to Count Georges Komaroffsky a Russiain General who had been in Manchuria during the contention over the right of Russia to occupy that province The trouble being settled he was now on his way home, via, India. In conversation with the Count I found that he was one of the few thinking men who did not condemn the Mormons for their [~~p~~] belief in the doctrine of polygamy, but on the contrary recognized the virtue of the principle and said that it would improve the moral condition of the human family if it were generally adopted.

After supper at the request of Mr. Sanford the acting manager of the hotel who had heard that Bro Ensign was a singer requested that he render some solos. Accordingly the parlor was prepared and Horace sang his way into the hearts of the guests and opened their eyes to the fact that there was something in the Mormon people which made them truly interesting. Thus we were favored of the Lord and won the respect of all and the way, we felt, was now beginning to open before us, and we had a very nice conversation on the teachings of Mormonism with a number of the guests.

Wednesday, 14 August 1901, Yokohama

We held our usual meeting before breakfast and had our customary morning prayer.

The Chinese Tailor to whom I had given an order for [~~some~~] /two/ light suits came in with one and it was an extreme pleasure to have on something cool. The Chinamen in this city are skilled workmen especially in tailoring and dress[~~ing~~] making, equal to any of the tailors in European or American counteries. They also are very rich many being bankers having as do the white men Japanese servants. They also make suits far cheaper than American dealers. I bought a pure duck suit (coat, dress vest, & pants) for 91/2 yen or $4.25 also a pongee silk suit for 20 yen or ten dollars, the equal of which in the U. S. would cost at least 30 yen or $15.00 and I doubt if it could be secured for that.

According to the appointment which we received Bro. Ensign and myself hired two rickshas and went out to Ponseforte's home or the Sheakspere Race Track. Mr. Ponseforte had at one time lived in Salt Lake City and was a member of the Church, but some twenty or twenty five years ago he came to Japan and married a Japanese woman. He also apostasied before leaving the U. S. He [~~had~~] died some two or three years ago but understanding that his wife and two children were alive and were keeping a boarding house we thought that perhaps they would have a kind feeling for us as we came from Mr. Ponseforte's former home and /some of us/ had seen him act upon the stage which was his profession. Bro Ensign and myself were received very kindly by Mrs. Ponseforte herself, but as her room charges were so high and it being nearly 2 miles from the heart of the city we could not as Mormon Missionaries stand the expense, and besides she kept a wayside inn where all kinds of liquors are sold and we did not care to jepordize our good name. Her son was 23 years old and had married a Japanese. Her daughter was 24 year old and had become a Catholic and had gone to a convent in France.

During our absence Bro Grant had found a place on what is known as the Bluff[16] but had not taken it as he wanted to consult us before doeing so. Bro Kelsch had called on a minister where he received a very cold reception but he succeeded in bringing [~~the~~] him to shame and reproved him for not being sufficiently charitable to give him the information which he wanted. Bro Kelsch made the call to get advice on securing text books on the Japanese language and the manner of studying them, but the minister refused utterly saying, "I cannot assist you in any way whatsoever." During the conversation this Rev. (?) gentleman betrayed the fact that all the preachers had, upon hearing that Mormon Missionaries were coming to Japan, united in the effort to crush us out. But Bro. Kelsch told the gentleman that we had come to stay and that we could get along without their assistance and could withstand their efforts to annilate us.

In the afternoon Bro Grant visited the editor of the "Herald"[17] (a Yokohama news paper) and they received him kindly and were anxious to learn of us and the cause which we represented. In the evening a Japanese editor of the largest Japanese newspaper /in Japan/ [came] published at Tokyo came from Tokyo to interview us. After an hour and a half's talk he went away with pictures of Utah, and leading men of our church also with a Book of Mormon and other matter pertaining to our people and Utah, their home. We also gave him the following address to the nation of Japan. . . .[18]

Thursday, 15 August 1901, Yokohama

Visited in company with Bro. Grant, a Mr. [Nappe] /Knapp/, the editor of the "Adveriser," also Mr. Stone an American Merchant.

In the afternoon we secured a suitable boarding place on the Bluff. The landlady on learning that we were the "Mormons" who had recently arrived in Yokohama, said that she was a little bit afraid of us, but that our money was as good as anyones [else] and, therefore, we could be made welcome. It seemed strange that we should be so suspicioned, yet her remark, that our money was as good as anybodies, showed a far less narrow mind than the man who refused /two days ago/ [us] /refused to take us/ in, because of our hard name, and was absolutely unwilling to hear anything good about us. We engaged accomodiation here for one month at $35.00 each, but as the rooms were not ready to go into we had to wait for [two] /one/ day[s]. The landladies name, we learned, was Parker.

Friday, 16 August 1901, Yokohama

Packed up our trunks preparatory to leaving the hotel for our boarding house on the Bluff. Left the hotel in time to take "tiffin" (Luncheon) at our new quarters. We found our home here to be quite pleasant. Situated in the midst of a profusion of vegetation with its mantle of green, our house appeared a monument in the centre of a garden sp[l]ot. The inconvenices of the place were few, but one could not expect to have all the comforts of home, especially in a land where civilization was far inferior to that of your native land. We rejoiced in having a place where we could sing and pray without being disturbed or without disturbing others, for our rooms were in a house separated a short distance from the main one and we were the only occupants of it.

Saturday, 17 August 1901, Yokohama

Very warm and unpleasant. During the afternoon we were visited by Mr. [Ushida] Koyama a Japanese laborer who came to see us (so he said, although he did not impress us favorably) for the purpose of "learning of our religion. We had a half a days talk with him during which he translated from the "Jiji" newspaper a long article upon the "Mormons."[19] He also translated two letters which Bro Grant had received from [other] Japanese residents of Tokyo. These letters all expressed a friendly feeling towards us but still there was a spirit /of insincerity in them/ [which they had] that did not appeal very strongly to us. In the evening again Bro Grant received another written in the Japanese characters. The translation has not yet been made because there was no one around the place sufficiently farmiliar with English to do so. The evening has been spent in singing; Horace as usual capturing the honors and winning the respect and appreciation of all the boarders.

Sunday, 18 August 1901, Yokohama

The first Sunday in Japan. The sun hot and the atmosphere oppressive. The entire day was spent in our rooms reading and writing.

Monday, 19 August 1901, Yokohama

During the day two Japanese call on us; one, Mr. Ushida who at one time went to school for about 4 months in the L.D.S. College.[20] His schooling, books, board, lodging and all expenses paid by the Church. He lived in the Bee Hive House[21] and was well acquainted with Thomaz Katsunuma who now lives in Honolulu, H. I. and is a member of the Church. Mr. Ushida is a simple laborer [and] at present painting ships for a living. He came with a Bible in his pocket and stated that he was a firm believer in Jesus Christ, and desired to know of our religion, for he was kindly disposed toward the "Mormons" because of the kindness which that had shown him while in Salt Lake City 7 years ago. He did, however, not understand English very well, so we were not able to make much head-way in explaining the plan of salvation to him.

The other gentleman who called was Mr. Koyama who had called to see us the day before. He did some translating for us and read the letter which Bro Grant had received the night before. We found that /the letter/ [it] was from Mr. Ketogi the brother of T. Katsunuma who was in Tokyo and very anxious to see Bro. Grant. Mr. Ketogi /wrote that he/ had been in Salt Lake City, and appreciated the kindness of the "Mormons" in helping him in the raising of silk. He also had lived (according to his statement) in the Bee Hive House.

During the day a number of other letters were received but it has been the experience of all foreigners, (especially missionaries) to have a great many gushing letters from the natives, and in most instances they have found them to be insincere, looking for work and for money more than for religion or friendship. I must confess that a majority of those which have called to see us, and claim to have desires to learn of our religion, have impressed me as fraudlent and absolutely devoid of an desires to assist us, but on the contrary that they are desireous of furthuring their own personal ends, for they are indeed a schreud and politic people. They impress me as being only skin deep and that their expressions of friendship and appreciation of our religious teachings come from their pockets rather than from their hearts. It is a recognized fact that the Japanese are a material class of people /generally/ [no]thing in which there is not a manifest gain in wealth or position or honor. And they put me in mind of the story told by Bro. Grant about the Indian, who said: "Lots of blankets, me good Mormon; no blankets me join the apostasize."

Tuesday, 20 August 1901, Yokohama

Another oppressive day. I have spent most of the time in my room conversing with a number of Japanese gentlemen, who have called on about the same business as the others had done. While I felt that it was a waste of time to /try to/ carry on a conversation with them and that I could more profitably be studying their language, yet I felt to make a friend by kindness and patience was preferable to making enemies because of a lack of charity. Besides the two gentlemen mentioned yesterday there was a Mr. Nakamura called to see us. He spoke very little English, and that was so peculiarly constructed that to understand what he did say was extremely difficult, but he seemed to be the most sincere visitor we [—] /have/ had so far.

In reading the papers for the last two or three days I find that the subject of Mormonism is being advertized extensively and that the different papers have taken sides and a heavy war is raging. In this, I rejoice, for we are getting advertized freely, and while many of the articles written concerning us are very severe and slanderous, yet it attracts attention [toward us] and the Devil in his efforts to malign us and bring to naught the work of the Lord is unconciously assisting materially to publish truth and righteousness to the inhabitants of this land as well as [in] all other lands where /he/ attempts to accomplish his evil purposes against the people of God.

Wednesday, 21 August 1901, Yokohama

We remained in our rooms practically all day; leaving only to get our meals and to make one trip in the afternoon to the tailors to see about some clothing which we had ordered. While in town we purchased a dressing gown each. These were made after the Japanese style and are called "Kamonas."[22] These "Kamonas" are made of a very thin fabric and serve as a very fine sitting gown during the extreme warm weather that is had in this country. So as soon as we returned with these Kamonas, we stripped off /all but our garments/ and sat around in these new articles of dress. The Japanese themselves, wear these Kamonas everywhere they go and in the interior towns a great many foreigners have adopted their use during the hottest days.

Thursday, 22 August 1901, Yokohama

The morning came cloudy and damp. Shortly after daylight the rain began to fall, and as showers are not common to Japan, it continued its downpour all day. The rain caused a cool wave to come in place of the hot one we had been having for so long, but the air became so fully charged with moisture that our faces and hands felt fully as wet and stickey as when we were sweating with the heat.

Not having anything important to do that would take us out into the storm we contented ourselves in studying the language and in reading and writing those things which we felt would be profitable to us. [He]I also assisted Bro Grant in preparing the following reply to an article which had appeared in the "Japan Daily Mail"[23] in which we were charged with preaching the doctrine of polygamy and which also stated that our proselyting in this land should be strictly prohibited by the government[al] officials. . . .

Friday, 23 August 1901, Yokohama

The receiving of letters from the native Japanese, aroused our desires to have the same kind of writing material that they use. So Bro. Kelsch and myself started in quest of it[,]. [and a] After visiting a number of Japanese stationary stores in which we found every kind of native souvenirs in the shape of writing material but the one kind which we had decided we would like to have, we were directed to a little "schack" looking place where were they manufactured paper. Here we found some Japanese who were unable to speak a word of English and we were fully half an hour getting them to understand what we wanted. They would nod their heads as if they understood what we were trying to explain to them but instead of showing us what we wanted they would pull down scrap-books, note-books, Account Books, blank newspaper sheets and infact [—] we saw /nearly/ everything in the store and were about to turn away in despair, when I spied a roll of paper on a top shelf. [and] Our trouble was over for it proved to be just the thing we were after. When the clerk took it down from the /shelf/ we nodded our heads and he broke into a hearty laugh as much as to say, "Who would of thought that a foreigner would have anything to do with Japanese writing paper."

This paper is purchased in rolls of about 25 or 30 yards and it is from 8 to 10 inches wide with a thickness about like tissue-paper, but it is very tough and durable. The Japanese unfold the paper off of this roll as they write, and instead of saying that they wrote a letter of so many pages, they measure it by the number of feet, yards, & etc. that they use. We purchased three of these rolls and also some Japanese [stamp] envelopes which are made of thin, tough paper and are long and narrow /in shape/ opening on the end instead of at the side.

Upon returning we found two representatives from the "Niroku Shimpo" newspaper published in Tokio. [this p] These gentlemen had called to learn more concerning our doctrines than what had been published already. This paper had published five successive articles on the Mormons and their history and they had come to learn particularly /of/ the difference in doctrine between our Faith and and the beliefs of other Christians. Upon hearing the interpetitation of the articles already published (which articles were indeed carefully prepared and just in their representation of our past and present /history./) we felt free to explain completely our standing concerning the principle of polygamy and the other doctrines peculiar to Mormonism alone. We also gave these gentlemen the /April &/ May numbers of the Improvement Era containing James E. Talmage's articles on the "Philosophy of Mormonism."[24] They took [dinner] tiffin with us and expressed themselves as being more than satisfied with their interview. We also had a call from Mr. Ushida. The day continued rainy and damp.

Saturday, 24 August 1901, Yokohama

One month ago to-day I left my home in Salt Lake City. I have been in Japan thirteen days and as a reminder of the day /when I left home/ I have written a long letter to my brother Samuel describing some of the things which are of interest to all who visit this wonderful country.

This evening I noticed an article in the "Japan Herald" stating that the government officials in the Department of Home Affairs, had under advisement the propriety of allowing the "Mormon missionaries" to proselyte in Japan, but as yet they had not decided what to do in the matter. This is a land of religious freedom, but the practice of polygamy is strictly against the law and because of the false reports that we intended to preach this doctrine, the government has been led to have some fears concerning us. "Rumor hath many tongues, but most of them lie."

Being away from home [and] in a strange land among a strange people, and being made an object for public comment much of which is extremely unfavorable, and lastly to become a subject for discussion /[suspicioned]/ by the government officials /and suspicioned by them/ [who officiate as /the/ head /men/ of the country, [would,] /is,/ perhaps, [be] sufficient reason to create in the heart of some a feeling of homesickness[nes] but with me I can go to my slumbers to-night with a happy heart never more joyous before, elated to think that I am in the world as a messenger of the Lord Jesus Christ and glad to suffer if need be for the glory of his name.

Sunday, 25 August 1901, Yokohama

This Sunday has been partly rain and partly sunshine, but quite pleasant throughout because of a gentle breeze which has blown softly all the day. We had breakfast about 8:30 am after which we held our regular morning meeting; singing the songs of Zion and praying unto Our Heavenly Father.

During the afternoon we were interviewed by two editors from Tokio representing the Japanese newspaper "Skakwai Shimpo." There names were S. Nakakuki and T. Yamasaki. In answer to their questions regarding our doctrines we gave them the following tracts: "A Friendly Discussion," by Ben E. Rich, "Morgan's Tracts" nos. 1 & 2, "Brief History of the Church" by Edw. H. Anderson, and Pres. L. Snow's "Greeting to the World."

They brought with them a letter of introduction from Mr. Katogi with whom Bro. Grant had become acquainted while in Tokio a few days ago. (This Mr. Katogi is [also] the same /person/ as mention heretofore in this journal.) These gentlemen told us that there was a great desire on the part of many [influential] /influential/ Japanese living in Tokio to meet us, and if we would go to Tokio that they wanted to call a large meeting and give us the oppertunity of addressing, through an interpreter, the Japanese people. They also said that the proprietor of their paper Mr. Oda told them that he would take great delight in introducing us to the people of his country. They also were the bearers of a message from Mr. Matsuoka, whom they said was a venerable gentleman of Tokio, telling us that he would furnish us a house without charging rent, if we would only come to Tokio. This great outpouring of hospitality so dazzles us that we pause to have the inspiration of the Lord on our acceptance of it, for no time in the history of our church has such a feeling been exhibited toward our missionaries in any land and the surprise is so great that we are almost led to suspicion the authors of it.

Is it the prayers of the [people of God] /Saints/ that is causing the Lord to turn the hearts of this people [of] unto us his servants? Is it that this nation is famished for the word of God, and have been seeking for it but found it not because it was not in their midst? Is it that the blood of Israel flows /so freely/ [largly] in their veins [and] /that/ they recognize /immediately/ the voice of the good shephard and their hearts leap with joy [at his words] /when they hear his/ call? Or is it that the Lord is testing us to see if we will follow after the gushing and flattery of men? Or is it the Evil One thinking to deceive the servants of God and cause them to fall into transgression or be ensnared in the traps of their enemies? These are questions which arise in our minds and [the beating of our hearts] we feel like consulting the Lord before advancing any further lest we do that which will be detrimental to our work in the future.

The Japanese are such a peculiar people that the gift of discernment is necessary to be able to understand the spirit [~~that~~] /which/ prompts their actions.

[~~Bros~~] Bros. Kelsch and Ensign who have been on other missions say that the interest manifested /in us/ is truly remarkable; entirely different to anything they have met with and consequently /they too are/ at a loss to understand the reason for it. We also gave tracts to Mr. Hiroi who called on us to learn of our doctrines. He is undoubtedly a well educated man and speaks good English.

Monday, 26 August 1901, Yokohama

A beautiful sunlight morning. Before breakfast I took a bath in a typical Japanese style.[25] The bath tubs, bath houses, and the manner of heating the water is very peculiar. A majority of the bath houses in the homes of the natives, consists of a room /or properly speaking a shed/ walled in on three sides, the other side being entriely open. This /room/ is some times covered over with a roof, but more often it is left open [~~to~~] during the summer months. The floor is made of boards, arranged after the style of a [~~wash~~] carriage washing platform, so that the water which is thrown onto the floor will drain into a sink or run into a little trough which conducts [~~the water~~] /it/ into one of the many drainage ditches so common to the Land of Japan.

The tub is oblong in shape and is made of wood bound together by hoops similar to those on /an ordinary wash/ [~~a~~] tub, in fact they are both made on the same principle, differing only in shape and depth—the bath-tub being about twice the depth of [~~the~~] /a/ wash-tub. The dimensions of the standard sized tub are about as follows: 4 ft. long, 2 ft. 3 in. wide, and 2 ft. deep. When in position, the tub is elevated from the floor about 6 [~~inch~~] inches by means of /4/ blocks of wood /which are placed under the bottom/ [~~one at~~] two on each side, and occupies a place next to the wall opposite the side which is open. In one end of the tub there is a little /iron lined/ cement stove [~~with iron lining~~]. This stove is round in shape, and about [~~the size of common American stove~~] five /or/ six inches in diameter. Four or five lengths of small piping is attached to the top /to/ convey the smoke, and there is also a part of the pipe petitioned off to carry a draft down to the fire box. When a warm or hot bath is wanted, a fire is started in this stove and the tub filled with as much water as may be desired. It takes about ten minutes for the stove to get hot and from an hour to an hour and a half for the water to be heated to the proper temperature. The slowness with which the water heats, enables one to [~~bathe~~] finish bathing before it gets too hot, but great care must be taken not to allow [~~your~~] /ones/ person to come in contact with the stove itself, for it is generally hot enough to blister the skin.

Fastened to [~~a hook to~~] one of the rafters in the roof, or if there is no roof to a bamboo pole put across from one side to the other, is a hook on which a bucket is hung [~~w~~] containing from 5 to 8 gals. of water. Attached to the bottom of the bucket is a tin sprayer very much like the head and /a/ small portion of the neck of a sprinkling can. [~~only larger.~~] The hole leading into the sprayer is stopped /up/ by a wooden or rubber cork to which a string is attached and put through a small pully hanging directly over the center of the bucket. This string hangs down on the outside of the bucket so that the person taking a bath can [~~regulate~~] regulate the flow of the water. [~~It is~~] It is quite pleasant after having a warm bath to finish up by taking a cold water shower [~~as~~] after this fashion.

The shower /bath/ is not original with the Japanese, but seeing it in other countries, they have adopted /it/ in their own. Where there is a water and sewerage system they have all the modern appliances, but in places where these things are not, the above has been substituted, and [~~it it~~] like many other little things it illustrates the genius of this people. Warm baths are seldom taken in the Summer, [~~but~~] the shower or tub of cold water, being far more in keeping with the intense heat.

The [~~aw~~] /atmosphere/ being so damp it is seldom, if ever, that the floor of a bath house is dry, and the result is that the wood moulds and rotts very rapidly. The tubs themselves smell musty, and at first I could hardly stand to bathe in them, but use has driven away that repulsive feeling, and I now feel myself becoming quite a Japanese. These bath rooms as well as all the rooms of the house [~~are do~~] are taken care of by native female servants, and among the /high and middle class/ Japanese [~~themselves~~] it is quite impossible for them to have a bath without the assistance of one or more of their servants. [It] /This/ is also true of many foreigners, [that] But as a rule /with foreigners/ these servants are taught to leave the room after they have prepared the bath, but to remain near /by/ in case their assistance is needed. The bath room connected with the place in which we are stopping, and in which I had my bath this morning, is entirely closed in, and has some other conviences besides those found in the ordinary Japanese home.

The first time I took a bath the servant came about 7:30 in the morning to my room, and informed me that my bath was ready. Accordingly I got out of bed, slipped on my pants and started, towel in ha/n/d, for the bath room. Just before entering the door I had to go through a narrow passage way, not large enough [to p] for two to pass without bumping each other, and to my astonishment I saw this servant standing /near the bath room door/ with her back closed up against the wall. I went right ahead, however, and squeezed past and entered the room, looked at the tub of water and nodded to her saying, "I am much obliged, it will do very nicely." She smiled, but evidently did not understand me, for she did not move a peg. I hated to shut the door in her face but as she did not move I had to. Locking this door I went over to the another which led out into the yard [but I co] and found it [unlocked] had nothing /with which/ to fasten it, [with] so I had to let it go, trusting that good luck would keep any body from coming in on me while I was bathing. After closing a window which /had been left/ [was] half open I ventured to undress /but/ all the time keep looking around to see if there was not some other place through which some one would be peeping at me. Finally I got into the tub and took a swift wash. [forgetting, however, /in the excitement/ to wash my face and ears.] When I got dressed again I bethought myself that I had not washed all my body,—not even [taken] cleaned the gum out of my eyes—so I turned loose again and finished my bath by washing my face and ears, which in the excitement I had forgotten were dirty.

When I came out of the bath room the servant was still standing in practially the same position. I smiled /as I passed/ and she smiled back, but since then, she has learned that her assistance is not needed in helping the Mormon Missionaries take their baths, so when the tub is filled now, she goes about other duties, and [I feel less timid in venturing to undress] things work more harmonously all around.

After breakfast we held our regular morning meeting and there being nothing for me to do /particularly/ I spent the greater part of the day in studying.

Tuesday, 27 August 1901, Yokohama

As I had been up quite late the night before, I felt very tired and indisposed to [get up] /leave my bed/, but Bro. Kelsch who is my bedfellow [is such] got up and made [an early bird] /such a noise/ that it was impossible for me to sleep. The custom in the morning is, for him to have his bath first [and] mine coming immediately after[w] so when he comes back into the room and finds that I am not up he starts to urge me out of bed and as I lie there listening to his repeated requests [for me to go and have my bath it reminds me of the] /which gradually grow into threats and commands,/ I am reminded of the many [times] /similar scenes/ at home when my mother has stood by my bedside [and urged] and urged for [half and then] /a quarter & sometimes a half an/ hour before I would respond to her wishes. This morning I told him that I wished he would not nag at me so much as he reminded me of home /and mother/ and there was danger of making me homesick. He replied that [I] my mother had told him on the evening of our departure to be both a father and a mother to me and I must confess that he fills mother's place quite well when it comes to [arousing me] /getting me up/ in the morning.

I did not eat any breakfast but devoted myself to fasting and prayer.

During a great part of the day I was occupied in altering or remodeling my garments.[26] [which] /They/ were so large for me that I had to undress in bed; fearing that in walking around [that] I would step in the crouch [of the garments] /of [the] garment,/ which hung down to my knees, and trip myself. This kind of a fit was too un[pleasant]/comfortable/ to be pleasant so I concluded to [take] /cut/ a strip about eight inches wide out, of the middle and attach the upper and lower ends together again thus making a better fit in length anyway. It looked easy enough to do but I found that it took me about four hours and then did not have a very artistic appearance, but [looked] perhaps quite in accord with a majority of batchelor's needlework. The general /appearance,/ however, was so much improved and the fit so much more comfortable that I felt no chagrin at the ackward stitches which I had made.

[~~Bro Grant returned from Tokio about 4 p.m. where he had been~~] Bro Grant went to Tokio in the morning to meet the United States Consul and also to secure from him any assistance or advice that could be given regarding the securing of a licence to proselyte in this land. He returned about 4 p.m. but had not secured the licence because the Government officer who issued them had gone away for the day. He, however [~~meet~~] met with Mr. [blank] the U. S. Consul[27] and [~~while~~] was received /by him/ with the greatest of courtesy, Mr. [blank] told Bro Grant that while [~~he was not of the same religious belief as himself and therefore he could not wish him success in his work of spreading "Mormonism," but that he~~] /the teachings of Mormonism were entirely contrary to his own religious belief[s] and that he, therefore could not concienciously wish us success in our work, yet he/ would see that [~~as~~] all [~~much~~] of the rights and privilages enjoyed by other sects should be accorded us and that his influence would be used at all times in securing for us the rights of American citizens.

We expected to have Mr. Clarke whom [‡] we had met while staying at the Grand Hotel, (see August 13th) call on us in the evening but he did not come. [~~but~~] About 8:30 or 9 o'clock his Japanese friend, "Mr. Genji Kuribara called to tell us that Mr. Clarke had received a telegram stating that the U.S. Transport "Grant" would sail for America from Nagasaki Aug 30˝ and that he had [~~to~~] left hurridly in order to be in time to take passage home on that ship and that he regretted very much not being able to say good-bye.

We found Mr. Kuribara a most interesting and talented man. He spoke English with most excellent grammatical accuracy. He had been anxious to see us and learn of our doctrines as he had been in Salt Lake City twice and had also visited quite often the town of Independence Missiouri from which he had heard the Mormons were driven many years ago. He possessed a spirit which appealed to us most force[~~fully~~]ably and altho he was a polished and refined Japanese gentleman yet he had a most genial and humble [~~spirit~~] /manner/ into which pride or selfesteem did not enter.

After he had gone we all symeltaneously remarked that at last we had found a man whose heart seemed right before the Lord, and that surely he must be one of the chosen seed. He listened with marked attention to the explaination of our doctrines and expressed a desire to receive some of our literature [~~when we obtain a licence to perform our work in this land~~] /as soon as we are permitted to distribute it./ He is a teacher in a large school in the northern part of this (the main) island. His address is: "Chugakko, Yonezawa Japan.

Wednesday, 28 August 1901, Yokohama

A severe rain storm continued during the morning, but the afternoon was very pleasant. Our morning meeting lasted from 9 [~~am~~] until 11 a.m. The question of whom to decide upon as a teacher of the Japanese language, was the main subject considered. [~~for out of the~~] /Altho/ many names [~~which~~] had been suggested [~~we had not had very favorable impressions but felt that~~] /to us, yet we had [~~not received had no~~] not been favorably impressed/ with the manner or apparent capabilities which they possess/ed/ as teachers, consequently we had not accepted the offers of any, but we feel now that our time is being almost lost and that some little assistance, even from a poor source, would be better than none at all. Bro Kelsch and Ensign were directed to try and find one of the gentlemen who had called upon us and had applied to teach us, and endeavor to secure his services as an [~~tutor~~] /instructor/ for the remaining two weeks that we expected to stay in Yokohama. (The opinion[s] of nearly all the friends that we have made is, that we would find it, by far more profitable to go to Tokio where there are fewer foreigners, a higher class of natives, a more religious sentiment, and by far better instructors in the language and much cheaper living. But as we had engaged our present quarters in Yokohama for a month we could not afford to leave here until we had received the full value of our money. Consequently, it will be still two weeks before our month will be up and then we intend to go to Tokio or some other strictly Japanese [~~town~~] place where we will come in contact with the language continually. But as time is money with the missionary and it is his duty to use every moment in efforts to spread the Gospel we feel that two weeks without any advancement in this language would be a serious loss and waste of time; hence the decision in our meeting this morning.)

Immediately after our meeting we were visited by Mr. Hiroi (See Aug 25") who had become much interested in us and our doctrine. He called to say good-bye to us before he left for a little town in the southern part of the country where he was engaged in school-teaching. This man is a Christian and [became] /was/ a preacher of the German Evangelical Church for many years, but [is now] /became/ disgusted with their teachings, and gave up the ministry. We gave him some tracts when he called on us some days ago, and he expressed himself as being well pleased and that they had started his mind into a channel which he felt would finally lead him to the acceptance of "Mormonism."

While at tiffin we received word from one of the boarders that a mail from America had arrived during the morning. The words "Mail from America" had a great significance to us and we lost no time /in/ dispatching [one] some of our party to the Post Office and to The "Brandenstein Tea Co's" office in whose care much of our mail would come, /to see if any letters had come for us./ This duty fell upon Bros. Kelsch and Ensign who had other things to do in town.

The mails which had [add] arrived heretofore had brought letters for all the other missionaries but I was left out in the cold. This, however, did not worry me in the least, for the time had past so rapidly since I left home, that I had none but the most favorable feelings concerning [their] /the/ condition and wel[l]fare of my folks; in fact I hardly seemed to realize that I was so far away from home, and had not seen any of my relatives or friends for over a month. [There] And as I had left no address to which they might send me letters I did not expect any by the mail which arrived to-day, but when the brethren came back and handed me two letters I took them with as much eagerness and joy as ever filled the heart of a Mormon Missionary on receiving his first news from home. [An efforts to describe those feelings would be useless for] The letters were from Mother and Sister Empey, conveying the messages of health, happiness, content, and love.

I saw also [by] /in/ a letter received by Bro Grant from Bp. Empey that the following had been chosen to fill [my] the vacancies caused by my departure. My brother Samuel was called to be First Councelor to Prest. Geo E. Woolley in the Mutual Improvement Association[28] and Malcolm Butter was chosen as Second Councelor, taking the place of Imer Pett who had moved from the Ward. Bro Leonard Ruckert was chosen [to] as acting teacher on the 6th Block together with my former companion, Christian Pieper.

The brethren who went in search of a teacher of the Japanese language, were unable to find the one they wanted so we were forced to let the matter rest for a day or two. I retired /about 10 p.m./ feeling thankful for the good news /which I had received/ from home.

Thursday, 29 August 1901, Yokohama

Pleasant sunshiney day. I spent /most of/ the day in study. During the afternoon we received the following card from Mr. Hiroi (See Aug. 28") written from Yokohama, Aug. 29th 1901: "My Dear Mormon Missionaries! Thanks to God to have had **a great pleasure** of seeing you again yesterday. I am leaving this city to-morrow for a while. May God bless you and your work here. Blessed are the messengers of Jesus Christ who are [appointed] persecuted for **the heaven appointed** mission. With best wishes, I remain, Very truly Yours T. Hiroi" (The parts in this letter with the black line underneath is to remind any who may read it [they is] /that they/ are not mistakes /made/ through copying, but that they are the [correct] /exact/ words of the author.)

This card made our hearts rejoice and we hope and pray that God will enlighten this man's mind that he may see the truth of the Gospel, and become a member of the fold of Christ. When Mr. Hiroi first called upon us, (Aug. 25") we were favorably impressed with the Spirit that he mani[fe]fested, and the receiving of the above card, makes our impressions of him more substancial.

During the evening I wrote a long letter home to my mother, in answer to hers of yesterday.

Upon [ree] reading the paper /(Herald)/ we discovered that the /editor of the/ Japan Mail" had published an article in the morning issue in which he made some severe attacks upon the "Mormons" and in the most unsavory terms referred to /the/ marriage relations of Apostle Grant.[29] The following is a sample of the lava which ran from his pen: "Whatever may be said for the industry and sincerity of the "Mormons," there is no gainsaying the fact that many of them practice polygamy and are consequently leading a life which shocks the moral susceptibilities of 999 Christians out of every thousand. No man who controls a hotel or a lodging house would be acting properly towards his ordinary guests if he gave accommodations to "Mormons." The entire article was written in defence of /the action[s] of/ a Mr. Staniland, [who was /is/] the keeper of a boarding house [in refusing to take us in because we were "Mormons."] /[who had refused] in refusing us accommodations because we were "Mormons."/ (See Aug. 13th)

Friday, 30 August 1901, Yokohama

Another beautiful day! The air has been so refreshing and cool that I have secceeded in overcoming much of the languid feeling which the warm days and caused to come over me. In the morning Mr. Uchida called on us and we engaged him as a tutor in the language. He returned again in the evening and gave us our first lesson.

The time between breakfast /and dinner/ was spent mostly in preparing a reply to the attack made upon us by the editor of the "Japan Daily Mail." The following is a copy of the reply as it appeared in the issue of Sept. 3rd 1901. . . .

While at supper I became acquainted with a Mr. Pierce who was a guest of one of the boarders. He did not Know that we were the "Mormons" until we had gone to bed, when the landlady told him. He expressed himself as much pleased to have seen us and was suprised at our /similarity to/ other men. [Meeting Mr. Pierce]

Saturday, 31 August 1901, Yokohama

Our teacher spent most of the [fore n] day with us, [Durin] but was not able to give much of a lesson because of so many [ea] visitors calling to see us. During the morning we had a long conversation upon the principles of the Gospel with two Japanese gentlemen from the Bible Society. There names were Mr. U. Yamasaki and Mr. [blank]. Mr. Yamasaki said that he was studying to become a preacher in the Baptist Church. They both could speak English fairly and seemed to be interested in the explaination of the principles of our faith. We extended to them an invitation to call as often as they desired and they accepted it kindly saying that they would be glad to meet with us again. They called on us to-day in response to an invitation given them by Bros. Kelsch and Ensign when they were at the Bible Society /some days ago/ in search of a /Japanese/ Bible written in roman letters.

In the afternoon I wrote [and] postal cards to the following of my [relatives] /cousins/: Perry, Little, Bp. Ed. Little, Geo. Little, Mrs Dean Young, Mrs. Howard Wallace, /[and]/ Mrs. Heber Bevins, and Mrs. Ted Paul; I also sent a card to my friend and neighbor Miss. Grace Frost. (See July 26")

About 4 o'clock in the afternoon we were visited by an old gentleman named /George/ Albert Allcot. He had been anxious to meet the "Mormon" missionaries and Mrs. Parker our landlady introduced him to us. He was a very talkative person and had but few good words for the Japanese people.

After supper we sat [in our room] /out in the garden/ together, talking over the future [as we then viewed it and the] /and the problems which it presented./ It was a beautiful moon-light evening and there [was nothing was not /which/ not broke the] came a gentle breeze from off the ocean that filled the air [[—] occasional cry of the beggar as he passed along the street] /with a freshness most delightful. As we looked from our elevated position out over the city/ below /we could see/ thousands of flickering lights which burned as if in rivality [with] to the starry brightness of the sky. Among the quivering branches of the trees the "katy-dids"[30] were singing with buzzing harmony their evening songs, and upon our ears [their] there fell the occasionl cry of [the] a blind beggar as he wandered through the streets below in search [for] /of/ alms. In the distance there [came] /arose/ the assuring [signal] sound of the night watch-man's signal, which as he came nearer grew louder & louder then died away /again/ as he passed along his beat. [The tranquility of the night /surroundings/ was reflected in an /us/ and we rejoiced in the past, drank in the joy of the present and].

As we sat there drinking in the beauty of the surroundings, our hearts were filled with tranquility; [and] our minds wandered [through] /back to the scenes of [of]/ the past; and our hopes hastened on to view the events of the future. We thought of home, with its familiar faces, its joys, its sorrows, and all its endearing features, [and] /but/ as the longing to be back /again/ amid those scenes crept over us, the path of duty [arose] /appeared/ before our eyes. And as we looked along its course, beholding in the distance the glorious future to which it led [us] the pleasures, joys, and brightness [of the past fled from before the contem /were lost in the contentempl/ plation ation of the happiness and blessings] of all that we had left behind/ faded from before the contemplation of that coming /day/ when our hearts would be made glad in the salvation of the [pe] souls of men. Indeed, the Happiness of the past [was] became as the darkness of night which flees [from before] /from/ the light and glory of the day.

We went to our rooms [with] and poured out our souls to God, expressing the thanks[giving] which we felt for his blessings and mercy. To the /sweet/ strains of music which came from a neighboring house we dropped off to sleep and in slumber [welcomed] /bid farewell/ to the Month of August and welcomed [with dreams] the dawn of September's morn.

Sunday, 1 September 1901, Yokohama

This being fast day we ate no breakfast, but went out into the woods about eleven o'clock to hold a prayer meeting. After about a twenty minutes walk from our rooms, we came to a secluded spot in a small grove situated on the south slope of one of the rolling hills lying to the south of Yokohama and about mid-way between the foreign residences on the Bluff and the bay.[31]

sitting down in a circle on the ground, we opened our meeting by singing, "We thank Thee Oh God for a Prophet." Bro. Grant offered the opening prayer which was followed with another prayer by Bro. Kelsch. Sang, "Now let us rejoice in the day of salvation", after which Bro. Ensign continued in prayer and without changing from our kneeling position our supplication was continued, myself being mouth. The principal features of our prayers were expressions of thanksgiving and praise to God; invocations for strength to preform the duties that rested upon us as missionaries in this land; and also that the Spirit of God would rest upon Apostle Grant to the extent that he would be able to offer up an acceptable dedicatory prayer: for the main object of our going into the woods was to dedicate this land unto the Lord for the proclaimation of the Gospel. After the four prayers had been offered up, we sang, "Come come ye saints." We again knelt in a circle and Bro. Grant offered up the dedicatory prayer.[32]

His tongue was loosed and the Spirit rested mightily upon him; so much so that we felt the angels of God were near for our hearts burned within us as the words fell from his lips. I never experienced such a peaceful influence or heard such a powerful prayer before. Every word penetrated into my very bones and I could of wept for joy. The following is an outline of the prayer, as I remember it:—

(a)—An appeal unto the Lord to hear the words that would be uttered.

(b)—An expression of thanks for the preservation of our lives; for the testimony of the Gospel which we had in our hearts; and for the great blessing of being considered worthy in the eyes of the Prophet of the Lord[33] to go a messengers of life and salvation unto a people who had never heard the Gospel.

(c)—An entreaty for the forgivness of our sins.

(d)—Dedication of the land for the proclaimation of the Truth and for the bringing to pass of the purposes of the Lord concerning the gathering of Israel[34] and the establishment of righteousness upon the earth.

(e)—By the power of the Priesthood and in the name of Jesus, Satan was commanded to release his hold upon the minds of the people, and rebuked in his efforts to overcome the work of the Lord in this land.

(f)—Words of praise unto God for preserving the people of Japan from the power of the Great and Abominable Church,[35] and that he had blessed them with sufficient knowledge to see the shallowness of the man-made Christianity which was sough to be introduced among them.

(g)—Petitioned the Lord to touch the hearts of the people that they might know that we were men of virtue, honor, and devotion, and that we had come among them to do them good; that their minds might be directed into channels of religious thought, and their hearts prepared to recognize the truth when it was declared unto them, being even as sheep, quick to recognize the voice of the shepherd.

(h)—Thanks for the talents with which we had been blessed and a dedication of them to the work of the Lord.

(i)—A request that we be endowed with ever, qualification needed in opening up this mission.

(j)—A prayer for the Church and the Priesthood.

(k)—A personal mention of the goodness of the Lord in preserving the life of Apostle Grant during the severe attack of sickness which he had, some years ago been called upon to pass through; when he was given up to die by nearly all his friends. He felt that the Lord had restored him to come upon this mission.

(l)—Thanks for the companions which he had. For the integrity of Bro. Kelsch who had been in the mission field for the past ten years, but was willing to come to this land and continue his labors for the salvation of souls; for the ready heart of Bro. Ensign in responding cheerfully to the call to go out and preach the Gospel, in spite of the fact that he had but lately returned from a mission to Colorado; and for his youthful companion "even Alma" who in spite of his youth had been favored of the Lord with much intellegence and knowledge, and a love for the truth which caused him to accept joyfully the call to come to this land and devote himself to the spread of truth. He asked his Heavenly Father to continue in blessing me with furthur knowledge and power to use the same in righteousness, that I might become as Alma of old, full of the Spirit and powerful in the Word of God.[36]

(m)—Words of gratitude for the love that we had for each other and the unity which existed among us.

(n)—A request that the Three Nephites[37] would visit us and assist us in our work.

(o)—Spoke of the righteousness of Lehi[38] and of the great faith of Nephi[39] in doing whatsoever the Lord commanded him. Also spoke of those, who because of iniquity, had been cut off from among the Nephites[40] and cursed with a dark skin like unto the Lamanites[41] their brethren, and said we felt that through the liniage of those rebellious Nephites who joined with the Lamanites, that the blood of Lehi and Nephi had been transmitted unto the people of this land, many of whom have the features and manners of the AMERICAN INDIANS.[42] Asked the Lord that if this were true, that he would not forget the integrity of his servants Lehi and Nephi and would verify the promises made unto them concerning their descendants in the last days, upon this people, for we felt that they were a worthy nation.

After this dedicatory prayer had been offered up, we sang, "The time is far spent." Following this, Bro. Grant read the prayer offerd by Apostle Orson Hyde when upon the Mt. of Olives dedicating the land of Palestine for the gathering and future home of the Jews.[43] Bro. Grant, Bro. Kelsch, Bro. Ensign, and myself, spoke in the order named; expressing the feelings of our hearts and telling of our love for each other and our earnest desires and determination to labor with all the zeal which we possessed for the success of the work of the Lord in this land. We then sang, "O my Father." Before dismissing we considered the advisability of separating into twos and going into the interior of the country. We all seemed favorable to this movement. Closing song, "God moves in a mysterious way." Benidection was offered by Bro. Ensign.

Monday, 2 September 1901, Yokohama

Cloudy, but close and oppressive. Held our regular meeting, in which we decided to change teachersof the Japanese language. Mr. Uchida who was giving us lessons seemed very incompitent so we decided to write to Mr. Koyama (see journal A Aug. 17th.) and secure his services if possible.

During the afternoon I wrote letters to my nephew Theadore Taylor and Mrs. Charles Strong. Bro. Grant went to Tokyo, expecting to stay over night so that he would be in time in the morning to catch the Secy. of The Religion Bureau in his office, and secure from him a a permit to proselyte in this land.

Tuesday, 3 September 1901, Yokohama

A severe rain had been falling during the entire night, and continued its downpour throughout the greater part of the day. I the forenoon Bro. Kelsch and myself took a walk into the city for the purpose of seeing if any mail had come from home, as a steamer had arrived from America during the night. We found mail for Bro. Grant and Bro. Ensign but none for us. Knowing that Bro. Ensign would be anxiously waiting for us to return with the mail, we thaught that we would take a walk around the town, and thus let him feel a little of the disappointment which we had done, in not receiving any letters. During our walk we went into a number of little Japanese stores to look at the numerous variety of trinkets which they kept for sale. I bought me a silk, ten-ribbed, steel rod umbrella for five yen, or two and a half American gold dollars. I also bought two silk flags, one the STARS and STRIPES, and the other a Japanese flag. I purchased them that they might be hung side by side in our room. For these I paid the paltry sum of five American cents. When we got back we found that Bro. Grant had returned from Tokyo, and he as well as Bro. Ensign were anxiously waiting our return, and the two and a half hours that we had been gone seemed to them as if it were an age. Of course we laughed at their suspense and felt partially repaid for not receiving any mail.

Bro. Grant had found out what was necessary for us to do in order to get permission to promulgate the Gospel in this land but had not received it from the officers of the government in Tokyo, as the power rested in the hand of the authorities in this city. Had he known this before, it would have saved this, as well as a number of other trips to Tokyo, but he having been told by what was considered good authority that licence must be obtained from the head officers of the government, having headquarters at Tokyo, had therefore acted upon their advice.

In the evening Mr. Koyama called on us in answer to the letter we sent to him yesterday. We told him that we would like him to teach us during the time we expected to remain in Yokohama. He accepted the offer and we arranged to receive our first lesson from him the following day at 2 p.m.

Wednesday, 4 September 1901, Yokohama

Weather fair;nobreeze and very warm. At two o'clock in the afternoon Bro. Ensign and myself attend-the marriage ceremony of one of our companion boarders. The marriage took place in Christ's Church (Church of England) before a small audience of about twelve people, and was attended by no great demonstration whatever. The bridegroom was a resident of China but had come to Yokohama to meet his bride, who arrived yesterday from America, where her home was and where she and her husband had met, while he was at college studying medicine. He is not only a practioner of medicine in China, but is also an officer in the Young Men's Christian Association[44] established there.

Being an active worker in this religious movement he had become so badly wrapped up Modern Christianity that he manifest but little love for the Mormons, and did not appreciate their society to any marked degree, consequently when he came to inviting the other boarders to attend his marriage he was forced to extend his invitation to us ("The Mormons"), still he did not care to have us accept, for he managed to invite us second handidly through the landlady. We realized the slight, but not desireing to have any comment on the part of the other boarders, or any criticism to be made because of not accepting the invitation, even though it was second handed, we decided that two of us had better attend, and the other two would favor the feelings of the doctor by staying away. The doctor's name is [blank]

During the afternoon we also took a number of pictures of ourselves, the rest of the boarders, and some of the surrounding of our home here.

Upon returning from the marriage ceremony, we had our first lesson in Japanese under the instruction of Mr. Koyama, and it proved very satisfactory indeed.

Thursday, 5 September 1901, Yokohama

We noticed that the "Japan Mail" of yesterhay had an article written in answer to our letter which we had published in that periodical the day before. (see journal A.Aug. 30th.) In their editorial they accused us of avoiding the main question of the discussion, viz polygamy, upon which they claimed to have based their opinion that no "Mormon should be admitted into a boarding house or hotel. To this editorial we prepared and sent to the paper the following reply. . . .

Most of the afternoon was taken up in reciting our lesson in Japanese. The lesson to-day has been a very interesting one, indeed, and with the blessings of the Lord I feel that I will be able to express myself fairly well in the native language of this people in two or three months.

Friday, 6 September 1901, Yokohama

In company with Bro. Grant and the other Brethren, I called on the U.S. Consul[45] in this city, to receive from him any advice that he might be able and willing to give, concerning the sending of an application to police headquarters to get permission to preach and distribute tracts in this country. We were received by the Consul very cordially, and after passing a few jokes concerning the manner in which the newspapers had been discussing the "Mormon" question, he told us that his advice would be to make our application in writing, and also to see that the answer was made in writing, so that we could have the evidence, that we had made proper application and had received licence from the proper authority, in case there should be any complaint made against us or any question arise that would need documentary evidence. Acting upon this advice we applied to the Chief of Police to find out just what kind of an application was required in order to comply with the requirements of the law. As there was no law specifying what particular form an application demanded, he said that he would have to consult with the Governor of the Prefecture, and that he would send us word when he had found out the particulars.

Brother Grant left us at the Police Headquarters and went off in another direction to fill an appointment which he had made with Mr. Stone. The other three of us went down to the warf and rode out to the steamer ("Empress of India") which was anchored in the harbor, to see the officers and take another look at the ship which had brought us to this distant shore, before it started on its homeward voyage. We saw and shook hands with the captain, 1st officer, ex-second officer, chief engineer, chief and assistant pursers, doctor, stewart, and a number of the sailors with whom we had become acquainted while on our voyage from America. They all seemed glad to see us, and it, indeed, felt good to be on board the ship which had become during our voyage, almost a home to us, and when we thought that it would soon be on its way home, it made us fell kind of sad to think that we were not going back, also,. We stayed on board for about an hour, but were forced to leave as the time drew near for its departure.

We rode back to the shore in a little launch belonging to the Grand Hotel. With longing eyes we stood on the shore and watched it as it moved gently out of the harbor, and we felt as though we were parting with a dear friend. But still we were happy in the thaught that we had come to this land for the purpose of winning souls unto Christ, and looked forward to the time when we would have accomplished our labors here, and be able to return in greater triumph then if we were returning now.

After dinner we had our regular lesson in Japanese.

Bro. Grant had been invited to take a ten days trip through the country with Mr. Stone who was going out to buy up silk. As Mr. Stone was going to be accompanied by a very proficient interpreter,[46] it was thaught by us all that it would perhaps be a long time before such an opportunity to see the country would be had again and that Bro. Grant would be about to observe much that would be of benefit to us in the future.[47] Consequently, as Mr. Stone was to leave in the evening,and Bro. Grant decided to go, we assisted him to get off in time to catch, the train. I wrote a letter to Mrs. Empey in answer to hers of Aug. 5th, received Aug. 28th. (see jou.A.Aug.28")

Saturday, 7 September 1901, Yokohama

The brethren all went out during the morning for a walk, and while I was writing up my journal, Mr. Kataro Okada, inspector in charge of the Bluff Police Station, called to deliver the message which the Chief of Police had promised to send us

We were also visited during the afternoon by Mr. Yamasaki (see journal A Aug. 31st.) who gave us an invitation to visit the Bible class which he belonged to. We said that we would be pleased to do so and asked him where and when it was held. He said that it would be held tomorrow between nine and ten o'clock a.m. at no.75 Bluff. He stated that the chief object of his call was to give us this invitation.

Sunday, 8 September 1901, Yokohama

According to the invitation that we received yesterday from Mr. Yamasaki to visit the Bible class of which he was a member, Bro. Kelsch and I went after breakfast to the place which we were directed (no.75 Bluff.) and found this class was being held in the home of a Baptist Missionary. The teacher of the class met us at the door and was quite surprised when we told her that we had come to visit the class in response to an invitation given us by one of the students. She said the she never had any foreiners visit her class before, and she thaught that it would make her students backward and timid, so she asked to be excused if she would have to deny us the privilage of attending, and also that the subjects considered were so simple that we would find nothing to interest us. We were invited, however, into another room where the head Missionary of the Church and another friend were sitting and were introduced to them. We of course explained to them the reason why we had come there and told them who we were. When he learned that we were the "Mormons that were creating such extensive comment, he appeared much surprised, and asked many questions concerning the peculiar points of our doctrine and the plan of our work in this land. The conversation lasted over an hour.

During our talk Bro. Kelsch had occasion to quote the words of the Savior: "I am come in my father's name and ye receive me not: if another come I his own name, him will ye receive," and stated that because we came in the name of Jesus Christ that the world would not receive us but if we had come in the name of men we would be received. After a while the Missionary arose and said that he would have to go to church, but as he could not sanction our doctrines he could not invite us, lest it be said that in so doeing he had given indirect approval to our work and teachings. To this Bro. Kelsch replied "Well, it is just as I told you a little while ago, if we had come in our own name then we would be received, but because we have come in the name of Jesus we are rejected." This was a hard slap for the Missionary and one which made him blush, but he took it gentlemenly and said nothing The other gentlemen, and the lady teacher, who by this time had dismissed her class, smiled at this remark, but showed their sympathy for their friend. We were much pleased with our visit, in spite of the fact that we did not get the chance to meet with the Bible class.

During the afternoon we went to a neighboring park and took some pictures with the Kodak.

While at supper we received three letters for Bro. Grant, but as they were from native Japanese we opened them to see if ther was anything in them that needed answering. The construction of two of them was so peculiar that I here insert a copy of them. . . .

Monday, 9 September 1901, Yokohama

A beautiful day, some what warmer than yesterday. After breakfast we held our regular morning meeting, in which we considered what steps to take regarding the finding of a suitable boarding place in Tokyo, where we expected to move next Monday. Bro. Grant had left this work for us to do, and we wanted to secure accomodiations in some private family if possible, so that we would come constantly in contact with those who spoke Japanese. We felt that it would be necessary for us to begin enquiry immediately as such a place would likely be hard to find. And as we knew nothing about Tokyo, nor any of its people, we decided to write to Mr. Katogi whom Bro. Grant had met while in that city, and see if we could not secure his help in hunting a suitable place to live. Accordingly I wrote him a letter signed for us all to the above effect, and requested him to answer immediately, so that if he could not help us that we could make some other arrangements.

I posted this letter and the one that I had written to Sister Empey on the 6th of the month. After dinner I went down town to the bank to get some money changed and on the way back I called at the Grand Hotel and had my hair cut. I went into the reading room to look at the local papers and found three copies of the Deseret News on file. As it was understood with the manager of the Hotel that these papers had come for us, I took them home with me, and found in reading the copy of Aug. 17th an account of the closing session of the convention of Western Undertakers which had been held in Salt Lake City, The account stated, to my great but pleasant surprise, that my father had been elected First Vice-president of the Association, the position occupied in the past by my brother Jos. Wm. Taylor. A day or two ago I notice in the paper from home that father was taking quite an active part in the Convention, having delivered the address of welcome and given a large banquet in the Knutsford Hotel for the members. Father had never before taken an active part in these Association Meetings and it has all come as a great surprise to me.

During the afternoon we were visited by a Mr. Frajuo Mogi Sato who had been a student in law at the University of Michigan, graduating from that institution in 1890. While at school he became acquainted with a number of Utah boys who were students also, among whom were J.H. Moyle, [blank] King, [blank] Thurman

He said that they were generally brighter students than those from any other part of the U.S. and that they were not proud and stuck up like the others, and that they were his best friends and with whom he took delight in associating. He said that their lives impressed him very much for they had no bad habits, and their example was a worthy one, indeed. We briefly explained the Gospel to him and he listened with intense interest, stating when he left, that he hoped that we would be successful in our work here for he felt that our doctrines would elevate his people. He also cautioned us against those Japanese, who would come to us and profess belief and say that they wanted to assist us in our work, for they would only be doing it for material gain.

We were also visited by Mr. Shigeaki Nishimura, a linen merchant and a follower of Buddha. He said that he knew all about Tokyo and that while he was there he would look around for a boarding place such as we wanted and let us know by Thursday if he could find one.

Tuesday, 10 September 1901, Yokohama

Spent most of the day in turning out my clothes and brushing the mill-dew off them. It got so damp during our last rain that it penetrated into the wardrobes and the trunks; making my clothes very musty. Not only does the dampness affect clothing but also shoes, books, and in fact everything, and it keep one constantly employed turning out his things to the sun and cleaning the mould off less they wrot and fall into pieces. Especially is this dampness hard on books. It causes them to swell and weakens the glue so much that it does not take long for them to come unbound. The books that are made here, however, seem to have better bindings for the are not affected like those that come from other places. They also seem to contian some kind of material that does not absorbe the dampness like other books, for when the two kinds are placed side by side, the one moulds very rapidly, while the other moulds slowly and but very little.

I received a letter from father via the Seattle mail. It contained the gratifying news that all were well at home. Father also wrote that the people seemed just as much interested in our work now as they did before our departure, and that they are waiting eagerly, to hear how we have been received by the people of this land. He also sent a clipping from the Herald containing an account of the proceedings of the Undertakers Convention held in Salt Lake City, but this account I had already received in the "News" which came yesterday.

After our lesson in the afternoon Bro. Ensign went down town and brought back with him some pictures which had been developed from those that we had taken some days ago with our Kodak.[48] They were very good but we hope to make them better in the future as we gain experience.

In the evening I wrote an answer to the letter which I had received from my father, and retired feeling grateful for the blessings of the day and the good news which had come from home.

Wednesday, 11 September 1901, Yokohama

A little rain fell during the morning, but the afternoon was clear and warm. After breakfast I took a walk to the Post Office, to post the letter that I wrote the night before, so that it would be in time to catch the steamer that left for America.

When I got back we held our regular morning prayer meeting, in which we also discussed some minor points concerning our work and what was to be done during the day. We also read the fourth and fifth chapters of the Book of Ether in the Book of Mormon. The rest of the morning I spent in study, prepareing my lesson for the class recitation that we have every morning.

Thursday, 12 September 1901, Yokohama

I spent the entire morning in studying my lesson in Japanese. Received an answer from Mr. Katogi to the letter which we wrote him on the 9th of the month in which we requested him to assist us in securing a suitable place in which to live in Tokyo. He state that he would be glad to help us, but that he would not be able to do so before Thursday the 19th. on which date he desired us to call on him, and he would be at liberty to spend the day in assisting us in our search for accomodations.

During the afternoon we took three pictures with the kodak; one of the little house used as the home of the servants, one of Bro. Ensign in a "rikisha," and also one of myself in a "rikisha."

After supper we took a walk down into the town to view the sights of a street fair, which occur twice in a month. The sights were, indeed, interesting. For about four or five blocks the street was hung on either side with hundreds of Chinese lanterns of all shapes and sizes. About twenty feet apart and reaching out considerably into the street were little spaces on which temporary stands made of packing boxes or other scraps of wood were erected containing thousands of little trinkets, in the manufacture of which the Japanese are particularly skilled. The street was thronged with people who had come out to see the sights and also to buy those things which were on sale, and which they might be in need of, for on occasions of this kind everything is sold at a sacrifice, in fact there is seldom anything that would be too dear for the poorest laborer, and the penny is by far more active than any other coin.

The shout of the auctioneer; the solicitating cry of the merchant as he invited the passers by to examine his wares; the shrill notes of the flute and the unharmonious music of Japanese fiddles, which had been purchased by a number who seemed to be overly anxious to display their musical ability; the excited chattering of the throng; and the scarping of the wodden sandals as the multitude moved to and fro, all united in creating such a deafening noise, that our ears rang with the sound after we had gone blocks away. We spent about two hours in viewing the sights, and observed with interest many a peculiar feature. With all, I should say, that while a Japanese street fair is not so elaborate as some in America (and this is because of their frequent occurance) yet they are as thoroughly enjoyed by a majority of the people, as any of which our country may feel proud—the Elk's Street Fair held in Salt Lake City, September 1901 included.

Friday, 13 September 1901, Yokohama

The atmosphere quite cool and refreshing. The day fair and bright. In the morning we were visited by Mr. Nishimura from Tokyo. (se Sept. 9th,) He called to tell us of his success in looking for a home for us in Tokyo. He said that it was impossible to secure accommodations in private families for the reason that foreigners were more or less suspected by the Japanese, both from a religious and political standpoint, and that they, therefore, could not think of inviting "a devil into their house." He had however found two places which he thought would be suitable to us and the rent was not high. We decided to go to Tokyo the next day and examine the places which he had recommended.

Our class recitation lasted from three o'clock in the afternoon to six in the evening.

Saturday, 14 September 1901, Yokohama

According to arrangements made yesterday, Bro. Ensign and myself to rikishas after breakfast and rode to the depot in time to catch the 9:35 a.m. train for Tokyo. We were met at the depot by Mr. Koyama, whom we had engaged to go with us as an interpreter. After a ride of an hour and fifteen minutes through the beautiful fields of rice which abound in this district, we arrived at our destination, where we were met my Mr. Nishimura, who had so kindly been hunting houses for our accommodation. He directed us to one very nicely finished Japanese home where we were met by the people who live in it with the greatest of courtesy. We were served with watermelon, pears, candies, tea, and smoking-boxes, all of which we thoroughly enjoyed, except the last two, which were of course contrary to our tastes. We were told that if we desired to rent this place that the parties who where now living in it would move out, and that it would be make comfortable for us. Leaving this place we were directed to two others which were recommend as suitable for us, but we found that there was some objectionable features connected with them all, and we could not feel reconciled in deciding on any of them.

Thanking Mr. Nishimura for his kindness we left this part of the city telling him that if we would decide on taking any of the houses that we would let him know by the following Thursday. We took rikishas and went into what is known as the Shimbashi district of the city. Here we found Mr. Katogi who received us kindly and promised to look for a home such as we explained to him we would like. He being a man of education and of considerable prominence in the community, would be able to help us very much, and he said that he would institute a search the following morning and as soon as he found anything that would be at all worthy of our consideration, he would send a messenger to us immediately, bringing us the terms and plans of the place.

Leaving Mr. Katogi we called on the editor of the "Shakwai Shimpo" who had visited us in Yokohama some days ago, and who told us of a gentleman by the name of Matsuoka who sent word by them that he would like to assist in securing a suitable place if we came to Tokyo: (see Aug. 25th, jou. A.) and in fact we understood that he had already found such a place and offered it to us free. The editor told us this gentleman's address. We spent some time in talking on the opposition that was being made against us by a majority of the newspapers. He also informed us that there was going to be a meeting helt that night in the hall of The Young Men's Christian Association in which the most prominent Japanese Christian was going to deliver an address against us and that all the newspapers that could be induced to printed it would be requested to place it in their columns so that the people all over the country could be warned against us and the damnable doctrine that we preached.

We called at Mr. Matsuoka's home but found that he was in Yokohama. Not desireing to return without seeing him, we concluded to to wait in the city until he arrived, which would be, so his daughter said, at 7 o'clock. It was then half past five, so we went down to the resturant at the R.R. Station and had supper, after which we went through a store called the "Bazaar." There are two doors in the front of this building about fifteen feet apart, each leading into what looked like a hall lined on both sides with goods from the floor to the roof. Entering the door on the west we followed the passage-way which winded around and around until it finally led up a slope which brought us to the second flat, then it winded and winded around again till it finally led us down another slope to the ground floor, where its irregular course continued for some time then led out on to the street through the door which which we found to our surprise was about fifteen feet from the one by which we had entered. When we looked at our watches, we found that we had been walking through the store for nearly one hour and had never passed the same thing twice. The most remarkable part of the circumstances was that the store itself was only two stories high and I should judge fifty by a hundred feet. The variety and the quality of the goods was also a feature which surprised us very much.

The the visit to this store proved to be a very interesting passtime, and we found after coming out that it was time to make our call on Mr. Matsuoka. We found him at home and were received with the greatest of courtesy. We explained through our interpreter who we were and what we had come to find out. He was quite surprised to learn that we desired if possible to live in a Japanese home and to adopt the Japanese style. However, he said that he would be glad to take two of us, and that he had a friend whom he thaught would take the other two. But as he expected to move from his present quarters to a more suitable place he would not be able to take us until after Sept 25th. We secured from him his terms and told him to write to us as soon as he had found out whewher his friend would give accommodations or not and what his terms would be, so that we could consider their propositions and let them know what our decision on the matter was.

We left his place at 9:15 p.m., having just five minutes to catch the train. We took rikishas and went rapidly to the depot, but were just one minute late, so we turned around and went back into town again to visit another bazaar, and thus while away the hour and fifteen minutes that we had to waite for the next train. The bazaar that we visited this time was not so elaborate as the one we went through during the evening, but was much after the same style.

We left Tokyo at 10:35 and arrived in Yokohama a few minutes before midnight. When we got home we found that Bro. Kelsch had gone to bed and we had to wake him up to get in. He was anxious to know what we had accomplished, so by the time we were through talking it was past one o'clock in the morning and when I did get into bed I felt almost too tired to sleep, but I was soon lost in dreamland, the bliss of which was broken long after daylight by the farmiliar morning cry of "Mother Kelsch."

Sunday, 15 September 1901, Yokohama

The morning was clear and cool, but the afternoon became very warm. We were exceedingly pleased to see Bro. Grant as he came walking into the room with his grip in hand at about two o'clock in the afternoon. He reported a very pleasant and profitable trip, and he was so much improved in looks that we all remarked immediately that he had gained a number of pounds in flesh. His face was sunburned and a decidedly improved appearence was manifest in his entire person. His travels had taken him into many a strictly Japanese village where he had received some experience in eating and sleeping in Japanese style. This close association had enable him to take a great many observations regarding the habits and feelings of the people; it also opened his eyes to some extent to the true life and character of the Japanese that will enable us to devise the best means of approaching them with the Gospel.

We reported to him all that we had done during his absence and he was perfectly satisfied with our work. He said that he felt that we should have an interpreter that could translate articles for newspapers and to read articles that are being written against us, so that we could be farmiliar with the things that are said against us, and be able, therefore, to intelligently defend ourselves. He also felt that we should have some of our smaller tracts translated so that the work might be progressing while we are studying the language. These propositions, however, were deferred until later.

Monday, 16 September 1901, Yokohama

The usual morning song and prayer meeting was held. The forenoon was spent in answering letters and in study preparatory to afternoon session of the language class. While at tiffin Mr. Nishimura came to see us and wanted to know if we would take one of the houses that he had shown us in Tokio when Horace and I were there the day before yesterday. We told him then, that we would be unable to give him an answer until the following Thursday. But as Mr. Koyama told us after Mr. Nishmura had gone, that the Japanese were a people who were nerveous and did not like to waite as the foreigners did, it seems that Mr. Nishimura had got overly anxious and wanted to know what we were going to do before we had come to any dicision ourselves. We told him that it would be impossible to give any definite answer for a day or two and that he must waite patiently until we could.

Tuesday, 17 September 1901, Yokohama

A bright and pleasant day. The usual routine of eating, studying, reading, and sleeping was about the only feature of the day. In the afternoon we held our regular class for the recitation of our lesson in Japanese. Toward evening Mr. Yamasaki called on us and spent about an hour and a half in conversing on different subjects pertaining to religion. After supper we were visited by a Mr. Y Tetsuka who was living in one of the little settlements just outside of Yokohama. He had heard of our arrival in Japan and also of our religion, through the newspapers. He also noticed that a majority of the papers were opposing us and he became anxious to know what there was connected with our faith that would cause so much comment. He listened with deep interest to our explanaition of the doctrines of "Mormonism" and asked many question concerning the charges that had been made against us. He stayed for nearly two hours and when he got up to go he asked the privilage of calling on us again in the morning, when he would like to continue in his investigation of our religion. We, of course, were glad to have a chance to talk to anyone on the Gospel so we told him that we would be delighted to have him come as often as he desired. He spoke English very well and betrayed in his actions a refinement that is not often met with in this land.

Wednesday, 18 September 1901, Yokohama

We held our regular morning song and prayer meeting immediately after breakfast. We had hardly finished when Mr. Tetsuka, who had called on us yesterday, came. He spent the entire morning with us and read through carefully one of our tracts, glanced through the Book of Mormon, and asked a number of questions that arose in his mind upon the subjects which he was reading. When he arose to leave he asked if we had any of our publications to distribute, and said that he would especially like to have a copy of the Book of Mormon, a strong testimony for which he had been reading in one of our tracts. We told him that we had plenty of literature and would mail him some as soon as we opened the boxes which contained it. He left one yen (fifty cents American money) and requested that we mail him a copy of the Book of Mormon. This, therefore, was the first Book of Mormon to be sold in Japan, and only one heretofore had been given away; that was to a representative of the "Jiji Shimpo" a newspaper published in Tokyo. (see Journal A. Aug. 14th.)

As there was considerable work to be done prior to our leaving for Tokyo we had to give up our lessons in Japanese as we would not have time to study them, so after the lesson which we received in the afternoon we told our teacher not to come regurarly any more but to call for an hour every other day so as to translate any letters that we may receive from native Japanese.

Thursday, 19 September 1901, Yokohama

In the "Japan Mail" of Friday, September 13th, there appeared a two column article entitled "The Mormon Menace."[49] Accompanying this article was a letter written to the editor of the "Mail" signed "American" requesting the publication of the article in the interest of the people of Japan, who, because of the late arrival of four missionaries from Utah, were entitled to a warning against the "dangerous Mormon plague." The article bears the name of Gen. John Eaton, "Ph,D., LL.D., Washington, D.C., President Sheldon Jackson College, Salt Lake City, Utah, formerly U.S. Commissioner of Education," and comes from the August number of the "Homiletic Review" published in New York. It is plainly seen from the article that Mr. Eaton was speaking for the purpose of raising means to support his school in Utah, which it seems has been established for the purpose of furnishing "higher Christian education" among the corrupt and depraved "Mormons." Being for this purpose, he evedently considered a rehashing of the old charges, such as "The Mountain Meadows Massacre,"[50] "The 'Danite' Band,"[51] "The arch-imposter Joe Smith",[52] "The continuation of plural marriages,[53] "The sorrowful conditions existing in the polygamus homes among the Mormons",[54] and a number of other falsehoods, a most excellent theme with which to work upon the sympathies of his hearers and cause them to donate liberally to the support of Christian institutions in Utah. And were it not that the people of this land did not know the truth about the character and practices of the "Mormons," we would have left these charges unanswered, but not wishing the peoples minds to become predijuced against us because of unfounded statements made by our enemies, we decided to write a reply to the article written by Mr. Eaton and have it published in the same paper. Accordingly much of the day was spent in getting the matter together that would be needed in making a full and complete argument that would entirely off set the charges that were made.

In the evening I wrote an answer to the letter which I received yesterday from my brother.

Friday, 20 September 1901, Yokohama

The day was clear and cool. After our prayer and song meeting was over we went to work and compiled in proper shape the matter which we had gathered together the day before in answer to MR. Eaton's article.

Mr. Koyama called in the afternoon and translated some letters which had been received. While he was with us, there came a letter from the Governor's office requesting us to call on him the following morning at 9 o'clock, to answer some questions regarding the application which we had sent to him requesting permission to preach the doctrines of "Mormonism" in Japan. During the evening we had the final reading of the article which we had prepared, and unanimously accepted it as a sufficient reply to the charges made in Mr. Eaton's article. . . .

Saturday, 21 September 1901, Yokohama

At nine o'clock in the morning we called on the Governor and were informed that we did not have to make such an extensive application as we had done in order to get permission to preach and establish a mission and that there were some points which the law required that had not been mentioned in the application which we had made. After asking some questions on points of doctrine that we had mentioned as a part of our teachings, we were told that we would be furnished with a blank form, on which to make a new application and that it must be filled out in Japanese. We were very much surprised that our previous application had not been satisfactory, as it was made out, and sent in accordance with the instructions that we had received from the Police Department, (see Sept. 7th.) but it seemed that such instruction was not in accordance with the law and we had to be content to waite until the proper forms were prepared and sent to us, before we could begin any active work in spreading the Truth.

The day was very rainy and miserable making it much more pleasant inside than out, so most of the afternoon was spent in studying, "Chamberlain on the Japanese Language"

Sunday, 22 September 1901, Yokohama

Immediately after breakfast we went out into the woods and held our regular morning meeting in the same grove that we had retired to three week before for the purpose of dedicating the land. When we had finished the meeting we took a number of pictures of the spot as well as of the hill and the grove. In the afternoon we had our Sabboth Sacrament meeting.

Monday, 23 September 1901, Yokohama

Received three letters from home. One from mother, containing also a note from Emma; one from Lutie, announcing her call to go as a missionary to Colorado in company with Fanny Wooley; and one from the editors of the "Era" thanking me for the contribution that I had given to that magazine during the past year and soliciting more contributions for the ensuing volume.

Tuesday, 24 September 1901, Yokohama

Another steamer arriving from America, I received another from home; this time from father. It contained the gratifying news of his good health as well as the health of all at home. In the evening I wrote a letter to Lutie in answer to hers received yesterday.

Wednesday, 25 September 1901, Yokohama

Spent the morning in study. In the afternoon Mr. Nishimura called on us. He came for the purpose of finding our whether or not we had found a home in Tokyo and if we could take him as our cook or house servant, as he wanted to study our religion and thaught that if he could be with us constantly that he would be able to learn more perfectly the doctrines of "Mormonism." He could not speak a work of English and we had to take him down to Brandensteins and get their interpreter to talk to him for us. We were surprised to think that this man should want to come and be a servant to us, when he had a business of his own, and from the style that he was able to put on, I should judge his business to be quite a profitable one, indeed. As he could not speak English we saw immediately the impropriety of accepting his proposition for it would be impossible to speak to him and consequently he would not be able to learn any of our doctrines and would not be able to understand what we wanted if we were to take him as a servant. We told him our feeling on the matter and he seemed to recognize the lack of wisdom in such act immediately

Leaving Brandentsein's Bro. Grant and I went over to the "Japan Gazette" office to get the copy of a paper which contained an article written against by the editor. We found on reading it that it was based upon a phamplet written by a Mr. Nutting who was a minister in one of the Christian churches in Utah. It was one of the kind which contained extracts from the sermons delivered by Brigham Young and other leaders in the church. The entire article was so absurd that we felt that it was unworthy an answer.

Thursday, 26 September 1901, Yokohama

Wrote a letter to Aunt Hattie. Devoted myself to study during most of the day. In the evening I listened to the reading of an article written by Bro. Grant in answer to the attack made upon us in the "Japan Gazette." We had practically decided the day before that the editorial was not worthy an answer, but it seemed Bro. Grant had changed his mind and prepared one. As it was getting late, we decided to leave the final criticism of it until the next day. Before going to bed I wrote a short letter to Rev. Nishijima of Sacramento, Cal. (see Journal A. July 28th.)

Friday, 27 September 1901, Yokohama

Weather rainy and cold. We received, by the mail, a letter from the Governor's office telling in Japanese and in English just the kind of form that we would have to follow in sending in our application for permission to preach. Mr. Koyama happened to come in and we wrote out our application and also a brief outline of our lives and gave it to him to translate into Japanese, so that we would be able to present it to the Governor as quickly as possible. In the evening I wrote an answer to the letter which I had received from the editors of the "Improvement Era" on the 29th. In my letter I told them that my labors as a missionary in Japan were of such a character that I did not feel I could spare the time to write for that magazine, but that my heart was in Mutual Improvement work and that I would be only too glad to help roll the work along, and if in the future any chance was presented and I had time and material with which to prepare an article, that I would be glad to do so, but did not wish to make any set promises.

During the day we reread and criticized Bro. Grant's article.

Saturday, 28 September 1901, Yokohama

Bro. Grants article was not re-written yesterday, so we re-wrote it today and submitted it for publication. Mr. Koyama brought back the translation of our application to the Governor, for which we paid him. We decided to submit it the following Monday. In the afternoon we received a card from Mr. Nakakuki editor of the "Shakwai Shimpo" living at Tokyo, in which he stated that he had been looking for a house for us and that he had found one which he thought would be suitable and requested us to come to Tokyo the following day and see it. We decided to do so and asked Mr. Koyama to go with us as an interpreter. . . .

Sunday, 29 September 1901, Yokohama

A dismal, cold, and cloudy day. We held our usual morning prayer and song meeting in which we discussed some matters pertaining to our work in the future. After tiffin we went directly to the depot and took the train to Tokyo as arranged the day before. We met our interpreter as per appointment, and after an hours ride through the beautiful green fields, we arrived at our destination. We took the horse car for about a thirty minutes ride, then engaged rikishas for the rest of our journey. Arriving at the home of Mr. Nakakuki we were immediately directed to the house which he had written to us about. We found it to be in a very disagreeable part of the city and the surroundings entirely opposite to anything that we would want. We were than directed to another place not far from the first, but this was unsuitable for the same reasons, that is, that we would bring disrepute upon ourselves by living in such a quarter and could never be satisfied to live where there was so much dirt and filth.

We told Mr. Nakakuki our feelings and he said that he would try and find us a more suitable place in a district where there were some foreigners and where the most respectable men would not hesitate to come and visit us, because of our pleasant surroundings. We thanked him for his trouble and turned our steps homeward. Taking rikishas, we decided to take a look through the foreign settlement and observe if we could see any place that might be for rent—at a price that we felt we could afford. While strolling through this part of the city, we were much impressed with it, and felt that if we could get a home in that part that we would be located in a district wherein the attention of the high class would be attracted.

Desiring to get back to Yokohama in time for supper, we took rikishas again and rode to the depot, but found that the train had just left and that the next one did not leave for an hour. To pass away the time, we made a call on Mr. Katogi, who, when Bro. Ensign and I were in Tokyo before, had promised to look out for a house for us, but evidently had not done so for we had received no word from him concerning any. We found him in and were received very cordially. He explained that he understood that we had already found a home and, therefore, he ceased his search for one. When we told him that we were still without one, he promised to begin search again immediately. Bidding him good night, we crossed the road to one of the big bazaar stores and went through to show Bros. Grant and Kelsch what immense places these were. (see Sept. 14th). By the time that we had walked through this store, the hour that we had to spare was well taken up and we had to hasten to the depot lest we lose the next train. We arrived at our boarding house in Yokohama just as the last course of supper was being served.

In the evening we sat and talked for a long time on what we had done and seen during the day and how to act in order to get the best and quickest results which would be for the good of the mission and the success of our own work in proclaiming th Gospel of Jesus Christ.

Monday, 30 September 1901, Yokohama

A bright and pleasant day We had our morning songs out in the arbor which stood on the edge of the bluff overlooking the city and from where a most excellent view of the bay could be had. As the words of the inspiring hymns which we sang were spoken in musical melody, in the production of which we seemed particularly blessed on this occasion, the sound was carried by the gentle breeze out into the distance where it seemed to blend itself harmoniously with the radient beams of sunshine falling peacefully upon the bustling city below. Our hearts were full of joy and peace, and the words of divine truth composing the songs we sang were as the bread of life unto our souls.

Leaving the arbor we went into our rooms and had prayer, following which Bro. Grant read from the Doc. and Cov. sec. 101. At the suggestion of Bro. Grant we arose, in turn, to our feet, and expressed the feelings of our hearts concerning the best plan for us to follow in the future. After a meeting of about two hours we were united in the feeling that it would be better for us to remain together during the winter and confine ourselves to hard study preparatory to going out among the people in the spring. We also felt that to secure the assistance of a teacher and live in Tokyo was the proper thing for us to do. According to these feelings, we agreed to begin laboring toward the desired end immediately.[55] The remainder of the day I spent in writing up my journal and in studying the language.

Tuesday, 1 October 1901, Yokohama

The mail which arrived to-day brot me two letters from home; one from mother the other from Bishop Empey. All at home were well. Bishop Empey's letter told that Clarance Patten had been called on a mission, but did not state his field of labor.

Much of the day was spent in study. In the evening we went to a concert held in the "Yokohama Public Hall. The concert was given by Herr and Madame Marquardt assisted by local artists. The invitation to attend this concert was given to us by Mrs. Warton, who also presented us with complimentary tickets. Mrs. Warton had come to Yokohama from Tokyo to spend a few days with her friends here, and made the boarding house at which we are stopping her headquarters. She is a woman who has devoted much time and means to the church to which she belongs. As we had only met her once or twice and did not even know her name, we were almost dumbfounded when we received an invitation to go with her and two other ladies (our landlady and Miss. Carrier one of the boarders) to this entertainment. The peculiar part about it was, that the other gentlemen boarders were not invited, but the despised "Mormons" received special distinction, and that too from a person to whom we were practically strangers. The fact that the "Mormons" had received special favor struck the other boarders as a peculiar problem, and one of them remarked that he wished he were a "Mormon," and could be among the chosen ones.

We told Mrs. Warton that we were looked down upon by a majority of the people and that us going with her would undoubtdly expose her to severe criticism by her Christian friends, but she did not care for that, and said, that she was the boss of her own actions and was not bound to act within certain limits prescribed by the opinions of others.

Being informed that those who attended this concert would all be dressed in their best, we decided to trim up ourselves, and when we had finished our toilet[56] we were just as much "hot stuff" as any of the rest of them. Horace was in full dress and the rest of us in P. A. with white vests. I had on a dress waistcoat and a pleated white front shirt in which I felt more dressed up than I had ever done before in my life, in fact I have been in places where more style and evening dressing has been done since I left home than ever before. In no instance have we allowed those with whom we have associated get the idea that we were common scrubs, but have dressed as well and conversed as intelligently as the best of them.

The concert program consisted mostly of harp and violin music which was very sweet and entertainig. As we sat in the hall we could see the people nugging each other and commenting on our presence, for whenever a "Mormon" goes into a strange crowd and happens to be seen by one who knows him, it does not take long before the entire assembly will have been informed of his presence and will have strained themselves to get a look at him.

One of the most graceful (?) and attractive features of the evening was the Rev. Mr. Staniland, landlord of Beverly House, where the "Mormons" were refused accomodations because it would not have been acting properly toward its ordinary guests if such corrupt and disreputable persons as the "Mormons" were allowed to come in and mingle with them. Mr. Staniland sat in his seat as he would in the pew of a church, moving only once, then he caught sight of the "Mormons" whose presence was evidently a damper destroying for him much of the evenings pleasure. I tell you it did me lots of good to sit there with my head up and look him in the face until he was ashamed to direct his glance in the direction we were sitting. He put me in mind of a dog which will bark as loud as ever as long as you are running from him, but which will turn and sulk away when you stop and look him in the eye. And like the dog which has its day our day had come, and we returned in triumph to our rooms.

Wednesday, 2 October 1901, Yokohama

Beautiful day in every respect. In the forenoon I went down to Brandenstein's to get some books and tracts out of the cases in which they had been shipped from home. Through the kindness of Mr. Brecker, the manager of the branch house here, we had been given the privilege of placing our boxes of books in their office for safe keeping.

The remaining part of the day I spent in my room. During the afternoon we prepered a short note for the "Japan Times," a newspaper published in Tokyo, to correct a slight error that had been made by the editor in commenting upon our application for permission to preach in Japan. Bro. Grant called on the Governor and submitted our Report which we had prepared according to the directions of the form which we had been furnished by the Goverment. (see Sept. 27th,). The report was filed in both English and Japanese.

Thursday, 3 October 1901, Yokohama

Warm bright day. The entire day was spent in my room. Wrote a letter to father enclosing a copy of the minutes of the meeting heldin the woods when we dedicated this land for the proclamation of the Gospel. (see Sept. 1st, 1901.) I also enclosed in the letter a newspaper clipping containing the answer written by us to a charge against the "Mormons" by Mr. Eaton. (see Sept. 20th, 1901.) I also sent home in the letter two photographs of scenes around our boarding place here in Yokohama.

Friday, 4 October 1901, Yokohama

A heavy rain fell during the morning, and the whole day was dark and dismal. After our morning prayer meeting, I went in search of Mr. Koyama our interpreter to get him to prepare a duplicate of the Report for Preaching which we had filed with the Governor. (see Oct. 2nd 1901.) This duplicate was for the Home Department at Tokyo. In the afternoon Mr. Koyama brot the duplacate form, which we signed preparatory to submitting it the following day.

A mail came in, bringing a number of issues of the Deseret News. In the issue of Thursday Sept. 12th, I was surprised to find a copy of a letter which I had written to mother on the 16th and 20th of last Aug. . . .

Saturday, 5 October 1901, Yokohama

Filed with the Governor a duplicate of our Report for Preaching. Received, by the mail from America, a letter from Florence. Wrote a letter to Mr. Yamasaki of Tokyo, who informed us that he had found two more houses in Tokyo that he would like us to see and determine if they would be satisfactory as a home for us in that city. We decided that we would waite until Mr. Hiroi was able to find a suitable place for us, and accordingly informed Mr. Yamasaki.

Spent the evening in chatting with Mr. Moss one of our companion boarders. We gave him some of our literature to read and also loaned him our scrap book containing Mr. Eaton's lecture on the "Mormon Menace" and Bro. Grant's reply. It seems that he had become much interested in the above controversy and was desirous of hearing both sides so that he could way the arguments intelligently.

Sunday, 6 October 1901, Tokyo

Rained all day. This being fast day we did not get up in time for breakfast, but were surprised to find that we had laid in bed until ten o'clock. We had desired to go out into the woods and hold our fast meeting but the weather was so bad that we had to content ourselves by holding it in our rooms. After partaking of the sacrament we expressed our feelings to each other and rejoiced in the peaceful spirit which prevailed in our meeting. During the meeting we sang eight songs and read four sections from the Doc. and Cov. 107–110.[57] Wrote a letter to Florence in answer to the one received from her the day before.

Monday, 7 October 1901, Tokyo

During the entire night the rain continued its downpour and there was not a moment of the day that the storm abated in the least. The consequence was, that we had to content ourselves by remaining most of the day in our rooms. I, however, was anxious to get out to some of the book stores and see if I could not find a text-book, which I had discovered was a good and simple treatise on the Japanese language; so in the afternoon I wrapped up and ventured out into the storm. While I was out I called at the "Japan Gazette" office to deliver a letter to the editor which Bro. Grant had written. This letter requested the editor to reconsider his objection to the article which we had furnished him as a reply to an unfair editorial written against the "Mormons." This was done in the hope of getting the answer printed in the same paper that had made the attack upon so that the same people who read the charges could also read the reply. (see Sept 28" 1901.)

Tuesday, 8 October 1901, Tokyo

The rain fell in one continuous downpour during the entire day nor had it ceased for a moment during the night. Our morning meeting lasted until noon. While together we listened to a reading from a little book known as "Nelson on Infidelity,"[58] the points in which we had decided to consider and see if we could glean from it any valuable matter that would assist us in the compilation of tracts upon subjects, such as "The Existence of God," "The Authenticity of the Bible, which subjects claim our first attention in the presentation of the Gospel to the Japanese. The afternoon I spent in study and research after the Japanese language, which seems at present an almost unsurmountable task, most discouraging to the mind of its young student. This discouragement, however, did not last long, for I paused to read the blessing given me by my father on the evening of my departure for this land, and the promise contained therein, that the Lord would bless every effort I made to obtain the language of this people, stimulated me in my determination to study earnestly and my faith was strengthened in the hope that I would be able to acquire this most difficulty tongue.

As the day was quite cold and there was no stove in any of our rooms, we lingered in the dining-room for some time after supper and listened to Bro. Ensign sing some of his charming songs.

Wednesday, 9 October 1901, Yokohama

Received by the mail from America, via SanFrancisco, a letter from my brother Samuel. His letter told of the harmonious working of all things at home, but told the sad news of the death of Alvin's little girl Florence, which was the result of her falling into a bucket of boiling water severely scalding herself.

In the evening I wrote a letter to mother in answer to hers written Sept. 9th. The storm which had been raging for the past three days lasted until noon to-day, thus making three and a half days and three nights of continual rain.

Thursday, 10 October 1901, Yokohama

Just as we were going to bed last night it started to rain a little, but later in the night the heaviest thunder storm that I had ever witnessed arouse me and kept me awake until about an hour before daylight. The peals of thunder were so loud and severe that one could easily have imagined himself on the battle-field where cannons were being fired off on every side. We saw by the papers published in the evening that many places had been damaged by the concussion which followed each report. The flashes of lightning were also startling and sounded like the shaking of tin. The rain fell in torrents as though it were being poured out of an immense watering-can.

As I lay in bed listening to the thunder and watching the lightning as it flashed in at the window and heard how the rain was beating down, I could not help thinking of the history of the flood in the days of Noah, and saying how easy it would be for the Lord to sweep the inhabitants off of the earth by lightning and by floods. It would not take many days if such a storm as we had during the night were to happen on all parts of the earth at once, to duplicate the flood which destroyed all the life which was upon the earth four thousand years ago.

By the time we got up, however, it had all cleared off and the sun was shining beautifully in a clear sky and the ground was hardened by the force with which the rain drops fell. It being a fine day, Bro. Grant went to Tokyo to see if he could not find a suitable home for us in that city. He returned in the evening after a long day of research and tiresome investigation, which had resulted in no satisfaction. Every home that he had visited was either unsuitable for the purpose for which we would have to use it or too high in rent for the limited means which we had. It seems a strange fact that we have been so unfortunate in our efforts to find a home in Tokyo the capitol of the nation, but thus far we have found it to be no easy task.

During the day I wrote a letter to Bishop Empey in answer to the one I received from him on the 1st of the month.

Friday, 11 October 1901, Yokohama

In the afternoon I went out on the American Launch to the steamer "Olympia" which was to leave for America at 4p.m. The purpose for going on board this vessel was to mail the letter which I had written the day before to Bishop Empey and which I had failed to get into the Post Office in time to go on board the steamer with the regular mail. This boat was an American vessel belonging to the Northern Pacific R.R. Co. As I walked around and through its different appartments, observing the great difference between it and the one on which we had crossed the Pacific, I was brought to a realization of the grandour of the Canadian Pacific Steamers as compared with this one which was dirty and so arranged that the passengers had to take quarters in the extreme stern end, where, if it was at all stormy, they would feel the motion of the ship most distinctly. My appreciation of the comforts which we had during our voyage grew much stronger as I compared them with those to be had by passengers on this ship.

The rest of the day was spent in my room studying. The weather during the entire day was warm and fair.

Saturday, 12 October 1901, Yokohama

Another pleasant day altho slightly cloudy. While at breakfast, a telegram came for Bro. Grant, which on opening he found to be from Pres. Jos. F. Smith announcing the death of Pres. Snow The Cablegram was dated at Salt Lake City, Oct. 11th and was received in Yokohama at 1:55 a.m. on this, the morning of the 12th. It was sent in care of M.J. Brandenstein & Co. and therefore did not reach us until near nine o'clock. It read as follows:—"Heber J. Grant, c/o M.J. Brandenstein & Co. Yokohama, Japan. President Snow just died. Pneumonia. Funeral Sunday. Joseph F. Smith."

This sad news cast a gloom over us all, and the rest of our breakfast was denied. Going into Bro. Grant's room we held our regular morning prayer meeting, but we also spoke in turn our feelings on the death of the much loved President of our Church and Prophet of God to the people. We sang his two favorite hymns, "Zion Stands with Hills Surrounded" and "Glory to God on High"; besides these we sang, "O My Father," "We Thank Thee Oh God for a Prophet,"&"Weep, Weep not for me Zion."

Immediately after the meeting Bro. Grant and I went down town to have a notice of his death together as an outline of his life and the greeting which he published to the World at the opening of the 20th Century published in the "Herald". The editor read over his life and also his "Greeting" but did not seem disposed to publish anything more than his death and name of the one who would be his successor. The following is what was published concerning the matter. . . .

Sunday, 13 October 1901, Yokohama

I over slept myself this morning and by the time I had my bath and dressed myself, it was too late for breakfast. Bro. Grant was also too late for his breakfast, whereas the other brethren were more fortunate, in that they were up in time to get something to eat before the morning meal was cleared away.

A very heavy rain fell during the morning, but the afternoon turned out bright and pleasant. About 10:30 a.m. we held our regular Sunday Fast Meeting in which we partook of the Sacrament and spoke extensively on the life and labors of President Snow. Bro. Grant told us many things concerning the character and administration of our much loved President, which we had never heard heretofore. The Holy Ghost resed upon us and we rejoiced in baring testimony to the work of the Lord and acknowledging the hand of Providence in all the blessings and sorrows which come to us from time to time. The afternoon was spent in study .

In the evening before supper, I took walk out on the Bluff. After I had strolled along eastward toward the part of the city where the most massive and beautiful homes of the foreigners were, I came to a place which looked out over the bay. The sight was a pleasing one, and my eyes seemed to long to gaze upon the surface of the water which was lit up by rays of light coming from thousands of lamps that burned on the native crafts and massive ships anchored along the port. The restless billows seemed to bare me home again, for before my mind there arose the loving and familiar features of my folks and the Wasatch Range with its canyons, its snow-capped peaks, its streams of crystal water, and its fascinating grandeur together with the beautiful and peaceful valleys which lie silently at their base. I thought of friends and the happy associations which I had left, to come out into this distant land. And why had I left the happiness of home? Why was I here traveling among those whom I knew not, and to whom I was a total stranger?

I am here to preach the Gospel of the Lord Jesus Christ to those who know not God and to lead men to a more perfect life which will entitle them to a joy and happiness that is everlasting. But why do this? The doctrine which you teach is mocked by men; your efforts are ridiculed by those whom you seek to convert; and your earnestness and sacrifice is not appreciated, but on the contrary, it is made a matter of sport and a subject for hilarity with those who see or hear of your labors. Why not return to your friends were your society and efforts will be appreciated? Because the Lord has called me to this land to proclaim the truth unto this people, and I have received the promise that if I do not succeed in converting one soul, yet am diligent in carrying out the duty that has been imposed in me by the Prophet of God, in spite of the ridicule and persecution of men, I shall in no wise loose my reward nor will the Lord fail to recognize my labor tho no soul is turned from darkness unto light. The path of duty is often rough, but the conflict lies before us and happy is the brave and unflinching soldier, for a crown of victory awaits him.

These are some of the thoughts which passed through my mind as I stood watching the sparkling water as it danced along the rays of light which fell in golden streaks upon the surface of the sea. The rain which fell during the forenoon had washed the streets; the gravely walks were hard and smooth; while the air was cool and refreshing; in fact it was an ideal evening for a walk, and the hour that I wandered musingly around was most delightful and exhilarating.

Monday, 14 October 190l, Yokohama

It being just sixteen hours earlier in Japan than in Salt Lake City, we got up early and held a memorial service at 6:30 a.m. in honor of Pres. Lorenzo Snow. As it was half past six here it would be just 2:30 p.m. yesterday at home or the hour of the funeral. We opened our meeting by singing "O My Father" Prayer by Bro. Ensign. Singing, "We thank Thee oh God for a Prophet." Bro. Grant was the first speaker; myself next; then Bro. Ensign and Bro. Kelsch. All the remarks were in reference to the Life of our

President and the lessons which his life teaches. Benidection was offered by myself. The meeting lasted one hour and three quarters.

When we had finished our breakfast, we read from the Doc. and Cov. concerning Celestial Marriage. We also read considerable from "Nelson on Infidelity." The entire afternoon was spent in reading and writing.

In the afternoon Bro. Grant went down town and saw that the "mail" had another two column article against the "Mormons." It was composed of extracts from sermons which some of the early leaders of the church had delivered and was much after the style of what appeared in the "Gazette" some days ago. (see Sept. 25th, 26th, 28th,) The article was over the signature of J.R. Birkelund M.D. of Tokyo.

Tuesday, 15 October 1901, Yokohama

A day of alternate cloud and sunshine. Wrote a letter to my brother Samuel in answer to his of Sept 17th. Bro. Grant went to Tokyo in the morning but was back in time for dinner. He felt inclined that we should go to Tokyo and had been up there to see what terms we could get from the hotel if we would register for a mont. He found that it would cost us 66 sen a day more than we were paying here in Yokohama and as we all felt that Tokyo was the place for us to be we decided to move to the hotel there, inside of one or two days, and accordingly wrote the proprietor of the Metropole Hotel[59] to expect us shortly and to reserve rooms for us.

This being the birthday of our landlady, an elaborate dinner was served in the evening, to which she invited besides those who were staying with her some of her old boarders. As this was an extraordinary occasion we all dressed for the evening and enjoyed very highly the savory and well served meal. For some time after the eating was over, we listened to singing and engaged in social conversation. Most of the amusement was furnished by the "Mormons," as it seemed that none of the others were able to sing or entertain much in any other way. I could not help but notice how much of the success was due to the solo work of Bro. Ensign, the stories and jokes of Bro. Grant, and the trio work of the four of us.

When we announced that we were going to Tokyo in a few days one of the boarders said, "Good God no, it will be like a grave-yard around here without you;" and I don't doubt for amoment but what it will for a time, anyhow. The "Mormons" in the eyes of most men are looked upon as ignorant and low, but we have yet failed to find a society in Japan where we have not been able to hold our own with the best of them, and many of the leaders have been forced to take a back seat, especially is this the case when Horace has come in contact with some of the recognized singers and musicians. Thanks be to God for his blessings. We recognize his helping hand and realize that he will not permit us to go down to disgrace or to become insignifant as long as we serve him and are humble.

This dinner was also a sort of a farewell reception to Mr. Sebenstein one of the boarders who was going to leave Yokohama on the 16th inst. Mr. Seibenshine is a good natured genial fellow whose frankness and gentlemanly conduct made him a favorite with us all.

Wednesday, 16 October 1901, Yokohama

Rained all day. Received a letter from father in which he spoke of a prophesy that had been uttered by Apostle John W. Taylor lately, while speaking in Mill Creek. During his discourse Bro. Taylor suddenly burst out in prophesy concerning the Japanese mission, and said that the brethren (meaning we four missionaries) would meet with great success; particularly among the enlightened and educated Japanese. This news was a great comfort, not only to me, but to all of us who were striving hard against much discouragement to establish the work of the Lord in this land. Especially were we delighted that an Apostle of the Lord Jesus Christ, who was particularly blessed with the gift of prophesy, should thus speak concerning the result of our labors here, and our hope was increased as our determination grew to perform well the part alloted to us in the fulfillment of Apostle Taylor's prediction.

Thursday, 17 October 1901, Yokohama

Another day of continual rain. It being so stormy and chilly, we had to sit in the dining-room all day where there was a fire so as to keep warm. The forenoon I spent in study and reading. After dinner I listened to an article which Bro. Grant had written in answer to several attacks that had been made upon us through the newspapers. After a half a day's discussion on what had been written and a correction of a number of errors had been made the article was still unfinished, and in fact was set aside sini di.[60]

Friday, 18 October 1901, Yokohama/Tokyo

A most unpleasant and stormy day. As we had written to the manager of the Metropole Hotel in Tokyo that we would be there to take tiffin, we packed up our trunks and started out in spite of the severe storm. With some little difficuly we got packed up and started our trunks for the depot; following after them, in a few minutes we arrived at the station just in time to get our baggage checked and catch the 12:20 train. When we arrived at Tokyo we secured a luggage cart for our trunks and valises and rikishas for us to ride in to the hotel. When we arrived, tiffin had been cleared off, but the manager ordered something for us to eat. The afternoon was spent in straightning things around in our rooms which were very pleasant except quite cold as a result of the storm that had been raging for the past three days.

Our stay at Yokohama had been quite a pleasant one, and we had come in contact with a great number of genial people who had come to board at the same place at which we stopped. The following is the names of those whom we met and had for companion boarders while we stayed in Yokohama: Mr. Fell, of Southern U.S. who was selling Rice Cleaning machines in Japan; Mr. Enberger, of New York, agent for The Singer Sewing Machine Co.; Mr. Carew, of New Zeland, engaged in the Pollock Trading House as a clerk; Dr. Berry from Shanghi, China, in Yokohama for his health and also to meet his prospective wife coming from Canada and who should have arrived on the same steamer that brought us; Miss. Carrier (an old maid) from New York who was touring the world; Mr. Siebensheine of Vienna, Austria, a traveling solicitor for several large Austrian firms; Miss. Hiron; Miss. Dr. Myers and Miss Brink of China, in the Far East performing missionary labor; Mr. Moss a native of Japan, engaged in the Pollock Trading Co.'s business; and Mr. Goodcell, an American missionary interested in the Y.M.C.A. in Shanghi and also engaged as a school teacher; in Japan on a pleasure and health tour.

By the time we had become settled in our new quarters and sit down to do some writing, we found it was very cold and unpleasant without a fire, so we ordered a fire made in one of the rooms. There was an extra charge for coal so we were told, and while it is the policy of "Mormon" missionaries to cut down expenses as much as possible we felt that it would be by far the cheapest to pay 25 sen a day for coal than to take cold and get sick. We went down to supper while the room was getting warm and when we returned we were able to spend a pleasant evening in our new quarters, for which we felt thankful to our heavenly father.

Wrote a card to mother telling her of our arrival here and for all the folks to direct mail to me in care of the Metropole Hotel.

Saturday, 19 October 1901, Tokyo

The day was cold and cloudy but very little rain fell. Most of the day was spent by me in sorting papers and other things which had become badly mixed through the packing and unpacking process which they had undergone. Towards evening Bro. Grant started again answer an editorial published in the "Mail" some days ago, in which Cap. Brinkley (the editor) renewed his advosacy of our expulsion from Japan. In the evening after supper I went into my own room and studied some one the Japanese language.

Sunday, 20 October 1901, Tokyo

A clear and beautiful day. I remained in my room all day, and devoted myself to fasting and prayer. In the evening, after the other brethren had eaten their supper, we assembled in Bro. Grant's room and held a prayer meeting; before doing so, however, we listened to a reading from "Nelson on Infidelity."

Bro. Grant spent most of the day in writing an article to the editor of the "Mail" answering some letters which that paper had published from correspondents who had taken it upon themselves to criticise the "Mormon" doctrine and suggest that its promulgation be prohibited in this land. I also assisted Bro.

Grant in correcting and re-writing his article preparatory to submitting it for publication. In the morning I also wrote a letter to Aunt Clara so as to catch the mail steamer which sailed from Yokohama two days later.

The following is a copy of Bro. Grant's article as it appeared in the "Mail" of Oct. 23rd 1901. . . .

Monday, 21 October 1901, Tokyo

A clear and pleasant day. Remained in my room practically all day reading and studying. In the evening Bro. Ensign did some singing in the parlor of the hotel for the entertainment of the guests. I received, via Seattle mail, a letter from Grace Frost, written for her by her friend Maud Baggerley. The announcement of the improvement of Grace's condition was gratifying and I thanked God that he had heard the prayer which Bro. Kelsch, Bro. Ensign, and myself offered in her behalf when we visited her and anointed her with oil for the recovery of her health, when she was in the Hospital at Portland.

Tuesday, 22 October 1901, Tokyo

Today has also been very pleasant. After breakfast we sat our on the upper veranda of the hotel and enjoyed a good sun bath, while we listened to Bro. Grant read from "Nelson on Infidelity." Immediately after tiffin, Bro. Grant and myself took a short walk for the purpose of having a little exercise and releiving ourselves for a little while of the close confinement of our rooms where we had been pouring over books and articles to newspapers ever since we came to Tokyo.

During the day Bro. Grant prepared an article to the "Jiji", a Japanese paper which had published the contents of a memorial to the government officials which had been gotten up, evidently by some Christian minister or ministers, and signed by the Presidents of the Japan and Tokyo Women's Reform Societies, requesting that the government would officially forbid us teaching the doctrines of "Mormonism" in Japan. As the "Jiji" had approved editorially this memorial and urged that the government would consider well its contents, we felt that it would be proper to defed ourselves through the columns of the paper which had attacked us.

The memorial urged the supression of "The Mormons" and their proselyting in Japan for four reasons: first, that while Mr. Grant had stated that polygamy had ceased as a prictice in the church and that the missionaries who had come to Japan did not intend to preach it here, yet such was not the case, for in Utah at the present time men were living with their plural wives, and that while we would not preach the doctrine on the start, still when we for some converts we would indulge them in this practice, and that our claim to the contrary was a falsehood; second, That the President of our church was possessed of great power and that he ruled as a king and all followers were as servants to him, and that allegience to the Priesthood was above allegience to civil power, and, therefore productive of great danger to this country politically; third, that "Mormonism" is characterized with bloody and foul murders and deeds so black that the people of Japan "shudder at their recital;" fourth, that wherever we go we exaggerate the resources of Utah and picture wonderful advantages that are to be had in the "Mormon" metropolis, until the minds of the people are filled with exictment and emigrate to Utah as rapidly as possibile, thus draining the country of its people and weakning the power of the government. Any one of these reasons was said by the memorialists to be sufficient to cause and justify the ejection of the "Mormons" and their heretical creed. This would have been a very strong appeal to the Government for the official forbidding of "Mormonism" in Japan if it were not for one thing; that is, that all the charges are false and their weakness easily shown. The final copying of Bro. Grants's reply to the above was left till the following day.

Wednesday, 23 October 1901, Tokyo

A delightful day. The rooms which we occupied both faced to the north and consequently at this time of the year were unpleasant to sit in without a fire, and still if the sun could shine in, it would not be necessary to use a store or a grate to head up the rooms as the sun was still sufficiently warm to moverate the atmosphere except where buildings cast a shadew unto which the sun's rays did not penetrate. We missionaries also being away from home upon our own resources as it were, therefore, felt that as long as the sun would keep us warm we could not afford to pay extra for coal, so we applied to the manager for rooms in the front part of the house where we could received the benefit of the sun. The result of our appeal was that we were given two very fine rooms in the front of the house and we were indeed grateful for the change for not only were we favored with the sun but with fifty per cent better rooms. The entire day, practically, was spent in moving and getting settled in our new quarters where we fell we will be real happy for the rest of our stay at this hotel.

The article to the "Jiji" was finished today and sent in for publication. Another short squib was sent to the "Mail" for the purpose of correcting an error that had appeared in its columns, concerning the visit of a Japanese Embassy to Salt Lake City in 1872.[61]

Thursday, 24 October 1901, Tokyo

Quite a strong wind blew all day. In our morning meeting we started to read "The Voice of Warning," as we had the day before finished Nelson's book on infidelity. In the afternoon I wrote a letter to Emma, and assisted in the final copying of Bro. Grant's short article to the "Mail." The evening and till after midnight was spent in talking over the things which pertain unto the work of the Lord upon the earth, and the particular endowments given to some of the men who have held and do now, hold prominent positions in the Church.

Friday, 25 October 1901, Tokyo

Considerable rain fell during the night and the day was cloudy and cool. Received via San Francisco mail a letter from mother. All well at home. Elais Ashton and Geo. J. Cannon had returned from their missions. Both were in good health and seemed to have improved considerably during their sojurn abroad. The day passed off quietly—nothing out of the usal happened.

Saturday, 26 October 190l, Tokyo

A bright and a most delightful day. Wallowed along in the same old rut. In the evening had a pleasant chat with Mr. and Mrs. Ourdan Mr. Ourdan was the inventor of an engraving machine and was now selling samples to the Japanese government. Their home is in Washington D.C.

Sunday, 27 October 1901, Tokyo

The day was cold and dismal. I spent the day in fasting and prayer. In the afternoon we had our regular Sabbath Sarcramental Meeting. At the request of the hotel'S manager, Bro. Ensign sang a number of songs for the entertainment of the guests. A young man from Portugal who was staying at the Hotel for a day or two and who was an accomplished musician, played the accompaiment for Horace's songs and also played two or three piano solos which were indeed beautiful. Bro. Ensign seemed to be particularly blessed of the Lord for he sang as he had seldom done before. The four of us sang a trio as a kind of benediction to the gathering. I was introduced to Mr. McCulla of "the Japan Times." He seemed to be well pleased with their singing of the evening, and as it is a good thing, generally, to make a favorable impression on newspaper men, I have felt since, that this meeting with Mr. McCulla would remove much of the projudice which the paper that he was connected with had shown aginst us in the controversy on "Mormonism."

Monday, 28 October 1901, Tokyo

It had rained considerabley during the night and the day continued cloudy and damp. Spent the forenoon in conversing with some of the Japanese guides who were always around the hotel. They having learned that we were anxious to learn the Japanese language said that if we would come down and talk with them that they would help us as much as they could and seemed to be quite pleased to think that we were sufficiently interested in their language to learn it. In the afternoon Bro. Kelsch and I took a walk around the adjoining neighborhood. We saw many odd sights as we walked along the streets. Little children carrying babies on their backs; women also with their children tied onto them going about their work, and in many instances on some of the boats which we noticed going up and down the river, these women were rowing equally as hard as their husbands and unloading and loading the cargoes of freight with the rapidity and strength of men, their babies undergoing different changes of position which to a white child would be a very unpleasant exercise.

We saw other children running around the streets with their bodies literally covered with large sores which in many instances had eaten most of the hair off of their heads. Ever since coming to this land I have been occasionally sickened with such terrible sights of skin eruptions which is undoubtly due to the immense amount of venarial trouble that exists as a result of the permiscus sexual relations among the people. Other children we saw with their heads shaved in all kinds of ways: some were shaved entirely; some heads were shorn of all but a little bunch of hair about one and a half inches long and covering a circular spot about an inch in diameter on the crown, other heads were only half shaved and indeed it seemed that some had been in too big a hurry to have more than half of their hair taken off at a time.

Tuesday, 29 October 1901, Tokyo

Cloudy and cold. In our morning meeting we completed the reading of the "Voice of Warning."[62] THis has been another day of study and other brain work, which is becoming more or less tiresome and tedious. In the evening one of the boarders in the hotel came to our room to spend a little time in chatting with us as he felt quite lonesome in living in a hotel without having anyone to talk to and thus relieve the monotony of hotel life which he had had for some months past. His name is Mr. Bowman, an Englishman who lived in India some time before coming to Japan, but who had to leave that country because of a breaking down in his health. He is a very liberal man and seems to be quite broad in his views, but has the weakness of drinking to much liquor.

Wednesday, 30 October 1910, Tokyo

It had rained quite heavily during the night and in the forenoon it was damp and dismal, but toward evening it cleared off and became rather chilly. Mr. Hiroi, the gentleman with whom we had been negoitiating to teach and translate for us, wrote a day or two ago that he would be unable to leave the school in which he was engaged as a teacher of English and philosophy, until some days when another instructor can be secured to take his place, and at the same time realizing that our time was extremely valuable told of another man whom we could hire until he was able to come. He mentioned his name and after considering the matter we decided to to secure his friend's services until such times as he was released from his present position. Today the alternate came and judging from the few moments talk that we had while arranging for our future work with him, he is a bright and intelligent fellow who will make our work very interesting. His name is Rev. Aoki and has been engaged as a poeacher in a German mission in this land for some time past. We arranged with him to call three times a week, beginning next Monday. The price to be paid is 2 yen (1.00) per day.

Thursday, 31 October 1901, Tokyo

The day was clear but cold. The weather at present so I am told is very peculiar for this time of the year. The cold and stormy season seems to have come ahead of time. Such cold weather is characteristic of Januar rather than October and November.

In our meeting we started the reading of the New Testament. In the afternoon I wrote a letter to father and enclosed some pictures which we had taken in Yokohama. Five of them were views of the hill and spot where we held our prayer meeting in the woods and dedicated the land of Japan as a missionary field for the proclaimation of the Gospel. (see Sept. 1st)

Friday, 1 November 1901, Tokyo

Rained most of the day. Bro. Grant went to Yokohama for the purpose of handing a letter to Mr. Eppinger of the Grand Hotel who was going to America and ekpected to visit Salt Lake City. The letter introduced Mr. Eppinger to Bro. Grants brother B.F. Grant and requested that all hospitality be shown Mr. Eppinger as long as he remained in Salt Lake City. The rest of us brethren remained in the hotel all day and passed the timr away in study and conversation with Mr. Bowman one of the boarders in the hotel who came to our room and spent mos of the afternoon with us.

Saturday, 2 November 1901, Tokyo

One of those half and half days. Some day or two ago Bro. Ensign received four tickets from Mrs. Warton admitting us into a concert to be held in the Y.M.C.A. hall at Uyeno Park. I did not know that these tickets had been received and was therefore quite surprised when the brethren stated that it was time for us to be getting ready to go to "That affair." It was announced to begin in the afternoon at 2p.m. Well what was it anyhow that they were talking about? I had not heard that I was expected to be ready to go anywhere. Why did'nt you know that we had received four complimentary tickets from Mrs. Warton to atted a concert to be given this aftrnoon? Why no, I had heard nothing about our going to a concert, and while I knew that Horace had received a note from Mrs. Warton I did not think it was anything that concerned me, for Horace has had so many Mrs. fall in love with him that I thought it was just a note telling him how much his singing had impressed one of his fair admirers and how much they hoped to have the privilege of hearing his wonderful voice again. What, can it be true that the ladies are falling in love with one of the "Mormon" missionaries? Yes, of course it is true. Some have become desperately smittin even some who are tied up to other fellows, and it is amusing how they purr over the magnificence of our singer's voice when they mean the singer himself.

But returning to the concert to which I have just been invited. It being quite a long way to Uyeno Park we had to leave the hotel three quarters of an hour before the scheduled time of the concert. After a ride on one of the Tokyo horse-cars (anybody who has been in Tokyo and rode on one of these snail-like moving excuses for cars which are used for the transit of passangers, can realize what I mean when I say that we rode on a horse-car) we arrived at Uyeno Park located in the North end of Tokyo city. We hastened through the park in search of the Y.M.C.A. hall for we were now behined time; and it was not till inquiry after inquiry that we finally arrived at the hall. We were directed up stairs to the second story and after giving up our tickets to a young Japanese who was stationed at the door we entered a large room which was well filled, mostly by Japanese. In fact the entire affair seemed to be in the hands of the Japanese and we were directed to our seats by one of the most beautiful Japanese women that I have ever seen—indeed I had trouble controlling my feelings of admiration when I saw her, but with an effort I kept in mind the fact that I was a missionary and much shut my eyes to the alluring beauty of the fair sex.

As we went in there was a strange mixture of sounds met our ears and looking down to the platform we saw four natives, dressed in the finest of black silk kimonas and squatted on the floor having their attention securely fixed on the instruments before them. These were playing and singing one of the difficult classical pieces in Japanese music, the name of which the program did not give; and they seemed to throw their whole soul into the notes of the music and it was evidently a great delight to the large number of Japanese who listened with the closest attention and applauded with enthusatism when it was ended. But to my ear it appeared to be the most complete jargon of notes that could possibly be brought together, entirely without harmony according to the foreign meaning of the term. The names of the instruments which they played are: "Koto,"[63] (there were two of these) "Samisen,"[64] and "Kokiu."[65] I will not attempt to give a discription of these instruments until some future time when I learn more about them.

Following this number was another performance which I guess would be known as a song, altho I would not swear to this as a fact. At any rate we were favored with some more Japanese music, consisting of three parts, a claranet sort of arrangement made out of a piece of bamboo about two inches in diameter and so large at the end into which the player blowed that it seemed to stretch his mouth a great deal farther than if he were eating soup with a table-spoon, the other instrument was a banjo arrangement, while the third part was made up by the jews-harp voice of the person who played on an instrument which looked like the counterfit of the banjo. In order to see how this sort of music appealed to the ear of a lover of music such as is heard in America, Europe, and elsewhere, I watched the expressions which appeared on Bro. Ensign's face. For a moment he would smile and look pleased as though there was a slight glimpse of harmony to be detected, but suddenly his countenance changed and he wrinkled his face like when a child is going to cry and I judged that such strains of music were to him more like the filing of iron than the delicate tones found in the lines that represent the fruit of a master mind.

Following this part of the program came some singing which was intellegable to us for it was rendered by some of the foreigners who were laboring among the Japanese in Christian Association work. These songs were not out of the ordinary, but quite pleasant when so far away from that part of the world where great artists are to be frequently heard. As I compared in my mind the tastes of the Japanese musician with those of the foreigners I would not help but feel that The music which we were now listening to, and in which we fould great delight, was equally as discordant to the native eat as their's had been to me. Therefore I felt a respect in my heart for the tastes of the Japanese who evidently considered their's as far superior to others as others thaught their's superior to the Japanese.

The class of Japanese which we saw in the audience make us feel that there was some thing for us to so among the educated in this land for there were truly many bright and intelligent faces, in fact some were so much after the style of foreingners that we felt somewhat inferior to many of the neatly dressed and keen looking fellows. As we looked upon this magnificent audience an and saw the signs of brain and perception that was depicted on the features of those present, we could not help but say to ourselves, "Oh if we could only have the chance to lift our voices in proclaiming the Gospel to people assembled here."

When we came out of the concert we walked leisurely through the Park enjoying the grandur of the scenery which surrounded us on every side. The gigantic maple trees which towered up like the massive pines on the Rocky Mountain forests were clothed to their very topmost branches with a mantel of green moss, while their immense arms furnished abundant foilage to shade the mossy earth beneath. Flying from tree to tree and chattering amid the branches were numerous crows whose boistrous cry often startled me as we strolled along the path below.

Scattered permiscously, through the Park were many little Japanese tea-houses whose pretty waitress tried with there dimpled smiles and courteous bows to persaude us to pause and rest ourselves while sipping from their dainty cups and tea which they serve with shigh glances and well chosen flirtations from their goo-goo eyes. Ah! it was too bad to disappoint those appealing smiles and spurn those graceful bows, but we were missionaries whose duty it was to to be blind, deaf, and dumb to the destroying nature of women. We passed on in silence not allowing even a smile to be given to the those lovely maidens; our faces were set as stone and like the monks of Africa showed no appreciation of their invitations.

We saw many ancient temples, and burial plots in which the headstones were covered with moss as if to remind those who might pause to look at them that here, some hundreds of years before, was laid the remains of a great priest of Buddha or a brave leader among their forefathers of the present race. As it was getting late we had to leave the pleasant surroundings of the Park and catch the first car so as to get back to the hotel before dark.

Sunday, 3 November 1901, Tokyo

The day was clear and beautiful. It being the first Sunday in November the "Mormons" did not eat break-or dinner, but remained in their room all day reading the word of God as it was spoken by men of olden time as they were moved upon by the Holy Ghost. In the aftrnoon about four o'clock we held our Fast Meeting and besides pertaking of the Sacrament we bore testimony of the goodness of the Lord to us and we bowed ourselves in humility before our Heavenly Father invoking him for his continued blessing unto us.

We recieved quite a number of papers from home and were delighted to see the accounts of the conference meetings and learn that Bro. Clawson had been appointed to act as second councelor to Prest. Snow in the Presy. of the Church. His appointment was however a great surprise to us all for we had thaught it likely that any other one of the Apostles would be chosen for this positon rather than Bro. Clawson, but he is a man who has been tried in the furnace and has stood the test for which God has magnified him. "He hath humbled himself therefore God has exalted him." The death of his Prest. however may make a change in the future, but the future is in the hands of the Lord and He will direct His servant Prest. Jos. F. Smith to call those to his assistance who will be the proper ones to labor in the First Presidency.

Monday, 4 November 1901, Tokyo

Our teacher, Mr. Aoki, came about 10:00 a.m. and we had a lesson which lasted for, I should judge, two hours. We found that this gentleman was somewhat better informed than Mr. Koyana[66] of Yokohama who had been our tutor in that city, but while he was a better educated man yet he did not have the nack of imparting his knowledge to others that Mr. Koyana had. In this we were very much disappointed, especially me, for I had hoped to be able to make rapid progress with his assistance. The remainer of the day was spent in studying and writing.

Tuesday, 5 November 1901, Tokyo

The morning was spent in conversation with our teacher. Bro. Kelsch and also Bro. Grant for a little while, preached the Gospel to him for all they were worth, but by the conversation we found that he, Mr. Aoki, was more throughly versed in the scriptures than a majority of those with whom we had come in contact, and he would not be convinced of what we said without some argument. I received a letter from home written by father and also containing a revised copy of the blessing he gave to me on the evening of my departure from home. I was much pleased to hear of the good health of all who were near and dear to my heart and from whom I had been separated for over three months. In the evening I wrote a letter to mother in answer to one which I received from her some time ago. Bro. Ensign has been having trouble with his stomach most of the day, and Bro. Kelsch stayed in bed during all of yesterday morning suffering from a severe headache caused by some rincid grease which some of the food had been cooked in and which his stomach refused to digest.

Wednesday, 6 November 1901, Tokyo

A dismal day having rained most of the time. Bro. Grant had been in bed all day with the lumbago which resulted from a cold he contracted the day before. Mr. Aoki called at ten o'clock and we had our lesson in Japanese. Spent the evening in conversation with Mr. Bowman a genial companion boarder which we have here in the hotel.

Thursday, 7 November 1901, Tokyo

Rained all day. Our teacher came in the morning a little easier than usual consequently we had a few moments more instruction (of the kind he was able to give) than heretofore. We had decided in our morning meeting to dismiss this gentleman as our teacher for we felt that we were paying an enormous amt. for the instruction which we were receiving, consequently we paid what we owed him and told him that we would be able to get along without his assistance in the future. He invited me to come up to Chiba and visit him at his home and if possible to come to-morrow. The proposition struck me very favorably and I arranged to visit him to-morrow.

Friday, 8 November 1901, Tokyo/Chiba

According to the arrangements made for my going to Mr. Aoki's home, I took the train at 12:00 m. for Chiba and after a ride of an hour through a beautiful farming district arrived at my destination. Mr. Aoki had met me at the station at Tokyo and during the journey from Tokyo to Chiba we had a friendly discussion on religious subjects.

Mr. Aoki I found was a believer in the bible spiritually, for every passage which I would quote I sub-stancitation of my side of the question would loose its literal interpretation and be as he claimed it should be translated as having reference to the spiritual man, thing, God, & etc. In speaking of the gifts of the Spirit as shown in the different actions of the Savior and the Apostles, he said that all the miracles wrought were upon the spiritual man and that the physical man was not healed of the palsy, blindness, lameness, and etc., To such statements as these I was able to reply successfully and forced him to acknowledge that he did not believe in those parts of the Bible which did not seem to correspond to his ideas. He did not doubt the vision of Jos. Smith, but it was the result of the mind working on spiritual things which caused him to become a religious genius just the same as Peter, John, Paul, and others were religious geniuses; to say that personages actually appeared to him just as one man might met another and converse with him was not true. He explained the conversation of Paul in this way: Paul had undoubtly been thinking on the claims of this man Jesus and the sincerity of the Christians, his followers, and the very fact that his mind was dwelling on these things caused him to be overcome and fall to the ground in a trance of spiritual thaught during which time his mind was active and he felt in his heart the words "Saul, Saul, why persecutest thou Me." Jesus Christ did not speak to him as one man might speak to another, but it was the result of a series of thoughts which worked to a climax. I remarked to him that Paul must of been in that condition into which the Methodists exite themselves at their revival meetings, when they rant around and shout until they become so worked up that the Devil takes possession of them and they faint into what they call a trance during which they see all kinds of things, such as snakes, lizzerds, toads, divils with pich-forks, and etc. When I asked him how it was that the men who were with Saul became frightened when they also heard the voice, he was silent for this was a part of the circumstances which he did not believe, I presume because it is a hard thing to spiritualize.

Mr. Aoki's house is about a half a mile from the station and we soon arrived where we were greeted with bows and welcoming smiles from the Japanese women who were sitting around on the floor. It being the custom to take the shoes off before going in on the matted floors of a Japanese home, I sat down and pulled off my shoes before going in. This house was one of the well built and well furnished places of the city. The first thing that a Japanese does for the entertainment of his guest is to furnish him with a cup of tea, just as in England it is etiquette to present whiskey or wine of some kind. Of course I being "Mormon" and taught not to drink tea or liquor of any sort had to decline the courtesy by making as neat a little speech as I could. An expression of astonishment stole over my host's face but he took the explaination kindly and ordered a cup of cold water for me. After a few moments I was invited to pertake of a Japanese meal in strictly Japanese style. I had to smile at myself as I sat there eating rice and fish with chop-sticks and being waited upon by a pretty Japanese maiden who did everything with such percision accompanied with the most exquisite smile imaginable.

Immediately after dinner we took a walk around the town and called at one of Mr. Aoki's friends who was a Buddhist Priest and lived on the outskirts of the town near the sea coast. A beautiful view and the air cool and exilerating. I was delighted with what I saw and the beautiful location of this little village (for it was not more than a village) which was so pleasantly located on the sea coast. Mr. Aoki teaches two classes of Japanese soldiers who are studying English and at his invitation I went with him by train to a little village known as Yotsukaido some five miles east of Chiba to where the Goverment barracks at which these students were serving was built. It was dark when we arrive there and consequently I did not see any of the sights in this place. A heavy rain had fallen the night before and the roads were quite muddy and as we walked along in the dark we often stepped into a puddle of mud which many times went nearly to the tops of our shoes. His first class of students consists of some twenty students, five only being present on this occasion. At his request I took the class for the evening and listened to their recitation of their lesson. They seemed to appreciate my efforts with them and thanked me very much. I left my cards with them and followed Mr. Aoki through the dark again until we came to another building in which his second class was held. These students were older than the first and were more advanced in their rank as soldiers. There were some ten or twelve in this class, and a brighter lot of fine looking fellows I had never seen. They provided us with cake and tea and paid the utmost attention to all that was said.

While here an earthquake shook the house until it rocked and cracked from roof to foundation. This is the most severe shock that I have felt and Mr. Aoki said that it had been a long time since such an one had been felt by him. When we were through with this class it was nearly ten o'clock and we had to hasten to the depot to catch the last train to Chiba. I had enjoyed myself immensely during this visit to Yotsukaido, and as I looked into the bright and intelligent faces of those students, my heart filled with a desire to preach the Gospel to them and I felt a love for them which I had not felt for the Japanese people before.

We got back to Mr. Aoki's house about eleven o'clock and were again welcomed by the women who bowed themselves upon the floor in courtesy to their master and his friend. A meal of bread, jam, and rice was speedily prepared and we ate heartily as we talked over the attitude of the "Mormons," past and present, on the subject of polygamy. After the meal the table was taken away and my bed made on the floor. A Japanese bed consists of two "footons"[67] (bedding which looks very much like comforters only containing much more padding) laid on the floor; a pillow a foot long and eight inches thick filled with straw or some other material equally as hard; and lastly as many "footons" on top as may be required for the comfort of the person. It is also the custom of the Japanese to sleep in "Kimonos" instead of night-shirts or gowns, so in order that I experience as much as possible of the native style I was provided with an unsavory-looking "kimono" which when I had put on made the inmates of the place laugh heartily. Also, according to custom, I was provided with a little tallow dip which was placed in a box the sides of which were of paper through which a dim light glimmered all night long. I said good night and the sliding door dividing my room from the others were closed and I was left alone to ponder on my condition and drink in more fully the surroundings which were so strange to me.

It would require a volume to contain the thoughts that passed through my mind in the two or three minutes that I spent looking around before getting into the Japanese cradle prepared for me on the floor. I noticed that the pillow was a little soiled by the grease from someone else's head which had lain on it before and not desiring to mix breeds, I took a sheet of writing paper which I found lying on a desk in one corner of the room and put it over the pillow as a protection against unpleasant feelings. My heart was full of gratitude to God for the experience of the day and for the prospects of the night, and I prayed to my Father in Heaven for strength to soon be able to proclaim the Gospel to this people in their own tongue and mingle with them constantly in their homes. I woke up a time or two during the night but the faint ligt which came form the tallow-dip brought me quickly to a realization of where I was, and I rolled over with an assurance of my safety and was soon asleep, again to dream of my future life in the land of the Mikado.[68]

A Japanese house presents quite a different appearence in the day time than at night. During the day everything is thrown wide open and as nearly the entire sides of the house are made of sliding doors, it looks, when open, like a skeleton of a building into which the sun shines and through which the breezes blow with perfect freedom; but at night the scene is different, the doors are all closed tight, and no air comes in nor does the moonlight or the feeble dawn of morn find its way beyond those cheerless walls.

It was half past eight when I got up and after nine o'clock when breakfast was ready. O what a breakfast! Warm condensed milk with rice and sweetened with a something which looked like a mixture of maple and white sugar and a very choice dish among the Japanese consisting of sliced raw fish prepared in some kind of a black sauce filled with horse-radish. The sight of this meal was sufficient to satisfy my appetite, but I, realizing that a Japanese would consider it a serious thing for his guests to refuse the food which he prepared for them, ate just as much as I could but, you bet, I left considerable of the raw fish uneaten.

When we had finished our breakfast we took a walk out to one of the ancient temples on the edge of the town and from where one of the most picturesque views of the ocean can be had. The temple was closed and therefore we were unable to see the inside save as we looked through the slat doors in the front of the building.

When we got back to the house again Mr. Aoki had some letter-writing to do, so I sat down and read one of his books for a few moments when the servant brot in some food the name of which I could not tell nor can I tell all the constituants from which it is made. This I do know about it, however, that it was by far better to look at than to eat. From the way in which the Japanese seem to enjoy this class of food I should judge that it was a sort of a delicacy among them. The pieces were about the size of a small biscuit and shaped very much like a biscuit. The outer coating was of uncooked dough while the inside was made of sugar and some fruit peculiar to Japan; and when you take a bite and start to chew it the dough and the sugar mixes into one of the mushiest messes that you ever had in your mouth. Fortunately Mr. Aoki was called away immediately after presenting me with the second piece of which I had taken one bite and while he was gone, I chucked the rest over the neighboring fence and made out when he come back that

I was just smacking my lips over the last mouthful of this most delicious (?) morsel of food. I was invited to have more, but I succeeded in escaping the ordeal by saying that my stomach was small and quickly filled and that I would be overloading it if I were to eat any more.

I had hardly finished my meal when a English gentleman came to see if Mr. Aoki would not take a walk with him during the afternoon, but as I was there as his guest, Mr. Aoki felt that it would not be right for him to leave me, but this difficuly was quickly obivated by the gentleman extending his invitation to me. Mr. Aoki, however insisted that we should have dinner before we went. I was surprised at this for I thot the ordeal through which I had just passed was quite enough for me and the thaughts of another meal made me nearly sick for there was no telling what would be presented, and I could not refuse for fear of hurting the feelings of my host. I was thankful when I saw food that I could eat and consequently enjoyed this meal quite well. Mr. Normon (the English gentleman) came into the room while we were eating and we started a conversation on the truth of Bible history, and it was quarter to four when we finished.

Mr. Normon said that he had traveled all over the Land covered by the Bible and said that the discoveries that have been made by scientific men as well as the observations made of the land itself is an evidence of the absurdity of the record that is now considered sacred. This statement surprised me very much for I had read the reports of scientific reaserches through that region and they all contradicted this gentleman's statements. I wondered how it was that he could come to such an opposite conclusion to that arrived at by world-wide professors of geology and the study of antiquity, and immediately there arose in my mind a doubt as to the truth of this man's statements concerning his deep study of conditions and discoveries in the Holy Land. With the blessing of the Lord I was able to refute his arguments at least so it was in my estimation, for I got him to a point where he had but little to say and reminded me that it was time to go.

Mr. Normon was living at a hotel known as "The Kaikikan" in the district of Inage R.R. Station, two miles west of Chiba. As it was only two miles to the hotel Mr. Normon invited us to take a walk out to his home which he assured me was very prettily located. The road led along the sea shore receding from which was a wooded bluff, thus making a most delightful path along which to stroll. It took us nearly an hour to walk from Mr. Aoki's place to the cottage of Mr. Normon. It was indeed a place, such as he had said, very beautifully located in a grove of pine trees through which the sea could be seen and the boats which played along the shore. At Mr. Normon's invitation I drank a glass of soda-water and looked through his house and observed the most pleasant surroundings of the place. After doing this I observed that it was time to go to the station and catch the train back to Chiba. Bidding Mr. Norman good-bye, I, with Mr. Aoki, started for the depot and arrived at Chiba at about half past six. As the train left for Tokyo at 6:15 I had to hurriedly tell the folks good-bye and thanking them for their kindness, I hastened to the train and arrived at the hotel in Tokyo at 8:45 p.m. finding the brethren all well. Bro. Grant had recovered from his attack of lumbago and was around as usual.

Sunday, 10 November 1901, Tokyo

A pleasant and bright Sabbath day. Our Sunday Sacrament meeting was held in the morning in which we also discussed again the subject of going out among the Japanese and living with them in their homes. There was an undecided feeling as to whether we would make more progress with the language, in its most perfect expression, out among the people of country settlements, than we would by staying here in Tokyo under the tutorship of Mr. Hiroi, who wrote us last Friday that he would be with us some day this week. In consequence of our lack of inspiration on this matter we decided to wait until Mr. Hiroi came and see what progress we could make with his assistance, but at the same time we regretted any furthur delays in our work. Bro. Grant expressed deep regrets (such as the rest of us felt) in not being blessed with the inspiration of the Lord concerning our movements in this land more than he had been. We all recognized that the hand of the Lord was over the work here still we desired to know His mind and will concerning it, in the execution of which we desired to labor with all the energy and strength that we possessed.

After dinner Bro. Kelsch and Bro. Ensign went out for a walk; Bro. Grant and I retired to our rooms where we were writing or otherwise busily engaged when the office boy came to the door with a card for

Bro. Ensign notifying him that Mrs. Parker, our Yokohama boarding-house keeper, was in the parlor down stairs and would like to see him. Of course we knew that no one of us could entirely fill the place of Bro. Ensign in the estimation of Mrs. Parker. Horace's voice and jolly disposition made him quite an object of admiration for our Yokohama landlady and he became her confident; indeed Horace has proved a successful heart crusher among the fair sex wherever we have gone and what was origanly a joke with us has become a very significant proverb—That Horace should never be allowed to go out alone lest he be kidnapped by those tender creatures known as women.

Bro. Grant hastened down stairs to act as proxy for Horace who fortunately for us was absent, as Bro. Grant soon came back with the information that Mrs. Warton was also there and that they had come to take Bro. Ensign out carriage riding, but he being absent had invited us to ride with them. It was too bad that Horace should loose this chance as it would have been a very appropiate celebration of his first birth-day in Japan, still I confess that I did not object to acting as a substitute for the prospects of carriage rides for "Mormon" missionaries were rather unfavorable and such treats would be few and far between. Bro. Grant and I hastily got ready and after some dispute with the carriage-men about four of us riding in a vehicle that was only strong enough, they claimed, for two, we started out, myself and the two ladies in the carriage and Bro Grant in a rikishaw. (the dispute as to the number that should ride in the carriage, having been decided in favor of the carriage men)

Mrs. Warton speaking in Japanese directed the driver to take us to a place in the northwest part of Tokyo where there was being held an exhibit of wax-work, such as is given every year during the chrysan-themum season. The place (park perhaps it is called) where this show was being given was about three quarters of an hour's ride from the hotel, which was made pleasant by descriptions given by Mrs. Warton of the different places and houses that we passed.

We were the guests of Mrs Warton and, you bet, we found it out before we had gone very far, for she alighted from the carriage and paid the the two rikisha-men who had been pulling Bro. Grant ten sen each as tabero (food) money and was just going to hand the driver a similar amount when I was brot to my senses and succeeded in paying the driver first. It was a source of great humiliation to both Bro. Grant and myself to have a lady pay our way and do the tipping of the rikisha-men, but we soon learned that we would have to submit to the ordeal without complaining. She had invited us and did not intend to have us pay out any money and after getting some change she insisted on paying me the amount I had hand-ed to the carriage driver, but I defeated her in this attempt.

First we went into a plant exhibit where Mrs. Warton bought and presented me with a very small cac-tus plant, which I could not help but feel was her way of getting even with me for paying out ten sen. Leaving this place which was not of much interest we followed like sheep after our shepherdress who led us next into one of the wax-work exhibits. Here we saw some of the most beautiful floral displays that I have ever witnessed, and which spoke in unmistakable terms of the wonderful artistic ability of the Japanese people. Figures in wax of the nobles, kings, princesses, warriors and others of the early fudual in Japan were to be seen in different attitudes on every side. Some represented scenes of bloody combat between man and man; others told of love scenes which happened long ago; others spoke of the manner of worshiping the idols of the past; others of court scenes; others of the heroic deeds which are now chronicled in history; while others spoke of the charm that music exerted on hearts of people in the days gone by. Each image was not a representation of the original actors of these historic scenes but of the recent depictors of the original characters as seen upon the stage to-day. Each figure was clothed in vest-ments emblamatic of the ancient garb, and made entirely with fresh flowers that are renewed every day. The gorgeous robes of nobility as seen in royal palaces the glittering armor of the warrior, the plain and simple vestments of the servant, the native costume of the musician, were all portrayed in perfect form and every color was produced in the most exquisite way and with the most delicate harmony that flowers in the hands of human beings can possibly be made to yield. Mountains, forests, gardens, palaces, and massive steps leading to them were also laid out with an exact art that was marvelous to me. To give such an exhibition as this required millions upon millions of flowers, and of a kind that would be considered rare as well as precious among the florists at home. The labor also that is required to do the work connected with such an enterprise is enough to dishearten the majority of men among the white races, but it seems that for such works of art the Japanese are especially adapted and take great delight in what they see as a result of their untiring efforts.

We went through two more exhibits similar to the first, and in all it was a mass of flowers arranged in different ways. By the time we had gone througt the third place it was almost dark and the others were closed so we found our way back to the entrance where we had left our carriage and rikisha.

Having rode to the place in the carriage I took the rikisha back to the hotel. As I rode along I thought over all that I had seen and I wondered at the extraordinary kindness of Mrs. Warton in giving us, who were almost strangers to her, such pleasant entertainment as she had done to-day and formerly. I felt that she was entitled to the blessings promised to those who treat the messengers of the Lord with kindness and administer unto their wants, so I offered up a silent prayer that God would bless her for her kindness to us as manifested in many different ways.

Mrs. Warton and Mrs. Parker came over to the hotel and had dinner with us after which we spent a very pleasant evening together in the parlor. Bro. Ensign sang the old songs which had appealed so strongly to Mrs. Parker while we were living at her house in Yokohama. The four of us sang together two of the old hymns and also entertained our guests by showing them the book of views which we had of Salt Lake City and vicinity Our little gathering broke up about 10:00 o'clock and we were all well satisfied with the hours we had spent in eachothers society.

Monday, 11 November 1901, Tokyo

This day I received a letter from Bishop Empey, which had been lost for some time here in the Post Office. It was addressed to me at Yokohama, general delivery, and judging from the number of tags which were attached to it when it reached me, I should imagine that it had been sent to not less than thirteen different places before it found the right one.

The mail which also came from America today, brot the news of the reorganization of the First Presidency of the church, and to say that I was surprised to see the name of Bro. John R. Winder as the First counselor and Bro. Anthon H. Lund as second counselor to Prest. Jos. F. Smith, does not in the least express the feelings of astonishment which the news aroused in me, yet I could not help but feel in my heart that they were God's choice and that he had truly chosen the proper men for the proper place. Bro. Lund I knew was one of the most intelligent men in the church as well as being full of great wisdom and judgment. Bro. Winder had been a man who was not very prominent in my mind yet his life is one of the most active, and at the same time humble, that has ever been recorded in the history of our people.

What an unassuming Presidency! yet, where in the world is there a stronger and better qualified triumph rate to rule over the church of God than is found in the newly organized Presidency of the Church of Jesus Christ of Latter-day Saints. Every man is broad and possessed with a strength and force of character which will push the work of the Lord along at what I feel will be, a marvelous speed, and that the Gospel will go forth to the inhabitants of the earth as it has never done before. I sustain with all my heart these three men as the Prophets of the Lord upon the earth, and pray earnestly that God will BLESS THEM FOREVER. Bro. Grant received a long letter from the new Presidency, telling of the actions of the Twelve in completing the organization of the church, and speaking of other matters pertaining to the work of the Lord in the future which, as Bro. Grant read, filled my heart with joy unspeakable.

I was led to rejoice in the appointment of Bro. Lund as one of the Presidency as it was he who blessed me, ordained me a seventy, and set me apart for this mission, in which he was assisted by Pres. Snow, Pres. Smith, and Apostles Teasdale, Grant and Smoot. It will ever be grateful recollection to me that I have been blessed under the hands of one of the Presidency of the church and also, that in that ordinance, the hands of two of the Presidents of the Church were upon my head. Thank God For Prophets and Apostles and the privilege of an association with them!!! May I ever be worthy of their confidence and esteem not only in this life but throughout all eternity.

Tuesday, 12 November 1901, Tokyo

Spent the day in writing up my journal and in writing a letter to Miss. Grace Frost in answer to one received from her some weeks ago. The day has been cold and piercing, making a fire quite comfortable.

Wednesday, 13 November 1901, Tokyo

Writing, reading, and studying occupied my time during the hours of daylight and in the evening I took a walk around the Tsukiji district, for the sake of a little exercise and a relief from the close confinement of our rooms out of which I had not gone for some days. Today has also been keenly cold.

Thursday, 14 November 1901, Tokyo

Loafed all day.

Friday, 15 November 1901, Tokyo

After tiffin Bro. Kelsch, Bro. Ensign, and myself took the train and went down to Yokohama. Bro. Ensign and I had been invited to have dinner and spend the evening with Mrs. Parker and Bro. Kelsch had some purchasing which he wanted to do in Yokohama so he went down with us for company. We spent most of the afternoon in purchasing things which the mission needed and also in getting some sundries for ourselves.

Bro. Horace and I arrived at Mrs. Parker's about an hour before dinner time. We chatted with Mr. Fell and Mrs. Parker during this wait and enjoyed a pleasant meal at the old table among those with whom we had become very intimate during the month and a half that we lived in Yokohama.

When dinner was over, we went with Mrs. Parker to the Van Schaich hall to listen to the program of the semi-monthly meeting of the Yokohama Literary Society. The program consisted of a lecture on "Carbon Photrogaphy,"[69] two piano solos, and a couple of Scotch ballads. As most of the entertainments in this country when compared with that which we have at home, this evening's program was executed in a very dry manner, but it was a change in the foreigner's monotonous life in Japan and consequently well received by those present. We got back to Tokyo just at midnight.

In the forenoon Bro. Grant received a letter from Apostle Lyman, now laboring in Europe. It was a most excellent letter and was full of advice and words of love which brot tears to the eyes of Bro. Grant.

Saturday, 16 November 1901, Tokyo

A pleasant day. The entire morning, nearly, was occupied by our meeting, in which we discussed quite freely on the different matters that pertain to the work here. In the afternoon about three o'clock, Mr. Hiroi, our long looked for teacher, came and we were indeed delighted. We arranged to begin work with him Monday morning at nine a.m. Mr. Hiroi's services to the school in which he had been teaching were highly appreciated by the President of the institution, and it was with reluctance that he parted with Mr. Hiroi. We felt happy that we had not insisted on Mr. Hiroi's coming to us before the school could find a teacher to take his place, for it had enabled Mr. Hiroi to leave with a good name and elevated us in the estimation of the officers of the school. We learned from Mr. Hiroi that some of his friends had been urging him to dissolve his contract with us for fear that his reputation would be forever blackened for having mingled with the much despised "Mormons." Among the friends who thus urged him, was Mr. Aoki, the gentleman with whom I spent so happy a day and night in Chiba last Friday and Saturday. The fact that Mr Hiroi had disregarded the warning from friends was quite a strong testimony to us that he had in his heart a firm belief that we were men of honor and that those who criticised us were in the dark concerning the true meaning of the cause which we represented. We were greatly rejoice to see Mr. Hiroi for we (or at least I) were for some months past building up considerable hope in what we would be able to accomplish with the assistance of a competent Japanese interpreter.

Sunday, 17 November 1901, Tokyo

Spent the day in fasting and prayer. In the morning Bro. Grant had occasion to correct some of us for the spirit of contention and argument that we had manifest for some time past. He had the spirit of the Lord resting upon him while reproving us and I rejoiced in the words which he spoke for the lessons taught appealed unto me as they had never done before. In the afternoon we held a sacrament meeting and spoke the feelings of our hearts with perfect freedom, expressing our appreciation of the advice which BRo. Grant had given us during the morning meeting, but at the same time we regretted that such a reproof of our actions had been necessary. Before the day had closed and even before our meeting closed our hearts, were filled with love one for another and we all asked each other's pardon for any injustice we had done.

Bro. Grant said that we should not discuss on those things in which their was no benefit or good of any kind whatsoever; of the necessity of exhibiting the greatest kindness in the word for each other, and be careful not to use harsh words that would wound the feelings of a brother, especially was it important that we should love eachother and be in the most perfect unity as we were out in a strange land as missionaries and needed the assistance of our Heavenly Father in our work and that we could not expect to receive any divine aid unless we conducted ourselves in a manner that would merit such assistance. He also spoke of the restless spirit which we had manifest in that we were not evidently accomplishing much and desired to get out and do more.

He said that if we had made the best of our time each day that we have been here that we would have been much farther advanced than we are and would be much better able to go out among the people, but as he had not received the impression from the Lord to send us out he felt that we were not justified in slighting the oppertunities which were before us here to learn the language, and that if we would from now on devote ourselves earnestly to our work that the Lord would bless us and make manifest unto us when it is time for us to go out among the people. Bro. Grant said that he did not want us to think that he desired to quench the testimony of the Spirit unto any one of us concerning our actions and that if we received from the Lord the desire to go out among the Japanese that it would be all right with him and that we could go with his blessing.

One of the ways in which the Savior taught the true principles of Christianity was by rebuking severely the wrong doing of the people and especially the hypocrisy and sin of the Scribes and Pharisees who claimed to be righteous priests to God, and I could not help but accept the correction from Bro. Grant as an act of charity on his part in setting us right before we got too far wrong. **I thank God with all my heart for Bro. Grant. and his kind words of council**.

Monday, 18 November 1901—Saturday, 30 November 1901, Tokyo

Nearly every morning from nine to twelve o'clock we received instruction from Mr. Hiroi our teacher, in the Japanese language, having for our lessons the study of the Japanese syllabary and the one hundred characters by which the syllables are represented. I am pleased to record that I have at this writing mastered these one hundred characters and can both read and write them though not very fast. Some translation has been done by Mr. Hiroi particularly letters and articles for newspapers also an article from the ERA regarding the conversion of Bro. Karl G. Maeser, written by himself.

Realizing that Christmas was approaching and that we would have to send our Christmas mail immediately, we have devoted much time in preparing letters for our folks at home and in sending little things as souvenirs of Japan I wrote a letter to father which, as near as we could judge without measuring it, was thirty feet in length. To mother I sent a silk handkerchief and four dozen views of Japan. To Aunt Clara, Aunt Hattie, and Emma I sent a silk handkerchief each. To Samuel I mailed a book "Things Japanese."[70] A Christmas card each to Bishop Empey and Bessie Badger. A long letter to J. A. McRae of the Colorado Mission and one of the same length to Will Erekson in New Zealand. A souvenir letter each to my sisters Jennie and Margaret. The mails from America have brought me two letters from Bishop Empey, one from my cousin J.A. McRae, and one from home. They all spoke of favorable conditions surrounding the writers. The Bishop, however, seemed to have the blues pretty bad over the loss of Lutie and Sister Woolley from the ward and at the same time Bro. McRae was rejoicing to think that he had been able to secure them as missionaries in his field. My heart leaped with joy when I read of the excellent condition of all at home and especially of the excellent health which father has been enjoying since I left. It is indeed encouraging to have good news from home for it seems to put renewed energy into me and I can go about my labors with a great deal more satisfaction and joy.

The weather has been very cold most of the time although there has been but little storm. The air being damp along the sea coast I feel the cold more than I did in the high altitude of the Rockies.

In a letter from Apostle Clawson we were told of a meeting of the Presidency and the Apostles in which it was decided to divide the Salt Lake Stake of Zion. This of course, means that father and the brethren who now form the Presidency of the Stake will be released and I feel that it will be a great relief to father for with his business and ecclesiastical labors he had too much to do for a man of his age. I thank God for the noble work of my father and I hope that the Lord will bless him so that he will feel well over the appointment of someone else to take his place for it will be a grand improvement to have younger men full of life and energy at the head of the centre stake of Zion.

Sunday, 1 December 1901, Tokyo

A clear cold day. Fast day in "Mormonville" Japan, and accordingly in the afternoon we held a testimony meeting in which we enjoyed a good spirit while speaking our feelings to eachother and before the Lord. Our remarks were more particularly on the things of the entire church than upon the special work which is before us here in Japan, but there was a good feeling manifest towards the work here and the spirit of unity was plainly felt. We expressed our love for eachother and our thanks for the health which the Lord had so abundantly blessed us with. Bro. Grant referred to the Thanksgiving day which had just passed an said that while there was no particular demonstration in this land on that day and that he himself had not manifest any particular thankful feelings before us, yet in his heart he was continually thanking the Lord for his manifold blessings; stating that he was never so full of gratitude before on any thanksgiving day for the reason that in the last year he had been blessed financially so as to be out of debt and free to come upon this mission, which, in itself, was a great honor that had been convered upon him.

In the evening while we were eating dinner, Mr. Moss one of our companion boarders while we were in Yokohama, came to see us and we spent a very delightful evening together. He is one of the oddest sticks that I ever met in my life and there is something about him that attracts the attention of others and those who become acquainted with him cannot help but like him in spite of the fact that he gets drunk very often and has other habits which are not of the best type.

Monday, 2 December 1901, Tokyo

A heavy rain fell all day. Devoted myself to the study of the language during the fore part of the day, but as I was suffering from a sore throat and headache, I did not accomplish much in this line.

In the evening Bro. Horace and myself went down town to select and mail 884 pictures of scenes in Japan which Bro. Grant ordered sent to his friends and fellow workers in the Priesthood and cooperations with which he was connected before he left for this mission. We brethren joined in sending a dozen each to the Presidency and Apostles as a Christmas box from Japan; accompanied with the season's greetings. The labor of selecting, sorting, packing, directing, and mailing so many views was quite a job and it took us so long that we did not get back to the hotel till ten o'clock, just one hour too late for supper. I was cold and did not feel very well so I went to bed right away after doctoring up a little. The rooms which we have here in the hotel are not at all comfortable as they are so drafty and I had taken a great cold from which I am not reaping the harvest.

To-day Bro. Ensign and myself decided that if it met with the approval of Bro. Grant that we would like to go out into the country or into some strictly Japanese quarter and see what we could accomplish by way of learning the language by being where we would have to make ourselves known as best we could by the use of what words we have already learned and what we would acquire by study and hearing others speak. Bro. Grant approved our feelings and we expect to look for a place immediately. W e had a day or two ago engaged rooms and board in another boarding-house but we countermanded the order making it for two instead of four.

Tuesday, 3 December 1901, Tokyo

A beautiful clear day. Before breakfast Bro. Grant received two letters from home; one from the First Presidency and the other from President Lund. In the letter from the Presidency, Bro. Grant found the advice which he had written for some seven or eight weeks ago and for which he was becoming very anxious. It was to the effect that he should learn the language and that we should separate and go out among the Japanese themselves to learn their language and not depend upon the instruction which we would receive from a teacher. The letter also read that it was the sentiment of the Presidency and Apostle that Bro. Grant should not send for his folks until we had been here at least a year and would have been able to form a thoroughly correct opinion of the method to be adopted in preaching the gospel to the natives of this land. This advice as seen, necessitated a change of proceedure and in an obscure way pointed out the fact that we were not pursuing the proper course to most quickly learn the language. I rejoiced exceedingly that Bro. Ensign and myself had decided the day before to go out and live with the people, as it is an evidence to me now that we were directed in our desires by the proper spirit. I had felt a little uncertain about our move and did not seem to be fully satisfied with the contemplation of living in a strictly Japanese way, but the word received from the First Presidency set my heart at rest and a peaceful influence was with me for the rest of the day.

After dinner Bro. Ensign and myself accompanied by our interpreter, Mr. Hiroi, started out in search of a Japanese hotel. We took the train to Omori, a little place kept as a summer resort, to see if the hotels at that place would take in foreigners for a month or so. We found one hotel, but the price was althogether too high. We started to walk to Shinagawa a little place closer to Tokyo than Omori. On the way we enquired at two hotels, but one was full and could not take us in and the other would not take boarders by the month but only by the day. When we came close to Shinagawa, we found another place where we could be accommodated with two rooms and meals for fourty five yen apiece. We took the address of this place in case we could not find anything better. This ended the search for to-day and we took the train back to Tokyo arriving at the hotel shortly before supper. Before going out on this house hunting tour, I wrote a letter to Bishop Empey in answer to three that had lately been received from him.

Wednesday, 4 December 1901, Tokyo

As soon as Mr. Hiroi arrived, we started out to spend another day in search of a house in which we could find accommodations. Thinging that we would be away from the hotel nearly all day, we took our lunch with us. First we went out into the Shiba district of Tokyo but were unsuccessful in finding what we wanted there. We then took rikishas to Azabu district and found one place, but were not favorably struck with what was offered us. At the suggestion of the rikisha men we went into the Conda district[71] where we found a place that struck us immediately as the one for us and to our surprise the price was not very high, being only fourty yen per month each, which in American money is $20.00.

We did not extend our search any farther, but directed our steps homeward. It was nearly two o'clock and we were begining to feel that it was time to eat, but we could not for looks sake eat as we walked along the street so we took the tram car into town where one of the largest Japanese restaurants is located. Here we went in and sat down on the floor in strictly native style and ate a Japanese meal which Mr. Hiroi ordered for us. It is very seldom that foreigners are seen in native restaurants and of course every eye was directed to us and the way we adapted ourselves to the Jap-style of sitting and use of the chop-sticks. Bro. Ensign being so fat it was extremely hard for him to sit on the floor with any degree of comfort and it was utterly impossible for him to double up like Mr. Hiroi and I. The meal consisted of fried eggs, sweetened eggs, two kinds of vegetables, roast chicken, chestnuts, and rice, including tea which Mr. Hiroi consumed for us all. Mr. Hiroi said that the way we handled the chop-sticks was very clever and I confess that I was truly surprised at Horace and myself in performing this feat although I had had the advantage over Horace by my visit to Chiba with Mr. Aoki. (see Nov. 8th,)

This was the farst experience for Horace with Japanese food and it was an excellent initiation for him into what he will receive as soon as we begin life on the strictly Japanese plan. When we left the restaurant all the waitresses came to the head of the stairs and thanked us with a bow and native word "Arigato."[72]

Mr. Hiroi told us that they were very glad to see a foreigner in their establishment and were expressing to us their feelings of joy. Before we went into this place we had to take off our shoes and leave them in charge of a person at the door who is hired to look after the footwear of the guests. I had two or three holes in my stockings and felt somewhat shy in taking off my shoes but I "grined and bore it" as best I could, all the time, however, trying to hid as much of my exposed feet as possible.

We submitted what we had done to the rest of the brethren when we got back to the hotel and they both approved of our actions and we decided to move to our new quarters in the forenoon of the next day and accordingly telephoned the owner of the Japanese hotel so that he could have things in readiness.

In the evening we criticed for publication an article which Bro. Grant had prepared in answer to a long article against us in the morning "Mail."

Thursday, 5 December 1901, Tokyo

In harmony with the arrangements made yesterday for Horace and myself to take quarters at the Japanese hotel in Conda district,[73] we prepared our things for transportation and bid farewell to the hotel Metropole. Mr. Hiroi went with us to see that every thing was done according to contract and write out the the aggreement with our landlord. It is the custom in Japan to report to the police the name, nationality, age, former place of residence of any person who may come to live at your house, whether public or private, so Mr. Hiroi proved to be of great assistance in seeing to the above matter.

It was some what after noon when we arrived at our new quarters and having left the hotel without having anything to eat, we ordered dinner or as it is called in Japanese, "hirumeshi." Oh! what a dinner!!! Ye crags and peaks, it was enough to kill a white man. For me to try to describe the meal would be folly, for words cannot well illustrate the horrors such grub gives to a person's stomach. We ate with chop-sticks and drank water out of the same bowl that contained our rice as it is the custom of the Japanese to drink tea with their rice and consequently a separate dish is not furnished for guests to drink from. It was a fortunate thing that Mr. Hiroi was with us for he led out in all things and taught us how to serve the meal after it had been brought. The servant stood looking on and laughing up her sleeve at the ackward manner in which we handled the chop-sticks and the looks of despair that crossed our countenances as we tasted with timidity the different dishes of food that were spread before us. Mr. Hiroi ate quite hartily and said that such a meal was truly a first class one from the native standpoint.

After the meal was over and the dishes cleared away Mr. Hiroi asked the landlord all the questions that felt were necessary to a complete understanding of the surroundings and a knowledge of how to lock the doors and find the necessary parts of the house. When Mr. Hiroi left us he said that he felt that he was leaving two babes and I felt that he was right for it seemed indeed that we were babes in very deed. Mr. Hiroi had not been gone long when the servant came to the door and started to ask some question or questions in Japanese which we did not understand in the least. The servants kept coming into the room and talked to us but we had to smile and keep our mouths shut for we did not know what to say in answer to the lingo which they jabbered away to us at an exceedingly rapid rate.

About four o'clock I went down stairs to have a bath which was an experience never to be forgotten. The room was cold and the windows looking out into the yard were without any covering but were perfectly open so that every one that passed could look in and see whoever might be bathing and it kept me dodging all the time to keep out of sight when the servants went back and forth on the path just outside. As is the custom in a Japanese bath, I washed off with cold water and soap and then got into a deep wooden tub which was full of water that was so near the boiling point that I thought I would surely cook and especially going from the freezing point to the boiling all of a sudden is not a very comfortable change. I succeeded, after considerable trouble, in finishing my bath and found it a happy relief to be dressed again so that those who passed the window would not if they happened to look into the bath-room see me in a nude condition. We had Mr. Hiroi tell the landlord to instruct his servants that we did not require anyone to assist us in taking a bath for we knew that if we did not that we would have to put up with the presence of an attendant. The landlord was very much surprised that we did not want help in taking a bath for he did not see how we could wash our backs ourselves, but we told him and it was heralded on the house-tops that the "Mormons" could wash their backs themselves.

In the evening we had another meal which did not set well on my stomach. After the meal we were visited by four of the students who were living in another part of the hotel. They were studying English and having heard of our presence here, they sought an early opportunity to make friends with us. They were delighted to think that we were studying Japanese and volunteered their services as helpers to us in our struggle for Japanese.

Later in the evening Mr. Oi, the owner of the house, came in to see us and being a good speaker of English we spent a very pleasant evening in speaking to him of the Gospel as taught by the Latter-day Saints. He had lived in America for ten years and had become so accustomed to the American way of living that he found it extremely hard to go back to the food and houses of the Japanese. In fact, he said that it was dangerous for a person used to the foreign food to change suddenly to the Japanese diet, telling us that one of his friends who returned from America at the same time as he did, died as a result of the sudden change of food and the quite different way of cooking. I spoke with him for some two hours and a half on the "Mormons" and it was the best Gospel conversation that I have had since my arrival in Japan. He was grately astonished to know of what the Latter-day Saints had accomplished and what the true meaning of "Mormonism" is. He said that he would like us to come to the school that he is teaching and give the students a lecture on our people so that the wrong impressions being made by the newspaper reports concerning us might be corrected in the minds of the students. This was a grand opportunity for us and we promised that we would be delighted to do so whenever he should desire. After all our visitors were gone and we were left to ourselves to reflect upon the conditions surrounding us, we felt to thank the Lord with all our hearts for the blessings of the day and to dedicate our quarters here unto him. Kneeling in prayer, I was mouth in expressing our desires to the Lord and my heart was full of peace and trinquility. The night was spent sleeping pleasantly on the floor where we were kept warm by four footons.

Friday, 6 December 1901, Tokyo

AFter breakfast we took a walk up town to buy some warm slippers as in is not the custom to ware shoes in a Japanese house and without them we find our feet get very cold. We kept walking until we found ourselves near to the hotel so we thought we would call in and see the brethren and find if there was any mail from home as a boat from America had arrived the day before. We found the brethren in and also a bundle of mail. I received one letter from father containing also a note from mother, a letter from Florence, and one from Bro. Edward H. Anderson of the Era. To my great satisfaction, all the folks at home were well and happy. Bro. Anderson had received my letter in which I tried to get out of writing to the Era, but he had refused to accept no for an answer and and his letter of to-day solicits me to write something for the magazine.

In the afternoon we were visited by the students who called on us the night before, they also came in again in the evening. During the day I finished a letter which I had started a day or two before to my mother and I also found time to write an answer to Bro. Anderson's letter.

After we had finished supper and were about to retire to bed, at ten o'clock, we were aroused by the sound of fire bells and at the suggestion of one of the students who came again into our room we went out on the porch in front of the house and some two or three blocks away we say an immense blaze, which spread very rapidly in the wind that blow with considerable force. The fire got so wild that the people of the hotel, became alarmed and started to attach the hose to the taps in case of an immergency. The sparks traveled for miles and for two hours the blaze leaped toward the clouds and when we went to bed at twelve o'clock it seemed to have quieted down considerable but it was not until the early dawn of morning that it was finally extinguished. Never in my life had I witnessed such a blaze before in my life. Eight or ten buildings were destroyed and being all built of wood the conflagration was rapid and rater picturesqe to those whose homes were safe from the danger of the flying sparks. As we watched we could see building after building turn into a massive torch and then in a very few minutes we would see them collapse and fall to the earth. What disaster fire can produce and in lands were the facilities for extinguishing it are as maeger as in Tokyo the destruction is something awful. It is said that if there is anything that Tokyo is noted for it is her fires and her quarrels.

Saturday, 7 December 1901, Tokyo

A pleasant day. I remained in my room all day, devoting myself to writing and study. In the morning, shortly after Bro. Ensign and myself had eaten our breakfast, some of the students with whom we had become acquainted came in to chat with us. They stayed until nearly tiffin time and during the hour or two that we were together we larned much concerning the Japanese language. After dinner, Bro. Ensign and I took a bath together, feeling that it would be better for us both to go in at one time so as to kind of shield eachother while we were exposed before the open window. I stood guard at the door while Horace took his bath and then he dressed and stood guard while I refreshed myself.

Hardly had we finished our suppers when some four or five new students came in to see us. We had thought of taking a walk seeing we had been closely confined nearly all the day, but with our new visitors we concluded to spend the evening. They stayed until nearly eleven o'clock. We sang, danced, talked both english and Japanese, and had a glorious time all around. The servants came in and sit on the floor around the "hibachi"[74] laughing hartily at all that was going on. The landlady came in with her baby on her back and before we closed, what got to be a circus, nearly everyone in the hotel had been in the room to see what was carrying on. The air became so stifling that I could hardly bare it so when the company dispersed, I put on my over-coat and started out to have a walk and get some fresh air. The Landlady did not seem to understand why I was going out at that time of night and I was absolutely unable to tell her, only that I would be back in ten or fifteen minutes. She had to go out and unlock the gate so that I could get out on the street.

I walked for some twenty minutes and enjoyed the fresh air immensely, but found that when I got back that the gate was locked, and not wanting to disturbe the landlady again I concluded to climb over the fence but there was some one coming down the street and I did not want to have them think that I was a thief trying to rob the house so I waited until the person passed and then with no difficulty I succeeded in mounting the gate which was some ten feet high. I then found the hotel door locked, so I had to ring the bell for the servant to come and let me in. They could not understand how I got into the yard, the date being locked, and I could not explain so the matter rested without them finding out how I got in. Bro. Ensign had been writing while I was out but quit as soon as I came in so we had prayers and went to bed.

Sunday, 8 December 1901, Tokyo

Another beautiful day. The morning we spent in conversing with some of our Japanese friends who came into see us. It being Sunday I wanted to fast and accordingly told the servants that I did not want breakfast nor dinner but I was a new thing to see people in health go without their food and they thought that we were not satisfied with the grub they were furnishing us. We had the students explain the matter to them but the more explaination that was given the more complicated the affair became, until the landlady rustled around and got some bread, fried some eggs after the American style, and also cooked some ham. This she brought into us for dinner. I looked at Bro. Ensign, he looked at me, and then we both looked at the ham and eggs and bread.

The sight of these things was indeed tempting after two or three days of Japanese meals, and seeing that they had evidently put their powers together to think of and prepare something that would suit us, I remarked to Bro. Ensign that I felt the Lord would forgive us for eating this meal even if we had intended to fast and pray. He said that he felt the same way so we started in. Never before in my life did fried eggs and break taste so good as on this occasion, and it was with the greatest effort that I succeeded in leaving the ham uneaten for it had never been such a temptation to me before since I swore off on pig meat some years ago. Bro. Ensign ate his and I doubt still whether the Lord don't think I was foolish for not pertaking of the "forbidden fruit" on this occasion.

After this meal (which was so delicious to my taste because of the trying food which we had had since coming to his hotel) we wrote a few lines home, telling briefly of our experience in living Japanese fashion, and also mentioning the meal we had just finished as one ever to be remembered during the rest of our lives. I wrote a letter to Florence in answer to one received from her last Friday. I took this letter and also the ones written Friday to mother and Bro. Edward H.Anderson and posted them when we went to the Metroplie hotel to meet with the other brethren in sacrament meeting. It was narly five o'clock when we reached the hotel, but found the brethren there, and began our meeting immediately. The principle subject spoken of, was the results, so far, of the separation of Bro. Horace and myself from the rest and our life in the place we were living. We only stayed with the brethren during the meeting as it was after dark when we dismissed and we expected callers in the evening so we had to get back in time to receive them. A letter from Lutie, now laboring in Colorado as a missionary, was received by me and read aloud to the brethren. She told of her experience during the first two days tracking among the houses of Denver. Her letter was interesting in the extreme and showed us that we were not the only ones who were suffering tribulation, but that in other mission fields, many hardships were to be met and overcome.

Very shortly after our return to the hotel some of the students came in to see us and remained with us till half past ten making it eleven o'clock or after when we got to bed.

Monday, 9 December 1901, Tokyo

Threatened rain all day, but none fell. Horace and I went over to the hotel to have our lessons from Mr. Hiroi. When we arrived we found that he had gone over to our place to give us our lesson. We were sorry to miss our lesson for we need all the instruction in the language that we can possibly get. We found that Bro. Grant had gone to Yokohama to see if his new typewriter had arrived from America. We stopped at the hotel and had dinner with Bro. Kelsch. It was a grand meal and we loaded up for all we were worth as we felt that the chances to have a good square meal in the future would be few and far between. Mr. Hiroi came back soon after we reached the hotel and we were able to take a short lesson before dinner. We met out old friends Mr. and Mrs. Ourdan and they were pleased to see us again, and asked Bro. Ensign to some to the hotel the next night and sing for them before they left for Germany. When we returned to our Japanese home we had our bath and spent the evening very pleasantly in conversing with some of the Japanese students who came in to see us.

Tuesday, 10 December 1901, Tokyo

The weather continued fine. Mr. Hiroi came to give us our lesson before we had finished our breakfast. Of late we have been rather late in getting up in the morning at the proper time. Mr. Hiroi stayed with us until after twelve o'clock. When we had finished our dinner four of the students came and invited us to take a walk with them through Asakusa Park. We did so and were gone all the afternoon. We visited the panamora in which was shown the battle of Tein-tein during the late war with China. The reproduction of this event was most wonderful, being painted on the canvas with the most accurate and life-like reality that I have ever seen produced with the painter's brush. There seemed to be a sort of a festival on at the park for all kinds of performances were going on in different parts of the grounds. We wandered around leisurely, visiting the temple and other place of interest in the park and then we started for home passing other temples which were almost as famous and ancient as the one we visited in the Park. We saw the manner of idolatrous worship. One of the little gods in the hall of the Asakusa Temple was all black and dirty Where the worshippers had been rubbing their hands. We stood and watched the men and women as they came in and bowed before this little piece of stone and then arose dipped their hands in water and rubbed their wet palms all over the face and limbs of the image, after which they would bow and leave the temple going about their business as though nothing had ever happened of a sacred character. It was dark when we got back and we were real tired with the walk for we had not stood still for more than ten minutes all the time we were gone. In the evening Bro. Ensign went over to the hotel to sing for some of his friends and I stayed at home entertaining the students until eleven o'clock.

Wednesday, 11 December 1901, Tokyo

The weather still excellent. Went to the Metropole after breakfast to receive our lesson from Mr. Hiroi. While we were there Mr. Hiroi translated an article from the leading magazine in Japan called the "Sun." This article was on the Mormon question and was an exceeding fair article on us, advancing parts of our belief with wonderful accuracy. The writer of the article was a Japanese by the name of Goro Takahashi the man who faught strongly for the Christians some years ago and who is looked upon as one of the strongest minds in the kingdom. In this article on "Mormonism" he overthrows all the slanders against us and, according to what Mr. Hiroi said, his sentences read like the strains of sweet music. This Mr. Takahashi had written to us while we were in Yokohama and wanted to know if we wanted any literature translated into the Japanese language and offered his services for such labor. He is one of the committee who translated the christian bible into the Japanese characters and has done considerable for Christianity. Bro. Grant told us that he had invited, through Mr. Hiroi, Mr. Takahashi to come and have dinner with us at the hotel, so we stayed at the hotel all day so as to meet Mr. Takahashi. In the afternoon we took a walk down town to buy some few things which the Brethren needed.

Mr. Takahashi came to the hotel an hour and a half before meal time so we had a very fine talk with him. He has the face of An American Indian and a head that is perfect in proportion. He talked well and seemed to take great delight in what he heard of our faith. After supper Bro. Ensign sang a song or two for the entertainment of our guest and we finally broke up our little part at about half past eight. We presented our friend with a Book of Mormon and a book of views, "In and around Salt Lake."[75] While we were still at the hotel a mail arrived from America bringing a letter to me from Lizzie Thomas. Horace and I got back to our Japanese quarters at ten o'clock.

Thursday, 12 December 1901, Tokyo

The day was fair and the air bracing. We were rather late getting up and were not through with breakfast when Mr. Hiroi came to give us our lesson. He stayed and had dinner at our expense, but we did not eat with him as we had told the landlady that we would note at dinner seeing we had eaten breakfast so late. In the afternoon we had our bath. It is not very often that a person writing a journal would record the taking of a bath, as such a thing is but the common place in ones life, but in Japan the baths are quite a feature of Japanese life and in them I find a great deal of pleasure, always looking forward to bath time with a great deal of joy for I find it to be a fine recreation. In Japan the bath-house are sometimes large and the tubs are also massive, making it easy to throw the water around and have a splash the same as can be had in some public pool. I wrote a letter to Lizzie Thomas in answer to the one received from her yesterday, enclosing in the same, two kodak pictures taken while we were in Yokohama.

There being a concert in the Metropole Hotel we left about seven thirty in the evening so as to be present to hear the music. Some of the students came in before we started and wanted to go with us do we took the them along. The music did not amount to much, so we did not stay long. We noticed in the Japan Mail two excellent articles in defense of "Mormon" missionary work in Japan. We also saw in the Japan Times an article in our favor and quite a slap at the critics of our doctrines. In the Japan Advertizer also there was a nearly a column of editorial thought on the agitation over our coming to Japan, all being rather for than against us. A day or two ago the Japan Herald had a short article in it holding up to ridicule the man who had lately written against the "Mormons" and signed himself as "An American Friend of Japan." Thus it can be readily seen that of late we have been brought quite prominently before the public and in a favorable light. These newspaper articles and the thoughts of Mr. Goro Takahashi as published in the "Sun" some time ago will without doubt do us a wonderful amount of good. Thank the Lord for his favors in raising up able defenders of the truth, and may the friends that we make always stand up for us and not be overcome by the lying statements made by the enemies of the Church.

Friday, 13 December 1901, Tokyo

The day was delightful—clear and exhilarating. This was our day to go to the hotel for our lesson, but I did not go, preferring to stay at home and study what had already been given me to learn and also to write a little on an article started for the Era according to the wish of Bro. Anderson received a few days ago. The students did not bother me at all, for which I was very thankful. Their help is a very fine thing to have and the instruction received from them is valuable, but it is necessary to have a change once in a while, so I thoroughly enjoyed being alone a little today. Bro. Horace went to get a lesson and when he came back he stated that he had read a letter received by Bro Grant from Mr. Takahashi, thanking us in the warmest terms for the kindness shown him to other evening. (See Wednesday Dec. 11th.) He also stated in his letter that we had treated him better than he expected, and even better then he had ever been received before. He gave us his opinion on what would be the best manner in which to present our doctrines to the Japanese people, and proposed to write a book on our doctrines and submit it to us for approval before publishing and then send it our over his signature. On this part of his letter their was some difference of opinion as to whether it would be well to accept this proposition. We all rejoiced that we had impressed Mr. Takahashi so favorably for the reason that he is a wonderful man among the Japanese and his writings are of the highest class, defending with great strength those things which he believes to be true.

In the evening we had the students again, who stayed till the "last dog was hung."

Saturday, 14 December 1901, Tokyo

Such beautiful weather as we are having makes life in Japan a great deal more pleasant than it was during the hot days and nights experienced shortly after our arrival. The weather for the last week has been equal in freshness and beauty to that experienced in the Rockey Mountain valleys during the month of September and the early part of November.

Mr. Hiroi came to give us our lesson about half past nine and stayed until after dinner, taking his meal with Horace—I was not eating.

Towards evening we went over to see the brethren and how they were located in their new boarding place. Mr. Horoi had told us that they were going to move to the central hotel in thefore part of the afternoon and we felt that we would like to see them in their new apartments. They had two rooms one for a bed-room and the other for a reception-room. They were in the part of the house that had just been erected consequently everything was bright and clean. Their rooms were on the south west corner of the house consequently they got the benefit of the sun and also had a neat little stove which seemed to be perfectly effective in giving out all the heat that could be desired. The electric light, good chairs, a nice centre-table, and a sofa and made the room look fine, while in where their beds were was equally well fitted for a sleeping apartment, having two excellent beds, rugs on the floor, dresser, wash-stand, and clothes-chest.

The mail coming from America, via San Francisco, had brought me a letter from Bishop Empey telling of the excellent condition of the ward and of some changes which had taken place and which would take pleace in the near future.

On the way back, we bought a pair of chop-sticks each, the ones we got at the hotel were very dirty and repulsive. We also purchased some little things which we needed, and some fruit and cakes to give to the students when they call. We generally treat them whenever they come in to see us and I remarked to Horace last night that I thaught we were buying them gradually into the kingdom.

Two of the students brought their teacher in Chinese in to see us and we had quite a pleasant evening talking with him. He said in his broken way that was very anxious to learn English and hoped that we would help him. He invited us to come and see him at his home and said that he would try and call on us every Friday evening. We arranged to call on him next Monday evening at 7:00 o'clock, inviting one of the students to go with us to assist us in conversing with him. It was interesting to contrast the difference between the Japanese students and their Chinese teacher, and I must give the Chinaman the greater credit for superior refinement and deportment in actions.

Sunday, 15 December 1901, Tokyo

Still the weather continues charming. It being Sanday Bro Horace and I fasted. In the morning I devoted myself to labor with the needle and thread, altering a pair of my winter garments. We also took a couple of pictures of the interior of our rooms. In the afternoon we had our bath, during which I took a picture of Horace in the tub.

As is always the custom on a Sunday, we met with the other brethren in the evening to pertake of the Sacrament and express to eachother the feelings of our hearts. We had a time of rejoicing while assembled together. Bro. Grant spoke of the advisability of sending for some more young missionaries, saying that he felt that there was no doubt about us being able to preach the Gospel to this nation just as soon as we could speak the language and that, therefore, there was no reason why more Elders should not be here studying the language. He also urge us in very strong terms to be more diligent in our own efforts to acquire the tongue of the Japanese. He spoke extensively of the difficuly men of advanced years would have to learn this most difficult language. He rejoiced in the fact that Bro. Horace and myself had been able to find such nice quarters among the Japanese and said that he felt that a better spirit had seemed to prevail than when we were all together. He felt to thank God for any improvement that we could make for his heart was in the work of the Lord and especially was he desirous to see missionary work in this land prosper and flourish as it has done in other parts of the world. The feeling expressed concerning the friendship of Mr. Takahashi, was that we were exceeding pleased to have met this man and that he impressed us as being a decedent of the Lamanites for we had never seen a face so much like the faces of the American Indians since our arrival in Japan. I do not believe one of us left the meeting without feeling that we had been exceedingly blessed of the Lord and renewed in the determination to do all that was in our power to accomplish the labor which had been give us to do.

Bro. Ensign and I stopped and had supper with the brethren. The meals served at their new boarding place are very fine and Bro. Grant remarked that it almost made him homesick to eat such meals as they were cooked after the same style as at home. It was nearly ten o'clock when we arrived at our rooms and as none of the students called to see us we went right to bed feeling that our labors in the future must be more earnestly preformed than in the past.

Monday, 16 December 1901, Tokyo

Weather fair—somewhat warmer. Went to the Central Hotel to take my Japanese lesson. Spent the whole forenoon with the brethren.

In the evening Bro. Ensign and I, accompanied by three of the students, called on Mr. Ho Pei Tung the Chinamen with whom we became acquainted the previous Saturday evening. We found him living in a very fine part of Tokyo, and in a house of excellent construction. He lived with four other Chinamen and one or two Japanese, and, judging from what we saw, this gentleman is not slovenly like most of the Chinese that I have seen, but in his room and person was clean and tidy. We were well received by him and his associates. They asked that we come and live with them stating that it would only cost us ten yen per month, but of course we did not accept this proposition as we did not feel like running into a place the reputation of which we knew nothing about. Altho we were delighted to find that we had found friends who would make us such a tempting offer. We stayed at this place for about two hours and then took the train back to the district in which we were living, arriving home at ten o'clock. Being tired we went to bed as soon as possible.

Tuesday, 17 December 1901, Tokyo

Part of the day was quite cloudy but the other half was clear and fine, and at night the stars shown as bright as ever. Bro. Kelsch came with Mr. Hiroi in the morning and stayed all day. We had our lesson in the forenoon and after taking dinner with us Mr. Hiroi went back to the hotel to assist Bro. Grant. While here with us, Bro. Kelsch got very sick with a terrible headache and sick stomach. We had the footons laid on the floor and doctored him up as best we could and toward evening he came around all right. While he was sleeping we took our baths and then took a photograph of "The Sick Man in Bed."" He had supper with us eating with the Chop-sticks and having one of the regular Japanese meals (except that it was a little better than we had been getting in the past). When we had finished our suppers Bro. Ensign and I walked over to the hotel with Bro. Kelsch and also walked back making a distance of about six miles. Bro. Kelsch's experience during the day had been quite a varied one and he expressed himself as more than pleased with all he passed through except the sickness. He had two Japanese meals, slept in a Japanese bed, drank Japanese tea, (as a medicine only) and in fact experienced everything that we had had except the bath. This we would have given him if he had been well.

Wednesday, 18 December 1901, Tokyo

The day was extremely cold, and threatened snow. Went to the hotel to met Mr. Hiroi. Spent the forenoon with the brethren. Received mail from home consisting of a letter containing nine pages from Aunt Hattie, and six pages from father, a letter from the Des. National Bank containing a draft for 201 Yen, and a parcel of books which I had written home for some months ago. All was well at home, for which I was very thankful. Spent the afternoon at home studying and in conversing with the students who called to see us.

Thursday, 19 December 1901, Tokyo

During the morning the first snow of the winter season fell, but in the afternoon it turned into rain which drizzled off and on for the rest of the day and during the night a severe thunder storm came up lasting for some hours.

Mr. Hiroi came to our rooms to give us our regular lessons. In the afternoon I wrote a letter to Sister Capener to comply with the request made by my father in his letter received yesterday. I also remember that I had made a promise to my cousin Lizzie Goodman in St. David Arizona to write to her when I got to Japan, so I took some time to write her a few lines, enclosing in her letter as well as in the one to Sister Capener some few pictures of the snap-shots we had taken with our kodak during our short stay in this land. In the evening we went to call upon a friend who lived about a half a mile from here. He is one of he students whom we met soon after coming to this hotel. The roads were very muddy and the trip was not all together satisfactory, but we had promised to make the call and did not want to destroy the good feeling which existed between us by any neglect on our part. When we got back the students came into our rooms and spent the entire evening with us . We had an orange festival, during which we devoured nearly a half a box of oranges.

Friday, 20 December 1901, Tokyo

The day clear but very cold. Spent the day at the Central Hotel with the brethren. We had our usual lesson in Japanese in the morning, and were occupied in considering the contents of a letter received from Mr. Takahashi in which he give an outline of what he thought would be the best plan for us to follow getting our doctrines before the people. He also proposed again to write the book for us if we felt that he was able to do us justice. We also arranged our financial affairs, finding our exactly how we stood in relation to the mission fund. Before coming back to our rooms we went over to the Metropole hotel to see Mr. and Mrs. Ourdan with whom we had become quite intimate during our stay at the hotel. They were going to leave for Germany in a day or two and we thought we would like to say good-bye.

Saturday, 21 December 1901—Tuesday, 24 December 1901, Tokyo

The weather during these four days has been pleasant and clear tho cold. A majority of the time during the mornings has been spent in studying the language and in receiving instruction from Mr. Hiroi.

Sunday afternoon we four missionaries assembled in the brethren's rooms at the Central Hotel and had just begun our usual Sacrament meeting when Mr. Takahashi came to speak with us, about the book that he had volunteered to write. He spent the afternoon and evening with us, taking dinner at the invitation of Bro. Grant. The favorable impression that this gentleman made upon us when we first met him still rested with us and we seem to like him more and more as we become better acquainted. The conditions upon which we were to be in any way responsible for the publication and sale of the book which he proposed to write were settled. We furnished Mr. Takahashi with considerable reading matter pertaining to Church History and the Doctrines of "Mormonism."

After he went, we held an informal meeting expressing our feelings to eachother and speaking our thoughts upon the conditions of our work here. During the evening a mail arrived from America in which I received a letter and Christmas card from mother, a letter from Emma, A Christmas card from Dear old Auntie Dale, A gold pencil as a gift from Emma, and a Silver match box from mother with best wishes for a Merry Christmas and Happy New Year. We also received word that a box of Christmas goods from America had been received in Yokohama for which we would have to pay custom duties and arrange for it to be forwarded to us. Bro. Grant thought that the best way to do was to go over to Yokohama the following day and get it ourselves. The next day, therefore, he went to Yokohama but for some reason he was unable to get the box through the custom house and he had to leave the matter in the hands of an Express Company who promised to forward the articles to us as soon as possible.

There was considerable consternation in camp when the box did not arrive the following day and we had given up nearly all hope of seeing the Christmas presents from home till some day after the cherished one had passed. On the morning of the 23rd I wrote a letter to father acknowledging the receipt of money sent me and all the Christmas gifts that had arrived the day before from home.

Wednesday, 25 December 1901, Tokyo

Realizing that we would not have to take a lesson to-day and feel-somewhat tired we laid in bed rather late. A drizzling rain fell during the entire day, making it a more unpleasant Christmas than if the sun had shown brightly to add cheer to the festivity of the day. We sat around in our own rooms reading until about noon when we decided that we would go and see the brethren with whom we had been invited to spend the day. The streets were very muddy and it was with considerable difficulty that we got to the Hotel without getting badly daubed with mud.

When we arrived, the brethren were eating their dinner which they had expected to share with us, thinking that we would be sure to come during the morning and be with them the whole day. Upon entering the room we found on the sofa some photographs from the gentleman with whom we had recently place so many orders for pictures. He had sent us a beautiful pictue each of one or more of the famous beauties of Japan. On the bureau we saw another parcel which on examination proved to be a present for each of us from Mrs. Warton This present consisted of a New Testament written in romanized Japanese.[76] This additional manifestation of the kindness of this woman made us feel very happy and while we were somewhat humiliated to have presents come from this unexpected source, yet we felt in our hearts to bless this lady in the name of the Lord and I don't believe there was any other incident of the day that so pleased us as these tokens of friendship which were accompanied by a note full of sentiments concerning our loneliness in this land and our sacrifice in leaving home, loved ones, and friends, to preach the Gospel as we believe it to be true. In return we sent her the best bound volum of the Life of Joseph Smith,[77] by George Q. Cannon, that we had, and wrote her a letter in which we expressed our appreciation of the gifts received as a token of her friendship.

The box from home which had been retained in the Custom-house had not yet arrived and we had decided to reconcile ourselves to forego the pleasure of opening it on Christmas day, but at about four o'clock the servant came into the room with a package under his arm which he said had been forwarded from Yokohama. We paid the bill and when the servant had gone we began to unfold the mystery that lay before us. I acted as the opener and when the deed was done Bro. Grant took the things out one by one reading the names of those to whom they belonged . "From Edith to Papa," "For Pa," "From Emily," "From Agusta to the Quartet," "For Horace from his wife," "To Louis A. Kelsch," and last of all "Alma, from Ma and Aunt Hattie." With excited movements we each hurridly unwrapped our portion, and oh, what a variety of articles we found had been sent on the long journey of 5,500 miles! Handerchiefs, wristers, neckties, suspenders, photographs, manicure ecquipments, card-cases,candy in abundance, and, for my share, a Christmas cake.

We now began to feel as though Christmas had really come. We spent the rest of the day in eating cake and candy until we had scarcely room for the supper which we were to forever remember as the first

Christmas feast in Japan. I wonder how many more I will celebrate in this land? If many, it will be interesting to note the comparison that future events will have with the scenes of yesterday. I hope that by the next Christmas that I will have received from my Heavenly Father that gift which I so much long for, namely, the knowledge of this language so that I may preach the Gospel of the man whose birth these days commemorate.

Though we four were the only ones that were assembled together, yet I never enjoyed a Christmas more in my life. We sang the songs of Zion, we laughed, prayed, and we feasted till our hearts rejoiced exceedingly. The events of this day are never to be forgotten and in recalling the scenes of Christmas 1901 in future years, I shall picture it only as a day of joy full of happiness and peace. Bros Kelsch, Ensign, and myself presented Bro. Grant with a gold-mounted fountain pen, as a token of the love which we had for our President.

Thursday, 26 December 1901, Tokyo

During the night the wind blew hard and a heavy rain fell. Went to the hotel Central to meet with Mr. and Mrs. Ourdan whom Bro. Grant had invited to have tiffin with us before they left Japan for their trip to Germany. Mr. Ourdan and his wife are Americans with whom we became quite intimate while staying at the Metropole Hotel. Their frank open spirits and their genial manner had caused us to think a great deal of them and they never failed to honor and respect the "Mormons." Mr. Ourdan told Bro. Grant that he had never met with anyone whom he liked better than we four men and while he had never heard anything but the blackest reports of "Mormonism" yet he now knew that they were all false and that no better class of people ever lived, if they were all like us. This acknowledgement from the man, made us like him the more and the meek, sweet spirit of his wife is charming in the extreme and we all said that we had seldom seen a more pleasant woman even among our own folks. I felt, whenever, I was in their company that they were one of my people and delighted to talk with them as much as though they were my own kin. Mr. Ourdan is a man of no small ability. He has invented a hydographic engraving machine which has been adopted in the U.S. and which has but recently been accepted by the nation of Japan. This invention has made its owner a barrel of money and he is still increasing the amount of his wealth as he goes from country to country introducing his machines with success wherever he makes the attempt. They gave the mission their photographs and said that they trusted we would met them again sometime in the wide world. We, at their request, gave them letters to the President of the German mission which they promised to visit while in that land. It seemed like parting with old friends when we bid them good-bye, but this world is filled with parting hours and as the song reads, "The best of friends must part."

In the evening, after returning to our rooms, I wrote a letter to Aunt Hattie in answer to the one received from her some days ago and I also made it suffice as an answer to the one from father received at the same time and the one from mother last Sunday. I also wrote a few lines to Dear Auntie Dale, who had kindly remembered me with a Christmas card on the first leaf of which mother had written, "This is from Auntie Dale, who is **almost** to "the end of the way."

Friday, 27 December 1901, Tokyo

The day clear but very cold. Mr. Hiroi came about nine o'clock to give us our lesson. Bro. Ensign had to go to the Bank and from there to the brethren's rooms at the Central Hotel to deliver some money to Bro. Grant and consequently I had the lesson all to myself. The lesson did not last long, however, as Mr. Aoki and one of his friends from Chiba called to see me and they stayed till after dinner. Bro. Ensign came back at about one o'clock bringing with him Bro. Kelsch. They had dinner and then went with Mr. Aoki to find a man's home whom Mrs. Warton had advised us to call on. Consequently much of the afternoon I spent by myself. Bro. Kelsch came back with Horace and spent some time with us leaving in time to get to the Hotel for supper. We walked down to the car with him so as to see that he did not get lost, but we learned the next day that he got lost at the other end of the line, and had quite a hunt to find the Hotel where he arrived rather late. In the evening Bro. Ensign and I copied the article written in the Japan

L. Kimball, "'This is the Place' Monument," *Encyclopedia of Mormonism*, 4:1476.

2. For an excellent treatment of Heber J. Grant's mission to Japan as mission president see Ronald W. Walker, "Strangers in a Strange Land: Heber J. Grant and the Opening of the Japanese Mission," *Journal of Mormon History* 13 (1986/1987): 20–43.

3. Canadian Pacific Steamship Company, Ltd. Beginning in the early 1880s, this company began offering steamship service from British Columbia to the ports of Asia. Subsidized by the British government, it quickly became the premier Transpacific mail and passenger courier. In 1890, it launched a new group of steamers known as the Canadian Pacific Railway's Royal Mail Steamship Line. Included in this group were the *Empress of Japan, India,* and *China.* E. Mowbray Tate, *Transpacific Steam: The Story of Steam Navigation from the Pacific Coast of North America to the Far East and the Antipodes, 1867–1941* (New York: Cornwall Books, 1986), 141–51.

4. Dr. Coe's Nervous Sanitarium in Portland. Dr. Henry Waldo Coe was born in Waupun, Wisconsin, in 1857. He completed his college course work at the University of Minnesota and studied medicine at the University of Michigan and Long Island College Hospital, graduating in 1880. In 1891 he and his young family moved to Portland, Oregon, where he became active in the medical community. In 1894 he established a private sanitarium for nervous and mental diseases. Eventually, his sanitarium became the largest private institution for nervous and mental diseases on the Pacific Coast. *History of Oregon, Volume II* (Chicago and Portland: The Pioneer Historical Publishing Company, 1922), 34–38.

5. Northern Pacific Railway. In 1864, Congress granted a charter for the Northern Pacific Railroad, a venture backed by American and Canadian financiers determined to create a transcontinental railroad route. Eventually, its lines (and affiliate railroads) helped connect Portland, Oregon; Seattle, Washington; and Vancouver, British Columbia, on the Pacific coast, with Canadian and other midwest American cities. William J. Wilgus, *The Railway Interrelations of the United States and Canada* (New Haven: Yale University Press, 1937), 124–27.

6. *Empress of India.* A 6,000-ton steamship operated by the Canadian Pacific Railway Company. This steamer, together with the *Empress of Japan* and the *Empress of China,* sailed routes connecting Vancouver, Hong Kong, Yokohama, Kobe, Nagasaki, and Shanghai. Shinji Takagi, "Mormons in the Press: Reactions to the 1901 Opening of the Japan Mission," *BYU Studies* 40, no. 1 (2001): 141.

7. Buddhist Mission in America. On 1 September 1899, Dr. Shuei Sonada, head of the Academy of Literature of the Hompa Hongwanji of Kyōto, and his disciple Reverend Kakuryo Nishijima, arrived in San Francisco to establish the Buddhist Mission of North America. These two men taught classes on Buddhism and introduced traditional Jodo Shishu rites and practices. Rick Fields, *How the Swans Came to the Lake: A Narrative History of Buddhism in America* (Boston & London: Shambhala, 1986), 143–45 and Donald R. Tuck, *Buddhist Churches of America: Jodo Shinshu* (Lewiston/Queenston: The Edwin Mellon Press, 1987), 2–3.

8. Cricket. An outdoor game played with a ball and a bat. Two teams of eleven players each face off, and the batsman (behind the popping crease) tries to successfully hit the bowler's pitch. "Cricket," *Microsoft Encarta 98 Encyclopedia.*

9. Deck Quoits. A game similar to horseshoe pitching in which players toss ring-shaped pieces of rope from a line or mark at a pin or peg that is one inch high. The object of the game is to ring the pin or throw the rope rings as close to the pin as possible. "Horseshoe Pitching," *Microsoft Encarta 98 Encyclopedia.*

10. Croquet. A game sometimes played on ship deck in which players attempt to hit large wooden balls through a series of wickets (hoops) using long wooden mallets. Whoever completes the quickest circuit of the series of wickets is declared the winner. "Croquet," *Microsoft Encarta 98 Encyclopedia.*

11. Jinrikisha. A two-wheel cart pulled by a man—a very typical form of transportation in Japan at the turn of the twentieth century.

12. Grand Hotel. The Grand Hotel was located at No. 20 Bund in the Foreign Settlement. According to newspaper advertisements it was the "largest and most complete hotel in the Far East" and "second to none either in Europe or America." Today, the Yokohama Doll House stands on the hotel's former location. Takagi, "Mormons in the Press," 141.

13. *Yokohama Advertiser* (Japan Advertiser). One of the several foreign language newspapers in Yokohama. It was founded in 1890. When the LDS missionaries arrived in 1901, it was under the editorial control of a Unitarian missionary, Arthur M. Knapp, who edited the paper from 1899 to 1902. Takagi, "Mormons in the Press," 144–5.

14. For another treatment of the LDS missionaries' Japanese media reception see Frederick R. Brady, *The Japanese Reaction to Mormonism and the Translation of Mormon Scripture into Japanese* (Master's Thesis, Sophia University, Tokyo, Japan, 1979).

15. Mr. Staniland, a former Protestant missionary and boardinghouse landlord, refused to house the LDS missionaries. This incident became known as the "Staniland Incident."

16. The Bluff. A boarding house located on #25 Bluff in Yokohama run by a Mrs. Parker.

17. *Herald Newspaper* (Japan Herald). The *Japan Herald* was founded in 1861 under British management and continued publication until September 1914. Although J. H. Brooke was both the owner (1870–1902) and the editor (1893–1902) of the *Japan Herald.* It seems that Grant may have spoken with a Mr. Harrison of the newspaper. See Taylor Journal, 2 February 1902. Takagi, "Mormons in the Press," 145.

18. "Address to the Great and Progressive Nation of Japan." Grant's editorial was most likely prepared by James E. Talmage. Takagi, "Mormons in the Press," 145–46.

19. *Jiji Shinpo* (Jiji Shimpo). A daily Japanese newspaper started in 1882 and first managed by Yukichi Fukuzawa. Jiro Hayasaka, *An Outline of the Japanese Press* (Japan: Kenkyusha Press, 1938), 3, 12.

20. The Latter-day Saints College, Salt Lake City, Utah, was founded in 1886 in the basement of the Salt Lake City Social Hall and initially attended by eighty students. Eventually, the school was relocated to President Brigham Young's old schoolhouse and then to the Ellerbeck Building in the 17th ward. Again, the college was moved to the Templeton Building on the southeast corner of South Temple and Main streets until 1900. Finally, it was relocated to a piece of land on North Main Street, opposite the Salt Lake Temple, and its name was changed to the Business College. Andrew Jenson, *Encyclopedic History of the Church of Jesus Christ of Latter-day Saints* (Salt Lake City: Deseret News, 1941), 416.

21. Beehive House. President Brigham Young built this two-story adobe residence in 1852 on the north side of South Temple Street, Salt Lake City. In time, the home was plastered in cement and a beehive was placed on its roof. Young and many of his family and friends lived here until he passed away in 1877. Jenson, *Encyclopedic History of the Church*, 55.

22. Kamonoas (*Kimono*). The Kimono, a robe-like dress, is the traditional garment of Japan for both men and women. A kimono is woven from silk and light cloth, materials that are very comfortable in the heat and humidity of Japan. These garments can be layered almost endlessly during the winter. "Kimono," *Microsoft Encarta 98 Encyclopedia*.

23. *Japan Daily Mail* (Japan Mail). A foreign language newspaper based in Yokohama that was founded in the 1870s. From 1881 to 1912, it was owned and edited by Captain F. Brinkley, a former member of the British Royal Artillery. Due to its Protestant missionary readership, the Japan Mail was consistently anti-Mormon. Takagi, "Mormons in the Press," 146.

24. James E. Talmage, "The Story of "Mormonism*,*" *Improvement Era* 4 (April 1901): 459–68 and "The Philosophy of Mormonism," *Improvement Era* 4 (May 1901): 497–506.

25. See Alma O. Taylor, "Life in the Orient," *Improvement Era* (February 1902): 288–90 and "Some Features of Japanese Life," *Improvement Era* (April and May 1902): 449–55 and 523–29.

26. LDS Temple Garments. Worthy Latter-day Saint adults, having made sacred covenants in temples, are issued white garments, which they are instructed to wear at all times under their normal clothing to help remind them of their covenants and obligations. Evelyn T. Marshall, "Garments," *Encyclopedia of Mormonism*, 2:534–35.

27. Grant had an appointment with Mr. Alfred E. Buck, "the minister from the United States." Grant, *Japanese Journal*, 19 August 1901.

28. Young Men's Mutual Improvement Association (Y.M.M.I.A). President Brigham Young created this organization in 1875 for the betterment of young men. He encouraged its leadership to help young men "develop gifts within them, stand up and speak, and bear testimony." Until 1900, all young men, regardless of age, met together to hear gospel lessons. Charles E. Mitchener and Mark E. Hurst, "Young Men," *Encyclopedia of Mormonism*, 4:1613–14.

29. Heber J. Grant was the polygamist husband to three wives—Lucy Stringham, Huldah Augusta Winters, and Emily Wells—and the father of twelve children. His second wife, Huldah Augusta Winters, joined him in Japan in 1902. Ronald W. Walker, "Grant, Heber J.," *Encyclopedia of Mormonism*, 2:566.

30. Katy-dids. Crickets

31. Most likely the present-day site of Yamate Kōen, Yokohama. Frederick R. Brady, "Two Meiji Scholars Introduce the Mormons to Japan," *BYU Studies* 23 (spring 1983): 169.

32. This is the only contemporary account of the Japan dedicatory prayer in existence.

33. President Lorenzo Snow.

34. Gathering of Israel. "Latter-day Saints 'believe in the literal gathering of Israel and in the restoration of the Ten Tribes; [and] that Zion (the New Jerusalem) will be built upon the American continent' (A of F 10). In the LDS perspective, gathering Israel in the latter days consists of the following: (1) the spiritual gathering, which includes coming to know that Jesus is the Christ and joining The Church of Jesus Christ of Latter-day Saints; (2) the assembling of Church members to organized stakes; and (3) the gathering of the descendants of Jacob's twelve sons—including the lost ten tribes (D&C 110:11)—to the lands of their inheritance. These gatherings are necessary because of ancient apostasies that resulted in the dispersion of Israel into all nations (Deut. 4:27; 28:64; Jer. 16:13; Hosea 9:17)." Terry L. Niederhauser, "Israel," *Encyclopedia of Mormonism*, 2:709–10.

35. Great and Abominable Church. "The phrase 'great and abominable church,' which appears in an apocalyptic vision received by the Book of Mormon prophet Nephi 1 in the sixth century B.C. (1 Ne. 13:6), refers to the church of the devil and is understood by Latter-day Saints to be equivalent to the 'great whore that sitteth upon many waters' described in Revelation 17:1. This 'whore of all the earth' is identified by Nephi's brother Jacob as all those who are against God and who fight against Zion, in all periods of time (2 Ne. 10:16)." Dennis A. Wright, "Great and Abominable Church," *Encyclopedia of Mormonism*, 2:568.

36. The Book of Mormon prophet Alma I or Alma II (Alma the Younger).

37. Three Nephites. During Christ's visit to the New World following his death and resurrection, he granted three of his Nephite disciples the same wish he had earlier granted to John the Beloved—to tarry in the flesh until his Second Coming as a special representative. According to the Book of Mormon, "And they [the Three Nephites] are as the angels of God, and . . . can show themselves unto whatsoever man it seemeth them good. Therefore, great and marvelous works shall be wrought by them, before the great and coming day [of judgment]" (3 Ne. 28:30–31). William A. Wilson, "Three Nephites," *Encyclopedia of Mormonism*, 4:1477.

38. Lehi. An ancient prophet led his family from Jerusalem to the New World about 600 B.C. to escape the destruction of Jerusalem. His posterity branched into two major Book of Mormon peoples, the Nephites and Lamanites. S. Kent Brown and Terrence L. Szink, "Lehi," *Encyclopedia of Mormonism*, 2:827.

39. Nephi. One of the righteous sons of Lehi who authored the first two books in the Book of Mormon. A righteous prophet and leader, Nephi had visions of Jesus Christ and significant future world events. His followers and progenitors were known as the Nephites. Noel B. Reynolds, "Nephi I," *Encyclopedia of Mormonism*, 3:1003–5.

40. Nephites. The group's majority were direct descendants of Nephi, the son of father Lehi. In other words, anyone who was not a Lamanite was a Nephite. John L. Sorenson, "Book of Mormon Peoples," *Encyclopedia of Mormonism*, 1:191.

41. Lamanites. Direct descendants of Laman, father Lehi's eldest son who was denied his birthright due to unrighteousness. Descendants of Lemuel and Ishmael were also classified as Lamanites, together with all Nephite dissenters. John L. Sorenson, "Book of Mormon Peoples," *Encyclopedia of Mormonism*, 1:191.

42. American Indians. According to the Book of Mormon, many Native Americans are the descendants of the Lamanites. Bruce A. Chadwick and Thomas Garrow, "Native Americans," *Encyclopedia of Mormonism*, 3:981.

43. Dedicatory prayer of Orson Hyde. The Prophet Joseph Smith called Orson Hyde, an early Apostle, to travel to Palestine and dedicate the land for the gathering of the Jews. On 24 October 1841, Hyde climbed the Mount of Olives and dedicated the land "for the gathering together of Judah's scattered remnants." American Indians. According to the Book of Mormon, many

Native Americans are the descendants of the Lamanites. Terry L. Niederhauser, "Israel," *Encyclopedia of Mormonism*, 2:711.

44. Young Men's Christian Association (YMCA). The YMCA was founded in London by humanitarian Sir George Williams to combat the "unhealthy social conditions arising in large cities at the end of the Industrial Revolution." Soon, chapter organizations spread throughout the world, including Japan. "YMCA," *Microsoft Encarta 98 Encyclopedia*.

45. Mr. Bellows, U.S. Consul General. Grant, *Japanese Journal*, 6 September 1901.

46. Stone's interpreter was a Japanese man named Sato. Grant, *Japanese Journal*, 6 September 1901.

47. For a description of Elder Grant's trip through Japan with Mr. Stone, see Grant, *Japanese Journal*, 6–15 September 1901.

48. Eastman Kodak Company. Known worldwide as "Kodak," this leading manufacture of photographic film, cameras, and imaging equipment, introduced its first portable camera in 1888. It became known as the Eastman Kodak Company in 1892. Four years later, the company had manufactured 100,000 cameras. "Kodak," *Microsoft Encarta 98 Encyclopedia*.

49. John Eaton, "The Mormon Menace," *Homiletic Review* 42 (August 1901): 99–105.

50. The Mountain Meadows Massacre. During the Utah War hysteria of 1857, a number of Native Americans and southern Utah Mormons massacred an entire wagon train of non-Mormon immigrants. Ronald K. Esplin and Richard E. Turley, Jr., "Mountain Meadows Massacre," *Encyclopedia of Mormonism*, 2:966.

51. Danites. "Following the violence in northwestern Missouri in 1838, the Mormon dissident Sampson Avard . . . charged that the Church had organized a band of armed men bound by secret oaths who had engaged in illegal activities against non-Mormon neighbors. With the 1841 publication of the court proceedings, Avard's account became the foundation for all subsequent non-Mormon 'Danite' accounts. Thus was born the legend of the Danites. Though no Danite organization was known in Nauvoo or in Utah, the stereotype persisted, becoming a part of national discussion about Utah and the Latter-day Saints and for decades a staple of dime novels. By 1900 at least fifty novels had been published in English using the Avard-type Danite to develop story lines of murder, pillage, and conspiracy against common citizens." David J. Whittaker, "Danites," *Encyclopedia of Mormonism*, 1:356.

52. The Prophet Joseph Smith.

53. The continuation of plural marriages. "Following a vision showing him that continuing plural marriage endangered the temples and the mission of the Church, not just statehood, President Wilford Woodruff issued the Manifesto in October 1890, announcing an official end to new plural marriages and facilitating an eventual peaceful resolution of the conflict. Earlier polygamous families continued to exist well into the twentieth century, causing further political problems for the Church, and new plural marriages did not entirely cease in 1890. After having lived the principle at some sacrifice for half a century, many devout Latter-day Saints found ending plural marriage a challenge almost as complex as was its beginning in the 1840s. Some new plural marriages were contracted in the 1890s in LDS settlements in Canada and northern Mexico, and a few elsewhere. With national attention again focused on the practice in the early 1900s during the House hearings on Representative-elect B. H. Roberts and Senate hearings on Senator-elect Reed Smoot, President Joseph F. Smith issued his 'Second Manifesto' in 1904. Since that time, it has been uniform Church policy to excommunicate any member either practicing or openly advocating the practice of polygamy." Danel Bachman and Ronald K. Esplin, "Plural Marriage," *Encyclopedia of Mormonism*, 3:1095.

54. The sorrowful conditions existing in the polygamous homes among the Mormons. "Contrary to the caricatures of a hostile world press, plural marriage did not result in offspring of diminished capacity. Normal men and women came from plural households, and their descendants are prominent throughout the Intermountain West. Some observers feel that the added responsibility that fell early upon some children in such households contributed to their exceptional record of achievement. Plural marriage also aided many wives. The flexibility of plural households contributed to the large number of accomplished LDS women who were pioneers in medicine, politics and other public careers. In fact, plural marriage made it possible for wives to have professional careers that would not otherwise have been available to them." Danel Bachman and Ronald K. Esplin, "Plural Marriage," *Encyclopedia of Mormonism*, 3:1095.

55. They decided to hire Mr. Hiroi as their teacher. Heber J. Grant Journal, 29 September 1901.

56. Toilet. The act or process of dressing, including bathing, arranging the hair, etc.

57. Of this meeting Heber J. Grant wrote: "I told the brethren that I felt impressed that a great work was to be done here but I had no impressions that we were to be the instruments in the hands of the Lord in doing that work but did feel that we would be successful in establishing the work of the Lord in this land that it would remain here and that many thousands of this people would yet embrace it. I feel in my heart that there are many of the Lamanites in this land and that the promises of the fathers would be made good to them by their coming to a knowledge of the Gospel." Grant, *Japanese Journal*, 6 October 1901.

58. David Nelson, *The Cause and Cure of Infidelity: Including a Notice of the Author's Unbelief and the Means of His Rescue* (New York: American Tract Society, c.1841).

59. Metropole Hotel. A well-known hotel for foreigners in the original Tsukiji foreign settlement of Tokyo. The Mormons made this their home for several months.

60. *Sini di* (Sine diē). "Without a day" (i.e. indefinitely, until an unspecified date).

61. For a thorough treatment of the 1872 Iwakura Mission to America (Utah), see Wendy Butler, "The Iwakura Mission and its Stay in Utah," *Utah Historical Quarterly* 66 (Winter 1998): 26–47 and Dean W. Collinwood, Ryoichi Yamamoto, and Kazue Matsui-Haag, *Samurais in Salt Lake: Diary of the First Diplomatic Japanese Delegation to Visit Utah, 1872* (Salt Lake City: US-Japan Center, 1996).

62. Parley P. Pratt, *A Voice of Warning and Instruction to All People Or, and Introduction to the Faith and Doctrine of the Church of Jesus Christ of Latter-day Saints By Elder Parley P. Pratt* (Liverpool, England: F. D. Richards), 1854.

63. *Koto.* A Japanese harp

64. *Shamisen.* A three-stringed plucked lute.

65. *Kokyū.* A long-necked bowed lute that was a combination of the Portuguese rebec and the Japanese *Shamisen*.

66. Actually Mr. Koyama.

67. Footons (*Futon*). A traditional Japanese mattress that is laid on the tatami at night and put away during the day.

68. Mikado. A historic popular title for the Emperor of Japan.

69. Carbon photography (Carbon Process). A method of making photographic prints by the use of a pigment, such as carbon, contained in sensitized gelatin.

70. Basil Hall Chamberlain, *Things Japanese: Being Notes on Various Subjects Connected with Japan* (Tokyo: Hakubunsha, 1890).

71. Should be Kanda District.

72. *Arigato.* Thank you.

73. Should be Kanda District.

74. *Hibachi.* A charcoal heater.

75. *In and Around Salt Lake City* (Denver: F. S. Thayer, c.1900).

76. Romanization of Japanese. The use of Roman letters to phonetically transliterate the Japanese language from Chinese characters into English.

77. George Q. Cannon, *The Life of Joseph Smith, the Prophet* (Salt Lake City: Juvenile Instructor, 1888).

Chapter 6

Alma O. Taylor Journal, 1902

Wednesday, 1 January 1902, Tokyo

It has been with·the feelings of utmost joy that I have spent this New Year's Day. My heart has been full of gratitude to my Heavenly Father for his preserving care during the year that has past and that I am able to look back and se the wonderful changes for good that have taken place in my life during the last twelve months. Words are inadequate with which to express my feelings to God for the health He has blessed me with and for the food that has been given me to eat and the clothing I have had to keep me warm and happy. In all these things I recognize the hand of the Lord for He is the giver of all things even life itself. Especially should I, and do I, thank God for the blessings which he has bestowed upon me in a spiritual way for never in my life have such gifts come to me as recently. In one year I have received privileges the value of which I cannot tell in words. The desire to go out into the world to labor for the salvation of the souls of men has been gratified, the blessings of the house of the Lord have been conferred upon me, the association with prophets and apostles has been my privilege and even beyond the hopes of my heart have I been favored with the intimate association of one of the Apostles of the Lord, Bro. Heber J. Grant who is practically a companion missionary in this distant land.

Having received such manifold blessings during the year that is past I desire to remain faithful and true to every covenant that I have made so that I will be continually favored of the Lord and my brethren in the church and Kingdom of God upon the earth. As the past year has been the greatest in my life in bringing blessings to me, may the present year be the greatest in my life, thus far, in using to the glory of my Heavenly Father these blessings which I now enjoy; particularly in the mission labor that rests upon me may I be able to perform my duties well.

The beautiful day made it very auspicious for the celebration of New Year's which with the Japanese the most famous holiday of the year. We did not get up until nearly nine o'clock. After breakfast we were visited by a number of the students all of whom looked a little the worse for ware as they had sit up all night to see the old year out and the new year in, accompanying their nights dissipation with considerable drinking of "sake"[1] the national intoxicant of Japan. In fact some that called upon us were so badly charged with New Year's celebration that they were what we called drunk to the extreme. There is one thing about the Japanese when they get drunk they are the happiest fellows I ever saw. As New Year's comes but once a year, it seems, from what we have seen, that all the men turn themselves loose to have a glorious time for on all sides they were reeling to and fro and the air was charged with the oder of liquor. Another feature of New Year's is that it corresponds with the Christmas in Christian lands, in that presents and the compliments of the season are exchanged as in America and elsewhere. The women and children throng the streets dressed in their best and powered like actresses on the stage. The children romped and played, the men drank their "sake" and the women stand and look on with a smile of contentment and joy. The streets are all decorated with evergreen, and bamboo trees, and on nearly every house there is seen hanging emblems of the years harvest and tokens of greeting for the dawning year, in fact, now is the time when Japan celebrates and the rest of the laborer is obtained, for with most of the people the New Year's holiday last for from three to seven days.

While all this merriment goes on around me I think of the joy that New Year's will bring to my loved ones at home, and with expectant thoughts I look into the future and wonder what the year will bring to me, mine, and to the labor which is to be preformed among the Japanese in presenting the truths of the Gospel.

In the afternoon Bro. Ensign and I according to the invitation of Bro. Grant went to the Central Hotel to spend the day with him and Bro. Kelsch. Bro. Kelsch was feeling quite badly as his head had been troubling him all the forenoon. The air was fresh and he thought that a little walk would do him good so we went out to see the sights on the "Ginza." After we had eaten supper with the brethren we went into their rooms and had a good time talking and singing together. Bro. Grant handed us a letter which he had written on the typewriter in which we wished us a Happy New Year and presented us with 100 shares each in the Woolley Furnace Co. as a New Year's gift. We were almost overcome at this presentation and, as it was make while we laughed and having a general good time, we wondered it if were not a joke, but soon we found that it was real and that Bro. Grant wanted to thus manifest his love for we his brethren. We all in turn expressed our thanks to him for this additional manifestation of his generous heart which has ever been the part of his character I have admired most.

The Woolley Furnace Co. was formed some time ago in lue of invention of a smoke consumer by Hyrum Woolley. After considerable demonstrations of the wonder of this invention a company was formed which secured patent rights in all the foremost countries in the World. The capitol stock is 200,000 shares at $1.00 each. The price per share has now advance to over $2.00 and letters received by Bro. Grant from his brother tells that the prospects are that this invention will, in a month or two, bring millions of dollars. This seems too great to be true, but the option is now pending to give Pennsylvania the patent rights in the state for one half million which means $2.50 per capitol. This option is now on for 60 days. New York has been offered for a million and it is absolutely without doubt that the rest of the United States will go for two or three millions. Hence according to the favorable estimate of the stock, given me by Bro. Grant, and the amount it will bring from the United States alone is $1750; according to the lowest estimate I will receive nothing but the amount of $10 which Bro. Grant originally paid for the one hundred shares. Whichever way this may terminate it matters not to me personally as I appreciate the feelings which prompted Bro. Grant to make me this present and I love him more for his generous heart than for any material benefit that he may bring me. These feelings I expressed to him and thanked the Lord that I had the privilege of an association with such a man as he.

Bro. Ensign and I returned to our rooms rejoicing over the events of the day and the demonstration of love that we felt in our hearts for each other as we realized that so long as we were united and at peace that the Lord would manifest himself in greater blessings unto us.

During the day Bro. Grant and I sent a joint letter to Bro. and Sister Empey Wishing them the compliments of the season and the peace of heaven to rest upon them with all the rest of the Saints in the thirteenth ward. . . .

Thursday, 2 January 1902—Friday, 3 January 1902, Kameari

About a week ago Bro. Ensign and myself were invited to visit the native province of one of the students with whom we had become quite intinate and whose attachment for us was so strong that he desired us to meet the members of his family who lived in the little village of Kameari. Since receiving the invitation we have looked forward with great pleasure for the arrival of the appointed day—Jan. 2nd.—when we would have the opportunity of going into the country and meeting with some of the humble, but highly respected farmer folk of Japan.

On the afternoon of the 2nd at about two o'clock we, in company with five of our Japanese friends, took the train from Uyeno Station having for our destination the home of Mr. Cano who acted as guide during our outing. In a direct course from Tokyo Kameari is only nine miles distant, but the round–about course of the railroad makes it almost an hour's ride. And in the winter season there is little to be seen along the way, save flooded rice fields and thatched–roofed cottages. But while the view from the car window was not at all interesting, we had a pleasant time singing Japanese songs and exchanging jokes in both Japanese and English.

Kameari is a place of no more than nine hundred houses most of which are small and rudely built. It is right in the centre of a farming district and with the exception of a few stores and an occasional tea–house all the buildings are the private homes of the people who own and care for the numerous fields in the vicinity, none of which are more than fifteen rods² square. The depot is a half a mile from the centre of the village and nothing but a little gravel path elevated two or three feet above the common level and four feet wide led to the home of our friend.

It had been four years since a fereigner was in the village therefore we were naturally looked upon as a curiosity, and as we walked along the children stopped their games and with a frightened look they shied off to one side as we passed and then followed after us till we found refuge inside the walls of the house to which we had been invited. The laborers in the fields paused and rested their chins on the handles of their digging–forks and the women in the houses turned from their work to get a glance at us. This was amusing to us, but at the same time somewhat embarrassing, as we had never realized before that we were so odd that our fellow men would look upon us with the same wonderment that they would view the features of a menagerie, and follow after us as the ordinary street urchin runs along with the clowns in a circus procession. In thirty minutes after our arrival the whole town had been informed that two foreigners were at the home of Mr. Cano and until ten o'clock that night the house was surrounded with old and young from all parts whose inquisitiveness led them to throw open the door of the house and pry into the room where we were sitting. This rudeness was repeated so many times that the people decided to leave the door open entirely until those on the outside had seen all they desired and viewed to their hearts content the strange caucations who had ventured into their midst. A crowd of not less than fifty people from babies in arms to old men and women whose race in life seemed almost run, stood for hours at the open doors gazing so hard that their eyes appeared ready to leap out of their heads. When one person had seen enough to satisfy him, he would leave and another would immediately crowd into his place and thus as I have said the throng lasted till ten o'clock and I guess it would have lasted longer had we not blown out the lights and gone to bed. Before leaving Tokyo we decided to take our kodak along with us in case an opportunity was presented to get some good snapshots. The sight which these people presented as they looked in at the door was too interesting to let pass without an effort to preserve it on paper so we took a picture which did not develop very well as it was too late in the evening when the film was exposed.

We were received with the greatest courtesy by the mother and brothers of Mr. Cano and all that could be done to make our visit pleasant was though of by them. As is the custom in Japanese homes, immediately upon our arrival we were provided with tea and cakes the former of which is the sign of hospitality in Far Eastern lands. Not being unable to speak much Japanese we were obliged to express our pleasure at meeting with this family through some of the students who acted as our interpreters. We were provided with the best that a country home can furnish. And let me say right here that in Japan it is like America where the thrifty farmer has in a crude but comfortable way the luxuries and necessaries of life. Mr. Cano's folks are among the highest in the village and consequently we had the finest food and the most comfortable beds that Japan is able to furnish. The house was large and surrounded by a high wall. The roof, like all the other places in this locality, was thatched with grass and rice straw two feet thick. The yard surrounding the house was large and very clean, having different kind of fruit trees planded promiscuously along the paths giving to the place a careless beauty which pleased me very much. We took a number of pictures of the place both in and outside the house. We also made a photograph of our friend' Cano's mother together with her little grandson, who before we left became very much attached to us.

The afternoon and evening of the 2nd, was pleasantly spent in conversing with the people and in having a general good time such as they are considered in this land. The evening meal was one which, for variety, I have never seen equalled in Japan. It being the New Year's celebration season a special kind of food out of the ordinary is provided and you bet these people were well provided. To us the food was quite palatable, but I dare say that for a foreigner who had never tasted Japanese food in would have been a very hard dose. After watching the young men play for an hour or so at Japanese cards we went to bed all sleeping in different beds but four or five in a room. At midnight or soon thereafter I woke up and saw our friend sitting by one of the "hibachi," but did not realize why he was doing so. It leaked out in the morning, however, that he feared we would be cold in the night and he has sit up all the time to keep the fires going for the comfort of we, his guests. Such a display of kindness and consideration found a soft place in my heart for him, and it showed to me that there was a pretty warm spot in his heart for us or he would not have taken so much trouble for our welfare.

Let people say what they will concerning the selfishness of the Japanese and the heathenism that prevails here, so long as they can demonstrate, by such actions as this, their appreciation of friends and friendship they can teach their more civilized neighbors how to be considerate of the comfort of the stranger traveling in their midst. I felt that this young man was entitled to thanks more than words could tell for this action, so I silently asked the Lord to reward his kind and sacrificing heart. I asked myself if I would be willing to sit up all night long to look after the comfort of a sleeping friend much less a comparative stranger and I feared that my disposition was faulty, so I tried to profit by the lesson which this incident taught me.

The following morning (3rd) we were provided with an excellent breakfast, after which we took a walk to a neighboring school–house where our friend received his early education. We had no sooner appeared on the street before the children began to gather around us as they had done the day before. They followed us wherever we went and to be able to give our folks at home a better idea of how many there were, we had them all stand up in front of the school while we took their pictures. This picture proved to be the most interesting one of the trip.

Laaving the village we took a walk through the fields to another settlement close by, where one of the oldest and most beautiful temples in the land is to be found. The name of the temple is Taishoku. We secured permission from the priests to go inside only on condition, however, that we remove our shoes. This was nothing unusual for us as we had been doing this at our own home for some time, so we quickly took off our shoes and entered just in time to see the priests enter and perform one of their ceremonies which I confess was the oddest worship that it has been my privilege to observe. It consisted of chants and the hammering of large brass gongs the solemn sounds from which are more death like than the tolling of any church bell in America. In all Japanese temples there are a certain number of merchants who sell curios, liquors, and other things to the people who are continually paying their pilgrimages to these ancient shrines. Connected with the Temple is a small but beautiful garden the shrubbry in which is of a superior and rare type. The alters, seats, and ledges are all made of gold, bronze, and other metals and the ornaments and trinkets seem countless. Large candles burn on the shrine all the time and at stated hours in the day the people come and pay homage to the different idols that sit mutely along the shrine. Just before we came out the priests began their chants and the people began to come in to worship in the presence of the priest who sat in a large chair surrounded by others of a more inferior class. He was dressed in white silk clothing which a king could wear without disgrace. We took a picture of the temple and also of the gate leading to it before we left.

We took a different course going back. One which led us along the bank of one of the large rivers emptying into the bay near Tokyo. One sight we saw which was very odd to us was, a man pushing a small car along a track which led from the temple we had just visited to the nearest railroad station. This car was about 1/3 the size of an ordinary electric car and it seemed with perfect ease that the man ran along at quite a rapid rate pushing his burden before him as tho it were a baby carriage. This is what is called in Japan, the push–car and we were told that in many parts of this land this mode of travel is used in going from the main railroad lines to outlying districts. We took a snap at this also considering it to be of interest among our collection of Japanese views.

As we walked on toward Kameari the people all along the line turned out to see us but the children seemed too much frightened to follow. Perhaps these children had never seen a foreigner in their lives and it is also possible that many of the older folks had never seen any of the white race and were therefore struck almost dumb with awe and wonderment to see such freaks as we. The "Mormons" attract attention wherever they go, but this trip can perhaps be considered among the record breakers for exciting curiosity.

We rested for a little while during which time the sister–in–law of our friend Cano provided us with a tasty lunch the dessert of which was a dish of oranges soon delapodated by our angry appetites. At a few minutes past one we said good–bye to those who had so kindly entertained us and left a "missionaries blessing" on the house and its inmates. In all this can be counted the most interesting outing I have enjoyed in the Mikado's Empire, and indeed a pleasant celebration of New Year's—the first spent in the Far East.

Saturday, 4 January 1902, Tokyo

Weather beautiful. Went to the hotel Central in the morning to take lesson in Japanese. Returned to my rooms at about two o'clock expecting to do some writing but met with some of my student friends who had just called to see me and spent the entire afternoon in talking with them. These students names I have not as yet learned but they are the most sensible and refined young men that I have become acquainted with in Japan. They are much interested in the study of Christianity and consequently our conversation was naturally along a religious line. Bro. Ensign stayed at the Central Hotel until evening. The students did not leave until after nine o'clock so I was baffeled in my work, still all for a good cause as I rejoice to find someone with whom to talk of the principles of Christianity and the manner in which the Church of Jesus Christ was established in this dispensation; especially is it a pleasure to met with Japanese who have already become imbued with a desire to learn of the Savior and the effect of t his teachings upon the destiny of mankind. The conversation with these young men to–day has been one of them most interesting and spirited discussions I have had in this land and I thank God for the opportunity given me to bear my testimony to the truth of his work.

Sunday, 5 January 1902, Tokyo

A pleasant clear day. Spent the morning in cleaning up, taking a bath, and writing up my journal. It being fast day I continued to abstain from eating—having eaten nothing yesterday. Went to the Central Hotel to meet Bro. Grant and Bro. Kelsch and hold, with them, the regular fast meeting. We had an excellent meeting; the spirit of the Lord was manifest and we rejoiced in the spirit of testimony that was manifest and partook of the sacrament with grateful hearts. Among other things, Bro. Grant said, that he felt that I would be the main instrument in the hands of the Lord in translating the Book of Mormon into the Japanese language and that he had been praying that this work would be given me to perform and that I should be assisted of the Lord to learn this language speedily so that the translation of this book might be made in the near future. He con–tinued to say regarding this matter that as Joseph Smith had become one of the greatest of Prophets by being the instrument in the hands of the Lord of bringing forth the Book of Mormon to the people of the earth so also do those men chosen to translate this Sacred Record into other languages pertake, to some extent, the same honor, glory, and blessing which rested on the Prophet as a result of the work of translation. In responding to this sentiment of Bro. Grant's I said that nothing would cause my heart such joy, if, in the providences of the Lord, I should be chosen and qualified for this labor, but that if it were the work of someone else that I would rejoice in seeing that person perform his labor well and faithfully.

While I had never thought seriously upon the probibility of such a work coming to me, yet I confess that the remarks of Apostle Grant have started more serious reflection upon this matter and I want to live to be worthy of such a glorious blessing which is also a great honor even though I am never called to this work. While Bro. Grant was speaking many things went through my mind. I thought of the prayer he offered in the woods wherein he asked the Lord to bless me with additional knowledge and wisdom that I might increase in power to perform faithfully my mission in life, that I might become EVEN AS ALMA OF OLD FULL OF THE SPIRIT AND POWERFUL IN THE WORD OF GOD. I thought of the name that had been given me at my birth and wondered if it should have any significence with my labor in the future and that I should indeed be called upon to translate the words of Alma one of the most striking characters in the history of the Nephites. All I want, is to have strength to do my part in bringing to pass the purpose of the Lord in the earth and in all things to submit unto His providences for I know that He doeth all thinks well.

We ate supper at the hotel after which Bro. Kelsch and I took a walk over to the Metropole Hotel to see if any mail had been received for us. It was almost ten o'clock when Bro. Ensign and I got back to our rooms.

Monday, 6 January 1902, Tokyo

As this was the day for Mr. Hiroi to come to our rooms, I did not go out at all during the day, but devoted myself to study and writing. The students did not bother us at all so the afternoon was quiet for a change, which fact I appreciated very much.

Toward evening Mr. Hume called on us to get some money that we had decided, at his request, to lend him. He stayed and ate dinner with us remaining for some time after. I had written a letter to Sam during the afternoon and as the mail closed at ten o'clock I had to leave Mr. Hume to chat with Horace while I went to the postoffice to mail my letter home.

The night was intensely cold and I had to walk briskly to keep warm.

Horace during the afternoon went down town to the photographers to get some pictures which we had taken while on our visit to the country the other day. They were exceedingly good; the best I believe that we have taken.

Tuesday, 7 January 1902, Tokyo

This day passed off as usual. Nothing out of the ordinary happened until evening when quite a funny incident happened to me. During the afternoon the landlady brought her sister in to see us and I was indeed surprised to see such a fine looking young lady and remarked to Bro. Ensign that it was not often that we saw such a handsome face in this land among the women. This visit did not last long as we could not speak enough Japanese to carry on a conversation for more than a moment or two.

Later in the evening, just before eating supper the landlady came in again and sit down in the chair as though she were going to stay for a while. She began to speak by making a slight reference to her sister. I then volunteered a compliment on the good looks of her family relative. She took up my remark immediately and said that her sister had become smitten on me and wanted to know if I would marry her. The landlady said that if I would take her for my wife that she would giver her concent and I could take her to America when I went. This was too funny to keep from laughing and indeed we had a harty laugh which did not seem to hit the feelings of the landlady at all favorably, as it seems she was in earnest when presenting the suit for her sister.

Not having come to Japan to place myself on the marriage market, I therefore declined the offer in as courteous a manner as possible, preferring to continue in that state which the old maids call, "single blessedness" until some future time when I either offer or receive a proposal of the kind from some sweet maid in Utah.

The landlady had not been gone long when one of the servants came into the room and kneeled down on the floor by the "hibachi" near which I was sitting. She took hold of my hand and began to comment on the beauty of my "soft white skin" when compared with the "dark dirty flesh of the Japanese." By this time I began to think that my time had come and that although I had been successful in turning away one fair maiden yet there were others whose suits I would have to hear. It kept getting more and more interesting until Bro. Ensign who was sitting at the table writing to his wife nearly went into laughing convulsions. The servant soon found that we were laughing at her and with a plagued look she left the room.

Wednesday, 8 January 1902—Sunday, 12 January 1902, Tokyo

In the night of the eighth it snowed a little and then cleared off, freezing the snow on the trees and other places until in the morning when the rays of the rising sun fell upon the ice robed trees the glittering effect was most beautiful and one is so rare in this land that some of the old residents of Tokyo say it was a scene which has not been observed here for the last fifty years. Since this storm we have had most delightful sunshine which, mixed with the fresh and piercing air of winter, has made the weather ideal, indeed.

The mornings have been spent with Mr. Hiroi who has given us our lessons either at the Central hotel or here in our rooms. The afternoons and evenings have been spent in various ways; study and entertaining guests being the principle features. I have also been busy preparing an article for the Improvement Era, giving a description of "Some Features in Japanese Life."[3] I finished the article on the evening of the 10th, and sent it off on the 12th, together with four snap shots of scenes that I had described, thinking that the reproduction of the pictures would greatly help the article to be interestion to the readers of the Era.

On the 9th, I received a letter from Grace Frost in answer to one written to her on Nov. 12th, 1901. The letter contained a silk handkerchief and Christmas card from Grace and a Christmas card from Grace's friend whom I have never met, but who has written to me for Grace, her name is Maud Baggerly. This letter was a complete surprise to me and coming from the source it did, I hardly knew what to make of it. I had attempted in my letters to Grace to encourage her to exercise faith in the Lord to heal her of her sore affliction. For my letters and the interest which I had manifest in her, she evidently liked to show her appreciation by this Christmas token. I rejoice exceedingly that I have the good wishes of my friends and if a line of encouragement from me can in any way help them to bear up under the burdens of this life, I hope always be ready and willing to give that word, for it costs me nothing, and is precious to those who receive it. I could not help but feel somewhat humiliated at receiving these tokens and being one of those who believes that, "it is more blessed to give than to receive," I sent home on the afternoon of the 12th, a letter and two Japanese photographs on silk cloth, one for each—Grace and her friend.

On the morning of the 12th, I wrote a letter to my Sister Lisadore, reminding her that it was five months to the day since the "Mormon" missionaries arrived in Japan, and that I was celebrating the day by writing to her. As the 12th, came on Sunday we met together in our usual Sunday Sacramental meeting to pertake of the Spirit of the Lord. We had a good time together and in the evening had Mr. Takahashi take supper with us. He showed a fine spirit towards us and we felt glad that he had become so warm a friend. It was decided in our meeting that we only assemble together once a week instead of every other day as we had been doing in the past.

Monday, 13 January 1902, Tokyo

Pleasant day. During the morning I was down town making some purchases. The afternoon was spent in study, while in the evening a number of the students came in to see us and we were occupied in entertaining them.

While on the car this morning an incident happened that illustrates the little regard the Japanese have for the women. Heretofore I had noticed with considerable regret that ladies always had to stand when the car was overcrowded and that a gentleman (if they can be called by this name) never offers to give a lady a seat no matter how old she may be or how beautiful. To the astonishment of all who have seen us, the "Mormons" have showed their superior breednig by getting up and offering their seat to a lady whenever occasion required. But I showed an American courtesy to a lady this morning that made all eyes fall upon me, and some seemed even to leap out of the heads of those who evidently had looked upon a woman as the slave of man. The car was not crowded but well filled and theire was room next to me for one person to sit down, so when a lady, very nicely dressed, entered, I drew her attention to the fact that ther was room next to me. In sitting down the shawl around her shoulders fell down her back and without noticing particularly what I was doing I reached around and put it up again in the proper place. The lady seemed much astonished and blushed exceedingly, at the same time making a very low bow and thanked me kindly. Those in the car who saw me do this looked thunderstruck, and I guess it was like a thunderbolt to their manner of treating women, and from that moment till I got off of the car I was the subject of conversation, which, judging from the expressions on the people's face as they talked among them selves, was partly ridiculing and party praising my action. Whatever may have been the opinion of others I felt quite proud of the fact that if I could not speak well enough to preach the gospel I could at least teach a lesson in etiquette.

Tuesday, 14 January 1902, Tokyo

After the morning had been spent in sleep and study mixed, I went to the central hotel to met with the brethren who were giving Mr. Hiroi and his bride a wedding dinner, Mr. Hiroi having been married the day before. The arrival of the bride and groom was rather late and we feared that as the bride had never been entertained in foreign style, that her courage had failed and that she had weakened during the last moments. The cause of the delay, however, was that Mr. Hiroi's mother–in–law had taken quite a sever cold and could not be with us, consequently, before leaving her, the bride had to prepare some food for her to eat while they were absent.

Mr. Hiroi is surely to be congratulated on the fine wife he has secured. She was so far superior to what we had expected to see that we were completely overcome with her beauty and refinement. She is only seventeen and quite small of stature, but has one of the sweetest faces that I have seen in Japan. Heretofore all the women had no charmes for me, but I'll declare a helpmeet in life like Mrs. Hiroi would not be very objectionable, even if she does possess those angular eyes so common to the Far East. She was elaborately dressed silks and her hair was arranged in a most tasty manner, being wrapped with gold braid and other choice head ornaments used by the Japanese women. Mr. Hiroi was the same old stick only that on this occasion he had on a clean shirt and new white tie, something quite unusual about his toilet.

The style of Japanese gallantry is not at all commendable in the eyes of the forigner who during his honey–moon gives strict attention to the comforts of his loving spouse. In going from the parlor to the dining–room, Mr. Hiroi rushed ahead of his lady, leaving her to get there the best way she could, which, of course, was rather awkward it being her first experinece in such a thing. At the table Bro. Grant allowed the couple to sit together thinking that they would be able to get along more comfortably if they were where they could talk together. This arrangement proved to be very unsatisfactory, as Mr. Hiori went strait on with his eating never seeming to think of his better half who had seldom seen knives and forks, let alone know how to use them and who was constantly, therefore, in a delemina to know how to handle her food. Noticing this lack of attention on the part of Mr. Hiroi, I felt like I wanted to kick him a time or two and bring him to a realization of what his duty was to his "persecuted" wife. Had I not been on the opposite side of the table and could have reached to her plate I surely would have at least broken her bread and shown a little more attention to her than that received from her husband. After all, Mr. Hiroi can not be blamed as it is the custom in this land to let the woman get along at everything the best she can, she not being supposed to encroach upon the time of her lord.

Considering the fact that this was the first time for her to eat at a fornign table, and that to in a hotel dining–room, I was completely captured with her genteel movements and the graceful manner in which she handled herself. The embarrassment which she felt while in the dining–room left her as soon as we got back to the parlor where we had an excellent afternoon singing, laughing, and talking in both Japnese and English. We also found to our astonishment that Mrs. Hiroi could speak one or two words of English which she used freely and without hesitancy.

It is considered a breach of good etiquette to put your cloaks on in the house, so Mrs. Hiroi started out with her wraps on her arm, but I stopped her and assisted her to put them on in the room where it was warm. She said in Japanese, "Is it not rude to do so," but being able to understand this sentence, I quickly retorted in the negative, In putting on a muffler she left on edge turned wrong side out and while her husband noticed this and reminded her of the fact, yet he did not offer to set it right. She tried to do it herself but could not, so I did it for her to the great amusement of herself, husband, and one other Japanese friend whom we had invited to celebrate the occasion with us. Before saying good–bye there was a feeling of the most perfect freedom and an absence of all embarrassment noticed in the beginning of the party.

The affair was voted a complete success, and we were well pleased with the results for we felt that a little show of kindness to our teacher and his new wife would forever be remembered by them and their friends and cause many favorable things to be said of the Latter–day Saints who are or will be in Japan.

Wednesday, 15 January 1902, Tokyo

My companion and I were very late in getting up, and had hardly finished our breakfast when Mr. Hiroi came to give us our lesson. Mr. Okamoto, the photographer, also came to get the money we owed him for some pictures we had him print, taken while we were in the country on the 2nd and 3rd inst.

Bro. Ensign went down town in the afternoon, but I stayed in the room all day, devoting myself to study. During the evening I read with intense interest the vision of Lehi and also the vison of Nephi[4] as recorded in the Book of Mormon. The style of reading in the Book of Mormon and the plainness with which it treats the principles of the gospel makes it, to me, one of the most, if not the first, book of interest that is found in the church. As I read of the faith of Nephi and the great blessings he received from the Lord in consequence of his faith, my heart swelled within me and I approached the Lord before going to bed with a spirit of prayer that I have not felt for some time. Would to God that I could exercise the faith in the Lord that was manifest in the life of Nephi and that I could have the desires of my heart gratified in regard to my labors among this people as his were gratified in early days! The greatest desire of my heart is to accomplish all things that it is possible for me to accomplish in brining to pass the purposes of the Lord in the earth according to His will and the ability with which He has blessed me. As Nephi in his youth turned unto the Lord so also do I wish to dedicate all unto Him and I pray that as Nephi was favored in his youth that the Lord will favor me in my tender years, even according to the work for me to perform on this earth that I may be found diligent in all things and worthy of an exaltation in the Celestial Glory of Heaven where my joy can be complete and the hours of eternity spent with the faithful of all dispensations.

Thursday, 16 January 1902, Tokyo

A most beautiful day. One of the best of spring, which seems to be already approaching. We have in our room a small plum–tree literally covered with blossoms, and which emit a fragrance that fills to air from morning till night and from night till morning. The plum blossoms are the first flowers of the year in Japan and in some districts there may be seen entire orchards all in bloom at the present time. This seems very strange to me as I have always been used to the long and cold winters experienced in the Rockies.

I stayed in the room all day long, reading and writing and studying. I wrote a letter to my sister Maggie enclosing some snap–shots of myself and some of the other brethren. The students were with us considerably, staying until eight o'clock in the evening.

Friday, 17 January 1902, Tokyo

Mr. Hiroi came about ten o'clock to give us our lesson. At a little past eleven, Bro. Kelsch called on us bringing mail from home. I received a letter from Father, one from mother, one from Bishop Empey, and a calandar from mother. The news was all good and encouraging for the reason that everything was moving along nicely at home and all those near and dear to me were well and enjoying immensely the scenes incident to an approaching Christmas and New Years. We also received a copy of the Christmas edition of the Deseret News This paper was very large having ten parts of eight pages each—80 pages in all.

Bro. Kelsch stayed and ate dinner and supper with us. During the afternoon we had a pleasant time talking with the two Mr. Kitada's. The older of these two boys seems very much interested in the study of Christianity and it was remarkable to us that his ideas were all good and harmonized with the teachings of "Mormonism," in nearly every part. Of all the students we have yet met, these two boys have impressed us most favorably as having sincere hearts in the study of religion and in whom there is hope of a final conversion to truth.

In the evening Bro. Ensign and I went with Bro. Kelsch back to the hotel. Having had but little exercise during the past week I felt that a good walk would do me good. At the hotel we had the privilege of hearing a letter from Apostle John W. Taylor received in the last mail from home. The letter was addressed to Bro. Grant, but it was practically for us all. . . .[5]

This letter came as an additional blessing to us and I felt in my heart to thank the Lord for the inspired words it contained, and to invoke Him to give me power that the blessing therein promised might be realized upon my head. Words cannot express the force with which the following sentence appealed to me, "He (the Lord) will open the mouths of the young elders and IF THEIR FAITH IS PERFECT they shall speak by the convincing power of the Lord." Nor could I help feeling that the true spirit of prophesy suggested the words, "The hour is at hand when the Lord will speak unto the heathen nations, AND THEY WILL BREAK DOWN THEIR IMAGES AND BURN THEM UP AND WORSHIP THEM NO MORE." Before closing my eyes in sleep I went before the Lord and prayed earnestly that the lives of all His representatives in this land might be such that the blessing pronounced upon them by one of the Apostles of Jesus Christ should be fulfilled and that they could all "return home again to the land of Zion, BRINGING OUR SHEAVES WITH THEM" and be welcomed by the prophets and saints of the Most High.

Saturday, 18 January 1902, Tokyo

Another beautiful spring day. Was in the room all day studying and reading. A time or two some of the students came in to see us but did not stay long. Bro. Ensign went in the evening to Mr. Humes house where there was to be a gathering of students and he had been requested to make a short talk to them on "Mormonism." He got back at nine o'clock after having no particular demonstration. . . .

Sunday, 19 January 1902, Tokyo

This being the Sabboth, Bro. Ensign and I went in the afternoon to the Central Hotel to meet with the brethren and hold a meeting with them as is our custom every Sunday. We partook of the Scrament and had a very pleasant, undisturbed, gathering. We sang the songs of Zion and expressed our feelings as led by the spirit of the Lord. No subject, however, of particular importance was discussed, save that we continue to pray for, and exercise faith in the Lord for, the blessings of Heaven to rest down upon Mr. Takahashi, who is such a powerful man in the nation of Japan, and who, at present is deeply interested in the study of "Mormonism."

After our meeting Mr. Takahashi called on us and ate supper at the hotel. Bro. Grant had an exceedingly pleasant talk with him and read considerable from the Life of Prest. John Taylor[6] wherein the ability of this prophet as a defender of the faith and a power against the enemies of the Lord is shown. Mr. Takahashi became very interested in the things of which Bro. Grant read and took some notes, a thing that he had not done on his previous visits.

Between six and seven o'clock Mr. Humes and three of his Japanese students called at the hotel to see us. They spent the rest of the evening and also ate supper at the hotel with us. One of the Japanese student was a sergant in the army, another the nephew of Marquis Ito to whom we have letters of introduction from Bro. Angus Cannon, who, with his Brother Geo. Q. Cannon, had met the Marquis a number of times.[7]

During the morning I wrote a letter to Aunt Lucy and one to Aunt Eliza, also a short note to my mother. The letters were explanitory of some pactures which I intend to send to them as birthday tokens.

Monday, 20 January 1902, Tokyo

Mr. Hiroi came in the morning at nine o'clock and spent the time till noon teaching us. As soon as he left I started to write up my correspondence. At this I spent the rest of the day and way into the night.

Tuesday, 21 January 1902, Tokyo

Spent the whole day in writing. I had received so many letters during the last few days that it required a long time to write answers, and as there were also some to whom I had never written and to whom it was my duty to write, i found that it took a great deal of time to get even with my promises. Some to whom I wrote were not members of the church and consequently I had to take more care in what I said, as I always try to put in a little gospel as effectivly as possible whenever I write to this class. One letter of six typewritten pages to Emma, another of three very closely written pages to Bishop Empey, another page and a half equally as close to all the folks at home, and six pages to Rev. H.C. Houston of Urbana, Ohio was the result of the day's work. A copy of the letter to him is herewith attached.

Mr. Houston visited the Thirteenth Ward Sunday School while I was a small boy in one of the Intermediate classes. On the occasion of his visit our class was studying the Articles of Faith and on this especial morning we were asked to recite them. I was the only one in the class who had learned them sufficiently to speak them without a mistake. This attracted the attention of Mr. Houston who observed the workings of the class for some minutes. After the school was dismissed, he came to me and asked for my name and address, saying that he was a teacher in a Baptist Sunday School in Ohio. I gave it to him and after some weeks had passed I received a letter from him. We corresponded for a little while. When I was called and had departed on my mission to Japan my mother found his address and sent him a copy of the newspaper containing my photograph, a short outline of my life, and an announcement of my call to this land. In answer to this newspaper notice my mother received from Mr. Houston a letter in which he expressed a desire to hear from me. The last mail brought this news from home and I have therefore embraced the first opportunity to renew the friendship which began some six or seven years ago. I have purposely dated all the letters which I have written the 23rd, inst., because the mail does not leave for America till the 24th, and I wanted my letters to appear up to date.

Wednesday, 22 January 1902, Tokyo

I was surprised on getting up, to see about two inches of snow on the ground and the day still dismal. It snowed and rained all day making it extremely unpleasant. Spent the entire day in the room.

In the evening according to an invitation received from Mr. Tilson one of the soldiers who went from Utah at the time of the war in the Philippines, but who stopped off in Japan when the batteries returned to America, Bro. Ensign and I went to the Metropole Hotel to eat supper. The hour set for us to met our friend was 7:30 p.m. but the host did not put in an appearance so at ten minutes past eight we went into the dining–room and treated ourselves to the supper which we had expected to eat at the expense of our friend. The four of us, Bros. Grant and Kelsch as well as Horace and I were once more at the table in the Metropole and we did indeed enjoy the meal immensely in spite of the disappointment from our host.

Thursday, 23 January 1902, Tokyo

A cold but clear day. The streets very muddy as a result of the snow the previous day. Except a short trip to the post–office in the evening I was in the room all day. I posted to–day the letters which I have written lately to my friends and relatives in America. In the morning we were visited by a yound man by the name of Hoshi whom Bro. Ensign had first met some days ago while taking a walk. This young man has a brother, whose photograph he showed us, living in America and publishing quite an exhaustive magazine in New York called "Japan and America."[8] This young man expressed a desire to talk with us occasionally on the subject of religion. Of course, this was a pleasant remark for us as nothing pleases us more than to speak of the workings of our Heavenly Father. We hope that the young man's remark will become a reality.

Friday, 24 January 1902, Tokyo

A beautiful day. Spent the day quietly in the rooms. Mr. Hiroi came and spent the morning teaching us. A friend of Mr. Hiroi's also called and spent nearly all the afternoon with us.

In the evening we had a pleasant time singing the songs of Zion. Since we have been living out in this hotel we have not done much singing. Perhaps the reason is, that we have not Bro. Grant with us to start the songs. When we were all together in the foreign hotel we were singing all the time. Our digression from the customary silence this evening has been indeed a pleasant change. . . .

Saturday, 25 January 1902, Tokyo

A pleasant day. Spent the day quietly at the rooms. During the afternoon Mr. Miazaki came to see us. Also we were favored with a visit from Mr. Kitada who in reading the New Testament had discovered some things that were not exactly clear and had come to us to have them explained. Bro. Ensign was out so I had to explain as best I could the passages which were hard for him to understand. He is one, if not the most, earnest young men that we have become acquainted with and there is always such a humble and good spirit with him that we delight to talk to him about the gospel for he is ever anxious to learn and his heart seems prepared to accept without much question the true meaning of the scriptures.

In the evening, according to previous arrangement, Bro. Ensign and I went to Mr. Humes' house where we spent a pleasant evening speaking to six or eight students on the principles of the Gospel as we viewed them. One thing that was very gratifying was, that there were a number of these students who could understand english well and it was with considerable ease that we made ourselves understood. Our remarks were principally upon the current slanders that are going throughout Japan concerning the "Mormons" and a warning to all to take the news papers reports with a grain of salt. We showed them our book of views "In and Around Salt Lake City." We also sang some of our hymns and left them all feeling kindly towards us.

Sunday, 26 January 1902, Tokyo

A beautiful day, somewhat warmer than the day before. Went to the Central Hotel to hold our usual Sundy meeting with the other brethren. Had an excellent time and enjoyed the spirit of the Lord. Mr. Takahashi came in the evening and ate supper with us at the hotel. He still seems to be interested in our teachings and is indeed very friendly. Mr. Tilson called and regretted that a mistake had been made in the evening with which we were to have eaten supper with him at the Metropole. (see last Wednesday) He invited us to rectify the mistake by coming to the hotel next Tuesday and eat the meal which he hoped to have furnished us last week. We accepted, and if another mistake is not made and other things are not pressing we will be at the Metropole again Tuesday evening as the guests of Mr. Tilson. Bro. Grant and Bro. Kelsch are also going to move on Tuesday afternoon from the Central to the Metropole Hotel. They have become dissatisfied with their present place and because of some recent scandal connected with their present boarding boarding–place, they think it wise to make the change.

Monday 27 January 1902, Tokyo

The day was pleasant and quite warm. Lesson in Japanese during the morning. In the afternoon wrote a letter to Aunt Clara and also wrote up my journal for the 2nd, and 3rd. insts. relating to the trip Bro. Ensign and I took to the village of Kameari.

In the afternoon we took one of those pleasant baths which are provided nearly every other day. The more I bathe in Japanese tubs the more I enjoy them. After studying or reading for a long time there is nothing more recreative than a good bath.

Tuesday, 28 January 1902, Tokyo

Went to the Metropole Hotel in the evening to meet with Mr. Tilson and the brethren and eat dinner with them. Had a very pleasant time as well as an excellent meal. Mr. Tilson seems to be a young man of good principle and of extraordinary reputable character for one who has been to war and away from his home for so many years. He is quite talkative and being familiar with many things that were also interesting to us, we had a very nice hour's chat after the meal was vinished.

Received two letters from home. One from mother written on Christmas and one from Liss, containing a note from father. All were well at home.

Wednesday, 29 January 1902, Tokyo

Spent the entire day at the rooms. The weather beautiful. In the afternoon had a pleasant talk with Mr. Oi the man who owns the hotel in which we are living. I spoke with him about the Gospel for a little more than two hours and also gave him one of our tracts.

Just before supper Mr. Kitada and his younger brother called to see us, but Bro. Ensign was away having left for the Metropole Hotel shortly after dinner. Bro. Kelsch called about noon and accompanied Bro. Ensign. Mr. Hiroi spent the morning with us. He had purchased a little book. Written and published on the "Mormons," by one of the recent graduates of the Imperial University.[9] If I am not mistaken the title is "Mormonism." It is not a criticism of our claims but rather a brief outline of our history. The Lord is moving on the hearts of some to write that which will help to place the truth before the people of this land, consequently when these men write or us it means that they are accomplishing that which our ignorance of Japanese makes it impossible for us to do at this stage of the work.

Thursday, 20 January 1902, Tokyo

Spent the entire day in the room. It being a holiday held in honor of the death of the present Emperor's father,[10] there were not schools in session and all day there was from one to five students in the room talking to myself and Bro. Ensign. Toward evening a young Japanese by the name of Nomoto came in to see us and as he had been drinking a good deal of "sake" he felt quite lively and created considerable fun for us. He invited us to take a walk with him to Uyeno Park, but I preferred to stay at home. Bro. Ensign, however, went with him. At this time of the year the people are flocking to the different parts to see the budding trees, therefore I was not all surprised when Bro. Ensign told me that thousands of people were at the part. Bro. Ensign ate dinner with this young fellow at the foreign restaurant consequently I ate alone.

Friday, 31 January 1902, Tokyo

A dark rainy dismal day. Went down to the Ginza to do some shopping Called at the tailors to have a new seat put in my pants. I have sit down so much since coming to Japan that nearly all of my trousers are like they had been patched with chaffon. Called at the Metropole to see if any mail had come from America. No had been received.

Saturday, 1 February 1902, Tokyo

Rained all day. Spent the entire day in the rooms. Had the students with us nearly all the time. In the evening Mr. Humes called on us and stayed for an hour or two. He said (but I do not always credit his words) that our visit to his house one week ago this night has caused considerable comment among the students living in that district and that their minds were much wrought up over what we told those who were present at his home concerning "Mormonism" and the slanders that have been circulated against us. All the conversation seeming to be the most favorable towards us. Not only, said he, are the students deeply interested in us, but they have told their parents of having met with us and the old folks are inquiring about us all the time, wanting, if possible, to see us and, if the reports of us from their children be true, to become our friends. The presence of the students during so much of the day made it impossible to do much studying, so the day was mostly spent in talking to them.

While looking over some of the old letters received from home I came across the following in one from Bishop Empey, dated at Salt Lake City Dec. 24th, 1901: "God is with you and will continue to open up the way before you and your labors will be great and the angles of the Lord will be with and go before you. Your tongues will be speedily loosened in the language of that great nation and your joy will be great and the manifestations of the Lord will be beyond your expectations. Your names will be held in remembrance not only before the Saints of God and the world, but before the Lord, and you will be preserved by His power." This, as will be readily seen, was a blessing promised to us all. The first time I read this letter the above did not appeal to me with any particular force, but to–day as I read it, I was struck with the feeling that such words were only written under the influence of the proper spirit, consequently I record them here that they may be preserved.

Sunday, 2 February 1902, Tokyo

Another day of rain and dismal darkness. After having a bath and brushing up a little in the morning, Bro. Ensign and I went to the Metropole Hotel to met with the brethren and hold our regular sacramental meeting with them. We enjoyed the same usual good spirit while thus assembled, and in the evening entertained at supper Mr. Harrison the editor of the Japan Herald. In the hotel's parlor we also had a pleasant time singing and conversing with the guests.

Monday, 3 February 1902, Tokyo

Spent the entire day in the room. Everything was very quiet and I therefore had a good opportunity for study. The day was clear and pleasant. The sun was warm and a very languid feeling stole over me. Mr. Hiroi was to have come to–day to give us our lessons in Japanese but we received a telephone message from the Metropole Hotel that he had mistaken the day and had gone to the other brethren at Tsukiji.

Tuesday, 4 February 1902, Tokyo

Spent the morning taking from Mr. Hiroi my lesson in Japanese. In the afternoon I wrote a letter to father in answer to his and Liss' and mothers received some days ago. I enclosed therein a copy of my journal for Jany. 2nd. and 3rd. also sent some pictures of the scenes that my journal of that date spoke of. After I had written my letter I went to the post office with it and did some shopping while I was out in town. The day was a perfect one in every way.

Wednesday, 5 February 1902—Thursday, 6 February 1902, Tokyo

Went to the Metropole hotel on the afternoon of the 5th, to spend the afternoon and evening with the brethren. Last Sunday it was decided that we meet at the Hotel every Wednesday and that Horace should give Bro. Grant an hour's lesson in music and I teach him for an hour in grammar. We enjoyed ourselves immensely and had an excellent supper. I received a letter from Aunt Martha, who lives in Teton Basin, Idaho.

Spent the entire day of the 6th at the rooms at the hotel. Mr. Hiroi was with us during the morning. In the afternoon I wrote a letter to Bessie Badger, in answer to one received from her during the forenoon. Th This was the letter which Bro. Grant had forwarded to us two weeks before but which had gone astray in transit. Both days have been beautiful and quite warm.

Friday, 7 February 1902—Saturday, 8 February 1902, Tokyo

Spent the entire day of the 7th, in the room. Wrote a letter to Aunt Martha in answer to the one received from her on the 5th.

On the morning of the 8th, took a short walk for exercise. The rest of the day I devoted myself to study. In the afternoon, however, I was occupied for an hour or two in entertaining some Japanese friends who called.

During the week I had been translating my testimony into Japanese, so that I could speak it when I got the chance. The few mistakes which I made in translation I had Mr. Hiori correct. We, Bro. Ensign and I, were invited to spend the evening at the home of Mr. Humes, where there was to be a gathering of students who wanted to hear of the "Mormons." I felt that this would be my opportunity to deliver the little address which I had prepared, so I spent the day in fast and prayer invoking the Lord to bless me with His Spirit that I might be able to remember the words and speak them under the proper influence. I felt somewhat condemned in making such a request of my Heavenly Father as I know that he does not expect His servants to prepare sermons, but I though that in this strange land where I knew but very very little of the language that He would pardon me for the course which I took. When the time came for the meeting, Bro. Ensign and I were prompt in our attendance, and as soon as we arrived I was called upon to speak first. I spoke my piece, but it was the hardest effort that I have every made in my life. I simply floundered for the words, and more than once was tempted to give up, but I fought it through to the last. This was the first time a Latter–day Saint elder had ever spoken in Japanese, and it was indeed a feeble effort, but I believe the Lord blessed me or I would never have been able to finish it.

Sunday, 9 February 1902, Tokyo

Visited the Brethren at the Metropole. Spent the entire afternoon there and had supper in the evening with Mr. Takahashi and Mr. Nakazawa, a priest in the Shinto church.[11] During the morning and until some time after our arrival a priest of the Mitake sect of the Shintoists and his interpreter visited Bros. Grant and Kelsch. Their visit, so Bro. Grant said, was the most satisfactory that he had had from anyone. The priest was very enthusiastic over our work here and said that he would translate immediately some of the literature that was given him. He said that his followers were anxious to know of our doctrines and he was desirous that they should. The interest that some are taking in our work here and what they think to be the final outcome of it is very gratifying and undoubtedly a Pentecost for the truth is not far distant. It almost makes my heart sick when I think of the opportunity there is in this land to preach the gospel not only to the low but more particularly to the high classes, if we could only speak the Japanese language. It is truly hell to want to, and not be able to.

Monday, 10 February 1902, Tokyo

Mr. Hiroi and Bro. Kelsch came in the morning about ten o'clock to see us. Mr. Hiroi gave us our lesson and stayed during the entire afternoon. Bro. Kelsch and Bro. Ensign went off shortly after dinner to hunt for a drug store where they kept bromo–seltzer.[12] Bro. Kelsch suffers with severe headaches quite often and he was extremely anxious to be prepared with an antidote for this trouble whenever he is attacked.

In the morning Bro. Grant telephoned from the Metropole that two letters had been received for me, therefore in the evening I took a walk with Mr. Hiroi to the Ginza and from there went to the Hotel. The letters were from Bishop Empey and his wife. Mrs. Empey spoke of a young lady who had come to Japan and was very anxious to see us but who had been deprived that privilege by a mere trifle. The Bishop's letter was full of a fine spirit, and told of many interesting things connected with the ward. He said that Samuel had been chosen President of the Young Men's in place of Bro. Woolley who had lately moved from the ward. The Bishop said that it had been presented to him that I would soon have this language given to me by the Gift of the Holy Ghost. I realize that all these promises will be realized by me if I am faithful and cease not to be diligent in my labor under all circumstances, and that if I am negligent and leave the Lord to do it all that I will be disappointed. Therefore I want to live so that I may be worthy of any blessing that the Lord sees fit to bestow upon me. I never want to feel that I am blessed for nothing, but I want to know that I have done that which merits reward, whether in dealing with my fellow men or with my Eternal Father. I let Bro. Grant read the letter and remarked to him that I intended to live for that which the Bishop said he felt was to be given me, and I ask the Lord to give me strength to do my full duty every day that I may not be counted a slothful servant in His vineyard. Before going to bed, my stomach began to pain me and about one o'clock I had to get up, as I was shivering and felt much like vomitting. I went to bed again, but had to get up almost the same instant, and I vomitted a terrible lot from my stomach. By morning I was much better and ready to eat my breakfast, which consisted of warm milk and toast.

Tuesday, 11 February 1902, Tokyo

Spent the day at the rooms. On account of having very little sleep during the night, I was very sleepy during the day. My stomach was also weak because of the eruptions that happened in it during the previous evening. We were visited during the day by our Japanese friend Mr. Tanaka and one other young fellow who speaks the English language very well indeed. The day was beautiful and warm for the time of year.

Wednesday, 12 February 1902, Tokyo

It is just six months today since we arrived in Japan. Last night after I had gone to bed, Bro. Ensign received a telephone message from Bro. Grant requesting us to met with him and Bro. Kelsch this morning at the Metropole hotel at 7:30 a.m. to discuss the matter of Apostle Grant's return to Salt Lake to attend April Conference. Bro. Ensign woke me up last night and told me the message that had been received, and I was so surprised that I could hardly believe what had been told me. "The idea" I thought to myself, "of Bro. Grant thinking of returning home. Why he has only been here it seems for a week or two." However, I rolled over on to my knees and asked the Lord to give me the inspiration of His spirit that I might be able to know His will regarding the matter so that I could council wisely with my brethren this morning.

We got up so early that we did not wait for breakfast, but did not get to the hotel until twenty minutes to eight. The brethren at the hotel were just going down to breakfast so we, on their invitation, ate with them. After breakfast we held a meeting for the purpose of deciding the matter mentioned the evening before, so that our dicision could be sent to the authorities at home by the mail which closed for America in a few hours. We had singing and prayer, myself being mouth. Bro. Grant spoke first telling why he had brought up such a subject for consideration and also read a letter which he had written to

Apostle John H. Smith the acting president of the Twelve Apostles.

In this letter Bro. Grant had advanced to the brethren at home all the reasons why he would like to return home for April conference, and the good that he felt would result for this mission from such an action. Then Bro. Kelsch who had heretofore talked this matter over with Bro. Grant expressed himself. Bro. Horace then spoke his feelings on the matter and the result of the meeting was that we all said that if Bro. Grant were permitted to return home now that the Japanese mission would derive great benefit. The principle reasons for this decision were that Bro. Grant could explain to the leaders at home the exact condition of affairs in this land if he were there and talked to them face to face better than could possible be done by correspondence. And as we were at present lying low as the saying is we could better afford to lose the presence of our president now than in six months from now, for by that time we will have begun to do active missionary work. And seeing that Bro. Grant intended to return in October we felt that he had better go now. These were the two chief reasons, and besides Bro. Grant has a daughter whom he wishes to marry and other things which he has to do in his home affairs that makes it more desirable for him to return now than in the fall. Thus not only for the good of the mission but also for Apostle Grant's convenience we felt to say "yes" to the proposition that was posented to us. The decision arrived at in our meeting was immediately written out and the letter posted in time to catch the departing steamer. If it is looked upon with favor by those at home, Bro. Grant will sail from Japan on the 11th of March.

Bro. Ensign and I stayed at the hotel for the rest of the day and took dinner and supper with the brethren. Every moment of the time was pleasant to me and Bro. Grant told me some things for which I can never be sufficiently thankful. I hope I shall every be worthy the respect and love which this good man now has for me. He handed me a letter which he had received from Lutie and invited me to read it. It was one of the sweetest things that I have ever read, full of love and praise for her father and breathing a spirit that is rarely found among the young of the present day. Lutie always did have a disposition and a faith in the work of the Lord which bound her to the affections of neary all with whom she came in contact, and I am glad to know that I have been privileged to be closely associated with her—almost as brothers and sisters—for I realise that her unswerving integrity to the gospel and simple obedience to the will of her parents has ever been a worthy example to me. No matter where she was she was always a Latter–day Saint, and now, while she is laboring as a missionary in Colorado, she is preforming her labor with excellent credit to the cause which she represents and the glory of her Heavenly Father. May the Lord bless her all the days of her life that she may leave a legacy to her posterity that shall be beyond the value of worlds.

The day was a pleasant one and Bro. Horace and I returned in the evening having had what was as good as a Semi–annual Conference celebration.

I received a letter from my sister Margaret who is attending school in Provo. She and her mother were well and school work this year had become quite pleasant. The family had moved from Heber City to Provo and consequently it was more homelike than it was last year when she had to board out with comparative strangers. The letter also stated that my sister Jennie and her husband and baby were getting along well in Park Cit. I answer this letter in the afternoon so as to be in time for the mail that leaves on the fifteenth.

Thursday, 13 February 1902, Tokyo

Yesterday I, with the brethren, was invited to meet Mr. Hiroi this morning at the Metropole Hotel at 9:30 a.m. and go with him to visit one of his friends who had expressed the desire to have the "Mormon" missionaries call on him at his home. It is not the custom for Latter–day Saint elders while traveling in the field to reject an invitation to meet with any of the people among whom they labor, so we quickly accepted Mr. Hiroi's invitation, little realizing when we did so that the event would prove such an interesting and profitable one.

Considerable snow fell during the day, but this only added enjoyment to our outing for it was the first good downfall that we had seen in Japan and we appreciated it as much as a pent up duck would appreciate a day's swim on a pond.

Mr. Hiroi, whose familiarity with locations in Tokyo is quite limited, said that it was about a twenty minutes walk from the hotel to his friends house, but it proved to be much farther than he thought as it took us just one hour and five minutes walking at a pretty rapid rate, to cover the distance. Having been pent up in our rooms so much this walk proved to be good and healthful exercise, and we did not regret that our guide had made a mistake in imagining the distance shorter than it was.

The house was situated in the Azabu district of Tokyo and located on a slight eminence. From the outside the building did not present a very comely appearance, and being low, nothing but the roof could be seen above the high wall which surrounded the place on all sides. But the beauty which the outside lacked was made up in the inner finish. There were perhaps ten or twelve rooms in the house and, according to the prevailing Japanese style, the poorest of these were in the front part. We took off our shoes and shook the snow off of our clothes and were immediately conducted to the rear part of the house where a room had been prepared to receive us. This room was not very large but of a class that told us immediately that the owner was a man of some means and undoubtedly of considerable prominence. The sliding doors dividing this room from the others were not the ordinary white paper ones that are found in most native houses, but were of cloth that had beautiful figures worked worked in it.

The little nook in the wall which the people of this land take great delight in decorating with the best they have, was full of the very choicest of wall ornaments, while in another corner of the room there were a number of little potted plum trees all out in full bloom and emitting a fragrance into the room that made the air smell like it had been charged with choice incense. To those who do not know the sweetness of plum blossoms in Japan, it would be hard to realize the beauty of these trees. In this land the plum and cherry trees are the pride of the people. The flowers come out in such great profusion that the tree bears no fruit whatever; the entire strength of the plant seems spent in its blossoms, and their fragrance rivels in my estimation the violet or the rose. In the centre of this room was a large table made of hard wood and for convenience to the native manner of sitting was made very low, not being more than a foot from the floor. On the floor Around the table mats were arranged upon which we squatted after the manner of our host. Besides the "hibachi" or Japanese stoves that were in the room we were each provided with a small wooden box in which glowing pieces of charcoal had been placed. We used these boxes to warm whatever part of our bodies might be cold. Through the openings in the The east side of the room we could see out into a small garden where the snow covered shrubbery duplicated a winter scene similar to those so common in our mountain home.

The host had invited two of his Japanese friends to be present and hear what they could of the "Mormon" question for it was to learn of our doctrines that this gentleman had requested us to come to his house. We learned the name of our host to be Mr. S. Ichiki who has figured prominently in many of the wars in Japan especially during the troubles of the Meji restoration. His friends were Mr. Miyasaki and Mr. Suyenaga. The first of a family whose record has been a famous one in the history of the nation, the second an editor of one of the influential newspapers. It was indeed interesting to look into the faces of these gentlemen and study the lines of their features. The editor, whose coal black hair hung in beautiful locks around his shoulhers, looked all the world like an indian brave dressed in citizens clothes. Mr. Miyasaki, whose hair was also long but done up in a bob, would have passed as a full blooded native of Armenia and were it not for the scant bunch of whiskers on his chin and the hair or two that outlined the place where a mustache should grow, I could have easily considered him a foreigner to the country, but such an attempt at a hairy growth upon the face is a sure sign of Japanese blood. Our host to me could have passed as a citizen of India, and with our interpreter Mr. Hiroi, who is the typical Japanese, we observed in the little gathering before us the features of four distinct nations.

The conversation soon found its way into religious channels and with Mr. Hiroi acting as interpreter we were able to explain to the satisfaction of all, our position and belief on the points most interesting to those present, the principle point being the "Mormon" doctrine of polygamy (of course). Judging from the animated talk had by the members of the company after we had answered their questions on this point I should judge our teachings regarding this religious law made some effect on them. They next wanted to know how it was that our people got the idea to send missionaries to Japan. They were answered that the President of the church was inspired to send Apostle Grant here, and while it is doubt-ful whether they believe in inspiration, yet after explaining a few incidents in connection with the call which go to show that a divine power directed the movements in this regard, they seemed to be perfectly satisfied on this point. In fact the conversation though intelligible to us only through a second party was indeed gratifying and resulted in the statement from our host that he regretted that we were so much mis-understood by the people of the world, and he offered whatever assistance his influence and position would be able to afford.

They all expressed the wish that we consent to deliver an address on our teachings before a literary organization composed of newspaper editors and members of the House of Commons, in the hope that some of the prominent speakers and writers would be able to assist us in correcting the wrong impressions of our cause. We expressed our willingness to appear before any organization that wanted to know the truth about us and the people whom we represented, but I doubt very much whether we will have any such a privilege as mentioned by these gentlemen, at least, for some time to come. But whether such opportunities as these come to us or not the fact that we can visit the same class of people in their own homes and sit down around their own "Hibachi" and talk to them in a quiet way gives, us the most intense joy in contemplating the future of missionary work in this land. It is by no means a doubtful con-clusion that their are thousands who would be just as glad to receive us and treat us with similiar respect to that which this man has shown us if we only had a sufficient knowledge of the language of to defend our own cause and work our way without having to depend upon an interpreter.

It being nearly eleven o'clock when we arrived at this place we could not get back to the hotel in time to eat dinner, and it was evidently not the intention of our host that we should, for very soon after our coming he stated that he desired us to eat dinner with him. We consented and expected that we would be provided with a Japanese meal, which did not give me any concern by which was the cause of many dubi-ous thoughts in Bro. Grant's mind for he was afraid that he would be forced to reject many of the kinds of food that would undoubtly be offered.

I was rather glad that we had got Bro. Grant in a position where he would have to, at least, try a native meal for Bro. Ensign and I had tried in vain to get him to mome out to our hotel and eat with us, but I was disappointed and he was favored. To the complete surprise of us all, we were provided with a foreign meal of very fine food all served in courses just as at the best hotel in the country. Bro. Grant said that it was the best cooked meal he had eaten in Japan, but I think that he was so much reloived in his feelings that he did not have to struggle with the imagined horrors of Japanese grub, that the food tasted better than it really was. Personally I have eaten many meals in Japan that pleased me much more and even in our Japanese hotel I have tasted dishes just as delicious. One thing that happened during the meal that pleased me very much was the presentation of a strictly native dish, which unfortunately was served at the close of the meal because it was not ready before. The host apologized for the irregular order in which it came and said its lateness could not be helped. I was sitting next to Bro. Grant and watched to see how it would affect him when he took the first mouthful. He did not take a mouthful, but only a nibble which was evidently enough for him. He put the cover on the bowl again and said, "It came too late eh?" at which I suggested the addition of the words, "Thank Heaven" to which he nodded a hearty "amen."

For perhaps two hours after the meal we sang and listened to Japanese music and there was such a pleasant spirit present that we were adverse to leaving but it would not be wise to wear out the kindness of a newly made friend. The mannerisms of our host were extremely interesting to us and his free easy way put us so much in mind of the big hearted farmer of Western America that we felt perfectly at home. To me our host is the man of the greatest character that we have yet met in Japan. He impressed me as being absolutely without hypocrisy and one who was not ashamed of his opinions and spoke them bold-ly whether to the high or the low. His manner did not indicate that he was wedded to the set rules of eti-quette, but that he had a manner that was his own from birth and which was so odd that it give him a facination which delighted me. His show of hospitality to us was beyond anything that we could possibly look for, and he was not satisfied with what he did to entertain us at his home but he put on the finishing touches by ordering rikishaws to take us wherever we desire to go. I fear his hospitality was too great for he indeed won our hearts and I am sure that there was not one of us who did not feel to bless him for his kindness. We voted our visit a complete success and upon the invitation of Bro. Grant it is hoped that we will meet the same Japanese gentlemen next Sunday evening at the Metropole Hotel on which occasion the "Mormons" are to be the entertainers.

We all went back to the Metropole Hotel from where Bro. Ensign and I went to our rooms in Konda district. On the way home I purchased some Japanese souvenir paper on which to write a letter to Sister Empey as per her request made in the tegami[13] received from her some days ago.

Friday, 14 February 1902, Tokyo

The day was very pleasant but rather cold after the snow of the previous day. Mr. Hiroi came to the hotel in the morning and was accompanied by Bros. Grant and Kelsch who had such a good time yesterday that they thought they would come out and see us while they had the spirit of visiting Japanese homes. We could not get hem to stay for dinner however as Bro. Grant preferred to draw the line on Japnese food. Mr. Hiroi gave us our lesson and then returned with the brethren to the Metropole.

In the afternoon Mr. Aoki from Chiba called and asked me to take a walk to Uyeno Park with him as he wanted to see the lion that had lately been imported from Africa. The lion has never before been seen in Japan and the people of this city have nearly gone crazy over this animal, while the officers of the zoological gardens are making barrels of money. After we had viewed the curiosities of the animal show at Uyeno which was interesting to me as well as to Mr. Aoki, we went to a Japanese restaurant and had a meal of "kisoba."[14] Mr. Aoki is a very friendly man, but his ideas of religion are the poorest that I have yet heard. He spiritualizes everything that he can concerning the teachings in the Bible and the account that is written upon which he can not put a spiritual interpretation he classes as fictional or allegoracal writing. We always have discussions on religion when we come together but in spite of our difference of opinion we are always on the best of terms. He invited me to come to see him at his home in Chiba, which invitation I hope to be able to fill in the near future.

Saturday, 15 February 1902, Tokyo

Spent the whole day in my rooms writing up my journal. The day was very pleasant and rather warm after the storms of the day or two before. Mr. Oi came in and I had a pleasant gospel talk with him for a little over an hour. He has read the tract I gave him the other day and dad come to ask a question or two about some of our teachings. I gave him another tract which I hope he will appreciate as much as the first.

Sunday, 16 February 1902, Tokyo

During the morning I shaved a little fuzz off of my face and streightened up my toilet preparatory to going to Tsukiji to meet in regular Sabboth Day services with the rest of the brethren. Our meeting was opened by singing on page 9 of the hymn book "The time is nigh, that happy time." Prayer was offered by Apostle Grant. Singing again on page 71 "Oh Say what is truth."

The first matter considered was the time for Bro. Grant to return home for conference. This matter was not definetely decided. In the following order we spoke concering the condition existing and the best method to be adopted in causing the progress of our work, Apostle Grant, Elder Kelsch, Elder Ensign, and myself. Bro. Grant made a special request that we exercise our faith and offer up our prayers in behalf of Bro. James McMurrin who is suffering much in consequence of a cancer on his face. In accordance with this request we united in prayer, Bro. Ensign being mouth. After singing "Ye who are called to labor," we partook of the sacrament. Benediction was offered by Bro. Kelsch who prayed that we might have the spirit of the Lord with us while entertaining those Japanese guests who had been invited by Bro. Grant to spend the evening and eat supper with us at the hotel.

Very soon after our meeting was closed Mr. Takahashi came to pay his regular Sunday afternoon visit. Bro. Grant had hardly become interested in conversing with him when Mr. Ichiki and his little girl arrived. We went down into the parlor to spend the evening where the conveniences were more fit for a night's entertainment. At half past five or quarter to six oclock all those who invited had arrived. The party consisted of Mr. Takahashi, Mr. Ichiki and his daughter, Mr. Miyasaki a friend to Mr. Ichiki and the one whom we met last Thursday, Mr. Suyenaga, Mr. Miyasaki a friend of our interpreter, our interpreter and his wife, and two other Japanese gentlemen whom we had never met, but who were welcome because they were firends of Mr. Ichiki, whose kindness to us last Thursday created a very warm spot in our hearts for him. Unfortunately our interpreter was the last to arrive and as most of the others could not understand English it was quite a trial for us to show them the proper welcome. Mr. Takahashi, however, soon became familiar with those present and at our request explained many things ot the company concerning our people whom Mr. Takahashi has been studying for some time.

The views of Salt Lake City and Vicinity proved to be very ineresting to our guests, as they have to all who have had the opportunity of seeing them. These views are particularly interesting and attractive to the Japanese people for they take a great delight in hearing of a community that has achieved so much in the material world as have the Latter–day Saints. The slight references that may be made to sociological conditions existing among the "Mormons" while explaining many of the views that we have with us also finds a fruitful soil for questions that oft times lead to good conversations on the gospel. The topics that appeal most to this people are, the material growth of the Church of J.C.L.D.S. and the manner in which it provides for its members. Such statements that there are no poor in the fold and that the destitute are especially looked after be an organization specially called to this work, that our officers work for the church for practically on pay, that we believe in opening up new countries and in subduing the soil, appeals to the Japanese heart more than any argument on the existance of a God or the revelations given to Jos. Smith could possibly do. I almost fancy that the channels through which we are going to lead people to the waters edge and get them to recognize the hand of devine power is through the wonderful things an organization has accomplished the whole system of which in not based at all on the wisdom of men. Mr. Ichiki whose interest was so much awakened in us last Thursday while we visited at his home, became more and more enthusiastic in his desire to have our cause set right before the public, after he had seen the views of Utah and had had explained to him some of the wonders of our city.

One of the first questions asked was whether we intended to announce our belief in polygamy and practice it in Japan. We told them that we would always believe in the doctrine but until the Lord told us to renew its practice we would not do so in any land or clime no matter whether the laws were in favor or against such a system. Too our surprise Mr. Ichiki and his friends suggested that as Japan was given over to the horrible custom of conqubinage that we should establish the practice of plural marriage in this land as it was the place of all others to do so. I might here record in my journal that nearly all, if not all, of the Japanese with whom we have had the privilege of talking have conceded that our position on this law is reasonable and have rather favored all that we claim for the principle. Mr. Ichiki and his friends tonight were not the first to suggest that we renew the practice of this rite in Japan for nearly everyone has conceded that many wives are better than conqubines and whores.

When Apostle Grant showed our friends the pictures of his wives and children they likewise made a profound impression for good. One of the photographs showing his little boy standing in a preachers atteitude, struck Mr. Ichiki very forcefully and he remarked that it looked just like an angel, and desired that he be given a copy of the picture. This fact illustrated that Mr. Ichiki must be a lover of children, which in this age of one–child–ism, speaks well of his ideals of what a home should be.

Mr. Ichiki on this occasion as well as at his home last Thursday was the star of all, and his odd manner together with the force he put to what he said, bore testimony to us that here was a man who realized that the "Mormons" were somebody and it was nothing but right that they be given a show with the rest of religions. He wanted us to get some of the things which he had heard from us before the public as quickly as possible for the reason that the people were now looking for our teachings, because we are late arrivals in the land and in a little while longer the interest will die away and our chance be lost entirely. We explained why we did not want to issue any of our doctrines for fear that the lack of a spirited translator would not do our beliefs justice and that in the long run would do us more harm than good and that therefore we would prefer to wait until one of the church members could at least have a slight idea of the translation as it was being made so as to make some few suggestions that would cause the original spirit of the writing to be maintained.

This did not satisf our friend, however, and he determined on another method which will undoubtly be a great thing for us. He suggested that we deliver a lecture before an assembly of newspaper editors that the aid of the press might be secured. He also stated that he would visit the editors himself and see that all those who were fighting against us should come and hear the truth by an authority on the teachings of "Mormonism." Bro. Grant told him that it would please him very much to be able to meet the editors or anyone else Mr. Ichiki said that it would be arranged immediately and I have little fears, but that it will come to pass altho when such a thing was mentioned last Thursday I doubted it very much. Mr. Ichiki grows on me and on all men with whom he comes in contact. Mr. Hiroi, our interpreter, who knows him well, says that in the circles where he mingles that he speaks and the rest obey, that he is a man that executes whatever he decides to do no matter how hard or what the odds. Words could not express our joy at finding such a friend as this for he is truly a strong man and a powor for or against any cause. Mr. Takahashi, whose opinion itself is not the opinion of a weak man by any means, said, as he watched the actionn of Mr. Ichiki and heard what he had to say, that Mr. Ichiki was a man such as is rarely found in Japan, and I would add or in any other country.

Our supper proved a very pleasant one, only to us, who could not talk sufficiently to entertain our guests with the usual table gab, the ocassion seemed very still. A number of songs were sung during the evening, and taking it all in all it was the most profitable few hours that we have spent in Japan. Our hearts burned in gratitude to our Heavenly Father for the way he had enable us to make sympathetic and earnest friends for the Truth.

Monday, 17 February 1902, Tokyo

Day rather windy. Mr. Hiroi came in the morning to give us our lesson in Japanese. Went in the afternoon down to the photographers to have a group picture made, which is to be painted on silk by Mr. Okomoto and taken home to Salt Lake by Bro. Grant as a sample of work done in Japan.

Tuesday, 18 February 1902, Tokyo

Went to the Metropole early in the morning to consult with Bro. Grant and Kelsch on some matters in connection with Apostle Grant's return to America. Had breakfast with the brethren. Held a meeting in which it was decided for Bro. Grant to cable the authorities that he would leave on Friday. Bro. Grant went to Yokohama to cable. Returned to the rooms at the Japanese hotel and spent the rest of the day in study.

Bro. Horace went to the Metropole in the evening to get some letters that had arrived for us. The one for me was from Florence Grant telling about different things which were happening in the ward.

Wednesday, 19 February 1902, Tokyo

Mr. Hiroi came to give us our lesson in Japanese during the morning Bro. Kelsch called a little before noon to say that Bro. Grant wanted us to go to Yokohama in the afternoon to have our pictures taken on the spot where the land was dedicated for the reception of the gospel on the 1st of last Sept. We left Shinbashi station at 1:40 and arrived in Yokohama about an hour later. Went to the photographer's who accompanind us to the spot in the wood where four different photographs were taken of the spot and surroundings. After the photographer had gone we remained and sang a hymn or two and offered up prayer. The songs were "Do What is Right," "Farewell all earthly honors," and "We thank thee oh God for a Prophet." I was mouth in prayer and enjoyed a freedom such as I seldom feel. On the way back to the depot we called on Mrs. Parker, our Yokohama landlady so that Bro. Grant could say good–bye in case he did not have to chance to see her again before leaving for home. Arrived in Tokyo about half past seven. We all went to the Metropole where we had supper together. I received a letter from my brother Samuel who had been sick for some time with the quinsy but had almost recovered at the time of writing his letter.

During the night I had been taken with some pains in the bowels and suffered more or less during the entire day. The diarrheal effect was somewhat alarming. This accompanied with the journey, came nearly exhausting me before night.

Thursday, 20 February 1902, Tokyo

The excessive discharge from the bowels continued all night and all day. I remained in the rooms entirely, feeling to weak to walk much. Prepared my lesson in Japanese for the following day's recitation. Wrote a letter to Aunt Hattie enclosing a copy of my journal for February 13th and 16th. Retired shortly after six o'clock.

Friday, 21 February 1902, Tokyo

Having spent quite a restless night and my grub box[15] still feeling bad, I concluded that the best thing I could do was to lay in bed and eat but a very little food to see if I could not starve my trouble out. With the exception of two cups of brandy[16] I took nothing . This seemed to do me a great deal of good, for by night I was feeling quite well save a little weak. I did nothing during the whole day but lie around taking it easy. Mr. Hiroi came to give us our lesson but I let this pass also as Bro. Ensign had enough questions to keep him busy all the time he was here. The landlady of the hotel is extremely kind and has wanted to do anything and everything she could for me. My sickness has taught me the lesson that I must watch what I eat more in the future than I have in the past.

Saturday, 22 February 1902, Tokyo

A beautiful day in every respect. In the morning I took a walk for the sake of getting an appetite after my sickness. Spent the rest of the day at the rooms preparing my Japanese lesson and in writing up my journal. With the exception of an occasional call from Mr. Bowman, we had no visitors. Being in Japan and out in the midst of the Japanese people we saw no signs of celebrating the birthday of Washington which is a National Holliday in America.

Sunday, 23 February 1902, Tokyo

The day one of the most charming of the year. A typical spring warmth and as clear as the water from a crystal spring. Spent the afternoon and evening at the Metropole Hotel. We had our regular Sabboth Day Sacramental Meeting after which we were busy entertaining friends. Mr. Takahashi came in the evening and also Mr. Nakazawa, the Shinto priest who haD called on us several times before. Mr. Nakazawa was not invited but he had a matter to lay before us which he wanted us to settle immediately. Mr. Nakazawa held the office of middle priest in the sect to which he belonged, but he confesses to be unsatisfied with the teachings of the Shinto faith, and has made himself a small Luther in his church. His former visits to us had become known to his superiors and realizing that he was an agitator in their ranks they were afraid that he intended to become a "Mormon." He was severely rebuked for his conduct but he defended himself by saying that he was seeking the truth, consequently had visited the "Mormons" to see what their teachings were. But when it became known to his superiors a little later that he had actually eaten dinner with us, he was expelled from his position and made an outcast from the folds of the church. The first Japanese to be put to death in effigy for the cause of truth in this land! The first one to be austercised from the company of his fellows for having anything to do with "the damned 'Mormons!'"

We were indeed sorry for this man's fate but we could not help but rejoice that he had manhood enough to stand out against such narrow-mindedness as that which faught against him. He now intends either to re– to his native province and become a farmer or to stay in Tokyo and study our doctrines in the hope of becoming thoroughly convinced that they are true. He wanted to know if we would help him to learn of our teachings if he remained in the capitol, where in the future he could become, perhaps, an ardent defender of the revealed truth as we accept it. He was told that our interpreter was with the brethren at the hotel every afternoon and that he could come as often as he liked to learn about our doctrines.

Mr. Ichiki, his little daughter and another friend whose name I do not recall, came about seven o'clock and had supper with us after which we spent a very interesting and pleasant evening with him. Mr. Takahashi acted as interpreter and the way they became interested in talking to eachother of our beliefs was gratifying. At the table Mr. Ichiki requested Mr. Takahashi to tell us that we need have no fears of any government intervention as the government would not interfere with us, hence the only thing that could be wielded against us was the pen. I suggested that the pen was mightier than the sword, at which Mr. Takahasdi[17] said, "I have a pen which I can wield in your behalf." This remark revealed a feeling which we had been trying to discover in Mr. Takahashi and our hearts rejoiced at such a friendship as he was manifesting towards us, for he is conceded to be one of the greatest and strongest men in the use of the pen that Japan can produce.

Monday, 24 February 1902, Tokyo

Beautiful day. So warm that it was not necessary to wear an overcoat when I went out for a little walk in the afternoon. The change almost gave me the spring fever. In the morning we had Mr. Hiroi with us, but the afternoon was quiet. Mr. Oi called for a few moments to have a talk on some religious topics, but we had only become interested when Mr. Bowman came in and spoiled the whole business.

Mr. Bowman is absolutely without the common amount of sense necessary to get through life in any respectable way. I feel sorry for his mental depravity, not only for himself, but for those around him as he is oft times an unpleasant annoyance. It is rather a misfortune that he has come to this hotel for we will undoubtedly suffer with his innocent mischief as much as we did when we were at the Metropole Hotel. It is indeed a sad thing to be robbed of the proper brain power, and every time I see a person who is thus deprived I cannot help but silently thank the Lord for his blessings to me and seek for power to live worthy of such choice gifts as Heaven has bestowed upon me.

Tuesday, 25 February 1902, Tokyo

With the exception of taking a little walk in the afternoon I stayed in the rooms all day, studying and reading. In the evening I went up into Mr. Bowman's room and had a discussion on the Existance of a God with a Japanese gentleman who lives in the hotel and who speaks English excellently. It was a sort of one sided affair as the fellow did so much talking that I could not get a word in edgewise. Every time I would open my mouth to say anything he would take me up on the first words and jabber away for a number of minutes, so rather than having a discussion, I consider it more proper to say that I listened to a fellow try to disprove the Existence of a Creator to which attempt there was no reply.

Wednesday, 26 February 1902, Tokyo

Rather windy today and yesterday. Mr. Hiroi came in the morning and gave us our lesson in Japanese. I took a walk with him when he returned. The afternoon I spent in reading from DR. Talmage's "Articles of Faith."[18] Bro. Ensign went over to the Metropole Hotel in the afternoon and as soon as he got there the brethren said they wanted him to eat supper with them and telephoned me to come and eat with them also. I did. We had a very fine meal and enjoyed a very pleasant quiet evening singing softly all the choice hymns that we knew.

Mr. Nakazawa, the Shinto priest who was cast out of his order a day or to ago because he called and ate dinner with the "Mormons," has called twice on the brethren and after considerable thaught on the subject says that he desires to be baptized. He said the very moment he read our articles of faith and saw that we did not believe men would be punished for the sin of our forefather Adam,[19] and read the other beliefs advanced by us, that he was struck very forcefully with the desire to investigate thoroughly for he felt in his heart that we had the truth in part if not entirely. He intends to call twice a week on the brethren and study the points with which he is not yet familiar, and as soon as he becomes a little clearer on some points he wants to join the church, and then return to his native province and work his little farm or labor for us if we want him to do so.

Thursday, 27 February 1902, Tokyo

Day rather windy and much dust. Spent most of the time in the rooms studying. In the afternoon I took a little walk around through the adjacent neighborhood. Wrote a letter to my brother Samuel in answer to the one received from him some time ago. Enclosed in the letter a clipping from one of the foreign newspapers in regard to how the foreigners look upon life in Japan.

Friday, 28 February 1902, Tokyo

Mr. Hiroi spent the morning with us. Quite a pleasant day but almost too warm. Went down town in the afternoon to post my letter and to order some pictures from the plates made in the woods at Yokohama a week ago last Wednesday. In the evening I prepared my lesson for the following Monday. Received a letter from the Bishop. He seemed quite worked up over Bro. Johnson's not geeting married and said there would have to be a change soon. All was well in the ward.

Saturday, 1 March 1902—Monday, 3 March 1902, Tokyo

Most of this time has been spent in study. The weather on Saturday was very rough. It rained most of the day and was almost as dark as night. Sunday and Monday however were real pleasant days.

On Saturday evening I received two letters from home. One from mother and one from Miss. Baggerly to whom I sent a Japanese picture some time ago. All was well at home. My brother Samuel had entirely recovered from his slight disaffection.

Sunday was spent with the brethren at the Metropole where I enjoyed an excellent supper. Mr. Takahashi was with us and we had with him the usual good time. He announced that his book was completed and in the hands of the printer, and would therefore be ready for the public in a week or two. We discussed a little regarding Bro. Grant's return home via the steamer which leaves on the 11th, inst., but this matter was not decided as we hope to get a telegram from the Authorities which will bring the matter to a final end one way or the other. I had the privilege of listening to a number of letters received by Bro. Grant from the Presidency and other officers in the church and also some from members of his own family.

Monday Mr. Hiroi came out to the rooms to give Bro. Ensign and I our lesson in Japanese. Bro. Kelsch came about noon and he and Bro. Ensign went for a walk. I also took a stroll in the evening before supper.

Tuesday, 4 March 1902—Friday, 7 March 1902, Tokyo

The time during these four days has been devoted mostly to study. The weather has been ideal all the time. A few friends have called which relieved the monotony of having our heads in books all the time.

On Tuesday evening at nine o'clock Mr. Tilson, our friend from America, came to stay all night with us. He spent all day Wenesday at our rooms and concluded on our invitation to stay over another night. He brought his camera with him and took some pictures which ought to be real fine when printed.

Thursday afternoon a telephone message came from Bro. Kelsch stating that Bro. Grant had gone to Yokohama to get a telegram from home. When Bro. Grant returned, he telephoned us that the message was in regard to the sale of Utah Sugar stock,[20] by which he made $12,000. (These figures were corrected later, however)

Friday about noon another cable was received from the Authorities saying for Apostle Grant to come home to Conference. Bro. Ensign and I went over to the Metropole to celebrate the arrival of the good news, and were additionally surprised to learn that on the following day Apostle Grant was going to baptize Mr. Nakazawa, who had become convinced that Mormonism was the truth. I received this day a letter from Bro. Geo. E. Woolley and a valentine from Miss. Baggerly.

Saturday, 8 March 1902, Tokyo

There are always some days in a person's life that are most important than others. not only are eventful days valuable for personal history or biography, but they claim their place in the record of families, societies, cities, states, nations, as well as in the history of the world. This day records events that brings such joy to my heart that can not be uttered in words, and I fear that I cannot realize the full meaning of what has transpired.

Not long ago I recorded in this Journal that a Shinto priest had called on Apostle Grant and Bro. Kelsch while they were living at the Central Hotel, and I later referred to the visits paid by this same man after the brethren had removed to the Metropole Hotel, and only one week ago last Sunday (February 23rd, 1902.) I spoke of the consequences of these visits to the priest himself. He was expelled from his former position and denounced as a deserter of his faith because he deigned to call on the "Mormons" for the purpose of learning what they taught. I felt then that as he had been made the first outcast for investigating after the truth, that in the providences of the Lord he would have the honor of being the first soul baptized in this great nation of Japan and become the first fruit to be gathered in, after the seed had been sowed by the servants of the Lord.

This thought of mine has been realized this day in the baptism of Mr. Hajime Nakazawa, the first native member of the Church of Jesus Christ of Latter–day Saints to receive the ordinance of baptism at the hands of a servant of the Lord in the populous nation of Japan. Who can tell what may be the results of this one conversion? How many hearts will this man be able to turn toward the gospel of the Lord Jesus? To how many heart will the action of this man give courage to wall the path which he has tread as an example for the fellows of his race? Will not his family soon join him in the fold to which he has entered? and will not his children follow the example of their parents? Will not some soul who has confidence in them be led to investigate for the truth and be caught up also in the gospel net? Where will the seed cease to spread if he lives worthy of the blessings which are his? May the Lord hear our prayers in behalf of this our brother that he may feel with all his heart that it is a far greater honor to be found fighting in the ranks of the Eternal God than to receive all the honor that the world can bestow. To me it seems something to be the first to receive the truth in a land which has never before heard the voice of the true shepherd—an honor among the saints and the priesthood and in the eyes of the hosts of eternity that have past the mortal stage centuries ago.

Bro. Ensign and I left our Japanese hotel in the morning before eight o'clock so as to get to the brethren's rooms before anyone came. We intended to have a short meeting. We had agreed to fast so had therefore eaten no breakfast. We were unable to have the meeting as Mr. Nakazawa (but whom I shall hereafter call Brother Nakazawa) came earlier than we expected. We had prayer together and then took the train from Tokyo to Omori a littl village just a few miles from Tokyo on the way toward Yokohama. It takes only twenty minutes by train. We decided to go to this place to perform the ordinance as the beach of the Tokyo bay was considered to be best in this district.

When we arrived we found the tide out and saw that it would be necessary to walk a considerable distance from shore before we could find water deep enough to perform the ceremony. While we were wondering what would be the best plan for us to follow in the matter, an old fisherman came up to us and asked if we did not want to take a ride on the bay. This struck us all in a heap and we saw immediately that it would be nice to engage a small boat and row out a little from the shore to a place where the water would not only be deep but where we could be all to ourselves. The party consisted of Bro. Nakazawa, we four missionaries, and our interpreter, Mr. Hiroi. We engaged an old sunburned fisherman to row us out in his little boat which has perhaps been used for some time as a fishing craft in which this man has spent many hours working with his net seeking to draw from the abundance of the sea sufficient to sustain himself, wife, and family. The name of our boatman we learned to be [blank]. He was not a small Japanese and his coal black hair which was nerly two inches long stood straight up from his forehead that crowned one of the most perfect indian countenances that we have been privileged to behold in this land, and I felt that we were really in the presence of one in whose veins flowed the blood of the great Lamanitish nation or the blood of that stalwart seed, the Jaredites.[21]

We rowed out about a block from the shore, singing as we went and our hearts full to overflowing with gratitude that we were this day privileged to witness the baptism of the first honest soul in this distant clime. After circling around for some time we found a suitabe place and by sticking the oar or paddle into the bottom and fastening the boat to it by a small rope the vessel was soon brought to a standstill.

Bro. Grant told Bro. Nakazawa how we generally proceeded on such occasions, and had Mr. Hiroi translate the prayer used in performing the ordinance of baptism. We then sang the hymn, "Farewell all earthly Honors." Bro. Kelsch prayed and then the ordinance was performed.[22] It was necessary to climb over the edge of the boat right into the water which came up around Bro. Grant's hips. Bro. Grant officiated. This was the first baptism Apostle Grant had ever performed in the mission field, consequently his joy was all the greater to think that the first person he ever baptized out in the world was the first convert in the wonderful Island of Japan.

There were no wonderful manifestations given. All was peace, and Br Apostle Grant's words were spoken slowly and with marked distinctness. Our bosoms swelled with emotion as the words of the prayer fell upon our ears and we could have shouted with thanksgiving when the waters parted and enveloped within their rippeling folds one of God's children who soon came forth from that "burial with Christ" unto a new life having taken upon himself the covenant of the everlasting gospel. As soon as the brethren had changed their wet clothes for dry ones we all laid our hands upon the head of our brother and Apostle Grant was also mouth in confirming our brother a member of the church and giving unto him the Aaronic Priesthood[23] after which in the same prayer he ordained his an Elder in the church to officiate in the duties of this calling according to council and the inspiration of the spirit. It can only be left to the imagination of others the feelings which passed through my mind and heart for this was the first time for me to witness the initation of a convert into the fold in the mission field and it was with the deepest sentiments of brotherhood that I welcomed this soul into the chosen fold of the Father.. We were rowed back to the shore after having spent nearly an hour in the boat. We were charge fifty sen (25¢) boat hire.

This experience of going out in a boat for the purpose of baptizing any one seemed rather odd and we were led to smile at the various ways the Elders were called upon to manage when receiving new members into the church and we though our experience one of the most novel recorded in Missionary Life. When we went out the tide was down and the boat rested upon the ground, still the little water lying between us and the boat made it unable to walk from the bottom of the steps which led down from the small pier to the vessel without getting our feet wet. And as the boat was then resting on the sand it was necessary to push it further out into water sufficiently deep to float it. It took two men to do this and we were wondering how we were going to cover the distance between, when our interpreter informed us that the men would pack us out. This was the most peculiar sight we have seen since leaving home and we regretted very much that we had not brought our kodak along to get some pictures of the difficulties connected with the first baptism in Japan. We rode on the men's backs like so many sacks of flour or sugar and a snap shot of us in this position with the men who carried us with their kimonos rolled up around their waist showing their bare legs to the hips would have indeed been an interesting relic of this day's experience.

Our regret that we could not get this picture made us decide to go back to Tokyo, eat our dinners, get a camra, and return in the afternoon and go through the same performances so as to get the pictures we so much longed for. To our great dissatisfaction, we found, on our return from Tokyo, that the tide had come in and the water was three or four feet deep where during the morning we were walking upon the pebbled beach. Not wanting the trip to be entirely in vain we got into the boat and had our photographs taken but the boats moved so much that we fear the pictures will be very poor. We got back to Tokyo about half past five, where we said good afternoon to our Bro. who ment to his home to tell the glad news to his wife while we returned to our several homes to reflect upon the happenings of this historic day in the history of the Japan Mission. We begun the day with four members in the ranks—ourselves—and ended with five all of whom hold the Melchisedek Priesthood.[24]

Sunday, 9 March 1902, Tokyo

The day has been quite stormy. The cablegram received by Prest. Grant last Friday had enabled us to definately decided the date of his return to Zion. As the steamer was scheduled to leave Yokohama at noon on the 11th, inst. we assembled at the Metropole to enjoy one more pleasant Sunday afternoon before saying good–bye to our chieftian. We sang, prayed, spoke, and partook of the sacrament. The spirit of love was made manifest and the expressions of all were an illustration of the brotherly feelings that warmed our breasts. The events of the past few days were fresh on our minds and the future unfoulding as it is in brightness and glory, caused us to be filled to the brim with praise and thanksgiving to the Lord for his blessings. It is indeed a comforting thought to know that as the seventh month since our arrival in Japan draws to a close we are privileged to witness the beginning of the hearvest in this mission.

Apostle Grant in warm terms left his blessing upon us and we in turn sought the protection of Heaven to shield him upon his journey that he if it be the will of our Father return unto us shortly having accomplished all that was in his heart to do while at home.

We had hardly finished our meeting, before some of our friends whom Bro. Grant had invited to come and eat a farewell dinner with us, began to arrive. By a few minutes before seven all the company had assembled in the hotel parlor. Besides we four missionaries, there were ten Japanese and one foreigner. They were, Mr. Hiroi, Mr. Takahashi, and Mr. Ichiki to whom I have so often referred in my journal and who are our principal friends, Mr. Koshiishi an editor of the "Tokyo Shimbun," a paper recently started in this city, Mr. S. Kikuchi, a Christian gentleman who holds open air meetings in Uyeno Park, but who supports no particular Christian creed for he had not been able to find any that seemed to him consistent with the Bible till he began to investigate "Mormonism," Mr. Shinsaburo Iwato, a doctor from Yokohama, whom we had never met before, Mr. Ito a distant relation of Marquis Ito, Mr. Humes, an english gentleman who is teaching school in Tokyo, Bro. Nakazawa and his wife, and the wife of Mr. Kikuchi.

Mr. Takahashi who has just finished writing a book about the Mormons and their doctrines, had sent Bro. Grant copies of the illustrations that the book would contain, and brought with him a copy of the content page. The illustrations were with but one or two exceptions excellent, and will surely do as Mr. Takahashi remarked when he first asked permission to reproduce them, dispel at a glance the charges that the "Mormon" people are ignorant, unprogressive, slovenly, and in most ways depraved. . . .

Considering the features of religion that appeal most strongly to the Japanese, this book will appeal to them with so much more force than an expianation on doctrine would do that the difference in its favor cannot be estimated. And also considering that this work is written by one whose name is so prominent and whose pen is so powerful and who has obtained all his information from reliable sources, there is no telling the immense amount of good it will do us.

The evening was one of the most lively and interesting ones we have had. More of the guests seemed to take part in the conversation, Mr. Takahashi let himself out in a gratifying way, and Mr. Kikuchi as well as Mr. Ichiki seemed particularly to get the spirit of the occasion. For variety we had some little singing and our pictures interested the new members of the company. the subjects discussed seemed interesting At the supper table, for most everyone as they laughed and chatted earnestly. The company did not all return till early ten o'clock. Bro. Grant and we brethren felt well satisfied with the evening for we knew that all had enjoyed themselves.

Monday, 10 March 1902, Tokyo

Very pleasant after the storm of yesterday. Bro. Ensign and I left our rooms early so as to get down to the Metropole and assist in packing Bro. Grant's trunks with the material he desired to take home. Surprises of late seem never to end, When we arrived at the hotel we found Mr. Kikuchi there also. He had come to be baptized before Bro. Grant went home. In replying to the questions asked by the brethren this man answered satisfactorily in every instance. Mr. Hiroi said that Mr. Kikuchi was remarkably well versed in the scripture, and knowing ourselves that he preached in public often on the teachings of the Bible we concluded that he was wise enough to know what he was doing when being baptized, therefore Bro. Grant decided to administer the ordinance as requested.

Just to the east of the Metropole the Samida River empties into the Bay. On the opposite side of the river a narrow strip of land covered with houses reached out for a short distance into the bay. We crossed the river in a "sanpan"[25] being charge for the passage the immense amount of one fourth of an American cent each. There were six of us. Mr. Hiroi, our interpreter, making the sixth. We preceded across this narrow promintory to the coast on the east side. The tide was out and it looked from the bank as though there were no suitable place within a mile or so from shore. Some small crafts however were floating around and many people were engaged gathering sea–weed. We haled one of the boats and rowed out for a short distance where fortunately we found water deep enough for the purpose. Bro. Grant and Mr. Kikuchi prepared their clothing on the shore before going into the boat. We also sang "God Moves in a mysterious Way." Elder Ensign offered prayer. A number of people who lived in the neighboring houses were attracted to the water's edge by our singing as well as our presence at so unusual place on the sea side.

The brethren redressed in the boat. The confirmation was not made till we got back to the rooms at the Metropole. Here Bro. Kelsch was mouth in the confirmation ordinance[26] and Bro. Ensign was mouth in ordaining our brother an Elder in the church. The same feelings of joy that characterize the baptism of Bro. Nakazawa last Saturday were experience on this occasion. We were additionally glad that there were two members instead of one for they can now be companions to eachother strengthening themselves against the temptations that will come to lead them away from the light they have now received. Before performing these two last ceremonies we sang "Truth Reflects upon our Senses."

After we had eaten dinner Bro. Grant was occupied in talking with Mr. Koshiishi the editor who was with us last night. Mr. Koshiishi had come also to receive baptism, but it was found on questioning him that he knew practically nothing of the gospel, and would be stepping blindly into the church. Bro. Kikuchi as well as Mr. Hiroi were glad that we did not allow this man to be baptized for they recognized that he was not sincere and they felt his motives were not the best. Bro. Kikuchi rebuked him for haughtiness and told him to be more humble before applying for so important a blessing as baptism.

While this conversion was being carried on by Bro. Grant, Horace was engaged writing letters and Bro. Kelsch and myself were working with the trunks wishing that Bro. Grant could be with us to say what he wanted done with this or that. Bro. Grant had only just finished with this man and a friend who came with him, when the office boy brough up the card of someone else who wanted an interview. We continued with our work as best we could. Bro. Grant had a long talk with his guests and came up to ask us to come down and met them. He was very much delighted with them and said he had never had such a satisfactory talk with any one except only Mr. Takahishi.[27] These gentleman were Mr. H. Wada and Mr. K. Fujiu, both Christian ministers who had graduated from a mission school here and who had been engaged in preaching Christianity fo some time, but who felt way down in their hearts that there was something wrong with the religions in this land. They were not satisfied with what they had and were hunting something more stable to fasten to. The peculiar point in their experience with other Christian Churches is, that they passed a successful examination in the ministery except on the subject of the Original Sin. This they refused to accept as it was taught to them, but still they were sent out to preach everything else which they had been taught but were forbided to discuss this subject.

We are surely getting little by little a knowledge of the shallow way the missionaries in Japan are carrying on their work. No wonder the Japanese are satisfied with a heathen religion when the Christianity that it offered to them is far worse than the wares they already have. The people of this nation are famishing for a religion. They are dissatisfied with the old form and their hunger is not quenched by accepting what assumes the role of Divine truth. In fact there are thousands in this land who are just like thousands in the days of the Prophet Joseph Smith, unsatisfied with all man-made systems because the spirit was not present in them to warm the heart and answer the stiritual longings. I feel that "Mormonism's" future in Japan will be WONDERFUL. As these gentlemen spoke excellent English, we presented them with some tracts pertaining to the Gospel which we all felt would be read and considered deeply.

Soon the callers ceased coming and the trunks were all packed and things all ready to the start next morning. We had supper and enjoyed a few moments peacefully together, after which Bro. Ensign and I returned to our "cottage on the hill."

Tuesday, 11 March 1902, Tokyo

Another beautiful day. At the request of Prest Grant, Horace and I went to the Metropole early enough to take breakfast with him and Bro. Kelsch which would be the last meal together for some time.

Bros. Nakazawa and Kikuchi came early to say good-bye, also. Mr. Koshiishi. All five of the "Mormons" went to Yokohama to see Prest. Grant leave. We left Tokyo on the 8:45 a.m. train. We were joined by Mr. Hiroi at the first station out of Tokyo. His wife was with him, having come to see Apostle Grant and to go to Omori to see the plum blossoms. Mr. Okomoto also went along to see that the pictures he had prepared for Bro. Grant were taken care of and secerely placed on the steamer. We called at a few places before going to the ship. Mr. Okomoto went and got a photographer to come with his machine and take some pictures of the departing scenes. Perhaps an hour or so before noon we took the tug boat and went out to the steamer which was anchored about a half mile from shore. We visited the cabin to be occupied by our friend and brother while recrossing the great Pacific. The sight of the appartments on the boat brought vividly before my mind the voyage from America to Japan yet I had no desire to return home, not even the slightest sensation.

The gong was soon sounded for the visitors to leave the ship. We said farewell with those same strong emotions that commonly fill the hearts of friends at parting. I had learned to love Bro. Grant very much and my association with him having been so close since leaving home, I felt those same happy but regretful feelings experience when I bid farewell to my loved ones at home. I paused to be the last to say good–bye and received a farewell kiss. The kiss of an Apostle of the Lord Jesus Christ! A kiss between a man and a boy whose affections have been linked together by the spirit of the Everlasting Gospel! A kiss of which I am not worthy, but one which I hope my increased faithfulness will merit. We walked along the bund watching to see the first movements of the ship, which is carrying the first of the original four back to Zion. Who will be the next?

Bro. Kelsch and I took the next train back to Tokyo. I went with him to the hotel to see, if any mail had some on the steamer which had arrived during the morning from America. Bro. Ensign came along later and as no mail arrived, we wended our way back to "Bachelor quarters." For the present at least Bro. Kelsch will continue to live at the Metropole and Horace and I will still be Japanese.

Wednesday, 12 March 1902—Saturday, 22 March 1902, Tokyo

These twelve days have been spent without anything particularly out of the ordinary happening. Most of the hours in each day have been devoted to the same old earnest research after a knowledge of Japanese. Our newly converted brethren have been with us a great deal. They are both anxious to become throughly versed in a knowledge of the religion which they have accepted. Bro. Kikuchi, having a little greater knowledge of English and a more perfect understanding of the Bible, has shown the most remarkable capacity for grasping the truths of the gospel. They both have expressed the desire that we Elders come and live with them so that they can be with us always and not only learn of the Gospel but learn a little english, at the same time causing a great reduction to be made in our expences, which, while we are living in hotels, are rather high. This desire of our brethren has received consideration from us but at present we are not yet decided as to what action we had better take in the matter. There are so many advantages and disadvantages connected with such a change that it seems rather difficult to know just what is the will of the Lord on the matter. This however will find a solution that will be proper and for the good of the mission.

The afternoon and evening of Sunday 16th, we met together us usual in the Metropole and held our sacrament and testimony meeting. In spite of the fact that Apostle Grant was absent, we were greatly blessed and enjoyed the same warm spirit that has characterized all of these meetings in the past. Mr. Takahashi, Mr. Miyasaki, Mr. Humes and three of his friends took super with us, as did also Bro. Kikuchi.

On March 13th, I received a letter from mother containing a draft for 198.02 yen. On the 16th, following I received another letter from mother containing the glad news that father was going with the Tabernacle Choir excursion to California and would take with him Aunt Clara and the two oldest girls. Changes of this kind have been so few and far between in father's life that it will surely be a pleasure trip in the fullest sense of the word. His life has been one of perfect devotion to the interests of home, but it is gratifying to see the burdens of business life lifted from his shoulders and carried by one of his sons whose heart is set upon doing the will of God. Rest from temporal labor is a boon for the aged, and my heart rejoices when I see the silver haired veterans relieved by the brawn and determination of that youth ful strength which at the same time fears the Lord and keeps His commandments. I also received, by the same mail, a message from Lutie which breathed a lovely spirit and showed plainly that her heart was in the missionary labor resting upon her. Undoubtly she will return from Denver to Salt Lake City for April Conference to meet her father who will be home at that time. Another note came from Bro. Edward H. Anderson saying the article I sent to the Era would be published in the April number.[28]

In the last letter from mother there was also a copy of a patriarchal blessing[29] given to me June 14th, 1894 by Patriarch John Smith many of the promises in which are being fulfilled in this mission.

During the last week many of the pictures we had taken shortly before Prest. Grant left have been developed and they are an interesting collection. Copies of most of them I sent home by the steamer which left for America yesterday. By this same mail I sent letters to my brother Samuel, Sister Ellen Capener, Sister Isabelle Erekson, Bishop Empey, Bro. Geo. E. Woolley, and The Thirteenth Ward Mutual. Also by a steamer leaving fro Australia I sent a letter to Elder William B. Erekson son of Sister Isabelle Erekson, both dear friends.

Of late Bro. Kelsch has made warm friends with most of the guests at the Metropole and last evening, on his invitation, we spent the evening with him and a nice party of these guests who assembled in the parlor to hear our brother Horace sing. The singing was beautiful and everyone was more than delighted. Much of the success of the evening was due to the good accompaniment played on the piano by Mrs. Cable, who, with her husband, is a regular boarder at the hotel. This nice warm feeling is quite a change from the cold atmosphere which had surrounded both Bro. Grant and Kelsch for some weeks before Bro. Grant left, and it gives a better chance to kindly drop a gospel seed occasionally. After the barrier of prejudice is removed a wonderful interest in "Mormonism" can oft times be aroused, and while we do not expect to convince any of the hotel guests, yet the good a single friend can do the cause cannot be estimated.

On the evening of 22nd, Bro. Ensign and I, accompanied by our two Japanese brethren, Elders Kikuchi and Nakazawa, went to the home of Mr. Humes to talk to a gathering of students he has there every other Saturday evening. As the students are not well versed in English and Bro. Ensign and myself not able to say mush in Japanese we allowed our native companions to occupy the evening in talking in the native tongue about the principles of "Mormonism." The students were particularly anxious to see the Shinto Priest whom we had converted and to their great surprise they were privileged to hear from his own lips his confession as to his belief in the work established by Joseph Smith. Elder Kikuchi demonstrated the fact that he was more or less used to speaking for he went at his job like an old hand at such work. We were very much pleased to hear them defend the Church into which they had so recently been initiated, and their defense was evidently a worthy one as the students seemed to be perfectly satisfied with what they heard. This was the first time we had been privileged to listen to our native brethren speak and it did our hearts good to listen to, (altho we understood but very little that was said) an address on the subjects pertaining to Everlasting Life by men who have been called to the Priesthood by the proper authority.

Sunday, 23 March 1902, Tokyo

Cold and stormy. Went to the Metropole to spend the afternoon with Bro. Kelsch. Bro. Kikuchi was with us to pertake of the Sacrament and participate in the exercises of our regular Sabboth Day Services. Bro. Nakazawa was to have been with us also, but the long trip through the rain of last night had undoubtly given him a cold as he was not feeling very well at that time. This was the first meeting we had ever held in Japan attended by any of the natives. It was indeed pleasing to have in our midst one whose heart beat in harmony with ours and who could thoroughly enjoy the spirit that we feel on such occasions. Elder Kikuchi spoke a few words in Japanese and also offered the closing prayer.

The evening was spent in a pleasant way among the guests of the hotel who assembled in the parlor to enjoy the singing furnished principally by Elder Ensign. Bro. Kelsch has truly found some among those who are boarding at the hotel, whose good sense has removed all the natural prejudice they may have previously entertained against the "Mormons."

Monday, 24 March 1902—Sunday, 30 March 1902, Tokyo

Rained nearly all the week. Tuesday 25th, I received a letter from my friend Will Erekson now laboring in the New Zeland mission. It was a very odd missive in appearance. He had gone to some newspaper–office and secured a strip about an inch wide and I should judge nearly 200 feet long (although I did not measure it) off of one of the big rolls of paper used in such places. He wrote quite a long letter on this one strip and rolled it on a little stick and sent it as an offset to one I had written him on a single sheet taken from a Japanese roll of letter paper. I also received a fine photo of himself which I will use for a weapon in defense of our belief in celestial marriage, and the manifestations of intelligence and morality and physical strength among the Latter–day Saints.

On the morning of the 29th we went out to Mr. Hiroi's home in Shinagawa and spent half a day visiting him and his wife. We were royally entertained and were glad to see the evidences of happiness and comfort that were portrayed in the home of our interpreter. His wife is a gem of rare type in Japan; accomplished, free from many of the many nasty habits existing so extensively among the women, humble, kind, and beautiful.

Some days ago one of the gentlemen at the Metropole with whom Bro. Kelsch had become particularly intimate, was taken with severe hemorrhage of the lungs and after two days of repeated flows of blood, the doctor came nearly giving him up. Bro. Kelsch had a dream on the second night in which he saw this man get better much quicker than his friends thought possible, and on the following morning he related his dream to the man's wife who seemed thankful for encouragement form some source. Yesterday we learned that he was progressing remarkably well and the doctor could not understand how such a great change could come in so short a time. The indications at present are that Bro. Kelsch's dream will be verified to the wonderment of all.

The 30th was spent pleasantly at the hotel where we had Mr. Takahashi as a guest for supper. It the afternoon we took a walk into Shiba district of Tokyo to look at a house some of our Japanese friends had recommended that we remove to. It was a long walk to see a dirty inconvenient place and more of a strain than a pleasure considering we had been fasting since the previous night.

Last night I posted a letter to my brother Mahonri and remailed Will's roll to the folks. The mail from America arrived about noon bring a letter from mother. It contained the sad news of my cousin–in–law's death (Heber Bevan). He leaves a wife and six children ranging from two or three months to perhaps thirteen years. The letter spoke as tho Miss Baggerly, a dear friend to one of our neighbors, would soon be baptized into the church, which fact makes me feel to rejoice, for, as this journal will show, I have written a letter or two to her in which I have referred to the advantages of becoming a Latter–day Saint. The following was written by mother in regard to my labor in trying to learn this difficult language: "I still think you are doing well in the language. I cannot get rid of the thought that if you would go to preaching you would receive the gift that has been promised you (the Gift of Tongues).[30] With a prayer in your heart get up and preach and if they understand you, thank God; if they don't, keep on preaching and the Lord will according to promise, come to your relief."

Monday, 31 March, 1902, Tokyo

Beautiful day. The cherry trees all over the land are putting forth their flowers and as I look out from my window, I see scattered irregularly over the city, clusters of the most delicate pink and white colors that nature in her spring time bestows upon this Oriental soil.

I spent an hour or two visiting Mr. Oi and his wife in company with Bro. Kikuchi. Elder Ensign went over to the Metropole to tend to some business with Bro. Kelsch. When he returned late in the evening, he brot with him a card from Apostle Lyman to me, written from Port Said, Egypt dated Feb. 19th, 1902. This, according to my recollection, is the first note or letter I have ever received from an Apostle. The reason he addressed one to me is undoubtly because he is personally interested in the welfare of his fellow Apostle, Bro. Grant, and the success of the mission to which he has been called; and I being accociated in the labor of the Lord in Japan with Apostle Grant, was undoubtly thought of when Apostle Lyman addressed a card to my President and fellow missionaries. The contents of the card as are follows: "A souvenir from Cairo, in Egypt, and from your friend and brother. God bless you forever. Kind greeting for your father and family. I am, Yours affectionately, Francis M. Lyman. Bro. Ensign also brought me a letter from Lizzie Thomas, written in answer to one I addressed to her nearly two months ago.

Tuesday, 1 April 1902, Tokyo

Mr. Hiroi spent the morning with us. I had the lesson all to myself as Elder Ensign was occupied in packing his trunk preparatory to changing his place of abode. Last Sunday evening Bro. Nakazawa came to the hotel and according to a desire which he had expressed some time before we decided that one of us would go and live with him from the 1st, of April. I proposed that Bro. Ensign go because to expense would be less and it would be better for him to be where he would have to practice what little he knew of the language and be with one whose heart was in harmony with us and who would naturally have more interest in our welfare than strangers. I would have liked very much to have gone myself, but I being younger than Elder Ensign, can get along a little better with my studies and I wanted him therefore to have all the advantages possible, for I do not want anything that my brethren do not share in.

Went down town in the afternoon after my companion had left to buy some books such as he had taken with him and which before we separated were used by us both. On the way home I met one of my Japanese student friends who returned with me to the room and spent the evening. Shortly after ten I blew out the lights and crawled into the futons to spend the first night alone since leaving Zion.

Wednesday, 2 April 1902—Tuesday, 8 April 1902, Tokyo

During this week I have had one or two opportunities to bear my testimony to the gospel of the Lord Jesus Christ and I have had other conversations in regard to religion with which I have been well pleased. Most of my time has been spent in the study of the language, and I have been able to get my lessons fairly well.

This being the famous cherry blossom season in Japan, I have been able to see considerable of the way in which the Japanese show their appreciation of flowers. Thursday the 3rd, in company with Elders Kelsch and Ensign and two Japanese friends I went to see the cherry trees in Uyeno Park The park was thronged with people, mostly out for recreation, and the men seemed to be generally too well filled with fire–water. The trees were pretty but no more beautiful than the spring flowers in a well kept orchard at home. I could see in them no special attraction. The crowded streets, the drunken men, the beautifully attired women, and the numerous people who bowed before the gods of wood and stone were the things that attracted my eye, and I learned a little of a side of human nature among the people of the East that I had never seen before.

In the evening of the same day I went to the Metropole to take dinner with Bro. Kelsch and Bro. Ensign who had come for a similar purpose, and for three or four hours after the meal we enjoyed a pleasant conversation, relieved occasionally by a song, in the private rooms of Mr. and Mrs. Godsey of the American Tobacco Trust Co. Besides us there was also Mr. Cable and his wife. These people during the last two weeks have manifested a wonderful liking for the "Mormons" and we have spent many pleasant hours with them. Mrs. Cable has become the regular accompanist to Horace in all his songs. Mr. Bowman who lives in the hotel here with me, has been sick for the last day or two and I have been quite busy taking care of him.

The separation from Elder Ensign has not left me in any state of melancholy, in fact I have hardly had time to think of the fact that I am living alone. The continual call of students and friends and the necessiary study of Japanese keeps me on the go.

Sunday the 6th, we held our usual meeting at the Metropole. We had Elder Nakazawa with us and he with us partook of the sacrament and in his own language bore his testimony to the truth of the Gospel. It is indeed a source of great joy to us to see our new converts take active part in the work. Bro. Ensign reported himself as being well pleased with his new home, and said Elder Nakazawa and his wife were doing everything they could for his comfort. It indeed looked cozy in his room the other day when I was out to visit him and the spirit of the people and the place is much more attractive than can be found in hotel life.

Wednesday, 9 April 1902—Wednesday, 16 April 1902, Tokyo

On the 9th, I wrote and posted letters to Emma, Lizie Thomas, Mabel Cunningham, Heber S. Goddard, and Apostle Frincis M. Lyman. I received on the same day letters from mother, father, Bessie Badger, and Bishop Empey. The news from Zion was all good and I was delighted to learn that father had gone with the choir to California. I had doubted when I heard that he intended to go whether he would not be hindered in some way or other as in the past he has had to cancel at the last moment many of his contemplated journeys. The Bishop's letter was full of good sentiments and love, and before closing he pronounced a strong blessing upon me if I would be faithful in the labor of this mission. The same mail brought a letter from Prest. Grant written on board the steamer and posted at Hawaii. Unfortunately he had according to his words, and from the style of his writing, been sick most of the way to the Islands. Long ere this however he has arrived in Zion and we are now awaiting anxiously a report on the effect of his presence in Salt Lake.

I have been spending most of my time as usual in the study of Japanese. Mr. Bowman the foreigner who lives in the hotel has been quite sick and I have spent some time in running around for him and in preparing his food, as the natives have but little idea about what is palatable to a sick man (and I know but very little more than they.) I succeeded in getting my patient out of bed and now he is perfectly well and has arranged to leave on Saturday morning (19th) for India, his former home.

Monday the 14th, I wrote a letter to father.

Sunday the 13th, I met with my brethren at the Metropole to partake of the Sacrament. All of the Mormons in Japan were present—the first time since we baptized our nitive brethren. A good spirit was present and we all in a brief way expressed the feelings of our hearts. In a feeble manner I bore my testimony in Japanese so that my native brethren could perfectly understand my feelings toward the gospel. They told me after the meeting that I made but few mistakes and they could understand all that I said. This was the second time I have ever attemped to say anything in Japanese in a formal meeting. In the evening we enjoyed ourselves for about to hours in the company of our friends at the Metropole.

On the fourteenth Bro. Ensign came and spent the afternoon with me. He also came the following day and together with him and Mr. Bowman I went over to Mr. Oi's, my next door neighbor, and spent a pleasant afternoon in what the Japanese call play.

On Tuesday I was to have moved to the home of Elder Kikuchi but for some, yet unexplained reason, he did not come to tell me whether the new house into which he intended to move was ready or not, which thing he promised Sunday evening to do. I had contemplated this change with considerable pleasure, but it seems that I am to remain where I am for some time yet.

Many students have called upon my during the past week, and with some of these I have had pretty good talks on the principles of the Gospel On the evening of the 16th, I ate dinner with Elders Kelsch and Ensign at the Metropole hotel after which we listened to some singing furnished by Bro. Ensign and an English lady who is stopping at the hotel.

Thursday, 17 April 1902—Monday, 21 April 1902, Tokyo

Thursday and Friday I spent the days quietly in my room, taking only a little walk for exercise. Saturday morning I got up early to bid Mr. Bowman good–bye as he left Tokyo for India at 6 a.m. Soon after he went away I received a note stating that he had gone off without his umbrella and wanted me to forward it to Kobe. In the afternoon I took it to Shinbashi Station and sent it off according to his request. On the way back I called at the Metropole and received two letters from Zion; one from Cousin Alexander McRae who had come to Salt Lake from the mission in Denver to attend Conference. He reported an excellent condition of affairs in the Colorado Mission. The other letter was from Sister Maud Baggerly to whom this journal will show I have written a number of letters. It conveyed the glad news that she had, after a hard struggle with self and others around her, been baptized into the church. This is a matter in which I have been deeply interested because the first time she ever heard any thing about the Gospel was from Sister Grace Frost who passed a long period of suffering in one of the Portland, Oregon hospitals, and being a neighbor and friend of mine I am interested in the success of her efforts to bring her associates to a knowledge of the gospel, for such success will be to her a great reward for her protracted suffering.

Sunday I met as usual with my brethren at the Metropole. We had a good meeting and spent a pleasant evening with our friends. I spoke a few words in Japanese for the benefit of my Japanese brethren and for the purpose of putting to use some of the knowledge that I have acquired of the language.

Monday was spent in the room talking most of the day with a foreign gentleman who has come to this hotel to stay a month or perhaps a little less. He is a Methodist Preacher on his way around the world and as he has but little money he can not afford to put up in foreign hotels. Yesterday I was able to hold my own in the discussions to my complete satisfaction and I thank the Lord for it is the first time I have ever been opposed by a minister.

Tuesday, 22 April 1902—Sunday, 28 April 1902, Tokyo

The weather during this time has been generally dismal. The same old routine of study, eating, and sleeping has been gone through. Once or twice I have spent a few hours in conversation with Japanese speaking in their own tongue. It is not a very favorable place to learn Japanese for the reason that servants and hotel masters are not always inclined to assist one who is endeavoring to learn another language.

A letter received on Thursday from father brought good news from home and told of the excellent trip he and Aunt Clara and Ruth and Liss had to California with the choir. He also spoke of the expected return of Apostle Grant. Newspapers received on the same day brought the report of Bro. Grant's arrival in Salt Lake where he was gladly welcomed by the people. I wrote and posted letters on this day to Aunt Clara and Sister Baggerly.

On Wednesday Mr. Koshiishi called on me to ask why we would not baptize him into the Church. I told him that we did not think he had a sufficient knowledge of the Gospel and that we did not want him to take such an important step blindly. He insisted that he was sufficiently versed and desired that we examine him and if he did not demonstrate a sufficient knowledge then he would be willing to stay without until he knew more fully what would be expected of him. Oh, if we were only like other churches! What a glorious record we could send home in relation to the number of converts made in six months. But I thank the Lord that the religion of Jesus Christ will stand investigation and requires the conversion of the heart.

Saturday Bro. Ensign went down to Yokohama to sing for a number of Mrs. Parker's friends and boarders. He had a real good time and met with nearly sixteen American war officers or their wives who are living at Mrs. Parkers for a few days. Mrs. Parker's home seems to have become the half way house to Manila for American Officers and their wives.

Sunday we had a glorious time at the home of Bro. Nakazawa where Elder Ensign is living. We assembled at this place to hold our Sabboth Sacrament and Testimony Meeting—the first ever held in a Japanese home Unfortunately the day was very wet and the streets were rivers of mud which condition undoubtly prevented Bro. Kikuchi from being present on this, the occasion of our first service in the home of a Japanese Saint—the beginning of cottage meetings in the Orient. I spoke a few words in Japanese to give as much encouragement as possible to my native Brother who could not understand anything that we said in English. To be able to say only a few words and them arranged in a crude form is indeed pleasant and I confess that it makes my heart glad to be able to say a little that is understood by those in whose welfare I am deeply interested.

After the meeting, I returned with Bro. Kelsch to the Metropole and ate supper with him. Shortly after supper the mail from San Francisco arrived via the ship in which Bro. Grant sailed to America—this being the steamers return voyage to the East. A letter from Aunt Eliza Smith thanking me for the picture I sent her for her birthday was received. Another letter from Samuel giving the news about home which in every particular concerning the immediate family was the most favorable. Some little trouble was being had in the Ward over the actions of some of the girls who held prominent positions in the Organizations in the Ward, especially in the Mutual.

One letter containing two parts from Bro. Grant was also received. He reported that he was sick nearly every minute of the way from Yokohama to San Francisco. Mother and father and his own folks were at the depot to meet him when he arrived over the O.S.L.[31] He had made report to both the Apostles and the Presidency and they were all delighted that he came home. He had not at that time laid the matters before the Brethren which he wanted considered by them in the interest of the Japan Mission. He had found all his business in a very favorable condition. Had met and had long talks with my father and mother and Elder Ensign's wife, but had only had the privilege of meeting and shaking hands with Bro. Kelsch's folks. All were well as far as he had learned. He sent his kind love and blessings to the native Brethren as well as to his fellow missionaries. Was glad that we had seen fit to dismiss Mr. Hiroi. He said that he had heard nothing against his coming back to Japan except from one brother who thought he could "run the mission as well from Salt Lake as from Tokyo." The newspapers spoke of the first session of the General Conference, giving the opening address of Prest. Smith in full. It was full of love for the Saints and praise for the excellent labors they had performed during the past year. He said it had been the record year in the Church's history and Zion was never so strong before.

Monday, 29 April 1902—Tuesday, 6 May 1902, Tokyo

During this week there has been a great deal of rain and in all it has been about the meanest weather that I have seen in Japan. So much wind has been blowing that even on the fine sunny days the dust filled the air like clouds of smoke.

Friday 2nd, I wrote a letter to mother answering the ones received from Samuel and father also wrote to Apostle Grant and my lady friend Bessie Badger. A number of steamers have arrived from home but thus far no new mail has come from the folks.

Sunday 4th, we assembled at the home of Bro. Nakazawa to hold our Sabboth Day Meeting. All the "Mormons" in Japan were present. The meeting was a pleasant one. After we had finished, however, Bro. Nakazawa had a little battle of words with Bro. Kikuchi which was not at all pleasant, and they parted without having the best of feelings toward eachother. There has been some slight manifestations of coldness between these two for some time, but we thought it would grow out of them in a short time yet the circumstance of this day was rather discouraging to our hopes. The evening was spent happily at the Metropole with our friends there.

On one of the last days of April, I in company with two or three of my student friends, went out to spend the afternoon with Elder Ensign. In going through Uyeno Park we met him coming toward the car on his way to Tsukiji. He gave up his trip to Tsukiji and returned with us. As we neared his place we met Elder Kelsch and two of our lady friends from the Metropole Hotel who had arrived at Bro. Ensign's house just in time to miss him. They joined us and we all had two or three hours of fun at the expense of Horace who treated us all to "kisoba" and other things which Japanese life calls quite choice dishes. The ladies had never seen such things before and it was indeed amusing to watch them handle the chop–sticks. The ladies were Mrs. Towell and Mrs. Cable with whom we have spent many pleasant hours at the Metropole. This event being on the 30th, of April we looked upon it as our May Day's outing altho celebrated one day too early.

Tuesday May 6th, was almost entirely taken up in discussing the personality of God with the gentleman claiming to be a Methodist minister who is not living at this hotel and with whom I have had a number of discussions in the past. The discussion this day was altogether unsatisfactory because all the evidences that I referred to were so spiritualized by this man that such words as man being in the form of God and Jesus in the form and image of His Father were constructed to mean alike in attribute and character and not in physical make–up. And the warnings that I cited him from the Bible against spiritualizing the words of the Lord and placing upon them private interpretations were not heeded in the least so all my talk was headed against a spiritualizing nothing.

Wednesday, 7 May 1902—Monday, 19 May 1902, Tokyo

This has been two weeks of practically all storm. Much of the time has been spent in diligently studying the language especially in asking all the questions that I could think of concerning it before our teacher, Mr. Hiroi, left us. It has been a long time since we have derived any practical good from his teaching and in fact ever since he first came to work for us we have had to draw out of him all that we received. And when strangers would come to hear of the Doctrines that we are in the land to preach he has not for a long time taken any interest in properly translating and interpreting for us. This being the case we gave him notice some sixty days ago that his services would not be needed after the 15th, of this month. We gave him a dinner at the Metropole on Thursday the 15th, and sent him away with as good a feeling as we could.

The following day, Friday, we went out to the Semmon Gakko[32] to deliver speeches before the English Speaking Society of that school. There were perhaps one hundred and twenty five very bright looking young men and we listened with intense interest to the program that had been prepared for the occasion. After the regular work was completed, we addressed the students, Bro. Kelsch being the first speaker. He spoke of the mission of the Prophet Joseph Smith and told how the Father and the Son appeared to him while still a small boy. I followed, hinging my remarks upon the subject "Abolition of Armies" which had been treated by one of the students who proclaimed that the time of peace would never be realized till the bloodshed caused by aries ceased. This gave me an opportunity to speak of the purpose of the establishment of the Doctrines of Christ as they are taught by the Latter–day Saints and show how these religious principles when property applied would finally bring about the condition of perfect peace on the earth. Elder Ensign spoke upon the necessity of keeping our word under all circumstances. We sang the Japanese national hymn which greatly pleased the students. After Elder Kelsch's speech we sang "Truth Reflects upon our senses" which was also greatly enjoyed by all present. This was the first opportunity we have had to stand before an audience in Japan and we delighted with the spirit manifested and the way in which what we did seemed to be accepted by the members of the Association. The day itself was a most miserable one, but we would go ten times the distance in much worse storms to have the same opportunity again.

Saturday evening, 17th., we had a very pleasant time at the Metropole in the apartments of Mr. and MRs. Godsey. They had invited their friends who live at the Metropole and some of the residents of Tsukiji to spend the evening with them. We met besides our old friends Mr. and Mrs. Pallister and Mrs. Pallister's sister. These are all English people and although we were "Mormons" we were gladly recognized as the equals of any. Gradually we are working our way into the foreign society as well as the native society and we will soon have so many friends among the good church members that the ministers will begin to wish they were out of sight. The party lasted till midnight. The "Mormons" did their share and the share of many of the others in entertaining during the evening. It being late when we said good night I and Elder Ensign stayed at the Metropole all night.

Next day, Sunday, we went out to Elder Nakazawa's to hold our Sunday Meeting. We had a good time, but were disappointed at not seeing Elder Kikuchi there. He was also absent the Sunday before and as there are only a few of us in this land we are partacularly anxious to have as much unity and activity as possible. Monday I called on Elder Kikuchi and found him busily engaged working with a number of people suffering from consumption. He has a medicine which he claims is especially good for this disease and has established a small hospital were people come to be treated. I watched the doctor make an injection in the back of the neck of one poor woman who looked like a mortal escaped from the grave. This sight took me back to the scenes of home and my work injecting chemicals into the bodies of the dead. It was interesting indeed to see something of the kind again. I talked with Elder Kikuchi about coming to his meetings and the good to be derived from activity in the work of the Lord. We expect to meet at his house next Sunday to hold our meeting. His place is pleasantly located on the south side of Shiba Park.

On Sunday May 11th, received a letter from Bishop Empey telling the usual news about the Ward. On the day before received a letter from Florence Grant. On 14th, mailed letters of Aunt Hattie, Bro. Willard Done, and Lutie Grant. On 19th, mailed letter to Elder William Erekson laboring in New Zeland. On same day received a letter from home written by mother. All were well and happy. Father had been especially strong since his return from San Francisco. The folks had been greatly pleased to see my picture on silk, dressed in a Japanese kimono.

Tuesday, 20 May 1902—Monday, 26 May 1902, Tokyo

The weather has been very pleasant during this week. Wednesday I went to Yokohama to express an album to mother which Bro. Grant had told me to select and send to her as a present from him. I arranged to send it over the O. & O.S.S. route to San Francisco per the "Gaelic," which was booked to leave Yokohama on the 27th.

During this week I have had two very good gospel conversations and some others which may do a little good but with which I was not particularly satisfied. One was with a gentleman who holds the position of secretary of a Buddhist Organization of considerable prominence here. He spoke very little English so I had to express a number of my ideas in Japanese which he evidently understood altho spoken in a most crude way.

The other Japanese with whom I spoke regarding religion is the student of the Semmon Gakko where we visited some days ago as will be seen from this journal of 16th, instant. This young man's name is T. Matsuda. He was baptized into the Church of England when a very small boy and he is better read on his religion than any Japanese I have met claiming to belong to Christianity. He seemed interested in what I had to say and, unlike the others who have called, he was not afraid to oppose me on those points which were contrary to his teachings. We had quite an argument regarding the responsibility of man for the sin of Adam compared with his responsibility for individual sin and the extent to which the Atonement[33] has effect in both instances. So many have come and immediately fallen in with every thing we say and then get cold and fall out of site, that it is refreshing to me to meet one who has a reason, which he respects, for being a Christian and a believer in the teachings taught by the Church to which he belongs. There is no doubt if we can get people to thinking earnestly upon our teachings that we will be able to get some believers who will say. As a general rule it is not the people who on the start say "yes" to everything said regarding "Mormonism" that make the ones who stand firm through thick and thin to last.

Friday morning I called , having been invited to do so on a very prominent Buddhist lecturer from India who is now in Japan addressing the leading societies and schools upon the more liberal conception of Buddhistic doctrines. He is a well read man and speaks excellent English. His very dark skin shows conclusively that he is a full–blooded native of India. He visited America some time ago and accidently met some Latter–day Saints whom, for their earnestness and purity of life, he learned to love. He is a firm believer in the doctrine of polygamy and in all a broad and open hearted man toward the truth of all religions. I spent perhaps some two hours with him and I was cordially invited to visit him again and he said he would call on me. He is extremely well read, so it is said, in the sacred and national history of all the peoples of Asia and the most ancient countries in Asia Minor and Africa, a subject about which the people of the Occident know but very, very little.

Saturday evening I was invited to go to the home of Mr. Pallister (see 17th, inst.) And spend another evening of song and social enjoyment with some new friend living in Tsukiji and our old friends at the hotel. I did not go however, but the other brethren were there and reported an excellent time. They met some ten or twelve new residents of Tsukiji—the foreign settlement.

Elder Kelsch reported in our meeting on Sunday held at the home of Elder Kikuchi that on Friday afternoon he began tracting among the foreigners in Tsukiji and that he had already visited some fifteen or twenty homes, five of them being the homes of ministers, with whom he had a good time and learned that they were all united to oppose us in our work with all the ability which they possessed and with all the force they could possibly muster. Amen. The quicker they begin the better it will be for us as the Lord has used them to advertize his gospel ever since Joseph Smith the Prophet told the world that he had received a vision from God, and such advertizement won't hurt us in the least in the estimation of the Japanese.

Bro. Kelsch never struck so many ministers all in a lump before, but as nearly all the foreigners in Tokyo are of the round collar type it is quite natural that he should. Monday it took him all afternoon to visit four places, three of which were the homes of divines. With this work of Bro. Kelsch's and our coming in contact and making friends in a social way with those who form the congregations of the different churches we will soon have the ministers of this land on the anxious bench. Won't it be fun! The people had the idea that we were afraid to meet their ministers and some could hardly believe it when Elder Kelch said he had called minister so and so to repentance. They had the idea that a people like we are reported to be and teaching a gospel as we are reported to preach could never stand for a moment before the wisdom and spirit of dear Parson. . . .

On Tuesday 20th. Received a letter from Bro. Grant that he expected to leave for Japan about June 17th. And it had been decided by the Authorities that he could bring his wife,[34] daughter,[35] Sister Ensign, and three or four more missionaries. This was glad news for us, not only that we are soon to see Apostle Grant again and Elder Ensign his wife, but that we are to have some other brethren to unite with us in preparing for the work in the important missionary field. The same day I received letters from mother, sister Ruth, and Sister Erekson. Ruth's was a minute account of the trip to California with the choir which was intensely interesting to me. All, according to mother's letter, were well at home and the business in all directions on the improve. Sister Erekson's letter was full of friendly sentiments and words of encouragement and blessing. On 26th. I posted a letter to Samuel enclosing verses written on Japan from both an Optomistic and Pessimistic view.

Tuesday, 27 May 1902—Tuesday, 3 June 1902, Tokyo

During the first of this week the rain storms were very heavy, but the last day or two has been almost hot. Nothing of any importance has happened in our midst during this time, and we have received no further news from Bro. Grant telling of what he is accomplishing in Zion for the benefit of the mission.

On Sunday we again met at the home of Elder Kikuchi to hold our usual Sabboth Meeting. Elder Kikuchi had invited a lady to be present on the occasion and observe what we did in our services and also to listen to whatever might be said that would be intelligible to her. This is the fist time we have ever had a stranger attend our meetings and we were particularly anxious to say something that would impress the heart of this lady with the fact that there was something in "Mormonism" and that our labor is characterized by a spirit that comes not with man's efforts alone. Bro. Kikuchi spoke with considerable earnestness and explained some of the principles of Christianity to this lady and I in a feeble way bore my testimony and said a few words in Japanese.

This was the first time I had ever aimed to say anything for the good of those who were not of us in the regular session of our meeting, for the reason that this was the first time anyone had been present with us. Such events makes me feel rather blue because of the disatvantage we are at not being able to speak to the people so that they can hear distinctly and understand fully the meaning of the words we utter. But no doubt the Lord is near on such occasions and makes up by the influences of His spirit that which is lacking, because of no fault of ours. On such occasions every breath is a prayer that the Lord will touch the hearts of the stranger and cause that no matter how poorly expressed or how weak the words that the meaning shall be made clear and the spirit of that meaning make the desired impression upon the hearts of those whom God sees, in His wisdom, are worthy to receive the Gospel. Bro. Nakazawa was not present.

Monday I was again in a long discussion with the preacher who lives in this hotel. Tuesday June 3rd. I went to see Elder Kikuchi and give him a brief translation of the incidents connected with the first vision of the Prophet Jos. Smith.

Thursday 29th. received a letter from the Des. Nat. Bank enclosing a draft for 200 yen. Friday 30th. wrote a letter to Emma Batt enclosing the the receipt for the album that left on 27th. directed to mother.

After the meeting at the home of Elder Kikuchi on Sunday, we all went to the Metropole where I found a package for me from America. It had come on the "Nippon Maru." I had received word that one had been forwarded by the express company in San Francisco, but there was no letter received which gave any information as to where it came from. On opening it I found it to be a large box of candy from the person whom I had imagined was the sender before the contents were revealed. It had come from Mabel Cunningham and was a strong evidence that former friendship was still alive among my associates from whom I separated with the kindest feelings. On the following day I sent a letter thanking her for the token which was also greatly enjoyed by my associates and our brethren and friends in this city.

Wednesday, 4 June 1902—Thursday, 9 June 1902, Tokyo

Wednesday evening I received a telephone message from Elder Kelsch stating that he had been invited to come on the following Friday night to the home of Rev. McCaleb and discuss with him on the points of difference in their religious beliefs and to use the version of the Bible that Elder Kelsch should choose. He chose King James' translation,[36] and accepted gladly the offer made by Mr. McCaleb as, according to the letter, some few were to be present and Elder Kelsch felt that it would be a fair way to present the Gospel to those who may be there to listen. I went down to the hotel to take Elder Kelsch some books that he wanted and which I had in my possession. I remained for some time reading passages to him as his eyes were rather weak and he therefore could not see very well at night.

During supper I received a letter from father containing much good news about those at home which was indeed gratifying to me. I seems that the Lord has been especially kind to them since I left them for according, to the letters I receive father's health has been exceedingly good of late which was not often the case for some time before I left home. In the letter there was enclosed a pamphlet giving some information about development of Mt. Olympus Farm in which father is deeply interested. This report was an excellent one indeed. Still however the industries of this place are still new and subject to the calamities which have carried from the heart of owners may a hopeful prospect.

A letter from Apostle Grant was received by Bro. Kelsch. It was short and told very little about what had been done in Zion.

The following day, Thursday, I spent the afternoon with Bro. Nakazawa. We had a pleasant talk concerning the Gospel and before leaving I ate supper prepared by his wife. She is a clever cook and though the food was entirely Japanese yet it had a flavor that seemed to satisfy a long ungratified appetite. Elder Ensign was absent, having gone to Tsukiji. I met him as I was on my way home. He reported that Elder Kelsch had been quite sick all day and during the previous night.

Friday evening we went to the discussion, if indeed it merits the name. Mr. McCaleb had invited some Japanese, some of whom I had met before. Rev. Snodgrass of the same religious ideas with Rev. McCaleb was also present. These gentlemen belong to the "Church of the Living God" and find no sympathy form the religious teachers of any other creeds in the realms of Christendom. They, like us, criticized severely the methods of the other preachers and consequently like us are ostracised. Mr. McCaleb in a very liberal man and a perfect gentleman in his arguments. The subject of discussion after the first two speeches found its way into the opportunities for man to hearing the gospel after death. The remaining four speeches which were fifteen minutes each, proved nothing and come wide of the mark for which they were intended. The reason for the roving manner was that this subject according to Elder Kelsch's References[37] (which was to be criticized by Mr. McCaleb) came up at a later date and they seemed evidently to been hiding their strong points behind a number of small shadowed ones. Thus the evening closed without a point being carried one way or the other.

The subject dicided upon for discussion the following week was the Name of the Church, Members Called Saints and, if time permitted, The Officers in the Church. After the discussion was completed One of the Japanese present gave a little talk in which he referred to our belief in polygamy and said in his opinion that a religious system that taught such a thing was in itself degrading. He told it in such a peculiar way that it was all right for him to say so and we told him we enjoyed his frankness and that at some future time the subject would be brought up for discussion between Elder Kelsch and Rev. McCaleb. Mr. Snodgrass stated that if we would not only give up polygamy as a belief as well as we had as a practice, but also change the name of the church he did not see why we then could not become a power in the earth. He stated that he could not see what good we had derived during the evening by discussing the subject that we had and he said that we should only care about those things which concern our salvation. He told of meeting with a Christian Minister the other day and saying to him that the Mormons were out visiting the people of Tsukiji and he asked the minister if they had called on him yet. The minister replied,

"No, and if they come I will not invite them in as I am now settled in my faith and I don't want it shaken." Mr. Snodgrass then suggested to the gentleman that perhaps he would be able to shake the faith of the Mormon who might visit him, but the minister still insisted that he would not ask them in if they came. Mr. Snodgrass said he could not see any depth in a Christianity that was afraid to met and compare its teachings the idea with other factions and it was an illustrated the terrible narrow mind of the person who was not sufficiently christian ask another preacher into his home. Elder Ensign spoke a few words in praise of the liberality of Mr. McCaleb in inviting us into his home and being willing to hear our side from our standpoint.

I made a few remarks on what Mr. Snodgrass said in the first of his speech and called his attention that there are two classed of sin—omission as well as commission and I told him that when we were convinced that such and such was our duty and a part of the plan laid down by God that we would be guilty of the sin of omission and until it was demonstrated that any of the doctrines we taught were nonessential would we be justified in giving up even the least of them. I wanted to propose to him that it might be just as well for him and other men to adopt the religion of the Latter–day Saints and receive divine commisson from the Lord and that then they might become a power in the earth for good; but I thought that this would be too direct a thrust at what he had said in a friendly way therefore I held it back. The discussion disclosed these facts that our belief in the universal effect of Christ's atonement, the responsibility of man in gaining by good works his own salvation are exactly the same and that there are those (the sons of Perdition) whose sins will never be forgiven in this life nor in the life to come. It is to be hoped that the result of the discussion next Friday will be more clearly marked and that the triumph of truth will be apparent to all. Elder Kelsch was not enjoying the best of health and all during the evening suffered with a terrible headache.

I received a letter from home written by mother and Sister Capener conjointly.

Saturday and Sunday Elder Kelsch continued to feel unwell and therefore did not venture out to the meeting at Bro. Nazazawa's. Elder Kikuchi was not there either. Mr. Koshiishi the man whom I have mentioned in my journal as being desirous of joining the church was on invitation from me present with us. The absence of our two brethren made the meeting rather short and there was some disappointment at the lack of interest Elder Nakazawa took in Mr. Koshiishi and our lack of ability made in rather hard to express our feelings so that this man would understand us.

My heart was sick at the thought that we have been here nearly a year and are still so lame in this matter and a desire filled my heart to have more fully the blessings of the Lord. It seems that our Heavenly Father is surely trying our patience and testing our endourance to the utmost for it is punishment of the severest kind to have people come and want to talk and learn of the Gospel and not be able to explain it to them. The blessing and the manifestations of the Spirit that have followed the Elders in other lands have not yet been felt or witnessed by us here and it seemes to me that if there is a spot on the earth where we need great strength from the Lord it is in this land where the people are either wedded to idolatry or infidelity, and where a language so difficult separates us from them like an unpassable chasm. But if the Lord is satisfied with our efforts and it is according to His will that this delay in coming to our relief be so long then I want power to abide the time of the Lord and ever be found ready and worthy to receive His power when it is to be bestowed.

A letter received from Prest Grant on Monday states that he will, with the rest of the company that is to come, sail from Tacoma on the "Duke of Fife" June the 19th. He said that he had been thinking seriously over the names of Fred Caine, Sanford Hedges, and Elias Ashton and had asked the President of the Alpine Stake to call a good young man from his Stake to accompany him to Japan. Nothing definately had been decided about these brethren consequently they may not be the ones whom the Spirit will finally designate. I know personally Fred Caine, and Elias Ashton; they are both my school mates; Elias being a bosom friend and as dear almost as a brother. But affections should not in any instance direct in things pertaining to the advancement of God's Kingdom on the earth, so while I would like to see and be associated with these brethren I will be happy to welcome any whom the Lord has designed to carry on this work.

Tuesday, 10 June 1902—Tuesday, 17 June 1902, Tokyo

Tuesday evening 10th. I took a walk and had it not been that I met some of my friends on the street I would have lost myself for I was going directly away from home all the time thinking however that I would soon find a familiar land mark. This is the first time I have been turned around in Tokyo.

Wednesday and Thursday I fasted. Thursday evening I went to the home of Bro. Kikuchi to have a talk with him but he was not at home. He had been away from the city for more than ten days and was not expected back for a day or two, therefore he was not present at our meeting last Sunday. We had been wondering why he did not come and felt a little bad because we thought he was manifesting in his absence more of the spirit of dissatisfaction which we have observed in him a time or two. While there talking with his wife, I met a gentleman who had many years ago joined the Catholic Church. He could understand English very well and I had a long talk with him. I presume I was explaining the Gospel to him for over two hours. At first he was quite prejudice and said he would not recognize anyone but the Pope, but after I had explained to him the Truth from the Bible he became interested and listened with eager ear to all that I had to say. I never felt more earnestly the spirit of testimony than on this occasion. I was quite weak when I got there having fasted for nearly forty–eight hours, but when I left I felt as fresh as though I had just come from an appetising breakfast.

Friday evening the second of the series of discussions between Elder Kelsch and Rev. McCaleb took place and was a fair improvement over the first. The subject concerning the name of the Church occupied the entire evening. Mr. McCaleb's only argument against the name of our Church was that we could not find it any one place in the Bible just as it reads: "Church of Jesus Christ of Latter–day Saints." Elder Kelsch on points completely triumphed, though Mr. McCaleb could not see the point which defeated him. Elder Kelsch clearly showed that it was not necessary to have a name that could be found all in one place without the interpolation of other words, and also showed that even in the days of the Apostles there were so many names used in reference to the name of the possessor of the Church that it would be impossible for man to decided from the Scripture alone, which, if any, of the names used by the New Testament writers was the correct one. The subject for the next meeting is the Officers in the Church and the necessity of Spiritual gifts today. One of the Japanese who was present on the occasion has since told us that he felt that we were right in adopting the name of "Jesus Christ" instead of only "Christ" "Firstborn", "Lord and Savior Jesus Christ," and other names applied in the scripture to the Church. This is the young man who said in the last meeting that he though any religious organization that taught polygamy was degrading. Since then he has read one or two of our tracts and has nearly repented of his doubts concerning our doctrines.

Sunday we went to the home of Elder Kikuchi to hold our meeting and expected to have some enquirers attend but the day being bad they did not come and Elder Kikuchi had not returned from his trip consequently we did not hold a meeting. We went to the Metropole and spent the afternoon with Elder Kelsch and ate supper with him before going home. I received a letter from my friend Will Erekson still laboring as a missionary in New Zeland. He wrote some very good advice and considerable encouragement concerning the study of a new language in the mission field, telling from the experience of those who have labored in New Zeland of those methods which with the help of the Lord have produced the quickest and also the best results.

A letter received from Apostle Grant on Saturday stated that he had postponed his departure till the 1st of July and would come over the Nippon Yusen Kaisha[38] route from Seattle, Oregon. On Thursday I wrote a long letter to father. Monday I wrote to Bishop Empey, and Tuesday 17th. I wrote to my sister Ruth, and my friend Chas. R. Pederson one of the faithful boys on the 13th Ward.

The weather has been irregular during the entire . week.

Wednesday, 18 June 1902—Thursday, 3 July 1902, Tokyo/Enoshima

Friday evening, 20th, Elder Kelsch discussed with Rev. McCaleb concerning the necessity of the same organization to be found in the church today as existed anciently and also that the same Gifts of the Spirit should be made manifest. While, of course, Mr. McCaleb could not see the point yet his side of the argument suffered extensively and the illustrations and evidences that he brought forth to overthrow this truth were the weakest he has presented during the entire time of the discussions. The victory was distinctly Elder Kelsch's.

Sunday we held meeting at the home of Elder Nakazawa. Elder Kikuchi being out of the city was not present. We had a very fine time and enjoyed the full influence of the spirit. Elder Ensign for the first time bore his testimony in Japanese.

Monday morning we left Tokyo on the nine twenty five train in company with Mr. Okamoto for Dzushi a small town on the sea shore about an hours ride from Yokohama. After calling at a certain place where a man lived with whom Mr. Okamoto was well familiar we were conducted by this gentleman to a suitable hotel built immediately upon the sea–shore and our rooms looked out upon the deep from off of which the refreshing and invigorating sea breeze blew almost continually. This was our home till the following Wednesday morning.

On Monday afternoon we took a sampan and rowed out to some large breakers perhaps a mile from shore. Here we spent some hours fishing with tackle which the boatmen provided. The waves as the swept past us and broke with deafening hoar and snowy beauty upon the ragged rocks reminded me of the poet's pictures of scenes which make the coasts of Norway the most fascinating in the world. As fishers we proved less skillful than the natives. Elder Kelsch as he stood or sit upon the edges of the rocks watching the movements of the little wire hook attached to the end of his line, presented as he looked over the top of his large glasses a more suitable picture for "Puck"[39] than a specimen of an up–to–date sportsman.

The evening we spent in the hotel where we had some new and rather novel experiences pertaining to Japanese life but it would not be wise to enumerate them here. In the evening we had the privilege of seeing the Crown Prince[40] who lives in this part of the country during the summer and who is so common a sight that the people do not stop to do any particular homage to him as he passes. He always, while in the country and upon good days, rides in a little open carriage drawn by one horse. He is a small insignificant little whipper–snapper with a mustache that is truly in harmony with the majority in Japan—composed of about a dozen hairs.

Next day we took a little larger sampan than the day before and went to the island of Enoshima. This island in about six miles from where we were staying and during the night a great storm had been raging, and the waves were still quite high but not high enough to cause any hesitancy in regard to taking the trip. The little craft danced around on the choppy surface with considerable irregularity, with the result that our friend Okamoto got very sick and cried out in despair a time or two. Once an extra gust of wind caught the sails and caused the boat to dip water on the side on which he was resting his head. But the splashing of the water in his face did not startle him in the least, as he said when we got on land that it being the first time he had been on the sea for such a long trip and the first time to be sea–sick that he thought he was surely going to die before he reached shore.

As we came near to the shore we could see dozens of boys and girls bobbing up an down in the water like muskrats. Their skins were so brown that they looked the same color as the rocks from which they jumped with childlike glee.

This island is noted for the natural cave in the south side which has in time been washed into the almost solid rocks by the angry waves of the sea. The night before these waves had been so high that the bridge or wooden path leading from the side into it had been completely demolished in two places. The tide being out, however, we were able by considerable climbing and clinging to the sides of the island to keep from sliding off into the water, to reach the cave and get in as far as the shrine but from there on it was dark and without lights we would be unable to proceed farther. This cave has been converted into a shrine for worship and at the entrance proper a little crude temple is erected in which, upon the floor before the image, were numerous pieces of copper coin left by the people who had donated to their God the night before previous to the coming up of the storm. In the dark part, which for lack of light we were unable to see, we are told there are hundreds of stone idols set in the walls on either side. The storm of the night before had sent in the waves as far as the little temple and piled up the debris from the delapodated brige in rather an irreverent way before his holiness the brazen god who sit in silence in this lonely place where the roar of the sea echoed and reechoed through the stony chambers with a voice that almost made my blood run cold.

On the return trip we visited a number of the shell stores where we also found many beautiful works in stone. But as the hour was late and the wind against our homeward trip we had to hasten back to the shore where our brownskinned, naked oarsmen were waiting somewhat nervously for our return. The trip was very delightful to us all, as we had not gone far when the wind changed and with the help of the sails we reached home an hour earlier that it would have been possible for us to do had the men been forced to row against the wind and waves all the way. The sea was rougher than when we came, but the sun being down the heat of the outward ride was replaced by a beautifl cool breeze. The Japanese who had gone with us as a guide lay down in the back of the boat and like Mr. Okamoto during the morning thought that the end had come. Mr. Okamoto returned from the island to Tokyo by train.

In the morning before taking this trip we all went out and had a swim in the sea. This was the first time I had bathed in the ocean.

Next morning at eleven oclock I and one of the Japanese returned to Tokyo, and Bros. Kelsch and Ensign went again to Enoshima. This time by train. The train arrived in Tokyo about half past two. This ended what may be called a three day's spree, but which also taught us much about the land in which we are laboring as missionaries and gave us an excellent chance to practice our Japanese on the people as every one we met could speak nothing else.

On going to the Metropole I received a letter from father telling about the result of the Oratorical Contest in which our ward came second with close honors, being represented in the battle by Bro. Allan Howard.

Friday, 27th., I wrote a letter to mother.

Sunday Bro. Kelsch was sick and Elder Kikuchi had not returned from his trip consequently we held no meeting.

Thursday evening, July 3rd., Elder Kelsch again met with Rev. McCaleb to discuss the Duration of the Marriage Covenant (Confined to this life or Eternal. Which?) And as to whether or not polygamy received or did not receive divine favor as proved by Bible law and history. This discussion was anything but decisive on this mater and indeed hardly touched upon. Mr. McCaleb in now going to try and prove through the public press that the Ethiopian woman and the daughter of Jethro whom Moses married are one and the same woman. I promised him that I would prove to the contrary and would give the name of the Ethiopian woman and the circumstances under which she was married to Moses. The outcome of this little conflab will perhaps be known in a week or two.

Friday, 4 July 1902—Monday, 21 July 1902, Tokyo

The weather during this time has been generally dismal. A letter from Apostle Grant requesting that we secure for him a house into which he could move as soon as he and the rest of the party arrived, was received about the 6th. For some days we were unsuccessful in our search, but finally found a small place which was suitable in every way except that the contract had to be made for three years.

On Tuesday 15th, sent letters to Samuel, Allan Howard, Brigham Clegg and Florence Grant.

On Thursday 17th, went with Bros. Kelsch and Ensign to Yokohama to meet the company from America. We arrived in Yokohama quite early in morning and at that time nothing had been heard from the vessel. On invitation from Mr. Towell we ate dinner with him and his wife at the Club Hotel. After the meal we were entertained listening to their phonograph.

We learned soon after that the ship had been sighted and would be in port in about an hour. We walked over to the wharf and were just in time to see her sail in. We took a number of pictures of the group of Saints as they stood on the deck. Indeed it was a great sight to see so many fresh faces from the land of Zion. We had been waiting with great expectancy to see those who had been chosen to come to Japan to assist in carrying on the work which we had already begun. For nearly a year we had seen only four faces of those, whose sympathies were with us and whose hearts were set upon accomplishing a mission on the earth for the success of their fellow men and the salvation of their dead relatives—ourselves.

We went immediately to the Metropole hotel at Tokyo as soon as the baggage had been passed through the custom house. The entire party remained at the hotel for one day. On the 18th. Bro. Grant and his wife and daughter and I went out to see the house on which we had decided. They were all pleased with the location and arrangement of the place. But the landlord being absent we were unable to settle on it defineately till the following day. In the evening Bros. Sanford Hedges, George Jarvis, Fred A. Caine, and John Stoker accompanied me out to the Nakai hotel were we expect to live together for some time.

The next few days were spent in getting the new Elders settled in their new quarters and in buying those things which are both handy and necessary to a pleasant life in a Japanese home.

On Sunday 20th. we all gathered to the Metropole Hotel to hold meeting and pertake of the sacrament. It was a lovely meeting and one which I will ever remember. Thirteen Latter–day Saints and one Japanese, (Mr. Koshiishi) were present. All expressed themselves in terms of the warmest feeling and there was a spirit present with us that melted more than one heart. It was a glorious feast for those of us who have been meeting in groups of three and four for the last year, and words are inadequate with which to express the intense feelings of joy that filled my bosom. The evening after supper was spent pleasantly in the hotel parlor with our old friends at the Metropole and with two or three of the Japanese who often called on us before Bro. Grant went to America. Bro. Kikuchi, his wife, and Mrs. Nakazawa were with us for supper.

Tuesday, 22 July 1902—Friday, 1 August 1902, Tokyo

On Tuesday I went to the Post Office with the Brethren and ordered our mail sent out to us at the Nakai. In the afternoon we all went to see the funeral of Admiral Saigo in Aoyama Cemetery. It was a grand affair. It is evidently only once in many years that such an elaborate funeral service is observed. The city of Tokyo contributed tens of thousands of spectators who thronged the line of procession and stood in immense masses around the burial plot and place where the ceremony was preformed. In a large open space in one part of the cemetery there were three marqee erected one for the casket and priests who preformed the funeral rites, one for the Ministers of State and prominent men who had come out to do honor to the illustrious dead, and still another for the relatives and particular friends of the deceased. I had been particularly anxious to see such a funeral as I was writing an article for father to read before the Unedrtaker's Convention to be held in September 1902 at Colorado Springs on the subject, "A Glimpse at the Funeral Rites of Japan." In that article I refer to some of the things seen at this funeral.

On the 23rd. went with Bro. Kelsch to Yokohama. He went to secure his passage on the steamer "City of Peking" to San Francisco, scheduled to leave Yokohama on 31st.[41] He purchased some kimonos for his folks.

Heretofore the brethren living with me had eaten everything set before them, indeed, they nearly exhausted the rice and hot water a time or two, a thing that is almost unheard of in Japan as these things are the principal diet of the people and they generally have an everlasting lot of it, but this evening 24th, I sent out and bought some kisoba for them and it nearly made them sick. after supper Mr. Yoshikawa and his friends came in to see us. We talked for some time about the Gospel, but it all seemed unprofitable.

Next day went out to Uyeno park with Bro. Kelsch who wanted to purchase some things to take home. It was the first time I had been in the Uyeno Bazaar and was much amused with the great variety of things they exhibited there.

On Sunday we met at the home of Bro. Grant in Yotsuya to hold meeting. Bro. Grant, his wife and daughter Mary, Bro. and Sister Ensign, and Bro. and Sister Featherstone had moved into the new house the Thursday before and had made it quite comfortable. There was a full attendance of every Latter–day Saint in Japan besides Mr. Takahashi and four Japanese visitors from the police department. I attempted to say a little in Japanese and Bro. Kikuchi was especially enthusiastic in his address which was an explaination of the first eight Articles of Faith.[42] The following day Mr. Takahashi wrote a letter to Apostle Grant and told him that I had been learning a bookish Japanese and that what I said would not be understood by the people. This is great encouragement I am sure. After spending a whole year studying the language and arriving at a condition where I thought I could express myself a little, to be told that any speech was as good as nothing at all, doesn't set well on my feeling.

Monday, word came that the steamer on which Bro. Kelsch was to sail was broken and would not sail for some weeks. On the 30th we all went to the Metropole to have dinner with Bro. Kelsch. On the 31st we went and had dinner with Bro. Grant and the folks. It was indeed a pleasure to eat an old style dinner once more. In the evening I finished my article concerning the Funeral Rites of Japan.

Aug. 1st was my 20th birthday. I received a call from Mr. H. Miganohara a Japanese just arrived from Salt Lake City. I went with him to see Bro Grant & the folks in Yotsuya, after which we had dinner in a restaurant. Sent mail home.

Saturday, 2 August, 1902—Sunday, 10 August 1902, Tokyo

With the exception of one day it has rained incessantly. The rice fields and gardens between Tokyo and Yokohama are flooded and it is reported that all the crops in this district are destroyed. This will cause no particular distress as far as the country is concerned as the big rice districts are all in good condition. Of course the people who own the little farms in this vicinity will suffer a slight loss.

Sunday I spoke in Japanese at the meeting held at Bro. Grant's. There was one stranger present and we all enjoyed the spirit of the Lord. We ate supper before returning.

Monday, went to Yokohama to see the Consul of the U.S. about making affidavit concerning a bill for the album I sent home some months ago. The express company had failed to send the bill I gave them and the Custom Officials at San Francisco estimated the value of the album to be about three times what I paid for it and consequently the duty was also very high.

Tuesday wrote a reply to an article written in the Voice by Mr. McCaleb against a letter I had sent concerning the marriage relations of the prophet Moses.

Wednesday Bro. Kelsch came to spend the day with us. He had a bath with us—his second experience in a Japanese tub. We enjoyed his company very much especially because it would be the last time he would be able to call on us before leaving for home.

Thursday spent the afternoon with the folks at Yotsuya in honor of Bro. Kelsch. We had a fine dinner and enjoyed eachothers society immensly The landlady of the Nakai Hotel came over to see Bro. Ensign and the place in which he was living. She took special notice of how the food was prepared and seemed to relish the same altho it was the first time she had eaten many of the dishes prepared. She promised to make similar dishes for us if she could learn how.

Friday spent the day at home. The landlady gave us Irish stew and boiled beans for supper. She had made them very well, showing that she had observed very closely how the folks out to Bro. Grant's had cooked the food.

Saturday went to Yokohama to bid farewell to Bro. Kelsch. Bro. Grant was suffering so with lumbago[43] that he could not go farther than the depot. We all went out to the steamer to see the cabin in which our brother was to sail. The steamer which took him away from us is the same as the one which took Bro. Grant back to Zion on the 11th of last March—"Gaelic." The day was rather an unauspicious one on which to make a start as the weather was very bad, but it being the day on which King Edward VII was coronated it will be a time easily remembered. I sent my journal home to the folks by him. It was hard to see him go home as I had, through close association with him, learned to love him for his good qualities, but I was glad in the contemplation of the fact that he would soon be with his folks from whom he has been separated so much during the last eleven years. He returned as the first Elder to be released from the Japanese mission and left with the blessings of the President and the love of all who were left to labor in the field. We came back from the steamer to the pier where we stood till it steamed out of the harbor. Not the slightest desire to return home crept over me. I felt then as I feel today that to labor in the field for some years yet will be more pleasant and satisfactory than to return so soon to loved ones at home.

Sunday, I, with my brethren, went to the home of Bro. Grant to hold meeting with them. There were four Japanese strangers present and for their benifit I spoke in Japanese as best I could, tho indeed on such occasions I feel weak and unfit to stand before anyone to speak of the Gospel. It will be a happy day indeed when my knowledge of this language will be sufficient to drive away the distress I feel when trying to say something in the defense of the cause I love in a tongue that I know nothing about. The others took a walk after supper but I remained and had a pleasant talk with Bro. Grant and his wife for about two hours.

Monday, 11 August 1902—Wednesday, 19 August 1902, Tokyo

On the afternoon of the 11th I went out to call on Bro. Nakazawa who was threatening to leave the church. I expected to be coldly received, but on the contrary I was welcomed as an old friend. Bro. Nakazawa of late has been wanting money first for one thing and then for the other. We were unable to advance it to him in all cases, first, because we did not have it to lend and, second, because we felt it would be unwise to do so. Bro. Grant of course as President of the Mission gave the answer in every case and because of his refusal Bro. Nakazawa got the idea that Bro. Grant had lost all love for him and he was not feeling warm towards Bro. Grant. In fact his hatred for him seemed to be so intense that he stated that if Bro. Grant should call on him that he would not welcome him to his house. I talked with him for nearly two hours but did not seem to phase him with anything I could say. I left feeling as though my visit had been a fruitless.one.

12th. was the first anniversary of our arrival in Japan. I went out to Bro. Grant's to tell him the result of my conversation with Elder Nakazawa. There was nothing done in celebration of the day.

13th. I received a telephone message from Bro. Nakazawa to come and see him. I went and found that he was in a penitent mood. Having talked with Mr. Takahashi and reflected a little on what I had told him regarding the error of entertaining such ideas and feelings as he did he felt as though he had hastily judged Bro. Grant and was now desireous of asking forgiveness. I was extremely glad to fine him in this condition and proposed that he go with me so as to be present in person while I acted as interpreter to Bro. Grant. He was glad that I was willing to go with him and tho late in the evening we took the train and went to Bro. Grant's house. After an hour's talk we returned in time to catch the last train. This is the first breach in the ranks of those who have accepted the Gospel and I hope we will not be called upon to contend with them often altho the Japanese are a very peculiar people and I feel that much trouble of this kind is ahead of us. Had my picture taken.

Thursday wrote and posted letters to Mother, sister Liss, and sister Margaret.

Friday was spent at home with my books.

Saturday we attended an exhibition of jugglery. The tickets to this performance were given us by Mr. Koshiishi. The tricks performed were astonishingly mysterious, illustrating that the Japanese are master tricksters. Sunday we organized a Sunday School class in which we expect to take up the study of Dr. Talmage's Articles of Faith. Bro. Ensign was chosen Teacher and Superintendent tnd and Bro. Fred Caine as Secretary and Treasurer. In the afternoon we held our usual meeting. Four visitors were present. Bro. Nakazawa spoke twice and I said a few words in Japanese. All the rest bore their testimony in English.

Monday went out to Bro. Grant's to get some money.

Tuesday wrote letters to Mrs. Ellen Capner, Mrs. Isabelle B. Erekson, Miss. Lizzie Thomas, and Aunt Eliza M. Smith.

Thursday, 20 August 1902—Tuesday, 2 September 1902, Tokyo

Wrote letters to Bishop Empey, Miss Baggerley, and Aunt Hattie. The weather during these few days has been generally fair. The heat on some occasions has been rather intense but not so much so as to make it as unpleasant as it was in Yokohama last year at this time. Perhaps I am becoming accustomed to the severe heat experienced in this land and therefore do not realize exactly how hot it is.

On the evening of the 26th, we all went out to see the fireworks at [blank] The most convenient way to approach this place is by boat to the Samida River where from the boat a fine view can be had of the display. We found after walking a short distance from the hotel a number of places from which small san–pans were starting with passengers to the fire–work's grounds. We tried at a number of places to get passage where we would not have to take off our shoes, but not until the third attempt did we get settled in a boat and then we had to take off our shoes to be considered gentlemen by the rest of the Japanese who rode with us. This is a peculiar custom among the Japanese; one which will do very well for those who can pull their feet out of their wooden shoes or "geta"[44] as they walk along but for foreigners who have a lot of laces or buttons to work with it is very inconvenient and unpleasant. The reason for the necessity of this is that the people sit in the bottom of the boat on a clean piece of matting specially placed for their comfort and it is not at all nice for them to sit down with their silk kimonos in large cakes of mud carried in on the soles of shoes or geta.

The display was good but the rapidity with which they set off the different pieces was like most of the things Japanese—terribly slow, in consequence of which it became very tedious. After the event was over the boatmen rowed us down the River for some distance. The scene on the water was beautiful. Thousands of boats all lit up in gay style shot around through the water and large boats bearing immense advertizements threw their light from shore to shore. Some boats were filled with foreigners who had tables spread and servants dispensing cold lunches.

On the way beck we came by a little out of the way canal. The experience along this course was frightful. It seemed to be the harbor for the boats that carry the sewerage from the big city of Tokyo. The stench was simply awful. Once one of the guests wanted to get off the boat as we were near his home. The only way he could get off was to row right up to one of these tanks which stood directly opposite an offing. The odor nearly put us all to sleep and had we not been kept awake yelling at the man to hurry we would certainly have swooned. His actions indicated that he was affected by the gas as he moved with the alertness of a snail, trying to go up stream.

On the 25th, I wrote another answer to an article of Mr. McCaleb's concerning the marriage relations of Moses.

Sunday 31st met with the rest of the colony at Prest. Grant's and enjoyed the subject discussed in Sunday School and the spirit manifested in the afternoon meeting. Mr. Takahashi and two other Japanese who can speak English very well were present at the meeting. Bro. Grant and Elder Ensign spoke in a very impressive manner.

The Thursday previous Mr. Takahashi's book had been completed and a copy was presented to Apostle Grant. Two days later Bro. Grant received the hundred copies which he had bargained to buy. The book is evidently very well arranged and written strongly in the defense of the Latter–day Saints. Mr. Takahashi had translated the first chapter into English so we could get an idea of the spirit and purport of the whole. He has certainly introduced the subject in a masterful and attractive way. The price is set at ¥0.75.

Monday 1st, I and the brethren who are living with me moved from the Nakai hotel to "The Nishō Kwan," a hotel only about a block from the old one and controled in a more business like manner. The food and other things at the Nakai having become poor we felt that it would be wisdom to seek other quarters as the price we were paying was sufficient to justify good food and the best kind of attention that a Japanese hotel can give. When we announce to the Landlord and landlady that we were going to move, they were greatly astonished and the Landlord became very angry, so much so that the night before we left (which was the time I told them we were going to leave the next day) while he was talking with me about it he simply shook, and threatened to call the police to assist him to keep us there because we had not given him longer notice. I smiled at his threats and when he saw that we could not be frightened, he cooled down and just as we were leaving came in with a smile and told us to call and see him often. It is wonderful how men's hearts are changed towards the Mormon Elders when once the come to know them.

The new place is more Japanese than the one in which we were formerly living but it is as nice a Japanese hotel as I have seen in the land. The woodwork is so clean that it shines like varnish and has not had a drop of paint on it. The servants are clean and attentive. The food is better and the dishes in which it is served are as clean as the ones I use to eat from at home. The price for the five of us is, ¥.151 per month. The reception room is larger than any that we had at the Nakai and so good in appearance that we do not feel at all ashamed to invite the best of our friends. It is quiet and the class of people who come here are the best, for th reason that the price is so high that students and the roughhouse class are not found here. In all the place is much better thus far than the former one and we feel quite satisfied with the action we have taken regarding a move. A foreigner of rather a bad character use to live her and the people are still a little bit suspicious of us but of course this feeling will soon wear away as the same feeling did at the Nakai.

Wednesday, 3 September 1901—Wednesday, 10 September 1902, Tokyo

On the third received a letter from Elder Wm. Erekson. He expected at the time of writing to be released on the nineteenth of this month to return home in company with President Magleby of the New Zeland mission. In the evening I and the brethren went over to the home of President Grant to have a choir practice. It had been thought advisable for us to practice a little singing so that our voices could be made to blend a little more than they had been doing and thus have better singing in our Sunday School and afternoon meetings. Wrote letters to my brother Samuel and Elder Louis A. Kelsch.

Thursday the fourth Bro. Nakazawa was with us all day.

On the evening of the sixth, I, with Bros. Stoker and Jarvis went to visit Bro. Kikuchi who has been very neglectful of his duties of late. It is now much more than a month since he came to meeting and his spirit seems to be practically asleep. In as kind a way as possible and still in a way that showed him that he would be deprived entirely of the Spirit of the Lord if he did not meet with his brethren and pertake of the influence of our meetings, I sought to awaken an interest in his heart for the Gospel.

Sunday being fast day, we dispensed with the regular class recitation and had a Sabboth School Testimony Meeting. In the afternoon there were only two strangers present and we did not hold a very long meeting.

Monday was another class day.

Tuesday did very little save write another letter to the Voice in conclusion of the discussion with Mr. McCaleb.

Wednesday the 10th, had another class recitation and in the evening went out to President Grant's and had supper. We all had a very fine time practicing the songs of Zion and telling of our experiences.

Thursday, 11 September 1902—Saturday, 26 September 1902, Tokyo

On the 11th Bros. Caine and Hedges went out to Yotsuya to have dinner, and Bros. Ensign and Featherstone came here to have a Japanese meal in exchange. Much of the afternoon was spent together and in all we had a very pleasant time. The brethren returned by way of the Ginza and while passing through a crowd Bro. Ensign lost his watch. Bro. Featherstone saw the watch go but did not realize what had happened till it was too late to get the man before he had given it to one of his palls They followed the man who took the watch and caught him but when they searched him they found that he hadn't it. This was a very unfortunate circumstance as the watch was not only a valuable one but a present from one of Horace's dear friends.

On the 12th Mr. McCaleb with whom I have been discussing in the Voice concerning the marriage relations of Moses, called to see us. We had a small discussion concerning the errors made in translating the Scriptures; I maintaining that men without special inspiration could not, no matter how learned, fail to make some serious errors in the text; he maintaining that the wisdom with which man was naturally endowed was sufficient to maintain in purity the full and correct meaning of all texts. As all the discussions with this man, this one was in no way profitable for he is of the kind that would not believe the truth of "Mormon" teachings if an angel from heaven should reveal it unto him. His salvation is in the money that he can make out of Christianity and the honor he can get by winning debates.

Sunday Sept 14th we had a fine Sunday School and afternoon meeting at Bro. Grant's. In the meeting I spoke in Japanese concerning the Gospel as a free gift. On our return to the hotel we found that half of the guests were intoxicated and there were many laughable sights as well as some disgusting ones. The Sabbath as we had observed it at Bro. Grant's and the Sabbath as it was being observed by this group of natives was sufficiently different to be considered an entirely changed day.

Mr. Oyama came to our meeting and desiring to speak he said that his investagation of the doctrines taught by the Latter–day Saints had proved to him that they were true and desired, if it be considered wise in the estimation of Apostle Grant, to be baptized. After considering the proposition it was desided that Mr. Oyama had better make a little deeper examination of the doctrines and then if his feelings were the same as he then exhibited that we would gladly receive him as a member of the church.

Sept 19th wrote a letter to father.

Sept. 20th received a letter from Bessie Badger. In the evening about twenty minutes to six Bro. Grant came in asking us if we did not want to go to Yokohama to see the Daniel Frawley company in "Secret Service." Foreign theatrical performances are so rare in this land that we gladly accepted his proposition. It was too late to catch the 6:20 train (the one he had decided to go on) and we thaught the next train went at 7:30 but were mistaken. It left at 7:00 and we got to the depot just about two minutes too late. The folks were all there waiting for us. It was a sad disappointment all around. Not wanting to return without seeing something we went to Asakusa Park where we saw a Japanese show of an inferior sort; indeed a poor substitute for a famous actor like Frawley.

Sept. 21st again assembled with the rest of the Brethren and sisters at "Grantsville." We had a good Sunday School and afternoon meeting. I spoke as best I could on the Value of History and Tradition as an Evidence of God's Existance.

On the 23rd bought a Japanese Bible and some Japanese National Readers.

On the 24th received a letter from mother enclosing a note from Emma. All were well at home, but there was considerable distress among our friends.

On the 26th a gentleman by the name of Nakamura came to enquire about the Gospel and as he could not speak a word of English, I had a good opportunity to see how well I could get along with the Japanese tongue alone. I felt quite satisfied with the interview, which however according to the logic of some is an indication that I did not make much of an impression on my hearer. It is said that the listeners are more deeply impressed when the speaker feels as though his effort was a failure. In the evening I wrote letters to Bessie Badger and Emma Batt.

Sunday, 27 September—Tuesday, 7 October 1902, Tokyo

On the 27th quite a sever storm swept over Tokyo, doing much damage to the houses and fields. A number of lives were lost. It being the day for us to go out to Bro. Grant's to hold meeting, we had to face the wind and rain as best we could with umberellas we had, there were no rikishas on the streets. Traffic had all ceased and the stores were closed up as tight as boxes. Out of the five umbrellas we had, three of them were broken before we arrived at the depot where we took the train for the rest of the distance. On arriving at Bro. Grant's we found them hard at work propping up the front of their house which had been loosened from its holdings by the wind. Much water had come in and they were in a general disturbed condition. In consequence of the storm and its wreckage, we held no Sunday School, but were sufficiently well settled to hold afternoon service. In the evening after returning to the hotel, I wrote another article for the "Voice" in continuation of the affirmative side of the question being discussed between myself and Mr. McCaleb. My last letter was written as a conclusion for the affirmative, but another letter from Mr. McCaleb arrived this morning.

On the afternoon of the 29th I had a very fair conversation with a Japanese friend, Mr. Tsuneda.

The following Thursday Oct. 2nd, the brethren and I went out to Apostle Grant's to have supper and the regular singing practice. When we arrived we met Messrs Mashimo and Nirayama with whom it had been decided the four brethren who had up to this time been living with me at the hotel should hereafter live. We went out to see the two places and were very well pleased with them. It was decided that Bros. Stoker and Jarvis should go to the home of Mr. Mashimo and that Bros. Caine and Hedges should go to the home of Mr. Nirayama. The date for the removal was fixed for Monday the 6th. I was asked to come and live with Prest Grant for a month or two and then it was thought that we (Elder Ensign and I) should go our to preach among the people.

Sunday the 5th. came again to "Grantsville" and held very good Sunday School and after noon meeting. I spoke in Japanese at both sessions. In the evening all the folks came over with us to have supper before we left our Japanese hotel to part and live in Japanese homes. It was perhaps the largest crowd of

Foreigners that had ever been in the hotel at one time. The landlord and landlady were greatly delighted and considered it a manifestation of good feeling which we all desired should exist.

On the following morning, we ate breakfast a little earlier than usual and packed our trunks in time to leave the hotel at about half past nine. Two hours later the brethren were nicely located in their new abodes and in the reports that they have since given speak glowingly of their new surroundings.

The change for me has been a peasant one in that I have the association of Prest Grant and the brethren and sisters who have been living with him ever since he came back from America. In fact I have been the bed fellow of the President.

Wednesday, 8 October 1902—Sunday, 12 October 1902, Tokyo

On the afternoon of the 7th Mr. Oyama came to visit us and after a chat which lasted for some time, he announced that he was thoroughly satisfied with the teachings that we advanced and desired to be baptized as he had expressed some two or three weeks before. This announcement greatly pleased us for we felt satisfied that this young man was sincere in his desire and had been diligent in the study of the Scriptures. That evening we took a little walk arund through the neighborhood to see if we could find a suitable place to perform the ordinance, but were unsuccessful. Mr. Oyama said that the following day he did not have to work and would look for a clear stream and let us know where it was.

On the morning of the 8th, he came quite early, but having just left the Post Office where he had been working all night he had not made any search. We decided to go with him in the hunt. Bro. Nakazawa acccompanind us and through his repeated inquiries we finally found a picturesque spot about two miles away from our home. Having only gone out to hunt a place, we had to return to the house and get some clothes to wear while preforming the ordinance. Mr. Oyama had dinner with us and about half past two the brethren who are living out in Japanese homes came and we all went back to the spot to witness the initiation of the third convert in Japan. The name of our new brother in Yoshiro Oyama, aged 25 years (according to Japanese figuring 26years), born in Tokyo on Nov. 11th Meiji 35.[45] The stream in which he was baptized is called [blank] President Grant performed the ordinance. At the riverside before the ordinance we sang "God moves in a Mysterious Way. Prayer by myself. Singing, "We thank thee Oh God for a Prophet.

On our return to the house we held a little meeting for the purpose of confirming Bro. Oyama a member of the church. Singing, "Guide us, Oh Thou Great Jehovah" Prayer, Elder Ensign. Singing, Now let us rejoice in the day of salvation. Remarks by Bro. Grant. He stated that it was his desire that I baptize Bro. Oyama as it had been through my efforts principally that Bro. Oyama had been led to investigate and seek the Spirit of the Lord which influence had converted his heart to believe the principles of truth that I had explained to him. But Bro. Oyama having expressed the desire to have Bro. Grant perform the ordinance, he had done so, but that I should confirm him a member of the Church. The confirmation then followed with mysefl as mouth assisted by Prest. Grant, Elders Ensign, Featherstone, Jarvis, Caine, Stoker, Hedges, and Nakazawa. This is the first person that I have ever confirmed a member of the Church and it was with unspeakable joy that I was permitted to officiate in such an ordinance. Singing, (quartet) "Truth reflects before our senses Prayer by [blank]

Bro. Oyama returned feeling well and we were indeed pleased with the labors of the day. Bro. Nakazawa manifested a fine spirit and was quite excited during the whole time to think that another of his countrymen was to join him in the fold. It was with considerable regret that we had to be conscious of the fact that our other brother, Bro. Kikuchi, was not with us and had for a long time manifested a dissatisfied spirit.

Thursday, Friday, and Saturday were rather quiet.

Sunday, 12th, was a joyous day for us all. In the afternoon meeting we enjoyed abundantly the influences of the Spirit and all who spoke, did so with considerable power. Bro. Caine bore his testimony in Japanese for the first time. Considering the fact that he has been in Japan hardly three months, his progress is something marvelous. All are doing nicely, for which I feel to thank the Lord with all my heart.

Monday, 13 October 1902—Wednesday, 22 October 1902, Tokyo/Nikko

Until the twentieth there was very little out of the ordinary happened. Bro. Hedges, while with us at "Grantsville," was taken with an attack of chills, but in the course of a day and a half entirely recovered. I received a letter from mother in which she stated that she and father had been on a trip to Colorado Springs to attend the convention of the Western Undertaker's Association, calling before they returned at Denver.

About noon on Monday, 20th, Bro. Grant, his wife, and daughter Mary decided to go to Nikko, the famous mountain resort of Japan, to spend a day or so seeing the sights which have made this place so attractive. They asked if I would not like to go along with them. I gladly accepted the offer, and in a half an hour later we were on our way.

From Uyeno Station it is just a five and three quarter hour's ride to the Nikko Station with only one change—at Utsunomiya. It was nine thirty by the time we reached the Utsunomiya Hotel. Supper was served and very much relished by us all; the trip on the train had given us, as it does nearly everyone, a strong appetite. The evening was spent in enquiring about the places of interest so that we would be prepared to use the following day to as much advantage as possible.

In the morning we went immediately to see the temples. These are considered to be the most beautiful in Japan, and indeed before we finished we felt that we had seen evidences of wonderful workmanship and architectural ability that to me is something marvelous. To attempt to describe the extent of the carvings and beautiful work displayed in the temple of Ieyasu, the first Shogun of Japan, would be folly. The yards surrounding, with there peculiar lanterns, bells, bell–houses, granite steps, Oriental gates, and a thousand other curiosities that the eye could not see in on visit; the exterior of the temples with their massive eaves, bronze trimmings all lately polished, and fantastic woodwork; the interior with its unsurpassed work in wood–carving, lacquer mountings, gold earns and sacred vessels, painted and inlaid walls, costly tapestries, all defy reproduction in words. Each temple is a large, wonderful, monument of art, which although erected in a land, but recently aroused into civilization, demonstrates beyond all question that the Japanese, of all people, are world beaters in ornamental decorating and that in their uncultured state possessed abilities that like the philosophies of the ancient sages defy all the modern products of its kind. The two principle temples of Nikko and the ones through which we went are the Ieyasu and Iemitsu, the former bearing the name of the first Shogun and the latter being named after his grandson, the third Shogun of Japan. We also went through the museum of the Ieyasu temple to see some of the implements of war and the home utensils of His Highness.

Shortly before we had dinner, Bro. Ensign, his wife, and Bros. Hedges and Caine arrived. In the afternoon Bros. Caine, Hedges, Grant, and I went up the river to a little garden that seemed to receive considerable credit for its beauty. To our great disappointment, the storm of Sept 27th had swept the garden and the houses entirely away and the men were busily engaged in digging away large banks of sand that has been piled up by the raging torrent. In the pile of sand that they were working at, at the time of our visit, they had found two of the bronze images that were in the temple which stood some distance away. On the way back we walked for a little way down the bank of the stream observing the outlines of the terrible stream of water that had gone down the river bed during the same storm that swept over Tokyo last month. Trees, telephone poles, houses, and anything that happened to be in reach of the swollen stream were like the little garden entirely destroyed.

Leaving the stream we went up a little revine on the left to what is known as the Deer Farm. After a long walk up a rough path we came to the gate and on enquiring of the people living in a little broken down house by the fence if we could go in and see the deer, found that there were only five left and judging from the extent of the canyon that was set apart as a deer reserve, we might spend a whole month looking for the deer and never see them. This trip, then, also proved to be a fruitless one, but we could say that we had been to the places which were so attractive to tourists in years past.

We retired early, and arose about seven o'clock. We had breakfast together. Bros. Caine, Hedges and myself, according to the arrangement of the night before, set out to see what is know as the "Kirifuri no taki" (Mistfalling Cascade). The distance was mapped out as three miles and rather an uphill climb. By nine fifteen we were seated on the rocks at the foot of the falls, admiring their beauty. To one who has been reared in the centre of the Rockies such a scene does not partake of the wonderful beauty that is ascribed to it by those who have live in lands where mountains are an unknown pleasure, but even to me the sigh was an attractive one, well repaying the hard walk it required to reach it. An ordinary mountain stream falling from a highth of perhaps one hundred and fifty feet in terraced form into a narrow gorge that cuts through the perpendicular walls on each side. A few stones were gathered as a souvenir of this pretty little spot.

As we climbed over the rocks on our homeward journey we occasionally looked back to catch a glimp of the falling stream and the beautiful autumn leaves that were to be seen in all their glory springing out from every crevice of the stony walls. The path led directly up from the stream to the ridge above from where the sight was almost as enchanting as at the bank below.

The two companions who were with me not having seen the temples, I took them to see the sights which I, with the Grant family, had seen the day before. We got back to the hotel in just four hours and a half from the time we left, making a record for time that has never been equaled by any of the foreigners that have ever been to Nikko before.

After dinner we took rikishas to the next station (Imaichi). The reason for this being that the road led through a long grove of Cryptomeria trees which was so famous that we desired to see it and enjoy the ride of about five miles by rikisha through them. It was a lovely trip. The storm which had done so much damage in Nikko had had its effect upon the trees—hundreds of them were blown down or broken off by the severe wind.

It was nearly eleven when we reached home. The outing was a delightful one and thoroughly appreciated by us all. There was a letter from Miss Maud Baggarly waiting for me when I got in the house. There was also a picture of mother taken while she was in Colorado attending the Western Funeral Director's Association's Convention.

Thursday, 23 October 1902—Friday, 31 October 1902, Tokyo

Our hearts were made glad on the evening of 23rd by the action of our young brother in the Church who was baptized so recently—Yoshiro Oyama. He came, and with one of the loveliest spirits that we have seen manifested since coming to Japan paid one yen and thirty sen as the tithing[46] of his months wages; the amount of his wage being thirteen yen a month. He said that he felt bad that his wages were not larger so that he could pay a larger tithing and that he took great delight in coming to our home to leave the money which the Lord has said should be given into His storehouse. As Prest. Grant took Bro. Oyama by the hand to pronounce a blessing upon him the tears were seen standing in his eyes. Nor was he the only one affected by the manifestation of Bro. Oyama's faith, for I could have wept for joy as my heart was filled to the brim in thanksgiving to the Lord for the joy He had caused to this day come to our hearts and a silent prayer went up from my heart to heaven in behalf of my young Japanese brother.

On the 24th the brethren living in the Japanese homes came to spend the afternoon and evening with us. We had a pleasant time. The lesson in Japanese which we received from Bro. Nakazawa was extremely interesting on account of the free discussion of the subjects carried on by all.

Sunday, the Sabbath School was a great success. The subject considered was "The Transgression and the Fall." In the afternoon we had a good spirited meeting. All those who spoke said something in Japanese except Bros. Grant and Jarvis. Lately we have pertaken to a great extent of the Spirit of the Lord during our afternnon meetings.

Tuesday the 28th, went with Bro. Nakazawa to see a church building spoken of by our Japanese acquaintence, MR. Koshiishi, in which he says a number of Christian natives hold meetings but have no special preacher so were anxious to have some of us come and preach "Mormonism" to them. After inquiring around in the neighborhood concerning the place and the time of the meetings and after investigating another matter spoken of by our friend we found that the facts were so different to what he had reported that we did not conclude to make any promises concerning preaching in a place where we were not sure but what we would be tramping on forbidden ground.

Wednesday evening Sister Featherstone was taken with severe pains in the abdomen and for some hours suffered intensely. We administered to her twice and before ten o'clock she had obtained some relief, so we retired the next morning finding her entirely free from pain but a little weak. By Friday she was up and around again. Friday morning all the soldiers in the capitol were out on parade on the big square in front of our place. The sight was and inpressive one. The forces of infintry, cavalry, and artillery were out in full blast; the united forces being about from 15,000 to 20,000 men. The occasion was a practice drill for the grand review of troops by the Emperor to be held on the 3rd of Nov. Thursday evening I wrote a letter to father including a description of the trip to Nikko which I had written a day or two before.

As will be noticed by the references made to the matter in the preceding pages of this journal that I have been carrying on a discussion with a gentleman by the name of J. M. McCaleb, as to the marriage relations of Moses. The discussion having been finished on the 11 inst. I will record a copy in full; the articles following in the regular order as they appeared in "The Voice." (The newspaper publishing the discussion). . . .

Saturday, 1 November 1902—Friday, 7 November 1902, Tokyo

Saturday was a day of regular weekly housecleaning. My part being the lamps, I spent much of the morning giving them a general polishing. IN the afternoon I found plenty of time to study up something to say on the following day, it being Sunday and a day of fasting and prayer.

There was an excellent spirit present at both of our meetings. As usual the Sabboth School was turned into a testimony meeting. In the afternoon meeting we sang a song in Japanese, the first ever sung at the services of the Latter–day Saints, in Japan. It was not one of our own, nor one that we were before familiar with, but being arranged to the tune of the "doxology"[47] we enquired into its meaning and found that there was nothing objectionable in the meaning and decided to sing it. Bro. Ensign prophesied that when our songs were translated and sung in the Japanese language so that the people could understand them that we would make friends much faster and the interest in the Gospel would increase.

Monday was the birthday of the Mikado and there was supposed to be a review of troops on the large parade ground in front of our home, but Sunday having been a very wet day there was considerable mud and the Emperor was like all of his subjects—afraid to come out in bad weather for fear he would get his feet wet. At noon a company of artillery drove up and fired one hundred charges in honor of the 50th year of the Soverign. We all had a holliday, doing nothing but play and tell jokes to pass the time.

The next day was a day of study.

Wednesday I went out to buy some bedding for myself. It had been discovered that the bed in which Bro. Grant and I were sleeping was too small for two and the change was suggested for the comfort of us both, tho indeed I have no objections to having an Apostle as a bedfellow.

Thursday I went in the morning to visit Mr. Nirayama and his wife. Two of the brethren have been living at this man's house for nearly two months and I had not been once to see them, so I felt it a duty to call on them and at the same time present my compliments to the family who had treated them and all the rest of us with the greatest respect and friendly consideration. We went over to a neighboring public garden to see the chrysanthemums which at this season of the year are so beautiful. This is the national flower of Japan and indeed the profonsion of their growth is something wonderful. About this time last year Bro. Grant and I, as will be seen by referring to my journal of about this time, went to one of the most famous exhibits of these frwers that is held in Japan. In the afternoon Bro. Grant and all the other folks together with Miss Mashimo came to Mr. Nirayama's and we went out to Asakusa Park to see the exhibition at that place, it having been reported to us that it was worth seeing. The one of last year was so superior to this one that I was not at all satisfied with the display and would have been disappointed with the trip had it not been for the great number of wild animals and birds on exhibition at the same place.

The weekly lesson in which we all participate was held Friday afternoon and we had a very good time discussing the rules governing the construction of the passive forms in Japanese. This is about as hard a part of the language to be able to use successfully as any that has yet come before us.

In the evening we had an enjoyable time together singing songs. **During the week I translated in**

connection with Bro. Nakazawa "We Thank Thee Oh God for a Prophet," and this evening we practiced the first verse as it has been set to music by Bro. Ensign. In the evening I sent a letter home to mother. A little later the mail from America arrived bringing me a letter from Florence Grant. During the week I received also a letter from father and a photograph of Sister Lizzie Thomas.

Saturday, 8 November 1902—Thursday, 20 November 1902, Tokyo

Our meeting on Sunday 9th was a very dry one indeed; no one seemed inclined to speak and the spirit was cold. This was a great change after the lovely spirited meetings that had up to that time followed in regular succession.

On Tuesday the 11th Bro. Oyama came to attend a sort of religion class which we have organized for the purpose of instructing our brethren more fully in regard to the Gospel, so that they will be able to defend its principles when opposed by their friends and enemies. The spirit of the Lord was upon me as I talked with them regarding the prophesies that spoke of the coming forth of the Book of Mormon in the latter–days, and they (Bro. Nakazawa was also present) seemed to pertake of the same spirit for their faces lighted with delight at the acquirement of new knowledge concerning the Truth they had received. As a first meeting of its kind it was truly a great success.

During the remainder of the week there was very little of interest. An occasional visitor was all that broke the monotony of continual study. **One feature of my studies that is perhaps worth recording in this journal is that the translation of the good old hymn, "We thank Thee, O God, for a Prophet" was finished and that to in a way that I felt quite pleased with, and sure of its correctness. On the following Sunday, 16th, we sang the entire song for the first time. This it the first Mormon hymn that had ever been sung in Japanese and the first time God's servants ever lifted their voices in praise to Him using the Japanese language to express ther praise that such an inspired hymn contains.** Sad to say, the meeting was a duplicate of the one pervious—no spirit and very few speakers. The Sunday School held in the morning was a very great success, the subject under discussion being "The Atonement." A slight change has taken place in the manner of conduction the School. Instead, as heretofore, of assigning lessons from Bro. Talmage's book we consider the lessons as marked out in the leaflets embracing the same topics as those in the book.

On the 13th or 14th a letter was received by Bro. Grant from Mr. Takahashi in which Mr. Takahashi proposed certain things to Prest. Grant concerning what he thought would be for the welfare of the mission. The style of the letter was selfish and a spirit accompanied it that made us feel like rejecting the propositions made, and Bro. Grant wrote him to that effect. On Sunday or Monday an answer was received that caused doubts to arise in our hearts as to the true friendship of this man. His words were not only insulting but revealed that he was mad because we would not submit to be led by him. The true motives prompting men to profess friendship to the Work of the Lord are always revealed to us sooner or later, and in this instance we are truly grateful to have revealed to us by the man's own words, the true sentiments of his heart towards us. Monday 17th, I wrote letters to Aunt Clara, Bishop Empey, and Lizzie Thomas.

In Tuesday's mail I received letters form Allan Howard, Bishop Empey, mother, and Bessie Badger. All the news was encouraging, everyone being well at home.

Thursday afternoon the second session of the Religion Class was held. Bro. Oyama and Bro. Nakazawa being present. The topic discussed was "Prophesies concerning the Work of God in the latter days." After the regular lesson was over, Bro. Oyama asked questions concerning some points in our Articles of Faith concerning some points not quite clear to him and it took till after dark to get him set right on the matter or two which he had been unable to understand.

Friday, 21 November 1902—Thursday, 27 November 1902, Tokyo

Friday the brethren were all at "Grantsville" for the purpose of taking their regular bath and lesson in Japanese. It is very inconvenient for them to have to come over here twice a week for the purpose of getting a bath but there are no accommodations at the places in which they are living and it is considered to be an improper thing for the Elders to go to the public bath–houses where sights of an unelevating character are far too common.

Saturday, Sister Ensign, Sister Mary Grant, Bros. Featherstone and Ensign, and I went to Yokohama to get some things to send home to our folks for Christmas. We were gone all day and found it very difficult to find just what we wanted. It is remarkable how few things there are in this land typical of the country and at the same time suitable to send home by the mail.

Sunday, there was an excellent spirit in our midst all day. The Sunday School and afternoon meeting were a great success. I have never enjoyed the Spirit of the Lord more in my life than I did when speaking in the meeting and it seemed that it required no effort at all to speak what I wanted to in the native language of the people. The comparison between the feelings that possess a person when they are speaking under the influence of the Spirit and when they are relying on themselves is truly marvelous. Surely God's power is great and without it as a help and stay, man can accomplish nothing in the missionary field.

Monday, I went with Bro. and Sister Featherstone to the bazar in Uyeno Park to see if we could find anything in the way of Christmas presents for our fathers, but we were unsuccessful. On the way back, we called at the Ginza and purchased a few things. I bought a vase for Sister Grant and a coffee cup and saucer for Mary. There were many other pretty things that I saw and wanted to buy but did not have any money with me. Judging from the great amount of secrecy that is going on among us there will be quite an exchange of presents at Christmas time. Rec'd a letter from Sister Maud Badgerly containing a short note from mother. All is well at home.

Tuesday evening Bro. Oyama called and we held a session of the Religions Class. The subject this time was Polygamy. The brethren have been asked a great many questions about this subject and being unable to answer all of them successfully, wanted to know what to say when brought in contact with the many queries that the enemies of the Latter–day Saints seem so prone to ask about this doctrine which was practiced by our fathers. The session was quite interesting and I believe profitable.

Wednesday was a day of preparation for Thanksgiving and an elaborate meal.

Thursday being Thanksgiving we celebrated it in true American style. Two turkeys graced the table and we were all filled to the brim ere we were aware of the fact that there was little left. Indeed how could there be when twelve hungry people, having forgone the eating of breakfast so as to be well prepared to do justice to the long expected dinner, sat around the board and suddenly came to a realization of the fact that, although they were in Japan, they were true Americans and should do perfect justice to the biggest feast in the list of Yankee customs.

After the meal we spent a very pleasant evening chatting and playing games. As the mail left for America the following day we had to see that our things were in the Post Office that evening so we sent some of our packages to the main Post Office by Bro. and Sister Grant and in the evening sent more to the branch office to go on the same boat. I sent a doily to mother, a card case to aunt Hattie, Two purses to Samuel, a fan each to my sisters Ruth, Lisadore and Margaret.

Friday, 28 November 1902—Friday, 26 December 1902, Tokyo

During this period of about one month there has been little happen out of the ordinary routine. On the 2nd of December I sent some more things home to the folks for Christmas, remembering this time father, Aunt Clara, Emma, and Sister Baggarly. Also sent season's greetings to Florence Grant and Bessie Badger.

We have had the privilege of meeting some new people and telling them a little about the Gospel. A captian in the army has been quite a regular caller for the last two weeks and while his motive seems to be to get the chance to talk in English, yet we have had great pleasure in talking to him and he makes himself so much at home that we find in no trouble at all to entertain him. Most of the natives who call to see us are very hard to entertain and it seems very dry and uninteresting when they are here. Very often in trying to explain the Gospel to the people in their own tongue, I have found that there are those who consider the poor words we use too uninteresting to listen to. But I rejoice that there are such people for their criticism of my efforts tend to keep me humble and not forget that I am dependent upon the Lord for all the good I can do in this land and that it is His Spirit and not the words of men that interest and convert others.

On the night of Dec. 24th we all went to Yokohama to attend a party given by Mrs. Bagnell. Her daughter had crossed the Pacific on the same boat that brought the last company of "Mormons" from America and became quite friendly during the trip. The house was beautifully decorated for the winter holidays and there was a beautiful Christmas tree in the parlor laden with presents for all those invited. We stayed to dinner but the rest of the pary returned early. We were entertained mostly by productions on the phonograph. The open frank manner of the hostess made us feel perfectly at home. When we reached Tokyo, it was after twelve and by the time we got home it was after one Christmas Morning. We stayed up till three putting the presents on the tree which we had purchased and decorated for the occasion.

Next morning we did not get up till late, but before doing anything else we assembled in the din-ing–room and took the presents off the tree. It was a glorious Christmas for the "colony." Every one had a present for his brothers and sisters, the result being that I received more presents than I ever did before in my life. A gold watch charm from Prest. and Sister Grant, two silk handkerchiefs from Bro. and Sister Ensign, a pair of silver cuff–buttons from Bro. and Sister Featherstone. A gold stick pin with a set pear from Bros. Caine, Hedges, Jarvis, and Stoker, a procket–book from Mary, numerous things from my Japanese brethren and friends, and, in the box which arrived from dear ones in America, I found hand-kerchiefs, ties, money, Christmas cards, book–marks with my name engraved thereon, and two boxes of candy. All the rest of the party fared about as well as I, so there was happiness in every heart. Many of our Japanese friends called to see the Christmas tree and were treated to candy, nuts, and something else good to eat and did not leave till every one had received a present by which to remember the occasion. We espe-cially remembered our brethren who had been baptized into the church and they also seemed very glad to present us with tokens suitable to the occasion. Bro. Kikuchi whose spirit has become cold and has failed to attend to his duties for many months, did not come in spite of the fact that I called at his place and left him a special invitation. We however remembered him and his wife by hanging their presents on the tree with the rest, and on Saturday I will take them to him and if possible have a chat with him concerning his neglect of duty.

Saturday, 27 December 1902—Wednesday, 31 December 1902, Tokyo

Saturday evening I went to visit Bro. Kikuchi and take the presents which we intended to give him on Christmas but he did not come to receive them. I hoped also to have a talk with him in the hopes of arousing him to a realization of the duties resting upon him as an elder in the Church but in this I was disappointed, for he was absent and I had to leave the presents with the servants who were taking charge of the place.

Sunday being the last of the old year all who spoke seemed to have the spirit of thanksgiving for the many blessings the Lord had poured out upon them during the year and expressed the desire to be able to accomplish much for the success of the work in this land during the year 1903. I spent the day in fasting and prayer to the Lord.

Monday, Tuesday, and Wednesday were spent in study. Wednesday Bro. Featherstone and I sit up to see the old year out and the new year in. According to the customs of this land none of the Japanese ever go to bed before the dawn of the New Year, for say they, "One who goes to bed on the night of Dec. 31st, will become grey headed at an early age." Just at midnight we went into the apartments of our Japanese brother and surprised him with the first congratulations of 1903. We stayed in his room for an hour and together with his wife we played a game which they say is specially dedicated to New Year's Day.

Notes

1. *Sake.* Although often referred to as rice wine, *sake* is actually fermented rice beer native to Japan.
2. Rods. A unit of square measure, 30 ¾ square yards.
3. Alma O. Taylor, "Some Features of Japanese Life," *Improvement Era* (April 1902): 449–55.

4. Vision of the Tree of Life: See 1 Nephi 8 and 11.

5. A portion of Elder John W. Taylor's letter read:

> My beloved brethren in far off Japan, my soul is filled with unspeakable joy as I contemplate the results of unlocking the doors of another nation, through the keys of the Holy Priesthood, and apostleship. For our Heavenly Father has given unto me a testimony, that in His own due time, it will be the opening wedge for the salvation of tens and hundreds of thousands of that race of people, both of the living and of the dead. The Lord will confound your enemies, He will open the mouths of the young elders and if their faith is perfect they shall speak by the convincing power of the Lord. He will send His angels before your face, and from this time forward His Divine Spirit will rest upon the people. They will see you in vision and when you speak, they will know the voice of the good shepherd. The dark cloud of superstition, the Lord will cause to raise and pass away, and the pure light of eternal truth will shine forth upon their understandings, for the hour is at hand when the Lord will speak unto the heathen nations, and they will break down their images, and burn them up and worship them no more. I feel to say to you my beloved brethren, "Peace be unto you all. Yea! your souls shall be filled with joy and thanksgiving. Your lives shall be spared and you will return home again to the land of Zion, bringing your sheaves with you.

Found under Alma O. Taylor, Journal for this date; John W. Taylor to Heber J. Grant, 18 December 1901, letter.

6. B. H. Roberts, *The Life of John Taylor, Third President of The Church of Jesus Christ of Latter-day Saints* (Salt Lake City: George Q. Cannon & Sons, 1892).

7. Angus M. Cannon first met Itō Hirobumi in the spring of 1871 at Ogden, Utah, and traveled with him onboard a Union Pacific train to Omaha, Nebraska, when he was traveling as a business manager of the *Deseret News.* Cannon met Itō again when Itō and a large Japanese government delegation spent some time in Salt Lake City in 1872. "Opening of a Mission in Japan," *Deseret News,* 6 April and 19 June 1901.

8. *Japan and America* (New York: H. Hoshi, 1901–3).

9. Uchida Yuu [Akira], *Morumon Shuu* (Tokyo: Bunmeidō, 1902). See Frederick R. Brady, "Two Meiji Scholars Introduce the Mormons to Japan," *BYU Studies* 23 (Spring 1983): 172.

10. Emperor Kōmei.

11. Shintōism. "(Japanese, 'the way of the gods'), Japanese cult and religion, originating in prehistoric times, and occupying an important national position for long periods in the history of Japan, particularly in recent times. During its early period, the body of religious belief and practice called Shinto was without a name and had no fixed dogma, moral precepts, or sacred writings. Worship centered on a vast pantheon of spirits, or *kami,* mainly divinities personifying aspects of the natural world, such as the sky, the earth, heavenly bodies, and storms. Rites included prayers of thanksgiving; offerings of valuables, such as swords and armor and, especially, cloth; and ablutionary purification from crime and defilement." "Shinto," *Microsoft Encarta 98 Encyclopedia.*

12. Bromo-seltzer. A dose of a proprietary effervescent headache remedy and antacid.

13. *Tegami.* A letter.

14. *Kisoba.* Buckwheat noodles.

15. Grub Box. Slang for stomach.

16. Brandy. For medicinal purposes.

17. Should be Takahashi (Gōrō).

18. James E. Talmage, *The Articles of Faith* (Salt Lake City: Deseret Sunday School Union, 1879).

19. According to the second Article of Faith, while "the transgression of Adam and Eve brought death into the world and made all mortals subject to temptation, suffering, and weakness, it denies that any culpability is automatically transmitted to Adam and Eve's offspring. All mortals commit sin, but they will be punished 'for their own sins, and not for Adam's transgression.'" Byron R. Merrill, "Original Sin," *Encyclopedia of Mormonism,* 3:1052.

20. Utah Sugar Company. Led by David Eccles, the Utah Sugar Company became the Utah-Idaho Sugar Beet Company. See Leonard Arrington, *History of the Utah-Idaho Sugar Beet Company* (Logan: Utah State University Press, 1973).

21. Jaredites. A group of people named for their original leader, Jared. They date back to the "great tower" mentioned in the Old Testament built near Mesopotamia. Like the family of Lehi, the Jaredites where led by God to the New World, where they established a major civilization. Eventually, they destroyed themselves by war between 600 and 300 B.C., Morgan W. Tanner, "Jaredites," *Encyclopedia of Mormonism,* 2:717.

22. Baptism. "The fourth article of faith of The Church of Jesus Christ of Latter-day Saints declares that 'baptism by immersion for the remission of sins' is one of the 'first principles and ordinances of the Gospel.' Latter-day Saints believe, as do many Christians, that baptism is an essential initiatory ordinance for all persons who are joining the Church, as it admits them to Christ's church on earth (John 3:3–5; D&C 20:37, 68–74)." Carl S. Hawkins, "Baptism," *Encyclopedia of Mormonism,* 1:92.

23. Aaronic Priesthood. The Church of Jesus Christ of Latter-day Saints recognizes two priesthood divisions: the Aaronic and the Melchizedek. The lesser Aaronic Priesthood "holds the keys [governing or delegating authority] of the ministering of angels, and of the gospel of repentance, and of baptism by immersion for the remission of sins" (D&C 13). By its authority, one can teach faith and repentance, and baptize. Verdon W. Ballantyne, "Aaronic Priesthood," *Encyclopedia of Mormonism,* 1:1–2.

24. Melchizedek Priesthood. The Melchizedek Priesthood is the authority and power to act in the name of Jesus Christ. Jae R. Ballif, "Melchizedek Priesthood," *Encyclopedia of Mormonism,* 2:882.

25. *Sanpan.* A small boat used for ferrying.

26. Confirmation Ordinance. "Two ordinances are required for admission to Church membership. The first is baptism. The second, confirmation, is performed shortly following baptism and is a type of priesthood blessing. Two or more men who hold the Melchizedek Priesthood place their hands on the head of the person who has been baptized and, with one of the men serving as voice, the baptized person is confirmed a member of the Church and given the gift of the Holy Ghost. Additional

words of counsel or admonition are then expressed according to spiritual promptings." Bruce B. Clark, "Blessings," *Encyclopedia of Mormonism*, 1:129.

27. Should be Takahashi (Gōrō).

28. Alma O. Taylor, "Some Features of Japanese Life, " *Improvement Era* (April 1902): 449–55.

29. Patriarchal Blessing. A special blessing given by ordained patriarchs to individual members of the Church. The blessing provides guidance, warning, encouragement, and reassurance to its recipient. Bruce B. Clark, "Blessings," *Encyclopedia of Mormonism*, 1:129–30.

30. Gift of Tongues. A gift of the Spirit often given to servants of the Lord to help learn foreign languages. H. George Bickerstaff, "Gifts of the Spirit," *Encyclopedia of Mormonism*, 2:545.

31. O.S.L. Oregon Short Line Railroad.

32. *Semmon Gakko*. A specialty or trade school.

33. Atonement. "The Atonement of Jesus Christ is the foreordained but voluntary act of the Only Begotten Son of God. He offered his life, including his innocent body, blood, and spiritual anguish as a redeeming ransom (1) for the effect of the Fall of Adam upon all mankind and (2) for the personal sins of all who repent, from Adam to the end of the world. Latter-day Saints believe this is the central fact, the crucial foundation, the chief doctrine, and the greatest expression of divine love in the Plan of Salvation." Jeffrey R. Holland, "Atonement of Jesus Christ," *Encyclopedia of Mormonism*, 1:82–3.

34. Heber J. Grant's wife Huldah Augusta Grant.

35. Heber J. Grant's daughter, Mary Grant. While in Japan, young Mary kept a regular journal of her experiences. See Mary Grant Judd Journals, Church Archives.

36. King James Version of the Bible. "The books of the Bible were originally written in Hebrew, Aramaic, or Greek. No original biblical manuscripts exist today, but they were copied and translated into many languages in antiquity. Many early papyri and parchments have survived. From those records, numerous modern translations have been made. From 1604 to 1611, some fifty-four scholars worked to produce the KJV of the Bible. . . . In an attempt to heal differences between Anglicans and Puritans, King James I appointed a body of scholars to produce a version of the Bible to be authorized for use in the English churches. . . . The resulting King James Version was published in 1611." D. Kelly Ogden, "Bible," *Encyclopedia of Mormonism*, 1:109.

37. Louis A. Kelsch, *A Practical Reference to Scriptural Passages on the Doctrines of the Gospel* (Salt Lake City: s.n., c.1899).

38. *Nippon Yūsen Kaisha*. Popularly know as the NYK line, this was the first modern maritime shipping company in Japan. It was originally part of the Mitsubishi Mail Steamship Company, created in 1870. Fifteen years later, the company merged with the Kyōdō Un'yu to become Nippon Yūsen. In 1893, NYK opened the first of its long-distance routes, the Bombay line, and in 1896 opened routes to Europe, the United States, and Australia." "Nippon Yūsen Kaisha," *Japan: An Illustrated Encyclopedia*, 2 vols. (Tokyo: Kodansha, 1993), 1097.

39. Puck. Likely Robin Goodfellow; a mischievous sprite in English folklore.

40. Crown Prince. A hereditary member of the Japanese Imperial family.

41. Elder Kelsch was honorably released because both he and the Church's leaders in Salt Lake City believed he could not learn Japanese.

42. Articles of Faith. "In 1842, in response to a specific request from John Wentworth (editor of the Chicago Democrat), Joseph Smith sent a succinct overview of his own religious experiences and the History of the Church over which he presided. At the end of the historical sketch, he appended a list summarizing the 'faith of the Latter-day Saints.' Later titled 'Articles of Faith,' these thirteen items were first published in the Nauvoo Times and Seasons in March 1842 and were later included in the 1851 British Mission pamphlet The Pearl of Great Price, compiled by Elder Franklin D. Richards. . . . The Articles of Faith do not constitute a summation of all LDS beliefs, and they are not a creed in the traditional Christian sense, but they do provide a useful authoritative summary of fundamental LDS scriptures and beliefs." David J. Whittaker, "Articles of Faith," *Encyclopedia of Mormonism*, 1:67.

43. Lumbago. Pain in the lower, or lumbar, region of the back or loins.

44. *Geta*. Wooden clogs.

45. 11 November 1878.

46. Tithing. The principle of tithing was revealed to the Prophet Joseph Smith. The Lord stated that all members should voluntarily pay "one-tenth of all their interest [increase] annually; and this shall be a standing law unto them forever" (D&C 119:4). Howard D. Swainston, "Tithing," *Encyclopedia of Mormonism*, 4:1480–81.

47. Doxology. A hymn often sung by the Latter-day Saints around the turn of the twentieth century: "Praise God from whom all blessings flow; / Praise Him, all creatures here below; / Praise Him above, ye heavenly host, / Praise Father, Son and Holy Ghost."

Chapter 7

Alma O. Taylor Journal, 1903

Thursday, 1 January 1903—Friday, 2 January 1903, Tokyo

The following day we had a number of Japanese friends call on us leaving their best wishes for our welfare during the coming twelve months. About noon the four brethren living in Japanese homes came and towards one o'clock we ate the first meal of the New Year. The day closed with some games in the evening which lasted till about eleven. This finished the celebration of the winter holidays as far as we were concerned, but according to the customs of the natives the festivities last till the 7th.

The contrast between the events of this Christmas and New Years to the same time last year may be to the same time lasting seen by referring to the account given of the former in my journal of a year ago. The presence of four of the sisters truly made it pleasant for all as it was due to their skill that we had good old time food to eat and they eclipsed the men entirely in making amusement for the colony. We are truly in comfortable surroundings in this land. Everything that the heart could long for is all around us. The love which exists to a great degree in every heart robs the absence of blood-relations of all power to produce home-sickness or blues. I hope the comforts are not hindering us from receiving the blessings promised when we left our homes. It is said that the missionaries who have to endure hardships get nearer to the Lord and receive more of His direct administrations than those who, morning, noon, and night, have plenty to eat, good clothes to wear, and comfortable beds and fires to keep them warm. If, therefore, the comforts that we have are hedging up the way, then I would like to exchange them for the hardships of missionary life, for I have not come to this land to seek rest and comforts for myself, but to tell the inhabitants of the land to turn from their idols unto the living God and have faith in His son Jesus Christ whose atonement saves those who obey the teachings of Eternal Life. But the Lord knows the feelings in the hearts of all those in this vineyard and we rely upon Him for assistance and direction when we shall do this and that instead of going blindly forth without consulting Him.

Friday we had a lesson in Japanese. Sister Grant acting as teacher. In the evening I wrote a letter to the Bishop.[1] The mail of the night before had brought me a letter from him containing five dollars as a Christmas gift. I also received a letter from father telling of the trip he took to Mexico and Arizona, which occupied the last of Nov. and until the 8th of Dec.

Saturday, 3 January 1903—Sunday, 8 February 1903, Tokyo

During this month there has been considerable trouble in the camps. It has all been caused over the failure of the rikisha-man to present his compliments according to the customs of Japan to our Brother (Nakazawa) who is living in part of our house. In trying to arrange the unpleasantness existing between these two we found ourselves severely criticized by other friends who thought we were acting unwise in taking the part of a rikisha-man and treating him with the same amount of respect and consideration that we showed to the Japanese friends and fellow believers with whom we are surrounded.

We being Americans and not accustomed to making distinction between the rich and the poor, high and low could not see wherein we were breaking any rules of civility by treating the servants around the house with that respect which we had been taught from childhood was due to even the lowest of our fellows. But according to the social rules of this land we have learned that we must, in order to retain the respect of the friends who have called upon us and who may call in the future, speak to the servants in terms that will tend to constantly remind them of their inferiority and unfortunate position in life. And, as repulsive as it may be to us to employ impolite words and phrases to the servants, yet it is absolutely essential to do so in order to be polite to those of higher rank. We are in Japan, and so far as the religion which we have come to preach will permit we must follow the customs of Japan, and this in obedience to the counsel of Prest. Lund.

Another disagreeable event that has risen is the lies one of our brethren has been telling to his fellow believer.[2] It required considerable counsel and earnest talking to reconcile the offended party and so peculiar are the emotions of the Japanese heart that it hard to tell when they have truly forgiven anyone who, perhaps unwittingly, offended them by word or action.

A number of letters have been received from relatives and friends and I have written about a half a dozen to that many of my correspondents.

Sunday Feb. 8th we had a very fine day in our Sunday School and afternoon meeting. The spirit was distinct in the meeting and everyone who spoke felt it to a degree that has seldom been experienced in this land.

Sunday, 9 February 1903—Wednesday, 19 March 1903, Tokyo

The principle subject that has occupied our attention during this time has been the construction of a tract introducing us to the people and giving them an idea of the message we have to deliver to them. Feb. 20th, after we had finished our regular lesson in Japanese and eaten supper, we had a council meeting to consider a suggestion made by me, that as we had completed the consideration of the text book on Japanese that we prepare to begin regular missionary labor. This I felt was the proper time for us to break away from the former routine of study and prepare to go out among the people and begin to labor in our feeble way for the spread of the Gospel. The decision of the meeting was, that after a review of the book just completed that missionary work should be begun. This review requiring a month or more it was thought well that the brethren who were living in Japanese homes should move to headquarters on March 5th; It being thought also that while we were all together we could practice singing and decide upon any literature that we would need in going out among the people.

On the fifth of March all the brethren came to headquarters and have been here till the present. The opinions as to what would be a good topic for the first tract were varied so at the suggestion of Prest. Grant we all wrote what we felt was proper to present as an introduction to the Gospel. The result was that many fine ideas were brought out but no one tract seemed to satisfy all. After repeated considerations, however, we finally decided that the first tract should contain no particular reference to any of the doctrines that we teach or a connected list of events in our Church's history but rather an introduction for ourselves and a general remark about our message and its importance. Consequently, altho, Bro. Featherstone and myself were appointed to write an outline of our history and a statement of our doctrines as brot out in all the essays written by the brethren, yet it was finally decided that these were not just the things we wanted for the first tract. On the evening of the 19th we listened to the final reading of the manuscript decided upon the authorship of which belongs to President Grant.

I neglected to record that at the meeting in which it was decided that we should prepare to go out the following appointments were made:—Prest. Grant and myself to remain at headquarters, Bros. Ensign and Caine to be companions in whatever field they might be called to labor, Bros. Featherstone and Hedges, and Bros. Jarvis and Stoker to be comp.

Wednesday March 11th., we having fasted from the evening before held a meeting in the afternoon for the purpose of administering[3] to Bro. Stoker who a little over a week before had sprained his ankle and in spite of the care and attention he gave to it did not recover. About three o'clock the meeting convened. After singing and prayer Bro. Grant, Caine, and Jarvis said a few words. Elder Ensign then anointed Bro. Stoker's foot and head with oil. Prest. Grant was mouth in the confirmation. Bro. Stoker felt the power of the Lord and after the administration stood up on his weak ankle. We also administered to Elder Ensign who had been troubled with a pain in his abdomen. Bro. Nakazawa was present and received a testimony that God does in very deed give power to his servants to call down blessings from heaven. I completed about March 1st the translation of the first chapter of Mr. Fukahashi's[4] book a work assigned to me by Prest

Thursday, 20 March 1903—Wednesday, 8 April 1903, Tokyo

The most important work occupying my time has been the translation of the second chapter of Mr. Takahashi's book, which I completed about April 4th.; and the translation of the tract, written by Prest. Grant, into Japanese. After I had completed this tract, I presented it to Bro. Oyama for him to criticize and after that, to be sure that no mistakes creep in, I had Mr. Takahashi go over it with me and make any suggestions that he might see fit to give. The afternoon chosen for this work was Monday April 6th, the seventy third anniversary of the organization of the Church.[5] I felt very much encouraged with the effort I had made to translate the tract as the criticisms were few and not of a very sever nature. I give the Lord the credit and pray for His continued blessings to enable me to speak and write intelligently to the people concerning the Gospel.

On the evening of the 6th., we held a meeting in which it was decided that the brethren prepare to leave for their fields of labor on the following Monday. This decision, however, was conditioned upon the possibility of getting a hall here in Tokyo in which to hold a meeting for the purpose of advertising ourselves before the brethren go out. it being thought wise for them to wait a day or two longer if we could get a suitable place to preach within a week or ten days.

The tract being completed and translated, it is now in the hands of Mr. Takahashi who is preparing it for the printer. Prest. Grant went to Yokohama on the 8th and ordered two thousand published in English for the purpose of distributing them to those who can speak English and as a test of the ability of the printer to do satisfactory work.

On the morning of March 28th Bro. Nakazawa moved from here to his former home in Negishi, Shitaya Ku, Tokyo. A little prior to his move he seemed to manifest one of the old disagreeable spirits and in talking to Bro. Oyama evidently told him something that grieved Bro. Oyama very much and excited his suspicions regarding the honesty of the Elders. This resulted in receiving a letter from Bro. Oyama in which he stated that he would leave the Church, but Bro. Grant called on him and prevailed upon him to come and have a talk with us and Bro. Nakazawa with the view to finding out what was the cause of his action. The result was that the mission was once more restored to apparent peace and Bro. Nakazawa manifested a nice spirit on the day of his removal. I and some of the others have been out to visit him in his present home.

On the evening of March 27th., all except me went to an entertainment given by the Japan-India Club at Kanda, Tokyo. Elder Ensign sang a solo for them and the papers of the following day gave him very favorable mention; laying stress on the fact that he was a Mormon with a musical talent without rival in Japan. This association with the Indians has proved very pleasing from the fact that they have been to see us many times since and they speak very intelligently on religious matters.

A friend, Miss. Baghell, from Yokohama, was a guest at headquarters from March 26th to 29th.

March 23rd went to Yokohama for the purpose of buying a wedding present for my brother and his girl who according to the news from home are to be married sometime between the middle of April and early part of May.

Thursday, 9 April 1903—Wednesday, 22 April 1903, Tokyo

Through the assistance of Mr. Hirai we were able to procure the hall known as the "Kinkikwan" located in Kanda district for the purpose of holding a meeting there on the night of the 18th. Prest. Grant made application for the Y.M.C.A. hall in the same district and received the promise that he could have it but on the following day a letter came stating that they were very sorry that they would have to cancel the agreement, and when asked for a reason stated that they were not aware of the church to which we belonged; Pres. Grant having reported us as missionaries of the Church of Jesus Christ of Latter-day Saints.

By considerable urging we were able to get the english tracts published in time to have them for our meeting. I made one trip to Yokohama on the 14th in the interest of this matter.

On the 15th. I went to the Shueisha Printing Co. in Ushigome Ku, Tokyo for the purpose of closing the bargain with them for the publication of the tract in Japanese. Two proof-sheets have

been corrected and it is expected that the work will be finished and the tracts be in our possession in the course of not more than a week from today (22nd.)

On April 13th we all went with Mr. and Mrs. Nirayama and Miss. Mashimo to Sakai to see what is called "The Cherry Tunnel." This is only a few minutes ride on the train and one of the pretty sights in the neighborhood of Tokyo. At this place there in a street with a beautiful clear stream running through the middle leaving a path on both sides by the side of which are rows of cherry trees, at that time out in full bloom. Some of these trees are very old and there branches arch so nicely over the paths and stream that it is fitly named "The Cherry Tunnel."

Our meeting in the "Kinkikwan was announced to begin at six but as the audience was late we could not begin till about six thirty. But in order that those who came on time should not be bored with waiting we entertained them by singing a song or two. . . .

This was the first meeting of its kind that we have held in Japan and it being the first time I had faced such a large audience, I was naturally a little timid, but having prepared my subject before hand I soon lost all fear as the Lord blessed me in calling to mind the words I had learned.

The following is the speech as it was originally written. I having taken for my topic the same as the one in Pres. Grant's tract the following is also decided to repeat the track as I had previously translated it and had it corrected. Therefore the following is the original of the track as I wrote it as well as being the first speech delivered before a public audience.

On Sunday 20th. one of our Indian friends was with us nearly all day attending both the Sunday School and the afternoon meeting. In lieu of the fact that the previous night had been occupied in the meeting at Kanda we postponed the regular Sunday School lesson and held a testimony meeting. A very good spirit was manifested. In the afternoon meeting there were three or four present who had heard our preaching in Kanda the night before.

In the evening four of the brethren went to the Unitarian hall[6] to hear Japanese lectures delivered by Messrs. Hiroi and Hirai.

Monday we held a meeting rather informal in its character, in which it was decided to send the brethren out. Two, Bros. Featherstone and Hedges, to leave on Wednesday morning for Chiba Ken not many miles from Tokyo. These brethren are expected to come in to visit us on Sunday and assist us in our services. Two, Bros. Jarvis and Stoker to leave Thursday morning for Naoyetsu over on the Japan Sea coast; one day's ride on the train from the capitol. The remaining two, Bros. Ensign and Caine to leave on the same morning and the same train for Nagano about three or four hours ride this side of Naoyetsu.

On Tuesday evening at nine forty we held a little meeting for the purpose of saying anything there was to say before the departure of Elders Featherstone and Hedges the following morning. Prest. Grant gave some very excellent instructions on how the brethren should act and labor.

The following morning, 22nd., Bros. Featherstone and Hedges took their departure from headquarters at 4:30 a.m. Mr. Mashimo accompanied them to their field for the purpose of assisting them to find a place to stay and introduce them to some of his friends in that section. According of arrangements made previously they went by boat from Tokyo across the bay to Nago. During the day I suffered considerably from a pain in my abdomen. Received a letter from mother and one from Bessie Badger.

Thursday, 23 April 1903—Sunday, 3 May 1903, Tokyo

On the 23rd Elders Horace S. Ensign, Erastus L. Jarvis, John W. Stoker, and Fred A. Caine left for their fields of labor. Bros. Ensign and Caine went to Nagano City, Nakano Ken, and Bros. Jarvis went to Naoyetu, Niigata Ken. The brethren went very early in the morning and altho I had been feeling unwell during the night yet I got up to see them off. During the day I suffered quite a bit, but through the administration of Prest. Grant I was able to get up twice.

The morning of the 24th I went with President Grant to the bank to have my name inserted in place of Bro. Ensign's as the secretary to Prest. Grant in the signing of checks. Since the departure of Elder Ensign I have been put in as sort of temporary clerk of the mission.

In the afternoon eight different Japanese came to enquire about the Gospel. I had never seen any of them before. One old man who seemed ready to be added to the list of the dead said that as he felt that his time to live was short that he wanted to find a religion that would give him peace in the hour of death. I had to smile for it was a verifacaiton of the statement that I had before read which said, "Most of the Japanese fancy that religion is a thing that comes into play only at funeral services."

On the 25 Bro. Yoshiro Oyama moved to headquarters so that we could have his help during the time that he was not attending to his duties at the post office. He refused to take any bargain in which we offered him money, saying that it was his duty to do whatever he was asked to do by the President and that he did not want to be paid for any help that he was able to render to his brethren. This is a fine spirit for a convert to have and we highly appreciate it after seeing Bro. Nakazawa's greed for money.

The 26th was Sunday and as there were only six of us present neither the Sunday School nor the afternoon meeting lasted very long. Both however were spirited.

The next week had nothing of particular importance attached to it. The tracts printed in Japanese were delivered to us on Tuesday 28th. In this edition there were 5,000 copies. On Saturday afternoon Bros. Featherstone and Hedges returned to the headquarters bring good news of their condition and work in the country. They had secured excellent quarters at the home of a doctor in one of the villages of Chiba Ken, called Funakata. Many of the older folks, so these brethren said, could not read or write and knew nothing about anything form a foreign land. They reported that they had been blessed in talking to the people and altho they knew little of the language yet they had held conversations on the Gospel which lasted more than two hours. The place in which they are living is beautiful for scenery. The brethren spent Sunday with us and their enthusiastic remarks added much to the lively character of the Sunday School and meeting. There were about nine or ten Japanese present, four of the number being women. It is a new thing to have women listeners and though not interesting to the natives I felt that they had a good spirit with them and enjoyed the words they heard.

Monday, 4 May 1903—Monday 18 May 1903, Tokyo

During this time I have been busy at headquarters assisting in housecleaning and tending to other matters necessary for the spread of the Gospel. I wrote a number of letters to the brethren in the field. Many letters have been received from them and it has been with regret that we have found it necessary for the Elders to make reports of their intentions to preach wherever they go with the intention of staying ninety or more days. It has also been found upon inquiry at the Home Department that the tract that has been lately published in both English and Japanese should have been reported to the library department of that office. They were very kind in the fact that they made no complaint about the ones we had already given to the people. In order to comply with the laws which up to this time were not known to us, I took the tracts to the printer on the 16th and wrote letters to the brethren to cease the distributing of them until the date of publication and distribution had been added thereto.

The house cleaning is all completed and the mission headquarters looks brighter than it did a month or two ago. One strange thing, however, about the changes made, is that the carpet the landlady furnished for the principle room in the house is all borders off the carpet that was used by the Emperor in his guest room. Our room is very large and it would have been very hard for the landlady to have found a carpet that would cover the floor and at the same time be attractive to the eye, without buying a new one, and such is not the policy of the lady who owns the house in which we are living. However while our carpet is not very nice to look at, it is clean, good, and soft; quite attractive to the inexperienced Japanese eye, hence we do not think ill of a carpet made of borders for it is not more than once or twice in six months that we have a foreign visitor—our quests are all natives.

Last Sunday, May 17 we bought some cushions to spred on the floor of the Japanese division of the house, as it had previously decided that we would begin holding our Sunday Meetings in the Japanese part, where those we come can have the pleasure of sitting down on the floor using one of the cushions for a seat. It was necessary for us to sing without a piano accompanyment as it is too much trouble to move the instrument from one room to the other. Besides, it is not good for the piano. After the close of the first meeting held in these rooms, we all felt that it was an improvement upon our former method and altho some of the students who were present said they would prefer to sit on a chair, yet they speak, no doubt, for the sake of making us think they are becomming expensively Westernized.

I received a nice letter from father about the 9th. and one from Sister Erekson of Murray, on the 12th. or 13th. **They both gave reports of the marriage of Samuel and Lucile.**[7] **The ceremony was performed in the Temple at Salt Lake City, April 15th. At 9:30 a.m. by father.**

Tuesday, 19 May 1903—Tuesday, 2 June 1903, Tokyo

All the errors we had made in consequence of our ignorance of the laws concerning the sending in of reports to the Home Department for the missionaries and the tracts published, have been corrected and everything now set up in a perfect working order. The brethren in the country were supplied with the corrected tracts and after a two days wait began as befor to distribute tracts among the people of their several districts.

Many people have been to headquarters to ask about our faith and on Sunday 24th. and Sunday 31st. we had a very good attendance at our meeting. On the afternoon of the 24th I spoke for perhaps thirty five minutes and on the following Sunday afternoon I occupied about the same amount of time. It is beginning to seem a little easier for me to express myself to the people than it has been. I feel as I did some months ago when I seemed to realize, all of a sudden, that I had been making a little progress. There are times in the study of the language when it seems to me that I am accomplishing nothing at all; then, all at once I feel quite the opposite. It is wise in the Lord that a person should feel this way for to him who is concious of the fact that each day he is progressing, the temptations to give the credit to himself appeal with considerable force, but to him who feels his weakness and only once in a long time feels that he has been doing something, the power of Satan is somewhat checked at least in the way of pride.

I greatly enjoy talking to the people about the faith we cherish so dearly and would that the opportunities to talk more were increased. But the work around headquarters is of such a nature that a person could not very well spend his entire time out among the people of the district with out slighting some of the clerical work imposed upon him.

I have received a lesson or two from Prest. Grant in book-keeping so that I could keep the accounts of the mission during the time I stay at headquarters, which, according to the present appeerences will not be more than a month or two longer. It has been decided that the brethren will all return to Tokyo for Sunday June 7th. There are to be a few changes made in the fields and companions of the brethren so as to make it possible for the wives of the Elders to be with them in the field where it is thought they can do a great deal of good.

About the 27th. I begun the translation of the third chapter of the book on "Mormons and Mormonism" written by our friend Mr. Takahashi. It seems that this work does not, as I expected it would, become easier as I progress in it. Each chapter presents almost as many new words as the first and peculiar constructions are constantly being met with. In the end, however, this work will no doubt prove of very great value to me.

I have received during these two weeks letters from the folks at home and also some of my friends. I have in return written brief letters to them. My health has been very good, and the weather, though occasionally stormy, is remarkable for this time of the year; it being much cooler than usual.

Wednesday, 3 June 1903—Sunday, 7 June 1903, Tokyo

Wedneshay spent most of the day working on the translation of Takahashi's book. In the afternoon visited Bro. Nakazawa at Negishi.

Thursday afternoon at about five o'clock all the brethren arrived from their different fields of labor. They all looked as if the experiences of the month they had spent in the country had caused but little change. We were exceedingly delighted to see them well and happy.

Friday I spent in study and chatting with the newly returned elders.

Saturday Bro. Oyama returned from the post office very late. He had been to the home of his mother where he found her suffering with rheumatism. He informed us that he would have to stay with her for a week at least. During the day the brethren made a great many purchases preparatory to their return to the field on Monday morning.

Sunday our fast meeting began at ten o'clock as usual. The following is an outline of the meeting and what was said: Singing, "My Sabbath Home." Prayer, Elder J.F. Featherstone. Singing, "Our Mountain Home so Dear." Roll call showed an attendance of all the missionaries and one of the three converts, Bro. Oyama. Minutes of the previous meeting were read and voted upon. Singing, "While of these Emblems We Partake." Sacrament administered by Elders Erastus L. Jarvis and S.W. Hedges. Elder Ensign said that he was never more blessed in his life than during the last six weeks spent in the field. Also remarked that he and Elder Caine, his companion had always been united upon all points and that it was found that when one would make a suggestion to the other about their work that the other had been thinking along the same lines. The purpose of the meeting being to bear testimony he did not feel to occupy the time in making a report but bore his testimony stating that it give him strength whenever he opens his mouth to speak of the mission of Joseph Smith. Encouraged the brethren and Sisters to occupy the time as the spirit dictated.

Sister Grant remarked that this day (Fast Day) was given us of the Lord for the purpose of expressing before eachother the gratitude that fills our hearts in consequence of the innumerable blessings received by each individual. She affirmed that we had no cause for complaint at the progress that had been made but that on the contrary we are daily obtaining encouragement which enables us to press on.

Bro. Featherstone was the next speaker. In his opinion, the only thing that gives us contentment so far away from home and relatives, is the testimony of the Gospel without which we would never have been persuaded to come to Japan in the first place. He stated that he was very grateful for the privilege of being here where the power of the Lord has been directly manifested to him and his companion, Elder Hedges, in enabling them to speak with comparative ease to the people. He felt that as it had been decided for his wife and Sister Ensign to accompany them into the field that they would find the women a potent power for good among the people. He invoked, in fervant terms, a blessing upon the Japanese nation and all those who had been sent here to instruct them.

Bro. Jarvis seemed pleased to be back to what he called "Our home" and partake of the influences which always seem to prevail. He exorted all to deepen their affections for eachother and be bound together in the bonds of love. He stated that his experience in Naoyetsu, his field of labor during the last six months, had been very valuable. He informed us that it was a Buddhist stronghold but the people being anxious to read everything simple that they could get a hold of that he and his companion, Elder Stoker had been able to give them quite a number of tracts. He paid a beautiful tribute to Bro. Stoker, saying that he was an honest upright young man with whom he felt it an honor to labor. Said that the fact that other Christian Churches in that place are crowded to the doors, gives evidence that there are many in that district who will listen to their message. The food of the hotel, he reported, to be inferior to that which the other brethren had been receiving, but at the same time it was eatable. Thinks that they have made no enemies and many friends among whom are the officers of that city.

I spoke next assuring the brethren that we were truly receiving the blessings of the Lord in rich abundance. I encouraged all, in my feeble way, to be diligent and contented with their lots, assuring them that it was not the Lord's will that we should be in any hurry to receive the gift of tongues or other manifestations that would speed the work more rapidly than it has been going up to the present for if it was His will, that He would have said so in bestowing those blessings. We know not what is in the heart and mind of our Heavenly Father until He reveals it unto us, hence do not realize His providences concerning this mission.

Elder Hedges felt very happy at being with all his brethren and sisters again. The Lord had answered his prayers in the fact that He had caused the people of Chiba where he had been laboring to listen to his and his companion, Elder Featherstone, when talking on the principles of the Gospel. But at times ridicule and indifference has been manifested. Inasmuch as he was not going to return to Chiba but go to Nagano with Elder Caine to take the place of Elder Ensign who with his wife will hereafter be the companion of Elder Featherstone and his wife in Chiba, expressed the hope that those who would labor in his old field would be greatly assisted by the strength of heaven. The ignorance of the people of Chiba was a drawback. Many however can read and among them there are those we have already investigated the subject contained in the tract, pronounce it good, but receive it not. Happy to go to Nagano alto he would have to part with friends in his old district. He stated that the Lord had been answering his prayers in behalf of his father at home who was now showing much more interest in religion than he had ever before done.

Sister Ensign said that humility would assure to us a continuation of the blessing that we had so abundantly received since coming to this land. Was glad that it was decided for her to go into the field with her husband where, with the help of the Lord, she felt that she would be able to do a little good.

Bro. Oyama, speaking in Japanese said that he was glad to be with us and pertake of the good spirit that was manifest. Has implicit faith that this is the true Church and knows that God is our Heavenly Father and that Jesus Christ is His Son. The brethren having been blessed in their several fields and manifesting joy on their return, caused him to rejoice with them. He stated that it was his belief that the work would become very prosperour in the future and asked the blessings of God to be richly bestowed to that end.

Sister Mary Grant manifesting a sweet humble spirit, stated that she felt as though she had not done much but believed in the promises of the Lord to those who are diligent. She assured all that her heart was made glad at the remarks of Bro. Oyama and hoped that the time would soon come when many more Japanese could stand up before us and bear the same kind of a testimony that he had uttered in our hearing.

Bro. Caine then said a few words. He had experienced a fine spirit in the little meetings held in the field. Especially was the meeting held in Naoyetsu five weeks ago one in which the spirit of the Lord was greatly manifest. He stated that he and Elder Ensign held a meeting every Sunday in a grove which they had dedicated for that purpose. He was happy to state that his memory had been strengthened. The unity of he and his companion was a testimony to him. Much indifference had been manifested by the people in consequence of the fact that they were satisfied with the teachings of Buddhism which claimed Nagano as one of its strongholds. He said that the ease with which he was able to speak to the people was a surprise to him.

Sister Featerstone testified that all had spoken under the influence of the proper spirit. She also felt that the spirit of the active missionary was always sweet. She was glad that the opportunity had come for her to go into the field and was very anxious to do some good. Of late she had been greatly favored in receiving strength to understand much more than heretofore. Especially one one occasion lately was she able to understand everything said in our Sunday Meeting. She said, "As our diligence is, so our success will be." Asked the blessing of health upon all.

Bro. Stoker said he felt weak in standing on his feet. Some of his recent experiences trying and others pleasant. Had met with people who wanted to hear them and others who wanted them to leave. Some had come to their rooms and listened attentively to explainations of the Gospel, feeble tho they might have been. The translation of the song, "Come, come, ye Saints" in Takahishi's book one of the most attractive things to the people. He bore a strong testimony saying that this mission had been a great factor in building his faith and especially was he strengthened in being healed of his lameness. (This instance of healing is mentioned in the previous pages of this journal.)

President Grant spoke at some length. He was satisfied with the remarks made. It was a happy time for us all when the Elders went out to begin their labors in the field. The Lord has prescribed that the way to preach the Gospel is to visit the people at their homes. Was glad that the suggested changes for Bros. Hedges and Ensign were satisfactory, and that the ladies felt happy in going out into the country with their husbands to engage in active work. Especially did he rejoice in the fact that the brethren had enjoyed the Spirit of the Lord and knew that it was with them [———] feel satisfied if the brethren were only able to make friends of the people. One of the purposes of calling young men on missions is to open up communication between Heaven and the missionary in order that when he returns home to Zion he may be worth something to the Church and the Lord. He stated that Prest. Kimball of the Thatcher Stake always kept as many of the young men in the mission field as possible for the reason that he needs strong men to help him in the building up of a new country and realizes that the best way to get them filled with the spirit is to send them on missions for two or three years. Even if we do not baptize a single soul yet we will be repaid for all the sacrifices made in the abundance of other blessings we will receive. When The power of the Evil One was threatening the Church, when many of the prominent men were apostising, when the Saints were receiving their bitterest persecutions, the Prophet Joseph Smith sent the Apostles on missions so that when they returned they would be filled with the power of God and be prepared for their mighty labors at home.[8] If we can do our duty and go home with the proper spirit we have obtained much and our labors will have been in no wise vain. It is our duty to listen to the councels of the officers of the Church and if they are satisfied with our labors then the Lord is satisfied with us. The Priesthood is the voice and representative of God. Bro. Grant stated that he was satisfied with what the brethren had done and that they have every cause to rejoice. If in the time that will intervene before our next gathering we have some converts, the Lord be praised. If not, still praise Him. Prest. Grant said the healing of Bro. Stoker was a source of joy to him, but wanted us to understand that it was through the power of God and not of man that Elder Stoker received his blessing. Man and his faith is but the instrument used to call upon God. God is our help and stay and stands at the head of this Church.

Bro. Ensign speaking for the second time said that his heart had been touched by the remarks made and his desire to do all that he could had been strengthened by what he had heard. He recited how at Nagano he was afflicted by a pain in his side by which he had been hindered somewhat from working as actively as he would have liked. While suffering he thought that as soon as he could come to Tokyo and be administered to by his brethren that he would be entirely restored. In order to place himself in a position to receive this blessing he had fasted since Friday night and would like the brethren to administer to him.

In answer to this request, Elder Caine anointed his head with oil and with Prest. Grant as mouth, we all united in the confirmation of the anointing. Singing, "Parting Hymn." Benediction, Bro. Oyama. (In Japanese.)

At twelve fourty five, Prest. Grant called a meeting for the purpose of hearing the opinions of the brethren regarding the work and plans for the future. I opened the meeting with prayer. Prest. Grant asked the brethren to express briefly their impressions of the places in which they had labored, stating if they thot any changes necessary. He stated that when traveling thro the Naoyetsu and Nagano districts two years ago that he was very much impressed with the places, but not knowing by experience would like to hear just exactly what the brethren who had been in those districts thot. He also desired to have their opinion about sending for more elders.

Elder Ensign was the first to respond to the request. He remarked that there was plenty of room for four elders to work in and around Nagano for there were 40,000 people in the city and in the hamlets all around there were many thousands more. When visiting Elders Jarvis and Stoker at Naoyetsu five weeks before, he was pleased with the spirit they manifested but depressed on account of the conditions that surrounded them especially did he feel for the brethren as his own condition in Nagano was so much better. He would, therefore, speaking in the interests of his brethren, suggest that their field of labor be changed from Naoyetsu to Nagano. He was hartily in favor of sending for more missionaries as soon as possible in order that double the amount of places could be worked. He also suggested that another tract be gotten out as quickly as possible as the one we already have is not sufficient by itself to fill the demand from the people.

Elder Stoker said that while he and his companion did not find the living accommodations at Naoyetsu quite so good as those had by the brethren at Nagano still they had no desire to change from one place to the other unless in the wisdom of the President it was thought best. He felt to go wherever he was sent but felt that there were many honest in heart in Naoyetsu who would receive their testimonies. Many articles of food are hard to get in that place and if they take three meals a day at the hotel, they will have to pay ¥.29.00 per month. The expense makes no different if through their labors some can be converted. The people ignorant and many unable to read the tract. He declared that another tract was just what we need, as the people who can and have read the present tract are constantly asking for something additional. He was heartily in favor of sending for more elders immediately as every day without them was a loss to the progress of the work.

Bro. Jarvis said he believed in staying with a work once commenced. The hotel life at Naoyetsu was not the most pleasant, but we are not here to hunt for comforts only. If more elders are needed in Nagano let them be sent for. He recited the incident of a certain man, who, when he first time them, laughed at their poor language and smiled when they presented him with a tract. But after reading the tract his manner was quite changed. Three days later he came to the rooms of the elders and had a long chat with them receiving a Bible which he is now diligently reading. This man now manifests a good spirit, is poor, makes baskets and is in no wise puffed up with pride. On the night the brethren left for Tokyo he came after nine o'clock in a big rain storm to say good-bye. Such a thing is strange in Japan. The people do not often go out in a rain storm on matter how binding a promise they may have made. This man wanted to know how to pray and the brethren after teaching him gave a practical lesson in the same. Many such people being in the neighborhood of this place makes Elder Jarvis feel like he did not want to leave for another field simply because the food and hotel accommodations were not quite so good as the rest are enjoying. The hotel conditions can be bettered by hunting another place.

Bro. Hedges not being acquainted with the conditions of the brethren in Naoyetsu and Nagano could say nothing about the change suggested by Elder Ensign. Heartily in favor of calling more brethren to labor in this land.

Elder Caine was of the opinion that it would be nice for four elders to be laboring in Nagano but was not inclined to favor the brethren's move from Naoyetsu. Let more Elders be called and sent to be companions of the two already in Nagano. Every Elder now in the field will be able to speak Japanese sufficiently well to break in a new elder by the time they would arrive.

Bro. Featherstone agreed with the brethren on the elder question and stated that as he stood on the top of a high mountain in the Chiba district and fiewed and land, he felt there was room for more workers. He and his companion had found three in the part in whom they had hopes. Often preached to thirty and fourty people in the fields at once. The old folks of that part of Chiba in which they have been living as a general rule uneducated, simple, and able to read the tracts only by the help of their children.

I remarked that I had been strongly in favor of calling more missionaries for a long time and that when Prest. Grant broached the subject to me some time ago that I felt it would be wise to at least have one report from the brethren then in the field and see what their prospects were before sending for more. But as the brethren's letters have from the first been full of good news and characterized by the proper spirit that I was converted that we needed more assistance. I also endorsed the idea of getting up a new tract and expressed my willingness to do all in my power to accomplish the work.

Prest. Grant stated that he understood from the remarks made that the united sentiment of the brethren was to have more elders and to get our another tract. This he said he would report by the next mail to the Presidency of the Church. He felt like allowing the Elders to remain in Naoyetsu as there was certainly something in not abandoning a field once opened. As the papers of that place had published some vile articles about us it seem especially proper to remain there and show that we can outlive such falsehoods. He stated that he would no doubt visit Naoyetsu before the current month was out. Prest. Grant then closed the meeting by prayer.

At two p.m. we met again in our regular afternoon meetings, holding it in the Japanese rooms. There were fourteen Japanese and twelve missionaries present. A good spirit prevailed. All the brethren spoke; also Bro. Oyama.

After the meeting most of the Japanese remained, as is their custom, as we chatted with them. It may be well to remark also, that, with the exception of Prest. Grant, all the Elders speak with the natives in Japanese.

In the evening a Mr. Yoshida who had been to see us a time or two before, called for a few minutes. Elder Featherstone and I went with him to his house. While pertaking of his hospitality a thief entered the yard and stole my shoes. The matter was reported to the police while I had to borrow a pair from my friend to get home with.

Monday, 8 June 1903—Friday, 10 July 1903, Tokyo/Nagano

Monday morning the 8th Elders Jarvis, Hedges, Stoker, and Caine started for their fields of labor, Elders Caine and Hedges going to Nagano and Elders Jarvis and Stoker returning to their old field,

Naoyetsu. Elders Ensign and Featherstone were busy with their wives in preparing for their start the following morning to Chiba.

For about a week after the brethren and Sisters left headquarters, the four of us left here, Prest. Grant, wife, and daughter, and myself, were feeling quite sick at our stomachs. We lost our appetites and became thoroughly indisposed to do anything. This affliction was caused, we thought, by eating strawberries that had been preserved with some kind of acid.

On June 15th, I finished writing a tract, entitled, "Thou Shalt Have no Other Gods before Me." Copies were sent to the brethren in the field for them to correct and alter according to their opinions. In the course of a day or two, letters containing the criticism were received and with the exception of the two brethren laboring in Naoyetsu, the reference made to the false gods of idolatry was thought to be to plain and direct an attack upon the forms of worship in this land. All united in saying, that according to their experiences, the subject should be presented in the simplest manner possible or the people would not understand it, therefore the ideas of my effort should be clothed in simpler words. Prest. Grant felt to sustain the criticisms of the brethren. Consequently I began the work of simplification immediately, but found as I wrote, that I was not adhereing closely to the run of the original. This however was not necessary. When I finished, I found that I have written practically a new tract about the same subject but with the title, "The True & living God. This second tract was likewise sent to the brethren after having been read to Prest. Grant. I did not wait for their replies, before beginning its translation, as Prest. Grant thought it was alright and that the brethren would approve of it. He was right. The brethren said they were satisfied. The original of both the rejected and approved efforts are found in the next ten pages of the journal.

On Sunday June 21st I spoke for forty five minutes in Japanese on the Resurrection of the dead.

About this time we received a letter from the folks in Chiba, stating that the sisters were having quite a time with the Japanese food. They had decided to move to a place where the sisters could cook their own food and desired us to look up a stove and send it out to them. I looked for one on July 1st and sent the prices of those I saw, but as Prest. Grant, his wife, and daughter and myself left on the following morning to visit the brethren in Nagano I do not know at this writing whether or not they sent for the stove.

The ride to Nagano was a very pleasant one. The train passes thro 26 tunnels within a distance of about ten or fifteen miles. The scenery was good, resembling very much at times the scenery of our mountain valleys in Utah. We arrived in the evening at nine o'clock, having left Tokyo in the morning at half past eleven. That night Sister Grant had her first experience sleeping in a Japanese bed. And the only thing that robbed it of its purely native style was a feather pillow she had taken with her. But be it said also to the credit of the hotel in which we stopped, the Gomeikwan, that their beds are the best native ones I have ever slept in up to this time.

The following morning was pleasant and we went out into the woods where the two brethren in that district were accustomed to go for prayer and song. It was a pretty little spot on the side of a mountain some thirty minutes walk from the hotel. A small spring of excellent water was what first attracted the brethren to the place when they were hunting a private spot. The water of Nagano being very bad and injurious to the health the brethren have to drink hot water except when they go to the spring. It is needless to say, therefore, that we filled up on this cool sparkling beverage. On the way back we called at a very famous temple, The Zenkoji,[9] and saw one of the signs that meet the eye of every observer that enters a shrine, whether Buddhist or Shinto, only that the terrible condition of those who are given over to idolatry seemed to be more plainly manifested in this country town of great fame than in any other place that I had visited.. From the temple we ascended a hill from the top of which we secured a good view of the surrounding country, then returned to the hotel.

After dinner, I went with elders Caine and Hedges to a little village which they said was five miles away and during the two hours that we were there, I had my first real missionary life. I assisted in distributing tracts, and tried my best to get a conversation with someone, but they were so busy with their cacoons,[10] for which the Nagano district is quite noted, that I failed in every instance. A rather amusing incident happened on this occasion. We accidently go separated and began going into houses alone. At one place I called at the front door to attract the attention of the people within, but they only looked through the glass at me and smiled. I thought that was very strange, but in a moment or two Elder Caine came around the corner of the house and told me that he had just that instant been talking to the people and leaving a tract at the back door. I was tired when I got back to the hotel. Ten miles is a long walk for one who is not used to it.

The next day was July 4th, but we did not celebrate. It rained hard so we stayed in the house till evening when three of us went to the depot to meet Elders Jarvis and Stoker who came down from Naoyetsu to be with us on Sunday. We had two very fine meetings Sunday. Pres. Grant gave much good advice and encouragement to all.

Next morning three of us brethren went to a little village close by and did some tracting. I had two good conversations and delivered six tracts. This day's experience was better than the first. The people were inclined to hear what we had to say.

Pres. Grant suggested that we return to Tokyo Tuesday morning which we did, arriving at four in the afternoon and found all in tact at headquarters which had been left in charge of Bro. Oyama.

On the evening of the 8th of July, I went to Mr. Hirai Kinza's home for the purpose of getting him to criticize and prepare for the printer the translation of the tract I had written. He refused to do it if we insisted on paying him for it, so it was arranged that he would give his time and assistance free. I have been going over the translation with him for the last three mornings and expect to compete the work next Monday.

Saturday, 11 July 1903—Monday, 31 August 1903, Tokyo

The translation of the tract I had written having been submitted to Mr. Kinza Hirai was criticized by him and so simplified that the majority of the less educated among the Japanese can read it and prepared by him for publication on Thursday or Friday July 16th or 17th. (After receiving it I handed it to Bro. Oyama to get his opinion on the manner in which it was gotten up. He read it and manifested a lack of enthusiasm, whereupon I asked him why his interest in referring to it seemed so slight. He said that it was elegantly written, but that the style was such that to those whom we had found were unable to understand the first tract that it would be still harder and to those who could understand the first tract it would be still simpler. This seemed to me a peculiar criticism and one that I did not like as my object in getting Mr. Hirai to criticize it was that he had had experience in talking to the people all over the country and would know how to make it so that a majority could understand it and at the same time mantain in it a superior form. If the exact opposite was the result then my failure to reach my object was strikingly manifest.)

I took it to our friend Mr. Mashimo and, after reading it, he showed it to his friend and they seemed to be of a different opinion to Bro. Oyama. This being the case, I took Pres. Grant's advice that it was not necessary to show it to any more as it was simply a matter of taste after all and that as we had solicited Mr. Hirai's assistance and got it that we could do nothing but publish it in the form he had arranged. I knew that there was no mistake in meaning and understood perfectly all the corrections made so had no fears as to the correctness of the text, so I took it to the printers. In giving a bid on 5,000 copies the same printer who had printed the first tract demanded what I thought was too much so I concluded to try elsewhere. The result of my search was that I got a bid of just a little less than half of what the first man gave me. I closed the bargain with the cheap house and in the course of a few days received and corrected the first proof sheet. There were so few mistakes in the second proof that I ordered it printed as corrected. This was done and the books delivered on August 7th. The tract when finished consists of twenty four pages without the paper covers. On the outside cover is the title, the author's name and the information that he is a missionary and the name of the mission by which the tract is published. On the inside of the front cover nothing was inserted. From page one of the tract proper the article began. On the inside of the back cover is the date of publication, distribution, etc, etc. which the law requires shall be inserted in all books. On the outside of the back cover is a picture of the temple.

August 1st, I laid aside the title of youth and donned the role of manhood, it being my twenty first birthday. To celebrate the event I accompanied Prest. Grant, his wife, and daughter to Hojo, in Chiba Ken. The purpose of our trip was to hold a fast meeting with the brethren and sisters laboring in that place. Elders Ensign and Featherstone and their wives had been laboring there for two months and had made very favorable reports of the conditions in that district. The trip is made by water in a little steamer which crosses Tokyo Bay. The ride was delightful, but would have been more so if we had had good places to sit or rest. A very large crowd was aboard.

As we slowed up to the anchoring place off Hojo we noticed what we thought looked like foreigners rowing on the Bay and as they came quite rapidly towards the steamer we soon recognized them to be the ones whom we had come to visit. A hearty handshake and exchange of friendly greetings soon placed us in touch with each other.

We found the brethren and sisters at this place to be very finely located and in the finest of health and spirits. It is needless to say that we spent the first hours of our visit in exchange of friendly ideas and narratives of experiences. But in the evening we were invited to go down to the shore and take a swim in the ocean. This delighted us all and though I cannot swim, yet I enjoyed the dip in the brine about as well as anyone. I concluded that my twenty first birthday had been well spent and fittingly topped off by a good toothsome supper made all the more palatable by the quantity of sea water I drank while trying to float.[11]

The next day was Sunday and we were blessed of the Lord in our Fast Meeting. All spoke with freedom and gave words of encouragement to their fellow laborers. In the evening at eight o'clock, as was written on a sign at the gate, we held a meeting to which the public were invited. The three rooms of six mats each were filled to overflowing and the people were jammed in the stairway and hall and were standing thickly around the outside of the house. This interest on their part was in no wise all due to the desire to hear Christianity but to see we curious creatures who had so recently arrived in town. But be the motive of the people what it may, we had a fine meeting, good attention, and a very good spirit present. Only once before in Japan had I had the opportunity of speaking to so many natives and that once was when we held our large meeting in Kanda, Tokyo where I made my first lecture in the Japanese language. I spoke for some thirty or thirty five minutes and the Lord blessed me in my effort.

The next day I went with Elders Featherstone and Ensign to a little village about four or five miles to the north of Hojo where I had the privilege of meeting many of their friends and assist in arranging for a meeting for the following Wednesday night. We were able to hire a lady's house for this purpose if we would pay her fifty sen. This we gladly promised to do and put up a large play card notifying the passers-by of what we intended to do. On the evening of Wednesday we rode over to the meeting in a boat. The name of the village in which we held the meeting was Nago. The people there were not so highly educated and acquainted with the foreigner's manner of speaking Japanese as are the people of Hojo and therefore we had some difficulty in making ourselves understood. The congregation was a large one and a little restless but on the whole our effort was a satisfactory one.

The following morning Prest. Grant and I returned to Tokyo to do some work which was waiting the publication of the second edition of tract No. 1. Sister Grant and her daughter were to have returned with us but they had become facinated with Hojo and surroundings and wanted to stay till the end of the month, so Pres. Grant and I returned to Tokyo with the intention of going back to Hojo as soon as the pending work was finished and remain in Hojo till after the quarterly conference of all the missionaries which we thought might just as well be held in Hojo as Tokyo, in view of the fact that there was plenty of room in the house out there and the brethren and sisters were so excellently situated. The ride to Tokyo was a little rough. On the boat I met a man who resided in a little village near Hojo and who had evidently been to our meeting the previous Sunday evening. He said for us to continue our work out there as it was only a matter of time before the whole nation would have to adopt Christianity and that he would be glad to help us build a church. The Japanese promises are like a lot of "hot air." Nothing.

Pres. Grant and I were in Tokyo till the morning of the 12th. **I added some Bible references to the first tract and made a few other corrections that were necessary preparatory to the publication of the second edition. Before going back to Hojo I corrected the second proof.** The weather in Tokyo we found to be very oppressive.

On our return to Hojo Elder Ensign and his wife accompanied us, they having come in from there to make some purchases. We took the cook along with us also. The ride over the bay was the best we had had. In the evening we went to the little village of Kawasaki to hold a cottage meeting.[12] The turnout was not so good as on previous occasions, the reason being because the place was not situated on a very prominent street. The feature of this meeting was the testimony born by Sister Mary Grant, the youngest of our colony. The spirit of the Lord accompanied her remarks and the people fully understood the words as they flowed from her mouth. My heart was touched and it was with difficulty that I restrained my tears.

The following Sunday we had an immense crowd to our meeting in Hojo. The landlord of the hotel in which we were stopping thought the floor would give way so great was the crowd. I spoke for thirty seven minutes on this occasion.

We tried to arrange for a meeting on the following Wednesday night at one of the near villages but were unable to find a suitable place. During the week I accompanied Elder Featherstone tracting and enjoyed my experiences in this line very much. One day I had a two hour's conversation with a priest of the Nichirin sect[13] of the Buddhist Church. I hah no difficulty in holding my own with him and whether he acknowledged it with a firm and settled conviction or not, he remarked that idols were not essential and after a while that they were false gods.

The next Sunday while holding a meeting among ourselves the mail arrived bringing a letter form a Mr. Stone in Yokohama apprizing Prest. Grant that there was a telegram for him in Yokohama that had been received from Salt Lake on the 21st. We tried to have its contents forwarded to Hojo, but in Japan they do not forward foreign telegrams especially when they are written with code words as this one was.[14] Prest. Grant therefore took the next boat to Tokyo to find out what the message contained. In the evening we held our regular Sunday service and as usual had a large crowd. I spoke first, addressing them for over forty five minutes on the resurrection of the dead. I presume they understood most of what I said. At least they seemed. to.

The next morning about eleven o'clock a telegram came from Prest. G. telling that the message form home was his release and that Elder Ensign had been appointed to take charge of the mission. I wired back that Sister Grant, Mary, and I would start for Tokyo on the first boat in the morning.

A day or two before leaving Hojo, I had a pimple come out on my face and as a result of my scratching it it got very large and sore. By the time I had been in Tokyo for a day my face began to swell and the sore to fester and run. I thought I had poisoned it with my nails and therefore took medicine to work it out and used salve to heal and draw the sore. To these applications there was no response, so upon the advice of Prest. G. I went to Dr. McDonald in Tsukiji and had him examine and prescribe for it He said that it was not poisoned but was only a boil. Inasmuch as Elder Ensign had been suffering with boils most of the time we were at Hojo and on their account was not able to get out I wondered if I caught them from him, but upon more serious reflection I attribute them to the bad water we had to drink. At this writing, Aug. 31st, the sore is fast healing up; the core having been entirely removed.

Friday afternoon, Aug. 28 all the missionaries in the field came back to Tokyo to be with Prest. Grant during the remainder of his stay, it having been definitely fixed for him and his wife and daughter to sail on Sept 8th per S.S. "Aki Maru." It is needless to say that we all regret the home-going of our president and his family all of whom we have learned to love. Especially have I been intimate with them as for the last three months I have been here alone with them at headquarters. In letters received from home some time ago Prest. G. received a hint that he was to come home and as the hint has been several times repeated the call home is not so unexpected after all.

Yesterday, Aug 30th, we enjoyed our meetings. All of the missionaries were present and two out of the three of our converts. It reminded us of the time before the Elders went out to their several fields. Sentiments of respect and love were heard from every lip.

Tuesday, 1 September 1903, Tokyo/Yokohama

Two years ago this day Apostle Grant, Elder Kelsch, Elder Ensign, and I went into the woods at Yokohama for the purpose of dedicating the land of Japan for the proclamation of the gospel. The account of the meeting held will be found in this journal under date, Sept. 1st. 1901. In order to celebrate the day in a fitting manner and enjoy, if possible, another outpouring of the Spirit similar to the one experienced two years ago, the entire group of missionaries now in Japan left Tokyo on the 10:30 train in the morning and wended their way to the hill near Yokohama, which because of its association with the dedicatory services, had become sacred to them all. It was with feelings of joy that I, as one of the party, was privileged to visit the spot again in company with my brethren and sisters.

We arrived at the secluded spot shortly after noon and after a few moments rest began the exercises of our anticipated meeting.

Singing,

"We thank Thee, O God, for a Prophet
To guide us in these latter-days,
We thank Thee for sending the Gospel
To lighten our minds with its rays;
We thank Thee for every blessing
Bestowed by Thy bounteous hand;
We feel it a pleasure to serve Thee,
And love to obey thy commands."

Prayer was offered by Elder Horace S. Ensign. Singing,

"Now let us rejoice in the day of salvation,
No longer as strangers on earth need we roam;
Good tidings are sounding to us and each nation,
And shortly the hour of redemption will come.
When all that was promised the Saints will be given,
And none will molest them from morn until even,
And earth will appear as the garden of Eden,
And Jesus will say to all Israel, Come home.

Prest. Heber J. Grant was the first speaker. He expressed his pleasure at being present—referred to the time when the four who first came to Japan were strangers in a strange land—they were not familiar with the customs of the people, opposed by the papers, refused lodgings at a boarding-house, and in every way opposed by those who wanted and tried to get them prohibited from preaching in Japan.—spoke of the particularly bitter attitude of the "Japan Mail" the editor of which wilfully lied about them and their position towards the doctrine of polygamy, which doctrine Prest. Grant had personally assured him they did not intend to teach or promulgate—asserted that the feelings that fill the hearts of pioneers can only be understood by the pioneers themselves—felt that the four first elders were abundantly blessed of the Lord and many times melted to tears by the manifestations of the Spirit of God. Prest. Grant said that he treasured sacred remembrances of the spot of ground upon which we were assembled, not only because it was the place of the dedicatory services, but because of having come there in company with Elder Kelsch and in the course of the prayers they offered up received many blessings and promises which dispelled the feelings of sadness that were then filling his heart. The proper time to tell what the blessings and promises are will be after they are realized as predicted.

Prest. Grant referred to the fact that he is only blessed with the spirit of prayer on rare occasions, yet nevertheless sincere in offering all supplications to the Lord. Remarkably blessed in making the dedicatory prayer two years before. On that occasion Elder Kelsch brought a copy of the prayer offered on the Mount of Olives when Orson Hyde dedicated that land unto the Lord for the return of the Jews, but Prest. Grant declined to read it feeling that he wanted to be influenced by the whisperings of the Spirit rather than by what someone else had asked the Lord, and felt to acknowledge the influences of the Spirit in enabling him to offer an acceptable prayer. Prest. Grant felt that since the time of the dedication much good had been accomplished. He referred to the home-going of Elder Kelsch and the little he seemed to have done here and to his own contemplated return and the slight labor he felt to have done, but stated that as in the case of Elder Kelsch all who come to this land and return in a short time will be interested in the progress of the work and do much by calling the attention of the Saints to this mission. "If left to

Sun by Mr. Takahashi on the subject of "Mormonism." This article was so fair that Bro. Grant had Mr. Hiroi translate it from the Japanese into English so that it could be sent home for publication in some of our Church periodicals.

Saturday, 28 December 1901, Tokyo

The chill bleak air of winter seemes to have come for the season. Went to the Central Hotel to meet Mr. Hiroi and take our lesson in Japanese. Went from there to the Metropole to read an article written in the "Japan Mail" by a man who signs himself "An American Friend of Japan." This gentleman wrote an article on the coming of the "Mormons" to Japan some time ago, and the criticism on what he said both by Bro. Grant and others not acquainted with us were so strong that it seems he needed to defend himself. But we noticed in his reply a much weaker attempt than the first to find fault with the teachings or works of the Latter-day Saints.

Before going to bed, I made some flannel belts to wear over my abdomen, as in this country a person is quite likely to suffer from pains in the bowels as a result of chills if the abdomen is not particularly protected by additional clothing. One foreigner has told us that he would not go without such a protection for a moment, and that he has worn them with good results ever since he has been in Japan. As health is one of the important things for a missionary to watch I thought I would take the advice given and make me some flannel belts to wear especially in the winter. One thing which leads me to believe that such belts are of value is that many times I have got so cold in this Japanese house that I have gone to bed chilled through and could not get warm for hours, and one peculiar feature of this cold is, that it affects the regions of the stomach more than I have ever noticed in America. Received a letter from Bishop Empey.

Sunday, 29 December 1901, Tokyo

Studies and read during the morning. Had our bath in the fore part of the afternoon then went to the Central Hotel to hold Sacrament Meeting with the brethren. Our meeting was interrupted a number of times by visitors calling, but we eventually finished with the best of feelings existing in the hearts of all. We stayed and had dinner with the brethren, it being the first meal I had had since Friday night—the time intervening was spent in fast and prayer to the Lord. Before coming back to our rooms we wrote out an answer to the article published in the "Japan Mail" by "An American Friend of Japan," which answer Bro. Grant had prepared during the day.

Monday, 30 December 1901, Tokyo

Mr. Hiroi stopped and ate dinner with us after which I occupied my time in writing on an article for the Improvement Era. The day was clear and cold and having nothing to do away from the hotel, I stayed in all day. The students came in a time or two, but when they saw us busy they did not stay long. Mr. Koyama, our Japanese interpreter while in Yokohama, came to see us and to borrow some money with which to celebrate the holidays. He had become particularly interested in our work and wants to help us in any way that he possibly can. Indeed, there seems to be an enthusiastic feeling in his heart for our welfare that we do not notice in the actions of others. We were also favored with a call from one of the students with whom Bros. Kelsch and Ensign had become acquainted some time ago.

Tuesday, 31 December 1901, Tokyo

The air cold and piercing, but the day bright and clear. Went to the Central Hotel to receive lesson in Japanese. On the way back purchased some cakes and fruit with which to feed the students who might call on New Years. Received a call from an English gentleman named Hume who has been in Japan for ten years off and on. Also visited by two students with whom we had a delightful time talking of the Bible and the saving principles of Christianity.

Notes

1. On 24 July 1847, Brigham Young entered the Great Salt Lake Valley and reportedly said, "This is the right place." James

act upon my own desires," said Prest. Grant, "I will visit this land again."[15] He felt that the Presidency and the Apostles were satisfied with what he had done here.—was glad that Elder Ensign, who had had some experience in missionary labor before coming to Japan was to be left in charge and that Elder E's wife was here with him. He said that all should give to Elder E. the loyal support which he himself had received while presiding here.

I was requested to read the synopsis of the dedicatory prayer as taken from my journal of Sept 1st 1901. I did as requested. Singing,

"Come, come, ye Saints, no toil nor labor fear,
But with joy wend your way;
Though hard to you this journey may appear,
Grace shall be as your day.
'Tis better far for us to strive,
Our useless cares from us to drive.
Do this, and joy your hearts will swell
All is well! all is well!"

Elder Horace S. Ensign then spoke. His mind went back to the meeting held on the same spot two years before, and he recalled the Prayers and supplications which were offered up on that occasion for the success of the work here. He referred to the mighty power of the dedicatory prayer offered by Prest. Grant and the remarkable way in which it affected him. Spoke of the shaking of the earth at the time the City of Enoch[16] was taken into heaven, and asserted that the actual shaking of the earth could be felt. To prove this he related an incident which came under his observation while on his mission to Colorado. He, Apostle John W. Taylor, and two others were traveling along the road when Apostle John W. Taylor had a revelation in which it was shown to him that one of the brethren was to be a Savior in his father's house. This brother had witnessed his father's excommunication from the church long before. Upon Apostle Taylor's suggestion the company stopped on the top of a summit which lay on their road and there knelt in prayer facing the temple, Apostle Taylor being mouth. The Holy Ghost descended upon him and under its influence he prophesied many things that should come to pass and many of his predictions have been literally fulfilled. Among other things he predicted the war between the U.S. and Spain and the manner of its beginning.[17] The ground around the kneeling brethren shook perceptibly. The same great power and influence of the Lord was manifested on the occasion of dedicating this land.

Elder Ensign testified that Pres. Grant is indeed a prophet of God. Asked the blessings of God upon all who are to remain in this land. The immorality and superstition of the people makes our work here harder than it otherwise would be. Determined that no neglect of his should leave a stone unturned in the interest of this mission. Assured all that he loved them and asked God's choicest blessings upon them. Especially desired that Sister Grant should be restored to perfect health. He stated that the labors of Sister Mary Grant had been a factor for good and hoped that she will some day be privileged to return to Japan. Spoke of a meeting in Kawasaki, Chiba where Sister Mary spoke under the influences of the Spirit and touched the hearts of all.

I followed Elder Ensign in making a few remarks. Said: Two years ago a time never to be forgotten; never felt the Spirit more plainly than at that time, but as I was young and without similar experiences could hardly understand the emotions of my heart; the angels of God were near us at that time; would rejoice if Elder Kelsch were present with us; recalled the time when the Elders assembled in the woods just prior to the former return of Prest. Grant to America; was much impressed by the words in Prest. Grant's dedicatory prayer which referred to me; those words helped me to be diligent, and desire to become a man of God. I spoke of my close association with Prest. Grant and the good counsels I had received from him, and said that his great care in advising me as a father had taught me to love him and desire to always put into practice his excellent teachings. I expressed the hope that he would be able to return to us, but at the same time felt that if he did not, other important work would be demanding his attention and time at home. Referred to the instructions of my father on the eve of my departure from home, to the effect that in all things I was to give strict heed unto the wishes of Apostle Grant and that it had been my desire to do so even if I had failed in any particular. Hoped that nothing would ever alienate the affections that I had for Prest. Grant.

I spoke of the kindness of Sister Grant and the admirable way in which she had taken the place of my mother in this far off land. I voiced my appreciation of the interest Mary had taken in me and my welfare and acknowledged that I had learned to love her as a sister and appreciate the lessons of humility she had set before all of us. Spoke of the times when I could have wept for joy at seeing her bear her testimony to the natives in their own tongue and listening to her humble remarks in our own little gatherings. Expressed my love for all my companions in this land and prayed that we might be united. Stated my desire to support Elder Ensign with all my strength as I had tried to support Prest. Grant. Expressed my belief that Elder Ensign will be filled with the Holy Ghost in presiding over this mission.

Singing,
"Let us oft speak kind words to each other,
At home or where'er we may be;
Like the warbling of birds on the heather,
The tones will be welcome and free;
They'll gladden the heart that's repining,
Give courage and hope from above,
And where the dark clouds hide the shining,
Let in the bright sunlight of love."

Elder Joseph F. Featherstone said that he was glad to be present with the rest on so sacred a spot, and while speaking desired the assistance of the same spirit that had prompted the remarks of the previous speakers; while not one of the first to come to Japan was still very pleased to be present on this occasion; loved all, especially those who are shortly to return to America. Elder Featherstone stated that in letters from his relatives and friends at home that he is often reminded of the great blessing of being in the company of an Apostle of the Lord. He desired to follow the example of perseverance set by Prest. Grant. He spoke his thanks for the kind and encouraging remarks made to him and his wife by Sister Grant. Was glad that Sister Mary had come to this land for she had been a sister to us and a good companion for his wife. Expressed his thanks for the kindness of Sister Ensign whose admirable qualities he had learned to appreciate more fully since their sojourn in Hojo. Was grateful that Elder Ensign had had many valuable experiences in his life.

Repeated his love for all and hoped to live so that he would be worthy to have his love reciprocated. Felt weak in performing his labors and said doubts and despondencies often arose before him, but by prayer and faith he had been able to stand. Stated that he was considered a rough fellow before entering the Brigham Young Academy at Provo, Utah[18] and in reality did not know the purpose of life, but now had a testimony of the gospel and the mission of Joseph Smith. Requested that all unite for the success of the work in this land. Expressed his desire to fill an honorable mission and stay as long as he was wanted. Would not object if called to spend his whole life in the mission field. Had received a testimony that he will yet visit other lands. Admired the excellent spirit exhibited by Sister Mary. Hoped that Prest. Grant and his family would have a pleasant journey home.

Elder Erastus L. Jarvis remarked that he felt weak in standing before his brethren and sisters. Said that all the sentiments of love and good feeling already expressed for Prest. Grant, his wife, and daughter were in harmony with the feelings in his own heart. Realized that without the Spirit of the Lord he cannot do anything in this land. The advice of his father before leaving home was to obey the instructions of Prest. Grant and all would be well. All of his companions knew how well or poorly he had followed this advice. Spoke his love for all and said he hoped to enjoy the association of those who were to remain as he had done in the past. Prayed that Prest. Grant and family might return in safety to America, and if they ever come again to Japan that they may see the fruits of the labors they have already performed. Said he loved Elder Ensign and gave to him his hearty support. Wanted to fill a good mission.

Elder Fred A. Caine next spoke. He said that it was a pleasure to be present. Hearing of our meeting held two years ago had long desired to see this spot. God's blessings had been received during the meeting. Entertained a strong love for Prest. Grant, wife, and daughter. All three of them are striving to do good in the earth. Looked upon Prest. Grant as a father and Sister Grant as a mother. Had never known the care and counsel of a father[19] and consequently Prest. Grant's instructions and advice to him had been cherished as fatherly. Praised Sister Grant for the way in which she had made things pleasant for all and thanked Mary whom he looked upon almost as a sister for what she had done to make him and all in the mission happy. Asked a special blessing to rest upon Sister Grant that her health might be entirely restored, and expressed his delight that she was able to be with us. Voiced his love for all who are to remain and promised to support Elder Ensign and obey his counsels.

Elder John W. Stoker was the next to speak. He stated that he was glad of the opportunity to stand on so sacred a spot. Knew that we had been greatly blessed in our meeting. Heart was full of joy for all the blessings—first, for the gospel; secondly, for this mission; and thirdly, for the privilege of laboring under the leadership of an Apostle of the Lord. Said he, "Prest. Grant is a man of God whose diligence and patience is a great lesson to us." Stated that his associations with all in the mission had been most pleasant and though not so closely connected with the Grant family as some of the rest had learned to love them. Felt that he had fallen short of living up to the instructions received, but such failure should be ascribed to the flesh and not to the desires of the heart. Realized that we must labor diligently for the gathering out of the honest and so the wicked would be left without excuse. Stated that blessings promised under the inspiration of God were always realized and that the Lord would therefore remember to keep the promises made unto Lehi and Nephi concerning their seed. Desires that all shall be free in asking him to give whatever assistance he may be able to bestow, little though it may be. Referred to the restoration of his weak ankle and acknowledged the blessing of the Lord in healing him. Desired that Sister Grant should be made strong, have a pleasant voyage, and meet with her dear ones in safety.

Singing,

"Ye who are called to labor and minister for God,
Blessed by the royal Priesthood, appointed by His word
To preach among the nations the news of Gospel grace,
And publish on the mountains salvation, truth, and peace."

Elder Sanford W. Hedges followed in making remarks. Asked that the Spirit might direct his thoughts and expressions. Said that his home environs had been such as to make a testimony of the gospel difficult. In youth had used tobacco and done other things common among young men, but as he advanced in age the turning point in his life came. Thankful for the one God raised up to reform him and reclaim him from the downward path and who had offered many prayers in his behalf. Said that no church works were found in his home till after he had become interested in the Gospel and purchased them. Felt weak and acknowledged his many failings, but thought they were only of the flesh. As it had been hard, very hard for him to get a testimony of the gospel, so it seemed to be hard, very hard to obtain a knowledge of the language. Felt that he was at the foot of the column, but had never been discouraged for a moment. The kind words which he had received from his brethren and sisters had been a great encouragement to him. Especially had he appreciated the kindness of Prest. Grant, wife, and daughter who are soon to leave us. All the sisters hold a prominent place in his heart. Had received much advice from Elder Ensign which he desired to put into practice. Thankful for all the assistance received and lessons learned from every one of his brethren. Inasmuch as the gospel is to be preached everywhere, glad to be engaged as one of its heralds. Asked special blessing upon Sister Grant whose presence was an evidence that the Lord had heard the prayers in her behalf. Asked to be remembered in the prayers of all.

Sister Augusta W. Grant spoke briefly. Said that was weak in both body and spirit but strong in faith. Her presence was due to the blessings of the Lord to whom she gave all praise and glory. Much good had been said during the meeting and a most excellent spirit manifested. Accepted all that was said as true and expressed the faith that great success would attend our future efforts and in the end this whole nation be Christianized. Prayed that we might all remain true to the covenants we had made.

Sister Mary W. Ensign said that she knew the spirit of the Lord was with us at so sacred a place and that her heart was filled to overflowing with peace and joy. Desired to unite with all the rest in performing the labor here and sought the Spirit of God to assist her in performing well her share. Hoped that Pret. Grant and family would reach home in safety and find all well at home.

Sister Marie S. Featherstone spoke next, saying that the angels of the Lord were present, and that all the remarks made found an echo in her heart. Told of her love for Prest. Grant, wife, and daughter and regretted that she had not shown her love more fully in greater efforts to make them happy. Spoke of their generosity in giving advice, assistance, and in many other ways. Stated that wherever they may be, their influence will be great and good. Wished them a pleasant trip home. Expressed her desire to do all in her power to assist in the work of the future and to support Elder Ensign and take his advice on all matters pertaining to the mission. Was very glad to be present and pertake of the spirt manifested.

Sister Mary Grant stated that she did not intend to speak, but could not resist the desire to express her feelings of thanks to the Lord for His blessings. Had read the synopsis of the dedicatory prayer, but upon hearing it read again desired to state her conviction that it was given by inspiration, and that a prayer from such a source would surely never fail to be heard and realized. Whether she would ever return again to Japan or not she could not tell, but after hearing what had been said and pertaking of the spirit of the meeting, desired very strongly to return and asked the Lord to grant her desire. Did not feel worthy of the love expressed for her, but wanted to live so as to merit event greater love if such a thing were possible.

Elder Featherstone expressed the desire that Prest. Grant would bless the elders before he returned; whether collectively or individually he might suit himself and if not there in the woods, at the home in Tokyo. It was decided that this be attended to at Tokyo, the brethren being united in the desire to receive a blessing and Prest. Grant equally happy to bestow it.

Prest. Grant spoke a second time. Appreciated all the expressions of love and good will. Looked upon all the young men in the mission as his children in whose welfare he had a deep interest. Understood the feelings in Elder Caine's heart, as, like him, had never known the love and care of a father.[20] His heart went out to every elder without exception. Because of the age of Elder Kelsch had looked upon him as a brother, but had always felt a fatherly love for Elder Ensign. Stated that his heart was large enough to overlook the little mistakes of the flesh so long as the intentions of the heart are good. Satisfied with the labors of all, and felt to censure none. Said that the doubts which had arisen in Elder Featherstone's heart from time to time were no cause of alarm, as the devil was constantly watching for opportunities to place such doubts in the hearts of those who stand in the most prominent positions in the church as well as those of lesser rank. By doing well the duty of today Satan's attempts will be futile and the arising doubts be overcome. Asserted that he would not exchange the testimony of the gospel and the sweet influences of the Spirit as manifested in the meetings of the Saints for all the honors of this world. He who sets his heart upon the things of this world will be shipwrecked in the faith. To receive the Melchisedek Priesthood and its powers is greater than being honored with the position of ruler over nations.

Said that his sympathies went out to Bro. Hedges, for he realized the struggle he had had in gaining a testimony of the Truth. Asked God's blessings upon Bro. Joseph H. Felt who had been an instrument in the hands of the Lord in touching the heart of Elder Hedges. Bro. Felt is a man of sweet spirit and possessed with power to turn the wayward young men unto God. When Elder Hedges was speaking his voice sounded like the voice of Bro. Felt, and seemed as though Bro. Felt were present with us. Asked God's choice blessings upon the heads of the parents and relatives of the Elders. Invoked the special favors of the Lord upon the Elders that they might be the means of turning the hearts of their wayward brothers, sisters, and relatives unto the Lord. Asked the Lord to bless me with power to touch the heart of my brother Ed whose mind was bright and heart good but who had wandered in the wrong path as had his brother B.F. Grant. Prophesied that the blessings of Heaven would rest upon the Elders and they be filled with the Spirit of the Lord to which end he blessed them in the name of Jesus Christ and in the authority of the Melchisedek Priesthood. As Prest. Grant pronounced these blessings the Spirit rested upon him in rich abundance and we were filled with joy and gratitude.

Singing,

"God moves in a mysterious way,

His wonders to perform;

He plants His footsteps in the sea,
And rides upon the storm."
Benediction was offered by me.

After the meeting we partook of an abundant lunch which we had brought along and made two snapshots of the scene. Some had a little shopping to do in Yokohama while others returned directly to Tokyo.

Sunday, 13 September 1903, Tokyo

Sunday morning services at ten o'clock. Dinner and afternoon services at two o'clock. In the evening had a pleasant time talking together before the departure of the following morning.

Monday, 14 September 1903, Tokyo/Chiba

Up in the morning at about four o'clock. Elders Jarvis, Caine, Hedges, and Stoker left at about five, the latter two going to Naoyetsu and the first two to Hojo. I ate breakfast and left at 6:45 for Honjo Station where I took the eight o'clock train for Chiba city in Chiba Ken. After a ride of about an hour and fifteen minutes arrived in Chiba. Took a rikisha from station to the Umematsu Hotel. The prices being high I concluded to move somewhere else so after enquiring of the police about the different hotels found one, the Kanoya, which suited me. Reported my arrival to the police and my intentions to do missionary. Visited Mr. Aoki and a Scandanivan preacher. Hunted a quiet spot in the woods and held a prayer meeting. Sang, "Ye who are called to labor." Read my patriarchal blessing, blessing received from my father at the time of my leaving home, and the blessing received from Prest. Lund when being set apart for the Japanese mission. Prayer. Sang, "The time is far spent." Again engaged in prayer. Dedicated by a third prayer the district of Chiba for the proclamation of the message which I bore. After this prayer meeting I ate two pears for lunch and returned to the Umematsu by way of the seashore. After taking a bath and having a supper at the Umematsu I moved my things to the Kanoya.

Tuesday, 15 September 1903, Chiba

Weather slightly cloudy and cool. Up at 5.00 a.m. Studied till breakfast and after breakfast till 8:00 a.m. Began the work of tracting from eight o'clock. By twelve thirty had distributed fifty tracts. Bought some pears and a small cake and went into the woods for lunch and prayer. Upon returning to the hotel, wrote a card to headquarters informing Prest. Ensign of my whereabouts. Walked out to an eminance on the east of the City where I obtained a good idea of the lay of the land. On returning to the hotel was visited by a native preacher of the Swedish Church and an editor of the Tokai News. Had a very fair interview on gospel topics. Bath, supper, study, bed.

Thursday, 17 September 1903, Chiba

Clear and hot. Up at 5:00 a.m. Breakfast and study till 8:00. After the day's tracting went into the woods for prayer. Studied till supper. Mr. Aoki and his friend called. Mr. Aoki is a man drunken with vain philosophies. Received a letter from Prest. Ensign in which he advised me not to overdo myself, a steady easy gait being the more profitable in the end. Bed.

Sunday, 20 September 1903, Chiba

Cool, rain. Up at 6:00 a.m. Studied, cleaned shoes. Did not eat breakfast. Had thought of visiting the morning services of one of the churches, but decided to stay in the room during the morning and hold a little meeting by myself. After singing and a silent prayer I read from the 4th to the 23rd chapter of Mosiah in the Book of Mormon. After taking dinner, Mr. Aoki called and I went with him to his home where I had a conversation of some length on the certainty of inspiration. Returned to the hotel and read again from the Book of Mormon (from Mosiah 23rd chap. to Alma 7th chap.). In the evening I went to the Swedish church to hear Mr. Bergstrom's sermon The excellent manner in which he expressed himself in the native tongue demonstrated that a foreigner can master the language sufficiently to make himself clearly understood if he stays in Japan long enough and is diligent. However, considering that Mr.

Bergstrom had been in Japan for ten years and during most of the time in parts where no foreigners resided he ought to do as well as he did if not better. On returning to the hotel had about half an hours talk with the landlord. Bed.

Sunday, 27 September 1903, Tokyo

Cloudy, moderate. Up at 7:00. Wrote a letter to Elder Kelsch and one to father before Sunday morning meeting. In meeting we read the second Lecture on Faith from the Doctrine and Covenants.[21] Was astonished to note that the way the Prophet Joseph traced the history of faith in God was similar to the way in which I had traced the testimonys for the existence, personality, and attributes of our Heavenly Father in the tract I wrote for the Japanese. I had once before read the Lectures on Faith but in was so long ago that at the time I wrote the tract I did not know that there was any writings in the church literature that handled the subject in the same style as I had done. This discovery was a surprise, but one for which I am grateful for having been sincere and honest in thinking my writings original and not borrowed, I am not at all ashamed to find them comparing with what I consider a strong argument used by the Prophet of the Lord many years ago. Again in the afternoon I wrote other letters to friends at home and part of my journal for the last two weeks.

In the evening from 7:00 we held meeting to which our friends were welcomed. About twenty five natives were present. The speakers were, Bro. Oyama, myself, Elder Featherstone and Prest. Ensign.

Sunday, 4 October 1903, Tokyo

Cloudy and cold. Up at 6:00. Finished writing my journal up to the last of September. So many visitors called in the morning that we had to pospone our sacrament meeting. Strangers keep coming and going all day, but before beginning the evening meeting we excused ourselves and went into a room privately and there partook of the sacrament and offered prayer. The evening meeting was well attended and altho our singing was badly impaired by the absence of Bro. & Sister Ensign, yet the Lord was with us. Mr. Matsushita spoke a few words in our praise. Bed.

Wednesday, 7 October 1903, Chiba

Fair, but cool. Up at 6:00. Breakfast. Studied till about 10 o'clock when a Mr. Takaya called to enquire about the church I was representing and at the same time get a little exercise in english, I thot. He was with me for two hours. I got the spirit of the talk and after speaking for a little while in english dropped it for Japanese, and was blessed of the Lord with great freedom. Went out tracting & visiting till 5:15. In the evening Mr. Iguchi of the "Chiba Daily News" called with one of his friends and we had a very fine two hour's talk on the Gospel. As the Lord blessed me in the morning while talking to Mr. Takaya so he blessed me with fluency in conversing with Mr. Iguchi and his friend. I might insert here, that Mr. Iguchi is a member of one of the Protestant Churches in Tokyo, and seems to be very much interested in our claims as we prove them from the Bible. He is also one of the editors of the "Chiba Daily News" and has written a number of very accurate articles about "Mormonism" as he learned through his interviews with me & reading our literature (what little there is translated into Japanese). Thus far he has manifested a very friendly feeling towards me and my work.

Friday, 9 October 1903, Chiba

Cloudy and cool. Up at 5:30 After two & a half hour's study and breakfast, left the hotel for my labors among the people. Was engaged in this way until 5:30 p.m. **For two hours in the morning I was engaged in conversation with a native preacher of the Episcapal Church. The Lord blessed me greatly in defending the Gospel in the native tongue before this man. This is perhaps the first Gospel discussion in Japanese that I have ever had with a preacher. We considered many principles of the Gospel and became particularily interested in the difference of opinion concerning the Godhead.**

Saturday, 10 October 1903, Chiba/Tokyo

Cloudy and cold. Up at 6:00. After breakfast went to the barber's to get trimmed up for Sunday. Revisited a few places, then went into the woods for prayer. Felt that I had been greatly blessed of God in the labors of the week not only in being able to speak with freedom, but with /being filled with/ joy at the companionship of the Holy Spirit. On the way back from the woods, I called at the Educational Society to see if I could get their hall to preach in, but they claimed to have rented it for two weeks ahead. Went from there to the preacher of the Presbyterian Church but found him absent. Returned to Tokyo on the 2:19 p.m. train and on the way to headquarters bought a newly written book on Japanese grammar especially arranged for foreigners. I paid ¥5.00 for it and hope it will aid in throwing some light on many of the obscure points in the language. The book is entitled "A Text-book of Colloqual Japanese"[22] by Dr. Rudolf Lange of Germany. Translated into English & revised for english students by Christopher Noso now Professor of Ethics & Apologetics in the North Japan College, Sendai. He is said to be a preacher of the Reformed Church Mission. Upon arriving at headquarters, found all well.

Sunday, 11 October 1903, Tokyo

Cloudy, slight rain, warm. Up at 7:00. Wrote a letter to mother also one to Apostle Grant. A great many visitors called during the morning. **At three o'clock in the afternoon we repaired to a little stream that runs through the fields not far from headquarters for the purpose of baptizing a young man who for three or four weeks had been diligently reading the Bible and investigating the Gospel. His name is Kenzo Kato, age 20; a student of law. For the past three weeks he has been asking for baptism, but feeling sure that he did not realize the importance of such a step all of his requests until yesterday were denied by Prest. Ensign. Our experience with two out of three converts in the past, has taught us the importance of giving the applicants for baptism a little trial before allowing them to enter the church.[23]**

This young man having heard most of the Gospel-teachings from Elder Featherstone Bro. F. was requested to administer the ordinance to what may be considered his convert. We stood on the bank of the stream and sang, "The Lord is my light" I offered prayer in Japanese, then Elder F. & Bro Kato went down into the water and according to the pattern given by Jesus one more of God's children was baptized into the fold. Bro. F. is to be recorded as the first person properly authorized of God to perform the ordinance of baptism in the native language, although the prayer was translated by me some nine months previous. We returned to the house and after the brethren had put on some dry clothes. Prest. Ensign, Elder Featherstone and I layed our hands upon Bro. Kato's head & Prest. E. was mouth in confirming him a member of the church and bestowing upon him the gift of the Holy Ghost. Quite a number were present to witness the baptism and some few friends were present at the time of the confirmation.

Among those who saw the performance of this rite was a young man (well not very young either) who is studying to become a preacher of the Greek Catholic church. For some time he has been a member of that church but while on his summer vacation he came to one of the meetings we held out to Hojo and was impressed with what he heard & saw. He has been carefully reading our teachings and comparing them with what is found in the Bible and after seeing what we did to and for Bro. Kato he acknowledged that he had felt the desire to join our church for he had ceased to be satisfied with Catholicism. I feel to write here that I am impressed our growth in numbers will be much more rapid during the coming year than in the past.

In the evening we held our regular meeting. I spoke first. The Lord blessed me. Bro Oyama followed, and for about an hour he spoke with strength and spirit such as he had never had before. Truly the spirit of his priesthood rested upon him and he defended boldly the Latter-day Saints & the Prophet Joseph Smith. He had been suffering quite severely with a cold hence rather than run the risk of catching more cold while going home in the night air, he decided, upon our persuasion to stay with us over night. We were indeed greatful for the day and its blessings & experiences and our evening prayer was made up of expressions of gratitude and petitions for many more such happy days in the near future.

Friday, 16 October 1903, Chiba

Cloudy and warm. Up at 6:15. Study and breakfast. Tracting from 9:00 till 10:00. Met Mr. Aoki while tracting and returned with him to the hotel for the purpose of arranging in verse form one of the songs I had translated a few days before, but a detective from the Police Department called to inquire into my plans for the future and stayed so long that Mr. Aoki had to return without giving me the assistance expected. Went out tracting in the afternoon and was very successful in getting conversations wherever the people were at home.

In the evening I went again to the home of a native preacher of the Presbyterian Church (Mr. Kawasaki) to enquire after his church building of preaching. He met me in a very cold stern way, and even before I could deliver my message, he stated that it was a trouble to him to have me come to his house so much for the reason that he did not want to hear anything from me about "Mormonism" When I informed him that the purpose of my visit was not to talk about my religion as he thought, but to ask the loan of his church for a night or two for the purpose of preaching the pure Gospel of life & salvation unto the people, he fell down a notch but was quick to reply that he was not the whole church and had not the right to loan the building to anyone. He furthur stated that in all Presbyterian bodies it would be necessary to hold a council and descide upon the matter of letting the preacher of any other religious sect use their place of worship. I thereupon asked if such a council could not be called to consider my request, but he answered with a haughty, "No, your religion is too vastly different." At that I bowed politely, thanked him for his refusal and returned to the hotel. Ate supper, studied till ten o'clock, then retired.

Sunday, 18 October 1903, Tokyo

Fair & Warm. Up at 7:00. Sunday morning class at 10:00. Read the 5th & 6th Lectures on Faith as recorded in the Doc. and Cov. After lunch spent some hours looking over the papers and periodicals from home. The mail which arrived in the morning brought a good long letter from Prest. Grant, wife, and daughter, telling of their trip on the ocean. During the first week of the trip they had a very serious time because of a typhoon which they encountered the second day out. The passengers were very badly frightened and Prest. Grant stated that he had his clothes on for 72 hours straight. The latter part of the trip being pleasant weather, they landed safely and in good spirits.

In the evening we held our usual meeting and had a goodly attendance—more women being present than on former occasions. A Mr. Yamasaki who has been a Christian for 18 years was present and there was something in my remarks which caused him to want to speak. Bros. Ensign & Featherstone having met and talked with him before, Prest. E. gladly gave him permission to address those present. He related his experiences since becoming a Christian and so interesting was his manner of delivery that the audience did not realize that we had been together for over 2½ hours. Bro. Oyama slept at headquarters.

Monday, 19 October 1903, Tokyo

Cool and Cloudy Up at 6:30. Feeling that it was a duty to pay Mr. Hirai a visit, I asked permission to stay in Tokyo till Tuesday morning. This was granted. In the morning I wrote a letter to the Editors of the "Improvement Era" (Prest. Jos. F. Smith and Elder Edward H. Anderson) in answer to their favor of thanks for past contributions to their magazines & solicitation for further manuscripts in the future. I promised to do something if the circumstances of this mission would allow and some interesting topic came to mind, but I declined making any definite statement as to the time & name of the article. In the afternoon read and conversed with friends who called. In the evening accompanied by Elder F. went to Mr. Hirai's and had a very fine conversation with him. He seems as excellent as ever.

Tuesday, 20 October 1903, Tokyo

Fair & warm. Up at 6:00. According to the desire expressed the day before **I stayed in Tokyo during Tuesday for the purpose of visiting Bro. Kikuchi our second convert in Japan, but who for the last**

year had not been to see us or written a line in explaination. In the morning just as I was getting ready to go, Mr. Yamasaki called and I spent two or more hours conversing with him about the gospel. After dinner I started to Shiba Park where I was told Bro. Kikuchi was located, but found him in Kojimachi Ku, quite a distance away. On the way back, (for Kojimachi is beyond Yotsuya) I called on Mr. Nirayama and after chatting at his home for an hour went on to Mr. Mashimo's and presented my compliments to them.

I called in to headquarters and took a bath before going to Bro. Kikuchi's. Upon arriving at his place, found him very fairly located and very busy administering his medicine to the sick who were gathered there. He, however, welcomed me quite heartely and talked to me while operating upon his patients. Quite a novel experience for me! The lack of privacy prevented me from talking as plainly to him as I should have liked, but I felt quite satisfied with my visit as it was, for the reason that I felt a better spirit than when I called on him some 6 months previous. He stated that he had no ill feelings towards any of us and was not dissatisfied with "Mormonism," but being busy with his newly invented medicine, he had set aside religious duties for a time, etc. etc. I earnestly invited him to bring his wife & visit us assuring him that while we regretted his past indisposition towards the religion that he had accepted, yet we had for him a hearty welcome, whenever he could find time to call.

Wednesday, 21 October 1903, Tokyo
Fair & warm Up at 6:15. Prepared to leave for Chiba, but concluded to stay a day longer in Tokyo, **for at the request of Prest. Ensign I began the work of translating some songs from the D.S.S. Hymn Book**[24] **and thought it just as well to work at this in Tokyo as Chiba. The two Elders laboring in Hojo having been successful in organizing a Sunday morning class for children, reported the great need of some songs for the young folks. Prest. E. requested that I arrange to go with him and his wife to Hojo Oct. 29th to assist in some of the meetings the brethren have arranged in that & neighboring places.** Mr. Hirai called in the afternoon. We had a pleasant chat with him about the B. of M. After spending the long evening in relating Gospel experiences, retired.

Friday, 23 October 1903, Chiba
Fair & warm. Up at 5:30. Met Mr. Toihura at the hotel He had been drinking and altho he knew I was in the room next to him, yet he was so ashamed of his condition that he had concluded to return to Tokyo without meeting me, but just as he was starting away I called to him and it was amusing to see his look of shame. Tracted from 8:30 a.m. till 5:00 p.m.

In the evening at 6:00, a young Buddhist came to convert me to Buddhism, but I believe he failed and he realized it also. However he is the most thoroughly converted Buddhist and the best prepared person to defend his faith that I have thus far met. Two others were present to listen to the conversation which lasted till 10:45.

Saturday, 24 October 1903, Chiba/Tokyo
Fair & warm Up at 6:00. After breakfast started out tracting and continued till a little before 1:00. Being close to the hotel, I dropped in for lunch. Left about 1:30 for an afternoon's work, but had only started when I met Bro. Ensign who had come from Tokyo to answer in person the card I had written him about holding meeting in one of the big halls in Chiba. We went immediately to the hall, but according to the statement of the owner (which I believed & still believe to be false) a telegram received the night before had engaged the hall for a week. We went to two other places but found them still occupied as when I first enquired about them. We went back to the hotel and chatted for a few moments. Then left to visit Mr. Aoki to solicit his help in translating some of our songs, but he was absent. It was then decided by Prest. E. that I return with him to Tokyo, and try and find some one there who could write poetry as there seemed to be no opportunity to get very much assistance from Mr. Aoki, he being so busily engaged with his own work. We left on the 4:19 train. After supper at headquarters, I went to find our friend Mr. Yoshida to see what he could do for us, but he had moved and it was so late that I did not attempt to hunt him. Bed.

Sunday, 25 October 1903, Tokyo

Fair, but rather cool. Up at 6:30. Prepared myself for Sunday School then took a short walk, buying on the way some things [~~necesary~~] /necessary/ to complete my set of toilet implements. We read in the Sunday School the 7th Lecture on Faith from the Doc. and Cov. After Sunday School, I went out to see Bro. Nakazawa for the purpose of getting him to help in the translation of some of our songs. I found him suffering quite badly with rhumatism with which he had been bothered for over a month. We chatted pleasantly about mission matters for about two hours, then I approached him on the song affair and found him willing to do what he can in the matter. I left three of the songs I had already translated, and returned to headquarters, quite tired and hungry, having been fasting during the day. I arrived just in time to receive a letter from Chiba telling me that the hall I had been trying to secure for preaching purposes would be unoccupied from the 1st to 4th of Nov. By the time I had eaten a little supper the hour for evening meeting had arrived—it convening at 6 instead of 7 as heretofore. I felt very weak in my attempt to speak to the people assembled and was rather depressed in my flow of ideas and ability to express them. Bro. Kato our most recent convert in making a short talk, acknowledged all his sins and went so into detail that I felt the cold chills run up and down my back once or twice. Had supper about 9 and retired at 10:45.

Monday, 26 October 1903, Tokyo

Fair but cool. Up at 6:30. Spent the morning partly in idleness & partly in study. Bros. Ensign and Featherstone with their wives went down town so I kept house Wrote a card to Chiba engaging, if possible the Hagoromoto Lecture Hall for one week beginning Dec. 7th.

After noon a gentleman[25] who was at meeting Sunday night called. He had been preparing the new testament in the ordinary spoken language, and wanted my opinion on it I declined to give a definite criticism because of my lack of knowledge of & experience with the Japanese language. He read the 1st Chap. of Mark in the reformed style, and it was so plain that anyone could not fail to understand it. I had a short talk with him on the relative values of the Bible and Book of Mormon He is now teaching a great many foreigners Japanese and according to his statement he is an officer of the Imperial Educational Society of Tokyo with considerable experience as teacher of Japanese at Foreign legations After eating a late dinner (3:00 pm) Bro. Featherstone and I went out to see Bro. Nakazawa. Found him much improved. He had written in verse form two of the translations I had left with him. Had a pleasant chat for two hours. After returning at supper and then read carefully Bro. Nakazawa's rendition of our songs and so far as the meaning is concerned found them all right. Bed.

Thursday, 29 October 1903, Tokyo

Fair. Up at 7:15. Mr. Yoshida called just as we were having breakfast. We gave him a few opinions regarding the improvement of a reader in english which was in course of printing. Afterward we asked his opinion on the hymns that had been translated into Japanese. He stated that the language was not good and after listening to Prest. E. sing one, he remarked, "I forget the vulgar words while listening to your rendition of the music." This is quite a severe criticism of Bro. Nakazawa's method of writing Japanese poetry. Such songs, he said, if published would be a laughing stock among the educated Japanese. I spent the afternoon studying Japanese. Bed.

Friday, 30 October 1903, Tokyo/Hojo

Stormy Up at 4:00. **Ate very early breakfast and left in company with Prest. E. & wife for Hojo. The rain fell quite steadly, but there being little wind the boat did not rock very badly. We arrived in Hojo at about 12:30, finding Elders. Caine & Jarvis in good health and spirits.** We went immediately to the Hayaskiya where the brethren were boarding. Ate dinner, spent the afternoon in conversation. After supper went to the neighboring village, Tateyama to hold a meeting previously arranged by the Elders. An audience of about 60 listened Elder Jarvis presided at the request of Prest. E. Elder Caine and

I did the speaking. Bro Caine spoke with far greater ease than I had ever before heard him. The meeting was rather short but interesting.

Sunday, 1 November 1903, Hojo/Tokyo

Heavy rain. Up at 7:00. Left Hojo on the 8:00 a.m. boat for Tokyo. It was a very unpleasant day for traveling on the sea, but Elder F. and his wife, being alone in Tokyo, it was necessary for someone to return to assist him in holding the regular Sunday night meeting and I was chosen for this purpose. The waves were quite high and although I tried to keep my mind off the rocking of the small steamer in which I rode by reading, yet I felt a little inclined to seasickness and could only ward it off by looking out of the window and singing for a pass-time. Reached Tokyo at 3:00 p.m. Arrived to Yotsuya a little after four.

We had a good attendance at Meeting in spite of the rain. The song we sang was so amusing that it is worthy of note here. I attempted to lead the first song—"Ere you left your room this morning" etc. I started the first line to an entirely different tune with the result that Bro. & Sister F. could not follow and when I arrived at the second line I discovered that there was something wrong for the words did not harmonize with the tune I had started. We all floundered around for about a second or two and suddenly I hit upon the proper music. Sister F. was asked to lead the next song and she pitched it just right, but in beginning "Do what is right" which we sang after Elder F. address she got it so low that we could not be heard. On the start of the second verse I raised the key a notch or two and all went well until the closing hymn which I got a little high and the way in which we forced & pinched our throats to reach the upper notes, must have been funny to the natives assembled.

Monday, 2 November 1903, Tokyo

Fair and cold. Up at 7:15. Spent the morning reading and studying. About noon Mr. Kojuna the man who is translating the Bible into the spoken language and of whom I have spoken in this journal under date Oct. 26th, called and we had a two hours talk upon the Bible—teachings concerning the Godhead[26] and the effects of Adam's sin. I also related to him the story of the coming forth of the Book of Mormon and its contents. **According to advice from Prest. E I started out to find a Mr. Owada, who in Japan is a noted Poet, to solicit his criticism of the songs already written, but** after inquiring at several places to find out where he lived. I was unsuccessful so spent about an hour chatting with Mr. Yoshida.

Upon returning received mail from home conveying the news that Apostle Grant had been called to preside over the European Mission[27] in place of Apostle Lyman who had been released to return home, to assume his duties as Prest. of the Council of the Twelve. The announcement of the call of Bro. Geo. A. Smith to fill the vacancy in the Quorum of Apostles was also received and the papers gave an account of the conference in which he was unamiously received by the people.

Tuesday, 3 November 1903, Tokyo

Fair & cool Up at 7:00. It being the Emperor's birthday, the large military review took place on the Parade grounds in front of our house, but I, having seen this review last year, went to visit Bro. Nakazawa. He was absent. When I returned—12:30—the crowds had left the parade grounds. The newspapers from home telling of the conference arrived. I read them with very much delight. Prest E & his wife returned from Hojo about 3:30. Among the letters to Prest. E was one from Prest. Grant containing missive from Sister Grant & Mary. We read the contents with eager appetites. In a letter from Bro. /Geo./ Reynolds it was stated the Bro. Grant had decided to leave for England Nov. 4th (tomorrow). Bro Nakazawa called in the evening and we did a little work on the songs.

Thursday, 5 November 1903, Tokyo/Chiba

Fair & warm. Up at 7:00. Prepared to leave for Chiba by the 10:00 am train. After arriving in Chiba went directly to the hotel where I ate lunch; then went into the woods to my usual spot for prayer. After singing and praying for about an hour and a half, I returned to the hotel, calling on my way at the

Hagoromote to see about renting the hall for a week in the early part of Dec. I was informed that it was the custom to rent the place for 15 days and that if we had it for only a week the remainder of the 15 days would not be taken by anything else. I reported the matter to Prest. Ensign by the evening mail. Having finished supper, I went to visit Mr. Aoki. Spent an hour or two at his place; then took a walk with him.

During the night I was greatly disturbed, by the drinking and revelry going on in the next room. The tenor of the conversation and the yelling of the servant girls together with the laughter of the two men who were guests of the hotel, sounded as though the place had been turned into a whore house. So disgraceful was the whole affair that I was completely sickened, and after enduring it as long as I could, I demanded in a loud voice, so that it could be heard above the din, that they cease so that decent people could sleep. This had the desired effect, but so indignant had I become that even after peace had been obtained I could not sleep because of reflecting on the horror of such affairs and their being countenanced in what is considered a respectable hotel. The fact that the boarders [of] /in/ Japanese hotels, the servants, and proprietors of the same, all smile at such things and refer to them the following day as very lively, and interesting evenings, speaks ill of the morals of this people. O God! are thy servants sent to give the pearls of the Gospel to such humans—far worse than swine? And why, O Lord, are we left without words and power to rebuke such rottenness, that its stench may pass from off the earth?

Sunday, 8 November 1903, Chiba

Heavy rain all day Up at 7:00. Being the Sabboth, I fasted till evening. About 9:30 Mr. Suzuki came. He stayed till 10:00. I went with him to a Christian church to hear Mr. Iguchi deliver a discourse on the "Benovelence of Jesus" The heavy rain had cause a postponement of the meeting.

Returned to the hotel, and held a little fast meeting by myself. Sang prayed, sang again. Then read from the Book of Mormon commencing with the 7th chap. of Alma. About 1:15, while I was still reading, Mr. Takeda called on me and after a short talk he returned taking with him a copy of Mr. Takahashi's book. I resumed my reading for a little while, then [of] sang a song and offered the closing prayer. A peaceful spirit filled my heart as I sang, prayed, & read and I know that God recognized my doings. I would have liked very much to have gone into the woods, but it rained so heavily that I could not.

Just before Mr. Suzuki called in the morning I received a letter from Prest. E. concerning the hall for preaching purposes Enclosed was a letter which had just arrived from America. So full of love and concolation was this letter from mother that the tears rolled in a perfect stream from my eyes. O Lord, would that I could express unto Thee the gratitude of my heart for the blessing of [shu] such noble, faithful, pure, & loving parents as Thou hast given me.

After my meeting I spent an hour or more talking to three students of the Middle School, who came to enquire about "Mormonism. One of them, a Mr. Tanaka had seen and read Mr. Takahashi's book. When these visitors returned, I went to the home of Mr. Suzuki to see him in his home. Returned to the hotel, ate supper, then went to the Presbyterian church services. Mr. Kawasaki, the man who refused me the use of the church building sometime ago, was the preacher. Thirty five people were present, most of them looked and acted like members. I understood the little stories he told pretty well. Upon returning I spoke about the resurrection to one of the hotel clerks, but /he/ being busy I did not have a chance to get any farther than the beginning of the subject. I read in the Book of Mormon till bed time.

Monday, 9 November 1903, Chiba

Fair and warm. Up at 6:30. Ate breakfast, then studied till about 9:00. Went out tracting and was engaged in the work from morning till 5:00 in the evening. The day being beautiful, I felt well and enjoyed my labors. The Lord blessed me whenever I got an opportunity to speak. After bath and supper spent the evening in study. Bed at 10:00. In the morning while on my way to my field of labor I called at the Hagosomote and told the landlord of the place what we wanted and inasmuch as he could not promise the house to us for a week for fear someone would come and want it for 15 days, I would call again in a few days and see if we could not have it as desired. He said if no one else engaged the house by the 26th or 27th of this month, that he would let us have it for a week, beginning Dec. 7th. I promised to call again on the 26th or 27th.

P.S. Today's work finished my second tour of the city. I have now practically visited all the accessible homes in Chiba twice.

Saturday, 14 November 1903, Chiba/Tokyo

Fair & warm. Up at 6:30. Breakfast. Prepared to leave for Tokyo. Went into the woods and had prayer. On the way did some visiting among friends. Went to the depot calling at Mr. Suzuki's on the way. Bought a ticket as far as Funabashi where I spent two hours looking around. Visited the only Christian preacher in the place. His name is Mizuguchi and had heard a little of us from a Mr. Adams who crossed the Pacific on the same ship with us. Was not very favorable impressed with the place A majority of the population being fisherman. Upon arriving in Tokyo, found all well. Bros. Stoker and Hedges had returned from Nagano a few moments before I arrived. They were well and in good spirits. It seemed very good to see them again. We spent a very pleasant evening relating experiences. The Brethren had been laboring in a very hard district and had had but little opportunity to speak with the people.

Monday, 16 November 1903, Tokyo

Fair and cold Up at 7:30. **In the morning went to visit Mr. Owada, but he was not at home. Made an agreement to call in the afternoon again about 2:00 pm After dinner when the agreed hour arrived I called again at the home of Mr. Owada and found him at leisure. I showed him the three songs that had been translated and asked what he would change to arrange them into good Japanese verse and found that he asked ¥1.00 a verse. This was a starteling price but having been to his home three times to see him about the songs I could not very well reject his assistance in the songs I had already read & explained to him I told him that I would request the right to criticize them after they were arranged and request that he rewrite any part wherein the meaning was at fault or overdone etc. I went from Mr. Owada's to** Bro Nakazawa's and found that he had finished three other songs & the Doxology. Bro. Nakazawa's hip had been bothering him again considerably.

We spent a pleasant evening chatting and singing. **Prest. E. descided to appoint Thursday Nov. 19th for a special fast & prayer concerning the contemplated meetings in Chiba from Dec 7th. He as well as many of the rest of us felt very uncertain as to the advisability of we who are so poor in the language to assume the position of lecturers especially before the intelligent audiences that are sure to assemble in Chiba.**

Thursday, 19 November 1903, Chiba

Fair and quite warm. Up at 6:45. **Prest. Ensign having set this day apart for a special fast and prayer concerning our contemplated meetings in this city. I ate no breakfast. After calling at a number of places and finding the people absent, I went into the woods for prayer. For about an hour & a half I sang and prayed and read from the scriptures. I received a letter from Prest. Ensign stating that they would hold a special prayer meeting in the evening at 6:00 so after calling at one, two places, I returned to the hotel and studied till that hour; then knelt in prayer asking the Lord to give to Prest. Ensign the proper inspiration about or meetings—whether they would be pleasing in the sight of Heaven and characterized with good results. The reason for such** a seemingly peculiar prayer, is that we all realize fully our own inability to interest the intelligent audiences that we are sure to have in this city and knowing that unless we have the support of the Holy Spirit our efforts will kill instead of advance the work begun, we all (especially Prest. E.) desired to know the will of the Lord on the matter before deciding definitely upon the [matte]/hall/ and time together with the manner of proceeding.

Saturday, 21 November 1903, Chiba

Fair and warm. Up at 6:15. Studied till about 11:00 am. Mr. Aoki called ate dinner with me and we chatted together till 2:00 p.m. I had him criticise some of the most difficult parts of the piece I had written the day before. At four o'clock I went out to call on Mr. Ōta the advocate for criminals in the Chiba Court House. He was not home, so I took a walk, going out about a mile on "fisherman's street." (Ryoshimachi). Called on the barber on the way back and got a shave for 2½ cents.

When I returned to the hotel I found a group of about twenty army officers in the Restaurant connected to the hotel. There were about the same amount of singing girls and of all the horrible yells and disgusting acts, there enacted by this group of what is considered "Japan's best type" were the most repulsive! The men, mad with wine, rolled on the floor or threw their arms around the girls, who, educated to such society, allowed themselves to be clasped and caressed in any manner that the wine-bibber's whirling brain might suggest. The scene of this party of feasters was directly across the garden from my door, but one glance of no more than a minute was sufficient to satisfy my curiosity and reveal the character of those assembled. The officers of the hotel and servants smiled and laughed at this picture of revelry and when I refused to comply with their behests to look at the "interesting and lively" company, they seemed to be incapable of understanding why I could not enjoy such merry making. They tried to tell me how sweet the maidens were and how beautiful the songs and music of the stringed-instruments [was] and point out the virtue in the yelling of the drunkards. I told them that no one liked to see sweet maidens better than I, and that I enjoyed music as an art and admired man of true dignity, but considered no female sweet who lacked virtue & common decency, no music artistic that was accompanied by the voice of intoxication, and no man an object for admiration who allowed himself to be victimized by wine. Words would fail me were I to attempt an[d] expression of my gratitude for my birth and education as a Latter-day Saint. Thank God for the teachings & example of noble, God-fearing and virtuous parents!

Monday, 23 November 1903, Chiba

Cloudy and cold. Up at 6:15. Studied till 3:00 p.m. Went out visiting friends till 5:00. Returned to hotel took a bath, ate supper, **then went to the Episcopal Church to hear a sermon by the Bishop of that mission. The gentleman was a typical English preacher, but had not learned Japanese sufficiently well to get along in speaking without an interpreter. He spoke in English and a young Japanese who had no doubt translated the sermon time and time again gave it in Japanese This was the first time I had seen a sermon delivered through an interpreter and they are not a great success.**

Wednesday, 25 November 1903, Chiba/Narita/Sakura

Cloudy & warm Up at 7:00. **Received a letter from Prest. Ensign stating that we would not attempt to hold the contemplated series of meetings in Chiba for the present at least.** He invited me to come to Tokyo for Thanksgiving Day and help devour the feast under contemplation. I took the 11:00 a.m. train for Narita to investigate the condition of that place. This is a very small place but has one of the most noted temples in Japan the devotees of which are renouned for their long fasts. I have seen the beautiful temples at Nikko (the paradise of Japan) but the surroundings of the Narita shrine[28] are the most attractive I have yet seen. The spirit of this religion was so strongly felt that I could feel it even as a breeze while walking through the streets. The many large festivals that are held by this sect attracts thousands upon thousands of people; with the result that every street is lined with hotels, restaurants, eating houses, and other things that conform to the spirit of Buddhism.

Off to the side of the main temples are lecture halls and the priests apartments. In one of the large rooms sat twenty two men all of whom were working with all the speed they could attain in an attempt to count the copper & iron coins that lay in large heaps before them. These men are daily employed in this work and the donations given into the numerous coffers before the countless gods is sufficient to keep them busy during the greater part of the day. This was a great sight to me and while it appeared as though there were hundreds of thousands of yens yet the value of each coin is so small that the wealth in these heaps of money is but ordinary. I asked if they would change twenty sen (10 cents) into the smallest coins they were handling. They assented & handed over 200 coins for the one I gave them. Truly as Frank Carpenter has written in his articles about Japan. "If one were to change a $5.00 gold piece into their smallest unit of exchange he would have to have a wheel barrow to haul it away."[29]

I left Narita feeling that any elder sent to that place would find his efforts fruitless unless he received a special dispensation of providence. On the way back to Chiba, I called at a fair sized place called Sakura and spent two hours walking around & enquiring into the faith, customs, and habits of the people. On asking at the Police Office, I was directed to the Christian meeting place but found that the preacher was a resident of Chiba City and only visited Sakura twice a week. He is my friend (?) Mr. Kawasaki of the Presbyterian church. Upon leaving this place I felt that an elder sent to Sakura would have a fair chance to deliver his message and perhaps with effect.

Arrived in Chiba about 6:30 and went straight to a friend's house to get a book that I had loaned him, but he was absent. After supper, Mr. Suzuki called. He corrected some of my writings in Japanese, staying till 11:30.

Thursday, 26 November 1903, Chiba/Tokyo

Rain and cloudy. Up at 5:15 a.m. Left Chiba on the 6:14 train for Tokyo, arriving at headquarters about 8:45. **Found the brethren from Hojo had come to Tokyo to [hold] spend Thanksgiving Day with the rest of the colony. They had been traveling all night and had had a very unpleasant time. We enjoyed being together and made things pretty lively during the entire day. The Thanksgiving Dinner was a most excellent and toothsome one.**

Friday, 27 November 1903, Tokyo

Rain Up at 7:45. Immediately after breakfast, I went with some of the brethren down town to see if I could find some nice Christmas cards typical of Japan. I had decided not to buy presents to send home, thinking it more wise to use the money for the purpose for which it was sent—viz. to pay my expenses from day to day. I was not very successful in finding just what I wanted.

Spent the afternoon in chatting with visitors and in writing Christmas letters. **I rode part of the way to town and back on the new electric cars.[30] This was my first ride on an electric car in Tokyo, and the first time I had been on one for over a year and a half.**

Sunday, 29 November 1903, Tokyo

Fair & cold **Up at 7:00. Prepared the room in which I and some of the other brethren had slept for the Sunday School we /were/ expecting to hold. One week before there had been about fifty little children come to the night meeting and thinking it a good chance to invite them to a meeting held specially for the young Prest. Ensign had them all assemble in a separate room where Bro. Oyama spoke to them a little while and got them to promise to come the next Sunday at 9:00 am. At 9 o'clock there were about 75 children ranging from 6 to 13 or 14 assembled and by the time we got the meeting started there were over 85 present and some 10 or 12 of those had babies strapped to their backs. There faces looked as tho they had been washed that morning all right, but there were two ugly looking streams flowing profusely from most of their noses into their mouths and the[ir] circumstances of the homes from which they came was such as to excuse the rusty looking clothing which all but a few wore.**

Prest. Ensign said, "Well, Alma, I think I shall put you in as superintendent of the Sunday School." It is needless to say that I felt funny for it was a calling that I would not be tempted to seek for, but having been thus asked I responded and did the best I could.

We sang [blank] in English. Bro. Feathersone prayed. The second song was "Jesus once of humble birth." (Katsute iyashiku umareshi Iesu) which we sang in Japanese. I then attempted to teach the little ones the first verse of this song, but had it not been for the musical ability of Prest. Ensign and his knowledge of how to teach the same to others my first attempt as a teacher of Japanese children would have be a failure. The little ones showed themselves very quick to learn and we soon had them singing the first verse. I next attempted to tell them what [I] we would teach them if they would be sure to come every Sunday morning. I spoke a little about Jesus and where

he was born all of which the majority grasped very quickly.

Thinking it would be very fine to have a picture of this group I told them that when we had sung one more song and prayed to put on their clogs and go out to the garden and we would take their pictures. This seemed to delight them very much. They all promised to come the following Sunday and bring their friends and also hand in their names on a piece of paper so we could make a roll. We sang "Katsute etc" once more and Sister Ensign dismissed the school by prayer. We were together for about three quarters of an hour.

Soon after Sunday School a Mr. Yamasaki who had visited Prest. Ensign & Elder Featherstone quite often came in and I talked with him concerning the Gospel for about 2½ hours. This man (according to his own story) is a member of a family that have been Catholics for over three hundred years, and had come over 30 miles to investigate our teachings. The first of this statement may be true, for he seemed quite conversant with Catholism, but the latter clause I doubt for the reason that his manner did not bear out its truth. He finally asked for baptism, but after explaining what one receiving baptism should know, sense, and feel with a whole heart he said "I guess I have asked for baptism too hurredly." He stayed to our evening meeting. While I was speaking he feel asleep and begin to snore. This started a laugh and I thought they were making fun of something I had said, and my embarrassment can better be imagined then told. But if they were laughing at some mistake of mine, I determined to keep on talking till I could win back their attention and sympathies. I did not know till after the meeting that the faces pulled by our friend Yamasaki was the cause of the laughter. This together with my experience with the children in the morning made the day quite eventful.

Sunday, 6 December 1903, Tokyo

Fair and warm Up at 7:30. Prepared for the Sunday School exercises. About 26 children were present. We continued to teach them the song, "Jesus once of humble birth" and talk to them about the life of Christ. Between the Sunday School and night meeting I was occupied in talking to visitors. Our evening meeting was exceedingly well attended over fifty being present. After the regular meeting we held a [fast] /testimony/ & sacrament meeting in which I was formally sustained as Superintendent of the Sunday School, a position which I am illy qualified to hold but perfectly willing to attempt with the help of the Lord to magnify.

Tuesday, 8 December 1903, Tokyo/Chiba

Cloudy & cold. Up at 6:30. During the morning read from the Era and studied up on the Japanese songs. Went to the home of Mr. Owada, the poet, in the early afternoon and looked over three songs which I had given to him to correct, or rather arrange in good Japanese verse. I found in his work two or three places where he had mistaken the meaning. He corrected these and promised to rewrite them and forward them to headquarters as soon as he could. Not being a competent judge of the merits or demerits of Japanese writing I was able to see but little improvement over the way in which Bro. Nakazawa had rendered the same songs. It will be amusing to show the two translations to some person fit to judge and see how they compare in the estimation of those who should be sufficiently learned to express a worthy opinion.

In the evening I left Tokyo for Chiba on the 6:00 p.m. train supposed to arrive in Chiba at 7:15 but owing to a down bound train being out of order ours was delayed for two hours at a little station about 8 miles this side of Chiba. The night was very cold and no arrangement in the car to keep a person warm except a small tank of warm water. So I got out and walked up and down to keep warm, finally landing in the station by the side of a good hibachi.

Thursday, 10 December 1903, Chiba

Cloudy and very cold. Up at 7:00. After breakfast went into the Sangawa district to do some tracting but found in making my second calls that the people had simply accepted my first tract but not even looked at it in a majority of cases. At two or three places I saw the tracts I distributed lying on the dirt pile or in the chicken yard. Rather encouraging! A majority of the people in the district being fisherman but few have enough intelligence to read the new names. I almost feel it a waste of time to labor among this class for I cannot make myself clearly understood. This class of people have a language all their own. In the evening Mr Suzuki called.

Sunday, 13 December 1903, Tokyo

Fair. Up about 7:00. Sunday School from 9:00 to 10:00. Class for Japanese children (Sunday School Proper) from 10:00 to 11:00. About 50 youngsters present. **After dinner I went according to previous appointment to the Law School at Kanda to speak before the English Society of the school. About twenty students were present. Out of those who had been appointed to take part on the program but four young men were prepared. I spoke in English about 35 minutes on "The relation of Law to Religion." Afterwards the students were given the privilege to ask questions on any point I had touched upon. Three of the most absurd questions I ever heard were asked. This showed me that no more than one or two out of those present were sufficiently acquainted with english to understand me. Mr. Hiroi our teacher of some two years ago was the president of this society and the one who requested someone of our mission to appear.**

In the evening our meeting was fairly well attended, 37 being present. Elders Hedges, Nakazawa, & Priest Oyama were the speakers. Bro. Oyama spoke for about 45 or 50 minutes and was very enthusiastic in criticising the lives & systems among the Japanese. A young man sitting in the rear being a little opposed to Bro. Oyama's criticism on Socialism and also being a little the worse for wine disturbed the meeting slightly by calling out once. Bro. Oyama discussed for some time after the meeting with those who had questions to ask.

Thursday, 17 December 1903, Tokyo

Fair & warm. Up at 7:00 a.m. Spent the day in the house. Felt quite unwell about 8:00 a.m. but as the day wore on I picked up in spirits and felt very well about bed time. During the evening I wrote a letter to the Officers & members of the Eight Quorum of Elders, Bro. Jno. Evans president.

After prayer I bid the folks good night and went into my room in the Japanese part. A lamp was burning (Elder Hedges having been in about fifteen or twenty minutes before to make the bed and shut the doors). [H̶o̶o̶] As I laid the letter I had written on a table in one end of the room, I looked toward the opposite end and saw the curtains forming a door into the neighboring room moving as though someone had just gone through them. "Is a door open and the wind coming in?" "Is a burglar in the house?" These are the thoughts that flashed quickly before me. I determined as quick as a flash to investigate and went to the curtains, parted them, and looked beyond into the next room.

All was dark but a ray of light coming through the parted curtains revealed a pair of white legs ahead which I decided were the legs of a robber and at the same time I did not feel like attacking him in the dark for fear he had a knife or some other weapon. Therefore as I held back the curtain watching the white legs that appeared in the darkness I called Elder Hedges. He did not reply so I called again. He did not reply to the second call so I called out his name very loudly. At this point the white legs began to come toward me and I was just upon the point of springing forth to meet him half way when he changed his course and darted out of a door on the left into an adjoining room with me in hot persuit. He made straight for another door but [f̶] it being closed he crashed against it. The room was dark as pitch and hence I was directed to my man by the crash. As luck would have it I secured both his arms at the first clutch and had about succeeded in getting him to the light when Elder Hedges arrived. With his help I soon rustled him into the light.

Imagine our surprise! Our brother in the Gospel Hajime Nakazawa—the thief!! Both Bro. Hedges and I were dumbfounded but we held on and rustled our captive into the dining-room and called to Prest. Ensign who had just gone upstairs with the light to bring [h̶i̶m̶] it down. Upon seeing what we had taken in hand he like us turned white with surprise. We (Elder H. & I.) held on to Nakazawa's hands while Prest. E. searched him to see if he were carrying any weapons. We discov-

ered on him pincers, chisel, and other instruments showing for what purpose he had come in the night and quietly stolen into our home. Besides these things he had a very large "furnshiki"³¹ and a rope in which to put [put] and carry off his spoils.

Prest. E. called up the other two brethren in the house (Elders Stoker & Featherstone) and after speaking for a moment or two we all raised our right hands and united our voices in cutting /him/ off from the Church. After this we descided to turn him over into the hands of the officers and let the law handle him as all other robbers. Elders S. & F. went for the officers while Elder H. & I still held him bound. [H] To hear his lies and pleadings and threats and see his face which looked like the face of a maniac was truly an experience that I do not want to have again. To attempt to write all he said would be a waste of time. Suffice it to say he tried to lie to us and seeing that we would not believe his tales he tried to work upon our sympathies. This means failing to change our determination to see him punished, he began to chide us and call us unkind and hypocritical brothers.

He whinned like a dog that bays the moon and after sticking out his tongue a time or two cooled off and tried to run a bluff on the officers and told them he wasn't a robber and would explain all at the Police Station. The officers seeing his tools laughed, bound him, and led him around inside the house and out while they made an investigation of how he entered the yard & house. He told them that his shoes (cloggs) were on the outside, but when we started out to find them he said as we were looking before one of the doors that they should be here, but on investigating further we found his geta at the foot of a tree in the immediate rear of the house and his hat in the crotch above. Thus the officers caught him in a lie. After giving the officers the outline of how we captured him, what we knew of him and where he lived they marched him off to the station just at 12:30 a.m.

We excommunicated him upon the motion of Prest. E. seconded by Elder F. just at 11:40 p.m. The ladyfolks were very much frightened and so astonished were we all to find one of our brothers a thief plotting against his brethren that we shook like taking a chill. After all was over we rejoiced greatly over the way in which the Lord had delivered him into our hands and revealed to us what a reptile we had for so long welcomed into [his] our house. After all was over we [all] breathed a sigh of relief and felt a great load lifted from our shoulders.

Friday, 18 December 1903, Tokyo

Fair, a cold wind. Up at 7:30. **Went in the morning in company with Prest. Ensign & Elder Hedges to the Police Station to respond to a request of the Chief of Police relative to the capture & arrest of Nakazawa.** Spent the rest of the day in the house and tried to study but found it very hard to do so because of the persistent manner in which my mind worked upon the affair of the night before. Retired early.

Saturday, 19 December 1903, Tokyo

Fair and very cold. Up at about 7:15. During the entire day we were explaining to our Japanese friends the circumstances of Nakazawa's arrest. **Every paper in Tokyo had a little squib about the affair and all who knew us and Nakazawa were very much excited over [the affair] /it/.** Having been up considerably went to bed about 10:00 p.m.

Sunday, 20 December 1903, Tokyo

Fair & cold Up at 7:30. Sunday Sacrament & reading exercises at 9:00. Regular Sunday School for the native children at 10:00. **At 2:30 p.m. we repaired to a small stream running near the house and had the pleasure of welcoming our first female convert into the fold. This Sister has and is working at headquarters as our cook and helper. Her name is Nami Hakii, still single but old enough to have been married long ago.** Elder Stoker preformed the ordinance of baptism after we had sung "We Thank Thee Oh God for a Prophet" and Bro. Oyama had offered prayer.

In the afternoon we were occupied till meeting time entertaining friends. Our evening services were very well attended. After meeting two of our friends requested that we consider the propriety of getting Nakazawa out of jail making as a basis for their request the statement that a person who has been in a Japan prision is so humiliated & disgraced that he generally turns out a far more dangerous character than when he went in and that the government refused to recognize the children, be they true or adopted, of such a person to the second generation. In lieu of this we promised our friends to consider their request which our brothers Oyama & Kato felt to approve.

After this we assembled in the dining room and confirmed our newly baptized convert a member of the Church. I was mouth assisted by Prest. E. & Elders Featherstone, Stoker, & Hedges. This was the first confirmation ever administered in the Japan Mission by the use of the Japanese language, and the first time the native tongue was ever used in conferring the Holy Ghost according [th] to the commands of God.

During the day the following letter was received from Mr. Takahashi Goro.

Dec. 20th 1903.

My Dear Rev. Mr. Ensign,—

I am very sorry to learn that Nakazawa has become a thief on account of his poverty. You know the fact better than any other in the world. I heartily sympathize with him. I read once Victor[s] Hugo's "Jean Valgean"[32] to learn [th] to sympathize with the forced thief. Of course, speaking intellectually, you have no responsibility for his doing, but intellect is not all and all. Everybody knows that Nakazawa lost his lucrative profession for sympathizing with "Mormonism." You cannot forget it, as no one can. But Mr. Grant quite cold-bloodedly, has left him destitute of help. Of course ordinary men can to that with impunity, but not an Apostle, who too, is not poor, not to speak of his Church's wealth. To help such helpless persons would be efficacious means of accelerating the spread of your honored religion. But, as it was and is, the sympathy of the good and kind for you persecuted missionaries has died away, and there you are! Mr Grant's sudden change of his proceedings and his non-fulfillment of his promises have contributed more than any other to check your progress, or rather to annihilate your prospects. When you retired to your present place your religion too has retired from the world. The public has forgotten you, and my book has sold only **a few copies**. Of this disasterous consequences have I often told you. We call such self-contradictory movement 'The head of a dragon with the tail of a snake.'"

"In short, some persons are now very angry with you for this unhappy issue of one of your "brothers," and ready to assail you to crush your prospects trumpeting your cold-bloodedness in respect of Mr. N. Of course, I shall and will endeavor to defend you, the consequence is to be much feared. I believe you remember what I have often spoken about Nakazawa's future. I was right to my great grief. I cannot write any more. Adieu! Yours truly Takahashi Goro."

The purpose for inserting this letter here is to record the sentiments of a soured friend. This man Takahashi's name appears many times in this journal of my mission /to/ Japan. He was our closest and most daring advocate just as long as the phantomistic idea he had formed concerning the wealth and position he would obtain by befriending and writing about us, lasted. In my opinion he is a man who loves foreigners so long as he can make a fat living off of them and turns traitor and [saurer] "sauerkraut" as soon as he finds they cannot be duped neither by his flattering speeches nor by his threats. His remarks concerning Bro. Grant's cold-bloodedness and non-fulfullment of promises are a reflection upon his own dishonesty and breach of promise.

In a word this Mr. Takahashi got it into his head that because Prest Grant welcomed him to the Metropole Hotel and talked to him about the wonderful achievements of Mormonism & Mormons in America, England, Hawaii, & other places, that millions of money was going to be spent in erecting schools, churches, hospitals, cooperatives, etc and he dreamed himself into the position of chief Japanese advisor, director, or something else with a mint and a name. Hence when he saw us go quietly to work and his dreams vanish like mist, he suddenly realized that he was still the same Takahashi Goro, a school teacher, a book writer, and newspaper critic. Oh how glorious was the ease, luxury, the honor and applause of men that the dream afforded! But, oh how stinging the druggery & disappointment of awakened reality!! Thus we go on from day to day learning little by little the characteristics of the people among whom we are called to labor. Oh the dishonesty, the lying, the insincerity of the world! Oft am I led to exclaim, "Where, O God, is a truly honest soul who is hungering and thirsting after righteousness?"

Monday, 21 December 1903, Tokyo

Fair and Cold. Some wind. Up at 7:15. Spent the day in the house. Did a little studying but a great deal more playing. **In the evening the brethren from Hojo arrived having returned to spent the holidays in Tokyo with the rest of us.** I was glad to see them and feel the good spirit they brought from their field of labor. I caught a cold during the morning and it developed into quite a soar throat by night.

Tuesday, 22 December 1903, Tokyo

Fair & Windy. Up at 7:45. Stayed in the house all day. In the evening popped some corn for Christmas tree. Wrote out a part of my speech for the coming Christmas entertainment.

Wednesday, 23 December 1903, Tokyo

Fair & cold. Up at 7:00. Spent the morning in the house. The brethren went to town to buy some gifts for our friends. Elder Hedges went with Prest. E. to Yokohama and while there purchased a satsuma plate which I intend to give to Sister Ensign for a Christmas token. In the evening I went to get my hair cut. **After returning I wrote a 9 page, typewritten letter to father; the longest letter I had sent home for nearly two years.** [H] In the evening the brethren and sisters popped some more corn.

Thursday, 24 December 1903, Tokyo

Fair & warm. Up at 6:45. After breakfast, Elder Featherstone and I went down town to buy some Christmas. We went all over town in search of something for Prest. E, but could find nothing that suited us. About noon we met Prest. E & Elder Caine on the Ginza and went with them to a kisoba shop for dinner. From the Kisobaya we all went to Yokohama—Elder F. & I in search of something for Prest. E; Prest. E & Elder Caine for some presents and two boxes from America which contained our presents from [f] loved one's at home.

When we got back we found the Christmas tree all decorated and we all went to work immediately after supper preparing the candy & nuts & books for the children whom we had invited to the Christmas entertainment. We made preparation to welcome 100 children.

Friday, 25 December 1903, Tokyo

Fair & cool. Up at 6:45. We all hurridly prepared for the distribution of presents which lay on a table before the tree. At about 7:50 we were all in the dining-room and knelt in prayer, thanking the Lord for his abundant mercies. Immediately after prayer, Bro Hedges was asked to take the presents [of] out of the boxes from America. Something was found for everyone in the mission. Elder Hedges folks sent a pair of warm knitted slippers /each/ to all in the mission. Cakes and candy were abundant. Elders Hedges, Caine, and I had a great supply of remembrances and Sister Mary Grant sent a novelly constructed calander to every one individually with sentiments on each suitable to the peculiarities of the receiver.

After the opening of the boxes from home the presents presented by the members of the mission were displayed. Everyone was remembered and we rejoiced exceedingly in the tokens of love so abundantly manifested. My portion for Christmas was Three pair of black cashmere hose, four linen handkerchiefs, one silk handkerchief, one pair of undressed kid gloves, two ties, a manicure set, a two pound /box/ of candy, a Christmas cake for the mission, a Christmas card and calander for 1904 (from Mary G.), all from home. Mother sent a number of things to Sister Featherstone which indicated that she had learned of Sister F's condition and /her/ prospects of becoming a mother soon. Besides the above I received a pocket nife & four white ties from Prest. & Sister E., a book from Bro Kenzo Kato, and a set of Japanese writing implements from Sister Nami Hakii also [two] /a/ purse & card case from the photographer—Mr. Okamoto. The above would indicate that so far as gift are concerned, I had an excellent Christmas.

Prest. E. having received a summons to appear in court at 9 a.m. as a witness in the Nakazawa case, went in company with Bro Kato to the court house. Elder Caine and I went to Bro. Kikuchi's to present him with a Christmas token. He nor his wife were not at home so we left the present with the person tending the house. Prest. E. & Bro Kato got back from the court at about 12:45 p.m. [~~They~~] Prest. E. had answered all the questions asked by the judges and had seen the prisoner, but was dismissed before finding out what the decision of the court was.

At 1:00 p.m. we all sat down to Christmas dinner. We had everything that the stomach could desire. An excellent meal! After dinner I started to prepare the rooms to receive the children who began to assemble from 4:30. A number of our Japanese friends called to see us in the afternoon, some staying to witness our evening exercises.

By five o'clock over eighty children had assembled. Having arranged to begin our exercises from 5:00 p.m. we invited our friends to sit up in one end of the dining room then invited the children who were waiting in the Japanese rooms to come in. Our large dining room was filled compactly and before the program had gone on very far our room was crowded almost to suffocation. The children all sat on the floor according to the native custom.

The first number on the program was a song in english by the missionaries ("Merry, merry, children sweetly sing.") Prayer was offered by Elder Hedges. We then drew the attention of the children to the Japanese rendition of "Jesus once of Humble birth" (Katsute, iyashiku umareshi Iesu") which we had written /on a large piece of paper/ & hung up [~~on~~] so all could see it. The children having practiced this quite often in Sunday School sang it with manifest enthusiasm. They seemed to have the spirit of the occasion. I then gave the children a brief talk on Jesus & Christmas. Then Bro. Featherstone & Sister Ensign gave a mandolin & guitar duet with Prest. E as accompanist on the piano. The next was a sort of prepared prayer of praise & thanks for Christ & His blessings unto the children of men. Bro Kato read this paper. Following was a duet by Elder F. (guitar) & Elder Hedges (Harmonica). These musical numbers seemed to please the children very much. Sister Featherstone then entertained the little ones by telling them what the American children do on Christmas and how Santa Claus[e] brings beautiful presents to them.

I then explained the decorations on the tree, finishing the talk by announcing the appearance of Santa Claus[e] who with long grey beard and snow covered /winter/ cap & coat entered by a door close to the Christmas tree. The children burst out in laughter which indicated their joy. Before this time however we lighted the tree & put out the lamps. After the arrival of Santa Claus[e] he and I had a little dialogue which tickled the children as well as the older ones. After this Santa Claus[e] took the presents from the tree and called out the numbers marked thereon. Each child was given a slip of paper with a number on it when they came in, so the person having the number corresponding to the one Santa Claus[e] called out arose & received the present. This was also great sport for the assembly. After this we sang a song invited all the children to be sure to come to our Sunday School so that Santa Claus[e] would be sure to bring them another present on the following Christmas. Elder Stoker offered the closing prayer and as the children went out we gave each of them an apple & an orange. There were about 120 present and by improvising a few more presents than we had prepared [‡] we were able to send all away fairly well laden with good things. The entertainment was a grand success and as the superintendent of the Sunday School and the director of the exercises I felt to acknowledge the blessings of the Lord and the earnest & effectual labors & advice of my brethren & sisters.

After the children had returned we passed cake & candy & fruit around and spent a very interesting two hours with them. They were all elated over what they had heard and seen, thanking us for the interest we had taken in them and the Japanese children.

After all had gone we sat around to review the day. We compared the day with the Christmas of the year before and decided it was more satisfactory than the last one. A year ago we were not able to entertain our guests as we have been this year for we could not then handle the language as now. At that time we had no Sunday School among the natives and but a limited association with the older people.

Thursday, 31 December 1903, Tokyo

Fair and cold. Up at 7:45. After breakfast, read from the Book of Mormon. Wrote a letter to Sam & Lucile. Mail arrived from America. Received notice that a package addressed to me had come per SS "China" from Salt Lake.

In the afternoon studied a little. In the evening went with the brethren & Sister Ensign to eat "soba" in honor of the last day of 1903. After returning to the house we had an informal molasses candy pull. In this role we welcomed 1904.

Notes

1. Nelson A. Empey.
2. Brother Nakazawa was apparently slandering the Latter-day Saint missionaries to Brother Oyama.
3. Administering to the sick. "Blessings of health or comfort are given to one who is sick or injured. Two Melchizedek Priesthood men normally give this blessing in accord with James 5:14. The head of the sick person is anointed with a few drops of olive oil consecrated for this purpose. The two priesthood bearers then gently place their hands on the head of the afflicted person and the one sealing the anointing expresses promises of healing or comfort as he is impressed. Many incidents of dramatic and even miraculous healings have been recorded in Church history. Any worthy Melchizedek Priesthood bearer, when requested, may give such a blessing." Bruce B. Clark, "Blessings," *Encyclopedia of Mormonism*, 1:129.
4. Should be Takahashi Gorō's book, *Morumonkyō to Morumon Kyoto*, published in 1902 by the author.
5. The Church of Jesus Christ of Latter-day Saints was organized by revelation by the Prophet Joseph Smith on 6 April 1830, in Fayette, New York.
6. Unitarian Hall. Place of worship and assembly for members of the Unitarian church.
7. Alma's older brother, Samuel M. Taylor, married Sophia Lucile Badger on 15 April 1903, in Salt Lake City, Utah.
8. Joseph Smith sent the Apostles on missions. "During the 1837–39 troubles of the early Church in Ohio and Missouri, the Prophet Joseph Smith received a revelation that the Twelve Apostles were to serve missions 'over the great waters' (D&C 118:4). After arriving in Great Britain, these faithful men enjoyed unparallel missionary success and eventually returned to the Saints endowed with great power and leadership abilities." David J. Whittaker and James R. Moss, "Missions of the Twelve to the British Isles," *Encyclopedia of Mormonism*, 2:920.
9. The Zenkōji. "Famous Buddhist temple in the city of Nagano. Established in 670, it at first belonged to the Tendai sect, then passed to the Shingon. Toward 1630, it returned to the Tendai-shuu and became a dependency of the great temple Tōei-zan of Ueno. It is dedicated to Amida, Kwannon and Daiseishi, whose statues according to legend have been miraculously carried there from Korea in the 7th century.—The town of Nagano is often called ZenKōji, on account of this temple." Edmund Papinot, *Historical and Geographical Dictionary of Japan* (Tokyo: Librarie Sansaisha, 1910), 2:763.
10. Silk industry.
11. There was no injunction against Mormon missionaries swimming at this time.
12. Cottage meeting. A small proselyting meeting.
13. Nichiren-shuu. "Buddhist sect founded by Nichren in 1253. The doctrine of this sect is that of the sutra Myōhōrenge-kyō, which contains the last instructions of Buddha; these instructions were preached for the first time by Nichiren. It is the doctrine of the 3 great secrets: adoration (honzon), law (daimoku) and moral (kaidan), which resume all the discoures of Shaka; it is however so profound that only the Buddha and the highest Bosatsu can comprehend it. It is no doubt on account of the excellent doctrines which they profess, that the followers of Nichiren have always been the most turbulent and fanatic Buddhists in Japan." Papinot, *Historical and Geographical Dictionary of Japan*, 1:439.
14. The First Presidency often communicated by coded telegrams with each other and members of the Quorum of the Twelve Apostles, to avoid the hostile anti-Mormons discovering their communiqué's contents.
15. Heber J. Grant never again visited Japan. The next Latter-day Saint Apostle to visit Japan was Elder David O. McKay in 1921, during his world trip with Hugh J. Cannon.
16. City of Enoch. Enoch was the "seventh in a chain of Patriarchs extending back to Adam." Under his prophetic leadership, his followers reached a level of spirituality, through faith in Jesus Christ, that enabled them live in economic and spiritual unity. After 365 years, the entire city and its inhabitants were taken up into heaven. Rulon D. Eames, "Enoch," *Encyclopedia of Mormonism*, 2:457–8.
17. War between the U.S. and Spain. "The Spanish-American War pitted the United States against Spain in 1898. The majority of the fighting occurred near the Spanish-controlled island of Cuba and the Philippines. The resulting destruction of the Spanish naval fleet signaled the end of Spain's colonial power and the expanding power of the United States military." "Spanish-American War," *Microsoft Encarta 98 Encyclopedia*.
18. Brigham Young Academy. Founded in Provo, Utah, in 1875, Brigham Young Academy was renamed Brigham Young University in 1903 and has become the largest private religious university in the United States. Harold R. Laycock, "Academies," *Encyclopedia of Mormonism*, 1:11–12.
19. Elder Caine's father, Alfred H. Caine, passed away at the age of thirty on 29 December 1890, leaving six-year-old Fred fatherless.
20. Heber J. Grant was born on 22 November 1856, in Salt Lake City, Utah, to Jedediah M. and Rachel Ridgeway Ivins Grant. However, his father died of "lung disease" nine days after he was born and his mother was left to raise him alone in Salt Lake City. Ronald W. Walker, "Grant, Heber J.," *Encyclopedia of Mormonism*, 2:564.
21. Lectures on Faith. The Lectures on Faith were seven theological lectures given to the School of the Elders during the

winter of 1834–35 in Kirkland, Ohio. Until 1921, these lectures were included in nearly all of the English-language editions of the Doctrine and Covenants. The introduction to the 1921 edition of the Doctrine and Covenants makes clear that the lectures were deleted because "they were never presented to nor accepted by the Church as being otherwise than theological lectures or lessons." Larry E. Dahl, "Lectures on Faith," *Encyclopedia of Mormonism*, 2:818–19.

22. Rudolf Lange, *A Text Book of Colloquial Japanese: Based on the Lehrbuch Der Japanischen Umgangssprache*, revised and enlarged by Christopher Noss (n.p.: n.p., n.d.).

23. This is in reference to Brothers Kikuchi and Nakazawa, who had become disaffected while Brother Oyama remained active.

24. Deseret Sunday School Hymn Book. This hymnbook may have been any of the following three hymnals published by the Church: "S. S. Union Music Book," (1884); "Sunday School Hymn Book," (1888); or "The Deseret Sunday School Song Book" (1892). Andrew Jenson, *Encyclopedic History of the Church*, 847.

25. Mr. Kojuna (See 2 November 1902).

26. Godhead. "According the first Article of Faith, Latter-day Saints believe in God the Father; his Son, Jesus Christ; and the Holy Ghost. The three Gods form the Godhead but are 'each an independent personage, separate and distinct from the other two, the three being in perfect unity and harmony with each other.' The majority of other Christians view all three members of the Godhead as being one and the same, thus creating one of the most defining characteristics of Mormonism." Paul E. Dahl, "Godhead," *Encyclopedia of Mormonism*, 2:552.

27. See Ronald W. Walker, "Heber J. Grant's European Mission, 1903–1906," *Journal of Mormon History* 14 (1988): 16–33.

28. Shinshō-ji. "Famous temple of Narita, dedicated to Fudō. It belongs to the Shigon sect. The statue of Fudō which is venerated there was, according to some, sculpted by Kōbō-Daishi, according to others, brought by him from China." Papinot, *Historical and Geographical Dictionary of Japan*, 2:577–78.

29. Likely Frank G. Carpenter, *Asia* (New York: American Book Co., 1897).

30. Electric trolley cars.

31. *Furoshiki.* A wrapping cloth used to carry objects.

32. Takahashi is referring to Jean Valjiean, the main character in Victor Hugo's novel *Les Miserables*, who is forced to steal a loaf of bread to avoid starvation.

Chapter 8

Alma O. Taylor Journal, 1904

Friday, 1 January 1904, Tokyo

Fair Up at 8:00. Spent the day in the house. A few friends called. Ate an excellent New Year's dinner. In the evening Mrs. Matsudawa and her two daughters called. We served them ice cream and lit the Christmas tree for their entertainment.

Saturday, 2 January 1904, Tokyo

Fair & cool. Up at 8:30. Spent the day in the house. Bro. Oyama called. Received a letter from Apostle Grant. Prepared myself to speak to the S. S. children

Sunday, 3 January 1904, Tokyo

Fair & warm. Up at 8:15. Prepared the rooms for Sunday School. S. S. from 10:00 a.m. Altho it was one of the New Year's holidays yet we had a fair attendance & a very interesting exercise. From 11:15 a.m. we held our fast & sacrament meeting. All the missionaries & three of the saints were present. Had a good spirited meeting to begin the New Year. In the evening our meeting was not so well attended as usual altho we had a fair crowd and they seemed interested.

Tuesday, 5 January 1904, Chiba

Fair & cold Up at 7:40. Left Tokyo on 10:00 a.m. train for Chiba. Went to the Kanoya, had dinner, did a little writing, then went into the woods for prayer. Called at several places then returned to the hotel. Bath, supper, study and bed.

Upon arriving at the hotel from Tokyo found a letter from Mr. H. Loomis, manager of the Japan Bible House awaiting me. It contained clipping /on Mormonism/ from "The Search Light" magazine.[1] The title of the piece was "The True Mormon Doctrine" and was written by Rev. [blank] the well known "Mormon" eater who for some time was stationed in Salt Lake. Mr. Loomis asked if the article was a correct statement of "Mormon" Doctrine. I sent a letter to Mr. L. telling him that I would answer the article in another letter when I had time.

Sunday, 10 January 1904, Tokyo

Fair & cool Up at 8:30. Cleaned the Japanese room for Sunday School. At 9:00 held our Sacrament Meeting; also read from the D. & C. From 10:00 till 11:15 had S. S. for the native children. A very large attendance and one of the finest classes ever[♥] held thus far. In the afternoon some visitors called.

From 6:00 p.m. our regular evening services were held. As a strong wind came up about 5:00 and the clouds began to threaten rain not as many as usual were in attendance. An excellent spirit prevailed. I presume I have seldom been blessed with greater freedom /while speaking/ than on this occasion. The Holy Gost was made manifest through me for which I praise the Lord.

Monday, 11 January 1904, Tokyo

Fair & cool Up at 7:30. In the morning after we had eaten breakfast, **Prest. Ensign called a meeting to hear the reports of the Elders on the condition of work in their respective fields and the prospects for the future. Our session lasted till noon. After dinner hour which was spent mostly in reading letters, & papers from home another meeting was held beginning just at 3:00 p.m. The purpose of the** meeting was to consider the writing of another tract. All were in favor of the proposition and decided that /something about/ Jesus Christ's life & mission [~~should~~] /would/ be /a proper/ subject. After expressions upon this matter it was voted that someone be appointed by Prest. E to write the tract and submit to the rest for their consideration. Prest. E. stated that he would seek the will of the Lord on the matter of appointing one and make the appointment later. He requested the brethren & sisters to consider it their duty to write on the Gospel topics whenever they felt impressed to do so and thus avoid the necessity of considering who should write special tracts as in the past.

He stated that he knew the time had come for us to begin work on the translation of the Book of Mormon and asked all the brethren to use their spare moments in translating any part they might desire and preserve those translations that in some future time they might be gathered and compared, revised, and eventually absorbed into the translation of that most sacred book. The announcement that the time had come for the work on this book to begin filled my heart with joy and unspeakable thanksgiving. Because I had been praying earnestly for the Lord to hasten this work to completion that the natives of Japan might receive the benefit of its glorious teachings and thrilling spirit. After going out to Chiba City I made this matter a subject of most earnest prayer. I fasted about it and went into the woods and cried unto my God that he would speed the work. I went so far as to ask Him to give Prest. Ensign the proper inspiration on the matter and if possible bless us all so that the work might begin with the new year—1904.

Hence when Prest. E. stood up and declared that he knew the time for the translation to begin had come and that altho our first efforts would be very feeble still the Lord would abundantly strengthen us and as a result of searching the B. of M and writing it in Japanese that the power of tongues would be made manifest. I say when Prest. E. said these things my heart fairly leaped within me, for I knew God had heard me when I went alone in a fasting condition before Him and supplicated Him with all my soul in behalf of the B. of M.

I offered the opening prayer of the afternoon session and, like a flash, the thought "pray for the translation of the B. of M." came to me and I did so. Prest. E. testified that he knew when I started to pray that I would pray as I did and hence he was suddenly impressed to call on me. Truly the Lord was with us in the great abundance of His Spirit.

P.S. The following appointments were made at the afternoon meeting. Jno. W. Stoker & Jos. F. Featherstone, Tokyo; Sanford W. Hedges and Fred A. Caine, Boshu; Erstus L. Jarvis, Nakano (west of Tokyo); Alma O. Taylor, Chiba City.

Tuesday, 12 January 1904, Tokyo

Fair & warm Up at 7:30. In the morning Prest. E. called another meeting and gave us valuable instructions on how to make reports, work, act[s], and administer the ordinances of the gospel. In the afternoon went to the Ginza to look after a package from America. On returning to headquarters found that the package had been delivered. It was three pair of garments. In the evening went with five of the brethren to have a "soba" feast.

Wednesday, 13 January 1904, Tokyo/Chiba

Cloudy and rain. Up at 7:00. Had breakfast, chatted with the brethren, bid them all good-bye and started for Chiba City. Elder Jarvis left for Nakano just an hour before I started out. After arriving in Chiba, went into the woods for prayer; then began a search for a new stopping place. The Kanoya Hotel has treated me with every kindness possible, but in lieu of the fact that my friends don't like to call on me there I find it necessary to get more humble quarters and a place with a better name than the Kanoya has. I have learned much about the character of Japanese people while staying here and while I now consider it no place for an Elder to stay, still I feel that I was directed and kept here buy the proper spirit.

Thursday, 14 January 1904, Chiba

Cloudy—cold—rain **Up at 6:30. Fasted all day. Spent the morning looking for another hotel,** the surroundings of which would be favorable to my missionary work. After visiting two places I was prompted to call in and enquire at a very small looking place. I found on going through the house that it was quite large and having been lately erected everything was shining with cleanliness. I decided to take the two rooms in the extreme East end on the ground floor.[2] These rooms are not so good as others but their being a rear enterance right by the door of one I concluded they would be very handy. One is 6 & the other 8 mats. The landlord said I could hold meetings if I desired.

Sunday, 17 January 1904, Tokyo

Clear—cold Up at 7:00. Cleaned out the rooms in the Japanese part for Sunday School. At 9:30 held a sacrament meeting. **From 10:00 a.m. the S. S. commenced. Following a suggestion from Prest. Ensign, I decided upon dividing the S. S. into two classes—a primary & intermediate grade. I appointed, with Prest. Ensign's approval, Bro Stoker to teach the older class and asked Bro. Jarvis to act as his assistant. I concluded to continue the position that I had been occupying ever since the school started—teacher,—so I called Sister Ensign to assist me in the primary class appointing her also as Secretary of the School.**

In the afternoon a young Japanese came to receive a lesson in music. Prest. E. was absent so I took his place playing the tune of one of our Japanese songs with one finger and instructing the student with the motions of my left hand as to the time of the hymn. The folks sitting around the room made great sport of the attempt, but the young native didn't know enough to detect my blunders so I rather enjoyed the attempt as a huge joke. Prest. E., fortunately, had gone to the Kanda Law School to deliver a lecture before the students of the English Society.

In the evening, our meeting was fairly well attended. The Lord again assisted me to say a few things in Japanese.

Monday, 18 January 1904, Tokyo/Chiba

Fair—cold Up at 7:00. Left Tokyo on the 10:00 a.m. train for Chiba. Went into the woods for prayer. Called on at number of places where I had been kindly received before. Wrote a letter to Prest. Ensign.

P.S. In the evening I began work on the translation of the Book of Mormon starting with the title page. With the blessings of the Lord and the sanction of His Spirit I hope to progress rapidly and accurately in this work.

Tuesday, 19 January 1904, Chiba

Fair & cold Up at 6:20. Study, breakfast, tracting Spent most of the day on Nobuto district. After returning I went out to buy some large paper for a sign announcing a meeting for the coming Friday night. A friend called in the evening.

Wednesday, 20 January 1904, Chiba

Cloudy—cold Up at 6:40. After breakfast went to Sangawa and Nobuto districts to tract. Spent the day at this work. On the way back called at a lantern shop to get a couple of signs which I had left to be painted—the lantern makers being very fine penman. These signs are to announce the meeting I intend to hold Friday night.

Thursday, 21 January 1904, Chiba

Clear & warm Up at 6:45. Fasted all day. Tracted in Nobuto district. Went into the woods for prayer. Supplicated the blessings of the Lord to be with me in holding a meeting the following night. Received a letter from Prest. Ensign stating that Elder Stoker would be sent to Chiba to help me with the meeting. Bath, Study, Bed.

Friday, 22 January 1904, Chiba

Clear—severe wind & cold Up at 6:40. After breakfast went to Nobuto and tracted till 12:30 then went to the station to meet Elder Stoker who arrived on the 1:15 p.m train from Tokyo. He had been sent by Prest. Ensign to assist me in holding the meeting appointed for 7 o'clock in my rooms at the hotel. We went into the woods and supplicated the Lord for His assistance.

Upon returning ate supper prepared the rooms for the reception of the contemplated audience. At 7 o'clock no one had arrived. The wind being very strong the people evidently did not feel like going out of their homes. We were greatly disappointed in this the first attempt at holding meetings in Chiba. We sang and made as much becoming noise as we could to see if [y] we could not attract at least some of the passers by but this means of getting someone to talk to also proved of no avail. At about 8 o'clock all the guests of the hotel came in and a little later some quests of the Umematsu Hotel came to spend the evening. There were not more than 12 in all. At 8:10 we sang a hymn "We Thank thee, oh God, for a prophet." I offered prayer. Sang "Kesu oki izuru sono mae ni inoru koto oba oboeshi ka" Elder Stoker spoke for about ten minutes. He then played Home Sweet Home on the harmonica to which tune I sang "Mid scenes of confusion etc."

I then spoke for about 20 minutes, feeling depressed and utterly left to myself. The reason for this failure to be assisted in my effort is now apparent. I spoke upon an improper subject, and the audience was made up of men whose characters are not to be regarded as very high—if they be judged by a majority of the natives who travel over the country and put up at big hotels. They had come with more of a desire to spend the evening than to hear the truth. We sang "Katsute Iyashiku yashiku umareshi Iesu." Elder Stoker prayed and the meeting closed. One or two immediately returned but a majority remained. Questions arose on polygamy and instead of heading them off as I could easily have done I foolishly encouraged them and got into a prolonged and profitless discussion directly in opposition to the advice of Prest. Ensign at our last conference at Tokyo. Bed at 11:30.

Saturday, 23 January 1904, Chiba/Tokyo

Slight wind—clear—cold. Up at 6:40. Spent the morning in the hotel translating the synopsis of the books of Nephi (I, II). Prepared to leave for Tokyo. Went with Elder Stoker to a [sh] "soba" shop for dinner. Intended to call on Mr. Aoki and spend an hour with him, but just as we got to his gate we met him. He was going to the funeral of a Shinto priest who had been burned to death in a recent fire which entirely destroyed the largest shrine in Chiba. Called at the barbers. Left Chiba on 2:19 train for Tokyo. Called at the Ginza for books containing suitable songs & recitations for S. S children. Found all well at headquarters. Wrote a letter to folks at home. Bath, bed.

Thursday, 28 January 1904, Chiba

Clear, cloudy, & warm Up at 7:00. Spent the morning informing the people of the meeting arranged for 6:30 in the evening. Went to Nobuto and finished revisiting that district. Through the blessings of the Lord I have been able to converse with more people, in porportion to the size of the place, than in Chiba proper. Returned to the hotel about 2:00 p.m & found Elder Stoker waiting for me. He had been sent out by Prest. Ensign to assist me in holding [a m] the evening meeting. We went into the woods for prayer. Returned to the hotel and prepared the rooms to receive the guests.

At 6:30 not many were present so we waited for 15 minutes. When we started we had an audience of about 20 or 25. As we proceeded with the opening exercises others came until we had the rooms dotted with listeners We sang, "Our God we raise to Thee etc" Elder Stoker prayed. One statement in the prayer caused some in the front to smile audibly. This rather disturbed me for in looking over the audience I notice that [they] it was mostly composed of students from the medical college and like the students of all higher institutions /of learning/ would no doubt hold in derision one whose language was no better than either Elder Stoker's or my own. To have them laugh in the middle of the opening prayer was not a very favorable sign of what they would do during the course of our talks. We sang again "O say, what is truth?" I then spoke touching upon the establishment of the Church through the Prophet Joseph Smith and the mission of the Church as a forerunner of Christ's kingdom on earth. All during my effort there were smiles passing over the faces of those before me and before I got through five young men right in the front row stood up and went out. Others would occasionally shift around as though disinterested but then quiet down again and give good attention. I spoke for at least 50 minutes. We then sang, "Do what is right." Elder Stoker spoke for some fifteen minutes. He was blessed of the Lord and was understood by those who listened. We sang again "Katsute iyashiku umareshi Iesu." I offered the benediction and invited any who had questions to remain. No one had any thing to ask. Just as the meeting was dismissed three Japanese came. We invited them in and conversed for nearly a hour and a half. After they returned [‡] we ate supper; neither one of us had taken anything during the day. In comparison to the meeting held a week before this one was a grand success and filled our hearts with joy. We gave and do still give all praise and honor and glory to God.

Thursday, 4 February 1904, Chiba

Fair—warm Up at 6:45. After my usual exercise went to Miyakonomura for the purpose of putting up posters announcing the meeting Saturday night at Mr. Kikujiro Nakamura's house. I also visited many of the houses inviting the people to the meeting. Found a home in a most deplorable condition and donated a little rice for the occupants. Returned to Chiba in time to meet Bro. Jarvis at the station. He arrived on the 1:15 train. We went into the woods for prayer; I having been fasting since the night before. Returned to the hotel prepared the rooms for the meeting ate supper and welcomed our friends. By 6:30 only three had arrived at 7:20 we had enough to begin on so we sang prayed and as we were singing the second hymn quite a number came in making 18 in all. I spoke for 50 or 55 minutes on the resurrection of the dead as an achievement of Christ in the interest of mankind. We sang again and then Bro. Jarvis spoke for about 25 or 30 minutes on faith & works.

Before the meeting began, Mr. Nakamura came from Miyakomura to say that the priest of his sect had come to him and told him it was wrong for him to let a Christian service be held in his home. Mr. Nakumura was influenced by the priest sufficiently to come all the way to the hotel to see if I could not cancel my arrangements, but having already visited every house in the village and invited the people I did not see how I could. I talked with him for some time about the matter and tried to show him why the priest opposed me and assured him that the priest did not know anything about the teachings I am spreading and consequently could not judge without hearing [me] whether we were right or wrong. I promised on his /Mr. Nakumura's/ request to call and see him the following morning.

Friday, 5 February 1904, Chiba

Cloudy—warm Up at 6:45. After breakfast went in company with Elder Jarvis to Miyakomura to see about the objections the priest of the temple there had made to holding a meeting in the home of one of his followers. He was afraid to come out with a full statement of his objections showing to us that he was only making baseless threats and causeless complaints to Mr. Nakamura to frighten him out of allowing a Christian meeting at his home. Mr. Nakamura called in a friend to consider the matter anew so we had to leave the matter unsettled [neither one way nor the other] I asserted with all my strength how detrimental it would be to me and my religion if I were to disappoint the people of the village all of whom I had by personal visit invited to be present. However, seeing the talk of the narrow-minded priest had frightened Mr. Nakamura, I consented to forego that part of the program which called for a discourse on Christ or religion and entertain the people with American songs. This brought a smile of approval over Mr. N's face and he said surely there could be no objection to a song service but even on that he would have to see the priest. He promised to send a messenger to tell me of the decision.

As we returned to [Tokyo] Chiba, we called at a temple belonging to another sect of Buddhism (Tendai) We met the priest and in the course of a short interview we sounded him on letting us use the assembly rooms of the temple for the purpose of instructing the people in the ways of the true God. He made some excuses and in order to predict what kind of a service we would have a lady working around volueneered the following excellent explaination of the character of their own services. **"The whole place is packed with men, women, and children who smoke, drink, and sometimes quarrel until there is nothing going on except confusion & noise which is certainly disagreeable." The priest evidently did not appreciate the frank way in which the old woman told us the character of the serv-**

ices conducted at his shrine but after awhile he confirmed part of her statement by saying "the people always smoke & drink."

Saturday, 6 February 1904, Chiba

Fair & warm Up at 7:20. After breakfast studied a little while. About 9:30 a messenger came from Mr. Nakumura's with the intelligence that we could hold our meeting as at first contemplated if we would do so under the name of "Song Service." The messenger stayed all day. A friend called with whom I had a very interesting conversation.

Went to Miyakomura arriving at the place of meeting just at 5:00 p.m. Only three were present at the appointed hour, but an hour more brought 80 adults and 40 children or more. With this audience we began our meeting. I have never stood before such an unsettled audience. For about 50 minutes I held them down as well as could be expected. Bro. Jarvis spoke for 30 minutes. The people were very much surprised at our request that they refrain from smoking the reason being found in the old woman's statement [found] given in the account of yesterday. While I was speaking a man a little the worse for "sake" interrupted me. When silenced he concluded to go away. Much confusion on the outside made it necessary for Bro. Jarvis to go out and put it down. While Bro. Jarvis talking the landlord came stalking through the crowd and presented him with a cup of hot water and then gave me one. Then he brought out a tray with tea and cakes and passed them around. A number kept going in and out all the time to have their smokes; they could not endure for an hour and a half without a puff. In all we felt blest in our effort and give the praise to God. Returned to Chiba, supper, bed.

Thursday, 11 February 1904, Chiba

Clear—warm Up at 7:00. Mended my clothing. Went out to Miyakomura to continue tracting that district. Was successful in getting a house in which to hold a meeting. Arranged for a meeting on the 12th beginning from 7:00 p.m. The man who kindly opened his house is named Takai Jihei evidently of very fair standing in his village. Went to every house in the village to invite the people out to hear our message.

Returned to the hotel at 3:15 p.m. just as Elder Stoker arrived from Tokyo. We went into the woods for prayer. I had been fasting since the night before. **Bro. Stoker brought me some letters which had come from America. One from mother announced the Samuel's wife had given birth to a boy baby on Jan. 18th and all were doing nicely.** From 7:00 p.m. we held our meeting in my rooms. A fair crowd came out to hear us and the Lord sustained the listeners as well as the speakers. There was a peaceful sweet, spirit; not the least tendency on the part of those present to mock our poor Japanese The subject discussed was "God, the Father of the human race." After the meeting my heart was filled with unspeakable joy and thanksgiving for the glorious blessings of the Lord unto us. After the meeting Mr. Aoki who came in during the course of my remarks assisted me in correcting the translation of the "Articles of Faith" and suggested how to improve our two songs.

Saturday, 13 February 1904, Chiba/Tokyo

Clear—warm Up at 6:30. Left Chiba on the 10:19 train for Tokyo. The reason for the early return was that **Prest. Ensign had arranged for Bro. Oyama to meet us at 2:00 p.m. and explain before us all his reason for withdrawing from us. He did not come till after three o'clock. In listening to his statement we learned that he considers us absolutely devoid of authority and while he had no power to judge whether or not we were once the true servants of the Lord he certainly [called] considered us shorn of all power now.**

The objections which he named in support of his argument were about as follows:—We come here to teach the people in the ways of the Lord but in writing [three] our doctrines we go to men without power or sympathy to get their criticism of our Japanese translation of the same. When Christ was born the wise men and scholars came to do homage to him. If we are the servants of the Lord the scholars should seek us out and we should not go to them for help as we had done. We dis-

tinguished between the poor & rich, the sick & the well, the scholar and the ignorant man which no man of God should do. We found fault with our native brethren in the presence of others etc. etc. We talked with him about his objections to us, but he was so set in his opinion that he practically refused to listen to us. At any rate he said all our attempts to answer him & show him his error were in vain only confirming him in the belief that we had lost our power and their was not spirit in our Japanese literature. He called us to repentance and asked us to cut him off from the church if we did not come to his terms & acknowledge our mistakes which he had attempted to point out. We saw that it was useless to try and reason with him for he practically scorned all we had to say. The conversation was peaceful and without any excitement or heated words. It is my opinion that the peculiar ideas Oyama holds on most subjects are the result of an impa/i/red mind, altho I hope I am misjudging his mental ability.

Thursday, 18 February 1904, Chiba

Clear—cold—windy Up at 7:30. Ate breakfast, studied a little while then went out visiting friends in Chiba. Ate dinner at a "sobaya" and returned to the hotel about 4:00 p.m. Found, to my great surprise, that Bro Katō had come out at the request of Prest. Ensign to help me with my meetings. I was delighted to have him with me and feel his spirit for he acted as though he wanted to do his duty. We went into the woods for prayer. He cannot speak English and we did not know the words to the Japanese songs so I did the singing all by myself. We prayed in turn then returned to the hotel. Took a bath, ate supper and then awaited the arrival of the audience Two men and one little boy came so we had to postpone the meeting, but I had a nice talk with the two guests. One returned about 9:15 but the other remained till 10:00. We were disappointed in our contemplated meeting, but I feel to thank the Lord for the pleasant time had with those who came.

The cold piercing wind was no doubt the cause of many staying away, but our poor Japanese sounds harsh to the Japanese ear so many who had come once or twice no doubt have concluded that it is a waste of time to listen to the terrible way in which we murder their mother tongue. **In fact one of the friends last night told me frankly that our language is so poor that many if not a majority have gone away from our former meetings disgusted with [——] us and everything "Mormon." Rather a flattering criticism after being in Japan for 2½ years & studying the language diligently.**

Friday, 19 February 1904, Chiba

Clear & warm Up at 6:20. Exercise, breakfast, study. **About ten o'clock went to the home of Mr. Aoki to see if he had corrected the songs I left for his criticism some time ago. He was at home. I spent two hours with him in going over the songs with the result that one song was entirely criticised and the first verse of another rearranged The completed song is, "See the mighty angel flying."**

Returned to the hotel had dinner with Bro. Katō then /we both/ went to Miyakomura /to hold a meeting/ according to previous arrangment. We visited a number of place on the way inviting the people to come out and hear what we had to say to them. The meeting was well attended—children, of course, being in the majority. A great number of women were present and had all the young and middle aged men who stood on the outside come in we would have had the house jammed. There is a terrible custom in this land of coming to everything in the nature of a meeting an hour or an hour and a half late. This custom prevented us from beginning the meeting at seven o'clock as designed. It was five minutes to eight when we sang the first hymn. Another agravating thing is that the people stick their heads in at the doors & windows and it is so hard to get them to come in as it would be to dig up so many posts and pack them in. The reason for this is that they have not had any training [about] in how to act when they come together to hear a lecture or sermon. Bro. Katō spoke first and did very well indeed. The experience seemed to do him good. Paid 50 sen for the use of the house. Returned to the hotel at 10:30. Bed.

Sunday, 28 February 1904, Tokyo

Cloudy—slight rain. Up at 7:00. Prepared the rooms for S.S. From 9:15 to 10:00 held Sacrament

Meeting. From 10:00 to 11:30 held S.S. In spite of the big storm the night before and the unpleasant morning we had a very fine attendance.

As we were singing the last hymn, we[re] were delightfully surprised to see Bro. Kikuchi come walking in. After an absence of over a year and 4 or 5 months it seemed almost as though he had returned from a sleep in the grave or somewhere else. He stayed with us all afternoon and spoke in our evening meeting making a very pleasing speech. He left feeling very well and said he would come again the following Sunday. He has been prevented by the law from practicing the theory of injection which he claims to have discovered and which he has been using for over a year past. He has not a doctor's license so when it way discovered that he was administering his medicine to the aflicted with /out/ legal permission a cry was raised and he was prevented from continuing in the development of his **great** plans. He says now that all he can do is to sell his medicine to those who can use it. This has given him much leisure time and, as he said, his body has grown fat & hale but his spirit has grown weak, and he intends now to devote more time to the nourishment of his finer feelings & sentiments. It is, of course, still to be seen how earnestly he feels on the matter of religion and his own church duties

Tuesday, 1 March 1904, Chiba

Clear—warm Up at 7:30. Spent the morning studying. Went out at noon to get some books and meet Bro. Stoker who arrived at 1:30 Returned to the hotel at dinner, then went into the woods for prayer. From the woods we went directly to Henda to hold the meeting appointed for 7:00 p.m. It was 8:00 o'clock before we got started and our audience was made up mostly of young people who were not quite so orderly as we would liked to have seen them. I felt rather depressed in talking to them. There were practically no responsive hearts in the whole audience. The day was rather an unaspicious one for the reason that the old folks of the village had been assembled here and there in small groups all afternoon for the purpose of observing some of the rites of their own religion. As a result most of them were so full of wine that they were no doubt ashamed to come out or at least found sleeping more easy than listening to a Christian sermon. I felt thankful that they had enough sense to keep away, for had they come we would have no doubt been greatly disturbed. As it was the young men assembled were very rude and loud-mouthed evidently taking the license for such conduct from the example set by their parents. After the meeting had a short conversation with a few of the older & most attentive. [I] I felt like any further attempts at holding a meeting in that district in the near future would be utter failures so I did not enquire after a place for future gatherings.

Wednesday, 2 March 1904, Chiba

Very heavy rain Up at 7:15. Ate breakfast then went in company with Elder Stoker to the home of Mr. Aoki to assist in finishing the translation and arrangement of the song "What was witnessed in the heavens?" We stayed till 1:00 p.m. but did not get it finished. Having an appointment to meet some friends at the hotel at 2:00 we hurried back and had dinner. The friends did not come till 3:15. We conversed with them for an hour and a half. We then held a short prayer meeting and started for Yahagi to hold the meeting appointed in that place for 7:00 p.m. A very severe rain storm had been raging ever since early moring and about 3:00 p.m. it seemed almost like a cloudburst, but by the time we were ready to leave the hotel it had cleared off nicely and everything became favorable to us. We walked through the village to let the people know that we had arrived and would hold services as announced. Quite to our surprise a large crowd had gathered at 7:00 o'clock, the appointed hour. We began to sing at 7:10 and held a most excellent meeting for a full[y] hour & a half. The rain had kept the people in all day so they were glad to get out in the evening. We had a house full of listeners and it was the best spirited meeting for a country village held thus far. The people were quiet and a majority fairly well educated. The house was large and the owner arranged it very comfortably. The walk home in the light of a full moon was delightful. Fully a hundred adults were present.

Thursday, 3 March 1904, Chiba

Clear—warm. Up at 6:30. Spent the morning in the hotel studying. About noon went out with

Elder Stoker, bought some cakes & baked sweet potatoes, and went into the woods for prayer and lunch. On the way back from the woods called at a place or two to see some friends whom I had been able to make. They were all absent but one. Returned to the hotel just as a Mr. Tamaru came to visit us. This young man lives a long ways from Chiba, but according to what he said, on passing the hotel he saw the sign announcing a meeting for 7:00 p.m. and, being very much interested in the Bible and Christ, he concluded to stay over a day for the purpose of attending the meeting. We talked with him for about two hours. He attended our meeting, which instead of beginning at 7:00 as announced began at 7:40. It looked as tho we would not be able to hold one at all, but when the number of visitors reached 7, we decided to start. Two medical students came in about 8:30. After the meeting had a short conversation with three who remained to chat after the meeting.

Friday, 4 March 1904, Chiba/Tokyo

Cloudy—warm Up at 6:25. Mr. Tamaru spent the entire morning with us. Including the two hours conversation and meeting yesterday, the man has certainly heard more about the Gospel than he will be able to remember unless wonderfully blessed by the Lord. He seemed earnest and I pray God, my Heavenly Father, that He will bless all that Bro. Stoker & I said in this man's hearing and sancitfy it to his good. In order to called at Mr. Aoki's to return a borrowed umbrella and eat dinner at a "sobaya" we left the hotel at 12:30, /and then catch the 2:19 train for Tokyo./ Upon arriving in Tokyo found all peace, happiness & health at headquarters. Supper, prepare to leave on the following morning in company with Prest. E & Bro. Katō, for Hojo, Boshu. Bath, bed.

Saturday, 5 March 1904, Tokyo/Hojo

Heavy rain all day. Up at 5:00 a.m. Dressed and left in company with Prest. Ensign & Bro. Katō for Hojo. The sea was smooth but a heavy rain made it more unpleasant than we anticipated and desired. Elders Hedges & Caine were out to meet us. They were well in body & spirits. The rain continued during the entire day spoiling the prospects for a good meeting at the place /in Tateyama/ selected by the brethren. During the afternoon, Elder Caine & I compared notes on the translation of the first chapter of I Nephi. Elder Caine has translated four chapters.

After supper we went out in a very severe shower and by the time we arrived in Tateyama everyone of us were soaked to the knees and would have been in a far sadder condition had we not been protected by long overcoats. In Japan the people have a poor record for coming out in a rain storm especially when the occasion is a Christian meeting held by foreigners who don't know how to speak Japanese. By eight o'clock there were fourteen prepared to listen. A few moments later we began the meeting Elder Hedges making the announcements. Bro. Katō and I did the talking. I felt free in my remarks & recognize the hand of God in sustaining me while I stood before the few assembled. On the way home we did not encounter so severe a rain as when we went. After talking a little while we went to bed. The change in temperature was so marked that we did considerable perspiring.

Sunday, 6 March 1904, Hojo

Rain during morning—afternoon clear. Up at 7:00. It being fast day we ate no breakfast. Talked about different subjects till about 9:30 when the S.S. children began to come. By 10:00 there was over twenty bright-looking little boys and girls seated on the floor ready to hear what their "sensei" (teachers) had to teach them. The regular S.S exercises were suspended in order to give the visitors from Tokyo a chance to speak to the children. I spoke to them for a little while, then Prest. Ensign taught them the first verse of the new song, "Love at Home." They seemed to enjoy it very much. Bro. Kato then spoke. The children were very orderly and seemed to appreciate seeing new foreign faces.

From 2:00 p.m. we held a fast & sacrament meeting. A peaceful spirit prevailed. In the afternoon we took a walk around the village & town. In spite of the heavy rain of the day before which lasted all night and ended in a terrible downpour about 9:00 am [this] in the morning we met a cloud of dust coming up one of the streets suffcent to make that part of our walk unpleasant. In other words this street, and in fact all of streets in the town, were changed from almost riverbeds [of n] to dust ways in seven hours.

Soon after supper the guests for the evening meeting began to come in. By 7:15 we had a fair crowd which grew larger as the opening exercises progressed. Elder Caine was the first speaker, Bro. Kato followed; a song was then sung after which I spoke for something over 30 minutes.

Saturday, 19 March 1904, Chiba/Tokyo

Rained all day Up at 6:45. Spent the morning in the hotel working on the Book of Mormon. Went out to Yahagi to thank Mr. Nagashima for his kindness in allowing us to hold a meeting in his house on the night of March 2nd. Called at the homes of two people whom I met /and had/ conversations with while tracting Yahagi. Returned to Chiba & went immediately to the depot to catch the 4:19 train for Tokyo. Upon arriving at headquarters was glad to find two letters from home and other good news. The "Millenial Star"[3] from England had a three page article about the "Semi-occasionally that we sent to Apostle Grant for New Years. Was greatly surprised at the confession of Bro. Katō. He announced to the folks at Tokyo that he was a married man and had been since September of last year, but for various reasons had kept the matter a secret until now. We had often seen his wife, but did not know who she was. Things have gone against him lately and he is in financial trouble and has asked to live with us at headquarters, for his wife's folks can't take care of her any longer so he wants to bring her along too. Surprises that are not pleasant are continually being sprung by our converts.

Monday, 21 March 1904, Tokyo/Chiba

Fair & warm Up at 6:45. Prepared to leave for Chiba. The time table of the Honjo-Choshi Line having changed, I left on the 10:35 train instead of the 10:00 as heretofore. At every station along the line the people of each little village were gathered to bid farewell to a large body of soldiers who were leaving the barracks at Sukura for the field of battle. It being a national holiday everyone seemed to be out in the streets for I could hardly get from the depot to the hotel without pushing my way through the throng. The name of the day is "Shinki Koreisai."

So many people being on the streets I concluded, that it would be about useless for me to do any visiting. Judging from the spirit of things even if I [did] should find people at home they would no doubt be celebrating the day by drinking wine etc. Therefore I worked on the Book of Mormon till 5:00 p.m. then went into the woods for prayer having fasted all day. Returned to the hotel, ate supper, studied a little, then went to bed.

Friday, 25 March 1904, Chiba

Cloudy, warm Up at 6:45. Spent the day visiting the people of Kasōri. It was just 5:50 p.m. when I called at the last house in the village. This day's work completed the third round of the village. Upon returning to the hotel found that a number of soldiers were there to stay over night. After supper they indulged in games and "sake" as a result of which the air was filled with obscene words far more objectionable than the tobacco and "sake" smells. Another evidence of the terrible degree of immorality and sin that prevails everywhere in this nation.

Saturday, 2 April 1904, Chiba/Tokyo

Cloudy, warm Up at 6:45. Went to Yahagi and worked in that village till 2:00 p.m. Returned to the hotel and prepared to leave for Tokyo on the 3:05 train. Found all well at headquarters, but was surprised to learn of conditions existing in Shirahama where Elder Caine is laboring alone. Evidently the Buddhists of that district have become much worked up over the presence of an active Christian preacher and they have found little trouble in exciting the ignorant and credulous who /perhaps/ had never seen a foreigner before Bro. Caine came among them. And at present, while war is going on with a foreign land the people of a little out of the way place like Shirahama can be easily made to believe any lie that a priest might concoct. The landlady of the house in which Bro. Caine is staying received the following unsigned letter March 29th

Kika ni oite chikagoro yosokyō wo hikikomi, taisetsu ni shite oru yoshi kiki, oyobi ikani mo kokoro ye chigai ni sōrō. Nippon koku no kisoku ni somuku shūshi nari. Yotte sassoku oiharaubeshi. Moshi nagaku oku [~~tosh~~] toki wa omaesama no [~~uchi~~] ie wo yakiharai mata yasokyō wo uchikoroshite shimau yae kakugo wo shite orubeshi soro. Ni san nichi no uchi oihasawanai toki wa kitaru kyū no hatsuka made no uchi ori wo mite hi wo tsuke, yasokyō mo kitto korosu kara shochi shiro.

"This sounds fierce" as Elder Caine says, but I don't think Bro. Caine is going to leave his field. The matter was at once placed in the hands of the police and Elder Caine, not wanting, in the case of trouble, to bring any evil upon the home of his landlady moved to a hotel after telling the [——~~of~~] owner fully about the reason for coming to his hotel. This is the first signs of active hatred toward us and is the only threat[s] made against any of the elders. As a change, it seemed very fine, but we pray earnestly for the safety of our brother. It is perhaps a good sign for the success of future work in that district. It is hoped that the attention of the honest in heart will be attracted and they converted to the truth.

In the evening we colored 95 eggs for the S.S. children for it was Easter Sunday the following day.

Sunday, 3 April 1904, Tokyo

A little cloudy but warm. Up at 6:45. Sunday School from 10:00 a.m. There was not more than half the usual attendance. The presentation of the Easter eggs was the unusual feature of the day. Before distributing them I spoke of Christ's death and resurrection drawing special attention to the fact that the Christian World was that day celebrating the 1870th anniversary of Christ's triumph over death. From 1:00 p.m. till 2:00 p.m. we had a S.S. teacher's meeting From 2:00 p.m. we held the regular fast & sacrament services. All but two of the speakers spoke in Japanese which reminded me of old times. Dinner followed the meeting. The night meeting was exceptionally well attended.

Friday, 8 April 1904, Chiba

Clear & very warm Up at 5:30. Spent the day tracting in a part of Chiba City. In the morning about 9:00 o'clock a Mr. Takeyama called. He is the interpreter for Chiba Ken & attends to all translating from English into Japanese or visa versa that the Ken authorities may require. **Soon after the advent of the "Mormons" into Chiba Ken he was directed by the State government to translate into Japanese the account given of the "Mormons" In one of the large English Encyclopedias. By reading & translating this he became very much wrought up over what appeared to him a most terrible sect. He had known that I was here in Chiba, but he felt like he did not want to associate with me. But while in Tokyo some time ago he came across a copy of Mr. Takahashi's book on "Mormons & Mormonism." and by reading it came to the conclusion that the encyclopedia article must have been written by our enemies and that there was much to be admired in our doctrines and manner of living. After his opinions had thus changed he concluded to call on me and make my stay in Chiba as pleasant as possible.**

Saturday, 9 April 1904, Chiba/Tokyo

Clear & warm. Up at 5:50. Went to Kusori and arranged to hold a meeting in the home of Mr. Sentara Hara on April 13th. Visited every house in the village and on the way back to Chiba called at Henda to see if I could not secure a place there. The owner of the house as which I enquired was absent. After gathering up a few deeds I started for the depot, calling around by Mr. Aoki's.

P. S. Learned upon returning to headquarters that Bro. Katsunuma from Hawaii had visited Prest. E on Monday the 4th. Bro. Katsunuma is the first Japanese to join the Church in all the world. He was converted in Utah many years ago. He has become an American citizen and is now in the civil service at Hawaii. He having received a month's furlough is in Japan visiting friends & relatives. He sought the "Mormons" out the first thing and seemed pleased with what they had accomplished & were doing. He was glad to see some Latter-day Saint Hymns in his native Language and gave the Sect. of the mission ¥10.00 towards further translation.

Another happy intelligence upon my arrival was the birth of a 10 pound son in Bro. Featherstone's family. The day was Wednesday April 6th the 74th anniversary of the /re/establishment of the Church. All were doing well and Bro. F & his wife were greatly pleased with their heir.

Wednesday, 13 April 1904, Chiba

Clear, warm Up at 5:30. Spent the morning in Yahagi. Secured the house of Mr. Toyozo Hara for the purpose of holding a meeting on the evening of the following day. Passed through Henda on the way to Docho Chiba City where I did a little tracting. Returned to the hotel about 3:45 p.m. and found Elder Stoker had arrived from Tokyo. We ate supper and went out to Kasori to hold the meeting appointed. The audience was principally composed of women. The men hung around on the outside. A rather annoying feature was that the men, women & children of the house were bathing right in front of the entrance doing the act of welcoming the comers at the same time. Certainly this land is still barbarous in many respects. There was very fair order observed. I have held better meetings but have no particular sorrows about this one. One noticable feature was that all those who were most anxious to have me hold another meeting in that village were not present. Quite illustrative of one phase of Japanese character. Returned to the hotel a little before 11:00 p.m. & went immediately to bed.

Monday, 18 April 1904, Tokyo/Chiba

Cloudy. Warm Up at 6:45. Left Tokyo on the 10:25 train for Chiba. Prest. Ensign on the first boat to Boshu to look over the country and see what the elders in that field are doing. Upon my arrival in Chiba I went immediately to the home of Mr. Aoki to eat dinner with him according to previous promise. One of the converts of his church was present. I had a fair conversation with him. Visited at Mr. Aoki's till almost 5:00.

On the way to the hotel called on a lady whom I had met and /with whom/ had had several conversations. She received me very kindly. I had a conversation with her which lasted over two hours. Before leaving I had prayer with her at my suggestion & her permission. This is the first time I have ever prayed under such circumstances.

Saturday, 23 April 1904, Chiba/Tokyo

Fair, warm Up at 5:00 pm. Went immediately into the woods for prayer. Returned to the hotel and had breakfast. Then went out to do some visiting among friends. **Left Chiba on the 4:29 train for Tokyo. It being my last day in Chiba City for a long time (it having been thought well to give the district a little rest) a number of my friends were at the depot to say "goodbye." Upon arriving in Tokyo found that** Prest. Ensign had returned from Boshu where he went the previous Monday morning, bringing back with him Elders Hedges and Caine, who together with all the rest at Headquarters were in good health.

Sunday, 24 April 1904, Tokyo

Fair, refreshing Up at 6:20. Sunday School from 9:00 Sacrament Meeting from 11:00. Wrote a letter to mother during the afternoon. In the evening our meeting was very well attended. Bro. Kikuchi and I did the speaking. We were delighted to have Bro. Oyama with us all day. He had come to the conclusion that he was in the wrong in judging us and upon the invitation of Elder Featherstone came & renewed his fellowship with us. The day was an exceedingly pleasant one, for the reason that every member of the church made in Japan & the full quorum of missionaries were together—the first time for over a year & a half. Had Bro. Katsunuma come according to this promise every "Mormon" in Japanese /nation/ would have been together.

Wednesday, 27 April 1904, Tokyo

Cloudy with rain Up at 6:15. Wrote till the evening meal, completing the letter to Mr. Loomis and started to copy it on the typewriter.

Thursday, 28 April 1904, Tokyo

Rain in the morning—afternoon fair. Up at 6:30. Spent the entire day pounding the typewriter. My head was going in a regular whirl by night. During the night my rest was greatly disturbed by terrible dreams, produced no doubt from the mental strain during the day.

Friday, 29 April 1904, Tokyo

Fair—a gentle breeze. Up at 6:00. Spent the day writing on the typewriter finishing the letter to Mr. Loomis at 11:00 p.m. Elder Caine & Prest. Ensign kindly read the letter which consisted of twenty two & a half pages of letter-sized paper closely typewritten.

Saturday, 30 April 1904, Tokyo

Cloudy, but very warm. Up at 6:15. Spent the morning looking after the letter to Mr. Loomis. **In the afternoon about 80 of the Sunday School children assembled at headquarters in harmony with previous arrangements for an outing to one of the parks. The weather being bad, we did not feel like risking a trip so we went out on the parade ground in front of the Mission House and had some races & other contests for which we gave small prizes. We then repaired to the garden on the south of the house where we turned the children loose. They certainly had a glorious time and didn't want to go home. We gave them a lunch, foreign style, which made them very happy. We were elated over the event, for it gave us an opportunity to learn the children and give them a chance to become better acquainted with us. The little ones we found to be very affectionate & we romped around with them with as much real taste for the sport as they. For 2 ½ years I had been studying Japanese and trying to teach the people but had not had time to play & romp with them before. It was quite a treat.**

Sunday, 1 May 1904, Tokyo

Rain Up at 7:45. Sunday School from 9:00. Being fast day, we held Sacrament & testimony meeting in the afternoon from 2:00 p.m. In spite of the rain our evening meeting was quite well attended. Elders Jarvis & Caine held a meeting in Nakano district.

Elder Featherstone blessed his babe giving it the name Horace Zentaro. The first after Prest. Horace S. Ensign, the second, a Japanese name quite common among the men. It means the first son. The blessing was given in Japanese. The first instance in the history of the Japan Mission.

Monday, 2 May 1904, Tokyo

Rained all day Up at 8:00. Went to the Ginza to buy a trunk. In the afternoon we held a priesthood meeting in which the brethren gave reports on their respective fields. Prest. Ensign gave some instructions & requested that we all pray for the inspiration of the Lord as to the place where the summer months should be spent. **Elders Stoker & Hedges were appointed to go to Boshu making their headquarters at Chikura. I was appointed to open operations in the eastern part of Tokyo. Bro Jarvis to continue in his present field—Nakano. Elders Caine & Featherstone in the vicinity of headquarters.**

Wednesday, 4 May 1904, Tokyo

Cloudy, warm Up at 7:15. After breakfast went to the Yotsuya kuyakusho to see about making a report on headquarters as a meeting house. **About 11:00 am. I left headquarters for Negishi; arrived at the Negishi kwan #90 Nakanegishi cho Shitaya Ku Tokyo, about noon. Went out to get a hair cut then walked around a little to see where it would be well to begin tracting and also to get my bearings. After taking a bath & eating supper I went out and tracted for about an hour. One of the young men whom I met was waiting at the hotel when I returned. While talking with him, a gentleman visiting one of the guests of the hotel sent in his card wanting to know if I was Mr. Taylor of #16 Kasumigaokacho Yotsuya. I sent word in that I was the fellow whereupon he called on me and conversed for a short time. He had heard my name from the nurse who took charge of Sister Featherstone during her childbirth period. He also knew Sister Hakii from whom he had received our tracts. I was very much surprised to see him at [so] /such an/ out of the way place.**

Sunday, 8 May 1904, Tokyo

Up at 6:00. Left the hotel about 7:00 for headquarters. Found all well. Sunday School convened at 9:00. It was almost a fizzle. Only 12 or 13 in all. Sister Ensign's and my class was the only one that could be held. Most of the little folks had gone off with their schools to play in the parks. They are not bound by any sense of duty to attend the S.S. of a church to which neither they nor their parents have any relation so they follow their likes as they please—play is more interesting than listening to a poor speaker relate a Christian story or ask questions concerning a strange God.

At about 11:15 we repaired to the stream that flows not far from the house and witnessed the baptism of two female converts. One Katō Tsuta wife of Bro. Katō aged 21 the other Kamiyama Rin 19 year old daughter of Mr. & Mrs. Kamiyama who have been regular attendants at our meetings for some months Prest. Ensign performed the ordinance in the native tongue, of course, Quite a crowd went along to see the baptism, among others, a Buddhist priest. The father & mother of Sister Kamiyama were present and seemed very happy to see their daughter take the step which she did. After returning to the house we held a /sacrament/ meeting in which we confirmed the Sisters into the Church & bestowed the Holy Ghost. I was mouth in confirming Sister Katō while Bro. Caine was mouth in confirming Sister Kamiyama. At the request of Prest. Ensign I spoke for about twenty minutes on baptism, laying on of hands, & the sacrament. In the afternoon wrote a letter to Samuel & received one from father. The evening meeting was very slimly attended. Elder Caine & I did the talking.

Tuesday, 10 May 1904, Tokyo

Clear Up at 6:00. Studied till about ten oclock. Started out to find a place for prayer, but was unsuccessful; the houses being so very close together that I thought every shady nook I saw too close to some house to permit of singing and prayer without being disturbed. I walked through Uyeno park and when I came to the cemetery I remembered being told there was a cre[a]matory in that district so I enquired about where it was and went as directed until I found it. It was nearly to the next village from Tokyo. The name of the place in which it is built is Nippori District and the cre[a]matory is called, Nippori Cre[a]matory and is owned by the Tokyo Hakuzen Kabishiki Kwaisha.

I asked the man in the office if I would be permitted to go through and see the arrangement of the building and witness the cre[a]mation process. I told them I was an undertaker and embalmer /by trade/, though just now interested in the spread of religion. One of the men came out from behind his cage & took me through the building, the biggest part of which is the large red-brick smokestack. The entrance is large in width but not very high. Passing through the door one enters into a room with brick floor, bare walls, high celing, and no ornaments except a metal Buddha & a few candle sticks around him. Around near the wall were little trucks about two & a half feet high, three feet long, & two feet wide with four rollers. The were very crudely made & had been used so much that they looked like freight stands.

We passed out of this room through an arched opening on the south into the furnace appartment. An avenue ran from east to west throughout the entire length of the long room. The furnaces were connected on each side of the avenue and were made of common brick very badly stained with smoke & grease. Most of the furnaces were loaded ready for the kindling of the fire. There were thirty-five openings capable of holding that number of bodies at one time. The guide kindly opened the only one that was empty and showed me the inside. First a large iron door swings back, revealing a space of about 1 ½ feet deep before coming to another iron door all rusted & red with heat. This door is only half the size of the outer one and opened right into the inner chamber where the fire consumes the contents. This was opened showing a square chamber about 4 x 4 x 4 ft. This particular furnace is made to receive the casket in which the corps occupies a squatting position. The furnace for the long shaped caskets were all full. In the bottom of the one opened was a large portable piece of flat iron, on this the casket containing the dead is placed and from it the ashes are scraped when the burning is completed. It seemed to me that quit a portion of the ashes of the last victim were left. In the carelessness of the scrape out.

While looking around a corpse was brought in and placed on the little truck, run into the furnace room and hurridly shoved into the furnace I had just looked at. After the occupant takes his position the inner & outer doors are closed a brass tag hung up on the side near the lock. The key is turned /and/ given into the hand of some representative of the deseased and he is instructed to be on hand at such & such a time the next morning to unlock the door & witness the taking out of the ashes so that a mistake shall not be made and he get the ashes of some stranger. Mud is plugged into the cracks around the door to keep all smell & smoke on the inside or rather to make it go out through the proper channel. There is a separate fire pot to each furnace and the fuel is put in from the rear. The fire tender must have a hardened nose or be an old had at his job, for from the looks of the arrangement he would have to open the door of the fire pot which is not over a foot & a half from the casket and put on fuel a time or two before the process would be completed.

The bodies [were] /are/ received during the day but no burning takes place till night so I did not see exactly how it [went] /goes/. I went up into an apartment of the smoke stack where a smoke burner [was] /is/ constructed. This is to kill all living germs and do away with much of the smell that comes /with the smoke/ from the ovens filled with dead.

I inquired about the price and was told that $4.00 was charged for the first class square shaped $5.00 for the long shaped. Second class square $ 1.75 long 2.75. Third class (no long places provided) ($1.00. Children under six year $.65. The only thing that makes the difference between the classes is the duration of time the[y] /corpses/ are allowed to "bubble, bubble, boil & bubble, in the caldron boil & bubble," fiz & frizzle, smoulder smoulder, boil, bake, then moulder, smoulder. The third class ovens cook two a night when the cre[a]matory is rushed—August. At present the average consumed in a day is 32, but during the latter half of July & all of August the average is about 56. There are six cre[a]matories in Tokyo & vacinity making the total average of cremations a day 192 (So I am told, though I doubt it). I thanked the guide for his kindness and returned to Nigishi about 12:30. Had "soba" for lunch and then went out tracting till nearly 7:00. A friend called in the evening.

Friday, 13 May 1904, Tokyo
Cloudy—cold Up at 6:20. After studying a little while went to Asakusa to visit at Mr. Inoye whom Elder Jarvis had met in Nakano. Visited at his place for about three hours. Had dinner with him. On the way back called at the Asakusa Park Aquarium and saw fish in all forms and stages of growth. It was so arranged that a person could see them as they lived in nature; the sea bottom being represented in every instance. From 3:30 to 7:00 I was engaged in tracting. In the evening studied.

Sunday, 15 May 1904, Tokyo
Rain in morning—Fair by evening Up at 6:00. Left the hotel about 6:45 for headquarters. A friend, Mr. Tsutsui, came early enough to accompany me out to headquarters which he said he wanted to see once. I called at a store on the Ginza to buy some things. It was 8:45 by the time we reached Yotsuya. The Sunday School was much better than usual. All the classes were conducted separately and a fair attendance in each. During the day visitors were very numerous. Held Sacrament Meeting about 11:30. In the afternoon I wrote out on the typewriter an article of three & a half pages on the existence of God. I had prepared it in story form and given it the title "Earth's Master Engineer." The evening meeting was late in starting but well attended.

Saturday, 21 May 1904, Tokyo
Cloudy, Warm, Rain Up at 6:00. After breakfast went out tracting for about three hours. Returned to hotel & ate dinner. Started to write a letter home, but a friend, Mr. Kato, called. I talked with him from two o'clock till after five. Just as he went out the door Mr. Egawa came in & I talked with him till after eight when Mr. Tsutsui called. He together with Mr. Egawa, kept me going as hard as I could talk till 10:15 making just 8 ¼ hours of continuous talk. This added to a two hours conflab I had in the morning while not tracting makes 10 ¼ hours speaking in one day. I was very happy & thank God for the opportunities [of] to explain the gospel.

Sunday, 22 May 1904, Tokyo

Cloudy, in the evening fair Up at 6:00. Left the hotel at 7:15 taking Mr. Tsutsui with me to headquarters. Held Sunday School from 9:00 to 10:15. Then conversed with a friend until nearly noon. Sacrament Meeting was held about noon. **After dinner I wrote a letter home & discussed with the brethren at headquarters about the translations of the two prayers on the Sacrament Mr. Takahashi had made one translation a year [ago] /before/ & Mr. Hiroi one nearly two years [ago] /before/. From these and some that I had made myself I managed to get a translation which the brethren decided to accept & begin to use.** The evening meeting was late in beginning, but a good crowd was present. I spoke for 55 minutes on God & His relation to man.

Sunday, 29 May 1904, Tokyo

Cloudy—Moderate Up at 6:00. Left for Yotsuya at 7:00 taking Mr. Tsutsui along with me. The children came out pretty well, so we had a fine Sunday School. Held Sacrament Meeting from 11:00 a.m. In the afternoon we had a little talk on tracts. The evening meeting was not so well attended as usual.

P.S. In the Sacrament Meeting Elder Caine blessed the bread using the Japanese translation. Prest. Ensign blessed the water also using the Japanese words. This is the first time the Lord's Supper has been performed in the native tongue. The translations referred to are mentioned on page 153 of this book.

Tuesday, 31 May 1904, Tokyo

Cloudy—Warm Up at 7:30. Spent the morning in the house studying. In the afternoon I went to the Shitayaku Police Headquarters to inform the officers of my intentions to hold meetings at the hotel in which I am living. On the way back I purchased some paper & card board for a large sign. Went out tracting in which work I was engaged until 7:30. Returned to the hotel and talked with a visitor until 10:30. Then retired having fasted all day.

Wednesday, 1 June 1904, Tokyo

Cloudy—Rather warm. Up at 5:45. Spent most of the morning getting a sign up on the front of the hotel announcing a Bible class for Wednesday nights and [a] meetings on Sundays. I the afternoon a Mr. Mochizuki called to ask about Christianity While he was here Mr. Tsutsui called. I was engaged in conversation with these two till 6:00 p.m.; took a bath and ate supper. Three friends called and we searched the scriptures till 9:30. Retired.

Thursday, 2 June 1904, Tokyo

Fair & warm Up at 6:30. After breakfast went to talk with Mr. Nakagawa. Was with him until shortly after noon. Returned to the hotel and found Bro. Katō waiting for me. He had come over from headquarters to tell me of being discharged from his position in one of the Government hospitals because he was a Christian. He was asked by his boss in the office if he was a Christian and upon informing him in the affirmative his boss suggested that he had better conceal his faith and make out that he was a Buddhist, Shinto, or something else in order to hold his job. Bro. Katō refused to disgrace his faith by such an act stating that he was not ashamed of his religion and would be condemned if he refused to confess the Savior before men in order to retain his work. The conversation that followed made Bro. Katō rather angry and he unwisely volunteered to quit before his discharge came, but he was informed that his services would be no longer needed so he sent up his completed work and left. That a person should be questioned because of his faith in Christ and practically forced to lose his position upon refusing to deny or conceal his belief does not speak well for the freedom of religious worship in Japan.

In the afternoon I wrote a letter to Bishop Empey, then went out tracting. Returned to the hotel before 7:00, but before I could get supper a friend called bringing with him two companions neither of whom I had before met. Upon the arrival of two more visitors the first three left. Later Mr. Tsutsui came in then another man called whom I had not met—Mr. Watanabe a Methodist. He had read the tract left at his place and seeing in it the name "Mormon" he recalled what he had read in the papers some two or two & a half years ago and also what the preacher in his church had told him concerning "Mormons & Polygamy." He wanted to know about this peculiar religion. He had long felt that there was something lacking in the Methodist system and his heart was hungering for truth & more light. But upon reading the Articles of Faith, he did not perceive any difference between what we announced as a creed & what his Church accepted. I talked with him till 11:15 p.m. He was astonished to note the differences I pointed out to him. I went to bed without eating supper. My heart was full of joy for the manifold blessings bestowed upon me during the day and I ask God in all the humility of my soul and in the name of his Son Jesus Christ to sanctify /my testimony/ to the good of all who heard it.

Sunday, 5 June 1904, Tokyo

Clear—hot Up at 6:00. Went to Yotsuya as usual. Mr. Tsutsui accompanied me. The Sunday School was fair. After Sunday School a Fast Meeting was held. Then a council was called to consider the advisability of suspending regular missionary work, that is, visiting from house to house and seeking conversations with the people, during the hot months and devote ourselves exclusively to the translation of the Book of Mormon and other literature necessary to the future activity of this mission. We who were assembled felt that it was a proper step. Ate dinner.

Elder Jarvis had arranged for two meetings in his district, I had one announced in my district and there was the regular meeting at headquarters so it became necessary to divide up the elders so as to have the [neeess] /meetings/ go off in good order. Elder Caine went out to Bro. Jarvis' district with him to assist in the 1st meeting announced to begin at 4:00 p.m. Then Elder Caine was to return to headquarters to assist Elder Featherstone in the meeting at headquarters. Bro. Katō was sent out to support Elder Jarvis in his meeting from 7:30. While Prest. Ensign accompanied me to my field to assist me in my first attempt at holding a meeting in Negishi.

Thirteen were present. We sang our Japanese songs, Prest. Ensign did the praying while I did the preaching. I held them down for 55 minutes on the subject "What and Why is Mormonism?" The Lord sustained me and I believe those present understood fairly well all that I said. Prest. Ensign returned immediately after the close of the meeting.

Friday, 10 June 1904, Tokyo

Fair—warm Up at 6:30. Worked on the translation mentioned on the opposite page till 2:00 p.m. Then went out tracting and was so engaged till 7:45 p.m. In the evening Messrs. Tsutsui, Watanabe & two other men called and were with me till bed time. I had fasted the entire day and prayed in behalf of the translation of the Book of Mormon.

Sunday, 12 June 1904, Tokyo

Rain—warm Up at 6:00. Went to Yotsuya and assisted in holding Sunday School, which was fairly well attended. Then had Sacrament Meeting. After dinner returned to Negishi bringing Elder Featherstone with me to assist in my evening meeting. Thirteen were present—5 females. The noise around the hotel was a little annoying during Elder Featherstone's talk. A hotel is not an ideal place in which to hold meetings but in the absence of something else is to be regarded as better than nothing.

While at headquarters I was a little surprised, not greatly, to hear that it has been decided for Sister Featherstone to return to America with her babe, leaving here July 10th on the Northern Pacific R.R. company's steamer "Tremont." Since the birth of the child its grandparents in America have been worrying about its welfare especially because it had to be raised on the bottle Hence they wrote suggesting that the mother & her babe come home. This led to serious reflection upon the matter and, upon the request of Elder Featherstone, Prest. Ensign discussed with him on the propriety of such a step. As a result it has been decided for her to go as stated and her companion on the voyage it to be a Miss Dyre of Yokohama whose friendship was very fortunately obtained some days ago. The passage for both is practically already secured.

Tuesday, 14 June 1904, Tokyo

Slight shower—fair—warm Up at 6:30 Spent the entire morning in the house translating [on] the tract I am preparing for publication. After dinner, I went out tracting until 7:00. In the evening Mr. Tsutsui called.

While out tracting, I met a man who had been to America, Germany, England & other places studying. Never in my life have I seen a person so conceited as he. He would ask me a question and then before I could get through with the answer he would be off on something else. I left feeling that I had just had a conflict with an arrogant fool whose own experiences had puffed him up so high that he referred to the ordinary educated Japanese & Americans & people of all countries as ordinary chaps not to be respected for their attainments by people like himself who have been abroad & graduated from the great schools of the world.

Monday, 20 June 1904, Tokyo

Cloudy, Slight Rain, Cool Up at 6:45. Spent the morning talking with a visitor about the Church and its present condition. After dinner, I devoted three hours to translation and then went out to do some revisiting. Returned, ate supper, and talked till after eleven o'clock with Mr. Watanabe. He told about what his preachers told him when he informed them that he had called on me and heard many things that impressed him. Of course, they tried to prejudice his mind against the truth and judging from some of the passages he asked me to explain they had attempted to overthrow our teachings by referring to the Bible. He left feeling very well and apparently with his faith confirmed that the church he has acknowledged so far is far removed from the truth and the Church of J. C of L.D.S. is the only one accepted of God.

Tuesday, 21 June 1904, Tokyo

Cloudy—Cool Up at 6:45. Mr. Tsutsui called in the morning We had rather an exciting talk on the war. In the afternoon I finished going over the translation of the tract on the existance of God which I have been preparing for publication. It is now ready to be criticised by some Japanese friend and made clear & interesting to the native mind. I went out about 3:30 to do some visiting among friends where I have been received on previous occasions. Met a friend on the street and returned with him to the hotel where we had an excellent time together. The Spirit of God rested upon us both and I was delighted beyond expression to hear him offer the first prayer of his life. I first taught him how to pray by both example and precept then to see if he had understood I asked him to pray. My heart rejoiced on hearing his simple yet earnest [pra] /expressions./ In the evening about 8:00 a visitor came & stayed till 10:30.

Wednesday, 22 June 1904, Tokyo

Clear—Hot Up at 6:30. During the morning I did some [f] visiting but in every instance but one found the people absent.

On my way back to the hotel I was unpleasantly startled at seeing Nakazawa He got sight of me before I did of him and used his umbrella to good advantage in hiding his face so I could not see it and detect who it was. This in itself gave him away. I passed by him and walked ahead for a chō or two, then to see if he was following me I turned into a cake store and while the lady was putting five cent's worth of cake into a sack, I looked back and saw him lurking in the rear. I saw his face and was sure of my man. When I stopped at the cake shop he slacked up and hiding behind his umberella went from on side of the street to the other like a disgraced animal. Poor Nakazawa! I feel sorry for him. The fate of those who attempt to make merchandize of the Gospel and defraud with lying & other sins these brethren is not to be sought for by anyone.

In the evening I went out again to make a visit. Returned, had supper and from 8:00 p.m held a meeting for the purpose of considering our teachings concerning God, Jesus Christ, and the Holy Ghost from a Bible standpoint. Nine were present I prayed, then spoke of Christ's prophecy concerning the downfall of Jerusalem etc. and its fulfillment as recorded in history: making this as a point in favor of the truth of the Bible writings. I then had those present read from the scriptures many passages explaining their meaning and pointing out their relation to the subject (Godhead) when ever they needed such additional comment.

Ever since the 1st of June, I had been trying to get enough people out on Wednesday nights to hold such a meeting, but on former Wednesdays only one two, or three came so I simply called the talk on those occasions /a/ conversation.

Sunday, 26 June 1904, Tokyo

Fair—hot. Up at 6:00. Left the hotel at 7:00 & went to headquarters. Found all well and in very good spirits. Read a brief letter from Prest. Grant. The S.S. convened from 9:00. A good attendance. Sister Ensign's & my class was particularily interesting. After S.S. I changed clothes then assisted in administering the sacrament. Had dinner. Afterwards went with Elder Featherstone to see the home of Sister Kamiyama's parents. Her father is not in the church, but recently called in the elders to administer to him that he might recover from his sickness (neuralgia of the hips). As a result of the blessings of God in answer to the prayers of the brethren he was very quickly healed & had gone off on a 250 miles trip so I did not see him. Prest. & Sister Ensign accompanied me to Negishi and assisted me in holding my meeting. They prayed, I prea/c/hed, and we all sang. /To/ Bed at 10:30.

Tuesday, 28 June 1904, Tokyo

Cloudy—Cooler Up at 6:45. Mr. Watanabe called in the morning and stayed till noon. After dinner, I went out to do some calling on my friends. Did not return to the hotel until 8:00 p.m. While eating supper Mr. Tsutsui and another Mr. Watanabe (different to the one above) called Mr. Tsutsui soon returned, but I talked with Mr. Watanabe till 11:30. Before bidding him good night I taught him how to pray and listened to him make the first prayer of his life. It is on such occasions that my heart rejoices beyond expression and the sweet peace of the spirit is abundantly felt.

Friday, 1 July 1904, Tokyo

Clear—Very hot **Up at 6:00. Left the hotel at 9:00 o'clock for headquarters, having finished my labors in Negishi district for some time. After dinner I wrote a letter home. Then took the five o'clock train from Shinanomachi Station for Nakano where I met Elder Jarvis. Together we walked to his field of labor. I found him located in one of the most facinating spots I have seen since coming to Japan. The house in which he was living is a large farm house with clean surroundings and right in the centre of a pine grove. The owner's name is Tamano Sokichi**

After eating a fine supper we went to the home of the head man of the village and held a meeting (the last of a long series Elder Jarvis had been conducting in his field). The home of the "soncho" [~~was~~] /is/ large and the people very kind, he being a dignified, refined, and pleasant old man of about 65 years. The audience was not very large but interesting. I enjoyed remarkable liberty of speech & thought while speaking. After the meeting, a young man had a question or two to ask about my remarks. Before going back to Elder J's lodgings the people insisted on giving us some cakes & fruit. This household had been acquainted with Elder J. for a long time and it being his last meeting till after the summer months they wanted to & did show their friendliness to him in a striking manner. As I observed the conditions of the district and looked into the faces of the people & felt their spirits, I felt very very happy and imagined myself in an ideal spot for a Mormon colony. Bed at 11:00 p.m.

Saturday, 2 July 1904, Asagaya/Tokyo

Clear & hot Up at 7:00. After breakfast assisted Elder Jarvis to gather up his traps preparatory to leaving for headquarters. We left Asagaya to catch the train from Nakano station, but were too late. Came in by rikisha & street car. Called at the barber shop and had a hair cut. Mr. Tamano having accompanied us to headquarters to see Elder Jarvis and the Mission Home he ate dinner with us. In the afternoon I did considerable cleaning up. About 4:30 Elders Hedges & Stoker arrived from Boshu. They had all their hair cut off short and look like escaped prisoners. But they had had it off for nearly two months and testified that they had not enjoyed such comfort for a long time. In the evening we had a bath, supper, & then a short visit before going to bed.

Monday, 4 July 1904, Tokyo

Clear—hot. Up at 7:15. Put up the American flag over headquarters in honor of the day. After breakfast sang patriotic songs. Read from the Era. Dinner. After dinner sang patriotic "Mormon" hymns. About 3:30. Mrs. Cresswell & Mrs. Kochi called. Later Mr. Roose called. We had ice cream served in the garden. Afterwards we went into the house and had some more singing. Mr. Roos favored us with an excellent reading from Tennyson. Our singing of national songs was so loud that a company of soldiers from the parade grounds were attracted and filled the yard in front of the house. We gave their national hymn with equally as much vim as we had rendered [their] our own. This pleased them greatly. After supper we talked & chatted till nearly 11:00. Bed.

Friday, 8 July 1904, Tokyo

Hot occasional showers. Up at 6:15. After breakfast went to the dentist. Had the amalgum[4] filling in one tooth taken out preparatory to putting in gold. The gold in Japan is so cheap that it is as economical, if not more so to have teeth filled with gold here than with [at] amalgum in America and the looks of gold is by far the best. On the way back looked around for something to give Sister Featherstone as a token of esteem but could not find just what I wanted. Returned, ate dinner and worked on the translation of the Book of Mormon. Bed at 10:30.

Monday, 11 July 1904, Tokyo

Rain in the morning fair in the afternoon Up at 7:15. Spent most of the day writing part of the tract I am preparing [in] /with/ the Chinese characters. After dinner I finished one chapter and went out to have a little exercise by playing ball with the brethren. **In evening I took the chapter I had completed [over] to Mr. Yoshida to get him to correct the faulty grammer. He was home and kindly consented to help me in criticising my writing. Returned to headquarters & spent the remaining moments with the others reading mail that had just arrived from America.**

Tuesday, 12 July 1904, Tokyo

Rain till 8:am. Rest of day fair **Up at 6:00. Prepared to leave for Yokohama with the rest of the colony on the 10:50 train to see Sister Featherstone and her babe leave on the steamship "Tremont" for America. Four of the brethren, Sisters Katō and Haru, and myself went to the depot on the street car. The others went in rikishas. Upon arriving in Yokohama went directly to the ship. Learned that it was late in getting in and therefore its departure would be delayed till the following morning at daylight. Some of the party arrived at the boat a little later than the rest of us as they went around by the stores to buy a vase as a present /to Sister Featherstone/ from Elders Jarvis, Stoker, Hedges, Caine, & me. As soon as they arrived I wrote a little letter to go with the vase. The brethren signed their names and the gift /was/ presented in a very rough informal way. After staying on the boat for some hours we decided to go ashore get something to eat, then come back to the boat and spend the evening, leaving in time to catch the last train back to Tokyo. This we did. We left Sister Featherstone feeling as fine /as could be expected/ under the circumstances. The baby too seemed to be enjoying his new quarters on the great ship. Elder Featherstone stayed on the boat with the intention of being with his loved ones till the departure of the ship the next morning. We caught the last train for Tokyo, and were fortunate in meeting the last car for our district. We arrived at headquarters a few minutes after 12 midnight. Sister Haru & Katō who had returned on an earlier train had supper all ready for us and by their kind hands the beds too were nicely made. Bed at 1:30 a.m.**

Wednesday, 13 July 1904, Tokyo

Cool—hot. Up at 9:10. No breakfast at headquarters. Devoted considerable time during the day to writing in Japanese. **In the evening Mr. Yoshida called and returned the part of my writings that I left with him day before yesterday for correction. I was pleased to note that only two grammatical mistakes had been made. However quite a number of words had been changed, not because the ones I had used were wrong but because they were a little hard for the ordinary person to understand.** Supper, chat, bath, and bed.

Thursday, 14 July 1904, Tokyo

Clear—hot Up at 7:15. Ate breakfast and went to fill an appointment with the dentist. I am having some of my teeth filled with gold. He filled one today and prepared another for the filling. Called around by the Ginza on my way home. In the afternoon I did considerable writing in Japanese. In the evening before supper, went out on the parade grounds and enjoyed an hour's exercise with the brethren playing ball. After supper wrote a little more. Bed about 10:30.

Friday, 15 July 1904, Tokyo

Cloudy—Cool—Slight rain Up at 8:00. Was at headquarters all day. **Spent most of the time writing Japanese for my tract on the Existence of God. Mr. Yoshida is kindly correcting my grammatical mistakes and calling attention to places where the words used are not clear. In order that he can read it readily and save as much time as possible he requested that it be written in the Chinese characters instead of the kana. Being unfamiliar with the Chinese characters as yet I find it very tedious to look up /in the dictionary/ almost every word [~~in the dictionary~~] & then copy it into my writings.**

In the afternoon I had a short conversation with some young students who called. Bed at 10:30.

Saturday, 16 July 1904, Tokyo

Cloudy, but very hot. Up at 6:40. In the morning I did a little writing before breakfast. After breakfast, a counsil meeting was held in which all the elders of the mission took part. After they had all expressed their feelings concerning the condition of the Mission and made those suggestions they thought fitting Prest. Ensign spoke encouragingly and referred to the ways in which we could make great improvement both collectively & individually. **He then advised that during the summer while we expect to be engaged in the work of translation that we endeavor with all our strength & faith to draw near to God. In order to do this he suggested Wednesday of every week as a special fast day and 12 noon as the hour for the missionaries to unite in special prayer.** Before Prest. Ensign said anything about this matter of prayer, I received an inspiration that such a thing would be of great benefit to all and determined in my own mind to make the suggestion before the meeting closed. A feeling like unto an electric shock passed over me when Prest. Ensign said that he had a proposition to lay before the elders for I knew before he mentioned it what it was going to be.

Prest. Ensign called Elders Featherstone, Stoker, Hedges and Jarvis to go to Hojo for the summer and instructed them to be ready to leave on the following Monday morning. Prest. Ensign & wife, Elder Caine & I were appointed to remain in Tokyo to carry on the Sunday School & Meetings in connection with our work of translation & writing tracts for translation.

The following work was assigned. Prest. Ensign to write something on the organization of the Church & Conditions of that time, Elder Featherstone to write /& translate/ a tract on Christ; Elder Jarvis to begin work on the translation of Geo. Q. Cannon's History of Jos. Smith for young People;[5] Elder Stoker to start the translation of Edward H. Anderson's Brief History of the Church;[6] Elder Hedges to write a tract on any subject he may feel led to [~~refer~~] /consider/ to and which from his experiences thus far would be suitable to the needs of this people; Elder Caine to continue with earnestness in the translation of Col. Thomas' tract "My Reasons for Leaving the Church of England & joining the Church of Jesus Christ of Latter-day Saints;[7] and I to the special labor of

working on the translation of the Book of Mormon until it is completed /or/ I for good reasons I be released from the work.

To say that my heart leaped with joy at being called to devote my time to the Book of Mormon does not express my feelings by far. It was the direct answer to the earnest desires of my heart and a fulfilling of the promises given me in blessings pronounced by Prest. Grant during his sojurn in Japan. And I praise & glorify God, the Father, for the glorious work he has entrusted to me and in the humility, weakness, & earnestness of my whole soul do I invoke Him in the name of Jesus Christ for the assistance of the Holy Spirit & gift of interpretation & translation that I may be successful in writing for the Japanese in their own tongue the great truths & powerful testimonies of the Book of Mormon. While my heart throbs with gratitue unspeakable for the honor conferred upon me yet every time I contemplate the magnitude and importance [f] /of/ the work before me and the responsibility it places upon me, I fear & tremble from head to foot and sense a weakness such as I have never before known.

O God, remember thy young servant. Magnify him in his new calling. Cause that his mind shall be lit up by the direct inspiration of Heaven that the task which now lies before him might be successfully accomplished by him in the time which Thou hast alloted and make Thine alloted time not too far distant. O Almighty God, forget not the way in which Thou didst support & bless Thy servant Joseph Smith in his weakness and didst make it possible for him to bring forth to the world the most glorious & authentic sacred record the world has, [ever ha] and, in this time, when that sacred record is to be written in a language made up of strange characters & expressions like unto the [E]strangeness of the Egyptian writings & language found on the Gold Plates, again open the windows of heaven and pour forth upon Thy young servant, Alma, the gift of tongues & translation to such and extent that the purity of the Book of Mormon may in no wise be lost, the clearness in no wise obscured, and the spirit and testimony that always accompanies it in no wise impaired. O Lord, draw near unto thy servants in this land that they may know Thee as they have never known Thee before. Sustain them in the performance of their several duties, make their minds fruitful in thoughts and their hearts abundant in faith & endurance. Lead, I pray, Thee, by the manifestations of Thy Spirit through Prest. Ensign, everything pertaining to this Mission. Thy name shall be praised and all honor & power & dominion shall be Thine forevermore. Through Christ Jesus. Amen.

After the appointments and labor assignments all expressed themselves as pleased with that which had been given to them to perform and desired that the faith & prayers of all be exercised in behalf of each. Elder Hedges offered a very fine prayer. **Prest. Ensign then spoke asking us to make it a special feature of our prayers that the Lord would bring us in contact with some bright, intelligent Japanese whose character is good and faith strong, and give us power to convert him that we might be assisted by such a person in our work of translation.** Prest. Ensign also advised the Elders as to how we should proceed with our work during the summer, laying special stress on the point that we should not allow our time to be occupied in long conversations with those who come to us for the sole purpose of learning English. The meeting was then closed by singing "The Spirit of God Like a fire is burning" Prayer by Prest. Ensign.

In the afternoon I cleaned my typewriter, took some exercise by playing ball with the brethren. In the evening went out with the rest to have supper at a "sobaya."

Sunday, 17 July 1904, Tokyo

Clear & very hot. Up at 6:30. Cleaned up the rooms for Sunday School. The attendance was not so good but the children were exceedingly interesting. After S.S. Sacrament Meeting was held as usual. All the elders & four saints present. In the evening meeting Elders Featherstone, Hedges, & I were the speakers. A fair attendance. **Before retiring Prest. Ensign blessed & set me apart for my work on the Book of Mormon. He promised me health & strengh for the arduous task and the power & inspiration to the Spirit for the successful accomplishment of the work. It was a beautiful prayer and rich with glorious promises regarding the Book of Mormon & my work in its behalf.**

Wednesday, 20 July 1904, Tokyo

Clear—hot Up at 7:00. After studying a little while, went to the dentist's, but found he being busy and there being an appointment at headquarters for 12 n., I returned without having anything done. Shaved. **A twelve o'clock the four of us at headquarters repaired to the room in the south east corner of the second floor and held a prayer meeting according to the appointment at our priesthood meeting on the 16ᵗʰ. We sang "Guide us O Thou great Jehovah." We then knelt in a circle & prayed in the following order: Prest. E, Elder Taylor, Elder Caine, Sister Ensign. Prest. Ensign dedicated, during the course of his prayer, the room for a prayer room and afterward told us to use it for such whenever we felt like calling upon the Lord in special prayer. The closing hymn was, "O My Father." Benediction by Prest. Ensign.**

After dinner I wrote /in the characters/ a number of pages of my tract on the existence of God. About 4:15 had dinner having fasted since the night before. Wednesday has been established as a day of special fast in the mission. Played ball for exercise. Entertained a visitor. Received a letter from father Bath. Bed at 12 m.

Friday, 22 July 1904, Tokyo

Very hot Up at 6:10. **During the morning wrote my journal and finished writing the tract on God which has occupied my time so much of late.** In the afternoon from about three to seven I worked on the Book of Mormon. Prest. & Sister Ensign went down town and did not return until quite late so Elder Caine and I ate supper without them. About 9:00 p.m. a very supicious tramp whom the entire neighborhood /had been watching/ came in, but a policeman who had been informed of the tramp's suspicious rambling around [here] and was therefore watching him came in and took the fellow in hand. With Nakazawa this makes the second victim hauled away from #16 Kasumi gaokachō by the police.

On account of distressing conditions as a result of the war now going on there are many more robberies than before and the people everywhere are keeping a strict guard on their things.

Sunday, 24 July 1904, Tokyo

Cloudy—cool Up at 6:05. The weather today has been in great contrast with that of yesterday. Yesterday was hot & very close; today was cool and breezy.

The Sunday School convened at 9:00 am as usual—The attendance very light. One class only /(the children's)/. **Since the four elders have gone out to Boshu our force here is a little short so one class has taken the place of two. Elder Caine was called to teach the Teological Class in the absence of Elder Featherstone.** At our Sacrament meeting only those who live at headquarters were present. In the afternoon about 1:00 p.m. we had dinner with a few extras in honor of the 24th of July. This day is celebrated by the Japan Mission not only as the anniversary of the coming of the Pioneers into Salt Lake Valley, but as the anniversary of the departure from Salt Lake of the 4 first missionaries to Japan. As one of the four, I feel to thank God for His abundant blessing during the three years that have passed since leaving home. His protection from sickness and temptation is a source of great joy to me and I feel to renew my efforts and apply to the utmost my energies in behalf of the work that has been set on foot in this land.

The evening meeting was well attended, and good attention was paid. Before supper & meeting I took a walk. After meeting I read for a little while then went to bed, feeling happy in the service of my Maker whose benediction I always hope to be worthy of.

Friday, 29 July 1904, Tokyo

Rain most of the day—hot & sultry Up at 6:00. After breakfast, went to the dentist's and spent the morning with him. My visit was a painful one. Having returned to headquarters & eaten dinner I devoted the rest of the after noon to the translation of the Book of Mormon. In the evening after supper until bed time I was busy correcting the errors in writing in part of my compiled tract on the existence of God. Papers arrived from home. In one we noticed the appointment of Bro Charles W. Penrose to fill the vacancy in the Quorum of Apostles occasioned by the death of Apostle Abraham O Woodruff. This great-ly pleased me, for I am an admirer of Apostle Penrose for his activity, devotion, and remarkable talents especially in literary lines. It is an honor to one who is fully worthy of it.

Sunday, 31 July 1904, Tokyo

Severe Electric Storm—Cool. Up at 6:15. Our Sunday School was rather small. Two classes however were held.—The primary & theological. From eleven o'clock we held our Sacrament Meeting with four saints & two visitors in attendance. Just as I was offering the opening prayer a most terrible peal of thun-der, preceded by a dangerous flash of lightening startled everyone in the room for it broke right outside and the house shook almost as moved by a slight earthquake. A second peal followed immediately upon the first frightening our Japanese nearly to death. They hid their faces, stopped up their ears and began to tremble. After the meeting which lasted but 30 minutes the storm continued to rage for an hour or more while rain fell nearly all day. In the afternoon we learned that the lightening struck in many places all over the city, one place being only a block from headquarters. I wrote a letter to mother. In the evening our meeting was disposed with as the five who came did not get here till 8:15. I engaged them in conversation for three quarters of an hour. Bed.

Monday, 1 August 1904, Tokyo

Fair—warm Up at 6:15. After breakfast I went to the dentist's and did not get back to headquarts till noon. Had dinner, then worked till supper time on my tract, correcting the copy of one article Bro. Katō had made for me. After supper I went and spent the evening at Mr. Mashimō's home. Returned at 10:00 and retired. This is my birthday. Twenty two years have elapsed since I came forth into the world and while I have done perhaps little or no good during that time, still I have tried to keep out of the way so that I would not be looked upon as a stumbling block to my fellows and thus do the world no harm by sojurning in it.

Tuesday, 2 August 1904, Tokyo

Fair—hot Up at 6:05. Spent the morning working on my tract & the Book of Mormon. In the afternoon was also engaged in translation till 5:00 p.m. Then went to Kanda and talked with Bro. Oyama till nearly 9:00 p.m. He was and had been for a long time worked up over the evils of war and having the idea that we were war advocates he did not cherish the best of feelings towards us. I attempted to show him that we were not and are not advocates of war, but see in the present strife the fulfillment of prophecy and a sign of Christ's Second Coming to the earth. Consequently while we deplored the slaying of men in battle yet we could not as believers of the Bible help rejoicing in their death as an evidence of the fulfillment of God's plans. I felt on leaving him that he looked upon war with a different view than before. Returned, had supper, & retired.

Tuesday, 9 August 1904, Tokyo/Hojo

Fair—very hot. Up at 4:15. **Left headquarters at 5:00 a.m. in company with Prest & Sister Ensign, Elder Caine & Sister Hakii and took the 6:00 a.m. boat from Reiganjima for Hojo. We had a very pleasant sea and made the entire trip without the least disagreable sensation. Found our four brethren in Hojo at the beach to meet us and were glad to see them looking so well.**

After a fine dinner we chatted a little then went to the sea shore and took boats for a ride on the brine. We rowed to an island not very far distant and took a plunge in the ocean. Rowed back and after eating supper retired.

Wednesday, 10 August 1904, Hojo

Fair—very hot Up at 6:30. Spent the morning working on the Book of Mormon. At ten o'clock went to the beach, thinking to take boats out to the island and hold our prayer meeting there, but the boats were gone so we returned to the hotel and at 12:00 n. had our regular Wednesday prayer circle. In the afternoon again worked on the Book of Mormon. At 4:00 p.m. we ate, having fasted since Tuesday evening's supper. After eating went and took a row and a swim. Returned about 8:00 p.m. Ate an improvized meal and then gave a diving exhibition for our own pleasure and to entertain the people who had gathered round. Bed at 10:30.

Thursday, 11 August 1904, Hojo

Clear again & very hot. Up at 6:40. After breakfast worked on the Book of Mormon till dinner. After dinner I continued translating till about 4:30. Then went with the rest of the elders & Sisters Ensign & Hakii down to the beach where we engaged two boats, took an hour's ride on the bay and then had a swim for about the same length of time. Returned to the hotel, ate supper, and read the newspapers from America.

Friday, 12 August 1904, Hojo

Fair—still very hot Up at 7:00. Three years ago today the first missionaries to Japan landed in Japan making the mission just three years old. Our original intention was to return the Tokyo today but remembering the anniversary of our arrival Prest. Ensign & I determined to spend the day with the rest of the missionaries at Hojo.

After breakfast word came that two large whales had been captured & brought into Tateyama (about a mile & a half from our hotel). Having never seen a whale. except at a distance and knowing nothing as to how they were cut up I with some of the others hurried over to see the proceedings. We were to late to see the actual cutting on the first but made an inspection of the parts as they lay around in the shed-like building prepared by the whaling company who had the two animals in charge. It was a wonderful sight and a smell that will not soon be forgotton. Around the entire whale is a coat of fat about 5 or 6 inches thick. Then comes the dark blood-like meat which is found in such quantities that the whole town could find plenty at about 10 pounds a family. The viscera are all preserved and used in various ways. In fact, [the] /an/ officer of the company told me that there was no waste whatever. Large caldrons for the rendering of the fat were heated and three men were busy watching the boiling masses of oil. The number of people employed in this of chopping, cutting, & boiling were about 50 or 60. The amount of oil secured from one whale about 35 or 40 feet long is said to average 1700 gallons and the profits on the entire fish about 3000 yen. We engaged a little boat and rode out around the second whale which lay dead in the water. Children were using the beast as a diving platform and seemed to enjoy slipping & sliding around on its smooth surface!

We returned to the hotel and had dinner and went back to see how the carving of the great fish was done. About twenty men [N] with large very sharp knives not less than a foot & a half in length & attached to a handle not unlike the handle of a pick. The head is soon cut off and dropped out of the way. After a little fat is taken away the fish is divided into three parts and as many groups of butchers cut & slash diligently for about 2 hours & a half, keeping a gang of women busy carrying off the severed pieces. The cutting is done in the water with the result that the ocean around becomes a sea of blood. Little children, no doubt belonging to the women & men at work, run around naked and seem to enjoy their paddling in the blood. They crowd around the busy knives so numerously that it is marvelous that some human blood is not mixed in with the whale's and some child's flesh carried out with the large hunks of fish meat. Whenever a piece of the bony carcas was left floating for a minute a flotilla of little children not over 5 & 6 /years old/ would attack it and tear off the stringy meat still clinging to the ribs and fill their

baskets to the brim. This sight has left such an impression upon me that time will never entirely obliterate it.

One of my friends in explaining how the whales are caught and brought in said that the fisherman along the sea could go out and discovering a whale in the vacinity get up a small party armed with harpoons. They speed out to the haunts of their victims and after a dangerous fight which sometimes results in the sinking of more than one of their little crafts and lasts a number of hours the great fish is conquored and as soon as it can be done a steamer is surrounded and their prize snaked into the whaling station. The company considers that they have done well if they get 4 or five fish in a year for when they do they make enough profit to declare a dividend.

In the evening we all went out boat riding and had a bath. Returned to the hotel to a good meal & fine beds for both of which we were well prepared.

Saturday, 13 August 1904, Hojo/Tokyo

Fair—Heat terrible. Up at 5:35. Ate an early breakfast and left the hotel to catch the 8:00 a.m. boat for Tokyo. Prest E & wife, Elder Caine, Sister Hakii & I returned to headquarters. The sea was uninterestingly smooth, nothing more than the slightest ripple being encountered. Arrived in Tokyo about 2:15. Sent our baggage home by rikisha. We took the car. **As soon as we got to headquarters, I changed clothes and went to see Mr. Yoshida about the tract he was reading over for me. Found him at home and spent an hour & a half with him looking over his suggestions. Found some of his corrections good but in other cases it was necessary to correct him.** I will be very thankful when we have someone in the church here whose soul will be in the work of God and who under the guidance of the Spirit will be a willing and thorough critic of our translation Returned. Ate supper & retired. Bro. Oyama called to inform us that he had given up his position in the Post. Office for one with the Singer Sewing Machine Yokohama.

Saturday, 20 August 1904, Tokyo

Clear & Oppres/s/ively hot. Up at 6:15. Spent the most part of the morning working on the translation of the Book of Mormon. Took a bath and ate dinner. In the afternoon continued to work on the Book of Mormon. In the evening I did some writing for the Sunday School children. During the day mail arrived from America bringing a letter from Sister Featherstone. We were greatly rejoiced on learning that she had a remarkably fine voyage and though not yet securely landed when she sent her letter out to shore yet everything pointed well for a most auspicious arrival in Tacoma and easy ride to her Utah home. Her babe had enjoyed the best of health on the voyage and had not needed so much attention as when here in Japan. Truely the blessings of the Lord were poured out upon them in great abundance.

Sunday, 21 August 1904, Tokyo

Hot—Clear Up at 6:40. Ate breakfast about 7:30. The S.S. was not well attended. Still we had a session Four saints were present at our Sacrament Meeting—Elder Caine did the speaking. At 1:00 p.m I went over to Sister Kamiyama's to talk with her father. For almost a year now this family has been coming to our Sunday meetings. The daughter has joined the Church and through the advice of the elders the father has ceased the use of tobacco & tea. On two occasions he called on the brethren to administer to him for his affliction—sciatica.[8] On both occasions he was healed and received a testimony that the power of God was with the elders. Still he did not show his appreciation of the blessings received, by obeying the Gospel so he was taken down again and suffered for quite a long time. During this attack he did not ask for the prayers of the brethren, but called in a doctor. He recovered slowly and today I learned from his daughter who came to Sunday School that he was able to get around. He asked his daughter to tell us that the doctor had said his condition was mainly due to the non use of stimulants and advised him to begin. the use of tobacco or tea or both. After thinking over the matter he had decided to break his covenant with himself never to use tea or tobacco again and take a little tea until he regained his complete health. But he instructed his daughter to tell us about his decision and get our permission to carry it out. This she reported to me and I felt it very strange that her father, not being a member of the church should ask us to permit him to encroach upon one of the commandments given to the Saints.

I visited the old man and told him as plainly as I could that we had no right to command him to do thus or so, but as his friends desiring his welfare we would suggest that he look to God who had blessed him in the past and reject the advice of the doctor to use tea or tobacco. But I pointed out to him that the manifestations of God's power in healing the sick were for the repentant baptized and faithful believer, and that if he had a testimony that we had the plan of life and salvation in our church that he was in sin by not announcing his faith and going down [it] into the waters of baptism and we could no longer assure him of blessings if he neglected to manifest /in abiding/ his gratitue for those favors already received from his Heavenly Father.

In the evening we had our meeting as usual and a good attentive audience. Elder Caine and I did the speaking. We sang the song "God moves in a mysterious way" as translated in the Methodist Hymnal. After meeting we had something to eat talked a little while then retired.

Monday, 22 August 1904, Tokyo

Fair—No breeze—Hot Up at 6:00. **Spent the morning looking over some suggestions made by Mr. Mashimo who called and returned the manuscripts of my tract on the existance of God which he had, at my request, kindly looked over. They were very few places where he considered any changes ne/ce/ssary and only one place where he said the meaning was not clear. By noon I had made what changes I considered proper and after dinner went to the printer's and ordered an edition of 1000 copies for which I agreed to pay ¥14.67.**

Mrs. Creswell and her daughter Mrs. Kochi spent the afternoon and evening at headquarters, taking both dinner & supper with us. They came as guests of Bro. and Sister Ensign. Mr. Yoshida also called and spent the evening. Prest. & Sister Ensign accompanied their friends home and while waiting for their return, I looked over the translation of three songs our Church has adopted from outside religions & which we find are translated in "Collection of Sacred Christian Songs." Found the translations in many cases to be most horrible, but still the sentiment in the Japanese rendition was in no wise opposed to Latter-day Saint beliefs.

Tuesday, 23 August 1904, Tokyo

Fleecy clouds—Slight Breeze. Up at 6:30. Spent the whole day working on the Book of Mormon. After supper looked over the translation of some more songs in the Sectarian Hymnal.

Sunday, 28 August 1904, Tokyo

Clear—quite hot again. Up at 6:15. Had breakfast at 7:40. From 9:00 till 10:00 held Sunday School. The slimest attendance of the year. However the tots in Sister Ensign's & my class were very attentive. From 11:00 we had Sacrament Meeting Two of my friends from Negishi were with us. I spoke on the 13th chap. of I Nephi reading a part of it from my translation. I did this to show the saints that the prophecies of the Book of Mormon taken together with their fulfillment as recoreded in history demonstrates the Divine Inspiration of the sacred record.[9] In the afternoon I read & wrote a little. The evening meeting was fairly well attended and we enjoyed a good spirit.

Just as I was going to bed two letters came. One from father, the other from Sister Maud Baggarlley The folks at home were reported to be in very fine health & spirits. Sister Baggarley's letter was extremely interesting. She has of late been marvelously bless of the Lord. At a meeting of the Mutual Conference she had the interpretation of tongues & in the temple had a glorious personage by her side for some minutes.

Monday, 29 August 1904, Tokyo

Cloudy—Cool Up at 6:45. **Spent the day correcting the proof sheets of my tract on the Existance of God. Elder Caine assisted me very much. After supper I went to Mr. Yoshida's to let him look over the proofs also, for he made the request some time ago that I let him see them. Found him at home and discussed a few points in the tract. He promised to look it over & return it next day.** Got home about 10:00 p.m. Went immediately to bed, but had not gone to sleep when Sister S[——] brought a large bundle of mail up. I had two letters; one from Mother enclosing some stamp pictures of Samuel's baby Harold, one from Apostle Grant containing expression of love & words of encouragment.

Tuesday, 30 August 1904, Tokyo

Rained all day—Very Cool Up at 6:30. Spent the day in the house writing and reading. At the request of Prest. Ensign I wrote a synopsis of my old tract "The True and Living God" and also an outline of my new one "Is there a God?" Prest. Ensign desired me to do this that he might send them to the Presidency of the Church, who from the tone of a recent letter received seem to have lost sight of the fact that we have already prepared literature for the Japanese on the subject of God. I also, at Prest. E's request, read over Elder Hedges article written on "Prayer." and made a few notes on the places which in my opinion would sound better if differently rendered.

In the evening Mr. Yoshida called and returned the proof sheet of my tract "Is There a God" (This being the title of the pamphlet I have been preparing on the existance of God.)

Sunday, 4 September 1904, Tokyo

Slight Rain—Then Clear—Then rain again—Cool. Up at 7:00 The Sunday School came near being a failure. There were only 11 in the childrens class & 4 in the theological. I spent an hour or two on Elder Featherstone's tract. From 2:00 p.m we held our fast & sacrament meeting. Bro. Oyama came in in time to say a few words. He confessed his mistake in drawing away from us and his desire to do right in the future. A friend (rather an acquaintance) whom I first met in Chiba called and sat through the meeting, then had dinner with us. The evening meeting was very slim but a fair spirit was manifested by the people present. A little food was served before going to bed.

Thursday, 8 September 1904, Tokyo

Clear—warm Up at 6:45. Spent the morning and part of the afternoon writing on the translation of the Book of Mormon. It takes almost, if not quite, as much time to write a chapter in the characters as it does to translate one, thus making the work doubly long. In the afternoon an old man called to ask about the Gospel. He is a man who has been here very often and more than once received assistance from us. He asked to be given an examination on the principles of the Gospel and see if he knew enough to be baptized into the church. I asked him about his ideas of God and found him very much mixed so far as truth is concerned so I told him he had failed on the first question in the examination and had better study more. I then talked and read to him about the God of Heaven & Earth, the Father of the Spirits of all men. In the evening Elder Caine & I took some exercise by playing ball and after dark walking across the parade ground to see a lantern parade. Before going to bed mail came. In it was a letter from Wm Erekson to me. **Bro & Sister Katō moved from headquarters**.

Sunday, 11 September 1904, Tokyo

Beautiful day Up at 6:45. Cleaned up the rooms for S.S. Had a good attendance. Elder Caine spent the afternoon's of Friday & Saturday visiting the people in the neighborhood inviting them to send their children to Sunday School and come them selves to our evening meeting. Our Sacrament meeting was poorly attended by the Saints. The evening meeting was a success. I was feeling very unwell having contracted a cold. Before going to bed I bathed by feet in hot water & mustard and took other of mother's oldfashioned but sure remedies. /During the day/ Mr. Yamasaki called with his little boy and stayed for about two hours.

On Saturday evening the girl at headquarters went into the bath and fell fast asleep. She found herself in that position the next norning when she woke up As a result she felt unwell all day.

Monday, 12 September 1904, Tokyo

Rain—Warm—Up at 7:00. Got up feeling much better than the night before. Spent the morning writing to father. **The order of 1000 copies of my tract "Is there a God?" was delivered at headquarters in the morning. In its completed form it looks quite fine. The one thousand copies cost /¥/17:70 ($8.85)*** Wrapped up three copies to send home as souveniors. The rest of the day & evening I spent working on the Book of Mormon.

*On page 16 it is stated that the agreed price for 1,000 copies should be /¥/14.67 but the figuring was faulty making when corrected the difference as noted above.]

Thursday, 15 September 1904, Tokyo

Fair in morning—Evening windy & threatening Up at 5:50. Got up with a cold and felt so miserable by noon that I didn't do a thing during the latter half of the day. **In the morning I wrote a little on the Book of Mormon finishing recording the translation of I Nephi in the characters.** My custom being to translate first into the Romajii, then go over it once carefully and if there are any mistakes correct them and on all points that I think might be a little obscure to the natives I consult with some Japanese around the place. Then I copy from the romaji into. the native characters using as many Chinese characters as I know. Mr. Mashimo & Mr. Yoshida called in the evening. Before going to bed I bathed my feet and took some medicine to raise a sweat. During the night I could hardly sleep it was so hot but I grinned and bore it.

Thursday, 22 September 1904, Tokyo

Fair—Cool Up at 7:00. Worked on the Book of Mormon till dinner In the afternoon, I was troubled so with the catarrah[10] that I couldn't do any work so I was idle most of the time. I had however a gospel conversation of over an hour with a man who came to hear our teachings. In the evening I tried to doctor my nose with a syringe Prest. Ensign bought for me, but this proved a failure. After going to bed, had a hard time to get to sleep.

Monday, 26 September 1904, Tokyo

Cloudy—Cool 7:30 a.m. Went down town in the morning to see if I could not get some catarrah medecine, but after a half a day's search I returned empty handed. In the afternoon I started to do some work on the Book of Mormon but my nose was so troublesome that I set aside all brain work and was idle the rest of the day. In the evening I went to the post office to mail some letters to the brethren in Boshu. Went to bed early. During the day I washed my nose with warm salt water and before going to bed snuffed some olive oil. During the night I was very restless.

Tuesday, 27 September 1904, Tokyo

Clear—Cold Up at 7:30. In the morning started to work on the Book of Mormon. **Mr. Tsukakoshi called had dinner and was with us till about 4:00 p.m. He assisted Elder Caine in looking over the translation of Col. Thomas' tract. On his return he took the translation home and promised to have it entirely looked over inside of a week. In the afternoon a friend from the Buddhist School called. In the evening Mr. Mashimo, his sister, and three friends called.**

The mail from America brought papers. On one the sudden death of Bishop Nelson A. Empey was announced. This was a great shock to me, for outside our family /& relatives/ there was no one for whom I had greater regard and affectionate love than Bishop Empey.

Thursday, 29 September 1904, Tokyo

Clear—Warm. Up at 7:00. During the morning I wrote letters Feeling it my duty, I wrote a letter of sympathy and condolence to Sister Nelson A. Empey. In the afternoon I worked a little on the Book of Mormon. In the evening I went up to the Post Office to post mail for America.

Sunday, 2 October 1904, Tokyo

Cloudy—Cool—Rain in the evening. Up at 7:15. Being 'fast' day ate no breakfast. The Sunday School was not crowded. Elder Caine's Theological class however was exceptionally well attended. The class over which Sister Ensign & I presided was very interesting; all the students seemed to take delight in the lesson presented & in reciting [the] some of the Beatitudes.[11] All took a very active part. Our Sacrament & Fast Meeting was held at 2:00 p.m. Only two saints were present. After meeting [we] /Prest Ensign & Elder Caine/ administered to Elder Jarvis who had been feeling indisposed for some days. Before the evening meeting [we] /Prest/ E. /& I/ administered to Bro. Oyama who for some time had been suffereing with a lung disease. The evening meeting was very fairly attended in spite of the bad weather.

Wednesday, 12 October 1904, Tokyo

Cloudy—Warm. Up at 7:15. Took a walk before breakfast. Assisted in pumping the bath. Compared eleven chapters of the Book of Mormon with eleven corresponding chapters in Isaiah. Took a bath and united with my brethren & Sister Ensign in prayer meeting. After dinner I spent two hours & a half or more talking with a young man named Suzuki who applied for baptism. In the evening Mr. Nishimura came and I spent the time talking with him. Mr. Sukakoshi spent the afternoon & evening at headquarters assisting Elder Caine with his translation of Col. Thomas' tract.

In a letter from the Elders in Hōjō received by Prest Ensign, we learned of a severe experience that came to Elder Featherstone. He and his companion, Elder Stoker, have been accustomed to using condensed milk at each meal, using a little out of the can & then setting it aside till the next meal. Elder F. poured some hot water into one of the cans thus used to get the little milk which clung to the bottom & sides. He then drank it. In an hour or so he had a strange feeling come over him especially in his head & stomach. He looked in the glass & saw his face flushed to a scarlet red. He took a walk which did a little good but his body swelled up and red spots covered him all over. It then appealed to him that he had been poisoned. His companion with the help of the hotel people gave him hot baths and succeeded in drawing all the swelling down to his feet. He got relief and at the time of writing the letter was restored. Thus the promise of the Savior "if you drink any deadly thing it shall not hurt you" was verified in behalf of our brother.[12]

A letter from Elder Hedges informed us that cholera[13] had broke out in his district & the maid of the hotel in which he was staying had showed symptoms of the diesase so he left his district in all haste and joined his brothren at Hōjō. But we wonder if he hasn't got things mixed and has mistaken the dread asaitic cholera for the cholera morbus. However, the people of his district seemed very much wrought up over the announcement of the appearance of the disease and the ignorant fishermen & farmers awakened to a memory of their old traditional superstitions were seen in large & small bodies following the priests to their respective temples and to the sea shore to offer prayers for deliverance from the threatening pestilence.

Tuesday, 18 October 1904, Tokyo

Rain—Cold. Up at 7:15. Spent the morning and part of the afternoon working on the translation of the Book of Mormon. **In the afternoon about five o'clock the elder's baggage from Hōjō arrived an hour or so later they arrived. All were in excellent health & spirits. We enjoyed a recital of their experiences. Bro. Katō was with us most of the day. In the evening after supper he went off, but came back all out of breath just as we were going to bed about 11:00 p.m. He said his wife's mother's house was full of guests and there wasn't room for him to sleep there so he came to get a bed for a night. We thought it a little strange but as he had requested Prest. Ensign during the day to allow him & his wife to come back to headquarters for a day or two while he looked for a house in this district we didn't suspicion anything.**

Wednesday, 19 October 1904, Tokyo

Cloudy—Changeable—warm. **Up at 6:30. Immediately after getting up, assisted in pumping water for the bath. Elder Hedges was going all over the house hunting & enquiring after his satchel in which he had put his watch and chain and diamond pin and other valuable articles. The satchel had been moved from where he put it the night before. Who had moved it and where had they put it? This was the question and no one could answer, but suspicion fell on Bro. Katō who during the night was up and around more than necessary and had left early in the morning before anyone else was up. As we investigated and thought on the affair our suspicions increased in spite of the fact that we did not feel right in incriminating a brother. However we decided to act quickly, for if the valise and its contents were not recovered Elder Hedges would be out over ¥300.00 and it was also discovered that five yen had been taken out of Elder Featherstone's purse which was in his coat hanging on the foot of his bed.**

We decided to act upon our suspicions and consequently set out in search of Katō. Elders Featherstone & Stoker went over to his wife's mother's house were his wife was staying and Elder Hedges & I went over to a distant relative's house where he & his wife were living until just recently. Elder H. & I learned from the people of the place to which we went that Katō had proven himself disagreeable & was discharged from his work with the family making it imperative for them to move. This information was in direct conflict with what Katō told us at headquarters. We thought all the time that he was an employee of the Meguro Beer Co. and was only living with his relatives. He had told us about his experiences with wicked men at the Company works & what a good position he had with chances for promotion. But upon enquiry later on in the day at the Beer company's office I found that he was not known to the company & never had been. Lie number one. Then he told us that he moved from his relatives partly on account of his wife's mother's sickness & /on/ account of the evil surrounding at his relatives who ran a foreign restaurant. But upon inquiry and evidence written in black & white we found that he was kicked out of his place because of idleness etc. Lie number two. He told us that he was getting ten yen a month but his relative stated positively that he only paid Katō seven yen. Lie number three. He said that he was only taking a rest from work and intended to start again as soon as he could get his wife located. But I found that he was discharged in disgrace. Lie number four. When Elder Hedges & I returned to headquarters we reported what we had learned. Later Elder Stoker came stating that Katō was not at the place where they went but was expected sometime during the day so Elder Featherstone waited for him.

Soon Elder Featherstone came in with Katō holding him as though he had had to bring him by force. Katō was white & shaking. We all gathered in one room. Prest. Ensign began by demanding an explanation of the reason why Katō had played the thief at our home. The suddenness of the question and the sternness of Elder F. in bringing his victim here had frightened Katō so that he acknowledged all and told where the stolen valise was. He had left it at a friend's house not a stone's throw from here. Two of the Elders went with him to the place and Elder Hedges opened the satchel and took out his watch before the people and put it on much to their astonishment. While they were gone three dectives from the Police Station called and we could have relieved ourselves of the remainder of the days work had we turned Katō over into their hands, but we had decided [to]and promised not to send him to jail if he would divulge & restore the stolen articles. We told them that we had apprehended the guilty one and made him return the stolen articles consequently did not feel like turning him over to the law Inasmuch as he had acknowledged his guilt and it was his first offense. We had infomed the officers of our loss in order that they could begin the search for the valuable articles before they were entirely out of reach. They accepted what we said and after spending a few minutes eating and drinking a little spread of tea, sandwiches, fruit, etc which we prepared for them returned.

Katō was then brought back to the house & questioned as to what he did with Elder F's five yen. He said he had paid it to his friend Fujishima of the house where he had put the valise. We called in Mr. Fujishima and asked him before Katō if Katō had paid the five yen to him in return for a five yen borrowed in the past. Mr. Fujishima denied and gave Katō the lie. Lie number five. Katō insisted upon what he had said about paying the five yen to Fujishima but when pressed he put his hand into his sleeve and pulled out a five yen and handed it to Elder F. saying it was not the same five that he had stolen But his only made this position that more critical. Lies number six & seven.

We then took action in his case and upon the motion of Elder F. seconded by Prest. E. We were unanimous in raising our hands to cut Katō off from the church divesting him of blessings, privileges and powers. We then charged him to guard his future acts lest he be taken and thrown into jail.

One peculiar thing about the action to cut him off from the church was that he requested us to cut his wife off at the same time. This, of course, was denied as his wife was in no wise a party in his falsifying & stealing. He went away disgraced and with his head hanging low.

When Elders F. & Stoker went over to Katō wife's mother's place to see if he was there they heard from them the real reason why Katō was not allowed to stay there last night. He had of late been acting exceedingly harsh towards his wife as a result, her mother had called her back home and determined to keep him out. He had deceived his wife, lied to her parents and been a lazy good-for-nothing husband. [E]The elders told them that he had done a very bad thing and it was to see about it that they had come for him. As soon as Katō came Elder F. who was waiting for him said nothing to the surprised mother & daughter but simply took hold of Katō and led him away. This revealed plainer than words that Katō's offense must be very serious so in the evening Sister Katō came over to find out about the matter. She was told all which frightened her and made her feel as though she and her mother would not be safe alone in her mother's house without the protection of a man—her father being gone from early morning till late at night. So after supper Elder F. & I accompanied her home and stayed there till the father came home. While there we learned of a great many more lies which Katō was guilty of and which he refused to acknowledge.

In the afternoon after the excitement was over we held our prayer & fast meeting. Mail came from America. Was glad to learn of the continued health of my folks.

Thursday, 20 October 1904, Tokyo

Clear—Warm. Up at 6:30. Spent nearly the entire day in the house working on the Book of Mormon and reading papers from America. **The mail from America yesterday brought a letter from the Presidency of the Church to Prest. E. In this letter they referred to the translation of the Book of Mormon and desired to encourage us in this great work. This is the first time that the presiding authorities have said anything about this work and I am delighted with what their letter to Prest. Ensign contains.**

In the evening, Mrs. Kamiyama came over to headquarters to request baptism for her husband who has been lying sick for a long time, but who through the blessings of the Lord has more than once been relieved of much suffering when the elders laid their hands upon him. Undoubtedly she also will be prepared to receive the ordinance by the time for its performance has arrived.

Friday, 21 October 1904, Tokyo

Fair—a slight shower—warm. Up at 6:15. Spent part of the morning translating A detective called to see what he could learn about the recent robbery, but I didn't tell him anything. Mr. Iwano was here nearly all day He and Elder Caine went over a number of songs and corrected the mistakes. In the afternoon, I worked again on the Book of Mormon for a little while. Mr. Suzuki called and I talked with him for quite a while. Mr. Yoshida & his friend called and spend a few minutes chatting with Prest. Ensign. Elder Featherstone spent some hours looking around in this neighborhood for some large tub or box that would hold water and could be made of service in baptizing Mr. Kamiyama whose sickness keeps him in bed most of the time. Elder F. was unsuccessful in his search. Elder Stoker took the afternoon train out to Nakano to meet Elder Jarvis & assist in holding a meeting in Elder Jarvis' rooms at Agagaya.

Sunday, 23 October 1904, Tokyo

Cloudy—Cold. Up at 6:30. **Fasted the fore part of the day in the interest of Elder Jarvis who felt indisposed.** The Sunday School went off pleasantly. The Sacrament Meeting was attended by all the Elders, Sister Ensign, & three converts. **Between the Sunday School & Sacrament Meeting administered to Elder Jarvis.** The evening meeting was well attended and the audience paid strict attention. After meeting took a walk with Elder. F. accompanying Sister Katō home at the same time.

Monday, 24 October 1904, Tokyo

Fair—Cold. Up at 6:00. Spent the morning working on the Book of Mormon. Part of the afternoon also was spent in translation. During the day united with my brethren in praying for and administering to Elder Jarvis who continued to feel unwell. **Mail from America arrived. I received a letter from Prest. Anthon H. Lund regarding the Book of Mormon. It is as follows:**

Salt Lake City, Utah. Sept. 30th 1904.

Elder Alma O. Taylor,

Tokio, Japan.

Dear Brother:

From Prest. Ensign's letter, which we received a short time ago, I learn that you are engaged on the translation of the Book of Mormon into Japanese. We are pleased to know that this work is being done. I am glad that you have succeeded so well in getting hold of such a diff/icult/ language that you can undertake the important labor[ing] of rendering the Book of Mormon Intelligible to those who speak it. You have our earnest prayers for your success.

Some time ago your father left a postscript to one of your letters, in which you refer to what Bro. Roberts says concerning the method that the Prophet used in translating the Book of Mormon. Our people have been satisfied with the explanation given by some, namely, that when Joseph translated the characters on the plates he saw the English text appear on the Urim & Thummim and that he had nothing to do but to read the words there appearing. This was the easiest way of answering the question, How was the translation done? But when a person has ever translated sentences from one language to another, he has learned how nearly impossible it is to translate it in the exact words that another person has done it. Then when the Book of Mormon passages, taken from Isaiah, are compared with the Bible as we have it today, one is struck with the identity of the two vers/i/ons. The difficulty increases when it is remembered that the Bible has been translated from a Latin version and that again from the original Greek. One of the strongest objections raised against the Book of Mormon has been the verbal similarity between it and the Bible. It was to meet this objection that Brother Roberts answered "Unknown" as he did. When you read the ninth section of the Doc. & Cov. you can see that Oliver Cowdery was rebuked because he wanted to translate and did not take thought upon the subject, but thought it would be given without any effort on his part. If he, Oliver Cowdery, was to study and receive the testimony of the Spirit as to the correctness of the work done, there is no doubt that the Prophet did translate in the same way the Lord directed Oliver Cowdery. If Roberts be right then we can understand how the wording in the Bible and the Book of Mormon can be so nearly alike. If he be wrong, then we know that nothing is impossible with God, and that he is able to give the writing on the Urim & Thummim verbatim. Whichever way it has been done we know that it has been done by the power of God. I do not see any objection to Brother Roberts' theory. It is consistent with the ninth section, with my own experience in translating, and it explains a difficulty which many investigators have met and turned into an objection.

In regard to your last question: "If a passage is found in the Book of Mormon corresponding to that in the Bible, how safe would it be to turn to the Japanese translation xxx and copy from that uninspired text the translation as it stands?" I wish to say that in revising the Danish Book of Mormon, when I found a passage that responded to a passage of the English Bible, I would compare it with the Danish Bible and if the latter did not differ in meaning from the English, I would use the text of the Danish Bible, the language being the best that could be used. If the text varied in meaning from the Book of Mormon I would translate with the variations, but where the texts were alike, I have chosen, as above stated, to use the words of the Bible, it being as a general rule the choicest language. I would suggest that where you find the Book of Mormon text similar to the English Bible, turn to the Japanese Bible, and if that is a good translation use the Japanese text, as no doubt those who translated their Bible were their best students and philologists, and hence would be better able to give the exact shade of meaning.

In the former German translation of the Book of Mormon our translators went too far in the direction I have suggested, and took the German Bible and followed it whether it agreed in meaning or not with the Book of Mormon, and hence many places are really faulty. This has been corrected in the last edition.

May the Lord inspire you, Brother Taylor, in doing this important work, as well as in all your duties. Give my love to all the brethren laboring with you.

Your Brother in the Gospel
Anthon H. Lund.

The receipt of the above letter gave me much joy for as will be seen it contains instructions & advice which will materially assist me in gaining faith for the work of translation as well as assisting me greatly in the method of my work. I might record here that the postscript referred to was written in one of my letters to my brother Samuel soon after I read in the Deseret News the controversy between Brother Roberts & "Unknown" Soon after writing it an article on the way the Prophet Joseph Smith must have translated the characters on the gold plates came out in the "Era." This article was by Brother Roberts he having been requested to write it /(it appeared as a letter)/ in answer to an investigator's inquiries direct to Prest. Smith Prest. Smith having committed the duty of answering the letter to Brother Roberts showed to me that the Prophet of God at least approved in a large degree Brother Roberts' ideas. I read the article, thought upon it, and became reconciled to it in exactly the way Prest. Lund expresses in his letter before the letter came.

Tuesday, 25 October 1904, Tokyo

Fair—Cool. Up at 5:45. Spent most of the day reading newspapers from home and from books on the gospel. Having been awake from about midnight till morning watching Elder Jarvis whose ill health still required us to nurse him, I felt a little sleepy so took a short nap in the afternoon. Before going to bed read from the Book of Mormon for two hours. In the evening assisted the other brethren in administering to Sister Ensign who was suffering a slight nervous shock. Fasted all day in behalf of Elder Jarvis.

Wednesday, 26 October 1904, Tokyo

Clear—Cold—Rain in the evening. Up at 6:30. Continued the fast for Elder Jarvis until 4:30 p.m. In the morning I started to translate a little of the Book of Mormon but other things came up and I had to set translation aside. Took a bath, tended to Elder Jarvis for an hour or so. Then united with my brethren in prayer, after which we united in administering to Bro. Jarvis. Sister Ensign's nerves being affected we also administered to her. In the afternoon I spent some hours talking to visitors. In the evening I again waited on Elder Jarvis and with Elder Featherstone slept just outside of our sick brother's door to keep watch through the night. Received a letter from mother during the day. She wrote interestingly of home and especially of my baby nephew Harold.

Thursday, 27 October 1904, Tokyo

Cleared off & became fair & warm. Up at 8:00 a.m. Was up tending to Elder Jarvis serveral times before eight o'clock but did not dress till then. My night's rest was not very good as I was thinking about my watch and could not sleep. Elder Jarvis was much improved during the day. In the morning I read over a part of Elder Caine's translation of Bro. Hedges' tract on "Prayer." In the afternoon I went to Shinagawa to visit Mr. Suzuki but after a long search for his house I gave up the hunt and returned. Ate supper and retired.

Friday, 28 October 1904, Tokyo

Fair—Warm. **Up at 9:00. The night was an eventful one. Elder Featherstone & I were sleeping** in the extreme far room in the Japanese half. Elder Caine was alone in a bed on the floor in a room next to us. Elders Stoker and Hedges were sleeping in the upper hall to keep watch on Elder Jarvis. Prest. & Sister Ensign were sleeping peacefully in their own room.

Having been on watch the night before I was fast asleep when I was awakened by a nudge or two from Elder F. who said, "there is someone in here do you hear them. I listened and heard footsteps plainly, but had not been awake long enough to distinguish in the dark the location of the person tho the noise indicated that he was on my side of the bed. I was hardly awake but thinking it might be some one of the brethren I said in English "Who are you." At this the person started to run and struck one of the paper doors. This was like an electric shock to me. I leaped up and all I know was that there was a terrible crash followed by Elder F grasping me out in the hall. I huridly told him that he had the wrong man. He released me & went to the end of the hall where he saw a window standing wide open. This made it plain that we had been robbed & the thief had made his escape from the window. The crash had been heard all over the house. Elder Caine suddenly jumped up out of a sound sleep and ran around in the darkness almost unconscious of what he was doing. Elder Hedges & Stoker appeared on the scene in great excitement. Prest E wisely remained up stairs to keep tranquil the sick one and passify his wife whose nerves received a severe shock.

The brethren who ran outside in persuit of the thief soon came back for some weapons to protect them in further search through the trees & shrubs of the garden. All we had was a pair of indian clubs so they took one each and a lamp & went in out to hunt up what traces there might be. The thief had escaped with two pair of pants, a coat, & a vest of Elder F's and a coat & pants belonging to me. In Elder F's vest was his /gold/ watch & chain and gold spectacles and in one of his pockets there was a purse containing something ~~over~~ /less than/ ¥2.00. Fortunately according to my custom, I had my vest containing my watch, fountain pen and other things under my pillow. In the clothes that were stolen I had nothing of particular value and no money.

After a little while the brethren on the outside came back, having found where the thief had taken down a part of the fence on the west to make an effective opening for entrence & retreat. They had gone into the neighboring yard and in the foundation of a new house that is being erected they found the empty purses, letters, books, papers & etc which were in our clothes showing that the robber was a deliberate fellow having taken the time to examine the things he had stolen and discard everything that was of no value to him and if caught would tend to convict him.

Elder F & I went over to the police & notified them of the affair also gave them a description of the stolen articles so they could begin to search for them immediately. A policeman accompanied us back to the house & we searched through the neighboring yard among the material for the new building to see if we could find no further clues or something that the thief had dropped. We then went back to the house, entered quietly so as not to disturb anyone and after doctoring up a few bruises I received as a result of going through paper doors & etc in the dark we went to bed & sleep for an hour or two before getting up. The thief was discovered at 2 a.m. We went to bed at 4:30 or 5:00 a.m. After looking over the affair and considering the great risk Elder F. & I took in making for the thief in the darkness we feel thankful that we were protected from all harm for the plans laid by the thief to rob us and the cool deliberate way in which he did it is evidence that he is a professional in his line and no doubt determined enough to use a knife in self defense if necessary.

After getting up I spent some time tending to Elder Jarvis. In the forenoon two detectives from the Yotsuya police force called to investigate /the/ particulars of the robbery. In the afternoon I looked over part of Elder Caine's translation of Elder Hedges tract, "Prayer." In the evening, in order to get a little exercise and make a long due visit I went to see Mr. Yoshida. Elder Stoker accompanied me. We spent about an hour chatting with Mr. Yoshida and a friend who was spending a few day's at his home. Returned to headquarters, united with the others in special prayer in the prayer room for Elder Jarvis' recovery. Elder Caine & I went on watch over Elder Jarvis who was much improved during the day.

Saturday, 29 October 1904, Tokyo

Clear—Warm. Up at 7:00. Feeling the responsibility of the watch I did not sleep more than thirty minutes all night. During the forenoon, I cleaned up my shoes & clothes and took a bath. In the afternoon I wrote my journal and spent two hours with Elder Jarvis whose condition was greatly improved. I then took a long nap. Got up and ate supper then read a little before going to bed.

Monday, 31 October 1904, Tokyo

Clear & Cold Up at 8:00. In the morning the brethren put the stove up in Elder Jarvis' room. His condition is much improved today. I devoted part of the day to work on the Book of Mormon. Spent an hour or two going over the translation or rather half of the translation of the tract "Prayer" and discussing with Elder Caine those points which I thought would be improved if changed. Retired about 10:00 p.m.

Tuesday, 1 November 1904, Tokyo

Clear & Warm Up at 8:30. Spent the morning shopping on the Ginza. Purchased a new hat and a pair of suspenders. In the afternoon Elder Hedges and I took Elder Jarvis out for a rikisha ride. On the way we called on Dr. Whitney and had him examine Elder Jarvis' condition. In the evening assisted in cutting tomatoes & onions which Sister Ensign intends to make into /pickle/ sauce.

Wednesday, 2 November 1904, Tokyo

Cloudy & Cold. Up at 8:15. Spent two hours in the morning tending to Elder Jarvis. Assisted by Elder Caine I took him out for a walk. I had a bath about 11:00 a.m. At noon we held our regular prayer meeting, all the elders except Bro. Jarvis were present. Sister Ensign was also in attendance. The main object of our prayers was that the Lord would be especially merciful unto Elder Jarvis and heal him as quickly as possible. After prayer we all repaired to Elder J's. room & administered to him myself & Prest. Ensign officiating. In the afternoon I worked a little on the Book of Mormon. Went on watch over Elder Jarvis from 7:00 p.m till 10:45. Then took a recess of about thirty minutes when I went to bed with him. Fasted till 4:00 p.m.

Saturday, 5 November 1904, Tokyo

Fair—Moderate Up at 8:15. Fasted all day in behalf of Elder Jarvis. During the morning did a few jobs and spent two hours with Elder Jarvis. Elder Caine & I took him out for a walk. In the early part of the afternoon took a bath and shaved. Mrs. Matsudaira and a gentleman companion called. I spent about an hour talking to them. Worked till 10:p.m on the Book of Mormon. Elder Featherstone and I went on watch for the night.

Sunday, 6 November 1904, Tokyo

Stormy and very cold. Up at 7:00. Continued fasting till four o'clock in the afternoon. The Sunday School was slim but spirited the lessons being very satisfactorily carried out. Only one Saint was present at fast meeting. After pertaking of the sacrament and bearing testimony the elders repaired to the prayer room each praying in turn in behalf of Elder Jarvis. We then went into Elder Jarvis' room and administered to him. In the afternoon I had a conversation with a young soldier. Tended Elder Jarvis for an hour then ate supper. The evening meeting like the Sunday School was not crowded but it was by no means a failure with four visitors & five missionaries present.

Monday, 7 November 1904, Tokyo

Clear & Cold. Up at 7:30. Spent most of the day in the house. Finished a letter to Aunt Clara. Worked on the Book of Mormon. Spent two hours with Elder Jarvis. In the evening I accompanied Elder Featherstone over to Mr & Mrs Kamiyama's. Mr. Kamiyama was very sick with his old disease. We did all we could to stir up in the hearts of the old man and old woman the necessity of being baptized and coming into the church as their daughter had already done. The old man and woman came to headquarters and requested baptism sometime ago, but his relatives not being favorable to Christianity pictured to him the great danger of going into the water in his weak condition and got the family to thinking that to submit to baptism under the present circumstances would be the same as inviting death. I hope the efforts of Elder F. & myself will allay all their fears & reawaken their former faith. Together with Elder Caine went on watch over Elder Jarvis for the night.

Tuesday, 8 November 1904, Tokyo

Clear—Warm. Up at 7:00. Assisted Elder Jarvis to wash and eat his breakfast. The mail came from America so I spent the morning reading letters and looking over the newspapers. In the afternoon I did a little on the translation of the Book of Mormon. In the evening I walked to the book store on Aoyama and back. After supper I spent two hours talking with Elder Jarvis, then went with Elder Stoker to the post office.

I have mentioned Elder Jarvis as ill a number of times but have not given the name of his ailment. For some months Elder J. felt discouraged in his work and he felt that he was not approved of the Lord, or he would be able under the blessings of Heaven to make greater progress in the language and promulgation of the gospel than he was. Prest. Ensign & his comapnions did all in their power to reason Elder J. out of his despondency and judging from the changed expression that would come over his face after the different talks with his brethren we all thought he would be able to control his feelings, but he kept getting worse so Prest Ensign gave him some changes in fields of labor and finally had him come & stay at headquarters.

He had only been here a day when is mind weakened and he collapsed mentally and lost his reasoning powers. We put him to bed and kept a vigalent watch over him having to give him medicine to keep him asleep at nights. Satan had wonderful power over him and in order to get the mastery over the evil one and cast him out we fasted twice for /almost/ forty eight hours and prayed most earnestly to the Lord. God heard our supplications and blessed Elder Jarvis little by little with the result that he is a great deal better now. Today he has accompanied Elders Featherstone & Stoker on an out to see the maple trees some miles from Tokyo. However his is not yet well and we continue to care for him and invoke God's blessings upon him in all humility and frequent fasting & prayer.

Thursday, 10 November 1904, Tokyo

Clear—Cool—Calm. Up at 7:00. **President Ensign's 33rd Birthday. Had breakfast at 8:00 a.m. did some coping into Japanese till 11:30, then prepared to eat dinner and take a trip out to Daugozaka to see the chrysanthemum flowers displayed there. Reference to my Journal of three years ago this time will give a good idea of the display. Although this year is much poorer than three years ago. On the way back four of us brethren /who were together/ went through a bazaar and then called at a "sobaya". After reaching headquarters, we had ice cream and cake which had been specially prepared in honor of Prest. Ensign**

Wednesday, 16 November 1904, Tokyo/Chiba

Clear and Cold Up at 6:45. Took a walk before breakfast. In the morning made the index to Journal E and for journal D. Took a bath in the morning and at noon joined in a prayer meeting with my brethren Elders Featherstone, Stoker, Hedges, and Caine. Prest. Ensign and Elder Jarvis were out in Hongo Ku looking at a foreign styled house which is for rent. Sister Ensign was feeling unwell so did not join with us in prayer. In the evening I worked on the Book of Mormon.

Thursday, 17 November 1904, Tokyo

Fair—Slight wind—very cold. Up at 6:30. Spent the morning working on the Book of Mormon. **It was decided by Prest. Ensign at the breakfast table that Elders Featherstone, Jarvis, Stoker, and Hedges leave for Choshi Chiba Ku the following morning and labor in that city till Christmas time. The principle purpose of this appointment was to get Elder Jarvis away from Tokyo & give him a chance to do a little work in the country and see if his mind would not get more strength. He is still**

in a very unsatisfactory condition mentally. In the afternoon I did some more work on the Book of Mormon and in the evening I had a conversation with two visitors.

Monday, 21 November 1904, Tokyo

Fair, Moderate. Up at 7:45. After breakfast Elder Caine and I went with a friend to the Yotsuya Police Station to see an exhibit of "jujitsu" (Japanese wrestling)[14] We watched the performance which was very interesting until noon. No professionals appeared. It was not a betting game; simply a friendly comparison of the skill of the policeman from the different districts in Tokyo. All policemen in Tokyo are required to practice this art or "kinjutsu" (fencing)[15] so that when necessity requires they can cope successfully with vicious men.

In the afternoon Prest. Ensign & wife & Elder Caine and I went to Hongo to look at a house. On the way back I went around by Negishi and visited some of my friends. Was greeted cordially wherever I called. Got back to headquarters at 8:30. Ate supper and retired.

Thursday, 24 November 1904, Tokyo

Fair—Slight wind—cold. Up at 6:45. In the morning after breakfast I went down town to do a little business for the mission and buy some Christmas cards to send home. In the afternoon about 1:30 I helped eat a very palatable Thanksgiving Dinner. In place of a turkey we had stuffed fish which in my estimation is equally as delicious as the former. In the afternoon I wrote Christmas Greetings on the cards I had purchased.

Friday, 25 November 1904, Tokyo

Cloudy—mild Up at 7:15. After breakfast I started out in quest of a house. I called at real estate agencies, police headquarters, building associations, newspaper offices, and friends houses. I tramped all over Ushigome, Koishikawa, Kanda Shiba, Ugabu, and Akasaka making a side trip on the car through the centre of town from Kanda to Shiba. I got back to headquarters at about 6:00 p.m. Had dinner at /a/ "sobaya" on the Fore.

Saturday, 26 November 1904, Tokyo

Morning rain—Warmer—Afternoon fair. Up at 7:30. After breakfast went over to the Aoyama Hospital to enquire of a specialists in mental diseases about what we had better do for Elder Jarvis who according to reports from his companions in Choshi City is getting worse. The doctor was absent so I returned to headquarters did a little writing then went to the hospital again after dinner. Had a long talk with one of the doctors who thought it would be best to take Elder Jarvis to the hospital. But in going through the place and seeing where our brother would be put I concluded that we could accomodiate him as well at headquarters. I returned and reported the result of my interview to Prest. Ensign. In the evening I wrote some Christmas letters.

Tuesday, 29 November 1904, Tokyo

Clear, Moderate, Up at 7:15. Mail came from America in the morning so I spent some time reading news from home. Did just a little on the translation of the Book of Mormon. In the afternoon, Mr. Tsuoka called and I had a conversation with him. Then one of the Sunday School children who is going to take part on the Christmas program came to say her piece. I then went with Prest. Ensign to the post office to send off the Christmas mail. I did not send any presents home this year. All I did was to remember relatives and friends with letters, cards, and calanders for the new year. I sent things as follows: Letter to the family through father a calander to father and mother, card each to Sara, Aunt Clara, Aunt Hattie, Aunt Jane, Bro. & Sister Nunn, Joseph Wm, Robert Mitchell, Sister Empey, Aunt Martha Aunt Margaret, Cousin Alex McRae; Letters to Miss Baggarley, Miss Grace I. Frost, Lizzie Thomas, Will Erikson, Emil Egli, Wm Seidenfaden, my brother Alvin V. and my brother Edward; and a calander to Bessie Badger.

In the evening Mr. Yoshida called with some proof sheets of an English Reader he is getting out.

Prest. Ensign looked over them for him and made corrections of all the mistakes he detected therein. Afterward I had a religious conversation with Mr. Yoshida.

Wednesday, 30 November 1904, Tokyo

Cloudy, Cold Up at 7:10. Pumped the bath water. Ate breakfast. Worked on the Book of Mormon for a little while. Took a bath and together with Prest. and Sister Ensign and Elder Caine, I engaged in special prayer. A young Christian called and I had about a two-hour's conversation with him. I then did a little on the Book of Mormon but some of the Sunday School children who are going to take part in the Christmas exercises came to review their parts so I had to be with them for some time.

Elder Featherstone came back from Choshi and reported Elder Jarvis in a very serious condition his acts become very peculiar at times and he attempts desperate things as well as profane and talk foolishness. This all indicates that he has become really insane. He can be controlled all right, so Elder Featherstone reports, and does not attempt to harm any of those around him. This report of the deplorable condition of our brother is certainly very painful to us. Prest. Ensign has decided to send him home on December 14th per S. S. "Kanagawa Maru" and has released Elder Jos. F. Featherstone to go home with him. This will be a very great loss to our mission, but it is something which, under the circumstances cannot be helped. The trip will be a very great trial to Elder F. for it will be necessary for him to keep a strict watch on Elder Jarvis almost day and night.

In the evening after dinner I did some more translating.

Thursday, 1 December 1904, Tokyo

Cloudy, Warmer. Up at 6:35. Took some exercises and a walk before breakfast. Continued during the day to work on the translation of the Book of Mormon. About noon I had a conversation on God as a personal being with a student who visits us quite often.

A Cablegram was received from President Joseph F. Smith. It read as follows "Release Jarvis. Money telegraphed. Smith." This was sent immediately upon the arrival in Salt Lake of President Ensign's letter telling of the condition of Elder Jarvis and asking for money in case he had to be sent home.

In the evening we decided to take a house in Hongo which we found a long time ago. We will according to our present plans move between Christmas and New Years.

Tuesday, 6 December 1904, Tokyo

Clear Cold wind. Up at 6:45. Took my exercises and a walk before breakfast. In the forenoon I wrote a letter in Japanese to a friend who was formerly in Tokyo but now in the west of Japan. After dinner I had a long talk with Mr. Sukukoshi. He also made a few suggestions as to how some of the difficult expressions in the Book of Mormon should be translated. After supper Mr. Yoshida called and I got him to help me a little in the rendition of difficult words & idioms into Japanese.

Tuesday, 13 December 1904, Tokyo

Cold—Rain and snow Up at 8:10. The morning was so black and dismal that everyone in the house was deceived as to the time so arose very late. During the morning I did some work connected with the translation of the Book of Mormon. There is much side writing to do and lots of notes to take when making as extensive a translation as that in which I am engaged. After dinner, I began the translation of the Book of Jacob but only finished about a page. In the evening Elder Caine and I went to the post office. Before going to bed I read a little in the book entitled "Japan in Transition."[16] Took a bath and retired. From about 5:00 p.m. the rain which had been falling all day turned into a snow storm—the first of the season. The falling flakes looked very cheerful to us who were born in a land of long winters and much snow.

Wednesday, 14 December 1904, Tokyo

Snow Up at 7:30. Spent considerable of the day translating.

In the evening the Elders from Choshi returned. Prest. Ensign mailed Elder Jarvis' release to return home, yesterday and called all three of the brethren in to Tokyo. Elder Jarvis seemed in pretty good spirits, but we could see that he was in an unbalanced mental state.

Thursday, 15 December 1904, Tokyo

Cloudy, Warmer Up at 7:15. After breakfast, went out to a gardner's to see if he had any Christmas trees. He was not home. I came back and read from "Japan in Transition" till noon. Then went to the gardeners again and saw the trees he had. There was nothing in his garden that just suited, but one tree that we can get along with if nothing better can be found. In the afternoon the Sunday School children called to practice the Sunday School songs and especially prepare for the Christmas singing. In the evening before supper, I went to invite the parents of one of the S. S. children to our Christmas exercises and ask the little girl to take part on the program. In the evening after supper, I wrote out a dialogue in Japanese for Santa Claus and the one who will welcome him and introduce him to the children.

Sunday, 18 December 1904, Tokyo

Very cold—Fair Up at 7:30. Did a little janitor work before Sunday School. We had a very large attendance. From 11:a.m. held the usual sacrament meeting. Elders Featherstone and Jarvis made their farewell speeches. Prest. Ensign spoke in praise of the labors of the returning brethren. In the afternoon I wrote a prayer for the Christmas entertainment. Translated it into Japanese and gave it to Yae Uesugi to learn. Later in the afternoon accompanied some of the brethren who went out to a certain garden near by in search of a Christmas tree. The evening meeting was well attended.

Monday, 19 December 1904, Tokyo

Cold—Clear— No wind Up at 7:15. In the morning went to Yotsuya to look around for Christmas presents for the Sunday School children. In the afternoon Elder Hedges and I went to Okulō to look for a Christmas tree. Found one and purchased it for ¥1.0 delivered. On the way home invited a number of people to the Christmas entertainment. In the evening practiced some songs with the rest of the folks at headquarters.

Wednesday, 21 December 1904, Tokyo

Clear—Warmer Up at 7:30. After breakfast, we all prepared **to go to Yokohama to bid farewell to Elders Joseph F. Featherstone and Erastus L. Jarvis. Before going however, I called on two or three families in the neighborhood and invited them to our entertainment. There was only one friend accompanied us to the railway station—Mr. Matsushita. We left Shimbashi Station at 10:20 a.m. After arriving in Yokohama I looked after the Elders' baggage until it was safely loaded onto the ship—"Kanagawa Maru." We all met at the boat and spent an hour or so together before the whistle blew informing the visitors that it was time to leave. We watched the boat until it stopped, just outside the port for inspection. It was hard to part with our two brethren but under the circumstances we were very glad to see them leave in good spirits and comparative health. Elder Jarvis, to our great joy, was almost himself again. After returning to Tokyo did a little more in preparation for the Christmas entertainment.**

Friday, 23 December 1904, Tokyo

Clear—Warmer Up at 7:30. After breakfast disolved some alum[17] and sprayed the Christmas tree. Then sprinkled the tree with pulverized starch. Did this at the suggestion of a writer in the Lady's Home Journal hoping to get a chrystalized tree as a result but was disappointed. In the afternoon I read from a little book entitled "Jesus Christ." In the evening I had a conversation with a student of the Normal School. The Sunday School children were here for about an hour in the afternoon to practice the songs for Christmas.

Sunday, 24 December 1904, Tokyo

Clear—Cold. Up at 7:15. During the morning we decorated the Christmas Tree. In the afternoon we cleaned up and made all the final arranement for the children's entertainment. In the evening I went out to invite one of the native sisters whose now engaged in the shipping department of the medical service of the army. After supper we fixed up 100 packages of candy & nuts for the S. S. children. Elder Stoker and I had a dress rehearsal of our part on the program. Took a bath and retired at 12 m.

Sunday, 25 December 1904, Tokyo

Clear—calm—cold Up at 9:00. Having been up quite late the night before we were all glad to sleep this morning. No breakfast was prepared as we had arranged for an early dinner. Had not been up long before visitors began to call and presents from friends began to arrive. There was no exchange of presents among the missionaries, which to my mind was very fortunate and in harmony with the spirit of missionary conditions. We remembered some of the saints with small tokens. From 11:00 a.m. we held our Sacrament meeting. From 12:30 had dinner. Mr. Ikeda ate with us.

Later in the afternoon we moved the table, side-boards, book case, and chairs out of our big dining room and laid cushions all over the floor for the children and guests whom we hoped would be present. The company started to come about 5:00 p.m. By 6:00 the house was full of Sunday School children and their parents & friends. In fact so many came that we could not find room for them inside. At 6:00 the program began and it did my heart good to look into the sea of faces before me when I arose to announce the first song. The children were dressed in their best and their sweet face's wore an expression of intense joy at the prospect of what the evening's exercises would bring to them. They had been living in expectation of this event for some weeks and the joy which the opportunity of being here tonight afforded them could be read in the sparkle of their eyes and smiles upon their faces. The old folks were as much pleased with the decorations and Christmas tree as the little ones for they had never seen such things before. The program was carried out as follows. . . .

Every one who took part on the program did exceedingly well. The little boy who offered the opening prayer is the son of a poor widow woman and is only 11 years old. The Takagi sisters are Christians and do exceedingly fine in the Theological Class, but both are quite young. The Katagiri girl is only 12 years old, but the ease with which she learns and recited her speech was remarkable. [~~Seh~~] Saito Hisa also is young (only 11 years old) and we count her one of the gems of the school. The little Ichikawa girl is only 10 years old but has a beautiful voice which won the special favor of the crowd. Hakii Nami is one of our lady converts. Her speech was interesting to all and led up to the coming of Santa Claus so nicely that the children were worked up to the last notch of expectancy.

The bells of Santa's reindeer could be heard 'way in the distance. The jingle grew louder as he came nearer. The children's eyes were almost springing out of their places by the time Santa's sleigh stopped outside the door and his cheerfull voice rang out, "Hello there." A great cry went up when Santa came in with his big basket load of presents—one for every child. Some of the smaller children were greatly frightened at first but they soon found that Santa Claus was the friend of all. The tree was lit just before he came in and all looked exceedingly fine. The old folks looked on with open mouths. After Santa Claus [~~had~~] finished distributing his presents we gave out at the request of three young Japanese friends 46 Christmas cards to those "who had been the most faithful in their duties to the Sunday School. Hakii Nami had provided special prizes for some of the children. These were given out also at her request. Then after the closing prayer the children were given an apple each as they passed out. The parents were thanked for coming and asked to assist us in making the Sunday School a success during 1905. Only one family out of the great crowd that was present are Christians and consequently the children and their parents are to be complimented. After the exercises we played and sang to some few who remained for an hour or two. I accompanied Sister Deguchi and her sisters home. We had a very light meal before going to bed.

I forgot to state that just before noon two packages from America arrived—one for Elder Hedges and the other for Elder Caine. In them were presents for these two brethren and the others in the mission.

Sister Hedges sent me a very nice white silk necktie. The Christmas cakes from home made our noon meal quite home-like.

Altogether, I received as presents the following: A tie, as stated, from Sister Hedges, a tray from Sister Deguchi, postal cards from Deguchi Tomi, a book from Sister Hakii and two book marks from Mrs. Kiyo Umeda & Miss Take Kogu. I united with Elders Stoker, Hedges & Caine in giving a bible each to Sisters Deguchi & Kamiyama and geta to sister Hakii.

Saturday, 31 December 1904, Tokyo

Clear—Windy—Cold Up at 7:10. Took a walk before breakfast. During the morning I did a little translating finishing the book of Jacob. It will take about a week's work to copy the translation into the characters. In the afternoon shaved and read a little. In the evening we all went to a "sobaya" and ate "soba" for supper in honor of the last day of the year. Elders Stoker, Hedges, Caine, and I went down to the Ginza to see what was going on. We got back at 10:00 p.m. We took a bath and thought of making molasses candy which Sister Ensign already had cooking on the stove. It was not quite done by midnight so after wishing each other a happy new year we went to bed leaving the candy for sometime in the future.

Notes

1. *The Searchlight: Devoted to the Interests of the Church of Christ in Zion* (Independence, Mo: Church of Christ in Zion) February 1896–March 1900.

2. Makimoya Hotel, Chiba.

3. *Millennial Star.* "From 1840 to 1970, *The Latter-day Saints' Millennial Star* was the official publication of the LDS Church in the British Isles. Its pages contained editorials, Church history and doctrine, and other administrative issues central to the mission of the LDS Church." Stanley A. Peterson, "Millennial Star," *Encyclopedia of Mormonism*, 2:906.

4. Amalgam. An alloy of mercury with another metal or metals used in dentistry.

5. George Q. Cannon, *The Latter-Day Prophet: History of Joseph Smith Written for Young People* (Salt Lake City: Juvenile Instructor, 1900).

6. Edward H. Anderson, *A Brief History of The Church of Jesus Christ of Latter-day Saints to the Present Time* (Salt Lake City: George Q. Cannon & Sons, 1893).

7. R. M. Bryce Thomas, "My Reasons for Leaving The Church of England and Joining The Church of Jesus Christ of Latter-day Saints."

8. Sciatica. Pain and tenderness at some points of the sciatic nerve; any painful disorder extending from the hip down the back of the thigh and surrounding area.

9. 1 Nephi 13. "Nephi sees in vision: the church of the devil set up among the Gentiles; the discovery and colonizing of America; the loss of many plain and precious parts of the Bible; the resultant state of gentile apostasy; the restoration of the gospel, the coming forth of latter-day scripture, and the building up of Zion."

10. Catarrah. A syringe used to get liquid out of nose.

11. Beatitudes. The "promises of blessings" given by Jesus in his Sermon on the Mount (Matt. 5:3–12). Thomas W. McKay, "Beatitudes," *Encyclopedia of Mormonism*, 1:98.

12. "And he said unto them, Go ye into all the world, and preach the gospel to every creature. He that believeth and is baptized shall be saved; but he that believeth not shall be damned. And these signs shall follow them that believe; In my name shall they cast out devils; they shall speak with new tongues; They shall take up serpents; and if they drink any deadly thing, it shall not hurt them; they shall lay hands on the sick, and they shall recover," Mark 16:15–18.

13. Cholera. A horrible, infectious disease marked by diarrhea and severe dehydration. Death can occur as quickly as several hours after the first visible symptoms. If untreated, the mortality rate is more than 50 percent; if properly treated the rate falls to less than 1 percent. "Cholera," *Microsoft Encarta 98 Encyclopedia*.

14. *Jujutsu.* A general description of many styles of Asian martial arts that involve kicks, choke holds, throws, and a variety of sorted weapons. "Jujutsu," *Microsoft Encarta 98 Encyclopedia*.

15. *Kinjutsu.* A style of Japanese fencing.

16. Stafford Ransome, *Japan in Transition; A Comparative Study of the Progress, Policy, and Methods of The Japanese Since Their War with China* (New York: Harper & Brothers, 1899).

17. Aluminum.

Chapter 9

Alma O. Taylor Journal, 1905

Sunday, 1 January 1905, Tokyo

Breezy—Cold—Fair Up at 9:00 Owing to the fact that all school children were expected to attend services at the schools in honor of the Emperor and to welcome the new year, we held no Sunday School. The three Katagiri children came and stayed an hour. From 11:00 a.m we held Fast Meeting with only one saint present. In the afternoon I read from the Bible and History of the Church. After dinner I talked with Bro. Oyama about the translation of the Book of Mormon. He thought my translation a little too colloquial. In the evening we expected to hold meeting but only three children and three adults came. We invited them into the dining room and lit the Christmas tree for their entertainment. Two of them stayed till quite late talking about Hokkaido.

Thursday, 5 January 1905, Tokyo

Clear—Warm—Up at 6:45. Took exercises and a walk before breakfast. Intended to put in a whole day on the Book of Mormon, but the Normal School student called and I talked with him from breakfast till dinner. After dinner another Normal Student came and I talked with him till **it was time to get ready to go to a party to which all the missionaries were invited. For some time past two ladies have been coming to headquarters once a week to get a few pointers in English. One is a teacher at a private girl's school, the other is the wife of a Japanese now a prisoner of war at Kiel. This evening we met at the home of the former Take Kogu San where the latter Kiyo Umeda San is living temporarily. We spent the evening very pleasantly. A number of games were indulged in and we had a little music both foreign and Native. Quite a toothsome Japanese supper was served.** We returned to headquarters about 11:00 p.m.

Saturday, 7 January 1905, Tokyo

Clear—Quite Warm Up at 6:30. Spent the morning and part of the afternoon house cleaning. **Received a card from Bro. Yochi Oyama now in the employ of the Singer Sewing machine Co. at Yokohama. He told of an experience he had a day or two ago at a prayer meeting held in Yokohama by the followers of the different Christian sects operating there. According to Bro. Oyama's card it would seem as though it was customary for such meetings to be held in the beginning of each year. As Bro. Oyama writes, he went to see the "theatre" (this is what he called the prayer meeting) and while taking in the different prayers, was rather surprised at being asked by the pastor to pray. He quickly consented and asked the Lord to remember and abundantly bless Prest. Joseph F. Smith, his councillors, the Twelve Apostles and Elder Horace S. Ensign, president of the work in Japan. The pastor evidently realized by this time that he had made a mistake or at least thought he had for he asked Bro. Oyama to close his prayer.**

In the afternoon three Normal School students called and I had conversations with them.

Tuesday, 10 January 1905, Tokyo

Fair—Cold Up at 6:55. Took exercises and a walk before breakfast. During part of the morning I did some work on the Book of Mormon. But mail arrived from America and the news was all so interesting and good that we discussed the contents of each other's letters for some time. It was the mail that should have reached us at Christmas time but got on a very slow boat. I received letters from Mother and

Samuel. Sister Featherstone sent me a neck tie and Elder Stoker's father and mother sent me a card with the season's greetings. I also received a good photo of Samuel & Lucile's baby Harold. In the afternoon and evening I worked again on the Book of Mormon.

Wednesday, 11 January 1905, Tokyo

Clear—Cold Up at 6:40. Took a long walk first thing in the morning. Returned and went to work on the Book of Mormon. During most of the day I was occupied by this work. Noticed in the Deseret News of Dec. 20th the account of the funeral of Heber S. Goddard the famous singer of Utah. His death was a very sudden one and being very intimately acquainted with him, the notice of his funeral was a great shock. Two days ago [we no] we noticed /in papers from home/ that he was taken with a bad case of pneumonia but I had not the least idea that he would die. Truly this life is an uncertain one and it is well to always live so that one is prepared to meet his God at any moment.

Saturday, 14 January 1905, Tokyo

Rain during forenoon—clear & cold in the afternoon. Up at 7:20. After getting up I pumped the bath water before breakfast. **After breakfast shaved and then went with Elder Caine to the printers. Elder Caine has finished the translation and correction of the tract "My Reasons for leaving the Church of England and joining the church of Jesus Christ of Latter–day Saints." Was greatly surprised when we approached the printer's place to see the building gone. The only thing remaining to indicate that there used to be a printing office was a heap of ashes and charred wood. We found where the office was temorarily opened and upon learning that the company was carrying on its business as ever through its branch offices and other firms we felt safe in placing our work with them. The compositor being out we had to leave the manuscript without learning the price of the 1,000 copies which the mission wants in the first edition. They promised to inform us /by letter/ of the price and particulars of the printing.**

On the way home I called in to the barber's and had a haircut. Returned to headquarters and had dinner. Hurriedly dressed to go over to the Aisumi Jo Gakko¹ to see and take part in some exercises which were given for the benefit of a regiment of soldiers who leave in a few days for the battle field. Prest. Ensign, Elders Stoker, & Hedges and I represented the Mission and sung and played to the amusement of the assembly. After the exercises we were entertained & feasted in the home of the head teacher of the school. After returning I looked up some points for the Sunday School lesson I had under contemplation for the Primary class the following day.

Sunday, 15 January 1905, Tokyo

Windy—Fair—Cold. Up at 7:30. Did a little cleaning up for the Sunday School. Ate breakfast. Sunday School commenced at ten o'clock. Heretofore it has commenced at 9:00 a.m. but owing to the shortness of the days and the coldness of the weather, we have decided it best to begin at 10:00 a.m. There were 34 children in the Primary class and about 10 in the Theological Dept. The sessions of both classes were extremely interesting. From 12 n we held our sacrament meeting with all the missionaries, two saints, and two friends in attendance. In the afternoon I wrote a letter to Florence Grant of Salt Lake City, ate dinner, took a walk with Elder Hedges and on the way home called in at Sister Kamiyama's. The evening meeting was very, very slimly attended, but we managed to hold one for the first time this year.

Tuesday, 17 January 1905, Tokyo

Fair, Very cold Up at 6:45. Took a walk and returned just in time for breakfast. Went down to the Ginza in the forenoon and purchased a copy of Chamberlain's "Introduction to The Study of Japanese Writing" for which I paid ¥10.00. I also bought some collars. Elder Hedges having business on the Ginza accompanied me and we met again after our shopping was over and came home together. In the afternoon I worked a little on the Book of Mormon, but spent quite a while looking through my new book. In the evening I took a bath before retiring. The mail from Hawaii brought a card to each of the elders from Bro.

Tomizo Katsuama. On the cards was printed in both Japanese & English the Seasons Greetings.

Wednesday, 18 January 1905, Tokyo

Clear—Cold Up at 6:50. Took a walk before settling down to the days work. All morning I worked on the Book of Mormon. From 12 n to 1:00 p.m. we held our weekly prayer meeting. In the afternoon I conversed with a student of the Normal School for about an hour & a half. At 5:00 p.m. ate dinner and took a little rest from study. **Worked again till nearly bed time finishing up to the close of the Words of Mormon. This completes the translation of the small plates of Nephi and Mormon's introduction to part of his abridgement, which introduction serves as the connecting link between the small plates and the abridgment of the larger ones.**[2]

Friday, 27 January 1905, Tokyo

Morning very cold—afternoon clear & warmer. Up at 6:45. During the night considerable rain and snow fell and towards morning it turned bitter cold freezing the snow on the trees in a way which made the scenery very beautiful. On account of the bad weather I did not take my morning walk but exercised by doing a little cleaning around the house. After breakfast, I worked on the Book of Mormon. In the afternoon talked a little with Mr. Sukakoshi who had dinner with us. He had only just gone when my friend from the Normal School came. I talked with him till nearly five o'clock. Worked an hour on the Book of Mormon. After supper went to the drug store to get some medicine for Sister Ensign who had quite a severe dizzy attack in the afternoon. I returned and read over with Elder Caine sixteen proof sheets of the tract (My Reason's for leaving etc) which he has translated.

Sunday, 29 January 1905, Tokyo

Fair—Warm Up at 6:45. Did a little sweeping up around the house. Ate breakfast. Sister Ensign did not feel so well, therefore she and Prest. Ensign fasted. The Sunday School was a great success. The largest attendance in six months and very interesting recitations. The two elders (Stoker and Hedges) from Azagaya came in while we were holding our Sacrament Meetings. In the afternoon I read a little. Ate dinner about 5:00 p.m. The night meeting was poorly attended. Sister Ensign had a very severe attack of nerv/e/ousness accompanied with dizziness just about 8:45 p.m. We administered to her. She went to bed feeling very unwell. For a long time past she has been taking medicine and using the electric battery for her nerves.

Monday, 30 January 1905, Tokyo

Cloudy—Cold Up at 7:00. Took a walk before breakfast. Mail from America arrived in the morning. I received a letter from mother and one from Sister Grace I. Frost. Wrote a letter to Aunt Harriet A. W. Taylor. **Having been invited to a musical entertainment given in the Young Men's Christian Association Hall at Kanda for the benefit of the volunteer fleet Elders Stoker, Hedges, Caine, and I spent the afternoon listening to quite an interesting program consisting of songs, musical selections, & speeches all in Japanese. In the evening I read articles in the newspapers & magazines from home.**

During the evening a letter came from Elder Featherstone written from the boat and posted at Victoria. He reported Elder Jarvis in good health during the first week of the trip but afterwards he became very bad and had to be locked in his room at night. The doctor's assistance was also necessary.

Tuesday, 31 January 1905, Tokyo

Cloudy—Cold—North breeze Up at 6:45. Took a walk and helped pump the bath water before breakfast. A letter from Elder Jarvis was received during the morning. His writing was clear and the letter would indicate that he was himself when he wrote it. It was also posted at Victoria.

During the morning I looked over some of my Book of Mormon translations. In the afternoon my friend from the Normal School called. After talking with him for a little while I continued to do a little on the Book of Mormon. In the evening, after eating supper, I went out and visited at the home of Mr. Komatsu the father of one of our Sunday School children. I was received very cordially and spent a pleasant evening.

Tuesday, 7 February 1905, Tokyo

Clear—Warmer. Up at 7:15. During the morning I conversed with Nobu Mashimo who came over to visit with us. After dinner I began /my day's/ class work on the Book of Mormon. I continued this labor till supper time. After supper I went to see Bro. Kikuchi who has absented himself from us for a long time. He is still so engrossed with his patent medicines that he thinks little of spiritual things. Although disturbed a great deal in our conversation by people coming and going, I endeavored to warm his spirit and make him feel like it was time for him to think more of his God. Returned to headquarters and took a bath.

Wednesday, 8 February 1905, Tokyo

Fair—Cold Up at 7:00. Took a walk. Swept the dining room. Worked on the Book of Mormon till noon. After prayer meeting I went and visited with the parents of Hisa Saito, one of our bright Sunday School children. Returned and ate dinner about 4:15. After dinner and a little reading from home papers I worked again on the Book of Mormon till bed time. During the morning I received letters from America. One from father, one from Aunt Margaret Goodman & one from Sister Maud Baggarley. The one from father was written on Jan 9th just after having a visit from Elder Featherstone who with Elder Jarvis arrived safely in Salt Lake City on the evening of Jan 8th. Bro. Jarvis was much improved but by no means himself. His father was at the depot to meet them. Bro. Featherstone had a long visit with the Presidency on the 9th & gave a very intelligent report of the condition of affairs in Japan.

Monday, 13 February 1905, Tokyo

Fair—Quite cold. Up at 7:00. Took a walk before breakfast. During the morning did a number of odd jobs and a little on the Book of Mormon. In the afternoon I worked on the Book of Mormon. The mission through Prist. Ensign received a copy of Bro. Reynolds' Concordance of the Book of Mormon.[3] It may prove of some little use to me in my work of translation. In the evening after supper I read twenty four pages of the proof of Elder Caine's tract.

Sunday, 19 February 1905, Tokyo

Clear—Cold north wind. Up at 7:00. Did a little sweeping in the yard before breakfast. The Sunday School was held from 10:00 a.m. with a large crowd in attendance. The Sacrament Meeting convened from 12:00 noon. In the afternoon I went with a young man named Komorita to the home of a young girl named Nomura. Both the young man and young lady have been attending our Sunday School, but it seems that they have been carrying on a very improper correspondance which fact was discovered by the parents of Miss Nomura. Neither are members of the church but as they are students in the Sunday School I went to the home of young Komorita last evening and enquired about the matter. I learned that he was guilty of writing improperly to Miss Nomura and as he confessed his fault and desired forgiveness, I arranged for him to go with me to the home of the girl and confess all before them. This he did today, so I feel that our Sunday School will not suffer for the actions of these two.

Today the elders from Azagaya (Elders Hedges & Stoker) returned to Tokyo having left their work in the country at the suggestion of Prest. Ensign. They expect to be here at headquarters for sometime.

The evening meeting was not large but a fair spirit was felt and we hope some good was accomplished through the efforts made.

After our dinner which we ate at 4:00 p.m. Elders Stoker, Hedges, Caine, & I went to Mr. Nobu Mashimo's home to say farewell to him before his departure to the front. He leaves early tomorrow morning. We presented him with a three pound box of candy to make his thoughts of his Mormon friends as sweet as possible.

Wednesday, 22 February 1905, Tokyo

Clear—Cold. Up at 8:50. Took a walk. Did a little translating in the morning. From 12 n; we held our regular prayer meeting. All the missionaries were present. **Elder Fred A. Caine was chosen and set**

apart to act as Secretary of the mission following Elder Featherstone. Prest. Ensign set him apart. In the afternoon did some more translating and ate dinner about 4:00 p.m. In the evening I called on Mr. Koza the father of one of the Sunday School boys. Returned & studied an hour before going to bed.

Sunday, 26 February 1905, Tokyo

Cloudy—Breezy—Very cold. Up at 7:40. Did a little sweeping around the yard. Ate breakfast. From 10:00 a.m. the Sunday School convened with the usual excellent attendance. The exercises were carried out interestingly. In the forenoon about 11:45 Messrs Tamano from Azagaya called on us. They brought us a present of 40 fine fresh eggs. They are of the family who so kindly received Elders Jarvis, Stoker, & Hedges during their stay in Azagaya. The attended our Sacrament Meeting which was held from about 12:30. They had only been gone a little while when the three Katagiri girls (Fuyu, Miki & Massa) and Saito Hisa (all students of the primary class in Sunday School) came to "play with their sensei or teacher. They stayed till dinner time, about 4:00 p.m. After dinner I built up the fires in the assembly rooms and prepared for the night meeting which was a little better attended than usual.

Tuesday, 28 February 1905, Tokyo

Clear—Windy—Cold. Up at 6:30. Took a walk before breakfast. Spent the morning working on the Book of Mormon. In the afternoon after dinner I called on Mrs. Furuuchi the mother of one of the Sunday School children. Found her to be a very interesting woman. He husband was not at home. He being a newspaper man, the family had read all the bad tales about the "Mormons" and had formed a very hard opinion of us. She said that when she read that the hotel refused to let us in upon our arrival in Japan, that she thought them justified in their actions and that she would certainly turn a Mormon down if they ever attempted to visit her home. She told me frankly that had she of known who I was when I came to the door that she would not have let me in but after hearing what I had to say for myself, she was glad to see me and know our side of the story. On going into the house I said, I was a missionary of the Church of Jesus Christ of Latter–day Saints and did not mention the name "Mormon" till it appeared that I had made a favorable impression upon them. The lady laughed heartily when she realized that a "Mormon" had found his way into her house in spite of the resolve she had made with herself to keep them out if they ever came. On leaving she invited me to come again. I asked her if she was not still somewhat afraid of us, whereupon she said "No, not now that I have heard the truth about you."

During the evening I worked on the B. of M. again, took a bath and retired.

Monday, 6 March 1905, Tokyo

Clear—Warm Up at 6:45. Spent the morning doing a few odd jobs. Read over an essay on "Faith" written by Elder Hedges. **In the afternoon we all went to the home of Mrs. Tanaka in Yotsuya to see a display of "hina" (small dolls) and other things which are used during the girls festival or "hina no sekku".[4] Our friends Miss Kogu and Mrs. Umeda had arranged to see the display at the home of Mrs. Tanaka for the reason that there are but few places in all of Tokyo where the decorations are so elaborate and ancient as those indulged in at this lady's house. There was a representation of the Imperial Palace of the Emperor Kaunin ("Shishiuden") with the Royal Persons and all the attendants of the Court. The building of course was a miniature affair but said to be a perfect representation of the actual Palace. The dolls which represented the persons were artistically made. Besides the palace there were numerous pieces of furniture made exceedingly small but in perfect proportion and excellently finished. Minute utensils of all shapes & styles represented what was used many hundreds of years ago by the men & women of old Japan. After viewing the display the lady showed her hospitality by furnishing us with light refreshments.** We left about 5:00 p.m. and returned to headquarters. In the evening I did some visiting among friends

Today 1000 copies of Elder Caine's translation of "My Reasons for Leaving The Church of England and Joining The Church of Jesus Christ of Latter–day Saints" were delivered at headquarters.

This is the size of the first edition, the price paid for which is ¥.31.00 This tract will be called throughout my journal "# 4"

Thursday, 9 March 1905, Tokyo

Clear—Quite springlike. Up at 6:30. Took a long walk before breakfast. During the morning worked on the translation of the Book of Mormon. **In the afternoon and evening did further translating. In the afternoon the first proof sheet of the new song book was received at headquarters. It was the translation and arrangement of the Sunday School Song "Come Dear Children Join and Sing." This will be the first song in the new book. It looked very fine to see "Mormon" hymns in Japanese print.**

Mr. Hiroi our old teacher called and spent an hour or two with us during the afternoon.

Friday, 10 March 1905, Tokyo

Clear & Warm. Up at 6:40. Took a long walk before breakfast. During most of the day worked on the Book of Mormon. However for some time in the afternoon I was exercising in the garden. The weather was so warm & the ground so sofft that I could not resist the temptation to try some jumping. Some of the brethren erected a swing in the garden. In the evening I wrote a letter to Aunt Clara then took the mail to the post office.

Tuesday, 21 March 1905, Tokyo

Cloudy—Snow & Rain—Cold. Up at 6:10. Was very much surprised to see everything white with snow when I got up. Swept and dusted the dining room. During the forenoon I looked over the last 6 chapters of Mosiah,[5] taking note of the passages the translation of which gave me considerable trouble. In the afternoon I did a number of odd things—looked over the translation of the title page of the B of M; took some exercises; played with some children who came around to see us; etc. In the evening went out to visit at an acquaintance's home, but found the gate locked and couldn't get in. Called at another place in the same district, but was not invited in so I returned and did some studying, before bedtime.

Saturday, 25 March 1905, Tokyo

Cloudy—Warm Up at 6:10. The streets being very bad, I did not take a walk. Swept & dusted the dining room. During the forenoon did a number of odd jobs, including sweeping, shaving, shoeblacking, darning etc. In the afternoon a number of Sunday School children called. I spent sometime with them and did a little reading. Took a bath before retiring.

Wednesday, 29 March 1905, Tokyo

Fair—Warm Up at 6:00. Took an hour's walk. Returned and worked a little on the Book of Mormon. We discussed and chose ten new songs to be translated and added to the Song Book now being printed. A new poet translator has been found and will translate the songs decided upon immediately. We thought it would be wise to have these new translations made by a different poet to the one who did the ones now being set up in type; to have a variety of expressions if possible. Our prayer meeting was held from 12 n. as usual. In the afternoon we discussed for an hour or so about the translation of certain words such as "Priesthood," ordain, confirm etc. I then did a little more work on the B. of M.

In the evening I went and visited at the home of Mr and Mrs Odan.

Friday, 31 March 1905, Tokyo

Clear—warm Up at 6:00. Took a walk before breakfast. Spent the morning and part of the afternoon working on the Book of Mormon. In the evening did a little visiting. **The proof sheets of the translation of Elder Hedges' track were received at headquarters last night. Elder Caine looked over them yesterday evening and I looked over them with him in the afternoon.**

Thursday, 6 April 1905, Tokyo

Cloudy, Rain Up at 5:55. Took a walk as usual before breakfast. During the morning a meeting of the elders was called for the purpose of considering Elder Hedges' essay on Faith. Sometime ago he wrote on this subject and was requested to rewrite from a different standpoint His second effort which we considered today was a great improvement on his first, but still we felt there were so many changes still necessary before it would be suitable to be given to the people as a tract that he has as a result of our discussion been requested to write on the subject again. In the afternoon I did a little on the Book of Mormon Translation. In the evening I wrote a letter to Samuel.

Saturday, 8 April 1905, Tokyo

Clear—Warm Up at 5:50. Taking advantage of the fine weather we all spent the day cleaning in and around the house. It was truly a day of odd jobs for all. My days work consisted of cleaning the largest stove pipe in our house, washing and repapering two windows, helping to shake bed clothes, helping in the removal of trees and rubbish, talking a little to a friend who called, scrubbing, shaving, darning and eating. The other brethren all had as equally varied work—housecleaning, taring down old sheds & planting trees in the stead others of, sweeping the garden, putting in a new bath & pumping the bath water, going on errands, entertaining guests & teaching English. There are perhaps few experiences in keeping house that we are not having here at headquarters. As it is an ill wind that blows no good we are happy in this kind of work occasionally in the fact that we hope to see the good in the future. Took a bath before retiring.

Wednesday, 12 April 1905, Tokyo

Clear—Warm Up at 6:30. Took a walk. Worked on the Book of Mormon nearly all day. Went to the Ginza to buy some liquorice for my cough. From 12:00 n. held our weekly prayer meeting. All the elders were present.

In the evening went over to the home of Sister Rin Kamiyama and was surprised to learn that she is to be married tomorrow. Her husband is not a member of the church so the ceremony, whatever it may be, will be according to the customs of the people without any religious rites. It will take years before the people of Japan will be educated up to proper forms of marriage so we have simply had to listen and endure in this the first experience of marriage among any of the saints.

Thursday, 13 April 1905, Tokyo

Clear—Warm Up at 6:30. Took a short walk before breakfast. During the morning worked on the Book of Mormon. In the afternoon took a little exercise jumping. The Sunday School children came to headquarters in the afternoon and from 4:00 p.m. we had a singing exercise for an hour or more. In the evening I went and spent an hour or two visiting with the Katagiri family. While talking with this family I enjoyed a peaceful, lovely spirit. My heart was made glad to hear the oldest daughter, Fuyu, say that she could not sleep well if she forgot to say her prayers before going to bed and that she also enjoyed praying in the morning. When I realize that this little girl never heard of God or Jesus Christ before coming to our Sunday School and her parents are not acquainted in the least with Christianity, I feel to thank my heavenly Father for the way in which He has confirmed the words of the S. S. teachers in the heart of this child.

Saturday, 15 April 1905, Tokyo

Clear—Cold wind Up at 5:40. Took a walk before breakfast. Swept and dusted one of the rooms up stairs. Translated a little. In the afternoon read a little and did a little cleaning up. After supper I went and visited for an hour or two at the home of Mr. & Mrs. Soga the parents of one of the S. S. boys. I was received very kindly. Returned & took a bath.

Today 3000 copies of Elder Hedges tract on "The Necessity of Prayer" were delivered at headquarters. This is the first edition. The tract is # 5 in the series and will hereafter be referred to in this journal by its number.

Sunday, 16 April 1905, Tokyo

Cloudy—Cold. Up at 6:15. The Sunday School commenced at 10:00 a.m. A fair attendance in both classes. From noon until about 12:45 we held our Sacrament meeting. Besides the Elders & Sister Ensign only one saint was present. In the afternoon did some reading. During the morning mail from America was delivered at headquarters in little batches.

A letter from Bro. Geo. Reynolds to Prest. Ensign conveyed the happy news that four young men had been called to come to Japan as missionaries & that some, if not all, of the four would sail from Seattle Wash. on May 16th per S. S. "Iyo Maru," a boat in the Nippon Yusen Kwaisha's service. The names of the four young men as reported by Bro. Reynolds were as follows: W. R. Fairbourn, of Sandy, Utah, George A. Hoopes, of Weston, Idaho, Burt Seely of Mount Pleasant Utah, and Daniel P. Woodland of Pocatello, Idaho. More help means more work accomplished for the salvation of the Japanese. The evening meeting was held with six missionaries and eight visitors and one saint present.

Monday, 17 April 1905, Tokyo

Rain—Cold. Up at 7:15. Helped the girl clean up the dining room before breakfast. During the morning we considered what Elder Hedges had written as a substitute for his former efforts on the subject of Faith. **It was decided that Elder H. make no further attempts of writing on this subject, at the present at least. He was asked to write a short tract explaining briefly who we are, why we are here and the origin of the church. It is designed that this tract when written and translated shall take the place of our first tract written by Prest. Heber J. Grant some two years ago.** In the afternoon I did some work on the Book of Mormon translation. In the evening we had a singing practice.

Saturday, 22 April 1905, Tokyo

Morning clear—Evening cloudy—Warm Up at 6:00. Took a walk before breakfast. Elder Caine went with me. We visited a little resort near the spot where we baptized Bro. Yoshiro Oyama over two years ago. This is the first time I have visited this place since that event. Spent the entire day cleaning up around headquarters. This place is the dirtiest house & lot that I know of. Most of each Saturday is spent sweeping, dusting, scrubbing etc and still every week ends as dirty as ever. These weekly clean ups are giving me a good deal of experience in the different duties connected with housekeeping. I am thankful that the Lord made woman to do housework and make home comfortable for man.

Monday, 24 April 1905, Tokyo

Clear—Warmer Up at 6:00. Took a walk before breakfast. During much of the morning I was sewing up holes in my clothes. This don't mean that I am poverty stricken and have nothing but worn & patched clothes to wear. Far from such a condition I am blessed with all the fine clothes I need to keep me warm and looking respectable. I simply have to close up a ripped seam or darn a hole in some of my sox or underwear occasionally to keep in practice for some time /in the future when/ necessity shall require that I know how to handle a needle & thread. During the rest of the day I worked on the Book of Mormon but could not make very good progress owing to the fact that I was troubled with drowsiness for an hour or two in the afternoon when I could hardly keep awake. After supper I went out and spent an hour or two at the house of Mr. & Mrs. Ichikawa.

Tuesday, 25 April 1905, Tokyo

Clear—Warm Up at 6:05. Took usual morning walk before breakfast. During the morning spent some time looking over papers & magazines from home. Was glad to notice the account of the harmony among the saints at conference and how united they were in sustaining the President of the Church[6] in his high and responsible position in spite of the fact that he has been so bitterly assailed and so many vile charges made against him not always by those outside the Church. There were only two dissenting voices in the whole conference. Considering this fact in connection with the zeal of agitators & storm—starters just at this time I certainly see how faithfully the Lord is watching over his people & how hard it is for men to "kick against the pricks." During the afternoon worked on the Book of Mormon. In the evening we had a song practice.

Friday, 28 April 1905, Tokyo
Cloudy; later, clear, cool breeze.
Up at 6:15. Took a short walk before breakfast. During most of the day worked on the Book of Mormon. The part translated was exceedingly difficult, containing many expressions in English the equivalents /of which/ if indeed there /are/ any in Japanese I am as yet unfamiliar with.[7] Owing to this difficulty, I did not get over much ground during the entire days work. In the evening we had a singing practice.

Sunday, 30 April 1905, Tokyo
Warm—Windy—Much dust. Up at 7:15. Ate breakfast. From 10:00 am. held Sunday School. The good weather together with the flower season and its temptations is causing a decrease in the attendance at Sunday School. The children have little or no encouragement from those at home to come to S. S for their parents are not Latter–day Saints—most of them not Christians even—so they naturally take advantage of the fine weather for playing. The day schools also give outings for the children on Sunday. For this cause the attendance of our S. S. is often greatly decreased. At 12:00 n we held our sacrament meeting. In the afternoon Elders Stoker, Caine and I went to a place near Shiba Park said to be noted for its beautiful cherry blossoms. We were disappointed. Returned and ate dinner. The evening meeting was held with an audience remarkable for its smallness. Only four visitors and one of them left before it was over.

Thursday, 4 May 1905, Tokyo
Clear—Cold North Wind. Up at 5:55. After breakfast began work on the Book of Mormon and continued it until supper time. After supper, I went out and called on some of the Sunday School children who have not been regular in their attendance lately. Also called on Sister Ota and her husband. Sister Ota is the young lady who was married on April 13th (see Journal page 159) and who up to that time was known as Rin Kamiyama. She was not home this evening, but her husband was so I got a good look at him. I feel sorry that one of our lady converts had to be married to an outsider and without the proper ceremony but under the circumstances she could not do otherwise as she was given away by her parents.

Friday, 5 May 1905, Tokyo
Clear—Warm Up at 6:40. Took a short walk before breakfast. Worked on the Book of Mormon. Took all day to go over the translation of Alma 13th Chapter[8] and correct & rearrange it. This is one of the most difficult chapters in the book so far as my translation has gone. One or two expressions used seems to be quite out of the reach of ordinary Japanese. In the evening we had singing practice.

Saturday, 6 May 1905, Tokyo
Cloudy, Southeast wind—Warm. Up at 6:00. Took a walk out into the fields. Discovered quite a grove of trees and selected therein a spot for prayer. There is something about prayer in the woods that gives me greater freedom in talking with my Heavenly Father and consequently greater satisfaction than prayer offered elsewhere. During the morning did some sweeping and dusting, shaved, brushed my clothes and did /other/ odd jobs. In the afternoon I worked some on the Book of Mormon. In the evening looked a lesson for the Sunday School. Took a bath and retired.

Sunday, 7 May 1905, Tokyo
Rain—Warmer. Up at 6:40. Being fast day, we had no eating till about 5:00 p.m. The Sunday School was better attended than a week ago. On a rainy day the children generally have no other place to go so they come to Sunday School better than in fair weather. Our Sacrament & testimony meeting was held with a fair spirit prevailing. Generally Prest. & Sister Ensign speak in English but today all the praying,

speaking, and singing was in Japanese. This according to my heart, is as it should be always. I would be delighted if English could be entirely done away with even in our every day conversations, for I realize that I am not here to study and practice English but Japanese that I might be qualified to speak under the influence of the Spirit to the edification of the natives.

In the afternoon I wrote a letter to my sister Lisadore. During the day I received a novel post card from mother. It was a piece of thin leather representing the sole of a shoe and upon it was printed, "Pon my sole, haven't time to write, Salt Lake." It conveyed the good intelligence that all at home were well and happy. For the blessings of the Lord to my loved ones I am exceedingly grateful. In the evening our meeting was not well attended but it was better than a week ago. I addressed those assembled, talking I believe for a little over an hour. After the meeting read a little from the "Millennial Star."

Thursday, 11 May 1905, Tokyo

Cloudy—Warmer Up at 6:30. Took a walk before breakfast. During the morning worked on the Book of Mormon. In the afternoon did several odd jobs preparatory to welcoming the Sunday School children who had been invited to come from 4:00 p.m. to practice some new songs. In order to please the children and encourage them to continue coming to the Sunday School we provided ice cream w cake for all who came to the singing practice. Most of the children enjoyed this very much. There were only two or three who did not like the ice cream and all seemed to "have a mouth for cake" of which there was plenty. After supper I worked for an hour on the Book of Mormon then retired.

Friday, 12 May 1905, Tokyo

Morning cloudy—later clear—Warm Up at 7:00. Took some exercises in the garden before breakfast. During the forenoon, I worked on the Book of Mormon.

In the afternoon a great many visitors called so I spent most of my time entertaining them. Among others was a man named Miyazaki who claims to be "The Christ." Some time ago this man was an inmate of a mental hospital and the indications are that his cure was not complete. This man first called on the "Mormons" about 3½ years ago when we were living in the Metropole Hotel, Tsukiji. He seemed to be quite facinated with the claims we made at that time to have prophets in our church. This seemed to give him a desire for fame in the religious world. So he first went crazy over the subject and was taken to an asylum from which place he has appeared as the Christ in fulfillment of the prophecies concerning the Saviour's Second Coming. He not only claims to be "The Christ" but Buddha, Mohammed, and Confucious. He says, "My business, is that of a Prophet," and, has published a book containing a number of his prohecies and also his claims to the Messiahship. I pointed out a number of facts concerning the Second Coming of Jesus which he has failed to manifest in himself and showed how excellently his claims corresponded with what the Bible teaches would be the claims of false Christs and false prophets. One of the two friends Mr. Miyazaki brought with him advised the would–by–Christ to examine the Bible more closely and make his claims and doctrines harmonize more closely to what is written in the Bible or he could not hope to succeed in his profession as "prophet." In the evening we had a singing practice.

Thursday, 25 May 1905, Tokyo

Clear—Warm Up at 6:00. Took a long walk before breakfast. Went down town to buy a summer hat and subscribe for the "Yomiuri" newspaper for 3 months. The subscription cost me one yen. During part of the afternoon I was busy cleaning my summer clothes. Did a little work on the Book of Mormon taking notes of the parts about which I have some questions to ask. In the evening I went and visited at the home of Mr. Taguchi.

Monday, 29 May 1905, Tokyo

Clear—Hot Up at 6:00. Took a walk first thing after getting up. Elders Stoker and Caine accompanied me. We went into the grove where I have selected a spot for prayer. We sang and prayed together. During the day did a little on the Book of Mormon. Some Sunday School children came and played in the garden during the afternoon. I romped with them for about an hour. In the evening I did a little visiting in the neighborhood of headquarters.

In the afternoon the first complete copy of our hymn book entitled "Latter–day Saint's Psalmody" was delivered at headquarters. It is printed on good thick white paper and bound in black cloth with gold letters in the title. Altogether there are 66 songs with new music for each. Mr. Y. Iwano arranged most of the songs into Japanese verse. Mr. Kosaburo Kawai was the poet in the arrangement of 10 hymns. Mr. [blank] Owada arranged 3 and Hajime Nakazawa arranged 1. The music in every case was written by Prest. Horace A. Ensign. The songs were selected from the L.D.S. Hymn Book, the Sunday School Song Book and one from The Children's Friend. Vol 2. Songs for the use of the saints in their sacrament and other meetings, songs for the children of the Sunday Schools, songs for use when performing the ordinances of the Gospel and songs for general missionary use are found in this collection. The book is in every respect satisfactory and we hope it will be the means of doing much good in this mission.

Tuesday, 30 May 1905, Tokyo

Clear—Hot. Up at 5:00. Having fasted since Sunday night I desired to have a special prayer before breaking my fast, so I got up early and went into the woods. Returned in time for breakfast. During the day worked on the Book of Mormon. In the evening after supper we held a singing practice. **During the afternoon 95 completed copies of our new psalmody were delivered so we used them during the practice. It is certainly very gratifying to see our hymns in Japanese and appearing in so nice a book as the printers have produced for us.** Elder Caine filed in the Home Department, Tokyo, the necessary papers for a copyright! In the morning and evening papers reports of the practical annihilation of the greater part of the Baltic Fleet in the Sea of Japan appeared in tones of great joy.[9] The Japanese Fleet so far as the reports go have ths far sustained no loss in boats which 19 out of 27 of the enemy's ships have either been sunk or captured.

Wednesday, 31 May 1905, Tokyo

Slight rain during morning—Afternoon cloudy, Hot. Up at 7:30 During the morning did some reading and one or two other side jobs. In the afternoon I tried to work on the Book of Mormon but the elders had so many discussions on and questions about this and that in their several translations that I accomplished but very little. Took some exercise in the evening. Mr. Watanabe a member of the Methodist Church whom I met in Negishi a year ago and with whom I had many conversations on the Gospel called and we talked about the teachings of our Savior till 10:00 p.m. Today at noon we held a prayer meeting as usual.

Today another delivery of song books reached headquarters. Twenty five bound in limp leather were received. One each for the elders with their name printed in gold letters on the cover was among the twenty five.

Thursday, 1 June 1905, Tokyo

Clear—Hot Up at 6:30. Shaved and did a little brushing up before breakfast. In the forenoon and also for an hour in the afternoon I worked on the Book of Mormon. At 3:30 a telephone message from the office of the Nippon Yusen Kwaisha informed us that the steamship "Iyo Maru" had been sighted and would be in Yokohama in an hour.

We all made hurried preparations to leave for Yokohama by the first train. When we arrived at the pier we found that the ship was in and of the four passengers who had made the voyage from America three were elders sent to do missionary work in Japan. We were exceedingly pleased to see new faces from Zion and I regretted that they had had to wait for over an hour for us. Elder Justice Burt Seely the oldest of the three is a fine specimen of a man he stands six feet two and /is/ well rounded out with flesh. The other two brethren, Elders /William/ Reuben Fairbourn and John Leroy Chadwick are also large husky young men who will make an impression on the Japanese wherever they go.

While in Yokohama I did a little shopping. We all returned to Tokyo by the 7:40 train. Before going to bed we had a late supper.

Friday, 2 June 1905, Tokyo

Fair—Hot Up at 6:30. During the morning wrote a letter to mother and one to my brother Samuel's wife. Sent three pieces of Japanese drawn work and embroidery to Samuel's wife. In the afternoon did a little on the Book of Mormon. In the evening we had a short singing practice. Elder Hedges and I went to the post office.

This morning just before breakfast all of the elders were in the garden. Sisters Ensign and Hakii were in the house preparing the food. I came from the garden with the intention of going into the house. At the front door I noticed a pair of strange native "zori."[10] I entered the hall and saw a strange cap on the table. On enquiring who had come Sister Hakii said, "nome."[11] My suspicions were aroused so I ran up stairs and found a man in the upper hall. I demanded the reason for his intrusion. He turned pale and shook a little. I recognized him as the same stranger whom I found in the house once before and who on that occasion also had entered without permission. The reasons he named for his freedom were so plainly false that we detained him while a policeman was called. When the policeman came we explained the conditions and requests that they investigate the man's character through the police office. The family living near our front gate and whom we call our gatekeepers saw the man approach our door, look inside a time or two and then enter /the house/ very quickly. He also went around by the kitchen door and acted in rather a suspicious way before he came to the front door. About 1:30 p.m. a detective came to the house and enquired after further particulars.

Friday, 9 June 1905, Tokyo

Clear—hot Up at 6:00. Swept and dusted the dining room. During the morning worked on the Book of Mormon. In the afternoon Mr. Miyazuki, the man who claims to be a prophet, the resurrected Christ, Buddha, etc, called and I wasted the greater half of the day conversing with him. Took a long walk in the evening.

Friday, 23 June 1905, Tokyo

Rain—Hot Up at 6:40. During the morning did some reading. Worked on the Book of Mormon for the major portion of the day. In the evening took some exercises. Just after breakfast today we held a short meeting. In this meeting we were informed of the places where Prest. Ensign thought it would be well to do missionary work and the elders were called and the date of their departure to their several fields decided upon. Elder Hedges and Fairbourn were appointed to go to Sendai a large city 11 hours on the railroad north of Tokyo. Elders Stoker, Seely, and Chadwick were appointed to go to Hokkaido and labor in what ever district the Spirit might point out to them. The date set for departure is July 3rd.

Sunday, 25 June 1905, Tokyo

Morning cloudy slight rain—Afternoon fair—warm. Up at 6:00 Swept and dusted the dining room. The Sunday School beginning from 9:00 a.m. was well attended and considerable interest shown by the children. Read a little. Sacrament meeting was held at 12:00 n. I spoke for a few minutes. In the afternoon wrote a letter to my brother Edward. Ate dinner /Entertained a visitor/. Read a little in the Bible. The evening meeting began with only a few present but before it was over we had quite an audience and just as we were discussing about seven or eight people came.

This evening 5,000 copies (the first editions) of Elder Hedges' tract "The Latter–day Saints" were delivered. As this tract will hereafter be used in place of #1 (after the present stack of #1 tracts are disposed of) I will call it #1a in this journal.

Monday, 26 June 1905, Tokyo

Rain—later, clear and warm. Up at 7:00. During the morning read from Japanese books & newspapers. In the fore part of the afternoon did a little on the Book of Mormon. Mr. Homma, Miss Kitahara, and Mr. Okada called. I spent sometime entertaining them. In the evening I wrote a letter to Mr. K Tokoyo in answer to a letter I received from him today. He informs me that he has found a Japanese family that will take me into their house if the place is suitable to me. I arranged by letter to call on the family in company with Mr. Tokoyo June 30th I received a card from Mr. Kinza Hirai today. He is also looking for a Japanese family where I would be received and treated with kindness. After supper we had a singing practice.

Tuesday, 27 June 1905, Tokyo

Cloudy—Hot Up at 6:00. Took a walk before breakfast. We had a singing practice before breakfast. During most of the forenoon I worked on the Book of Mormon

But a cablegram from America stating that Prest Ensign's release had been mailed and that I was to be his successor upset me so much that I did not make much headway in translation during the rest of the day. Prest. Ensign went down to the Nippon Yusen Kwaisha office to secure berth /for himself and wife/ on the "Iyo Maru" which sails from Yokohama for Seattle Washington, July 8th

After supper we had another singing practice. The elders are taking turns conducting these exercises and starting the songs so that before Prest. Ensign leaves us we can sing any song in the book (Psalmody in Japanese) and pitch it correctly.

Just while we were eating breakfast a gentleman called and I conversed with him for an hour or so.

Wednesday, 28 June 1905, Tokyo

Cloudy—cooler—Rain Up at 6:00. Took a walk. Worked on the Book of Mormon till noon. Held our regular weekly prayer meeting. All the elders were present. Worked again on the Book of Mormon till dinner time. After dinner had a little talk with Prest. Ensign about the books of the Mission. Took some physical exercises. We had a song practice. Retired at 10:00.

Thursday, 29 June 1905, Tokyo

Clear—Hot Up at 6:15. Took a walk before breakfast. Had a singing practice. During the forenoon and most of the afternoon worked at the Book of Mormon. In the evening took a walk calling at my place of prayer in the woods. Returned and took some physical exercises.

Elders Stoker and Hedges went to Yokohama in the forenoon to welcome two new elders from America. They returned to headquarters about 8:30 p.m. bringing Elder Daniel P. Woodland and Elder James [A.]Anderson two fine looking and seemingly–intelligent young men. We had supper, then discussed American and Japanese topics for an hour or so before retiring.

Friday, 30 June 1905, Tokyo

Rain—Cooler Up at 6:35. During the morning worked on the Book of Mormon. At 1:30 I left headquarters to visit Mr & Mrs. Totsuka who live in Korshi Kowa Ku. Some days ago I received a letter from Mr. Tokoyo /informing me/ that he had found a home where I would be welcomed & well treated if I wanted to get out in a Japanese family. For in the past two or three months I have been exceedingly anxious to find a native family that would receive me as a boarder in their home. I felt that I would get along better living with the people than at headquarters and asked some of my friends if they could not find a place for me. As a result Mr. Tokoyo found that Mr. & Mrs. Totsuka would be delighted to have me live with them. But as Prest. Ensign is released to return home, I will have to be at headquarters and cannot take up my abode at the home of Mr. & Mrs. Totsuka. I called on them today in company with Mr. Tokoyo and thanked them for their offer and explained how it was that I could not come & live with them. They expressed regret and seemed to be truly disappointed. I stayed at their place for nearly two hours. Returned to headquarters & did a little more on the Book of Mormon. **After supper I with the other elders spent about an hour practicing our hymns. The first installment of the new hymn book was delivered at headquarters this evening.**

Saturday, 1 July 1905, Tokyo

Unsettled—Cooler Up at 7:40. After breakfast gave Elders Woodland & Anderson their first lessons in Japanese. Did a little cleaning. In the afternoon worked on the Book of Mormon. Mr. Homma called and spent to evening at headquarters.

Sunday, 2 July 1905, Tokyo

Fair—Hot Up at 7:00. Sunday School was held from 9:00 am. A good crowd of children were present. Prest. Ensign and his wife made their farewell talks. At noon we held a fast and sacrament meeting Two saints were present. In the afternoon I wrapped up and mailed a copy of our new psalmody to an acquaintance in Hokkaido. Had a short nap. The evening meeting was well attended and a very fine spirit prevailed.

Monday, 3 July 1905, Tokyo

Clear—Very Hot Up at 6:00. Took a walk before breakfast. Gave Elders Woodland and Anderson a lesson in Japanese. Wrote a letter in Japanese to Mr. Hoshi/i/shi. In the afternoon went down town and enquired for a Japanese house as present unoccupied. Met the rest of the missionaries at a photographer's and we had our picture taken in a group. Returned to headquarters. In the evening we all went out to a sobaya for supper.

Tuesday, 4 July 1905, Tokyo

Clear—Very hot. Up at 6:15. Took a walk before breakfast. **Spent the forenoon down with Prest. Ensign. We went to the bank and had the account turned over to me. We also went to the head office** of the Nippon Yusen Kwaisha where I was introduced to Mr. Mizukawa the passenger agent. On the way back looked for a Japanese house suitable for a mission headquarters. After dinner I went out and searched till 7:30 pm. for a house but was not successful in finding anything at all satisfactory. We had ice cream for supper in honor of the Fourth and Old Glory has been floating in the breeze all day from the top of the highest tree in front of the house. In the evening before taking a bath and retiring sang some songs—patriotic & religious.

Friday, 7 July 1905, Tokyo

Clear—Hot Up at 7:30. It being the last day Prest & Sister Ensign would be in Japan I did not go out any where. Some of the brethren went to the Ginza to purchase a book to be presented to Bro & Sister Ensign as a token of love & esteem from all the missionaries. During the day I did several odd jobs and got out my books to do a little work on the Book of Mormon but I did not do much. In the evening we had a few songs and received some few instructions from Bro. Ensign. We seized upon this opportunity to present the book we had purchased. I made the talk in behalf of the elders.

Saturday, 8 July 1905, Tokyo

Clear—very hot Up at 5:50. Ate an early breakfast. Last evening when Prest. Ensign was talking to us I expect him to say something about my succession to the presidency of the mission and speak of the necessity or now necessity of setting me apart, but he said nothing so I went to bed feeling anxious about the matter. This morning I approached Prest. E. about the matter and he was in doubt as to the propriety of setting me apart for he did not know whether or not he held the authority to do so without receiving special instructions from the First Presidency. This made me feel as though it would be well if Prest. Ensign had seen fit to postpone his departure till after the arrival of his release which the cable gram a few days ago stated had been mailed. I too wondered in my own mind whether or not Bro. E. without a special commission to do so could set me apart as his successor.

After Prest. E had his morning prayers, he said he thought he had better set me apart for there was surely no one else in this land who would be authorized to do it and a special officer would not be sent from Zion to do it, so not knowing exactly whether or not setting apart was necessary he decided that before his departure he had better lay his hands upon me and set me apart /for fear it was necessary/. I confess that I did not feel exactly right about this decision and still I feared that if I was not so set apart that something would be lacking so submitted to Prest. Ensign's decision and was set apart this morning just before leaving for Yokohama. I would have been more happy if Prest. Ensign had waited till his release came and my appointment reached me for as it is I have to assume the position of President of the Mission till the properly signed appointment comes. Prest. Ensign's early return has appeared too premature.

We all went to Yokohama on the 10:20 a.m. train. Prest. & Sister E went straight to the boat while the rest of us had dinner at the station restaurant then went to the steamer to say goodbye. A number of friends & three converts out of the five in the church in Japan were at the boat to bid our president farewell. The raised ancor a little before three o'clock and were soon out of sight. The steamer on which the sailed is called the "Iyo Maru" and is running on the Nippon Yusen Kaisha's American service between Yokohama & Seattle. An hour after the departure of the "Iyo Maru" the "Minnesota" having on board Baron Komura peace plenipotentiary for Japan sailed from Yokohama for Seattle. He goes to Washington D.C. to represent his country in the peace conference between Japan an Russia.

After the departure of these two ships we returned directly to Tokyo. Ate bread & milk for supper and were soon in bed.

Sunday, 9 July 1905, Tokyo

Clear—Hot Up at 6:00. Did some cleaning up before breakfast. In the forenoon held Sunday School as usual. At 12:00 we held sacrament meeting. At 2:00 p.m. we held a short meeting in which I gave the elders some instructions prior to the departure of five to new mission fields in the northern part of Japan. Later had dinner and then in the evening held our regular public meeting.

Monday, 10 July 1905, Tokyo

Clear Very hot. Up at 6:00. After breakfast went to New Station to bid farewell to Elders Stoker, Seely, and Chadwick who left for Hokkaido and Elders Hedges and Fairbourn who left for Sendai. Elder Anderson went with me to the depot. We met Mr. Tokoyo at the station and we went with him to the home of a lady whose sister (a woman about 45 years old) was desirous of getting a position as house keeper. Since the return of Prest. and Sister Ensign I have been anxious to have an elderly lady look after our home here in Tokyo it not being wise to continue with Sister Hakii Nami as cook without someone older in the house. The Japanese are adept in the art of creating and spreading scandal. Found the lady home and arranged for her to come on Wednesday 12th and try the work.

Mr. Tokoyo came and had dinner at headquarters and assisted me in correcting and translating reports for proselyting to be sent in to the Home Department for the brethren who have gone north to do missionary work. Mr. Tokoyo has been assisting us very much lately and seems to be a regular bureau of information all by himself for he seems to know about anything we want and which we discuss with him. I thank the Lord for the few friends we have in Japan and pray my heavenly Father that he will touch their hearts and cause them to be converted to the truth.

Tuesday, 11 July 1905, Tokyo

Cloudy—Rain Up at 6:30. Spent an hour or more in the morning giving Elders Woodland and Anderson a lesson in Japanese. The rest of the day I spent cleaning up and rearranging the pictures throughout the house. In the evening I prepared copies of reports to be filed with the Government relative to the missionary work of the new elders. These copies I intend to send to Bro. Oyama at Yokohama and have him write the real report to be handed to the Home Department through the [Ku—] Gunyaku shō where the elders reside.

Wednesday, 12 July 1905, Tokyo

Rain—Hot Up at 7:30. Spent the morning teaching Elders Woodland and Anderson Japanese. In the afternoon and evening I worked a little on the Book of Mormon. Being fast day we held prayer meeting at noon. First thing in the morning I went to the home of Mrs. Nachie to see if I could not employ her to work at headquarters. She was not in when I called, but came to see me about the matter later in the day. She is a cook of long experience among foreigners and has received a much larger wage than what I offered her so it is doubtful if she will decide to come.

A letter was received from Elder Hedges stating that he and Elder Fairbourn were safe in Sendai but found the hotels all very high priced. Through the influence of Mr. Yoshida's mother they expected to find a cheaper place in a day or two.

Friday, 14 July 1905, Tokyo

Clear—Oppressive heat. Up at 6:20. Worked a little on the Book of Mormon before breakfast. After eating gave Elders Woodland and Anderson a lesson in Japanese. Went to Hongo to look for a house. Did not succeed in finding one. Called on Mr. Takahashi and requested him to deliver at headquarters 219 copies of his book "Mormon and Mormonism" the balance of 700 copies purchased by Prest. Grant. Returned to headquarters and found that the old lady who has been engaged to work at headquarters had not arrived. She should have been here on the 12th. I went immediately to find the cause of her tardiness and found she had concluded not to work for us because the pump attached to the well is too hard to work. Hearing this I felt it would be just as well not to have a woman who gives up at a little thing like pumping water occasionally. I went out in search of another woman but will not know whether or not she can come till day after tomorrow.

Just before starting out in the morning American mail was received. A letter releasing Prest. Ensign and wife and one appointing me to the Presidency of the Japan Mission were received from the First Presidency of the church. From my letter of appointment it is clear that the action of Elder Ensign in setting me apart to the labors of Mission President by the laying on of hands was unnecessary. Having now received the official appointment I begin to feel for the first time the real weight of the responsibility resting upon me. In my weakness I rely upon the Lord for strength and wisdom to make me to fully discharge the duties of this office—the most important one thus far in my life.

Monday, 17 July 1905, Tokyo

Fair—very hot Up at 6:00. Spent most of the day writing letters and preparing reports to be sent into the church officials. Answered the letter from the First Presidency appointing me to the presidency of the Japan Mission.

Tuesday, 18 July 1905, Tokyo

Fair—Windy—Dusty—Hot Up at 6:15. Before breakfast went over to Yotsuya to see a house which a friend told us was for rent. We found it but the owner does not intend to rent it for some time. During the morning I did some writing. Received a card from the three elders who went to Hokkaido stating that they were well and had arrived without experiencing any trouble. A letter from the two brethren who went to Sendai states that they are living in a very fine Japanese family, having a room of 15 mats[12] and very find food for ¥15.00 per month. This is good news. I gave Elders Woodland and Anderson a lesson in Japanese. Did a little on the Book of Mormon. In the evening had a singing practice.

Just after breakfast Mrs. Nachie came and I engaged her and her 14 year old daughter to come and keep house for us at headquarters. She promised to begin her work on the 20th of this month her daughter being a day or two later as she is now living in another family.

Wednesday, 19 July 1905, Tokyo

Windy—Rain—Cooler Up at 7:00. Spent the morning working on the Book of Mormon and teaching Elders Woodland and Anderson Japanese. At 12:00 n. we had prayer meeting. In the afternoon I went to the Ginza. Among the business I transacted was giving an order for the delivery of 219 copies of Takahashi Goro's book on Mormons and Mormonism the balance of a purchase of 700 copies made by Prest. Grant about two and a half years ago. In the evening worked an hour on the Book of Mormon

Thursday, 20 July 1905, Tokyo

Windy—Cooler Up at 7:00. Spent nearly the entire day working on the Book of Mormon. Wrote a letter to Elder Horace G. Ensign. Went to Azabu to see what the landlord of a house would do in the way of repairing and cleaning up if we decided to move into it. Today Sister Naomi Hakii (Staru) left us. She has been doing the cooking at headquarters for over two years. In her place we have an elderly woman who began her work today. In a day or two more we will also have this lady's fourteen year old daughter at headquarters to help her mother do the work.

Friday, 21 July 1905, Tokyo

Clear—Cool Up at 6:45. Spent the greater part of the day reading over my recent translation of some chapters in the book of Alma in the Book of Mormon. Wrote a letter to Goro Takahashi relative to the purchase of more of his books on Mormonism and the copyright of the same. In the afternoon went out to look for a house and do some shopping. Called at the home of Mr. and Mrs. Katagiri to see how one of the little girls was getting along; having heard that she was sick.

Monday, 24 July 1905, Tokyo

Clear—Cool. Up at 7:00. In the morning I went to the home of Sister Hakii Nami to see if she would not like to do some visiting among the people whose children come to Sunday School and she if she couldn't arouse in the hearts of the mothers and father a desire to earnestly investigate the teachings of him whose life and great deeds are being taught to their children. In the afternoon I worked on the Book of Mormon translation. Received a letter from Elders Hedges and Fairbourn by which I learn that they are busy and happy in the work.

Tuesday, 25 July 1905, Tokyo

Cloudy—Cooler. Up at 7:00. Mail came from America soon after breakfast. A letter from Dr. James E. Talmage was received. In it he enclosed an article written in compliance with the request made for the same by Prest. Ensign some months ago. The articles is entitled "In the Lineage of the Gods" and considered the the points: "What and who is man?", "Why and from whence did he come?" "After death, what?" Dr. Talmage stated in his letter that the article is meant only for an introduction leading up to the consideration of the conditions and way of salvation in other papers he has been requested by the First Presidency to write for us. These articles when carefully considered will be translated into Japanese and be used as tracts in this mission.

Mr. Tokoyo came and talked for an hour or two during the morning. He asked if he couldn't come and live with us for a month and a half from Aug 1st. He has been so very kind to us lately that I could not refuse his request so he expects to move here on Aug. 1st.

In the afternoon I received a newspaper from Sendai where Elders Hedges and Fairbourn are laboring. In it was an article relating a little of a conversation with one of the elders wherein some questions put by the writer about polygamy were answered and commented upon in quite a sportive way. The afternoon was spent reading to Elder Woodland a part of the discussions I had with Mr. McCaleb a long time ago in the marriage relations of Moses, and part of an article written in answer to Rev. J.D. Nutting's attack on our articles of Faith. In the evening we sang the songs of Zion, then took a bath and retired.

Friday, 28 July 1905, Tokyo

Clear—Very hot Up at 5:50. Spent the day writing letters. Wrote one home, one to the elders in Sendai one to the elders in Hokkaido and one to Dr. James E. Talmage. The one to the Dr. required a great deal of time as I offered my opinion on his article "In the Lineage of the Gods" and gave what pointers I could about the best way to write for the Japanese on religious subjects.

Sunday, 30 July 1905, Tokyo

Clear—Morning hot—Evening cool Up at 5:45. Swept and dusted the dining–room to show the new servants how it should be done. The Sunday School was quite well attended and interesting sessions of both classes were held. At noon none of the saints being present we four elders here at headquarters assembled in the prayer room and held a short sacrament meeting. In it I called Elder Fred A. Caine to assist me in copying into Chinese characters the translations I make from the Book of Mormon in Romaji.

In the afternoon I went to the house of Mr. Iwai and had a pleasant talk with him. Just as I went into his home I noticed a soldier watching me to see why I went. After I got seated and was talking with Mr. Iwai I noticed this same soldier pass the window (the house being on a line with the public thoroughfare). About five minutes later the soldier appeared at the door and requested the privilege of asking me how to write his name in English on his name cards. Mr. Iwai asked him to come in. He did and when I had given him the information he wanted, he begged our pardon for breaking in upon our conversation and went out. The soldier was a total stranger to Mr. Iwai and likewise a stranger to me. This I insert in my journal to show how much gall (or what shall I call it) some natives have and how well they show it.

After eating dinner did a little reading. The evening meeting was quite a success. We hung up a large lantern at the gate with the word meaning "sermon" written on it in very large characters. This no doubt attracted a number of people who had come out for a walk and they were drawn into the meeting.

A letter received from Elders Stoker, Seely and Chadwick stated that they were well at the time of writing but Elder Stoker had suffered severely for a few days with convulsions of the stomach and finally found relief through the blessings of the Lord in response to the prayers and administration of his two companions. Two worms; one a foot long and the other seven inches long passed from his body. I am gratful to the Lord for his mercy and blessing bestowed upon my dear brother to his entire recovery.

Monday, 31 July 1905, Tokyo

Rain—Cold. Up at 6:30. It has been so cold all day that I have been quite comfortable with heavy clothes on. Spent the morning hemming napkins. In the afternoon gave the new elders a long lesson in Japanese. Did a little cleaning preparatory to welcoming Mr. Tokoyo who came to headquarters this evening intending to live with us for a month and a half. After supper I taught the two little girls who are working here at headquarters how to sing one of our Sunday School hymns.

Tuesday, 1 August 1905, Tokyo

Clear—hot. Up at 6:45. After breakfast I received a letter from Sister Rin Ota saying that her father died on July 31st at about 3:00 p.m. I went immediately to offer my sympathy and learned that the funeral was for 3:00 p.m. today. I went down town and did considerable shopping. Returned in time for dinner. Asked Mr. Tokoyo what the custom was in attending the funeral of a friend. I learned that it was a rule to present some gift, which might be, flowers, cakes, or money. The last named being closest to hand, I decided to give a yen and the other three elders at headquarters did likewise so I went to the home of the deceased and presented my gift and excusing myself from going to the graveyard returned to headquarters. This man as has already been stated in the previous pages, at one time was healed by the administration of the elders and later desired to join the church but he became sick again and lost his faith. He was buried yesterday according to the Buddhist rites.

Being the 1st I celebrate my twenty third birthday. This had in connection with the fact that we expected to have at least two of the saints present at the class held for their instruction in the principles of the gospel suggested the celebration of the day by eating ice cream and cake. Only Sister Hakii was present. In the evening after supper I went out to do some visiting. Took a bath and retired.

Saturday, 5 August 1905, Tokyo

Clear and very hot. Up at 6:15. Went to Yotsuya to do a little business and get a shave. In the afternoon looked over the Mission Books and accounts for July. Wrote out the prayer used when administering baptism and also the prayer used when confirming members into the Church. I then had Mr. Tokoyo go over them and see if they were grammatical and written in the proper Chinese characters. In the evening I did a little visiting.

Monday, 7 August 1905, Tokyo

Fair—Very hot Up at 6:45. Spent the morning doing odd jobs. In the afternoon talked with Mr. Tokoyo for a while. Decided that it would be good to have Elder Woodland go and live at the home of Mr. Totsuka who offered to take me before I was called to preside in this mission. After supper Elder Woodland and I went to Mr. Totsuka's home and discussed the matter with him. He is going to his native place on the 15 inst. and after spending a week will return to Tokyo. At that time he says he will be pleased to have Elder Woodland in his home for a month or so.

Tuesday, 8 August 1905, Tokyo

Hot—Very oppressive. Up at 6:10. Spent nearly the whole day on the Book of Mormon. During the forenoon received a letter from Prest. Ensign giving a detailed story of their ocean voyage and arrival in Seattle, July 21st. Prest. Ensign's beautiful voice soon won over the passangers. Everyone on board became their friends and they had the opportunity to bear testimony to the great latter–day work with perfect freedom. A concert was given in which Prest. Ensign figured centrally. Owing to a calm sea they made the voyage without any sickness. Sister Ensign had a dizzy spell the first night on board which disabled her till the following day from which time she enjoyed herself perfectly. The quick trip brought them to Seattle nearly two days ahead of time so their relatives and friends from Salt Lake had not yet arrived. They had no trouble with the customs everything being passed through without a charge. In the afternoon I walked to Yotsuya to show Sister Hakii where one of the Sunday School children lives, and to post some letters to the elders.

Wednesday, 9 August 1905, Tokyo

Clear—Hot—Windy Up at 7:00. Worked on the Book of Mormon till noon. Went out to our prayer ground in the woods to hold our prayer meeting. Upon returning did a little more translating. Wrote to Elder Stoker instructing him to make a tour of Hokkaido for the purpose of discovering the best place for missionary work and get a knowledge of the country and some idea of the conditions of the people. Gave the new elders a lesson in Japanese. Received mail from home. All well.

Thursday, 10 August 1905, Tokyo

Clear—hot Up at 6:45. Spent the morning reading home news and writing letters. In the afternoon Mr. Kuwana, a gentleman who lives in the home of our neighbor Mr. Yokoyama, called. He stated that Mr. Yokoyama had friends and relatives in Hokkaido to whom he would give Elder Stoker letters of introduction. In the evening I went over to Mr. Yokoyama's to get the letters but they were not written. He promised to hand them to me the following day. I spent the evening at his house. He is a member of the lower house of Parliament, but not a leader in that body.

Friday, 11 August 1905, Tokyo

Clear—Hot Up at 5:30. Went out to the prayer ground before breakfast. During the forenoon I did a very little on the Book of Mormon, wrote a letter to Elder Stoker sending some letters of introduction to some of Mr. Yokoyama's (See yesterday's journal) friends and relatives in Hokkaido, and gave the new elders a lesson in Japanese. In the afternoon I did a little more on the Book of Mormon and spent some time entertaining a guest.

Sunday, 13 August 1905, Tokyo

Cloudy—Oppressive Up at 6:15. Ate breakfast. Sunday School was held from 9:00 a.m. There was a fine attendance. Sacrament Meeting was held from 11:00 a.m. with four elders and one sailer present. In the afternoon read a little. About three o'clock went to Bro. Kikuchi's and talked with him for about an hour and half. I tried to show him how his was breaking sacred covenants by failing to live in a line of his duty as an elder in the church. Returned to headquarters and ate dinner. The evening meeting was quite well attended—a great number of women being present.

Tuesday, 15 August 1905, Tokyo

Rain—Very cool Up at 6:10. Worked on the Book of Mormon all day. I am thinking of using most of the time that Mr. Tokoyo is living at headquarters, collecting together the difficult expressions I have found during the course of translation and submitting them to him to see if my rendition is good. In the evening I helped Mr. Tokoyo a little with an essay he is writing in English. Received a letter from the brethren in Hokkaido. Elder Stoker having received my letter requesting him to make a tour of Hokkaido expects to start on the 15th inst. (today).

Wednesday, 16 August 1905, Tokyo

Cloudy—Cool—Slight rain Up at 7:30. Spent the morning teaching the elders Japanese and doing some shopping. At noon we held our regular prayer meeting. Today the special object of our prayers was that the special blessings of the Lord rest down upon Elder Stoker during his travels over Hokkaido that he might discover where the honest in heart are and begin missionary work among them. In the afternoon did a little work on the Book of Mormon and also distributed a few tracts in Aoyama Minamichō. In the evening Sister Hakii came and I talked with her for quite a while about the laying on of hands for the reception of the Holy Ghost.

Sunday, 20 August 1905, Tokyo

Rain—cold Up at 7:00. Ate breakfast. The Sunday School was an excellent success. The children and young folks seem to be progressing very nicely. At 11:00 a.m. held sacrament meeting with one saint, one friend, and four missionaries present. In the afternoon I read from the Book of Mormon and took a nap. The evening meeting was fairly well attended. Through the efforts of Sister Hakii a great many women are beginning to attend our meetings. This fact makes us very happy for the presence of women seems to give a more peaceful spirit to our meetings than when there are none in attendance.

Tuesday, 22 August 1905, Tokyo

Rain—Cold Up at 7:00. Fasted all day. During the morning, I gave the elders a lesson in Japanese. Then I corrected half of a translation from Japanese into English made by Bro. Yoshiro Oyama. During the afternoon worked on the Book of Mormon. In the evening had a long conversation with Mr. Iwai. He listened to my explanations of the necessity of prayer and before going home united with the rest of us in supplication.

Elder Caine had a conversation with our cook, Mrs. Nachie, who said she is convinced that the Latter-day Saints have the truth as taught anciently and that although she has been a member of the Church of England for many years yet she has heard during her short sojourn with us so many things that has given her new light that she realizes that her faith so far in the other church has been poorly placed. If after we test her sincerity a little more and teach her further about the church and its laws she is found worthy we will be greatly pleased to have her join with us. Took a bath and retired.

Wednesday, 6 September 1905, Tokyo

Clear—Very hot Up at 6:00. Gave Elder Anderson a lesson in Japanese. Corrected the remainder of Mr. Tokoyo's English composition. At noon we went to the neighboring woods and held our weekly prayer meeting. In the afternoon and evening I worked on the Book of Mormon a little. Took a walk up to Aoyama after supper.

Owing to the great dissatisfaction with the terms of peace mobs have /been/ operating in full black in Tokyo since yesterday. The have entirely overcome the police, /destroyed the plants of/ the one newspaper which defends the action of the government and have burned down or destroyed most of the police boxes in the main part of town and here made howling demonstrations before the homes and offices of the government officials who are connected with the war. There purpose it to force the nullification of the peace treaty and continue the war till Russia will pay all the indemnity asked and make way other concessions which the Japanese might make.[13]

Thursday, 7 September 1905, Tokyo

Cloudy—Rain—Hot Up at 6:30. Gave Elder Anderson a lesson in Japanese. Worked on the Book of Mormon the rest of the day. In the evening after supper, I taught two of the servants of headquarters how to sing some of our hymns.

The reports of the mischief done by the mob yesterday and last night took up the entire space of the newspaper. The situation has become so serious that the city has been placed under military control and the troops are stationed at all points where the excited citizens are liable to make further displays. The paper states that some Christian Churches in the other part of town have been burned by rioters. Today /armed/ soldiers came to headquarters and inquired about our safety. This made us wonder if there was any danger for us but I don't feel in the least troubled about the situation believing that we are perfectly safe in the hands of the Lord so long as we are wise and mind our own business.

Friday, 8 September 1905, Tokyo

Hot and Clear Up at 6:00. Gave the most part of the forenoon to teaching Japanese to Elder Anderson and reading about the disturbance now on in Tokyo. Spent a little time working on the Book of Mormon. Received a letter from Elder Stoker relating the particulars of his trip over Hokkaido. He states that in his opinion, after seeing the most important towns, cities and villages of the Island that Sapporo the capital of the island is the best place to operate the headquarters of the mission there and according such for money to rent and furnish a Japanese house. I wrapped up a number of books and sent them to the elders in Hokkaido by freight.

About 2:00 a.m in the night a small squad of soldiers came to protect our house and the neighbor's (a member of Parliament) from any likely attack by some suspicious looking men discovered in the neighborhood. We don't feel the least fear, for we have done nothing to incur the hate of anyone and God is our friend.

Sunday, 10 September 1903, Tokyo

Clear—Hot Up at 7:00. Ate breakfast. Held Sunday School as usual and in spite of the agitation about the destruction of eight churches in Tokyo the children came out very well. One saint was present at sacrament meeting. In the afternoon I did some writing. The evening meeting was almost a failure. Not many people ventured out. The fact that Christian Churches have been attacked and in many instances demolished during the recent excitement will no doubt keep the people away for some time. A company of 12 soldiers was dispatched to guard our neighborhood during the night. Due to the fact that they patrolled up and down in front of our place no doubt some few people were frightened away.

Wednesday, 13 September 1905, Tokyo

Clear—hot Up at 7:10. Ate breakfast. A Japanese called and spent most of the morning talking with me. Gave Elder Anderson a short lesson in Japanese. In the afternoon worked on the Book of Mormon. About 4:00 p.m. went and visited Mr. Uchimura Kanzo who while believing the Bible does not belong to any one sect. He is a very gifted man in literary lines. He is held by some as the most able writer in Japan and he speaks well in both Japanese and English. I had a hour's conversation with him. Returned to headquarters and read the newspaper from home. I received a card from Dr. Talmage who accepts the changes I suggested in his article "In the Lineage of the Gods."

Friday, 15 September 1905, Tokyo

Clear—hot Up at 6:50. Ate breakfast. Gave Elder Anderson a short lesson in Japanese. Elders Woodland, Caine, and Anderson and I went out to see the Tamagara River which is located twenty odd miles west of Tokyo. This river is noted for its clearness. From this river Tokyo takes its water for the water works. We found it a barren place with not a single tree or shrub along the bank to make a shade. We hoped to find on this river a suitable place to perform baptisms but the barrenness of the neighborhood dispelled the desire. Elder Caine went on to Hachiooji while I and the other two elders returned to Tokyo. We alighted at Shinjuku and hunted for a good place to baptize in the vicinity of the Juniso summer resort. We found quite a good place. We walked home. The trip in the sun was too much. I was sick and ate very little supper. Wrote two letters before going to bed. Retired early.

Saturday, 16 September 1905, Tokyo

Clear—Hot Up at 6:50. Spent part of the morning teaching Elder Anderson Japanese. In the afternoon Elder Caine and I went to one of the Red Cross Hospitals located in the Sendagaya Tokyo Fuka and had the privilege of holding two meeting for the benefit of the convali immates. It is very monotonous for the soldiers to remain in the hospital without any special change or recreation, so the authorities of the place are, so we were told, pleased to have Christian preachers or others come and talk and sing to the wounded. Wednesdays and Saturdays are days in which such visits can be paid to the hospital. An acquaintance working at the hospital informed us of the opportunity to preach to the soldiers and we took advantage of it. In the ward where we held the first meeting the soldiers sat upon their beds in their hospital clothes and listened. In the second ward we went into, benches were arranged and we had a large crowd seated before us. It was quite a beneficial visit and while it was with peculiar feelings that I entered the room where the wounded were lying I soon felt at home and enjoyed myself very much.

After returning to headquarters, I talked with two of the Takagi children for some time. In the evening, after supper I read a little and then retired.

In the morning wrote a long letter home and a short letter to Bro. Jos. F. Featherstone, one of our former missionaries.

Monday, 18 September 1905, Tokyo

Rain—Cold—Northwest wind Up at 7:00. Taught Elder Anderson a little Japanese. Finished writing my letter to Alvin V. Had a talk with Mrs. Nachie in the evening. During the day she went and called on the preacher of the church to which she has hitherto belonged and told his wife (he was not at home) that investigation had led her to believe in the teachings of Mormonism which she intends to embrace. I trust God will give her faith and strength to become a staunch member of His kingdom.

Tuesday, 19 September 1905, Tokyo

Rain—Very cool Up at 7:20. So cold this morning that I found it comfortable to wear winter clothes. During the morning taught Elder Anderson Japanese and did some reading. Last evening having received a letter from Mr. Totsuka stating that he was at last ready to receive Elder Woodland into his home. Elder W and I went to Mr. Totsuka's house this afternoon. On the way we called at Kanda and did some shopping. I stayed with Elder W till a little after eight o'clock and then left him at the home of Mr. Totsuka to begin his real Japanese life. As Mr. Totsuka's house is only about two miles from headquarters we expect to see Elder W at least once a week.

Thursday, 21 September 1905, Tokyo

Fair—Warmer Up at 6:30. Spent part of the morning working on the Book of Mormon. Taught Elder Anderson a little Japanese. Wrote a letter to the First Presidency. Received a letter from the elders in Hokkaido which told of the conditions in that island. The elders are now located at Sapporo where they are looking for a suitable home in which to live. They have been mistaken for Russian spies and are constantly watched by detectives. If the detectives watch closely enough and are the least bit susceptible to truth and virtue they would be converted to Mormonism. In the afternoon had a singing practice for the S.S. children. After supper Mr. Homma talked with me for some time. When he left, I taught one of the servants and her friend a song or two. During the day I was greatly distressed with my nose. I seem to be afflicted with quite a case of catarrah.

Tuesday, 26 September 1905, Tokyo

Clear—Hot Up at 7:20. Mrs. Tsune Nachie the lady who is now living at headquarters doing the cooking for us stated that she was ready to be baptized For some time she has been investigating the gospel and asked for baptism some weeks ago. (see page 117) I went and invited two of our sisters to come and witness the baptism. Then went to the little stream where it was to be performed, and selected a quiet spot. During the morning gave Elder Anderson a lesson in Japanese. In the afternoon I did a very little on the Book of Mormon.

At about four o'clock we left headquarters to go to the place of baptism. Elder Woodland came from where he is living to witness the ordinance. Sister Tsuta Deguchi was in the party; also a /lady/ friend of Mrs. Nachie. We went on the electric car from Sendagaya station to Shinjuku and then walked to the stream which runs in the rear of the water works near a little resort called Jūniso. We were allowed to pass through a private garden to the bank of the stream and were not disturbed or looked at during the service. We sang "Lo on the Water's Brink we stand." I offered a short prayer. Then Elder Fred A. Caine led Mrs. Nachie into the water and baptized her. As soon as they had put on dry clothes we returned to headquarters. During the evening I taught the Japanese living at headquarters and Sister Deguchi how to sing one or two of our songs.

Saturday, 30 September 1905, Tokyo

Cloudy—Cold Up at 6:30. Spent the morning teaching Elder Anderson Japanese and translating the Book of Mormon. In the afternoon Elder Caine and I went to the Red Cross Hospital and held a meeting for the wounded soldiers. Returned to headquarters and looked up a lesson for the Sunday School children. Read a little Japanese and took a bath.

Today's work on the Book of Mormon completed the translation of the Book of Alma.

Sunday, 1 October 1905, Tokyo

Rain—Cold Up at 7:50. The Sunday School commenced at 9:00. Not a very large attendance but an interesting session. At our fast meeting which convened from 11:30 a.m. we enjoyed a good spirit. Sister Nachie Tsune was confirmed a member of the church and given the Holy Ghost by the laying on of hands. In the afternoon I did some reading. Sister Hakii came with a bottle of oil for us to bless. We were delighted to see her do this for it showed her faith in the ordinance of anointing. The evening meeting was held as usual.

Thursday, 5 October 1905, Tokyo

Clear—Warmer Up at 6:20. Spent the morning teaching Elder Anderson and working on the Book of Mormon. After dinner, I walked to the post office. I began the translation of Dr. James E. Talmage's article entitled "In the lineage of the Gods" written for this mission. In the evening after supper I talked with a young man named Ikeda.

Thursday, 12 October 1905, Tokyo

Fair—Warm Up at 6:00. Taught Elder Anderson a lesson in Japanese. Went down town to do some business and called on Elder Woodland on the way. After returning taught Mrs. Umeda and Miss Kogu English. Wrote a letter to Elder Jarvis and selected from old films 120 to be printed and placed in an album for him.

Monday, 13 November 1905, Tokyo

Clear—Warm South Wind. Up at 6:30. Spent part of the morning teaching Elder Anderson Japanese. Wrote a letter to Miss Richardson who, I am informed by Prest. Woolley of the Hawaiian

Mission, is in Japan for treatment. She is a member of the Church, and according to Bro. W's. letter is now in Kusatsu Jōshū. In the afternoon I taught Miss Kogu and Mrs. Umeda English. I took a walk after supper and called on Sister Deguchi. I had a pleasant talk with her mother. Worked on the Book of Mormon till bed time.

Tuesday, 14 November 1905, Tokyo

Clear—Warm wind—Very dusty. Up at 6:10. Spent the greater part of the day working on the Book of Mormon. Taught Elder Anderson a lesson in Japanese. In the late afternoon I went to the barber shop, and from there to the house of Mr. Totsuka where Elder Woodland is living. I arranged for Elder W. to move back to headquarters this coming Saturday. The main reason for this move is that Elder W. does not feel as though he was getting the proper assistance in the study of the language.

Saturday, 18 November 1905, Tokyo

Clear—Warm— Up at 6:10. Spent the greater part of the morning cleaning house. Went over to Mr. Totsuka's to take some money /to Elder Woodland / and thank Mr. & Mr. Totsuka for their kindness to Elder W. while he was living in their home. Elder W. moved back to headquarters today. Ate dinner and spent the afternoon pasting new paper on the shop. In the evening Elder Caine and I spent an hour on the proof sheets of the third edition of #2 Tract. Took a bath and retired.

Today, when I returned from Mr. Totsuka's, I found our friend Nobu Mashimo at headquarters. He was released from service in the army and returned home on the 10th of the month. He is looking well and strong.

Thursday, 30 November 1905, Tokyo

Fair—Warmer Up at 4:45. The alarm that got me up so early this morning was the noise of a burglar leaving the house and the cry of the cook which immediately followed the crashing of doors. Last night our yearly night visitor entered the house by pulling out one of the kitchen doors. He ransacked the house down stairs. He sprung the lock on my trunk and went through the contents. He evidently only wanted money very little of which he got as we keep our money pretty close to us both night and day. He passed over good clothes and jewelry and silverware. I had a little relic money not over one yen and a half in value in my trunk. He took this and three sen out of Elder Woodland's trunk. He must have been in the house for a long time as he left things in a muddled condition. Sister Nachie discovered a light and thought it was one of the elders, but after a while she discovered that it was not anyone who had a right in the house so she called out. The visitor made his escape into the darkness. We are thankful for the little loss, for our visitor was not the kind who wanted everything he could get hold of [us], so he left practically without my pay for his risk. Sleep was about the only thing he deprived us of.

I swept the dining room. During the forenoon I taught Elder Anderson a lesson in Japanese. Worked on the Book of Mormon translation. In the afternoon two of the little girls who have been quite faithful attendants at S.S. during the year came to say good–bye before leaving for Kobe. We gave them small gifts as a token of the love we held for them.

Sunday, 3 December 1905, Tokyo

Clear—Cold. Up at 8:15. Sunday School was held as usual. After school, I practiced a little on the piano. Sacrament and testimony meeting was held at 2:00 p.m. I took a walk calling on Sister Deguchi. In the evening we ate dinner and there held a night meeting. Having decided that we can do much better by holding meetings in the afternoon instead of the evening during the winter it was announced that hereafter we will hold our public meeting on Sunday afternoon at 2:00 p.m.

Tuesday, 5 December, 1905, Tokyo

Cloudy—Rain—Cold Up at 6:50. Spent the morning contriving a means to secure the doors in the Japanese part of the house so no more burglars will get in. In the afternoon I read mail from home. Was terribly surprised to read of a great victory for the American Party in the Salt Lake City elections.[14] It means that the Anti Mormons have a complete sway in the city administration. Worked a little on the Book of Mormon and wrote a prayer for the S.S. Christmas entertainment. In the evening before going to bed practiced with Elder Anderson some of the songs for Christmas. Elder A. is preparing to play the piano.

Sunday, 10 December 1905, Tokyo

Clear—Colder Up at 7:00. Sunday School commenced from 10:00 a.m. a fair attendance. Talked with Mr. Imai who wanted to rent a room and live here with us. I told him we had not room for him. We prepared to welcome our audience for the 2:00 p.m. meeting, but not a single soul came. We have distributed invitations to about 700 houses in this vicinity reaching at least 2,500 people, but not one came in answer to the invitations. In the evening some came and we conversed about the Gospel. I walked to Sister Deguchi's after sacrament meeting which we held at 3:00 p.m.

Tuesday, 19 December 1905, Tokyo/Yokohama/Tokyo

Clear, then cloudy—Cold Up at 6:50. After getting up, I went immediately to Yokohama to make some purchases. **I called on Sister Richardson (see page[s] 14). She is a young Hawaiian 18 years old and evidently a daughter in quite a well–to–do family consisting of father & mother and 13 children. Sister R. would not tell me how she happened to come to Japan or what the nature of her disease is for which she has evidently come here. She received me with evident pleasure. I ate dinner with her, talked with her, and counseled her for about two hours. Her aunt (also from Hawaii) is not in sympathy with the Mormons and refused to see me. Upon leaving Sister Richardson handed me ¥5.00 for the Mission, ¥1.00 for the Christmas entertainment fund and ¥1.00 for my own use.**

Returned to Tokyo and spent the evening practicing the dialogue I have with Santa Claus. Took a bath and retired.

Friday, 22 December 1905, Tokyo

Clear—Cold Up at 5:50. Swept the rooms down stairs. Spent part of the morning writing letters. Went to the barber shop. In the afternoon arranged the Christmas presents and gave the children their last practice in the songs for Christmas. In the evening held a little meeting for five young people who came to learn about Jesus (see last Friday's journal).

Sunday, 24 December 1905, Tokyo

Clear—Colder Up at 7:00. Sunday School convened at 10:00 a.m. We conducted a final practice of the songs /for Christmas/ at the close of the school and I listened to the speeches of those who are on the program. From 2:30 p.m. we held a public meeting after which we held a sacrament service. In the evening I went around with invitations to the Christmas party.

Monday, 25 December 1905, Tokyo

Fine—Warm Up at 7:00. Yesterday being Sunday we had to do all our decorating and preparation for the Christmas party today. I went immediately after breakfast to buy some evergreen. Elder Woodland made this into a rope like decoration and hung it on the ceiling. Elder Anderson sacked the candy and pop corn. Elder Caine decorated the Christmas tree. We all worked as hard as we knew how till about 3:00 p.m. when we ate a hurried dinner. I dressed up to receive the guests after going out to buy some little ornaments. Elder Caine was still working on his Santa Claus make up when the first children arrived. By 6:30, the hour announced for the party to begin the large dining room was almost full, but guests kept coming till about 7:00 p.m. when the program began. It was a delight to us to see the S.S. children dressed in their best and smiling from ear to ear in anticipation of the evening's program. About 30 adults, mostly parents of the children were present. The children numbered between 55 and 60. The program was as follows. . . .

Every one in the program did well and it was carried out without the slightest hitch. It was 9:45 when the company returned and it was not till then that we felt tired from the day's work. This year the first prize for attendance at S.S. was awarded to Miss Hisa Saito who was present during the year 49 times out of a possible 51. This little girl got the second prize last year. The second prize was awarded to Miss Yae Uesugi who last year won the first prize. Master Motoi Ouozawa took third place. In the large class Miss Ai Takagi won the prize for best attendance and her sister, Miss Ei Takagi, won second prize. All the children received a present of some kind and a bag of candy and a bag of pop corn each. We felt satisfied with the day's work and thanked God for his assistance bestowed upon us and the children.

During the day received presents from Mr. Tokoyo (silk handkerchief), Miss Umeda (sofa pillow), Miss Kogu (silk handkerchief & furushiki), Sister Deguchi souvenir wine cup). The mission received a picture & two small vases from Sister Hakii and a box of candy from Sister Nachie.

Sunday, 31 December 1905, Tokyo

Clear—Cold Up at 7:30. The Sunday School was held with a small attendance. Today being the last of the year the natives are just completing their preparation for the great New Years feast, which in this land is the largest and most elaborate for both old and young, our meetings were, of course, not very largly attended. I enjoyed reading with my brethren the minutes of the second day of the General conference.

The past year has been one of important changes in this mission affectiong all the missionaries but having the greatest effect upon me. The year's experiences have given me strength to meet the vicissitudes of the new year more successfully than I could hope to do without them. The Lord has blessed me in my special work on the translation of the Book of Mormon. As I have progressed in the translation my joy in the divine record has grown until it is unbounded and my appreciation of its value as a book for the salvation and exaltation of the human family has grown from day to day. I prize the blessings that have come to me on account of the translation in which I am engaged and my prayers are ascending constantly to the Father for the speedy and entirely successful consummation of the work on the translation.

I am grateful for my companions in the mission over which I have during the latter part of the year been called to preside. They have sustained me and done their duty as servants of the Lord. May He bless them abundantly during the new year. I thank God for the soul that has been added to our little ranks [and] during the year and look forward to the future when I believe many will join the church and be faithful to the covenants they make with their God. I am grateful for the integrity of some of the native saints in paying their tithing and doing what they can with the limited means at their demand to further the work of the Lord in the earth. I have felt to praise my heavenly Father often for the faithful testimonies born by two of our sisters especially and I only regret that all of the six native members of the church are not so confident of their faith as these two. I feel to give thanks to the Lord for the work we have been able to accomplish in the Sunday Schools among the children. I pray ever for the rising generation in this land.

I am truly grateful for the year 1905 and all that it has afforded me and my relatives, friends, brothers, and sisters. Let the God of heaven and earth be praised for it all. May he continue in 1906 to open the windows of heaven and pour out upon the heads of his children in this and all lands the blessings which will best suit we who are battling with the things of an inclement and wicked world.

Notes

1. *Aisumi Jo Gakko.* Aisumi Girl's School.

2. Small plates of Nephi. About two decades after starting the large plates, the Book of Mormon prophet Nephi was commanded to create another set of plates. On this second set he was to record the spiritual ministry of his people—"preaching which was sacred, or revelation which was great, or prophesying" (Jacob 1:2–4). These small plates were recorded on for over four hundred years by nine writers: Nephi, Jacob, Enos, Jarom, Omni, Amaron, Chemish, Abinadom, and Amaleki. Grant R. Hardy and Robert E. Parsons, "Book of Mormon Plates and Records," *Encyclopedia of Mormonism*, 1:199.

3. George Reynolds, *A Complete Concordance to the Book of Mormon* (Salt Lake City: s.n., 1900).

4. The Doll Festival. A popular girl's festival celebrated every year on 3 March. As part of the festivities, each family with a

young girl displays a group of dolls representing the ancient Japanese imperial court. On the top shelf are the Emperor and Empress, and below them are placed their two important lords, three ladies, five musicians, and three servants. Sometimes miniature furniture and foods are also displayed. Nobuyuki Honna and Bates Hoffer, eds., *An English Dictionary of Japanese Culture* (Tokyo: Yuhikaku Pub. Co., 1986), 88.

5. Mosiah. The eighth book in the Book of Mormon.

6. President Joseph F. Smith—during the Reed Smoot congressional hearings.

7. See Book of Mormon, Alma 12:13–37, 13:1–5.

8. Alma 13. A synopsis of this complex chapter: "Men are called as high priests because of their exceeding faith and good works—They are to teach the commandments—Through righteousness they are sanctified and enter into the rest of the Lord—Melchizedek was one of these—Angels are declaring glad tidings throughout the land—They will reveal the actual coming of Christ." Book of Mormon, Alma 13 chapter heading.

9. The Battle of the Japan Sea. The Russian Tsar sent the Baltic fleet around the world to defeat the Japanese Navy during the Russo-Japanese War. In May 1905, the Battle of the Japan Sea ensued during which Admiral Tōgō Heihachirō's navy destroyed the Russian fleet. Pyle, *The Making of Modern Japan*, 141.

10. *Zōri*. Japanese sandals.

11. *Nome*. Unable to discern meaning.

12. *Tatami*. Tatami mats—made of straw and rush and measuring roughly 6 by 3 feet—are used as floor-coverings in traditional Japanese rooms. As all tatami mats measure the same size, they are often used as a unit of measurement. Nobuyuki and Hoffer, *An English Dictionary of Japanese Culture*, 296.

13. Although victorious in the Russo-Japanese war, when the peace treaty was signed at Portsmouth, New Hampshire, in 1905, many Japanese were displeased with the terms of settlement. Although they had hoped for much more, Japan was awarded the southern half of Sakhalin, the recognition of its Korean interests, a lease of the Liaotung Peninsula, and railroad rights in southern Manchuria. Pyle, *The Making of Modern Japan*, 141.

14. The influence of the dominant Republican Party in Utah was challenged in 1904 when former Republican senator Thomas Kearns helped organize the American Party, which opposed the LDS Church. Helped by Kearns' *Tribune*, the American Party was successful in dominating Salt Lake City and Ogden politics for a time. John Sillito, "Republican Party," *Utah History Encyclopedia*, ed. Alan Kent Powell (Salt Lake City: University of Utah Press, 1994), 461.

Alma O. Taylor mending his clothes.
Courtesy John W. Welch.

Horace S. Ensign sleeping on the floor of the Tokyo
mission home. Courtesy John W. Welch.

Chapter 10

Alma O. Taylor Journal, 1906

Monday, 1 January 1906, Tokyo

Clear—Cold Up at 7:30. Spent the greater part of the day talking with visitors who came to make New Years calls. Wrote a letter to my brother Samuel and one to the elders in Sapporo, Hokkaido. Totaled up the work I had done during 1905. In the morning gave Elders Anderson and Woodland the sacrament prayers in Japanese to learn by next Sunday.

Wednesday, 3 January 1906, Tokyo

Clear—Cold Up at 5:00 Went down to the Ginza and to Kanda on business. Returned a little after 12:00n, and we immediately held prayer meeting. Received letters from America. **In the afternoon a box of sweet-meats containing three pound boxes of candy made by the Grant family and a fruit cake made by mother were found on the inside. I had known that the box was coming but keep it secret and worked a great surprise on my companions, who with me enjoyed the sweets very much. A number of children called and two grown persons whom we entertained taking up most of the afternoon. After supper we read the last of the Conference sermons and we feel greatly blessed by the timely and important remarks of all who spoke. We enjoyed the spirit of the sermons even though they came to us in cold type.**

Sunday, 7 January 1906, Tokyo

Clear—Warmer Up at 8:00. The S.S. was well attended we had a most interesting session. A good beginning for the new year. Our afternoon /meeting/ was better attended than usual. **One of the audience left after the first speech and on his way out stole our big Standard Dictionary and Mr. Tokoyo's overcoat. We made a search for the robber but he had been gone over 30 minutes before we discovered the loss. The search for the thief threw our fast meeting rather late, but we enjoyed** a good spirit and were edified by bearing & listening to testimonies. Just before meeting Mr. Hiroi my old Japanese teacher and interpreter for the Mission during our first year in Japan called and we had a pleasant chat. In the evening I read a part of "The Brief History of the Church" with the view of making suggestions as to what parts might just as well be left out of the translation now being made by Elder Stoker.

Thursday, 11 January 1906, Tokyo

Clear—Warm Up at 7:00. During part of the morning I taught Japanese to Elder Anderson. Spent much of the rest of the day working on the Book of Mormon. In the afternoon I taught some of the children of the Sunday School a new song and we practiced one of the old ones. The mail from America brought the Christmas News a magnificent and exhaustive paper of 116 pages full of excellent illustrations and articles [—-ming] Utah, Idaho and Nevada. I worked again on the Book of Mormon a little before going to bed.

Thursday, 18 January 1906, Tokyo

Clear—Mild. Up at 7:00. Taught Elder Anderson a lesson in Japanese and continued the work on the Book of Mormon finishing the translation of III Nephi About 5:00 p.m. Miss Kogu and Mrs. Umeda called and spent an hour or so at headquarters.

Regretted to learn by the papers from Zion that Bro. Christian D. Fjeldsted one of the Seven

Presidents of the Seventies died in the L.D.S. Hospital at Salt Lake City Dec 23rd 1905 after a lingering illness and operation for kidney trouble. The papers also gave full accounts of the centennial services in Utah of the 100 anniversary of the birth of Joseph Smith, Prophet and founder of the Church. An account also of the unveiling of a magnificent granite monument on the spot where the Prophet was born.[1] The ceremonies were conducted by Pres. McQuarrie of the Eastern States Mission and were attended by Presidents Joseph F. Smith, Anthon H. Lund, a member of the Apostles and other leaders & members of the church numbering all about 50.

Friday, 19 January 1906, Tokyo

Cloudy—Rain—Warmer. Up at 6:15. Swept and dusted the downstairs rooms. Spent part of the morning teaching Elder Anderson Japanese. During the rest of the morning and for about two hours in the afternoon I worked on the Book of Mormon, finishing IV Nephi. I wrote a letter to the elders in the field sending a copy to Sendai and one to Sapporo. Requested in this letter that the elders observe Wednesday, Feb. 7th as a day of special fast and prayer in behalf of the translations of the Book of Mormon and The Brief History of the Church together with other works of translation important to the work of the Lord in Japan. Practiced singing and then walked to the post office.

Thursday, 1 February 1906, Tokyo

Cloudy—Afternoon rain—Milder. Up at 7:00. Spent part of the morning teaching Japanese to Elder Anderson. Did some sewing. Read over the rest of the manuscript referred to in yesterdays journal. In the afternoon did a little work on the Book of Mormon, but spent most of the time reading the Millennial Star (Joseph Smith edition) In it was the article I wrote entitled "The Holy Spirit Bears Witness" (See [blank]).[2] I wrapped up a number of copies which I intend to send to some English speaking friends among the Japanese. Received, today, a little book entitled "Great Truths"[3] from Prest. Heber J. Grant as a Christmas gift.

Wednesday, 7 February 1906, Tokyo

Clear—Mild. Up at 7:00. Went down town to tend to some business and have my teeth filled. Returned to headquarters in time for the prayer meeting at 12n. Today all the elders in Japan are fasting and praying especially for the way to be opened up for the correction and careful revision of the translation of the Book of Mormon and the translation of the Brief History of The Church both of which are rapidly nearing completion. In the afternoon I taught Elder Anderson a lesson in Japanese and then worked on the Book of Mormon till bed time. For about thirty minutes in the evening I talked to Mr. Okada who called inquiring about the church.

Friday, 9 February 1906, Tokyo

Heavy snow storm lasted all day Up at 7:00. Spent /most of/ the day indoors. Taught Elder Anderson a lesson in Japanese. During /most of/ the rest of the day worked on the Book of Mormon and spent some moments admiring the snow, which driven by the wind, fell in true home-like style. It is the only snow storm I have witnessed since coming to Japan which reminded me the winter storms in the dear old Rockies. After breakfast I went to the dentist's to have the repairing of my teeth finished.

Saturday, 10 February 1906, Tokyo

Clear—Warm—Big thaw. Up at 6:30. Swept chimnies and polished stoves for an hour or two. Ate breakfast, and spent the rest of the morning sweeping and dusting the upstairs rooms. In the afternoon conducted the singing in the Bible Class. Had a conversation with a representative of the Derupō Tsushinsha. Read the papers from America. Prepared a lesson for Sunday School. Took a bath and was about to retire when Sister Hakii came and asked some questions in answering which I was up till 11:30. The home in the which Sister Hakii is working is not, of course favorable to "Mormonism" being Episcopalians and they are conducting a proselyting work directly aimed at our sister in the hope of winning her from the true fold of Jesus. May God give our sister wisdom to withstand all attacks upon her and strength to defend the cause she has espoused.

Monday, 12 February 1906, Tokyo

Cloudy—Mild Up at 6:45. During the morning I taught Elder Anderson a lesson in Japanese, took a walk, and did a little work on the Book of Mormon. After dinner I had a brief talk with a Japanese who called on us. Elder Anderson and I had a singing practice. It is necessary for us to keep practicing every day so that when we have singing in our meetings neither the pianist (Elder A.) or the leader (myself) will get off and thereby spoil the effect. Received a letter from the First Presidency enclosing a draft for ¥200.00 to be subscribed for the relief of the famine sufferers in the northern part of Japan. Wrote a letter to Elder Hedges and his companion.

Tuesday, 13 February 1906, Tokyo

Clear—Colder Up at 7:00. Went down town to see where it would be best to make a donation to the relief of the famine sufferers. Returned and taught Elder Anderson a lesson in Japanese. In the afternoon I worked on the Book of Mormon. After supper talked with grandma Takagi and her granddaughter, Ei. Ei is going to enter a Methodist Girls School from which she will have very little opportunity of going out to other places, so she came to say good-bye to us. I went out to visit a gentleman who called at headquarters sometime ago, but after a long hunt, I failed to find his house.

Wednesday, 14 February 1906, Tokyo

Clear—Cold wind Up at 7:45. Did some sewing. Taught Elder Anderson a lesson in Japanese. Held our prayer meeting at noon. Worked on the Book of Mormon in the afternoon. Just before supper I took a walk to find the house I failed to find last night. After supper I visited Mr. Okada.

Today I received a letter from Joseph H. Thomas of Manasaw, Colorado. He states that he has been called on a mission to Japan and expects to leave about May 1st.

Friday, 16 February 1906, Tokyo/Yokohama/Tokyo

Clear—Not severely cold. Up at 6:35. After breakfast I wrote a letter to Elder Hedges in reference to the use of ¥120.00 for the relief of the famine sufferers. Took the 11:00 a.m. train for Yokohama where I took out a fire insurance policy for ¥1600 covering the furniture at headquarters & the clothing owned by the elders. Called on Brother Yoshiro Oyama and had dinner with him at a "sobaya."

Went to the home of Sister Richardson (see page 51) and spent an hour or two with her. Her aunt came out of hiding and I met and talked with her for a little while. Some time ago I received a letter from Sister Richardson asking that I come to Yokohama again and see her. It developed today that the aunt wanted me to come again for the reason that she is getting worried over Sister R's condition, and wants me to help them. When I called on Sister R. last December, I inquired about her sickness, but received no direct answer, so I was left to judge what it was by what I saw. I decided her affliction was leprosy[4] and when I saw her today I knew before I was told that my opinion was correct. The aunt wants the girl placed in the hands of a compitent doctor and wants me to find the best I can. I have promised to do my best for them. At the request of Sister R., I administered to her before leaving. I came directly back to Tokyo and made inquiry at the largest drug store in Tokyo about where the best treatment for leprosy can be attained. I wrote a friend to introduce me to the head of the Medical Department of the Imperial University,[5] to whom I may apply for advice regarding the matter. Before retiring, I wrote out a short prayer in compliance to a request from Mr. Okada.

Saturday, 17 February 1906, Tokyo

Clear in forenoon—Afternoon cloudy & warm. Up at 6:50. Spent the morning reading, writing and talking. Mr. Okada called to borrow some money—another scrub who has great pretenses! In the afternoon I delivered an address to the students of the Bible Class and then conducted the singing. Had a talk with one of the students. Went to see Dr. Whitney to find out, if possible, from him what would be the best thing to do with a person suffering from leprosy. I learned from him, the names and addresses of two prominent doctors in treating this disease. Returned, ate supper, read a little and took a bath before retiring. Received a letter from Sapporo telling of the good health of the brethren there.

Sunday, 18 February 1906, Tokyo

Clear—Strong wind with dirt & dust. Up at 7:15. Ate breakfast. The Sunday School held quite a successful session. This morning we presented to the children the matter of donating for the relief of the famine. The students of both classes received the proposition enthusiastically and we gave each student a small envelope on which was printed, Tōhoku San Ken Kyosakuchi Kyūsai Gun no tame (For the relief of the three Kens stricken with famine) In these they were instructed to place the amount they desired to give & bring it next Sunday. The missionaries and saints will join in this movement and all be sent as a contribution from the S.S. of the Church of J.C. of L.D.S. at Tokyo.

The afternoon meeting was a failure—no one came. We held a sacrament meeting at 3:00 p.m. I looked over a part of the Brief History of the Church making a few suggestions in writing in regard to the readition of some parts. After supper had a long talk with a Japanese. Just before supper Elder Woodland who is suffering with a boil[6] asked to be administered to. We attended to the ordinance.

Wednesday, 21 February 1906, Tokyo/Yokohama/Tokyo

Rained all day—Very Cold. Up at 8:00 Taught Elder Anderson a lesson in Japanese and with him practiced singing. Did a little on the Book of Mormon. At noon we held our fast and prayer meeting. We offered special supplications in behalf of Sister Richardson. We decided that rather then turn her over into the hands of a doctor and let her take chances for her life that we would prefer to plead with God in her behalf and give her into his care. Hence next Wednesday all the elders will fast for her and continue their fast until Thursday afternoon. Two or all four of the elders will go to Yokohama on Thursday and at 12:00n will pray for and administer to her. After our meeting today, I went to Yokohama to instruct Sister R. in what I want her to do for herself and report to her what I have learned about the treatment of leprosy in this land.

I returned to headquarters and after eating a late supper, wrote a letter to Elder [~~Hedges~~]. **Today I received from Sendai or thereabouts a letter signed by two people telling that [~~"Hedges"~~] a preacher of our church in Sendai has since his arrival in that region last July been associating with singing girls, harlots, and students of the Girl's School. They claim that the papers of that district have called attention to his actions in the hope of reforming him but he does not seem to be repenting of his way any as just recently he was seen in a certain district associating with the "geisha"[7] of the place. I don't believe a word of this terrible report about my brother, but in order that he might know what has been charged against him, I wrote, before retiring, a long letter enclosing the letter I received and instructed him what course to take in investigating the origin of this charge that has come to me and if true what to do to refute and deny it for his own protection and the defense of the work we represent.**

Friday, 23 February 1906, Tokyo

Rained and hailed all day Up at 6:50. Taught Elder Anderson a lesson in Japanese and had a singing practice in the forenoon In the afternoon wrote my journal and translated some of the Book of Mormon. In the evening, I continued the work of translation and wrote a letter to the elders in Sapporo. In the evening we had a very strong earthquake which rattled the house severely.

Saturday, 24 February 1906, Tokyo

Cloudy—Colder Up at 7:00. Intended to spend the morning translating but Mr. Tokoyo came and I talked with him for sometime. He informed us of a performance in the largest theatre in Tokyo by the best actors in Japan for the benefit of the famine sufferers. Elder Caine and I decided to take advantage of the opportunity and through Mr. Tokoyo ordered two seats for Friday night (March 2nd). I worked on the Book of Mormon during an hour in the forenoon and during all the afternoon. At supper time I ceased translating and spent the evening reading up on a lesson for the Sunday School.

Received a letter from Elder Hedges in relation to how he used the ¥120.00 sent to him and Elder Fairbourn for the relief of the famine sufferers. He also wrote in full about the letter mention on /page/ 121 of this journal. The author of the letter is supposed to be a person who has often tried to dupe the brethren and at one time stole paper and envelopes from the brethren's house during their absence. Failing in his attempts to persuade the brethren to adopt his plans he has manifested a wicked and vile spirit towards them and is supposed to be the author of all the bad things published against them. The brethren are accumulating testimony against him, which they will use if he does not cease to lie about their personal actions.*

*This morning at a little after nine o'clock we had a very strong earthquake. It shook two small vases off from the top of the piano and gave the house a severe test. The papers in reporting the matter later recorded a number of instances where parts of godowns and house had been shaken down. A rumor was started that in the night a still more sever shock would be felt so most of the people who heard the rumor didn't sleep well and some had their chattels ready to move outside.

Sunday, 25 February 1906, Tokyo

Clear—Cold Up at 7:15. As Sister Richardson is fasting today in order to obtain the blessings of God to assist her in overcoming the dread disease that is upon her, I also fasted and prayed for her. The Sunday School was a good success. The students brought their envelopes with the money in them for the famine suffers. Including the amount subscribed by the saints, the amount collected during the day was ¥7.80. There are two or three who have not yet brought in the donations and the elders have not subscribed yet. All the money will be in by Monday night so that it can be handed to the officers who handle the relief money on Tuesday. Our afternoon meeting was a failure, but by 3:30 we had enough callers to hold a meeting which we did. After the meeting we held a brief sacramental service. In the evening mail and papers from America arrived. I spent the evening reading the news.

Tuesday, 27 February 1906, Tokyo

Snowed & rained all day—Cold Up at 5:45. Swept and dusted the dining room hall and office.

After breakfast I went to the Department of Education to see the Minister of Education or his Private Secretary and propose to them a plan for the raising of money through the school to relieve the famine suffers. The minister was out and his private secretary also but I saw their representation and suggested that all the /pupils in all the/ schools in the nation donate one, two, three, four or five sen to the sufferers, and that it be done unitedly on one day thus bringing the attention of the entire nation to the scheme and making nearly every family in Japan a party to the relief of the distress, and teaching millions of people a lesson in sympathy and sacrifice. I showed the gentleman the little envelopes containing the donations of our Sunday School children and told him how gladly every child responded to the request for help. I and my suggestion were received with courtesy and I was promised that the matter should & would be presented to the Minister of Education and all the officials whose duty it would be to direct such a movement. I then called on the mayor's office and talked to one of the officials—the mayor himself being absent—about the same matter.

From the mayor's office I went to the "Jiji Shinpo's" office and handed the money collected in the S.S. to the editor who is handling contributions for the relief of the distress /the amount donated as ¥36.00/. The editor took special note of the manner in which the money was collected and states that he desired to give it special notice. I returned to headquarters just in time for dinner. In the afternoon and evening I worked some on the Book of Mormon.

Wednesday, 28 February 1906, Tokyo

Wind and heavy rain all day. Up at 7:45. Taught Elder Anderson a lesson in Japanese and with him practiced some songs. At noon we held our prayer meeting the special object of our fast and prayers being that God will bless and heal Sister Mabel R. Richardson from the terrible disease of leprosy from which she has been suffering for sometime. We intend to continue our fast until tomorrow. In the afternoon I worked on the Book of Mormon finishing the translation of Ether before bedtime.

Thursday, 1 March 1906, Tokyo/Yokohama/Tokyo

Clear—slight wind. Up at 7:00. **This morning dawned most beautifully. It was so clear that Fujisan[8] and surrounding mountain ranges seemed near neighbors. We were greatly delighted with such an ideal day as we were still fasting in behalf of our afflicted sister—Sister Richardson—and left Tokyo on the 10:00 a.m. train for Yokohama. I say we; there were four of us—Elders Woodland, Anderson, and Caine and I.**

After a pleasant ride we arrived at the station in Yokohama and went immediately to Sister R.'s house. We found her feeling happy and looking better than I had ever seen her before. Just at twelve o'clock we began a little meeting. The elders in Sendai and those in Sapporo were no doubt holding special prayer meetings for our sister at that hour for so I had instructed them. We sang "Did You Think to Pray." I offered the opening prayer; all kneeling. Prayer was followed by singing, "How Firm a Foundation." Elder Woodland then anointed Sister R. with oil and all four of us—I being mouth—layed our hands upon her sealed the anointing and invoked the healing power of God to rest upon her. We then sang "How Great the Wisdom and the Love" and Elders Caine and Anderson administered the sacrament. I then spoke for a moment or two. We sang "Do what is Right" and Elder Caine dismissed the meeting which lasted about an hour. We visited for about thirty minutes and then left to catch the 2:15 p.m. train for Tokyo. Just before we left however Mrs. Lurs the aunt of sister R. and her daughter came in. We were introduced to them.

On the way to the depot, I called in and thanked Bro. Oyama for his donation to the famine sufferers. We bought a Jiji of Feb. 28th and noticed therein a short complimentary account of the way in which our contribution from the Sunday School for the famine sufferers was collected. After arriving at headquarters, we broke our fast, which had been observed since Tuesday night. Spent the evening doing nothing.

Friday, 2 March 1906, Tokyo

Cloudy—Warmer. Up at 6:45. Ate breakfast. Taught Japanese to Elder Anderson for an hour. Wrapped up some books to send to Sister Richardson. Shaved and got dressed up to go the theatre.

After dinner Elder Caine and I went to the Kabukiza, the largest and best theatre in Tokyo and saw a part of the performance.[9] There were 7 acts billed but with the exception of the second which was a continuation of the first each act was a complete play. We arrived in time to see the second and stayed till the end of the fifth. All we say was exceedingly interesting and acting seemed to be of the very highest class. However the manner of expression on the stage is so different from anything heard in daily life that we being so far away that the sounds did not reach us clearly and there being so much confusion around us we could not understand enough to know the plot. The fact that this performance was given for the benefit of the famine sufferers may have made the general behavior of the audience and officials in charge rather offensive for while the performance was going on people in the body of the house were heard yelling and talking to each other and the waiters who were constantly bringing food to the guests were a decided bother to all but the one they served. The performance lasting from 12:30 to 8:30 p.m. it is necessary that the people eat their meals in the theatre. The result of this is most unpleasant to the foreigners, but no doubt quite stomach-satisfying to the natives—especially if they have enough charge to pay for a "gochiso—."[10]

Although we had tickets for first class seats, there being no reserve—first come first served—we were lodged in the second class circle and in such a position that we could see the tobacco-smoke-laden air which filled the auditorium like a fog. Our close are smelling still from the odor they gathered during our three hours experience. The pit is the third class, the first circle is first class

and the second circle is the second class. This arrangement gives the nobles and monied people to be looked up at by the poor and more lowly but the smoke and odors from the commoners below rises like a cloud from the top of a smoke stack into which the silk-attired, jewel-bedecked, and powerfaced /upper classes/ have to stick their heads simply for the honor, I guess of the higher position. A peculiar feature of the Japanese theatre is that running through the pit to the stage are two passages one on a side by which many of the actors approach the stage. Another feature which disfigures the performance for we foreigners is the freedom with which the stage hands & scenery shifters appear in full view to hand something or take something from the actors or arrange something on the scene. They wear black clothes and black hats & masks to hid their faces but this don't remedy the evil in my sight. The stage of the Kabukiza is very broad and is a revealing one which turns around when the scene changes. No women act upon this stage all the performers are men some of whom made most graceful and beautiful women. The play itself was an ancient one but I understood so little of its plot that I will say nothing of it here.

In the evening I went out to make a call but did not succeed in getting into the house as there was sickness in it. Returned, read a little, and retired.

Sunday, 4 March 1906, Tokyo

Clear—Windy Up at 7:30. The small class in Sunday School this morning was more poorly attended than usual but the Theological Department was very large. Enough came in the afternoon to justify a meeting, following which we had a fast and testimony meeting.

In the evening mail from America arrived and I noticed by the Deseret News that Apostle Merriner W. Merrill died at his home in Richmond, Utah, at 10:00 p.m. Tuesday, February 6th. Apostle Merrill had been ailing for two or three years and his death was not a surprise but a cause for great regret among the saints /for/ whom, as a faithful servant, he had labored well and long. How blessed it is to serve the Lord to the last and die having the esteem, love, and trust of God's people! How sad the condition of those who, after years of service in the church, are dropping away into the nests of the ungodly, breaking their covenants, lifting their voices against the Lord's anointed, and fighting truth with falsehood. Many men are a present turning against the Church. It is a serious time for those who are not living in strick obedience to all the laws of God.

Tuesday, 6 March 1906, Tokyo

Clear—Warmer Up at 6:30. Spent the morning teaching Japanese to Elder Anderson, practising singing, writing my journal, and correcting some of my Book of Mormon translation. In the afternoon I continued to correct the translation. Took a long walk just before supper. After supped did more work on the Book of Mormon, took a bath and retired.

During the forenoon I received a letter from Sister Mabel K. Richardson saying that she has been feeling very much better since we fasted and prayed for and administered to her. The night after our little meeting (see page 131) at her home she says she prayed, as usual, in the Hawaiian language but after getting into bed, she began to pray in a tongue unfamiliar to her. We rejoice to know that she is being thus blessed and ask God to continue His Holy Spirit with her that she may be strong against evil and cleansed every whit from the disease that is upon her.

Wednesday, 14 March 1906, Tokyo

Clear—Warm Up at 7:30. Taught Elder Anderson a lesson in Japanese. Worked a little on the Book of Mormon. At noon we held our usual prayer meeting In the afternoon I took a walk. Worked again a little on the Book of Mormon. Had a long talk with Mr. Chiba. After supper I worked again a little on the Book of Mormon.

Received a letter from Sister Mabel K. Richardson stating that she is improving in health for which blessing I thank the Lord continually.

Thursday, 15 March 1906, Tokyo

Clear—Strong wind with much dust. Up at 7:00. Taught Elder Anderson a lesson in Japanese. Sang a little, then worked on the Book of Mormon. In the afternoon at 5:30 I finished the translation up to the last of the book and after supper I started to look over the translation of the book of Moroni which is the only part I have not corrected. It will be two or three days before I will have this looked over and then the first and original translation will be completed. Today when I wrote the last lines of the translation, I felt a thrill of joy run through me and I did not forget, in my evening prayers, to thank the Lord for the progress on the work which, before finally completed and the translation ready for publication, will require many more months of hard and pains-taking labor. My prayer is that the work of revision and correction will begin soon and be carried on without delay or interruption, as the present translation has been, to the end.

Saturday, 17 March 1906, Tokyo

Up at 6:10. Spent the forenoon cleaning house. In the afternoon I took Elder Caine's place in the Bible Class. We had for the lesson "Baptism for the dead."[11] **After the class, I learned that Hisa Kato (female) desired to be baptized she being convinced that the truth and power of God is with the L.D.S. She is a friend of Sister Nachie's and has been staying with Sister N. for sometime. In the evening I had a long talk with her about the Gospel and what is expected of those who receive baptism, and enter the church and what also they most expect /who take upon them the name of/ L.D.S.** After the class also I had a talk with a young man who is a student and already a member of another Christian church. Took a little exercise before supper. Had a bath before retiring.

Monday, 19 March 1906, Tokyo

Clear—Warm Up at 7:00. Spent part of the morning working on the Book of Mormon. The other part I spent teaching Japanese to Elder Anderson and singing. In the afternoon I went over to Yotsuya and called on Sister Deguchi. After returning I did some sewing which took two or three hours. After supper I had a long talk with Hisa Kato about the gospel. Mail from America arrived just before we went to bed. I received a letter from Bro. Geo. Reynolds in behalf of the First Presidency. Received a letter from mother written from Ocean Park, Cal. mother having gone there for a rest. She is staying with Aunt Eliza on the sea shore. I was happily surprised to received this letter for I am always made glad with news telling of my parents taking a rest.

A letter to Elder Woodland from his sister brought the sad news that his father, who has been suffering with cancer of the liver for some time, died at Salt Lake City Feb. 19th.

Wednesday, 21 March 1906, Tokyo

Clear—Warm Up at 6:45. **Worked on the Book of Mormon for a few minutes finishing the correction up to the last of the Book. It was just 9:30 a.m. when I finished. The work of copying, which is being done by Elder Caine is a little behind due to the fact that he has been working on the tract "Life and Message of Jesus Christ." I began work on the translation Jan. [blank] 1904 and worked when I had a open hour or so; most of my time being occupied with tracting and other missionary labor. For six months the work was carried on in this way and I only got, during that period, eight or nine chapters of I Nephi translated. This process was too slow, so, on the 16th of July the same year, I was appointed to the special duty of making the translation, letting other work be secondary. From that time until this morning I have worked diligently on the translation and through the help of my heavenly Father completed the work today. However, when I began the translation I did not know as much about the language as I do now therefore I am aware of many places in the first of this translation which I can improve myself. I have enjoyed good health since beginning the translation and have had nothing but joy and satisfaction in the work, being worried only about making mistakes. It is my earnest prayer that the way will be opened up for the entire translation to be carefully and well corrected and revised.**

After finishing the translation I had a singing exercise with Elder Anderson. I then wrote a letter to the elders in Sendai and those in Sapporo. At noon we held prayer meeting. In a council after prayer we decided to present each member of the House of Peers with a copy of Goro Takahashi's book "Mormons and Mormonism." Took a walk before supper calling at Sister Rin Ota's to thank her for her donation to the famine relief fund. After supper I went to visit Bro. Kikuchi. He was not home. I had a chat with his wife and two gentlemen who were there. Read a little before going to bed.

Thursday, 22 March 1906, Tokyo

Cloudy—Cold. Up at 5:40. This morning after breakfast I went of to Mr. Yokoyama's (our neighbor's) and inquired about the method of presenting literature to the members of the House of Peers (Mr. Y. being a member of the lower house I thought he would know about such matters). Mr. Kuwana who is living with Mr. Y. volunteered to go with me to the place where the Peers are in session and introduce me to those who could answer my inquiries:

After waiting a long time we met one of the members who referred us to the head of the department of Miscellaneous Affairs, who after looking at the book said that it would be gladly accepted and that it would require 362 copies. As the Parliament disolves on the 27th of the present month the books should be taken to the Hall no the 23rd or 24th where they will be distributed to the members by the proper officers. I secured a ticket for admittance into the Chamber where I watched the Peers in session for about forty five minutes. The arrangement of the chamber is quite different to anything in American but similar to those in the old world. It being the first time for me to see this body and its hall, I enjoyed the experience very much. I went from the House of Peers to the printers and ordered suitable wrappers for the books. I attended to several other matters before returning to headquarters.

Today 5,000 copies (the first edition) of Elder Joseph F. Featherstone's tract, "The Life and Message of Jesus Christ," were delivered. It consists of 61 pages and three pages of advertisements.

In the evening got out the books to be presented to the members of the House of Peers and put the mission stamp in them. The book is the one written over three years ago by Mr. Goro Takahashi entitled "Mormons and Mormonism. It has great strength in allaying prejudice and placing the Latter-day Saints in a good light, hence, its distribution. As the Mission paid thirty sen a copy for them the gift represents (including eight extra copies for the secretaries, etc.) ¥111.00 Before retiring had a long talk with Sister Hakii who spent the night with Sister Nachie.

Friday, 23 March 1906, Tokyo

Clear—Cold. Up at 7:00. Taught Elder Anderson a lesson in Japanese. Practiced singing for thirty minutes. Wrote and read a little. After dinner I went down town to get the wrappers for the books to be presented to the members of the House of Peers. They were not quite ready so I did some other business and called at the printer's again. Upon returning to headquarters began immediately to wrap up the books. This work kept me and the other brethren at headquarters busy until bed time.

Saturday, 24 March 1906, Tokyo

Rainy—Cold Up at 6:45. Ate breakfast and went down to the Ginza and called at the House of Peers to see that the 370 copies of "Mormons and Mormonism" were properly handled and delivered to the officer who has promised to see to their distribution among the members of the body. 362 copies were given for the members 5 copies for the chief secretaries to the house and the President and 3 copies for the use of the officer who will look after the distribution. After dinner I went to Koishikawa to look for a house advertised for rent. I found that it was located in a low dirty part so didn't take the trouble to look at the inside. Returned in time to conduct the singing in the Bible Class. In the evening I read and took a bath.

Mr. Tokoyo called during the Bible Class so I had a talk with him afterwards.

Tuesday, 27 March 1906, Tokyo

Cloudy—Warmer—Rain Up at 5:45. After breakfast I taught Elder Anderson a lesson in Japanese.

We sang a little. I went down town to enquire at the Home Department concerning the laws in relation to foreigners holding land in Japan and also building homes and churches. I learned regarding the land at the Home Department but was advised to see the Tokyo Fucho-[12] regarding the churches etc. I learned that the law forbids a foreigner to hold land anywhere in Japan, but it does not interfere with contracts between natives and foreigners for a lease of land to the latter and places not time limit upon a lease a foreigner may purchase land, if he allows the deed to be made out to native. But if the native proved untrue and claimed the property the foreigner of course holding no deed in his name would not be respected in a law suit. Hence the only means for a foreigner to get and hold land would be by lease from the owners of the same. Leaving the Home Department I went to the bank to make a deposit. From the bank I went to Hongo to see an empty house. Then I called on the Nippon Yusen Kaisha and ordered a state room /reserved/ on the company's steamer leaving Otaru for Yokohama April 18th. Called at the Tokyo Fucho- and learned that a foreigner filing the proper application for a building permit, may on an equal with the Japanese, build and hold a house or church and that a church and all the land in actual use by the church building is exempt from taxes, but any residence in connection with a church building will be taxed. Went back to a "sobaya" and had buckwheat soup for dinner. After calling at the Ginza, returned to headquarters. Wrote a letter to Elder Hedges enclosing ¥65.00 for the expenses at Sendai. **Learned from Elder Caine that Mr. Chiba, a student from the Normal School who has been to headquarters a great deal to learn about the gospel, called and asked to be baptized.** Read the American newspapers, talked with Mr. Homma went to the post office, took a bath and retired.

Tuesday, 3 April 1906, Tokyo/Yokohama/Tokyo

Cloudy—Later, clear—Warm Up at 6:00. Ate breakfast at 7:00 a.m. and went to Shimbashi from where I took the 8:30 train to Yokohama. At Yokohama I spent two hours with Sister Richardson. She looked happy and much brighter spirited than I had ever seen her. She says she is getting strong and feels like the Lord is blessing here. I attended to some odd business at Yokohama and returned to Tokyo on the 2:15 p.m. train. I did some purchasing at the Ginza and got back to headquarters just in time for supper. In the evening I talked with the brethren and took a bath.

Wednesday, 4 April 1906, Tokyo

Clear—Warm. Up at 7:15. Spent part of the morning teaching Elders Woodland and Anderson a lesson in Japanese. Wrote a letter to my sister Ruth. At noon we had prayer meeting in which, as is our custom, we offered prayers concerning those things uppermost in our minds. We discussed some points relative to our work and decided what we could. In the afternoon I went to Aoyama to buy a few things needed for my trip to northern Japan. Packed up my things and after supper talked with the brethren a little before going to bed.

Thursday, 5 April 1906, Tokyo/Sendai

Clear—Cold. Up at 3:15. Washed and prepared for my journey which began at headquarters at 3:45 a.m. rode into Ueno Station were I took the 5:00 a.m. train for Sendai. After a tiresome uninteresting ride I arrived in Sendai at 6:00 p.m. The elders laboring in Sendai came as far as the first station out from Sendai to meet me. They looked well and seemed to be real happy which made our meeting a most pleasant one. After arrival went immediately to the elders' home at #5 Shimaza Koji and found them living in a large well-arranged, new clean Japanese house. The situation of the house, however did not strike me favorably as it is back a long ways from the street with houses in front on each side of the path. The walk from the depot and ride together from Magamachi station had given me time to ask and answer several questions so after looking over the house I joined the elders in a good meal of Japanese food served very well by a pleasant looking middle-aged woman who keeps house for the elders. After supper, two young men came to receive a bible lesson in English. Elder Fairbourn conducted the lesson part of which I listened to. We took a bath and prepared for bed talking, of course, all the time. Not having slept in a Japanese bed for a long time it seemed strange to me to get into the futon. It struck 11:00 p.m. before I went to sleep.

At Shirakawa Station the train stopped for a few minutes during which I took a walking exercise around the station. To the west and not over a block away are the ruins of an old Daimyo's castle the scene of a battle during the Restoration. The castle is now called "Shirakawajo-."

Saturday, 7 April 1906, Sendai

Clear—Warm Up at 7:00. Ate breakfast and spent the morning writing. For about an hour however was with Elder Fairbourn at the eye doctor's. Elder F.'s eyes have, he tells me, been very sore and painful for some time. Yesterday, after the trip to Matsushima they began to pain and by this morning his suffering was great. The doctor said he had chronic cataract of the conjunctiva[13] and should rest his eyes until they are well. He prescribed some medicine and advised the use of colored glasses. After dinner Elder Hedges and I walked around the town calling on Mrs. Hayaski the lady at whose home the elders found good quarters after their arrival in Sendai. Also called on Mrs. Yoshida the mother of our friend Mr. Yoshida in Tokyo who has assisted us in getting out two tracts. In the evening, Elder Hedges conducted an English Bible Class. Six were present. Took a bath and retired.

Sunday, 8 April 1906, Sendai

Clear—Warm Up at 7:00. Ate breakfast. At 10:00 a.m. the elders held their Sabbath School which I attended. After school we held a sacrament meeting in which we read two chapters of the Book of Mormon. In the afternoon I talked with the brethren and read a little to refresh my mind on the subject about which I intended to speak in the night meeting.

Yesterday morning Elder Hedges went around the neighborhood and put up posters announcing a meeting for tonight. This afternoon he went out for a walk and noticed the poster on the front gate all torn. He noticed that another was down also. We wrote another for the front gate but in an hour after we put it up it was half torn off. In the evening we put out a large lantern but while the meeting was going on some rude boys destroyed it.

The meeting was held with six grown people and two children present. I spoke with good freedom for an hour. Today two of the Christian churches have had special meetings and the speakers at those meetings are all famous lecturers from Tokyo. The people of Sendai have read all kinds of slander about the elders here and are therefore quite prejudices against them. This city is perhaps the strongest Christian center in Japan, at least there are more churches here than in any other city of its size and nearly half of the educational work is being directed by Christian missions. This makes the opposition to the "Mormons" rather keen. The elders are not situated in the best part of the town and their house is a long way back from the street so it is not seen by many people. These facts make it rather hard for them to get the people out to their meetings.

Monday, 9 April 1906, Sendai

Rain—Cold. Up at 6:30. Ate breakfast. Read the newspapers and wrote my journal. In the forenoon we held a council meeting in which I made the suggestions I felt necessary and attempted to encourage the elders in their labors. Elder Hedges and Fairbourn expressed themselves regarding the work. In the afternoon I read a little out of the papers from home and talked with the brethren previous to my departure for Sapporo. After supper Mr. Okayoto an old acquaintance from Tokyo called and I had a short conversation with him. We left the house for the station at about 8:20 p.m. I bought a second class ticket to Hakodate but after saying "goodbye" to the brethren and riding a little way, I saw that there would be no chance for me to lie down so I paid a little extra and went into the first class car where I had plenty of room to stretch [-] out. However I did not sleep.

Tuesday, 10 April 1906, Sendai/Aomori/Hakodate

Cloud—Very Cold. Up at 5:00. This morning when I woke up and looked out of the car window, I was surprised to see the train passing through a region of snow drifts that were from one to four feet deep. I washed and brushed up and after my fellow passengers had roused I talked to them about the country until the train arrived at Aomori. I went to the hotel for breakfast and then rode out to the Higo Maru in a fish-tail.[14] At 10:00 a.m. our ship (1400 tons) started for Hakodate. On the way I had the opportunity of explaining the origin of the Church to Mr. Uno a resident of Sapporo. I also had a long talk with Mr. Kintaro Ojima a professor in the Agriculture College at Sapporo. He speaks English well and was well acquainted with the name of Dr. John A Witsoe having been a student of the same teacher in Germany. This man seemed to know considerable about Utah students etc. He asked about polygamy (of course), tithing, the support of the poor, church government, Senator Smoot, and the position of the Church towards Christianity. At a little past four [w] left the large boat and took lodgings for the night in the Katsuda Hotel. I had a good bath, good supper, and a good bed underneath me.

Wednesday, 11 April 1906, Hakodate/Sapporo

Clear—Warm Up at 6:00. Being fast day I left Katsuda Hotel about 6:30 a.m. without eating breakfast and went to the depot where I took the 7:20 a.m. train for Sapporo. On the way I got into conversation with some of the passengers which helped to pass away some of the hours of a long tiresome day. The distance from Hakodate to Sapporo is 180 miles but the road is new and passes through a very mountainous region so the speed is about 14 miles an hour.

The mountains were not unlike those of old Utah and the pine trees growing on the highest mountains are the same as those beautis in the Rockies. Snow still lays in deep drifts and the trees and shrubs, which in summer must be very numerous, are all leafless and death like, thus robbing the scenery along the road of much of the beauty it possesses at other seasons of the year. As I left Hakodate I saw the farmers driving farm wagons pulled by a team just as in America. As I neared the end of my journey I saw the men in the fields working with American plows in American style. The sight did my eyes good.

From the station called Kuromatsunai I sent a telegram to the brethren in Sapporo telling them that I expected to arrive in Sapporo that night at about 9:00 p.m. This left me with only 8 sen in my pocket with which I could buy no more food than enough to aggreviate my stomach so I continued my fast till I reached the elders home where I had a nice bread and milk supper they had prepared for me. I was pleased to be welcomed by two of the native friends of the elders. After talking with both sides of my mouth for an hour or more I took a bath and went to bed.

Thursday, 12 April 1906, Sapporo

Clear—Warm Up at 6:30. After breakfast this morning, we elders had a brief song practice. The morning was spent talking with the brethren. After dinner I took a walk with Elder Stoker and Seely. In the evening an English Bible Class was held; eleven bright looking young men were in attendance and the session was quite interesting. The class continued till 10:00 p.m.

Friday, 13 April 1906, Sapporo

Cloudy—Colder Up at 7:00. After breakfast I wrote my journal and then worked on the Book of Mormon for two hours. In the afternoon I talked with the brethren for sometime and later with Elder Stoker went to the Sapporo Agriculture College and introduced him to Prof. Kintaro Oshima of whom I have written on page 180. Elder Stoker then took me to the Middle School and introduced me to Mr. Zemba a gentleman who was introduced to Bro. Stoker by a letter from Mr. Tokoyo our Tokyo friend. In the evening Mr. Kawanaka one of the two Japanese who met me at the station came and spent the evening. I talked with him for a little while and then left him to continue his conversation with Elder Stoker. I had a chat with the old lady who is keeping house for the elders.

Saturday, 14 April 1906, Sapporo

Clear—Cold Up at 6:10. After breakfast to a walk with Elder Stoker. Returned and worked a little on the Book of Mormon. Did not feel very well all day. Have a cold and my head is heavy. Took a walk in the evening. Read the Bible a little before bathing and going to bed. Today is, Elder Seely's 24th birthday. We had a chicken dinner prepared mostly by Elder Seely himself.

Sunday, 15 April 1906, Sapporo

Clear—Warm Up at 7:00. After breakfast I walked to the post office to send a letter to the office of the Nippon Yusen Kaisha at Otaru telling them that I would call on Wednesday the 18th and pay for the passage which Mr. Mizukawa had promised to secure for me on the [M——] Maru from Otaru to Yokohama. I enjoyed the session of the Sunday School conducted here by Elder Stoker. Here were forty boys and girls present and the School seems to be doing quite good work. About noon I received a letter from Elder Fairbourn telling me that his eyes are worse and giving him great pain. I sent a telegram telling him to go to Tokyo and see a reliable doctor.

In the afternoon at 2:00, Elder Stoker conducted a Bible Class in Japanese. The subject was "Resurrection of Christ." In the evening the special preaching meeting was held at seven o'clock according to the advertisement. An audience of forty mostly men listened with marked attention to the discourses. Elder Stoker made a few remarks by way of introduction. Then I spoke for nearly an hour. Before the meeting the elders knelt in prayer and asked God to assist them in their efforts to teach the gospel to those who assembled and I know that I was upheld in my remarks by the power of the Holy Spirit, so I give all the honor and glory for the success of our meeting to the Lord. This meeting marks the beginning of a series of weekly meetings to be held from now on by the elders in this city. The announcement [that] hereafter a Bible Class conducted in Japanese for young women would be held every Saturday afternoon at 2:30 was received with evident approval. These meetings in connection to the ones thus far conducted will make five each week.

Today I met three Aino[15] who came to the Bible Class. One gave a picture of his family. Since coming here I have seen a number of these aborigines of Japan. They are better looking men physically than the Japanese.

Monday, 16 April 1906, Sapporo

Clear—Warmer Up at 7:15. After breakfast, I talked with Elders Seely and Chadwick till about 10:00 a.m. at which hour I held a priesthood meeting for the purpose of making suggestions about the work here and giving some advice to the elders. Our meeting lasted for an hour and three quarters. I took a walk before dinner. After noon I had a talk with Elder Stoker about what he learned of Hokkaido while making his tour last fall. Elder Stoker and I then went to the home of Mr. Yasutaro Uno, the gentleman I met on the train between Sendai and Aomori and with whom I conversed on the boat between Aomori and Hakodate about the Church. Mr. Uno was not in so I could not introduce Elder Stoker to him. I left him a copy of Mr. Takahashi's "Mormons & Mormonism." We took a walk around the town. In the evening before supper I had a talk with Elder Seely. After supper a young man came who was hunting employment. Of course we turned him down.

Tuesday, 17 April 1906, Sapporo

Rain—Very Cold Up at 6:50. Ate breakfast. During the forenoon I talked with my brethren and at 10:00 a.m. we held a priesthood meeting in which I gave instructions to the elders regarding their work. After dinner I went out to buy a few Aino trinkets. Elder Chadwick accompanied me. Mr. Katogi, nephew of Bro. Thomas Katsunuma was at the mission house when I returned. I had a short talk with him. After supper Elders Stoker and Seely took me to see their friend, Mr. Kawanaka who seems to be earnestly seeking after the truth. I enjoyed my visit very much. Returned to the Mission House and took a bath before retiring. Received a letter from the Nippon Yusen Kaisha at Otaru stating that the "Miike Maru " would be delayed a day. While I was contemplating a trip by steamer to Yokohama this delay caused me to decide to return by rail.

Wednesday, 18 April 1906, Sapporo

Snow—Very Cold Up at 8:00. Being the weekly fast day of the elders, ate no breakfast nor dinner. During the forenoon I wrote a little. Mrs. Kawanaka and her children called and spent the greater part of the morning. At 12:10 we held a prayer meeting. In the later afternoon I gave Elders Seely and Chadwick a lesson in Japanese. Ate supper about 4:30 and at 5:40 left to catch the 6:13 train for Otaru where I expected to make connections with the night train to Hakodate. The train from Sapporo to Otaru was so late that it would not reach Otaru in time to meet the 8:10 train to Hakodate so I returned to the mission house to spend the night. Mr. and Mrs. Kawanaka and their two little children in spite of the inclement weather were at the station to see me off. We invited them to spend the evening with us at /the/ mission house where we tried to make it as pleasant for them as possible.

Thursday, 19 April 1906, Sapporo

Cloudy—Cold. Up at 7:00. Taught Elders Seely and Chadwick a lesson in Japanese. Did a little writing and then we had dinner. Immediately after dinner I went to the depot and took the 1:47 train for Otaru. On the way to the depot I called on Mrs. Kawanaka and said "good-bye." Left the brethren at the depot feeling happy and in the enjoyment of good health. Mr. Kawanaka came and saw me off.

The ride from Sapporo to Otaru was very interesting. Especially from a little town called Zenibako on as the train goes right along the sea shore where I saw the results of the recent herring catch of which the papers in Hokkaido have had so much to say. The sight was the first of its kind I had ever seen and was indeed very interesting. I must of seen 1000000000000000 or more fish. The fishermen—men, women and children were so very busy that the passing of the train didn't attract them from their work. In talking to some of the people about the fish I learned that the greatest part of the enormous catch would have to be used as fertilizer as there was no market for all of the fish in spite of the billions dried and smoked. After arriving in Otaru, I took a walk around the town to pass away the time I had before the departure of the 8:00 p.m. train for Hakodate. I went up on to the top of a hill in the middle of the town and saw the steamship "Miike Maru" on which I intended to go to Yokohama, leave Otaru. I called into a hotel just before dark and had supper. My walk around the town gave me an idea of its character. The people say there are two foreign families in the place. They are the families of Christian ministers. I saw two churches both small. Left Otaru for Hakodate at 8:00 p.m. as a second class passenger. Tried to get a little sleep but there were so many passengers I could not stretch out so I found myself still awake at midnight.

Friday, 20 April 1906, Train

Clear—Cold As I didn't go to bed last night I was already up at the earliest hour a.m. The ride on the train grew more tiresome as the hours passed and I grew steadily sleepier. About 6:00 a.m. I went to sleep and spent the happiest hour of the long ride. At 8:30 the train arrived at Hakodate. I went into the waiting room of the Nippon Yusen Kaisha at the railroad station and had something to eat before going on board the steamer for Aomori. All the 1st and 2nd class tickets had been sold so I had to buy a 3rd class ticket, but I was permitted to be in the 1st class appartment where I did a little talking with some passengers. The greater part of the voyage was very unpleasant because of the rough sea and the severe rocking of the small steamer. Therefore I spent most of the time on deck where the cold wind helped me keep down the breakfast I had eaten. The name of the steamer is "Suruga Maru". It took seven and a half hours to go from Hakodate to Aomori a distance of sixty miles. After arriving at Aomori I sent my chattels to the Kaguya hotel just opposite the railroad station. I went to the station and secured a berth so that I would not have to endure the long hours sitting up between Aomori and Sendai. At Aomori I ate supper at the hotel and boarded the 7:40 p.m. train for Sendai. From the hotel I sent a telegram to Elder Hedges telling him I would arrive in Sendai the next morning and stay with him for two days. It felt good to get my clothes off and get into bed.

The miles traveled up unto midnight I do not know so will write in tomorrow's journal the miles traveled from Sapporo to Sendai.

Saturday, 21 April 1906, Sendai

Clear—Warm Up at 5:00 a.m. Got up and washed myself and had a short conversation with a companion passenger. At 5:55 a.m. arrived at Sendai. Met Elder Hedges at the station and was glad to see him looking and feeling well. I learned from him that my telegram to Elder Fairbourn from Sapporo reached here last Sunday night and Elder F. left for Tokyo the following morning. A letter from Elder F. to Elder Hedges states that he is under the doctor's care. Ate breakfast. Spent the forenoon writing and talking. After dinner took a long walk with Elder Hedges. We went up on top of a hill where we could see the entire city. In the evening I wrote a little. Took a bath and was in bed by 9:30 p.m.

Sunday, 22 April 1906, Sendai

Cloudy—Warm & Close Up at 7:00. Ate breakfast and expected to attend the Sendai Sunday School but was disappointed as not one child came to the school. Read and talked with Elder Hedges until noon. Ate dinner and then went out to call on the richest and largest householder in Sendai. We called on this man's residence to enquire if he had a house suitable to our needs in a good location. The gentleman whom we met told us that none of the master's houses are empty at present. He gave us the address of another landholder on whom we called but were again informed that all the houses are full. We purchased some edibles and returned to the Mission house where Elder H. and I partook of the sacrament and read from the Book of Mormon. After supper we waited again in vain for our audience to preach too. I fear the failure of our meeting was partly due to a failure to advertize it properly. Elder H. & I sang the songs of Zion for an hour and a half and then I prepared my baggage for the trip to Tokyo.

Monday, 23 April 1906, Sendai/Tokyo

Clear—Warm Up at 4:45. Ate breakfast and left Sendai on the 6:10 a.m. train for Tokyo bidding Elder Hedges goodby at the station. The ride from Sendai to Tokyo was very interesting for the train went over the coast line which passes through a beautiful country we passed through over twenty tunnels on the way. Arrived at Ueno station at 3:15 p.m. exactly on time. I went from the station home by electric car. Found all the elders at headquarters enjoying good health and happy. There seemed to be nothing out of the ordinary. Was pained to learn that Sister Nachie had been and is still in the hospital having undergone an operation for piles.[16] She is now very well and will soon leave the hospital as I hear. Spent the evening talking to the brethren and retired about 10:00 p.m.

Upon my return read letters from father, mother, and Prest. Grant which had been waiting for me some days. The news was all good.

Tuesday, 24 April 1906, Tokyo

Clear—Warm and a little oppressive Up at 7:00. Conducted a two hours lesson in Japanese for Elders Fairbourn, Woodland, and Anderson. After the class Elder Fairbourn came to me and stated that he felt it his duty to tell me of some things he has observed about the work in Sendai and the actions of Elder [Hedges] which he feels are not proper. I was closeted with Elder F. during the rest of the morning and a great part of the afternoon. That which Elder F. said was of such a serious nature that I telegraphed for Elder [Hedges] to leave Sendai on tonight's train and instructed Elder Caine to go to Sendai on tonight's train to take charge of the Mission House during Elder [Hedges] absence. Elder Caine left to catch the 9:10 p.m. train. We sang a few songs before going into the bath.

In figuring up today the expenses of my eighteen day trip to Hokkaido I see that R. R. fare amounts to ¥40.85; jinrikisha hire ¥1.10; Telegrams 65 sen; the day's trip to Matsushima for three of us ¥4.88 Miscellaneous expenses including food and lodging on the way and courtesies to the brethren and a few souvenirs ¥12.74. The total of miles traveled is 1,396.

Wednesday, 25 April 1906, Tokyo

Clear—Cooler Up at 6:00 Taught the elders a lesson in Japanese. Before the class was over Elder [Hedges] arrived from Sendai having traveled all night. After the class I did some reading and thinking. At noon our weekly fast and prayer meeting was held. We enjoyed a good spirit much being uttered in the prayers of the brethren that gave me satisfaction.

At 2:00 p.m. Elder [Hedges], Elder Fairbourn, and I went into a room and I began to question Elder [H.] about his actions in Sendai and especially about those actions which Elder F. had observed and considered improper for a missionary to indulge in. This questioning lasted for perhaps an hour and a half or more. Elder F. was asked to retire as Elder [~~Hedges~~] desired to talk to me privately. After Elder F. left the room Elder [~~H.~~], with a terrible struggle and pangs of heart that shook his entire body confessed his sins and pleaded for forgiveness. This confession confirmed all the suspicions that were in my heart and the heart of Elder F concerning what Elder [~~H.~~] had done and revealed much more. In short Elder [~~H.~~] confessed to having fallen from virtue, misused a large amount of money entrusted to him for the famine relief work in Northeastern Japan and for the maintenance of the mission house in Sendai, and in order to keep his wrong doing concealed from his companion and the President of the mission, lied with word and deed.

The pain this confession brought to me, the sadness that I feel over the downfall of my brother cannot be expressed. This is the greatest sorrow in my life. But, having seen the agony and terrible remorse of my brother in his confession and cries for forgiveness I feel convinced that he has opened his heart and he after a terrible struggle of nearly an hour succeeded in controlling his feelings and thought sufficiently to listen to what I had to advise him and in humility he has promised that, with the help of His Heavenly Father, he will not repeat such grave offences and devote his remaining life to the effort of showing to his relatives, friends, and his God that his repentance is sincere. Brothers Woodland, Anderson and Fairbourn were asked to come in and Elder [~~H.~~] confessed to them and asked their forgiveness. This the elders freely gave and in speaking before my brethren the Spirit of God came upon me to the extent that /I/ shook from head to feet. I promised the mercies of God upon my fallen brother if he would go home, and bearing up under the sorrow and shame that he must feel in meeting his mother, father, brother, relatives, and friends, carry out his promise to keep the laws of God hereafter. We all shed tears freely.

At night I wrote and posted a letter to Elder Caine telling him to gather up Elder [~~H.~~] things, discharge the cook and get someone to watch the house for a week or ten days and then come to Tokyo as quickly as possible. Elder [~~H.~~] slept with me

Thursday, 26 April 1906, Tokyo

Cloudy—Warm—Dusty. Up at 6:00. Swept and dusted the dining room, hall and office. After breakfast, I went down town to see about steamers leaving for America. Found that the N. Y. K. Co's S. S. "Tango Maru" sails from Yokohama May 1st at 2:00 p.m. The Great Northern R. R. Co's steamer "Dakota" sails from the same port on the afternoon of May 8th I returned to headquarters and held a council with my brethren (Elders Woodland, Anderson and Fairbourn) and we decided to send Elder [~~Hedges~~] home on the first steamer "Tango Maru" and it being the opinion of all that Elder [~~H.~~] should not be permitted to go home alone and be left to brood on the way over his condition and the ordeal he will have to go through upon arriving home, [~~so~~] I appointed Elder Daniel P. Woodland to accompany Bro. [~~Hedges~~]. The loss of Elder W. is great to us as he has been here nearly a year and is getting along very well in the language. The duty assigned to him to companion Bro. [~~H.~~] home is one which he has accepted without an objection and with faith in the outcome, but parting with the work here is almost heartbreaking I know.

I will release Elder Woodland and leave the question of his returning to Japan to continue his mission in the hands of the First Presidency. After dinner I went down town to arrange for the passage on the "Tango Maru." I called at the shirt store and ordered some shirts for the brethren in Sapporo. Returned to headquarters and wrote about Elder [~~H.'s~~] release & also the return of Elder Woodland to the First Presidency. I wrote to Elder [~~H.'s~~] parents. I dropped a short note to Sister Woodland and sent a request to Bro. W. C. Spence to have him arrange the passage for the brethren from Portland to Salt Lake City. Went to the Post office to mail the letters which go by an Empress steamer thus reaching Salt Lake City about six or seven days ahead of the brethren.

Friday, 27 April 1906, Tokyo

Cloudy—Sprinkling rain—Cooler Up at 6:30. After breakfast I went to Sister Nami Hakii's home to give her an Aino tray I brought from Hokkaido and interpret two letters to her from the Grant family. I requested her to teach the children's class in Sunday School next Sunday. She gave me two bowls of soba. In the afternoon I went to the barber shop. I called on Sister Ota and was greatly surprised to learn of the death of her baby. I invited her to come to the house and view the Military Review /next Monday/ from our upstairs windows. I sent a telegram to Elder Caine. I also had a short conversation with the brethren concerning Elder Hedge's case. In the evening I wrote up the Mission Journal before retiring.

Sunday, 29 April 1906, Tokyo

Clear—Slight wind Terrible dust Up at 6:00. Swept and dusted the downstairs Elder Caine returned from Sendai before 9:00 a.m. He being tired and desiring to have a talk with Elder [~~Hedges~~] before the meeting, I conducted his Sunday School class and Sister Nami Hakii took my place in the Primary Department. After Sunday School the Elders (Daniel P. Woodland, [~~Sanford Hedges~~], James Anderson, Fred A. Caine and Wm R. Fairbourn) met to try Elder [~~Hedges~~] for his fellowship in the Church. The meeting opened with singing. Prayer was offered. I then stated the purpose of the meeting and requested Elder [~~Hedges~~] to give a complete recital of his downfall with the causes leading up to the same. He did so. I then spoke giving my feelings.

All the other elders spoke in turn then Elder [~~H.~~] was asked if he had anything to say. He spoke for two or three minutes stating that he wanted the brethren to do just as the spirit prompted them and allow not their affection for him to influence their vote. He said he thanked God he had not lost the testimony of the Gospel even if he had lost all else and he declared that his tongue and lips should never utter slander against us and the church. He repeated his desire to rectify his mistake and regain the position he was about to lose. On the motion of Elder D. P. Woodland which was seconded by Elder James Anderson to the effect that Elder [~~H.~~] be excommunicated from the Church of Jesus Christ of Latter-day Saints all the elders except the one receiving trial arose and united approved the motion by lifting their right hands.

At 2:00 p.m. a meeting was held with one saint and five visitors present. Elder Caine and I did the speaking. At about 4:00 p.m. Sacrament Meeting was held in which I explained to the two sisters present the reason for Bro. [~~Hedges'~~] sudden return and why Elder Woodland would accompany him.

Monday, 30 April 1906, Tokyo

Clear—Slight wind with terrible dust. Up at 4:45. Today being the great military review which had been talked of for two or three months and for which they have been preparing the parade grounds for the last month, I got up early to get swept and dusted up before our saints and acquaintances came to view the event from our up stairs windows. In spite of the fact that I got up before five o'clock and Elder Woodland was also up helping, our neighbors (Yokoyama family) came over. We had promised this family that we could entertain nine of them but they keep coming till there was nearly nineteen of them among the number being part of the family of Count Makino Koji a member of the House of Peers. Mr. Yokoyama is a member of the Lower House. Only one of the saints, Sister Hakii, was present. Mrs. Katagiri and her three children, Mr. Chiba and a relative, and some of the people around the house viewed the passing of the Emperor around the troops. In all there were about 36,000 soldiers & officers who took part in the parade. We provided fruit, cakes, and candy for our guests.

In the little crowd at our home were people with titles, people without titles but in high positions in the government and people of the ordinary walks of life and some of the servant class. I looked at them. I tried to study them. I listened to what they talked about. I watched their actions and I decided that, so far as one could judge by the few before me, title and position was entirely outclassed by the people of the humbler environments so far as physical appearance and deportment are concerned. I couldn't help up think of the fact that comparatively few of the nobles & titled accepted the gospel; the true word of God seems adapted to the humble, "The poor have the gospel preached to them" and they accept it. As I looked on our guests I felt in my heart "The Lord certainly knew what he was doing and what he is now doing in choosing his people from among the meek and lowly in life. Praise be unto his name." By noon our guest had all returned. I devoted the afternoon and evening to writing letters and preparing statements of the money misappropriated by Sanford W. Hedges. Had a short talk with Elder Woodland and retired about midnight.

Tuesday, 1 May 1906, Tokyo/Yokohama/Tokyo

Cloudy—Cool Up at 6:00—After breakfast went down to the bank and got enough money to pay for Bros. [Hedges] and Woodlands' tickets to Portland. I took the 10:00 a.m. train for Yokohama. The other brethren went to Yokohama on the 9:30 a.m. train. Arriving at Yokohama, I went immediately to the Nippon Yusen Kwaisha office and secured the tickets. From there I went directly to the steamer "Tango Maru" and gave the brethren their tickets. I looked through the ship. It is a beauty—the best in the N. Y. K's. service and everything being new made one feel like travel. Gave the brethren some parting advice, a good hand shake and "God bless you" before getting of the ship. We watched the steamer for about forty minutes. Sister Hakii went from Tokyo to Yokohama to see them off. Sister Nachie and some of our friends went as far as Shimbashi to bid them farewell. Bro. Oyama called at the steamer to give a last hand shake.

After the departure of the steamer I took Sister Hakii up to met Sister Richardson but she was not home. Sister Haku went to call on a Yokohama friend. I went immediately to the station where I met the brethren and returned with them to Tokyo. A good supper awaited us at headquarters. I felt tired and worn out and very thankful that the eventful week had closed and the brethren safely departed with every prospect for a pleasant and successful voyage. May the blessings of heaven be upon [Hedges] to strengthen him for all that awaits him upon his arrival home. May the Lord be with Elder Woodland to help him in his mission as companion, comforter, and counselor to Bro. [Hedges].

Thursday, 3 May 1906, Tokyo

Cool—Rained all day Up at 6:45. Before I got out of bed I read a letter from mother who was still in Ocean Park, Cal. and a card from Bro. Horace S. Ensign. Mother was well, Bro. Ensign wrote as though he was. Did some reading and a little writing. In the afternoon the papers came giving an account of the Annual Conference at Salt Lake City. Was greatly surprised to read of the resignation of Apostles John W. Taylor and Matthias F. Cowley from the Quorum of Apostles. The resignation of these men were handed into their quorum and accepted Oct. 28th 1905 at which time also the resignations were reported to the First Presidency. This announcement to the saints assembled in the large Tabernacle Sunday afternoon was a great surprise to them. Prest. Lyman of the Quorum of Apostles made the announcement and gave the reason that they were out of harmony with their brethren of the quorum. Their resignation made three vacancies in the quorum as Apostle M. W. Merrill had died on Feb. 6th. George Franklin Richards, son of the late Apostle Franklin D. Richards and First Counselor in the Tooele Stake Presidency, Orson F. Whitney whom in my younger days I called "Uncle Orson," and whom I know well as a strong defender and expounder of the faith, and David O. McKay, principal of the Weber Stake Academy were chosen and sustained as apostles to fill the vacancies. Bro. Charles H. Hart, of Logan was chosen to fill the vacancy in the Presiding Quorum of Seventy caused by the death of Christian D. Fjeldsted on Dec. 23rd 1905.

Later in the afternoon I wrote a letter to Elder John L. Chadwick, calling him to labor in Sendai with Elder Wm R. Fairbourn. In the evening, after supper, I had a long talk with Mrs. Hisa Kato regarding the resurrection and final judgment.

Saturday, 5 May 1906, Tokyo

Clear—Cooler Up at 7:00. Ate breakfast. Spent the day writing letters. Wrote to Horace S. Ensign, Rulon S. Wells, and Mr. and Mrs. [Hedges]. Before supper I went down town to attend to some business. As I started late, did not get back till after 7:00 p.m.

About 11:00 a.m. Mr. Shintaro Kato the husband of Mrs. Hisa Kato of whom I have written a time or two in this journal (See Book H. page [blank]) came to see his wife—Mrs. Kato has been living with Sister Nachie for two or three months at headquarters, and over a month ago requested us to baptize her. We told her to continue her investigation longer. It seems that she has already told the church to which she has belonged (Church of England) that she is going to join this church and has everything in readiness to be baptized. The other night in talking with her I told her that we could not baptize her without the consent of her husband, so she wrote for him to come here. Today I told him of his wife's request to be baptized and gave him an idea of what would be expected of her after she enters the Church. He stated that he has no objections whatever to her changing her faith and when she understands the teachings sufficiently to baptize her. Mr. Kato is also a member of the Church of England but had not been doing much at religion lately.

It may seem strange that he and his wife are not living together, but the explaination is this. In Japan it is a very common thing for the man and the woman to separate when the man can't make enough to support both himself and wife. This separation is not a breaking of the marriage agreement but simply a means of getting a living by each rustling for him and herself. When the man, or, perhaps the woman, gets in a position to again support the two they live together again. Mr. Kato has had hard luck and they are rustling for themselves. Another feature of this custom is, if the husband has a wife of a fairly well-to-do family and ill luck hits him he may send his wife back to her parents while he gets in a position to support her again. The man seems to have the best of the bargain and must certainly find this custom a very convenient one!

Monday, 7 May 1906, Tokyo

Clear—Cold Up at 6:40. Taught Elder Anderson a lesson in Japanese. Spent most of the day looking over the Book of Mormon to take note of the points about which I intend to write to the First Presidency. I began this work while I was in Sapporo and finished today so I will write the letter ere long. Before supper I took a walk to Yotsuya street and also went to Aoyama street before returning to headquarters. After supper I talked with Mrs. Hisa Kato about the gospel. I asked her several questions in an endeavor to find out how much she knows about the Church and the teachings we are promulgating.

Tuesday, 8 May 1906, Tokyo

Cloudy—Cool Up at 6:30. After breakfast I taught Elder Anderson a lesson in Japanese. During the rest of the morning and until 3:30 in the afternoon I worked on the revision and correction of my Book of Mormon translation. This is the beginning of this great work and I humbly pray that the Spirit of the Lord will be given to me in great abundance that the work of correcting the translation may be faithfully, spiritedly and well done. Before supper helped clean a carpet and pump the bath water. This gave me good exercise. After supper I wrote a little more to an article I am preparing about the Japanese children for the Juvenile Instructor. Took a bath and retired.

Today received a letter from Elder Fairbourn reporting him in good health.

Saturday, 12 May 1906, Tokyo

Clear—Warm. Up at 6:30. Wrote letters to the elders in the field. Mr. Tsukakoshi called. I had a pleasant talk with him. Met a man today who professes to be seeking after the truth in religion, but after listening to him for some time I concluded that if he is not a hypocrite he has good purposes. The odds, in my estimation, are against his sincerity.

After dinner **I got ready and went down to the bank and then to Mr. Hirai's. I had a very pleasant visit with Mr. Hirai. I talked with him for about two hours. Mr. Hirai having written me that he would not be able to correct the translation of "In the Lineage of the Gods," I took it to Mr. Hirai today and asked him to correct it and charge whatever he wanted for his time and labor. He refused to make the criticisms with the understanding that he would afterwards be compensated materially. He would gladly do it if he could take his time. I left the translation in his hand.** In the evening after eating supper, I did some mending. Took a bath and retired.

Today Elder Caine finished copying into Japanese characters my translation of the Book of Mormon, which I made in Romaji.

Tuesday, 15 May 1906, Tokyo

Clear—warm Up at 6:00. Ate breakfast taught Elder Anderson a lesson in Japanese. Sent a telegram to Sendai concerning a P.O. Order sent to the elders on Sunday. **Mail from America having arrived yesterday, we received a large bundle of papers today. All the details of the terrible earthquake and fire at San Francisco were reported. I spent almost the entire day reading the accounts given. At the time of the disaster there were 122 saints and elders in San Francisco.[17] This does not include Utah people who were there for pleasure, business and study. Not one of the saints or elders received a scratch although there were, many of them, in buildings terribly shattered. Nearly all of the Utah people in the earthquake district had hair lifting experiences but up till the 27th, nine days after the shock, no Utahn had been found among the dead or wounded. The San Francisco saints who were renting lost nearly all they had, but those who owned their homes are unharmed. The headquarters of the California Mission was blown up by dynamite to prevent the spread of the flames, but not until all the Mission books, records and a majority of the furniture were moved to a safe place. The protection of the Latter-day Saints from bodily harm was in some instances miraculous and shows the special interposition of God in behalf of his people. The relief work seemed to be carried on with remarkable system and speed. Utah being the nearest state on the East (Nevada being unable to do much) where supplies and support for the homeless, foodless, and clothesless thousands /should come from/ naturally stood in a position to show her ability and charity. According to the papers Utah was making a remarkable record in the work of relief. The Church immediately subscribed $10,000 and the saints through the various organizations were appealed to and liberally, cheerfully and quickly responded.**

Just before supper, I walked to the Aoyama post office and took a little exercise playing ball.

Friday, 18 May 1906, Tokyo

Clear—Warm Up at 6:30. Ate breakfast. Taught Elder Anderson a lesson in Japanese. Elder Caine and I read the translation of the Book of Mormon towards dinner time. In the afternoon I prepared an announcement for our meetings the hours of which will be changed June 3rd because of the hot weather. I looked over some old "Juvenile Instructors" in search of Christmas songs for children. We want to have some new songs for Christmas this year and as we will have to send them to America to have the music written we are looking them up early. Spent an hour or more before supper playing ball for exercise. After supper, I walked up to Aoyama and before returning, I called on Sister Ota, but couldn't get to talk with her. Called on old lady Kamiyama and said "yoroshiku"[18] at the door. Did just a little on the Book of Mormon before going to bed.

Thursday, 24 May 1906, Tokyo

Clear—Cool Up at 6:45. Ate breakfast. Received a letter from Sister Mabel K. Richardson saying she was sick at Yokohama and would like to have the elders go and administer to her. I wrote a card saying two brethren would visit her tomorrow. After giving Elder Anderson a lesson in Japanese I went downtown. I called at the Tukoku Insatsu Kwaisha[19] and ordered a thousand cards announcing the hours of our meetings etc. during the summer. I called at the tailor's to try on a suit I am having made. I went as far a Kaineya's and ordered some olive oil and a bottle of syrup. I went to the post office and to the bank. Wrote letters to Elders Stoker and Seely and to Elders Chadwick and Fairbourn. Did a very little on the Book of Mormon translation.

Wednesday, 30 May 1906, Tokyo

Clear—Cloudy—Cooler Up at 6:30. **Spent an hour after getting up teaching Elder Anderson Japanese. Spent the next hour with Elder Caine reading the translation of the Book of Mormon. This reading brought us up to the end of the book. Elder Caine has been very careful in his work of copying and in but a very few places did he omit any of my manuscript.** The next hour I spent working on the correction of the translation. At noon we held our regular weekly fast and prayer meeting.

I spoke to my companions taking for my text Ether 12: 23–27. In the afternoon I continued to work on the Book of Mormon. Took a walk before supper. Today the jinrikisha men have been beating carpets for us. After supper I worked again on the Book of Mormon. This afternoon Elders Caine and Anderson distributed printed announcements of our meetings.

Wednesday, 6 June 1906, Tokyo
Clear—Warm Up at 6:00. Did a little more carpet laying. Went to Yotsuya and bought some things needed in the childrens party tomorrow. At noon we held prayer meeting. In this discussion afterwards we came to a conclusion on many points. **Among other things, I appointed Elder Caine to look over the translation after I revise it. He will be expected to read it carefully and make any suggestions he desires. I will afterwards hear his suggestions and consider them.** After meeting I went down town and spent half a day going here and there to attend to mission house needs. Returned about 7:00 p.m. Ate supper. Wrote a letter to mother. Took a bath.

Thursday, 7 June 1906, Tokyo
Clear—Hot Up at 6:30. Spent the morning moving some of our furniture back to where it was before repairs on the house began. After dinner, I walked over to Yotsuya street to buy a few things for the children's party announced to begin at 4:00 p.m. It was 4:30 o'clock when the party began. We sang "Love at Home" I offered prayer and then we began the games. The first was to guess the number of beans in a jar. The one guessing the closest received as a prize the jar of beans in which twenty sen was put. Uesugi Yae San got the prize guessing within five of the exact number. We then had the children try to put a tail on the donkey blindfolded. A fan was the prize for the girl getting the tail nearest and a look sack was the prize for the boys. Miss Shika Sakazaki and Master [blank] were the winners. We then put a ring on a string and had the children sit in a circle and slide the ring around while one in the centre of the circle tried to locate it and catch the person with it. After this we gave the children strawberries and cake. The last game was the "fishpond." This was great sport and delighted the children more than anything else. We had provided live fish, seaweed, lobsters, devil fish etc and as each child pulled out his catch all the others laughed heartily. The children were given what they caught. After this game, I offered prayer and the children returned so as to get home before dark. The party lasted just two hours and twenty minutes. After the children returned we ate supper and I beat a mattress and set up a bed in my room. It was eleven o'clock before I got to bed.
Today the corrected translation of "In the Lineage of the Gods" was received from Mr. Hirai. Just glancing over the pages, I see a great deal of red ink and judge that Mr. Hirai has given it his best and careful consideration.

Saturday, 9 June 1906, Tokyo
Cloudy—Cool Up at 6:15. Spent the forenoon looking over Mr. Hirai's criticisms of the translation of "In the Lineage of the Gods." Before the Bible Class at 4:00 p.m. I had finished reviewing the criticisms. I attended the Bible Class taking charge of the singing. Bro. Oyama called just before the class. After the class I talked with him till supper time and then till about 9:00 p.m. He had received a letter from Bro. Horace S. Ensign at Salt Lake in which Bro. E. invites Bro. O. to make his home with him "if he ever goes to America and gets as far as Salt Lake City." Bro. Oyama had misunderstood this letter thinking it was an invitation to go immediately to Salt Lake City. I explained the meaning of the letter and advised him not to be in a hurry to leave Japan but to continue his work here till he can make enough money to pay his fare and get through without trouble. I talked with him about his failure to pay his tithing and do his duties in the church. He confessed his neglect and promised to do his duty to the Church and his God.

Sunday, 10 June 1906, Tokyo
Rain—Cool Up at 7:00. Ate breakfast. The Sunday School held at 9:00 a.m. was not so large as a

week ago but good interest was shown in the lessons presented. At 11:00 a.m. we held sacrament meeting. In the afternoon I had a conversation with Mr. Tokada. I read in the presense of Elders Caine and Anderson the minutes of the second day of the general conference of the church held at Salt Lake City April 6, 7, 8. Took a walk with Elder Caine. Ate supper at 5:00 and prepared to hold our evening meeting. Only one came. I engaged this lone listener in conversation. It seems almost impossible to get the people out to our preaching meetings. Naturally it is very discouraging to see the indifference of the people, but we have faith in the future even if we have to move somewhere else to find audiences.

Monday, 11 June 1906, Tokyo

Clear but cool Up at 6:15. Spent the whole day going over the translation of "In the Lineage of the Gods" and giving careful thought to all the criticisms made by Mr. Hirai. Many of his corrections did not suit me. Before supper I called on the home of Mr. Azuma a poor man whose children come to our Sunday School. He was not home. After supper he came to headquarters and I gave him the job of writing the translation as corrected by Mr. Hirai and myself. The corrections are so numerous that this rewriting is necessary before sending the manuscript to the printers. I talked with Mr. Azuma till prayer time. Had prayer and retired. This morning I received a letter from home in which mother told of the safe arrival of Elder Woodland and Sanford W. Hedges. The news of their safe arrival is very gratifying for I realize that Sanford has had a great struggle against his feelings and the temptations of evil and there was considerable fear that he would not reach home in safety without [✲] special protection from above for which I have most earnestly prayed.

Thursday, 14 June 1906, Tokyo

Cloudy—Slight rain—Cool Up at 6:30. Ate breakfast. Spent the morning writing a letter to Sister Justus B. Seely, wife of one of the elders in this field, and in correcting some of the Book of Mormon translation. After dinner, I walked up to the Aoyama post office. I spent the greater part of the afternoon working on the correction of the Book of Mormon translation. Took a short walk before supper.

After eating I started to read more of the conference proceedings but Mr. Azuma came in with the copy of the corrected translation of "In the Lineage of the Gods," and I talked with him about it. This kept me busy till bed time. It will be seen by referring to page 69 of this journal that I gave the corrected manuscript translation to Mr. Azuma last Monday night and he copied it as corrected and brought it this evening according to promise. There is an incident connected with his copying this translation worthy of mention here. Mr. Azuma's oldest child, a daughter of about 21 years, has suffered with a severe mental disease since last November. She talks all the time when awake and is given to sudden attempts to go he and there. Her insanity is a very pitiable one. The day following the night I gave the manuscript into Mr. Azuma's hands, this girl seizing upon an opportune moment went to the cupboard where the manuscript was put and was discovered with it by her mother. The mother realizing the importance of the manuscript began immediately to try to recover it from the girl. The girl refused to give it up and a lady from a neighboring house came in and finally after a struggle the manuscript was taken from the girl, but it was torn into small pieces and all crumpled up in the scuffle. After a long tedious effort Mr. Azuma succeeded in pasting the torn bits together and brought the new copy with the delapodated one this evening. The fact that the manuscript was saved and a good copy secured is a cause for rejoicing to me. It seems that this demented girl acted entirely under the influence of the evil one in her effort to destroy the translation for she did not see the translation put in the cupboard and she had never attempted to destroy anything of this kind before although her father is constantly writing and translating.

Saturday, 16 June 1906, Tokyo

Clear—Warm Up at 6:00. Ate breakfast. After breakfast, I went to Mr. Hirai's and spent the whole forenoon with him. I asked him all the questions I had on the translation of "In the Lineage of the Gods." Being satisfied with the suggestions made I took the translation to the Teikoku Ensatsu Kwaisha and arranged for the publication of the first edition of 5000 copies. On the way home I purchased a five pound box of sweet mints to send to Mr. Hirai and family as an expression of thanks for his kindness. The Bible Class which should have been held today was not held because only one young man was here on time and one other came about 45 minutes late. I engaged the latter, Mr. Chiba in conversation. Ate supper. Prepared a Sunday School lesson and took a bath before retiring.

Sunday, 17 June 1906, Tokyo

Clear—Very warm Up at 6:15. Ate breakfast. This morning our Sunday School convened promptly at 9:00 o'clock and there were so many children present that the seating capacity of our large room was greatly tested. At 11:00 a.m. we had sacrament meeting. In the afternoon we read the rest of the conference minutes.[20] We have greatly enjoyed the spirit of the discourses and feel blessed and strengthened by the excellent reports, counsel and warnings given by the speakers. I took a walk before supper. The evening meeting which should begin at 7:30 did not get started till 8:00 o'clock and then we only had four present besides the little girl who lives with Sister Nachie at headquarters. Last Sunday only one came. Since then Elders Caine and Anderson have been tracting nearly every day in this district. Their weeks labor brought out three. Another week's work may bring out two or three more.

Thursday, 21 June 1906, Tokyo

Clear—Cool Up at 6:30. After breakfast, I went down town to inquire for a real estate agency in the hope of finding through such a company a suitable house for headquarters in a good part of Tokyo. I found the Shintakusha and left a request for them to look up a suitable house which they promised to do. I called at the principal newspaper offices to find if they could give me any information about reliable agencies holding houses for rent. It seems that besides the one I mention above that there are no respectable companies in this great metropolis! I returned to headquarters. Read a newspaper from home. In it was the account of the death of Brother John A Evans who was the president of the 8th Quorum of Elders when I was a member of the quorum. After dinner, I wrote a letter to Elders Chadwick and Fairbourn. I had a short chat with a member of the Methodist church, who is a poor excuse for a Christian. Spent the rest of the day and evening working on the Book of Mormon.

Friday, 22 June 1906, Tokyo

Rain—Cold Up at 6:00. After breakfast Elder Caine and I read over the second proof sheets of "In the Lineage of the Gods." I took them back to the printers and told them after making the corrections indicated to go ahead and print the first edition of 5000 copies as agreed. I attended to other business before returning. After dinner I worked on the Book of Mormon and wrote a letter to the Takiwasha enclosing a check in payment of their bill against us for a dozen and a half books purchased for the Sunday School children. I made some changes in the books so that the children would not learn false doctrine when they read them.

Sunday, 24 June 1906, Tokyo

Rain—Cold Up at 6:15. Ate breakfast. At 9:00 a.m. our Sunday School began. The attendance was not so large today as it was a week ago, due, no doubt, to the fact that the weather was not favorable. At 11:00 a.m. we held our sacrament meeting. Only one saint and three missionaries present. In the afternoon I read papers & magazines from America.

Received today a letter from Bro. [Hedges] and /one from/ Elder Woodland. The former wrote that after meeting President Smith in company with his father and Uncle Rulon S. Wells that President Smith gave Bro. Wells authority to act in [Hedges']case and rebaptize him. After the rebaptism, he was confirmed and the authority of the priesthood which he held before his excommunication was again conferred upon him so I understand from his letter although the account of events was very brief. Bro. Woodland writes that after a talk with President Smith he was told that our action in [Hedges'] case was approved by the Presidency. This is good news altho I am anxiously waiting to hear directly from the First Presidency.

I received a letter from Prest. Samuel E. Woolley of the Hawaiian Mission. He gave some interesting information about Bro. Thomas Katsunuma who is in Honolulu. He enclosed a sealed letter to Sister Richardson which I have already forwarded to her. I read considerable from Orson Spencer's works. At 7:40 p.m. we began our evening meeting with 8 Japanese in attendance. After meeting I engaged a young man in conversation. Today Mr. Chiba called. He had kindly secured the criticism of two of his teachers in the Normal School on five songs which we have had translated and arranged recently. The purpose for preparing these songs is to teach them to the Sunday School children for the coming Christmas. We intend to send them to Bro. Horace S. Ensign at Salt Lake and have his make the music for them as soon as possible.

Tuesday, 26 June 1906, Tokyo

Clear—Hot. Up at 6:00. Spent the morning writing letters and doing several odd jobs. **Today the first edition (5,000 copies) of the Japanese translation of Dr. Talmage's "In the Lineage of the Gods" was delivered at headquarters. It is a tract of 26 pages in all. The body of the tract consists of only 17 pages but the inspiring hymn /"O My Father"/ which has a fitting connection to the theme is added and then the "Articles of Faith" with scriptural references, a page for the advertizement of church literature and one for meeting announcements** and invitations have been placed in the tract. The appearance of the tract is good and entirely satisfactory. This afternoon I prepared a box of tracts to be sent to the elders in Sapporo. I wrapped up two hundred of the new tracts and sent them by mail to the elders in Sendai. Received a letter today from Elders Chadwick and Fairbourn. They are well and progressing in Japanese. Worked on the Book of Mormon for about two and a half hours.

Thursday, 28 June 1906, Tokyo

Clear—Hot Up at 6:30. Spent the entire day working on the revision of the Book of Mormon translation. While we were eating breakfast a woman came wanting to know if we could teach her English and she stated that she desired to study Christianity and become a Christian. No doubt she does if it will help her in her English. There are too many such students of Christianity. But few ever amount to anything. After supper I took a walk.

Saturday, 30 June 1906, Tokyo

Rain—Warm. Up at 7:30. Spent the forenoon working on the Book of Mormon. In the afternoon I shaved, picked some fruit off from a tree in the garden. Then I attended the Bible Class. After class I had a talk with Sister Nachie about her work, calling her attention to some of her unclean ways. This made her rebel and she wanted to quit but I had a talk with her which perhaps will do her some good. After supper, I prepared the S. S. Primary Class roll for the third quarter and looked up a lesson to teach to the children. Took a bath and retired.

Wednesday, 4 July 1906, Tokyo

Clear—Hot Up at 6:00. The first thing I did this morning was to put the American flag on a pole which I tied to the topmost branch of a tall tree in front of headquarters in our garden. This tree has served as our flag mast for three years. I then draped the American and Japanese flag over the entrance. We froze some ice cream. I read the Declaration of Independence and did several odd jobs during the forenoon. At 12:00 n. we met in the prayer room and had our prayer and council meeting. In the afternoon Elders Caine and Anderson went down town to see some Russian guns and to attend to some business. I wrote letters to the elders in Sendai, Sanford W. Hedges at Salt Lake, and Daniel P. Woodland at Oneida, Idaho. I looked up some old "Contributors"[21] and read two stories about the Fourth. Received a letter from Sendai and one from Sapporo during the day. Ate supper at 6:30. We had ice cream, chocolate cake, stewed prunes, and plain cake in addition to a native meal. Before going to bed I read an article on "America," wrote a letter to Elders Stoker & Seely and took down "Old Glory." Mr. Arai called with his two children just after supper. He invited us to go and see a fencing contest at the Yotsuya Police Station next Monday.

Monday, 9 July 1906, Tokyo

Clear—Cool Up at 6:10. Ate breakfast. Spent the morning doing odd jobs and working a little on the Book of Mormon. After dinner, I did some sewing. About 3:00 p.m. I suddenly remembered that Mr. Arai had invited us to see a fencing match at the Yotsuya police station today. Elder Anderson whom I intended should go had already gone out tracting and although I had not thought of going myself Elder Caine and I went and enjoyed looking at the exhibition for about an hour. The fencing art in Japan is vastly different to the French art. It is however equally as difficult as the latter but far more uncouth. It being the first time I had ever viewed a fencing match, I enjoyed it very much. After returning and eating supper, I worked again on the Book of Mormon till bedtime. Mr. Mano came this evening to tell us good-bye before leaving for his home to spend the holidays.

Tuesday, 10 July 1906, Tokyo

Cloudy—Cool breeze Up at 6:45. Ate breakfast. Spent the morning working on the Book of Mormon. Also worked on this book in the afternoon. But immediately after dinner, I read an article in the "Elders' Journal,"[22] then had a singing practice with Elder Anderson for about forty five minutes. Before supper I took some exercise. A letter came to me from Elder Woodland bearing the news that he had been informed by the First Presidency that he would be expected to return to Japan just as soon as they could find some more young men to accompany him. After eating supper I took a walk. I called on Sister Rin Ota. Sister Hakii called this evening and paid her tithing. She is a good girl.

Saturday, 14 July 1906, Tokyo

Rain—Oppressively hot. Up at 6:15. Immediately after breakfast I went down to the Ginza then to the Hakubunkwan Printing Co. in Koishikawa. This printing company is printing 10,000 copies of our tract "Batsu Jitsu Seito" the second edition. On the way home I just dropped in on Mr. Hirai and said "Yoroshiku" to him and his family. **On the electric car between Ushigama and Shinonomachi I met Rev. J. P. Whitney who on hearing my confession as a "Mormon" drew a deep sigh and said "How in the world could you be connected with such a church?" I replied that the first reason was "Because I was born a "Mormon" He shouted and said "O no! No man is born a natural believer of that sect." During the five minute chat following I learned from this man First, that I am not a child of God; Second, that Mormonism doesn't require people to repent in order to be saved;" and, third, the Mormons in Sydney, Australia are practicing polygamy. "Not openly. On the quiet, you know."** Owing to the heavy rain no Bible Class was held. I prepared my Sunday School lesson. Read a little took a bath and retired.

Wednesday, 18 July 1906, Tokyo

Cloudy—Hot Up at 6:00. Today being our weekly fast day I ate no breakfast. Wrote a letter to Elders Chadwick and Fairbourn. Took the mail to the post office after our prayer meeting. The rest of the day I spent working on the revision of the Book of Mormon translation. In the evening I wrote a letter to Aunt Clara. A lady, with very peculiar features called today about 2:15 p.m. and wanted to know if this was a shrine were Christ is worshipped. I talked with her for a few minutes.

Thursday, 19 July 1906, Tokyo

Hazy—Hot! Up at 6:00. Went down town immediately after breakfast. I called at the Yomuri Shinbun Office and left a copy of our last tract "In the Lineage of the Gods." My purpose in doing this was to see if the editor wouldn't publish the tract in the paper as it will certainly be interesting to the readers at this time for recently a great deal has been written about the relationship of man with a Supreme

Being and the sorrow and pain man undergoes by not having a knowledge of that relationship and the purposes of life. I named these reasons to the editor's representative and told him we would be glad to see the truths portrayed in the tract given to the public through the Yomuri's columns. I called on a dentist, Dr. Obata and made a date with him. I have two badly decayed teeth. In the afternoon I did a little on the Book of Mormon revision but it was so very hot that I didn't get in much good hard labor. After supper I worked again on this revision.

Saturday, 21 July 1906, Tokyo

Clear—Hot. Up at 6:45. Spent most of the forenoon at the dentist's (Dr. Obata). My teeth seem to be made of lime covered over with the thinnest and poorest kind of enamel. In the afternoon I worked on the Book of Mormon. The Bible Class was a failure again today. After supper I took a short walk and then thought over a lesson for the Primary class in Sunday School.

Sunday, 22 July 1906, Tokyo

Fair—No breeze—Terrible Heat. Up at 6:30. Ate breakfast. Sunday School was well attended and the class exercises were carried out with spirit and unusual interest. I have rejoiced over the good school this morning. At 11:00 a.m. we held Sacrament Meeting. Sisters Nachie and Hakii were present. I talked for their benefit upon the evils of the custom among low class Japanese of going naked or nearly so during the hot weather. I told them that it was their duty to respect their persons by keeping them covered in the presence of others and avoid associating with people who didn't have enough decency to cover up their ugly nakedness. In the afternoon I read some in "Orson Spencer's Letters" and looked up some points on faith. Ate supper.

At 7:45 our evening meeting began. Before we had been in session long we had an audience of fourteen. I occupied all the time. After meeting held a long conversation with a young man named "Takagi. This young man has been to our meetings before and I have had two talks with him before this evening. He impresses me as being a pure young man and hence I feel particularily interested in him. The struggle with him as with the big majority is to love goodness and truth and God more dearly than all else—even life itself. He was impressed with what he heard and I think left for home with grave thoughts passing through his mind and strange feelings in his heart. May God be merciful to this young man and give him faith and courage to obey the truth in this life that he may be exalted in the future life. This evening just before meeting I wrote a card to Elders Fairbourn and Chadwick telling them to remember Sister Mabel K. Richardson in their fast and prayer this coming Wednesday. I wrote Sister R. also telling her to join her brethren in fasting and prayer on that day. Her leprosy is about as usual.

Monday, 23 July 1906, Tokyo

Clear—Hot Up at 6:30. Spent the morning washing windows, sewing, and cleaning. After dinner I went to the Yotsuya Police Station to complain about the scavanger man not coming around to clean out our dirt box. From there I went down town to the dentist's. For two hours I suffered most terribly while gold was being pounded into my front teeth which were exceedingly tender because of the separating operation. I called at Okamoto's picture store and had the finished kakemons[23] sent to Sendai to help decorate their home there. The kakemons is one containing verses 38 and 39 of the 22nd chapter of Matthew. This was written some time ago by a good penman. I called at the umberella shop. Returned to headquarters. Continued my sewing. After super I wrote a letter to the elders in Sapporo.

This morning I received a letter from Elder Stoker containing the good news that a Mr. Okafugi a teacher in the Normal School at Sapporo who has looked over the part of Elder S's translation which was corrected by Mr. Yoshida here at Tokyo, has expressed his willingness to look over and correct all the remaining part of the translation and be satisfied with what we feel proper to pay him. My letter in answer to Elder Stoker's told him to accept Mr. Okafuji's offer. No doubt, by the time the summer vacation is over Elder S's translation of the Brief History of the Church will be corrected and practically prepared for the printer. Elder S's letter also conveyed the

good news that some seemingly very earnest investigation of the principles of the gospel is being carried on by two or three of the natives at Sapporo.

Tuesday, 24 July 1906, Tokyo

Clear—Very Hot—Not even a slight breeze Up at 7:00. It is just 59 years ago today since the "Mormon" Pioneers entered the Salt Lake Valley and began the building of a city in the midst of the Rockies and sage brush which grew in that uninviting plain on the shore of the Great Salt Lake. It is just five years ago today since the pioneer missionaries, Heber J. Grant, Louis A. Kelsch, Horace S. Ensign and myself, left Salt Lake City for the Orient. The time has certainly flown on wings of lightening but many changes have taken place during these five years. Three of the pioneers have returned and have no doubt, almost forgotten their associations in this land. Other missionaries have come and gone. The seed sown has so far brought forth so little fruit that our fields are not dotted with sheaves of ripened grain. Much labor has been performed in getting out literature in the Japanese language. We have published one English tract, eight Japanese tracts, a psalmody and a hymn book. The translation of the "Brief History of the Church" will, no doubt be finished ere many more months go by. The Book of Mormon translation is being revised and criticised with hopes that two more years labor on this work added to the two and a half years work already performed will bring the translation forth in its printed garb. I have enjoyed health and happiness and abundant manifestations of the goodness of my Heavenly Father. My experiences have been varied and instructive. I have seen considerable of land and sea and humanity.

This morning I looked over Elder Caine's suggestions and criticisms of the first part of the corrected manuscript of the Book of Mormon translation. In the afternoon I worked on the work of revision. After supper, I took a short walk. Worked again on the Book of Mormon revision. Took a bath and retired. Today the Kato family who have lived in the little house at our front gate moved away. Their removal is the result of a discussion we held on the matter. Their presence had gradually become unpleasant and a worry.

Wednesday, 25 July 1906, Tokyo

Heavy showers—Slightly cooler Up at 7:00. Spent most of the day working on the revision and correction of the Book of Mormon translation. At 9:00 a.m. I taught Sister Nachie's daughter Ei an hour's lesson in English. During the summer vacation I have promised to teach this little girls English for an hour each day; using the hour just after breakfast or dinner—the time when my food is settling and I have nothing particularily to do. At noon we held a prayer meeting. Today we remembered Sister Mabel K. Richardson especially, asking God our Father, to continue his mercies unto her until she is entirely free from the poisons of her terrible affliction—leprosy. All of the elders in the mission have no doubt specially prayed for this sister as I wrote them asking them to do so. I also asked Sister R. to fast and pray. Before supper, I took a little exercise. After supper, I took the house cat and turned it loose quite a distance from home hoping that it will find another boarding house. The cat is no good; don't catch any rats and makes things unpleasant. Received a letter from the Elders in Sendai. They are well and in good spirits.

Thursday, 26 July 1906, Tokyo

Cloudy—cooler—Later rain Up at 5:20. Read the newspapers before breakfast. After eating, went immediately to the dentist's. Attended to mission business. Returned to headquarters just at dinner time. Ate dinner. Wrote a letter to the elders in Sendai. Worked on the Book of Mormon translation. Took some exercise just before supper. Worked again on the Book of Mormon after supper. Received a photo of mother. This is the first I have had from her in four years. She has grown grayer but is much more robust than when I left home. Her trip to the Pacific coast and a long rest has done her much good. I delight in the health and happiness of my parents.

Wednesday, 1 August 1906, Tokyo

Clear—Very Hot. Up at 6:30. Today I pass my 24th mile post. These twenty four years have been years of great opportunity. My parents—"goodly parents"—have given me all the advantages of education, progress, and development that a young man could wish for. The priesthood of God and God himself have conferred upon me honor and blessings more precious than the honor of kings and queens and far more valuable than the riches of this temporal world. In a word, I have been blessed of God and man. The questions are; how have I grasped the opportunities afforded? How have I appreciated superior advantages and blessings? How have I honored those who have honored me? How have I magnified the priesthood I hold? How have I labored in the interests of God and man? How have I honored my parents and blessed them in return for all they have done for me? I trust that after making allowance for my weaknesses that I will be considered worthy of both human and divine favors during all my future years. I have spent nearly the whole day working on the correction of the Book of Mormon. At noon we held our fast and prayer and council meeting. In the evening, after supper, I took a short walk. From 8:30 a.m. to 9:30 a.m. I taught English to Sister Nachie's little girl.

Thursday, 2 August 1906, Tokyo

Clear—Intense heat. Up at 6:30. After breakfast I went to the dentist's. From there I went to the bank and from the bank to Azabu to look at a house advertized for rent. The house, as usual was in a bad location. Spent the afternoon writing letters. Received a letter from Prest. Ralph A. Badger of the South Africa Mission. **In the evening I talked with Mr. Chiba about copying the corrected part of the Book of Mormon. He has agreed to come to headquarters and do the work here as requested. This will keep the books in a safe place and give him an opportunity to ask any questions he may have directly.**

Received a letter from Elder Woodland tonight stating that a company of Elders for Japan would be leaving Salt Lake about Aug. 6th. I note that the steamers of the line generally patronized by us leave Seattle Aug. 7th and 18th. No doubt the company will sail on one of these dates getting to Japan on the 23rd of Aug or Sept 3rd.

Saturday, 4 August 1906, Tokyo

Cloudy, then clear, then rain, always hot. Up at 6:30. After breakfast, I went to the dentist's and had the last work on my teeth finished. On the way home I called at Harajiku and looked at a house for rent. Spent the afternoon teaching Sister Nachie's daughter a lesson in English and correcting the translation of the Book of Mormon. In the evening I did nothing but sit and think. My eyes are getting weak and I have to be careful how I use them at night. Took a bath and retired. Today Mr. Chiba spent three hours copying the corrected portion of the B. of M. translation.

Received a letter today from Sister Mabel K. Richardson saying that she is improving and growing stronger each day. This is certainly gratifying news and indicates that God is answering our prayers in her behalf and will in the end cleanse her entirely from the dreaded leprosy with which she is smitten. I wrote to the elders in Sendai.

Monday, 6 August 1906, Tokyo

Cloudy—Cooler. Up at 6:00 Swept and dusted the down stairs rooms. After breakfast I read over that part of the Book of Mormon translation which Mr. Chiba copied last Saturday. I found a number of places about which I made suggestions to him. I wrote out a prayer for one of the children of the Sunday School to learn and recite in our next session. Mr. Katogi and the son of Bro. Katsunuma who is in Hawaii called and I chatted with them for a moment or two. I learned that Mrs. Katsunuma is now in Japan on a visit. In the afternoon I worked a little on the Book of Mormon translation and taught Sister Nachie's daughter a lesson in English. After supper I visited Sister Rin Ota and tried to show her the necessity of attending her meetings occasionally. Before going to bed, I read a letter from the elders in Sendai and was pleased to learn of their good health and condition. Received a long interesting letter from Bro. Horace S. Ensign and a pleasing missive from Sister Marie S. Featherstone.

Thursday, 9 August 1906, Tokyo

Cloudy—Cool Up at 6:45. Spent all the morning and afternoon writing letters. I wrote to mother,

Prest Smith and Counselors, Sanford W. Hedges, Millennial Star Office, Elders Stoker and Seely, and Mrs. Matsudori. In the evening I had a little chat with a doctor in the army. **After this gentleman left I received a letter from Elder Seely in which was written the good news of the baptism of Mr. Aritatsu Kawanaka who received the ordinance at Sapporo, on Aug. 3rd at the hands of Elder Seely. He was confirmed in the elders little fast meeting the next day, Elder Stoker being mo/u/th. This man and his wife impressed me very favorabley when I was in Sapporo this spring. They were indeed very kind to me. This is our first fruit in Hokkaido and may God bless this man with faith and strength to endure to the end.** Elder Seely reports the work of revising the translation of the Brief History as progressing nicely and gives a good account of the interest taken by Mr. Okafuji. Mr. Chiba called this evening. Sister Hakii was here to hear the good news.

Sunday, 12 August 1906, Tokyo

Clear—A little hot. Up at 6:15. Today has been a delightful Sabbath. The Lord has given his abundant blessings to his servants. This morning our Sunday School was attended by forty five students old and young. The exercises were pleasant and interesting. At our sacrament meeting there were three saints present. This is the greatest number of native saints we have had together for a year. In the afternoon, Elder Anderson and I went to see a house in Kojimachi. The house itself was very good but the location was so poor that we can not think of moving into it. I read a little in "Orson Pratt's Works."[24] Took a nap. The evening meeting was blessed with the presence of the Holy Ghost. I felt it plainly and enjoyed speaking under its influence. Ten natives were present. They gave strict attention. Just five years ago today I, in company with the other pioneer missionaries arrived in Japan. The spirit that has been present with me all day makes me rejoice in the blessings of God to me since I came to Japan and for the work that has been accomplished for the salvation of the people of this nation.

Monday, 13 August 1906, Tokyo

Cloudy—Just a little hot Up at 6:30. After breakfast, I went to the Yotsuya post office to see about sending and receiving some money. I then went to Dr. Whitney's to have my eyes examined. He was very busy and could not make a thorough examination but he said that he thought I have a slight stigmatism. I procured an eye wash and expect to have a thorough examination before long. For some weeks my eyes have been weak and I have not been able for the last few days to do any reading at night. After dinner Elder Anderson and I went to Azagaya Mura to visit the Tamano families who were so kind to Elders Jarvis, Stoker and Hedges which they were doing missionary work in that village. Found both of the families at home. After a pleasant chat at each place, we returned to headquarters in time for supper. After supper a young man who had been here before called. His manner is so disgusting that I excused myself from conversing with him. Sang a little. Mended some sox and retired.

Tuesday, 21 August 1906, Tokyo

Clear—Oppresively hot. Up at 6:45. Spent most of the forenoon writing part of a letter to Elder Jno. W. Stoker regarding some points in his translation of the Brief History of the Church. Worked on the Book of Mormon during the afternoon. Pumped the bath water before supper. Took a walk after supper. Had a talk with Mr. Chiba. He stated that after investigating and considering deeply the teachings of Jesus Christ and the claims of the Latter-day Saints, that he had been able to over come his doubts and believed with full satisfaction the Messiahship of Crist, the Fatherhood of God, the truth of the atonement and resurrection and the divinity of the Church of Jesus Christ of Latter-day Saints and asked to be baptized. Believing that Mr. Chiba's investigation has been honest and earnest and that he fully realizes the sacredness of the obligations he will have to make, I consented to his request for baptism and suggested one of the three days Aug. 29, 30 & 31.

Thursday, 23 August 1906, Tokyo

Cloudy—Hot Up at 6:45. Spent the forenoon working on the Book of Mormon. Also continued this work in the afternoon. After supper I took a walk to Aoyama. **When I returned, I was happily surprised to find Elders Daniel P. Woodland and John H. Roskelley at headquarters. They had arrived at Yokohama in the afternoon about 4:00. Having received word that Elder Woodland was going to return to Japan and bring other elders with him, I had figured that they would arrive on Aug. 23rd or Sept. 3rd but as the exact date of the departure of elders has always heretofore been communicated to us by letter I expected such a letter and because it did not come, thought the 3rd of Sept. would be the day of their arrival, consequently they were not met by anyone. They came in on us without warning.** Elder Woodland brings good news from the Authorities of the Church and from my parents. He was in fine health and his companion Elder Roskelley is young and large, looking as though he would be a good missionary after the essential training.

Friday, 24 August 1906, Tokyo

Heavy rain—Violent Wind Up at 6:30. Today the most violent storm of the season raged. It is a long time since I have seen such a heavy rain accompanied with such a strong wind. The rain came into our house and in places through the poorly made plaster walls destroying the whiteness of our walls. I wrote letters today. One to Elder Stoker answering some of his questions regarding the translation of "A Brief History of the Church," one to Bro. George Reynolds, one to Edward H. Anderson of the "Era" and one to Sister Woodland and quite a long one to Dr. Talmage proposing a theme for the next tract he will write for the mission. In the evening I had a talk with Elder Woodland about the progress and conclusion of his mission taking Bro. [~~Sanford H. Hedges~~] home. He reports that the First Presidency were more than pleased with all that was done in Bro. [~~Hedges'~~] case saying if they had been here the same action would have been taken. Not having received any word direct from the First Presidency regarding the matter, I am greatly pleased at Elder W.'s report and am at rest on the matter.

Saturday, 25 August 1906, Tokyo

Clear—Hot. Up at 5:40. Spent the morning and part of the afternoon working around headquarters. Read a little from the "Era." Elder Roskelley took a walk and was gone so long that we wondered if he had lost his way. We went out and walked around the neighborhood, but Elder Roskelley beat most of us home. He had walked a little too far and by the mere fortune of remembering the Japanese word "rempeiba" which means "parade ground," he found his way back. After supper Mr. Chiba came. I taught him how to sing one of our hymns.

Wednesday, 29 August 1906, Tokyo

Clear—Very warm Up at 6:15. Spent the morning working on the Book of Mormon translation. Did not fast today as we intend to observe a special fast day next Saturday it being just five years since Prest. Grant, Elders Kelsch, Ensign and I held services in the woods near Yokohama and dedicated the land of Japan and its inhabitants for the reception of the Gospel. This event marked the opening of the Japan Mission.

After dinner today we all prepared to go with Yasubeie Chiba to the Tama River near Yaguchi [~~fordy~~]. Elder Caine left early to attend to some business on the way. We were late for the train so he went alone to Kawasaki . We took the car to Omori expecting to find Elder Caine there waiting for us. He was not there. We waited a moment or two for the next train; he was not on it so we went without him to the river, a walk of about three miles & a half from the station. The river bank was quiet and we prepared to enter the water then sang the Baptismal Hymn and I offered prayer. I then led Bro. Chiba into the water and baptized him. When we got through dressing we sang "We're not ashamed own our Lord," and started for home we had only gone a few steps when Elder Caine arrived all out of breath. It was nine o'clock when we reached headquarters. Ate a bread and milk supper. On the way home, while changing from one street car to another on the Ginza, I had my pocket picked and lost a purse with nothing in it—A valuable experience for me without loss and a dangerous move without gain for the thief.

Thursday, 30 August 1906, Tokyo

Clear—Hot Up at 6:45. Spent most of the morning writing. After dinner I taugh some of our hymns to two ladies. Later I talked with Bro. Chiba. Accomplished only a very little on the Book of Mormon. After supper I went to Dr. Whitney's and had my eyes examined. He said I should wear glasses and I ordered them.

Saturday, 1 September 1906, Tokyo

Cloudy—A sprinkling of rain—Hot Up at 6:00. Today is the fifth anniversary of the dedication of Japan for the promulgation of the Gospel and the opening of the Japan Mission. The elders in the Mission are observing a fast today and at noon we all joined in special prayer, especially in behalf of the people of this land. At Tokyo there were five of us who took part in the services. After singing and prayer we all expressed our feelings. We sang again then knelt and took turns in prayer. We sang again. I spoke. Then the meeting was dismissed by singing and prayer. We enjoyed a peaceful influence and were greatly strengthened in our feelings regarding the work in this land. After the meeting I wrote an article on Japan, and the Japan Mission intending to send it to the Era. The purpose of the article being to correct false impressions about the mission and its chances for success and inspire in the hearts of the young men in Zion the desire to take a mission to Japan, for it is evident that the number of young men willing to come to this land is very small. During the forenoon I worked around the house. In the evening I taught Japanese to Elders Woodland & Roskelley.

Sunday, 2 September 1906, Tokyo

Cloudy—Cool Up at 7:00. Continued the fast began Friday night. Had a fair-sized Sunday School this morning. After school we held a sacrament and testimony meeting. **In this meeting Bro. Yasubeie Chiba was confirmed a member of the church by Elder F. A. Caine. The ordinance of laying on hands for the healing of the sick and the ordinance of consecrating oil was explained and performed for the first time in the fast meetings of the Japanese saints. After meeting we administered to Elder Caine who was suffering from summer complaint.** In the afternoon I read a little, talked to Mr. Okonogi and rested. About 4:00 p.m. I ate a little bread and milk to break my two day's fast. The evening meeting was fairly well attended and I enjoyed a good spirit while talking. Elder Caine was unable to attend the meeting, so I led the singing did the praying and all the preaching.

Monday, 3 September 1906, Tokyo

Clear—Cool Up at 6:30. Today Sister Nachie left headquarters to take a little rest so most of the afternoon and evening was spent washing dishes and cooking food. Elder Caine was not so well today so I spent some time giving him interval baths and oil injections. I wrote an addition to the article commenced Saturday "About Japan & the Japan Mission." In the evening Mr. Mori the private secretary of the Minister of Finance came to get an hour's practice in speaking English. This gentleman is a friend of our friend Mr. Tokoyo and at the request of Mr. Tokoyo we have consented to help Mr. Mori whose position requires that he shall be familiar with English.

Thursday, 6 September 1906, Tokyo

Cloudy—Cool Up at 6:45. Spent most of the day writing a preface for the translation of "A Brief History of the Church." Elder Stoker wrote one and sent it to me for consideration the effort of Elder S's was good but left out some important facts which I felt should appear in the preface so I wrote my ideas by writing a preface. I also spent much time answering some questions submitted by Elder S. in regard to points in the above-mentioned translation. Today Elder Caine was much improved. He dressed and came downstairs. In the evening I taught Elders Roskelley and Woodland a lesson each in Japanese. Last night Sister Nachie returned, so we have had no dishwashing or cooking to do. This morning in family prayer Elder Anderson was mouth. He meant to say that we were happy our Sister returned without accident or unpleasant experience but he left the latter part of his sentence off and simply said we were happy because she returned; the reason to be assumed was because we wouldn't have to do the kitchen work or worry about cooking any longer.

Friday, 7 September 1907, Tokyo/Yokohama

Rained nearly all day—Cool Up at 6:50. After breakfast I went to Yokohama calling at the Ginza on the way to the depot. After arriving in Yokohama, I went to the Bible House, made some inquiries about the men who translated the Bible into Japanese and purchased some Bibles. Went to the office of the company where I thought Bro. Yoshiro Oyama was working, but found he was no longer an employee there. I asked for and learned his address. Went and visited for thirty minutes with Sister Richardson. She seems to be about the same. Her disease still shows in her face very plainly. I gave her all the encouragement I could. After leaving her home I attended to some purchases and then began what turned out to be a long hunt for Bro. Oyama's home. Finally, I found his place but he was not home. I left two Eras which were sent over to his old address and returned. I also wrote a note telling of my call. Returned to Tokyo on 2:50 train.

Wednesday, 12 September 1906, Tokyo

Chilly—Continuous rain—Northwest wind. Up at 7:15. Spent the day working on the Book of Mormon and reading papers, letters, and magazines from Zion. At noon we held our prayer meeting. After prayers we discussed a few questions regarding the mission. Before supper, I took a little exercise in the house and then in spite of the rain, went out for walk. While I was out, Mr. Tokoyo called to stay good bye before leaving for Kobe where he expects to enter the Bank of Formosa. After learning that Mr. Tokoyo was expecting to go to Kobe we tried to arrange to have him spend an evening with us before his departure. We could not get any definite answer from him but rather expected him to eat supper with us this evening so we ordered a good foreign meal, but he could only stay thirty minutes. We enjoyed the foreign meal ourselves. After the meal, I spent the evening teaching the elders Japanese.

Monday, 17 September 1906, Tokyo

Cloudy—Rain—Cooler Up at 7:00. Spent the forenoon writing and reading. Received a letter from Prest. Heber J. Grant of the European Mission. After dinner I went down town to get some bids on the printing of the translation of the Brief History of the Church. I got one from the Shueisha Company. In the evening I taught Japanese to Elders Woodland and Roskelley. Before going to bed received and read a letter from Bro. Geo. Reynolds written in behalf of the First Presidency; one from Sister Augusta W. Grant expressing an earnest desire that Sister Nami Hakii be sent to America if she will consent to go; one from mother giving good news about home.

Tuesday, 18 September 1906, Tokyo

Rain—Cold Up at 6:50. Spent the morning writing a letter and doing a little on the Book of Mormon. After dinner Bro. Jacob Schulthess of Salt Lake City called on us. He is on his way to Manila where he holds the position of clerk in the Bureau of Justice of the Philippine Islands. He has been in the government service on the islands for some years. He went back to the U. S. on a vacation in March of this year. He is no returning to his post at Manila. He is brother to Bro. Schulthess who is in the Liberty Stake Presidency, Salt Lake City. He spent the afternoon and evening with us and then we gave him a bed to stay all night. Having just come from Salt Lake City he had much to tell us of home and having had a long experience in Manila had considerable to tell about the Philippines. We had an opportunity to tell him a great deal about Japan. Today's visit with him has been very pleasant.

Wednesday, 19 September 1906, Tokyo

Clear—Warm Up at 6:45. After breakfast, I talked a little with Brother Schulthess. **Then he and Elder Caine went to see the sights in the neighborhood. I did a little work on the Book of Mormon. After dinner Elder Caine, Bro. Schulthess and I went and saw the garden of Count Okuma. We received a letter to one of the officials in the Count's estate and were conducted through the gardens**

& hot houses by a young man who is studying horticulture in the count's gardens. The hot houses in which many peculiar varieties of tropical plants were growing as well as the yard were very interesting the inner garden or one just surrounding the house is the most beautiful thing I have seen since coming to Japan. The grass, the shrubs, the large and small trees, the artistic pines, the graveled winding paths, the running water and bridges and stepping stones certainly produced a picture worth seeing.

From the Count's place I went to the Printing Office of the Hakubun Kuan to get a bid on printing the translation of "A Brief History of the Church." This company refused to take the job as it was too insignificant. I returned to headquarters in time to get ready to go to the Metropole Hotel where Bro. Schulthess gave all the five elders in Tokyo a fine supper. On the way to the hotel, I called at the optician's to have him alter my glasses. After supper at the hotel, I accompanied Bro. Schulthess to the station where he took the 8:30 p.m. train for Yokohama. He sails on the S.S. "Dakota" at noon tomorrow for his destination—Manila. I went from the depot to the car and happened to board the same car the brethren were on. We returned to headquarters had prayers and retired. It is good to see "Mormons" from abroad **occasionally.**

Friday, 21 September 1906, Tokyo

Rain—Mild Up at 7:00. After breakfast I took Elder Woodland to the doctor's to have the doctor prescribe for his eyes which have been troubling him for sometime. Read the American newspapers and the Era till dinner time. In the afternoon I worked on the Book of Mormon making very good headway. In the evening I taught Elder Roskelley a lesson in Japanese and then had a talk with Sister Nami Hakii about getting to Zion.

Saturday, 22 September 1906, Tokyo

Rain—Cool Up at 6:00. Spent nearly all of the morning working on the Book of Mormon. Went to Dr. Whitney's about noon to have him examine my nose and prescribe for the catarrh with which I have been bothered for the last two years. The disease is a very light kind and one that give me little or no distress but keeps my nose running too freely. In hot weather I am not at all troubled but from now on during the winter I will certainly have more or less bother if something is not done. I rely upon the blessings of God, for without these I have no hope whatever in the skill of feeble man. After returning from the doctor's, I worked again on the Book of Mormon till supper time. After supper I taught Elders Woodland and Roskelley lessons in Japanese. This evening between 6:15 and 7:15 I taught Elder Woodland the lesson in Japanese I was unable to give him last evening.

Sunday, 23 September 1906, Tokyo

Rain all day. Up at 6:30. After breakfast welcomed the S. S. children. In spite of the heavy rain the children came out much better than last Sunday. After the school talked with Mrs. Umeda and Miss. Hijikata for some time. Mrs. Umeda will soon leave Tokyo for her home in Tsusugo on the west coast. Held Sacrament meeting and in the afternoon wrote a long letter to Bro. Horace S. Ensign. I talked with Sister Nachie about trying to get our four native sisters working together in a sort of women's relief society-like way. We only have four women in the church here in Japan but if they have a little to do it will be good for them and the work. In the evening our meeting was fairly well attended. We enjoyed a good Spirit.

Monday, 24 September 1906, Tokyo

Cloudy—Clear Up at 6:45. Spent the morning writing. Went up to Aoyama to attend to some business. In the afternoon worked a little on the Book of Mormon finishing the revision up to the end of Jacob. My catarrh has given me considerable trouble today. After supper I went and visited for about an hour with Mr. Okuno gentleman who took a prominent part in the translation of the Bible into Japanese being Dr. Hepburn's assistant and native advisor. Mr. Okuno is now 84 years old. I called on him to inquire about the manner in which the work was carried on, but learned nothing more than I had already been told by Rev. Loomis of the American Bible Society. Mr. Okuno became enthusiastic in relating his experience in connection with Christian work. He is an advocate of the Independent Japanese Christian Church movement but not quite so radical in his views as some who are churning for a Japanese Christian church to be run exclusively by Japanese. The old man does not speak any English and is quite a remarkable speaker for his age. He received me cordially and asked me to call again.

Friday, 28 September 1906, Tokyo

Clear—Milder Up at 6:00. Spent the forenoon working on the Book of Mormon. By dinner time, I had finished looking over Elder Caine's suggestions and criticisms on the second book of the translation manuscript. In the afternoon I worked again on the Book of Mormon. Before supper, I took a little exercise and after super had a thirty minutes walk. Taught Elders Woodland and Roskelley a lesson each in Japanese. Before going to bed, I had Elder Woodland rub my chest with oil and was then administered to.[25] All day my lungs have been feeling as though my catarrh had gone down into the bronchial tubes.

Saturday, 29 September 1906, Tokyo

Cloudy—Mild Up at 5:50. Did a little sweeping in the garden just before breakfast. Worked again in the garden during the forenoon. In the afternoon we expected to hold a Bible Class. Only one came and Elder Caine engaged that one in conversation. I went and called on Mr. Hirai. I meet at Mr. Hirai's home Baron Makimura who was also visiting Mr. Hirai. After supper, I taught Elders Woodland and Roskelley a lesson each in Japanese. Took a bath and after having my chest anointed with oil went to bed.

Sunday, 30 September 1906, Tokyo

Cloudy—Warm Up at 6:30. Fasted today. The Sunday School was well attended. An interesting session was held. At 11:00 a.m. we held sacrament service two native saints were present. I spoke on the subject "Be ye doers of the word, not hearers only." In the afternoon I read a little. Then took a nap. After my nap, I took a walk. Ate supper. The evening meetings was attended by five elders, one saint and eleven non-members. I spoke on "This is life eternal, that they might know thee, the only true God, and Jesus Christ, whom thou has sent."

Thursday, 4 October 1906, Tokyo

Cloudy—Cold Up at 6:30. After breakfast, I went down town to settle the matter of having the translation of "A Brief History of the Church" printed at the Shueisha Printing Company. It will be next year before they will be able to begin on the work and it will take about forty days to finish it. Returned to headquarters and worked on the translation of the Book of Mormon. In the early part of the afternoon I had a conversation with Mr. Tamura who was very kind to the elders when they visited Nago in the Boshu district. Spent the rest of the afternoon working on the Book of Mormon translation. In the evening I taught Elders Woodland and Roskelley a lesson in Japanese.

Monday, 8 October 1906, Tokyo/Sendai

Clear—Warmer Up at 5:00. Ate an early breakfast. **Went to Umo Station and took the 7:30 a.m. train for Tokyo. Nothing very interesting happened till I reached the home of the elders at Sendai. They not knowing when I was coming were nearly speechless. I ate supper with them and after quite a chat, I retired. Recently I read a statement in the Tokyo papers to the effect that this year the people in Northeastern Japan were threatened with bad crops again. All that I saw on the way to Sendai indicated that the people in the district I passed would have plenty of food at least, if some blighting storm or weather change did not come to destroy their fields of ripening rice. I inquired of a man who lives in Sendai about the prospects and how the farmers felt, and he replied that there was not the least concern and everything indicated a sufficient yield.**

Tuesday, 9 October 1906, Sendai

Clear—Warm Up at 6:00. Ate breakfast. Spent the forenoon working on the Book of Mormon. I intend to read over while here in Sendai the part of the translation I corrected last week at Tokyo. It is my custom to read over the corrected portions and compare them carefully with the original before I consider the work of correction finished. After dinner I talked for a long time with two young men whom I met nearly five years ago while living in the Kirin Kwan, Surugadai Kanda, Tokyo. Another young man was also present and took part in the conversation. Took a walk purchasing a hibachi on the way. After supper I taught the elders a lesson in Japanese and then we held a little meeting for about an hour. Retired about 10:00 p.m.

Wednesday, 10 October 1906, Sendai

Clear—Cooler Up at 7:00. Spent the forenoon working on the Book of Mormon. At noon we held a prayer meeting. The meeting was thoroughly enjoyed by me. I gave the elders instructions in regard to their work referring especially to some of the mistakes an elder is liable to make while out tracting. After meeting we took a walk for exercise. Returned and gave the elders a lesson in Japanese. Ate supper. Spent the evening talking with the elders.

Thursday, 11 October 1906, Sendai

Rain—Cold Up at 6:30. Spent the entire day in the house. My nose has been a bothersome member today. Spent the morning reading over the records being kept by the elders in this mission. In the afternoon I did a little on the Book of Mormon translation revision. In the evening I instructed the elders regarding their records and accounts. I also taught them some words & phrases in Japanese. During the day I took considerable exercise in the house.

Friday, 12 October 1906, Sendai

Cloudy—Rain—Warmer Up at 6:45. Spent the early part of the forenoon working on the Book of Mormon. Took a walk with Elders Chadwick and Fairbourn. Purchased some things for their home. In the afternoon we held a meeting in which I gave the elders parting instructions. We practiced some of the songs with which the brethren did not seem to be very familiar. An old gentleman called and we had a brief talk with him. In the evening a number of people came in and I conversed with them at length upon the Gospel.

Saturday, 13 October 1906, Sendai/Tokyo

Clear—Warm Up at 5:00. Ate an early breakfast and took the 6:10 a.m. train for Tokyo. The elders came with me to the station. On the train I worked a little on the Book of Mormon. Spent the rest of the time of the trip thinking, viewing the scenery, eating, and sleeping. Arrived at Ueno station Tokyo at 3:10 p.m. exactly on time. Went directly to the Mission Headquarters. On the car I met Rev. Whitney who told me one time that I was unsaved and not a child of God. I partly got even with him today before the car came to my station. Found all the brethren at headquarters in good health. In the evening I taught Elder Woodland a lesson in Japanese. Took a bath and retired.

Tuesday, 16 October 1906, Tokyo

Cloudy—Warm Up at 6:30. After breakfast I went down town and attended to a little business for myself and the Mission. Returned to headquarters and ate dinner. In the afternoon I worked on the Book of Mormon. In the evening I taught Elder Roskelley a lesson in Japanese. Mail from America arrived and the news was all so good that the hour to be devoted to teaching Elder Woodland went by discussing new elders from Zion and many other interesting subjects suggested in the letters received. A letter from Bro. George Reynolds says that two missionaries are booked to leave America on the S. S. "Dakota" which sails from Seattle Nov. 28th. Another has been notified to make preparations to leave in Jan. 1907 and his companion is now being sought after. By this mail the music to three of the five songs gotten out for Christmas was received from Bro. Horace G. Ensign who promises the music to the other two very soon.

Wednesday, 17 October 1906, Tokyo

Cloudy—Rain—Warm Up at 5:45. Swept and dusted the downstairs. Worked on the Book of Mormon during the forenoon. **We held prayer meeting at noon. After prayer we discussed a number of things. We decided to hold a English Bible Class every Wednesday evening. Elder Woodland will have charge of it.** In the afternoon I read the papers from America. I worked again on the Book of Mormon and then took a walk before supper. After supper practiced the music to two songs we have had prepared for the S. S. Taught Elders Woodland and Roskelley a lesson each in Japanese. Retired.

Saturday, 20 October 1906, Tokyo

Clear—Cool Up at 6:45. Spent the forenoon working on the Book of Mormon. After dinner I wrote a letter. At 2:30 p.m. we held a Bible Class at headquarters. **After the class I asked Mr. Mori if he had time to copy up some of the corrected Book of Mormon translation he conscented to begin next Monday doing about two hours work each day.** After supper I taught Japanese to Elders Roskelley & Woodland. Took a bath and retired.

Monday, 22 October 1906, Tokyo

Rain—Cold Up at 7:05. Spent all the forenoon reading over the copy of the Book of Mormon translation as far as the end of I Nephi chaper seven. This copy was made by Bro. Y. Chiba last August and had never been compared with my translation. **This afternoon at 2:30 p.m. Mr. H. Mori came to headquarters and worked until 5:00 p.m. copying my translation of I Nephi 8 chap. This gentleman expects to come nearly every day and do a little copying each day until about one or two books of the translation are copied. Before supper I took a walk. After supper I taught Elders Woodland and Roskelley a lesson each in Japanese. After retiring Elder Anderson brought me a letter from Elder Stoker in which he states that all of the corrected translation of the Brief History of the Church is copied up and in the hands of Dr. Kintaro Oshima who is now reading it and making suggestions.** A card from Mr. S. Okafuji, the gentleman who corrected Elder Stoker's translation states that he will visit us tomorrow.

Saturday, 27 October 1906, Tokyo

Clear—Cool Up at 6:30. Spent part of the forenoon sweeping the garden and cleaning up myself. Walked up to Aoyama. After dinner, I went and had my hair cut. Before returning I bought a poison to kill some of the rats around headquarters which have become so numerous and bold that it is very unpleasant to live with them. A Bible Class was held with one saint and three strangers present. After class I worked a little on the Book of Mormon translation. In the evening I taught Elders Roskelley and Woodland a lesson each in Japanese. Took a bath and retired.

Wednesday, 31 October 1906, Tokyo

Cloudy—Slight rain—Cold Up at 6:15. Spent nearly the entire day working on the Book of Mormon, and succeeded in correcting the translation of 8½ pages of the original. This is a big days work. Besides this I taught Japanese for an hour to Elder Woodland in the early morning and gave Elder Roskelley an hour's lesson in the evening. At noon we held prayer and council meeting which lasted from 12 o'clock to 2:00 p.m. Today we decided on the program for our Christmas entertainment. Papers from home giving the conference news arrived today. Politics are red hot in Utah and the devil is working hard against the Church. The time is near when the Church will lose its weak members—those only who have the testimony of Jesus who stand on their own bottom and are strict in keeping God's commandments will escape unscathed.

Saturday, 3 November 1906, Tokyo

Cloudy—Cold Up at 5:50. Today is the Emperor's birthday so I put the Japanese flag up on the flag pole (pine tree) and decorated the gates with the American and Japanese flags. But notwithstanding this patriotism on our part when we attempted to view the military review from the upstairs windows the police informed us that we could not **look down on** the emperor so it would be necessary for us to stay down stairs while his Majesty reviewed his troops. We hoped to hold a bible class in the afternoon but no one came so the session [~~was~~] ended in an attempt. I worked on the Book of Mormon, finishing the revision of the fifth book of the translation which reaches to the end of Mosiah 23 chap. In the evening I took a walk. After supper I taught Japanese to Elders Roskelley and Woodland. Took a bath and retired.

Wednesday, 7 November 1906, Tokyo

Clear—Warmer Up at 6:40. Spent part of the morning teaching Japanese to Elder Woodland, together with Elder Caine read over part of the translation copied by Mr. Mori. Had a conversation with a young man named Sugiyama. At noon we held our prayer and council meeting. **The brethren were asked for their opinion on the question of asking Mr. Hirai to contract for the correction of the Book of Mormon translation. The all expressed themselves as being in favor of the request and also gave it as their opinion that one versed in English would be able to give a better criticism than one not versed in English.** I stated that I wanted Elder Caine to read over the translation of "A Brief History of the Church" before that translation is printed. In the afternoon I worked on the Book of Mormon translation. After supper an English Bible Class was held under the direction of Elder Woodland. I taught Elder Roskelley a lesson in Japanese.

Saturday, 10 November 1906, Tokyo

Clear—Cold Up at 6:00. Ate breakfast at 7:00 a.m. and then went to Ushigome to see a house advertised for rent. The house was very well located and very attractive but altogether too small. **Went from Ushigome to the home of Mr. Kinza Hirai. My purpose in going to his home was to see if I could not persuade him to give most if not all of his time to the work of criticising the translation of the Book of Mormon. I met him and had a long talk with him about the matter. He is willing to do the work, but about the matter of giving up his several positions and devoting his whole time to this criticism, he will have to reflect deeply. I accepted his request to look over the English translation of the "Imperial Edict on Education" and make what corrections I considered necessary.** After returning to headquarters ate dinner and then spoke to the Bible Class on the "Deliverance of the Israelites from Egyptian Bondage." After supper, I taught Elders Woodland and Roskelley lessons in Japanese. Took a bath and retired.

Monday, 12 November 1906, Tokyo

Cloudy—Cold Up at 6:00. Until breakfast time I was occupied /cleaning house/. After breakfast I dusted the downstairs rooms. The rest of the forenoon and part of the afternoon I spent with Elder Caine going over his suggestions on book three of the Book of Mormon translation. In the afternoon also had a conversation with Mrs. Yoshimura who came to get some "religious consolation." After supper I taught Japanese to Elders Woodland and Roskelley.

Today Mr. Mori began copying Book III of the Book of Mormon translation. He finished Book II last Friday. I tried to reward him for his work on Book II but he absolutely refused saying that he considered it work for God and he didn't charge for work of that kind. I appreciate this feeling in him.

Wednesday, 14 November 1906, Tokyo

Cloudy—Cold. Up at 6:30. Spent the early morning teaching Japanese to Elder Woodland. The rest of the forenoon Elder Caine and I read over part of what Mr. Mori has copied. **At noon we held prayer meeting. Just as the meeting was closed Mr. Kinza Hirai called. I had a longer discussion with him about the criticism of the Book of Mormon translation.** After he left, I had a short chat with Mr. Mori. Then I turned my attention to the work on the Book of Mormon. After supper, I took a walk. Then I taught Elder Roskelley a lesson in Japanese.

Sunday, 18 November 1906, Tokyo

Cloudy—Cold. Up at 7:15. Ate breakfast. There were forty two present at Sunday School this morning the sessions of both departments were successful in every way. After school I read a little. A young lady from Shinonomachi came to see if we would allow representatives of her father's family to attend our meetings. It is a custom among well-educated people to enquire beforehand if it will be all right for them to attend meetings before they come to meeting. At 2:30 p.m. we held a Sacrament meeting in which I gave some instruction regarding the Sacrament. After this meeting, Elder Caine and I took a walk. Upon returning I ate supper. Evening meeting was well attended and the audience paid very good attention. After meeting I engaged in a conversation with Mr. Takada a military officer who attended or meeting. Later I talked briefly with Sister Hakii.

Thursday, 29 November 1906, Tokyo

Clear—Cold. Up at 6:15. During the morning I wrote letters and my journal. Just before dinner Mr. Norda came and I had a long talk with him about the Church and its relation to the commercial world. This man is a miner who has discovered a sulphur mine and a gold mine and being exceedingly anxious to develope them, entered into a contract with some Japanese who failed to keep their promises regarding money. He has approached a number of his countrymen for loans but their is so much red tape about getting money and he has so much fear that the capitalists will do him out of his possessions that he had been thinking that if he joined a Christian Church perhaps the church or one of its monied members would help him. I talked very plainly to him about our position in regard to such schemes on the part of his countrymen and I think he will not think of embracing religion for the purpose of getting money to start his mine. In the afternoon I did a little more writing. After supper, I taught Japanese to Elders Roskelley and Anderson.

Friday, 30 November 1906, Tokyo

Clear—Cold Up at 6:30. Before breakfast I taught Japanese to Elder Woodland for thirty minutes. After breakfast I wrapped up some photos to send to America. Mail from America brought the news of the defeat of the American Party in Utah at the last election. Also the news of the utter defeat of Senator Dubois of Idaho in spite of his active and vicious attack on the "Mormon" Church. In the afternoon and evening I wrote eight short speeches about the Beatitudes to be learned by the S. S. children and recited at our coming Christmas Party. Today I sent my Christmas letters and cards home.

Sunday, 2 December 1906, Tokyo

Clear—Windy—Moderate Up at 7:00. Before Sunday School I wrote a number of questions and answers regarding the visit of the Wise Men at the dwelling of Mary & Joseph in Bethlehem. After the regular session of the School, a song practice was held and I gave the speeches on the Beatitudes to some of the children. They were more than delighted with the call to take part on the Christmas program. I read in the "Era" till time for Sacrament & Testimony Meeting. After meeting I took a little exercise and rested till supper. Our meeting this evening was very well attended, but the number of females were very few. After meeting we had prayers, Sister Nami Hakii being present. This Sister manifested her love for the Gospel by paying her tithing and giving a donation of ¥5.00 to the Christmas Party Fund. Considering the fact that she is simply a servant girl who gets only ¥10.00 a month it is seen that her sacrifice of ¥6.00 (her tithing being but ¥1.00) represents eighteen days labor. When I see a brother or sister willing to sacrifice like this to God's cause I rejoice greatly and know they are worthy of and will receive Heavenly blessings in return.

Tuesday, 4 December 1906, Tokyo

Cloudy—Cold. Up at 6:30. Before breakfast I taught Elder Woodland a lesson in Japanese. After breakfast I went to look up a house advertised for rent. Upon returning I worked some on the Book of Mormon. After dinner I went over to the Akasaka Hospital to see how much it would cost to have Sister

Nachie's eyes tested and gold-filled glasses made for her. I made this inquiry with the intention of giving her this examination and glasses as a Christmas present. Returned and did some more work on the Book of Mormon. After supper I taught Elder Roskelley a lesson in Japanese. Took a bath and retired.

Wednesday, 5 December 1906, Tokyo

Cloudy—Very cold. Up at 6:15. Swept & dusted the down stairs. Spent the forenoon doing various odd jobs. At noon we held a prayer & council meeting. In the afternoon I did some writing and thinking and figuring in the interest of the events to take place this coming Christmas. **I also wrote a letter to Mr. Hirai relative to the criticism of the Book of Mormon translation.** I called on two of the Sunday School children to get them to take part on the Christmas program. After supper, I taught Japanese to Elder Roskelley. This evening Elder Woodland conducted an English Bible Class. There were eight young men present.

Thursday, 6 December 1906, Tokyo

Clear—Warmer Up at 6:30. Taught Elder Woodland a lesson in Japanese before breakfast. Read the newspaper and worked on the Book of Mormon. After dinner also I worked on the Book of Mormon. Before supper I took some physical exercise. After supper I taught Japanese to Elders Roskelley and Anderson. **This evening I received a postal card from Mr. Kinza Hirai in which he informed me that he cannot accept my proposition to him in regard to criticising the Book of Mormon translation. I feel perfectly satisfied with this decision on this question for I have prayed and felt that if he was not the man whom God has chosen to make this important criticism that God would prevent him from accepting my offer of the work to him. Mr. Hirai's refusal is a satisfactory answer to my prayers.**

Monday, 10 December 1906, Tokyo

Clear—Cold Up at 6:15. Taught Elder Woodland a lesson in Japanese. Ate breakfast. Spent the forenoon reading papers and magazines from America and writing to Bro. Y. Chiba. In the afternoon more mail came and I received a letter from Bro. Geo. Reynolds stating that two elders were set apart for the Japan Mission on November 23rd. Two of the Sunday School children who take part on the Christmas program came and rehearsed their parts. I did more reading this afternoon. Took a walk before supper. After supper I practiced the tune to one of the Christmas songs, and taught Japanese to Elders Roskelley and Anderson.

Thursday, 13 December 1906, Tokyo

Cloudy—Cold Up at 6:30. Taught Elder Woodland a lesson in Japanese before breakfast. Telephoned to the Nippon Yusen Kwaisha to learn if the steamer "Dakota" had been sighted or not. It had not been seen but the company informed Elder Caine, who later called at the office, that it would certainly arrive so he went down to Yokohama. I worked on the Book of Mormon during the forenoon and in the afternoon. I went out on Mission House business. Returned and conducted a singing practice on the songs to be sung at Christmas. Ate supper. Walked to Aoyama and then taught Elder Roskelley a lesson in Japanese. This evening I, on behalf of the elders here at headquarters, presented Sister Nachie with a pair of gold-filled spectacles. We had her go to the doctor and have her eyes examined some time ago thinking that the glasses would be done just in time for Christmas. The glasses coming so soon made it necessary to present them today. She seems well pleased and will be sure to enjoy reading and sewing as she has not done for a long time. Elder Caine returned without the new elders because the steamer didn't get in.

Friday, 14 December 1906, Tokyo

Warm—Fair. Up at 6:05. Taught Elder Anderson a lesson in Japanese before breakfast. During the forenoon I worked on the Book of Mormon. After dinner, I went and visited with Mr. Mori. **Today, about five o'clock, Elder Caine returned from Yokohama where he went to welcome two elders from**

Zion. He brought with him Elders Joseph H. Stimpson and Joseph P. Cutler the former coming from Riverdale, near Ogden, Utah and the latter from Salt Lake City, Utah. The addition to our force is greatly appreciated. During the evening I taught Elders Roskelley and Woodland lessons in Japanese.

Sunday, 16 December 1906, Tokyo

Cloudy—Colder Up at 6:45. Ate breakfast. This morning we had another large Sunday School. After the school we enjoyed a successful rehearsal on the Christmas program. I had a long conversation with a Mr. Suga. Held a short sacrament meeting. Took a walk before supper. Our meeting this evening was well attended. We had quite a disturbing spirit present. A man a little the worse for liquor came in while we were singing the first song. Elder Caine offered the opening prayer during which this man put in a number of sectarian "A—mens." During the singing of the second song his made some unharmonious variations. Immediately after the song, he came up to the front made a bow to the audience and was just getting his mouth open when I thought it was time to put him out. I took him by the arm and led him out. The elders saw that he got his clogs and started off, but he came back to the door and announced that he had something important to tell the people. He was again escorted out of the yard and told to go home, which he promised to do. I should have said that after the close of Elder Caine's prayer, he uttered a prayer which was such a conglomeration of repetitions that the audience began to smile out loud. This is the first experience of this kind we had ever had and after we got rid of the stranger our meeting passed off nicely.

Wednesday, 19 December 1906, Tokyo

Clear—Warm. Up at 6:15. Fasted all day. During the forenoon I went up to Yotsuya Street and also to Kojimachi street to buy some things for Christmas. At 12:00 n. we held prayer and council meeting in which it was decided to have Sister Nachie assist in the Primary Department during part if not all the year 1907. It was also decided that the Life of Christ should be the course of study in the Theological Department during the coming year. In the afternoon I did some more buying for Christmas and conducted a song and speech practice for some of the Sunday School children who have parts to render on Christmas. In the evening I wrapped up presents. Today Sister Nachie went down town and purchased most of the presents we intend to give the children this year.

Sunday, 23 December 1906, Tokyo

Fair—Cold Up at 7:00. Ate breakfast. At 10:00 a.m. Sunday School was held. The final practice (a sort of dress rehearsal) on the Christmas program was held. It was one o'clock before the children got through. At 2:30 p.m. we held Sacrament Meeting. Today being the birthday of the Prophet Joseph Smith, we held a little longer meeting than usual and spoke especially of his life and the church he founded under the direction of heavenly messengers. After meeting I wrote a letter or two in Japanese and then visited some of the homes of the S. S. children to invite them to the Christmas Party. After supper we held a special meeting in honor of Joseph Smith. The attendance was quite small but we enjoyed bearing testimony of the divinity and importance of the mission of the Prophet of the latter-days.

Monday, 24 December 1906, Tokyo

Clear—Very Cold Up at 6:00. Spent nearly the whole day working around headquarters decorating for Christmas and preparing for our Parties. I made a trip to Aoyama and one to Yotsuya to buy a few articles and leave admission tickets at the homes of some of the children. Retired very late in a very tired condition.

Tuesday, 25 December 1906, Tokyo

Clear—Cold—Ideal Christmas Day. Up at 6:30. Put the finishing touches on the house decorations and made a trip to Aoyama to buy one or two necessary articles. Ate breakfast at 10:30 a.m. Shaved & dressed preparatory to receiving the Sunday School children and their friends. By two o'clock, the hour appointed for the children's Christmas Party to begin nearly all of the children had arrived but the Party did not get started till about 2:40 p.m. There were 57 members of the S. S. and about 14 or 15 others in attendance. There were only three of the Sunday School members who received tickets and did not come, but the small number of guests was a great disappointment for we were anxious to have the children's parents with us and issued tickets for them. The reason for their non-attendance is given that they were very busy and could not get out to the party in the day time. The following program was rendered. . . .

It will be noticed that the Primary Department furnished the music. In fact every part of the program performed by the natives was taken by children of the Primary Department. The children acquitted themselves very well and the Lord is to be praised for the way he sustained them. This year Miss Miyo Mizuno of the Primary Department got the first prize for attendance having attended 48 times out of a possible 51. Miss Hisa Takahashi got second prize with a record of 47. Miss Hisa Saito got third prize with credit marks for 46 Sundays. The children were all given presents in porportion to their worthiness. All were given a bag of candy and package of crispets.

After the close of the Children's Party, which lasted not quite two hours, we arranged the seats and prepared for the Evening Christmas meeting which we announced would begin at 7:00 p.m. We were able to get a little bread and milk eaten before the meeting commenced. Six of the Sunday School children (all girls) had supper at our home and sang for us in the meeting. Their laughter and delight over their presents and their sweet voices gave our home just a taste of Christmas such as it has never had /before/ since we have been in it. Children certainly bring sunshine with them and this home of ours had some of that sunshine today.

The evening program was carried out as follows. . . .

After the benediction the audience again took their seats and the Christmas /Tree/ was lighted. Elder Caine explained some features of the tree and its use and object. After this I announced that we had a little booklet (Madonna) to present to each of those present with our Christmas congratulations. Elder Caine distributed the booklets and the audience dispersed. There were about 43 present besides the seven elders and the six little girls. Leaving out the Sunday School children who sang there were only two children in the congregation and two very small babies who were tied on to their mother's backs. The Lord blessed us again and I praise Him for his goodness. After the night meeting I relaxed and indulged in some laughter with some saints and friends. Three of our saints have put in an appearance today. They were all cordially invited to attend, but some seem to have entirely gotten out of the habit of coming to Mission Headquarters.

Today I received an embroidered cloth picture frame from Mrs. Umeda and a set of small vases from Misses Hayashi and Hijikata (two Sunday School students). A number of presents in the shape of cakes, candy and fruit were received for us all. This year the elders here at Tokyo (seven of us) /together/ bought presents or cards for all of the native saints, our friends and acquaintances. In all, the day has been a very busy one, a pleasant one, a profitable one full of experience. The Lord has sustained us in all of our efforts. I hope the seed sown today will bear much fruit—good fruit.

Wednesday, 26 December 1906, Tokyo

Clear—Cold Up at 8:15. Spent the forenoon sewing and doing nothing of consequence. At a little after noon we held prayer and council meeting. During the rest of the day I wrote my journal and indexed Journal I. After supper I walked up as far as Aoyama to order chicken for Christmas dinner which we intend to have tomorrow seeing we were too busy to eat on Christmas Day and today we have fasted. This evening I attended the English Bible Class. Retired in good season.

Sunday, 30 December 1906, Tokyo

Fair—Very Cold Up at 7:00. After breakfast I did an odd job or two. The Sunday School was well attended considering the fact that day after tomorrow is New Year's, the greatest feast and celebration observed by the Japanese. The exercises in the Primary Department which I teach were very interesting. The children all had very bright smiling faces this morning. The smiles from Christmas had not yet worn off. After school I talked with Miss Hijikata for about thirty minutes. Ate lunch. Had a violent headache. At 2:30 p.m. we held Sacrament Meeting. I did the speaking. After meeting I laid down for a while but the headache didn't ease up, so I took a walk. Elder Cutler accompanied me. Returned and ate supper. My headache left me before meeting began. After meeting I talked with Mr. Mori about a Sunday School Membership Application Card which I had conceived. I also wrote a brief letter to Mrs. Kiyo Umeda acknowledging the Christmas presents she sent to Elder Caine and I and also extended New Year's greetings.

Monday, 31 December 1906, Tokyo

Clear—Cold. Up at 7:00. Spent the day in the house writing, reading, teaching, and working on reports. During the year which closes at midnight I have been greatly blessed in body, spirit, mind, and work. The Lord has heard my prayers. I have been in the hollow of His hand. Good news has come from loved ones at home showing that a Divine Hand is over father, mother, brothers, sisters and all dear ones. While my father was called upon at one time to suffer a great deal, he was raised from his bed of affliction by good nursing directed and assisted by the power of our Heavenly Father. I have been able to lead one into the waters of baptism, bear testimony to others, work from day to day, as my limited strength and ability permitted, for the translation of the Book of Mormon and the general welfare of the Japan Mission over which I have been permitted to preside. If there is anything I have accomplished of merit, the praise is all due to God and upon Him I rely in humility for strength to do His will and my duty wholly and well during 1907. The following is a summary of the work done during 1906 as far as it is possible to estimate it in figures.

Notes

1. Joseph Smith Memorial. "To commemorate the 100 anniversary of the birth of the Prophet Joseph Smith, President Joseph F. Smith and a number of Church leaders and Smith family members traveled to Sharon, Vermont (Smith's birthplace), in 1905, to dedicate a memorial cottage and large granite obelisk. The Joseph Smith Memorial was one of the first historical sites maintained by the Church." Steven L. Olsen, "Centennial Observances," *Encyclopedia of Mormonism,* 1:260.

2. Alma O. Taylor, "The Holy Spirit Bears Witness," *Millennial Star* 67 (21 December 1905): 815–16.

3. William George Jordan, *Great Truths: Individual Problems and Opportunities* (London: Hutchinson & Co., 1904).

4. Leprosy. "A chronic, infectious disease that primarily affects the skin, mucous membranes, and nerves. It is caused by *Mycobacterium leprae,* which is similar to the bacillus that causes tuberculosis." "Leprosy," *Microsoft Encarta 98 Encyclopedia.*

5. Imperial University. Located on the old Maeda estate in Hongō, the Imperial University was started as a place of study of Westerners and Chinese by the shogunate. Edward Seidensticker, *Low City, High City: Tokyo from Edo to the Earthquake* (New York: Alfred A. Knopf, 1983), 241.

6. Boil. A collection of pus "accompanied by inflammation in the skin and its underlying tissues. Boils are also called furuncles and often look like large pimples. Roughly circular in shape, boils usually block the small cavities, or follicles, from which hair grows. They occur most frequently on the scalp, in the armpit, and in the groin. People who have lowered resistance to disease-causing agents, diabetes, or very oily skin are especially prone to boils. Boils are usually caused by a type of bacteria known as staphylococcus, which enter the skin through pores or small wounds." "Boil," *Microsoft Encarta 98 Encyclopedia.*

7. *Geisha.* Professional dancing and singing women of Japan, not prostitutes as commonly held. Geisha attended parties and entertained their male guests with songs, dancing, poetry recitals, and conversation. "Geisha," *Microsoft Encarta 98 Encyclopedia.*

8. *Fujisan.* Mt. Fuji or Fujiyama is the highest mountain (12,285 ft) in Japan and is noted for its conical form. Although recently dormant, it is an active volcano. It is revered by the Japanese as a sacred mountain. Nobuyuki and Hoffer, *An English Dictionary of Japanese Culture,* 46–48.

9. *Kabuki.* A form of traditional Japanese theater that combines acting, dancing, singing, and spectacle. It represents scenes from three kinds of plays: jidai-mono (histories), sewamono (domestic tragedies), and shosagoto (dances). Nobuyuki and Hoffer, *An English Dictionary of Japanese Culture,* (**[publisher?: place?, year?]**) 112.

10. *Gōchiso.* A dinner or a treat.

11. Baptism for the Dead. The proxy performance of the ordinance of baptism for one deceased. The Prophet Joseph Smith restored this biblical practice in Nauvoo in August 1840. H. David Burton, "Baptism for the Dead," *Encyclopedia of Mormonism,* 1:95.

12. Tokyo *Fucho.* Governor of Tokyo.

13. Chronic cataract of the conjunctiva. An abnormality of the mucous membrane which lines the inner surface of the eyelid.

14. Fish-tail. A small boat.

15. *Aino.* The aboriginal race of Japan, known in Japanese history as the Ebisu (barbarians). They were driven out of southern Japan to Hokkaido and finally conquered in the eighteenth century. Papinot, *Historical and Geographical Dictionary of Japan,* 1:4.

16. Piles. The condition of having hemorrhoids.

17. See William G. Hartley, "Latter-day Saints and the San Francisco Earthquake," *Ensign* 28 (October 1998): 22–29.

18. *Yoroshiku.* A greeting used to convey best wishes.

19. *Tukoku Insatsu Kwaisha.* Tukoku Printing Company.

20. Semi-annual general conference of The Church of Jesus Christ of Latter-day Saints.

21. *Contributor.* First published in 1879, the *Contributor* was a monthly periodical published by Junius F. Wells for the LDS Mutual Improvement Association. The publication continued until 1896. It was the forerunner of the *Improvement Era* and the present *New Era.* Jenson, *Encyclopedic History of the Church,* 158.

22. *Elder's Journal.* The *Elders Journal* was first published by the Church's Southern States Mission in 1903. By 1907 this periodical had been combined with the *Liahona* and adopted the same name. It featured sermons of Church leaders, doctrinal explanations, missionary correspondence, poetry, and news. Jenson, *Encyclopedic History of the Church,* 218.

23. *Kademono.* A hanging picture (scroll).

24. Orson Pratt, "Orson Pratt's Works" (published as proselyting pamphlet; recently reissued: Orson Pratt, "Orson Pratt's Works," [Orem, Ut: Grandin Book Company, 1990]).

25. At this time, it was common practice for priesthood holders to anoint the specific body part in need of healing of the person being blessed.

Four missionaries in Japan, c. early 1900s. Left Louis A. Kelsch, third from left Horace S. Ensign, the other two are unidentified. Courtesy John W. Welch.

Elders with Japanese Sunday School children in Tokyo. Courtesy John W. Welch.

Chapter 11

Alma O. Taylor Journal
(1907)

Tuesday, 1 January 1907, Tokyo

Clear—Cold Up at 7:20. Spent the morning doing little things. The afternoon also was spent making estimates of the work done during 1906. In the evening I taught Elder Roskelley a lesson in Japanese. I also taught Elder Woodland a lesson during part of the forenoon. Took a bath before retiring. Today several people called with New Year's congratulations.

Wednesday, 2 January 1907, Tokyo

Cloudy—Very Cold—Snow Up at 7:00. Today I made a number of New Year's calls. Called on Bro. Kikuchi and had a talk with him about doing his duty more fully. He accepted my advice and admitted that he was not doing right. I hope the Lord will impress my words upon him and stir him up to diligence. I found Mr. Kinza Hirai still in bed suffering with stomach trouble. At noon we held prayer and council meeting. In the evening after supper, I taught Japanese to Elders Roskelley and Anderson. Received mail from America.

Monday, 7 January 1907, Tokyo

Clear—Cold as usual Up at 7:00. Spent part of the forenoon reading part of the minutes of the Conference held last October. Mr. Mori came to write the names of the children in the Primary Department of the Sunday School so I spent some time arranging them in their proper order. Mr. Mori ate dinner with us.

In the afternoon I went down town to attend to some business. Among other things I called on the editor of the Jiji Shimpo and had a talk with him about the present position of the Church in regard to the subject of polygamy. The reason for this talk is to correct the errors in an article which appeared in yesterday's paper regarding Prest. Joseph F. Smith and his family relations. The editor received me cordially and I had quite a talk with him. Returned in time for supper but before eating I had a brief talk with a man who called asking about the gospel. After supper we read the rest of the minutes of the October Conference.

Tuesday, 8 January 1907, Tokyo/Kawagoe

Clear—much warmer Up at 6:30. Ate breakfast. Left Tokyo for Kawagoe on the 10:16 a.m. train from Shinjuku Station. Changed cars at Kokubunji. Between Kokubunji and Kawagoe I met a gentleman with whom I conversed for a little while about current topics.

Arrived at Kawagoe on scheduled time, 12:04. Took a rikisha to the Imafukuya Hotel. Ate dinner. It was not much of a meal and poorly prepared. Called at the Mayor's office, but the mayor, Mr. Shochin Nakai being ill I met his assistant Mr. K. Hirata with whom I had a brief talk and to whom I made many inquiries. From him I learned the names of the principal of the Middle School and the principal of the Higher Girls School. From the mayor's office I went to the home of Mrs. Tai, Sister Nachie's sister. I had a brief talk with her asking about the conditions of the mission work of the Episcopal Church in Kawagoe as she is the organist in the church and has been interested in her church affairs for a long time. From her home I went to the house of Mr. Macbara the principal of the Middle School and had a brief talk with him about the condition of the people religiously. I took a ride and walk around the town calling at the home of Mrs. Hirose the head of the girls Higher School but she was not at home. I returned to the hotel at 4:00 p.m. Took a bath. Ate supper. Thought awhile about mission affairs and about what I had learned during the day about Kawagoe. Retired about 9:00 p.m.

Wednesday, 9 January 1907, Kawagoe/Kōfu

Clear—Cold—Slight Wind. Up at 6:00. I gave orders last night for the hotel people to wake me at 5:30 this morning so that I could catch the 6:30 train for Kōfu. They forgot to wake me, but I heard the town bell strike six. I hurried my clothes on, washed my face in a minute, combed my hair in the dark and nearly ran over the servant as I was going down to get my shoes. A rikishaman was aroused from his slumbers and I got to the station at 6:20, ten minutes before train time.

The trip from Kawagoe was not only cold, but very dirty and of little interest. The train passed through 37 tunnels and some of them were so long that the tunnels altogether make up quite a part of the way. On the train, I met a gentleman who knows all about the country through which I intend to go. He told me that Iida in Shinano Kuni is a day's ride from the nearest railroad station so I have concluded to forgo visiting the place for want of time. After arriving in Kōfu at a little after noon I took a rikisha to the Daurokwan Hotel where I had dinner. The weather being quite cold and I having ridden half a day on an empty stomach, I felt like it would be unwise to fast any longer.

After dinner I took a rikisha and called first at the Kenchō (Governor's Office) and met Mr. Keiichiro Shibata who is the chief of the first department ([Chinese characters]). I asked about the growth of Christianity in Yama [blank] Ken and was informed that there are about 1000 Christians in the Ken and nearly one half of that number perhaps are in the city of Kōfu and the surrounding villages while the valley in which Kōfu is located may be said to contain the entire number of Christians. The people of this Ken were said to be very non-religious not even caring much for the traditions that have come down to them for centuries. The sentiment in favor of Christianity seems to be stronger [and] now than formerly, of course. From the Kenchō I went to the Shiyakusho (The Mayor's Office) and met the assistant Mayor. I enquired more particularly about the condition of the people religiously in the city of Kōfu. I enquired about rents etc. The Assistant Mayor is [blank] there being no mayor in office just at present.

After getting all the information I could about the educational condition of the people of the city, I called on Mr. Oshima the principal of the Middle School. I had a long talk with him. He is a friend of Mr. Kanzo Uchimura the famous Independent Christian in Tokyo and is also acquainted with Mr. Kintaro Oshima of Sapporo, Hokkaido, the gentleman who read over Elder Stoker's translation of "The Brief History of the Church." He also gave me an idea of the condition of Christianity and its prospects here from his point of view. He thinks the churches are not making any noticeable progress, but thinks the proper kind of missionary work would bring many to believe in Christ as their is no particular sentiment against Christianity. Mr. Oshima said he was one of the founders of the Independent Church in Sapporo. Before calling on Mr. Oshima I rode around the town and saw all of the principal schools and parts of the city. There are in this city over 40,000 people and there is one Middle School, a Normal School, a Commercial School, a Higher Girls School, and a Girls English School, the latter being a private institution established by the Canadian Mission Board. From Mr. Oshima's I walked to the hotel and ate supper. I wrapped up and addressed one copy each of "Mormons & Mormonism" by Takahashi Goro to Mr. Shibata and Mr. Oshima. I sent these books by a messenger. Before going to bed I had a little chat with the landlord about the country and the places lying between here and the next large place—Matsumoto. Retired about 9:30.

Thursday, 10 January 1907, Kōfu/Kamisuwa/Shiojiri/Tatsuno

Clear in some places—Snow in others—Cold! Up at 5:15. Ate a breakfast consisting of three glasses of hot milk and a loaf of bread. I took a rikisha to the station where I boarded the train going to Kamisuwa.

Upon arriving at the place I left my satchel at the station and went directly to the mayor's office and met the assistant mayor. I learned all I could from him about the town and vicinity and then I walked around the town twice. Kamisuwa is famous for its hot springs and the little fresh water lake named Lake Suwa. In the winter this lake freezes over and skaters from Tokyo and other large cities visit Lake Suwa for winter's sport. There is a Middle School and a Primary School in the town which has about 20000 inhabitants and lies in quite a pretty valley with many rural villiages surrounding it. The people are earnest followers of the Buddha according to the traditions of the Sodo Sect.[1] In the valley there are said to be one or two Christians and two or three foreign missionaries. I bought some cakes for dinner.

I took the 1:08 p.m. train and went to Shiojiri. On the way I met a naval officer who lived only a little ways from Iida. From him I learned about the road to Iida, the ways of travel and the charges. He said the people of Iida were honest and sincere. In fact, everyone has given a good report of them. After arriving at Shiojiri I was disappointed with the place which is still too small to be called a town. But I had just a little over an hour to talk and do so I called on the headman of the village (Village Chief) and learned that altho this mura[2] is only two stations away from Matsumoto, a Christian stronghold, the chief didn't know of a single Christian. I took the train back to Tatsuno the place where I have to take stage or rikisha for Iida. Arrived at Tatsuno at 5:05 p.m. I called [in] at the Minowaya and arranged to stay over night. Today it has been very cold.

Friday, 11 January 1907, Tatusno/Iida

Clear—Bitter Cold Up at 6:30. Last night it snowed a little so the morning scenery is truly wintery day. Ate hot milk and rice for breakfast. After breakfast I took a rikisha for Iida. We left the hotel about 8:00 a.m. and went as far as Akaho before stopping. At Akaho I ate dinner at the Kokuya. Continued the journey by rikisha from Akaho to Iida without a stop. Arrived at the latter place at 6:10 and stopped for the night at the Shōdō Hotel.

There was nothing of particular interest on the way besides the remarkable strength and endurance of the human horse that pulled me over the long 37 mile mountain road of hills and hollows. He is only half as large as I am but he is easily blessed with ten times as much endurance. His feat today has been very wonderful in my eyes. One interesting comparison is that we overtook the stage-coach that left about an hour ahead of us and I needed no change of men while the stage had to change horses four times on the way. Or in other words my man was faster than the stage and as good as five horses; if we consider that a rikisha with me and my valise in it as much for a man as a wagon with five people in it is for a horse. Ate supper. Wrote a little and then went to bed feeling very tired although I had done nothing but ride in a rikisha all day.

Saturday, 12 January 1907, Iida

Clear but very cold Up at 6:45. Ate breakfast. Before breakfast however I walked to the post office and sent a telegram to Elder Caine asking him to send me $50.00 by wire. After breakfast I walked to the barber shop and had a shave. From the barber shop I went to the Gunyakusho[3] and had a talk with the Guncho[4] about the condition of Christianity in this part. They didn't know much in fact they said there was not much about Christian work here to know. I went from the Gunyakusho to the mayor's office and saw the assistant mayor. He was very pleasant and told me all he could about the religious condition of the people. He also said that in Iida there are about 16,000 people and they observe their old religions with considerable diligence. I returned to the hotel and ate dinner.

After dinner, I went to a little village about two miles from Iida to see a Mr. Horiguchi of whom I had learned on this journey. I found him, but contrary to what I had been told he is not a Christian—only studying it. He introduced me to someone else but that someone else was not at home so the card of introduction did no good.

From this village I returned to Iida and then went to a place called Kamiuda and met the preacher of the Methodist Church. He told me that the Methodist mission in Iida was first opened 30 years ago and that during that time one hundred and twenty four had been baptized. Many of that number have moved to other places leaving only 70 in this part. Out of the 70 there are many who have grown indifferent and fallen to sleep spiritually so that they count only 30 or 35 active, live members of their church in this part. All of these are not in Iida. The large majority of them are in outlying districts. I had quite a long talk with him on religious topics. Returned to the hotel and had supper. I read the Bible for a while. No answer having come from Elder Caine, I sent another telegram asking the reason why. Retired at 8:30.

Sunday, 13 January 1907, Iida

Cloudy—Warmer but still very cold. Up at 8:00. Went to the doctor's in the forenoon to get some medicine for my eyes. My right eye has been inflamed for some days and has been running quite a bit so I thought it wise to have a little medicine for them. I also called at the post office to see about some money I telegraphed to Tokyo for Saturday morning. By some mistake on the part of the post office clerk the money order had been sent to the wrong place and was going all over the country to find me. I took a walk.

After dinner I went to the Sunday School held at the Nihon Kirisuto Kyōkwai.[5] Nothing much but noise and discord was manifest. I was surprised. I met the preacher Mr. Hiroshi Akasu. He knew Bro. Caine having met him many times at Tateyama Boshu. I took another walk in the afternoon and then went to the post office again in regard to my money. The order had at last reached me but the hour for payment was long past. I desiring to leave for Nakatsu early the following morning asked that the order be paid, seeing that it was the post office's fault that it had not reached be long before. Just after supper a messenger came from the post office and paid the money.

I walked with him as far as the post office and then went on to the Nihon Kirisuto Kyōkwai and attended their meeting. Six natives were present and it required that the preacher wait an hour to get that many. It reminded me of many like audiences at our mission headquarters in Tokyo. The sermon was anything but a gospel sermon. After the meting I went for a brief chat with Mr. Akasu and his audience. One old man and a young man came to the hotel with me and I talked with them till 11:00 p.m. Retired expecting to get up very early and take rikisha to Nakatsu.

Monday, 14 January 1907, Iida/Nakatsu

Cold—Calm—Snow Up at 5:30. Instead of being aroused at 4:30 by the hotel people as I requested I was allowed to wake myself at the above hour. I got up and had to wash in cold water that was only one degree warmer than ice and then I stood and had a general chill till I could get the cook to bring in some fire. After the hotel people got to moving they did very well and I can't complain for I and my guests keep them up till nearly midnight last night. I ate breakfast and at about 7:30 I left Iida for Nakatsu.

This trip has been quite an experience. I left the hotel in a rikisha moved by three men. It required this number to push and pull me up to the summit of the range of mountains lying between Iida and Nakatsu. As we neared the summit of the first ridge I got out and walked. Between this ridge and the next we rested at a mountain crest hotel and had dinner. It was only 11:00 a.m. The snow at this place outside of the beaten road was nearly two feet deep. As we came in sight of the summit of the second ridge the road was so heavy that I had mercy on my human studs and got out of the rikisha. I having alighted the men thought they could easily take the rikisha through a short cut where there was only a foot path. I followed and saw the experience. It was more work to get the rikisha through this place than it would have been to draw me over the regular road. At one point in this cut off the ascent was so deep and the snow so deep that it took all four of us to pull the vehicle along. When we got to the top of the last ascent one of the men said sayonara and I went on with two. Due to the fact that freight wagons are constantly going over the road it was very rough. The de/s/cent therefore nearly jarred all my joints loose. Before we had gone far the buckle on my trousers had rubbed so much between my back and the back of the seat that I had a blister on my spine. Five and a half ri (about 12 miles) from Nakatsu my human horses had to have a rest and a smoke. I found is very comfortable sitting by a kotatsu[6] in the meantime. The ride from this stop to Nakatsu or rather till it got dark was very interesting as the road lead along the side of the hill and below was the Kisō River where about 100 men were floating logs. The river is one of the clearest and most picturesque that I have seen in Japan.

At 7:10 p.m. we arrived at the Hashiriki Hotel in Nakatsu. Just before reaching the first summit it began to snow and continued till we were very close to Nakatsu when it turned into rain. Had the weather been fair the pleasure of the day's journey would have been greatly increased. The same rikisha man who drew me from Tatsuno to Iida was the principal runner on this trip also. The days journey cost me 40 sen for food and ¥9.50 for my carriage and "horses." This journey covers a distance of 36 miles of very hard road. This together with the 37 miles from Tatsuno to Iida makes 73 miles I have journeyed by the power of human flesh. Considering that it has been accomplished in the mid-winter and over mountain ranges I look upon it as quite an experience. I have been protected from harm & accident by the hand of my Father in Heaven for which I am very thankful. At the hotel at Nakatsu I ate supper wrote my journal and retired about 9:00 o'clock.

Tuesday, 15 January 1907, Nakatsu/Nagoya/Okazaki

Fair—Warmer Up at 7:00. Ate breakfast. Took a little walk around Nakatsu. Took the 9:12 a.m. train for Nagoya. A great many tunnels were passed through on the way. The scenery was far inferior to what I have been seeing on this tour. For a short distance where the train passes through a short narrow canyon by the side of a crystal stream there was a scene worth looking at. This was between Tajimi and Kōzōji.

Arrived at Nagoya at about 12:30. I took the street car and went as far as the City Offices. From there I walked to the Aichi Kencho[7] and was permitted to look over the list of Christian churches established in the Ken. In the city of Nagoya there are 16 Christian churches & preaching stations. The Roman Catholics, the Universalist, Methodists (two sects), Christian Church, Japan Christian Church, and the Japan Episcopal Church are represented. There are 30 foreigners working in the Ken and outside of Nagoya the next largest place, Toyohachi, has the most churches there being three in that place. Besides these two places there are 13 towns and villages in which either a church or mission house is maintained. The gentleman in the Kencho said that thus far the greatest amount of Christian missionary work had been done in the south east part of the Ken and remarked that it was no doubt in a better condition to receive Christianity than the other half of the Ken. I took a rikisha and saw the Nagoya Castle[8] which is now turned into a barracks for the third and fourth Nagoya Divisions of the army. There being nothing else of interest or value for me to see or learn about the city I left on the 3:30 train for Okazaki where I arrived at about 5:30. The town is a long ways from the station. I took a rikisha to the hotel. Ate supper, wrote my journal and had an hours reflection on the knowledge gained thus far on the trip and also on the condition of the mission. Retired at 9:00 p.m.

Wednesday, 16 January 1907, Okazaki/Toyohashi/Hamamatsu

Clear—A little milder Up at 7:50. Washed and packed up my valise and paid my bill at the hotel. Did not eat breakfast as today is the day all the elders fast. Walked around the town to get an idea of the place. I never have seen a place with so many temples and shrines for its size. I learned that Okazaki is a stronghold of the Shinshu sect of Buddhism.[9] I called at the Mayor's office and learned about the condition of the Christian Churches here. There are two one the Greek Catholic and the other the Japan Christian Church. The former has been here the longer and is said to have between 80 and 90 members. The latter has about 45 members. I met one of the members at the Mayor's office. I walked around a little more and called at the Gun offices where I learned that there was no place besides Okazaki in this gun where Christianity was being preached. I went from the Gun offices to the old castle (or rather what is left of the old castle) where Tokugawa,[10] the famous Shogun in power before Meiji[11] was born. Nothing remains except a few stones around the mote and the well where the new born babe was washed. The remains of the castle have been turned into a park.

I went to the hotel and got my valise and umbrella and took the horse cart to Okazaki station which is about one ri from the town. Left Okazaki on the 12:05 train and arrived at Toyohashi a little after one o'clock. I took a rikisha to the City office and enquired about the Christian missionary work in the city. I found that there are three churches. The oldest is the Greek Church which has been in the city for about 20 years. The Methodists also have a church but it is a hard looking place. They have been working in the city for a long time. The Japan Episcopal Church has a Mission House and I found on riding around the city that the Japan Christian Church has started a preaching station. The Greek Church had 154 converts the last of Meiji 38. The Methodists at that time had 32 converts and the Episcopal church had 51 as a result of 7 or 8 years work. Buddhism is the strongest religion but according to the information I received the people are not devout and the condition of the few temples I saw would prove the statement. The city was considered a town till last September when its rank was raised. Most of the people are merchants. There are a number of Primary schools, a Middle School, a Commercial School, and a Higher Girls School. In approaching the city I noticed a number of good sized villages in the valley which valley was very striking for appearance.

From the City Office I went to the Gun Office and was informed that there was only one place out-side of Toyohashi in the Gun where Christian missionary work is being carried on. The name of the vil-lage is Irogozaki; it is about 11 ri from Toyohashi. The Methodists have been doing a very little there for 10 years and have a following of 12. The name of the division of the mura in which the house used is located is Koshiozu. I learned that the population of Toyohashi is 37,200 or 9,200 families. Left Toyohashi on the 2:50 train and went to Hamamatsu. The scenery on the way was very interesting. A very small arm of the sea is crossed by the train between the two places. Arrived at Hamamatsu at 3:32. I went to the Hanaya Hotel. Took a bath, ate supper read and wrote and retired.

Thursday, 17 January 1907, Hamamatsu/Shizuoka

Clear—Quite Warm. Up at 7:30. Ate breakfast. Then I went to the Town Office and made inquiry about the town, its people and their doings and the condition of Christianity. I found that the town con-sisted mostly of Merchants and that so far as religion is concerned they have little time and less disposi-tion to dabble in it. The Zenchu sect of Buddhism[12] has the strongest influence over the minds of the people but as I have said religion doesn't cut much figure. The population of the town is 27,500. The Catholics have been working in the town for over twenty years and at the end of 1905 they had 190 members. The Methodists also have been working for over twenty years and in 1905 had 72 members. The Bifu Church (some sect of Methodists) have been operating for 7 or 8 years and have 23 members the Japan Episcopal Church has 37 as the result of between 4 & 5 years work. I walked around the town a little. I called on the Gun Office and learned that there was no place outside of Hamamatsu in the Gun where Christian missionary work is being carried on. I called on the preacher of the Japan Episcopal Church. He was not enthusiastic about what he saw and heard and experienced in Hamamatsu. I left two tracts with him so that he would find out who he was so "delighted to see."

I took the 11:40 train for Shizuoka City. Arrived here at 2:04. I took a rikisha to the Ken Office and was allowed to investigate what was carrying on in the Christian ranks in this entire prefecture. The Greek Catholics, the Roman Catholics and the Methodists seem to have the field in this prefecture. The two strongholds are Shizuoka and Numazu. In Shizuoka City there are 12 Christian churches. At the end of 1905 the enrollment of the Methodists was 315, the number of Roman Catholics was 190 and the num-ber of Greek Catholics was 170. The total of the rest of the churches was 104 making for the city 779 Christians. This is said to be the Methodist's headquarters. Their church is the largest and in the most prominent place. I will visit Numazu tomorrow so will write about it then.

The city of Shizuoka is the best place outside of Tokyo that I have seen. There is a hill near the city. I went up on top of it and had a good view of the country. The location is very fine; surrounded by hills on three sides and the ocean on the fourth side, the city may be said to have an ideal position. Quite differ-ent to the other places I have seen on this trip, the city seems to have special divisions for private dwellings and commercial enterprises thus bringing each class of people together so they can easily be reached. There is a division of the army located here. All the schools except a university are established here and the people generally seem to be greatly advanced. The population is about 50,000.

After walking around the town for some hours, I concluded to spend the night in the city so dropped into the Daitokwan Hotel. This hotel is very famous because the Emperor has stayed here on three different occasions and all the national guests from foreign lands are lodged and fed here when traveling through this part. I may be worth while to note that Shizuoka City is considered of enough importance and interest to be shown especially to the nation's foreign guests. I had supper, wrote my journal, read a little and retired.

Friday, 18 January 1907, Shizuoka/Tokyo

Clear—Warm Up at 6:15. Ate breakfast and left Shizuoka and went to Numazu. The scenery between these two places is very interesting. For a short distance the train goes along by the sea shore. Then by the foot of Mt. Fuji. The view of this famous mountain is perhaps best between Iwabuchi and Suzukawa.

Arrived a Numazu at 9:40. I walked all around the town which is very small. There are six Christian sects at work here. The Catholics (Roman) have a church building and 233 followers. The Methodists also have a church building and 75 converts. The Japan Episcopal Church has no meeting house. There membership is 65. The Japan Christian Church has 28. The Gospel Evangelists have 23 and the United Brethren have 5. I called on the preacher of the Gospel Evangelist's and had quite a chat with him. From his place I went to the Town Office and met the mayor. I made a few enquiries about Christianity in the town. The town is considerably smaller than Hamamatsu. They don't seem to be overly anxious about the welfare of their souls. It is located in a farming and fishing district.

Left Numazu on the 12:40 train and returned direct to Tokyo arriving there at 5:12. When viewing /Mt./ Fuji from Iwabuchi I thought a better view of the Mt. would be impossible, but I think at this time of the year perhaps the view from Gotemba is best because there is more snow on that side of the Mt. The ride to Ofuna was quite interesting. The scenery is good. I read the book of Revelations on the way. After arriving at Shimbashi station, I went immediately to headquarters. Arrived just in time for supper. Found all the brethren in excellent health and spirits. I received an autograph letter from Prest. Joseph F. Smith, also some interesting pictures of home from my brother Samuel.

Monday, 21 January 1907, Tokyo

Cloudy—Rain—Warm. Up at 7:00. Spent the morning fixing up the report of the Mission Sunday Schools. Also wrote a letter to my brother Samuel and his wife. Wrote a brief missive to Bro. Tomizo Katsunuma who recently sent half a dozen naval oranges from Hawaii to me. Read some of the Christmas News during the day. Also taught Japanese to Elders Woodland and Roskelley.

Wednesday, 23 January 1907, Tokyo

Clear—Warm Up at 7:20. After getting up I taught Elder Woodland a lesson in Japanese. During the rest of the forenoon I read and thought of the questions which rose in making up the annual reports of the mission. At noon we held a prayer meeting. I called the attention of the brethren to the fact that the elders who are in Sendai and Sapporo will be down to conference next week and we should prepare our minds and hearts for the outpouring of the Holy Spirit which I sincerely trust will be with us. After meeting I took a walk calling on the Takagi family. In the evening Elder Woodland's English Bible Class was held with a large attendance. I taught Elder Roskelley a lesson in Japanese and then visited the Bible Class for a few minutes. I went to bed early feeling quite unwell.

Thursday, 24 January 1907, Tokyo

Clear—Warm. Up at 7:20. Today I have been very unwell. My entire system has felt exceedingly weak. I have been taking chills all day. My head seems all stuffed up. I have done a little of a great many things, but I have not felt like work. Before going to bed I took a dose of medicine soaked my feet in hot water and prepared for a sweat.

Friday, 25 January 1907, Tokyo

Forenoon clear—Afternoon cloudy—Warm Up at 7:30. After a long night's sleep and sweat, I am much better today through the blessings of the Lord. I taught Elder Woodland a lesson in Japanese this forenoon. I looked over some of Elder Caine's suggestions on the fourth book of the Book of Mormon translation. Today I have carefully gone over all the annual Financial and Statistical Reports of the mission for 1906. The reports were sent to the Presiding Bishop's Office this evening.

Saturday, 26 January 1907, Tokyo

Rain—Colder Up at 7:20. During the forenoon I read the Era and then did a little on the Book of Mormon. In the afternoon a Bible Class was held at headquarters. I attended the opening exercises and then went to Dr. Wun/s/ch's to have him look at my nose again. I had to wait for quite a while for him. He also examined my chest and pronounced it strong. I have had a sore throat and disagreeable cough for some time so I wondered if my lungs were getting weak or diseased, hence the examination above mentioned. Returned and after supper had a very pleasant talk with Sister Hakii. Took a bath and retired.

Monday, 28 January 1907, Tokyo

Cloudy—Cold Up at 7:00 Spent the forenoon looking up a few facts regarding the amount of money spent by the elders in the Japan Mission during 1906. In all the personal accts. of the elders show that they used ¥4,839.17 during the year. This is a large amount and shows what a material sacrifice the elders' parents and relatives are making for the spread of the gospel. This amount represents the money used by 12 elders but two elders were only here during the last half of December. One came in the latter part of August and one went home on the 1st of May so the remaining eight have used most of the amount. During the rest of the forenoon I taught Japanese to Elder Woodland. In the afternoon I worked on the Book of Mormon and took some exercises. In the evening I taught Japanese to Elder Roskelley.

Tuesday, 29 January 1907, Tokyo

Cloudy—Rain Up at 7:00. Spent an hour after breakfast teaching Japanese to Elder Woodland. Thought a little regarding the Saturday Bible Classes. After dinner I cleaned and pressed my clothes. In the evening I took some physical exercises. Ate supper. Taught Elders Roskelley and Anderson Japanese. Took a bath and retired.

Had been in bed for about 30 minutes when I was awakened by the cry, "Fire." I sprang out of bed and looked out of the window and saw the flames in the large foreign house recently built by Mr. Taniuchi just across our neighbor's lot from us—not over 100 ft. away. I hurridly put on a few clothes giving an order or two to the elders in the meantime, ran out and put a ladder up to get on the roof by. Took a bucket of water up on the roof. Two more elders did likewise. The rest keep a patrol around the house. The Lord protected us. The flame and sparks from the burning building made direct for our house for a little ways and then, as though in a channel, they turned a right angle so that not a spark lit on the house or in the yard.

Until the building was entirely burned and the flames nearly extinguished a large crowd of onlookers and sympathizers were in and around our home. Our friends and acquaintances came running in all out of breath to offer any assistance to us if we were in danger. Many came and after seeing that we were in practically no danger, left their cards and returned. This way of rushing to the homes of friends who are in the neighborhood of fires to help and sympathize is a praiseworthy one. Our viligent patrol around the house kept us from falling victims to burglars & thieves who undoubtly were present in good numbers as the fire was without doubt an incendiary as there was no one living in the house—the tenants had promised to move in tomorrow. At 1:15 I returned to bed and after my nerves quited down a little I fell asleep. Praise is due to the Lord for his kind protection over our home.

Wednesday, 30 January 1907, Tokyo

Cloudy—Rain—Colder Up at 7:00. Spent the entire forenoon cleaning house. After noon I did a number of odd jobs and held a prayer meeting with my brethren. **At about 4:15 the elders arrived from Sendai and Sapporo. They were all looking quite well and seem to be in the proper spirit. The rest of the day was spent chatting and singing together.**

Friday, 1 February 1907, Tokyo

Clear—Cold Wind. Up at 6:30. Spent the forenoon doing a little on the Book of Mormon and thinking about matters to be presented to the Elders for their consideration. **After dinner we held a meeting, the first one of the conference in which the health and physical condition of the elders was reported and our duty to our bodies discussed. The meeting lasted three hours. In the evening I talked and sang with the brethren a little then Elder Stoker and** I took a ride and walk as far as Bro. Kikuchi's to invite him to be present at our testimony meeting on Sunday.

Monday, 4 February 1907, Tokyo

Clear—Cold Up at 7:10. Ate breakfast. From 9:30 we held conference. The meeting lasted till after 12:00 n. The elders gave a report of the condition of their fields. They all feel that the prospects are brightening and that those who continue the work in the fields will have great cause to rejoice. I spoke for some time. Ate dinner. Doctored Elder Anderson who is not well. He is suffering with a sore throat and cold. In the afternoon we held another meeting in which the elders were instructed regarding their use of money received from home. The matter of keeping records and also keeping a good, correct account of the mission money sent to the different fields were discussed. After meeting I took a walk with some of the brethren. Ate supper and prepared my mind to discuss the problems to be presented tomorrow.

Tuesday, 5 February 1907, Tokyo

Clear—Warmer Up at 7:00. After breakfast, we held another meeting of our conference. The matter of tracting was considered and a number of questions decided. The meeting lasted till about noon. Had a little rest then ate dinner. At 2:00 p.m. we held another meeting at which time I did most of the speaking. This being the last session of conference I sought to impress upon the minds of the elders the necessity to work with great zeal, for the time for the proclaimation of the gospel is growing short. The signs of the Second Coming are multiplying and the nations must have an opportunity to accept or reject the gospel. The Lord sustained me in my remarks and all seemed to rejoice in the meeting.

After the remarks I made the following appointments. Elders Wm R. Fairbourn and Joseph H. Stimpson to Kōfu the capitol of Yamanashi Perfecture. I called Elder Stoker to accompany these two brethren and assist them in starting the work in this field for no missionary work has ever been done in Kōfu. Elders Justus B. Seely and Joseph P. Cutler were appointed to Sapporo and Elders John L. Chadwick and Daniel P. Woodland were appointed to labor in Sendai. This leaves Elders Fred A. Caine, James Anderson and John H. Roskelley and I in Tokyo. I took a walk after the meeting. After supper I wrote an announcement for the brethren in Sendai to use in beginning their meetings. Took a bath and retired.

Wednesday, 6 February 1907, Tokyo

Cloudy—Very Cold Up at 6:15. After two hours work I succeeded in getting the house cleaned up a little. Elder Stoker and I spent the rest of the forenoon down town buying various articles. Returned and at 1:00 p.m. we held prayer meeting. The burden of our prayers today has been that God will move upon the hearts of the people and lead them to accept the gospel in sincerity of heart. In the afternoon I read letters from home and chatted with the elders. We took some snaps with the kodak.

After supper a Bible Class was held. As Elder Woodland has been assigned to labor in Sendai he was released from his position as teacher of the English Bible Class and was succeeded by Elder Anderson. The four young men present this evening were very much surprised and in a short speech one of the students told of the respect the class had for Bro. Woodland and expressed their hearty thanks for his kind teachings.

We were pained today to read in one of the papers from home the death notice of Elder Stimpson's father. No letter announcing his illness or death had been received by our brother so the news came as quite a shock. Bro. Stimpson's father has lived an active life of more than four score years and has set a good example before his large family. Realizing that his father has lived a long useful life and keep the faith our brother is reconciled to this separation. This incident just at the close of our conference and on the eve of the last day before the elders leave for their fields made a

feeling of sadness come over us. But God's hand is over us all and His will is righteous in all things.
Thursday, 7 February 1907, Tokyo

Clear—Still Cold. Up at 7:00. Ate breakfast. **At 9:45 Elders Stoker, Fairbourn and Stimpson left for Kōfu. At 10:30 Elders Seely and Cutler left for Sapporo and Elders Woodland and Chadwick left for Sendai the last four brethren traveling together as far as Sendai.** After their departure I straightened things around a little and did considerable writing in the afternoon. In the evening, after supper, I had a little time to think and teach Elder Roskelley a lesson in Japanese.

Sunday, 10 February 1907, Tokyo

Cloudy—Cold wind Up at 6:45. Before breakfast straightened things up a little around the house. After breakfast I welcomed the Sunday School children. We had a very large Sunday School today. Two or three had to stand up during the opening exercises. We are blessed in our Sunday School work. After school I put some stars on the roll and then ate dinner.

In the afternoon we held a sacrament meeting. Sisters Nachie and Kanabe were present. Sister Kanabe has been mentioned heretofore as Sister Deguchi, but recently she surprised by the announcement that she was married to Mr. Kanabe last November. Mr. Tsukakoshi came while we were holding meeting. He brought the June 4th number of the "North American Review"[13] in which there is an article on Senator Smoot and Mormonism. The article manifest no love for Mormonism but maintained that Senator Smoot cannot lawfully be deprived of his seat in the Senate.[14] Our evening meeting was not so large but a good spirit prevailed. I read a little of "Orson Pratt's works before going to bed.

Saturday, 16 February 1907, Tokyo

Fair—Cold and dusty. Up at 7:00. After breakfast, I worked on the Book of Mormon. Also wrote a letter to Elders Woodland and Chadwick asking them to see Bro. Yoshiro Oyama who seems to have become disaffected in his faith due perhaps to mental weakness. I also gave Elder Roskelley an hour's drill in Japanese. After dinner I again worked on the Book of Mormon. No Bible Class was held today as no one came. Elder Caine had, however, a profitable talk on the gospel with three students of the Normal School who dropped in an hour late. I looked up a little on the scriptures to sort of get my mind upon some subject to present to the people who might come to our Sunday Services. Pumped the bath water and took a walk before supper.

A letter received today from Elder Seely states that he and his companion, Elder Cutler arrived in Sapporo on the morning of the 12th inst. instead of the night of 9th as expected. The delay was caused by bad weather and a snow blocade. The brethren intended to leave Hakodate on the night of the 9th but their baggage did not reach the station in time so they waited till the next morning. They passed the train that left the previous night as it was piled up in a heap beside the track. It had been wrecked, so it was providential that the brethren's baggage was delayed and they did not take passage on the doomed train.

Wednesday, 27 February 1907, Tokyo

Fair—Still warmer. Up at 6:45. Took a walk. With Elder Caine I read 16 pages of the proof sheets of #3 Tract "Is there a God?" which has to be set up again as the plates were destroyed in the fire that burned the Hakushin Sha. I worked for an hour on the Book of Mormon and taught Elder Roskelley an hour's lesson in Japanese before noon. At 12 o'clock we held a prayer meeting. In the afternoon Elder Caine and I read 16 more pages of proof sheets. I worked about two hours on the Book of Mormon. Ate supper. Attended the Bible Class held by Elder Anderson. Today at about 3:00 p.m. two of the Sunday School children came and practiced a song which sometime in the future we will have them sing in our night meeting.

Thursday, 28 February 1907, Tokyo

Clear—Strong wind and terrible dust. Up at 6:00. Swept and dusted the downstairs. Ate breakfast. Taught Elder Roskelley an hour's lesson in Japanese. Wrote out a list of the pictures that I have thought suitable to go with the Japanese translation of the Brief History of the Church. This list I sent to Elder Stoker to get his suggestions on it before definitely deciding. Read the proof sheets of the revised edition of #1a Tract "The Latter-day Saints." Also read the first proof sheets of the last third of the new edition of the #3 Tract. This work keep me busy till after five o'clock. I took some exercise by throwing some water around the front yard and the street to settle a little of the dust. Ate supper, then looked up some of the books to see how many pictures we have here which can be reproduced for the brief history.

Monday, 4 March 1907, Tokyo

Colder—Cloudy. Up at 6:50. Ate breakfast. Taught Japanese to Elder Roskelley. Corrected a brief composition written in English by Mr. Mori. Ate dinner. Read the newspapers and studied a letter from Brother Chiba who because of misfortunes coming upon his parents is very much distressed in spirit.

Had a talk with Mr. Yoshijiro Watanabe a man I met while laboring in Nakanegishi, Tokyo three years ago and with whom I have had many talks on the gospel. I have felt that he has been impressed with the truth of "Mormonism" and I have also felt that I had discharged my duty towards him. He is about to leave for London, England and came this evening to say farewell. He confessed that he has never been able to discharge from his mind the testimony I bore to him and that he has reflected upon our teachings and compared them to the teachings of the Methodist Episcopal church to which he belongs and felt that the Church of Jesus Christ of Latter-day Saints is the true church and that he was connected with a church having no authority. However, he having been taught and nourished in that church so long and having formed such familiar relationships with the preacher and members of his branch he had not been able to sever the cords binding him to that society and come out boldly against the ridicule and opposition that would surely come upon him if he joined the true fold. This confession reveals a truth which explains why the Japanese do not come forth and unite themselves with God's Kingdom. They are cowards without strength to face the world for the sake of truth. This weakness has not only prevented Mr. Watanabe from going down into the watery grave to be born again but it is preventing many who have received just as strong impressions about "Mormonism" as he has. May God be merciful with this people and give them courage to follow their convictions of the truth and endurance to stand firm to the end of life.

Sunday, 10 March 1907, Tokyo

Cloudy—Still quite warm. Up at 6:30. Ate breakfast. Read up on a lesson to present to the children of the Sunday School which was attended by a good number of children and four or five adults. After school I talked for an hour with Mr. Sugahara who desires to be baptized. I then ate dinner and started a letter to mother but a young man called and I talked with him till time for sacrament meeting. After meeting I finished my letter to mother and wrote a brief note to the elders in Sendai who inquired about administering to people outside of the Church. Ate supper. At 7:00 p.m. we began our evening meeting which was not very well attended. The subject discussed was "Prayer." After meeting I read a little. Then we had prayers and I retired after a brief visit with Sister Hakii.

Tuesday, 12 March 1907, Tokyo

Cloudy—Warm Up at 6:00. Spend about an hour throwing water on the street in front of our house and in the yard to lay the dust, which has become very offensive lately due to the lack of rain. After breakfast, I taught Japanese to Elder Roskelley for an hour. I talked with Mr. Miyazaki the fake prophet and false Christ who has lost his good sense. He received no consolation from me as I told him he was false in every claim and was in transgression. Because of this delusion he is following he has become very poor and today had to beg for assistance to help himself and his wife. I gave him a yen. Spent the afternoon working on the Book of Mormon. Took an hours exercise before supper. After supper I taught a little Japanese to Elder Anderson and worked for an hour on the Book of Mormon. Took a bath and retired.

Wednesday, 13 March 1907, Tokyo

Cloudy—Warm Up at 6:30. Took a little exercise before prayers. During the forenoon I taught Japanese to Elder Roskelley and worked on the Book of Mormon. In the afternoon I wrote a letter to the Presiding Bishop's Office asking some questions about the Annual Reports. Took a walk for exercise. Ate supper and did a little more work on the Book of Mormon. Commenced an article on the subject of polygamy which will be put in the Brief History translation as an appendix. The reason for discussing this subject is to declare briefly and clearly the present position of the Church on this question in order that something final and official may be present/ed/ to the people of Japan who, like the majority, consider Mormonism and polygamy synonymous.

Today at noon we held a prayer and council meeting at which it was decided to begin an active search for someone with ability and character to criticize the Book of Mormon translation.

Monday, 18 March 1907, Tokyo

Clear—Warmer—Slight Breeze. Up at 7:00. Ate breakfast. Today I have worked on my article relative to polygamy in the "Mormon" Church. Today the good news of the victory of Reed Smoot in defending his right to his seat in the U.S. Senate reached us.[15] Inasmuch as his fight has been the means of bringing around a thorough investigation of the "Mormon" Church and able defenses of our stand, the victory of Bro. Smoot is a great victory for the cause of truth. His case has given "Mormonism" an advertisement in the United States which will result in many souls coming into the fold. Thus the opposition of our cousins will result in the increase of our strength. This great victory has caused my heart to rejoice exceedingly and thinking this a fit opportunity to declare a few things about the present position of the Church regarding the question of polygamy. **I wrote this evening a four page article for the newspapers. During the day** I took a little exercise. Retired very tired and weary in mind.

Tuesday, 19 March 1907, Tokyo

Clear—Cold Up at 6:00. Read a little of my article to Elder Caine who copied it on the typewriter. Ate breakfast and went to Waseda University where I met Mr. H. Hirai; Mr. Kinza Hirai's brother, a teacher of English at the University. I asked him to translate my article on polygamy for the newspapers. He consented and promised to have back four or five o'clock the next day. The article is entitled "No fears for polygamy." I returned to headquarters and taught Elder Roskelley a lesson in Japanese. I mended my overcoat. Ate dinner and then continued to dress up my article on Polygamy in the Mormon Church which will form the appendix of the "Brief History of the Church" in Japanese. Before going to bed I finished the work on the article which Elder Caine will copy on the typewriter tomorrow. I took a 30 minutes walk after supper.

A card from Elder Stoker states that the elders in Kōfu moved into their house today and are ready to begin their work.

Wednesday, 20 March 1907, Tokyo

Clear—Windy—Terrible dust—Cold. Up at 6:45. This morning I read over my article entitled "Polygamy in the 'Mormon' Church" and Elder Caine started to copy it on the typewriter. It took him one day to do this as there were 17 pages. In the afternoon I wrote a letter to the First Presidency and part of one to Elder Edward H. Anderson. In the latter I gave a list of the pictures we want sent to us so we can reproduce them in the translation of the Brief History. I went to the home of Mr. H. Hirai and read over the translation he made of the article wrote for the newspapers about the present conditions of polygamy in the Church. It took me till nearly 8:00 p.m. to look over the translation and have him correct an error or two that I found. He has made a very satisfactory translation. Returned to headquarters. Ate supper, read over the seventeen page article, finished the letter to Bro. Anderson, attended prayers and retired.

Thursday, 21 March 1907, Tokyo

Clear—Warmer—Calm. Up at 6:30. After breakfast I copied the translation made by Mr. Hirai I made a carbon copy at the same time and by the use of blotters and press got two good copies from the one I wrote. After dinner Elder Caine took the copies and gave one each to the Jiji, Mancho Asahi, and Hochi. These papers may publish the article in the course of a week or ten days. I talked with a gentleman who called asking about the Church. I then talked to the Sunday School children who had come today in answer to my request last Sunday. I asked six of them to take part in a program I desire to present to our audience Sunday night, April 7th. Then I went with Elder Andersen to see some houses in Koishikawa which from reports appeared to be about what we want for a mission headquarters. About 75 lbs of mail arrived from America this evening. All good news. Zion is growing. Retired at 10:00 p.m.

Monday, 25 March 1907, Tokyo

Rain—Colder Up at 7:00 Spent the forenoon writing and talking with Mr. Hayakawa a young man who has been attending our meetings for some time and who came today asking for "permission to receive the Holy Ghost." I talked with him during the rest of the forenoon. After dinner I worked on the Book of Mormon and taught Elder Roskelley a lesson in Japanese. In the evening I continued working on the Book of Mormon.

In a letter to Mr. Hirogaro Hirai I enclosed ¥10.00 for his work translating the article on polygamy for the newspapers. I also asked him if he would favor us by translating the article "Polygamy in the 'Mormon' Church" which I wrote recently as an appendix to the translation of "A Brief History of the Church."

Wednesday, 27 March 1907, Tokyo

Rain—Cold Up at 7:00. Spent the forenoon teaching Japanese to Elder Roskelley and looking over some of the Book of Mormon translation. After [dinner] noon, I did a little more on the translation then taught some of the children of the Sunday School some songs which they have been asked to sing at our meeting Sunday night April 7th. After supper I wrote a letter and then did some more on the Book of Mormon. **Today at the prayer and council meeting held at noon, we further discussed the case of Yoshiro Oyama and, upon the motions of Elder Fred A. Caine, seconded by Elder James Anderson Oyama was excommunicate from the Church for apostasy. The vote on the motion was unanimous. The letter I wrote this evening was to him informing him of the action which severed him from the Church of God.** Today Bro. Yasubeiye Chiba came and began copying the part of the Book of Mormon translation continued in Book [III] IV of the manuscript.

Thursday, 28 March 1907, Tokyo

Clear, Windy, Warmer Up at 6:45. Spent the forenoon correcting the copy of my article about polygamy in the Mormon Church and copying the same. I also wrapped up some literature to send to Sendai and Sapporo. After dinner all of the elders at headquarters went to the Aisumi Jogakko to witness the exercises in honor of the completion of a new building. I only stayed an hour. **I left the school and took a jinrikisha to the home of Mr. Hirogoro Hirai with whom I talked for about an hour. I asked him to translate my article mentioned above. He consented and will perhaps be able to finish it in a week or ten days.** Returned to headquarters and after supper prepared some things to take to Kōfu. Today Bro. Chiba has copied some more of the Book of Mormon translation.

Friday, 19 March 1907, Tokyo/Kōfu

Cloudy—Rain—Cold Up at 6:45. Swept & dusted the down stairs before breakfast. **After breakfast I looked over the papers. In this morning's Jiji I noticed with pleasure the article I had written about the present stand of the Church in regard to the practice of polygamy and which was translated and handed to the editor sometime ago. I left headquarters at about 9:15 and took the 10:16 train from Shinyaku for Kōfu. Arrived at Kōfu at a little before four o'clock and met elders Stoker, Fairbourn, and Stimpson at the station. I went with them to their house. Wrote and sent to the newspaper an advertizement of the meetings we intend to hold while I am here.** Wrote my journal, ate supper, after supper I had a talk with the elders telling of our doing at Tokyo and also read my article of "Polygamy in the 'Mormon' Church" to them. Had prayers and retired.

Saturday, 30 March 1907, Kōfu

Clear—Warmer. Up at 6:45. Spent the forenoon eating, writing, and cleaning house. After dinner I reflected a little about something to say to those we expected to attend our meeting advertized to begin at 2:00 o'clock. Only three came and no meeting was held. This was a great disappointment to me. At about 4:00 p.m. I took a walk with Elder Stoker. Ate supper. At 7:00 o'clock the time for our evening meeting, no one was here. Elder Stoker and I sang some songs and succeeded in getting four grown people and a number of children. At about 8:00 we started a brief meeting. I was the speaker. Again I was disappointed in the turnout. We have advertized the meetings through the papers and otherwise but the people do not seem to have heeded the call.

Sunday, 31 March 1907, Kōfu

Cloudy—Warm Up at 7:05. Ate breakfast. **At 10:00 a.m. a large crowd of children were assembled at the mission house. They were called to order and the Kōfu Sunday School of the Japan Mission was organized with Elder Wm R. Fairbourn as teacher. I spoke to the children and assisted a little in other ways.** Ate bread and milk for dinner. At 2:00 p.m. the hour announced for the afternoon meeting not a soul had come. Later Mr. Monor called. I talked with him about the Book of Mormon. After this conversation I had a private talk with Elder Fairbourn which lasted for about two hours. I gave him very plain advice about the way he should act in the presence of the Japanese, especially females and also cautioned him against becoming familiar with the people. Some of his actions in Sendai were not in harmony with his position as an elder and teacher and therefore he has been criticized somewhat. Ate supper.

The last hope for a meeting vanished when 7:00 o'clock came and not a single soul put in an appearance. We waited till eight, but no head got inside the door. We sang and made a noise to attract someone, but our petition was not heeded. We took down the lantern, closed the gates and held a sacrament meeting among ourselves. At this meeting I gave the elders what instructions I had to impart and then listened to their remarks. Retired tired of disappointment and disgusted with the people of Kōfu. The papers had written articles about us and announced the meetings, a hand bill had been printed and one placed in the Saturday morning's paper so that one of these extended every home that the paper extended. Fifteen posters had been written and posted up in conspicuous places and the neighborhood had been informed of the meeting by the Elders personal visits.

Monday, 1 April 1907, Kōfu

Cold—Rain and snow. Up at 6:15. Ate breakfast at 7:00 a.m. Took the 8:10 a.m. train from Kōfu and after a long, cold, lonesome ride arrived at headquarters in Tokyo about 2:00 p.m. Found all the brethren in good health. Spent the afternoon reading newspapers etc. After supper, I worked till bedtime on the Book of Mormon.

Wednesday, 3 April 1907, Tokyo

Clear—Colder Up at 7:05. Spent the forenoon teaching Japanese to Elder Roskelley, reading the papers, and correcting the Book of Mormon translation. At noon we held our prayer meeting. After meeting the children who are going to perform next Sunday night came and practiced their parts. I looked over a newspaper or two from America. After supper I took a walk calling at the homes of some of the Sunday School children. Visited for sometime with the Aguma family. They are in very distressed circumstances. Returned and worked on the Book of Mormon till bed time. Today Mr. Misumi who is writing a book on "Colonization among the Mormons" called. Elder Caine and I talked with him. Bro. Yasubeiye Chiba has been here most of the day copying some of the Book of Mormon translation. His work today finished what we expected him to do—that is, down to the end of the fourth book of the manuscript which is as far as the end of Mosiah 1st chapter.

Friday, 5 April 1907, Tokyo

Fair—Warm Up at 6:00. Spent the time before breakfast looking over the statements for last months receipt & disbursements and reading the newspapers. During one hour after breakfast I taught Japanese to Elder Roskelley. A young man named Katō who is now living with General Kawamura in Harajuku came to see if we would not teach him English. I arranged for him to assist Elder Roskelley in Japanese and for Elder R. to assist Mr. Katō in return in his English. Spent the rest of the forenoon working on the Book of Mormon and writing a letter to Mr. Hirogoro Hirai relative to the translation he is making for us. In the afternoon, I listened to some of the Sunday School children recite their parts on the program to be given Sunday night. The rest of the time I worked on the Book of Mormon.

Saturday, 6 April 1907, Tokyo

Cloudy—Slight rain—Warm. Up at 6:00. Spent all the forenoon cleaning house. After dinner I cleaned up and attended the Bible Class which was a success. After the class I wrote a long letter to Bro. Aritatsu Kawanaka in relation to tithing and the support of missionaries instructing him that it was wrong for the saints to ask the elders to lend them money or to try to get loans from the Church funds. It is very hard for the people to realize perfectly the great sacrifices the parents and relatives of missionaries make to support them in the mission field. We are looked up as men of means. They imagine that anyone who can afford to come so far and live in a large house must be wealthy. Took a bath before retiring.

Sunday, 7 April 1907, Tokyo

Clear—Warm—Windy. Up at 6:30. Did a few jobs before Sunday School which began at 9:00 a.m. The days having become longer, we have started today to begin the school according to the summer schedule. The children turned out in large numbers, but the theological department would have failed completely had it not been for the attendance of the two Mr. Moris. After school the children who are going to take part in this evening's meeting remained long enough to have their final practice. I walked to Aoyama and back and called at the home of one of the children who was not present to practice her part on the program. I found that owing to the death of a little girl in one of her relation's families she had gone to that relative's home and would not be able to take her part. My disappointment was great as she was the main prop in the singing force. At 2:30 we held our fast and sacrament meeting. After meeting I had a talk with Bro. Yasubeiye Chiba who has been very much distressed in his mind and purse lately because of misfortunes to himself and parents. This misfortune has led him to neglect paying an honest tithing and neglect many of his duties. Having heard the remarks during the meeting and being distressed in his mind because of his neglect he confessed and promised to do better no matter what straits he may find himself in. Ate dinner. At 7:40 our evening meeting convened. We had many unoccupied seats, but the attendance was fair. The following program was rendered. . . .

The children acquitted themselves creditably and to my full satisfaction. This departure no doubt was appreciated by our audience which consisted of those who have heard Elder Caine and I discourse regularly for nearly two years.

This afternoon I wrote a letter to Mr. Tokoyo our old friend and valuable helper. He is now in the Bank of Formosa, Kobe.

Monday, 15 April 1907, Tokyo

Clear—Calm—Warm Up at 6:50. Spent the forenoon teaching Japanese to Elder Roskelley and working on the Book of Mormon. In the afternoon also I continued my criticism of the Book of Mormon translation. **I was pleased to receive the translation of my article on "Polygamy in the 'Mormon' Church" which translation was made by Mr. Hirogoro Hirai. The neatness with which this work is prepared indicates that he has worked hard on the translation.** After supper, I called on Sister Ota and tried to encourage her to attend her meetings and perform her duties as that the blessings of heaven might rest upon her. Returned and talked with Mr. Sakuraba about copying some of the corrected translation of the Book of Mormon. He consented to copy a book and promised to begin tomorrow copying for about two hours each day till the work is done

Wednesday, 17 April 1907, Tokyo

Clear—Warm—Calm Up at 6:40. During the forenoon I taught Japanese to Elder Roskelley, read some of the copy Mr. Sakuraba is making of the Book of Mormon translation and wrote a letter Bro. Horace S. Ensign. At noon we had our prayer meeting. I went and called on Mr. Okuno to ask him about some of his friends who are capable writers and literary critics. He could only recommend one man Mr. Umehara the pastor of the Fujimichō Christian Church, Tokyo. **Returned to headquarters and had a long chat with Bro. Frank /J./ Hewlett who came to Japan from America day before yesterday. He is here in the interests of Hewlett Bros. business firm. He had a little to say about home but more to hear about Japan. He is going to China and then on his way back will spend about two or three weeks in Japan. We were glad to see a new Utah face.**

Today Mr. Sakuraba came and worked a little copying the translation of the Book of Mormon.

Saturday, 20 April 1907, Tokyo

Cloudy—Warm—Later, rain. Up at 6:10. Spent the greater part of the forenoon sweeping the yard and cleaning up myself. Bro. Frank Hewlett dropped in on us again. He had dinner with us. Having received an invitation from Mr. Mori to attend the Field Day sports of the Azabu Middle School I had Elder Caine & Roskelley take Bro. Hewlett and go, being unable to go myself as I had to conduct the exercises in the Bible Class. The class began at 2:45 with six in attendance. The subject discussed was the Apostasy of the Primative Church. Had a conversation with some Normal School students after the class. Then walked to the post office. Returned & helped pump the bath water. After supper I read the scriptures and wrote my journal.

Tuesday, 23 April 1907, Tokyo

Clear—Warmer Up at 6:10. Taught Japanese to Elder Roskelley, then spent the rest of the day working on the Book of Mormon. Mr. Sakurabu came today and copied a little of the translation He also copied some yesterday afternoon.

After supper, my companions and I went to the Y.M.C.A. Hall and heard General Booth of the Salvation Army speak. His speech was to Christian workers and urged the necessity of getting the spirit, character and purpose of Christ before doing the work and then working diligently and fearlessly for the salvation of the Japanese, especially those in Tokyo. He called upon the preachers to "drive the Devil out of Tokyo." The meeting ended in appeals to the emotions of the people to get them on the penitent seat which was prepared up front. One Japanese offered a prayer which sounded like a heathen calling upon a god of stone and he jumped up and down like he was taking electric treatment with an extra current coming into him through his feet. The surprise of the evening (and still it should not be a surprise) was the discovery of Kenzo Kato playing the bass drum. He discovered our presence and fearfully avoided looking at us. This shows that he beats the drum not for the glory of God, but to make a living. Kicked out of our Church for stealing, lying and gross hypocrisy he has succeeded in working himself into the Army where he no doubt gets plenty to eat and a uniform to wear. The shallowness and rank sensationalism of the cry for sinners to come forth and pray at the sinners bench is certainly repulsive to one who knows the true spirit of the Everla/s/ting Gospel. The General is a remarkable, venerable old man and in his speech much correct thought was presented, but there was also revealed a childishness that accompanies age. Six or Seven souls were saved!! This morning, before breakfast, I took a walk.

Sunday, 28 April 1907, Tokyo

Clear—Almost Hot Up at 6:15. Ate breakfast. Sunday School commenced from 9:00 a.m. The children's class was large but the adults class was very small. I caused a great laugh in my class by making a serious mistake in the use of Japanese. **Today we had an experience that is very valuable for it teaches** us the necessity of care in the administration of the ordinances of the Gospel. **For about six months there has been a man named Sugahara who has been taught the Gospel as carefully and fully as any Japanese. During the present year Elder Caine has called on him once a week and last year for a long time he came to Sunday School. He applied for baptism but at the time we knew he had not heard enough about the Church so we had him wait till he could be taught more fully. And we have done our duty faithfully in teaching him. Recently he was instructed about the law of tithing. He is a poor man and the law seemed hard. Today he came and brought back all the books we had given him and a pair of logs we gave him on Christmas and said that he could not receive the law of tithing and that he could not join the Church and not joining the Church his conscience would not allow him to keep the things he had received from us. I thank my Heavenly Father that he has provided such a good test of the faith of men as we find in in law of tithing. I thank Him also, that we found out that Mr. Sugahara has little faith in the Gospel and did not baptize him. Allowing people in the land to join the Church on a passing emotion is a great mistake. They must be taught. Their faith in the teachings given must be tested or all that is done will be regretted and no doubt have to be undone by excommunication.** At noon I ate bread & milk. At 2:30 p.m. we held sacrament meeting two saints were present. After meeting I cooled off in the garden. Ate supper. At 7:30 or evening meeting began the audience was small and half asleep. My mistakes in the use of Japanese were enough to make ordinary wide-awake people smile but not even an impression was made on the slumbering spirits. After the meeting I talked with Miss Ishikawa.

Tuesday, 30 April 1907, Tokyo

Cloudy—Warm Up at 6:15. Spent the most of the day working on the Book of Mormon translation. After breakfast, I taught Elder Roskelley a lesson in Japanese. After dinner Bro. Stoker arrived from Kōfu. Mr. Sakuraba came today and completed the work he bargained for on the Book of Mormon. Bro Chiba called and I had a pleasant chat with him. This evening I received a fine letter from home reporting all the folks in good health. Also received a letter from Prest. McRae of the Western States Mission asking me to get a bid on the printing and binding of 50,000 Books of Mormon. He stated that the Missions in the United States are making special effort to get the Book of Mormon into the homes of the people and their efforts were being greatly rewarded with success and the book was producing a good spirit in the hearts of the people.

Sunday, 5 May 1907, Tokyo

Clear—Strong Wind—Dusty Up at 7:00. Fasted today. The Sunday School was held as usual at 9:00 a.m. **The Primary Department was divided today making out of the oldest, largest, and most active members a new Department to be know as the 1st Intermediate Department.** After school we discussed the party to be held for the girls next Thursday afternoon. Read a little before fast meeting. The fast meeting began at 2:30. After meeting I spent an hour in the garden getting a little fresh dust together with a little fresh air. Ate supper. At 7:30 the evening meeting commenced. At this meeting Elder James Anderson made his first speech in a public meeting in Japanese. He did well enough to give me perfect satisfaction with his effort. The Lord has /blessed/ and is abundantly blessing him in the study of the language.

Monday, 6 May 1907, Tokyo

Cloudy, Clear—Wind & Dust. Up at 6:00. Swept the downstairs rooms. During the forenoon I was attending to mission and personal business down town. Ate an early dinner and went to Mr. Hirogaro Hirai's. I discussed with him about the translation of "Polygamy in the Mormon Church," until 5:30 p.m. Returned to headquarters. Ate supper Went with Elder Stoker to Mr. Matsui's to attend to some business in connection with the maps we are having made for the Brief History of the Church. This evening Sister Nachie's daughter Ei was a mouth in family prayer. This was the first attempt at vocal prayer in the family circle and her effort gave me great joy.

Saturday, 11 May 1907, Tokyo

Clear—Warmer Up at 6:15. Spent the forenoon talking with a printer who came looking for orders and finishing the work on the translation of my article "Polygamy in the Mormon Church." This translation is now ready for the printers. After dinner I took Bro. Frank J. Hewlett and two of the elders to a bazzar given by the students of the Aisumi Girl's School. In the evening I read a little.

Sunday, 12 May 1907, Tokyo

Fair—Calm—Warm. Up at 6:00. Ate breakfast. Sunday School was well attended. A good session was held. Today the first session of the First Intermediate Department was held. The division of the Primary Department into two will no doubt prove a great success. The theological students all seemed satisfied with their new room. Ate dinner. Read a little. At 2:30 p.m. the sacrament meeting was held. Bro. Hewlett spoke through Elder Stoker as an interpreter. After meeting I spent an hour or two in the garden. Had a brief chat with Mr. Homma who called. Ate supper. Evening meeting was fairly well attended.

Monday, 13 May 1907, Tokyo

Clear—Warm. Up at 6:30. Spent the entire day discussing questions connected with the Brief History translations. Took a little exercise before supper. After supper began work on the Ninth book of the Book of Mormon translation. Bro. Chiba came today and did some copying. My heart has rejoiced exceedingly over the action of Sister Kawabe who came today and paid her tithing for the first time. Her husband is supposed to support her but she does some sewing to assist in the family support and today came and paid one tenth of her earnings last month. I thank the Lord for this manifestation of her faith.

Thursday, 16 May 1907, Tokyo

Clear and Warm. Up at 6:45. Spent a little while in the forenoon talking with Elder Stoker about the Brief History translation. Taught Japanese to Elder Roskelley. Spent the rest of the day working on the Book of Mormon translation. Took a little exercise in the evening before supper. After supper sang a little, joked a little, grew fat and wasted time.

Sunday, 19 May 1907, Tokyo

Clear—Hot. Up at 6:00. Ate breakfast at 7:00. At 9:00 a.m. Sunday School commenced. A good sized school today and quite interesting exercises. After school I talked to Bro. Hewlett who with Elder Anderson returned late last night from Sendai. Ate dinner. At 2:30 sacrament meeting was held. Bro. Hewlett talked. I interpreted. This is the first time since Bro. Grant left Japan, that I have interpreted a speech into Japanese. After meeting we took a walk and a car-ride to Nakano and back. Ate supper. At 7:30 P.M. our meeting commenced with quite a fair sized audience. A special feature of the meeting was a duet by Elder Stoker and I. Talked with Bro. Hewlett again and retired quite late.

Thursday, 23 May 1907, Tokyo

Cloudy—Calm—Warm. Up at 6:00. This morning Elder Stoker and I arranged for the Sunday School boy's entertainment. Ate dinner. Some of the children came early. At 3:15 the entertainment commenced. Most of the exercises were held in the garden where the boys played the games with all their might. Before the went home we gave them fruit, sandwiches, cake, nuts, and candy to eat. After the entertainment we ate supper. We were then entertained by Bro. Hewlett who recited a number of pieces.

Friday, 24 May 1907, Tokyo

Clear—Warm. Up at 6:30. Spent the forenoon consulting with Elders Stoker and Caine concerning questions on the Brief History translation. **At noon I had a consultation with a gentleman from the Shueishi Printing Co. about the printing of the History. I ate dinner. Then went to the Daichi Koba of the Shueisha Printing Co. (a branch of the former Shueisha but run independently). They said they could begin on the printing of the Brief History after the middle of June. Their bid was**

no higher than the main store so I practically decided to have the printing done at the branch which is admitted to be the largest and most up-to-date Printing concern in Japan. Returned to headquarters and consulted

again with Elders Stoker and Caine about the History translation. After supper I read a part of a book in Japanese entitled the "Story of the New Testament."

Friday, 31 May 1907, Tokyo
     Clear—Hot. Up at 6:15. Spent the forenoon teaching Japanese to Elder Roskelley and writing letters. After dinner I chatted a little while with a young man whose home is in Kōfu, also talked for a few minutes with Mr. Sakuraba. **Went with Elder Stoker to the printers and gave into their hands the first part of the Brief History translation manuscript and a number of photographs and pictures which are to be reproduced for the history.** On the way home we called in to the barber shop and got a hair cut. After supper I called on the Kawana family and had an hours chat.

Sunday, 2 June 1907, Tokyo
     Clear—Warm—Calm. Up at 6:30. Spent the day at headquarters. At nine o'clock our Sunday School commenced and a fair session was held. After school four of the children practiced one of the songs. I read for an hour and a half. At two thirty o'clock our testimony meeting was held. The only regret was the non-attendance of the saints. Only one was present. After meeting I spent a little time in the garden getting some fresh air. Ate supper. The evening meeting was held with a fair sized crowd. Today the Lord has sustained the efforts of his servants and some good has been accomplished. After meeting I soon retired.
     Just before fast meeting I walked as far as Aoyama to buy some paper and bread and send a package of tracts to Hokkaido.

Monday, 3 June 1907, Tokyo
     Clear—Warm—Wind & Dust. Up at 6:30. Spent the forenoon teaching Japanese to Elder Roskelley, writing a letter to Heber J. Grant and working on the Book of Mormon. The afternoon also was devoted to translation work. After supper I received a letter from home that was not all good news. My brother Samuel is reported to be very disagreeable in his attitude towards the business methods of his father and though he is a son old enough to know his place and keep it, he assumes a dictatorial air and when his plans are not executed he becomes very angry and unkind in his manners. This disposition of my brother's is unmanly, uncharitable and unchristian. I worked again on the Book of Mormon before going to bed.

Wednesday, 5 June 1907, Tokyo
     Cloudy—Slight Rain—Cool. Up at 6:30. Swept & dusted the downstairs rooms gave the bath room a good cleaning. Taught Elder Roskelley a lesson is Japanese. At noon we held our prayer and council meeting. Today I expressed my feelings about the matter of getting someone to criticize my translation of the Book of Mormon and stated that I could not think of any name but Kinza Hirai the gentleman who when approached last year refused to do the work. During the past six months Mr. Hirai has been sick and I have greatly progressed in the review of my own translation so that I am in a better position to receive the criticism now than last year. And Mr. Hirai, because of his serious illness would have be able to do practically nothing on the translation had he accepted it. So his refusal last year has proved to be a good thing. And inasmuch as I cannot think of anyone else as suitable to the important labor, I asked my brethren today what they thought of renewing our request to Mr. Hirai. They all approved the idea, so I went to Mr. Hirai's today and presented the situation to him. He is very busy because of new duties that have recently come to him and because of the accumulated labor before him on account of his sickness. Still he manifested a willingness to give the criticism using his spare moments for the same. He could not estimate the time it would take to complete the criticism but feared it would be more than two years. This long period was rather chilling to me, but I told him that if the work could all be finished in two years

and the book in the hands of the public that I would be satisfied. He decided to take one of the books containing the manuscript and correct three or four chapters so that he can make a better estimate of the time required for the whole. Returned to headquarters, ate supper and taught the singing exercise in the Bible Class. Told my brethren the result of my interview with Mr. Hirai and retired.

Monday, 10 June 1907, Tokyo

Clear—Hot Up at 6:30. Spent the forenoon holding the final discussion with Elders Stoker and Caine in relation to the Brief History translation. After dinner I went to the printers to inquire about the publication of an edition of the Book of Mormon in English for the American Missions of the Church—having received a letter from Prest. Alex McRae of the Western States Mission requesting a bid on 50,000 copies. Attended to a little business in connection with the Brief History at the same time. Returned and taught Japanese to Elder Roskelley. After supper, did some work on the Book of Mormon.

Friday, 14 June 1907, Tokyo

Cloudy—Wind—Slight rain. Up at 6:25. Spent the forenoon working on the Book of Mormon and teaching Elder Roskelley a lesson in Japanese. In the afternoon I went to Hongo to see a house advertized for rent. When I got there the man who was supposed to have the place in charge couldn't find it. Called at the printers on the way back and attended to some business. Ate supper and then wrote a letter to Prest. J. A. McRae of the Western States Mission in relation to printing 50,000 copies of the English Book of Mormon, for use in the American Missions. Wrote a letter to Elders Seely & Cutler. Retired. Today's work on the Book of Mormon finished the revision of the translation down to the end of the 9th Book of the manuscript which goes up to the end of Alma 62.

Wednesday, 19 June 1907, Tokyo

Rain—Cool Up at 7:15. Spent the forenoon proof-reading the copy of the Book of Mormon translation and teaching Japanese to Elder Roskelley. In the afternoon I did a little more proof-reading and then started the revision of the tenth book of my manuscript. Received a letter from Mr. Hirai saying that the part of the Book of Mormon translation I sent him arrived all right but that he had not started to look over it. He promised in this letter (a postal card) to let me know in a few days whether or not he can undertake the work. At noon we had prayer meeting. After supper I took a walk calling at the homes of some of the Sunday School children who are on the program to be rendered the first Sunday in July. Also called at the carpenter's and ordered two tables for the kitchen. Elder Caine took the walk with me. Bible Class (English) was held tonight. Today Mr. Mori came and continued his work for us.

Thursday, 20 June 1907, Tokyo

Cloudy—Cool Up at 4:30. Spent the forenoon teaching Japanese to Elder Roskelley and proofreading the copy of the Book of Mormon translation. In the afternoon I went down town to see about the map plates which we are to have in connection with the Brief History. Attended to some other business on the way. At different times during the day, I did a little correcting on the Book of Mormon translation. Today a number of Sunday School children called and we had them practice their parts on the program being prepared for July 7th. I was absent so Elder Stoker took charge. Before they went home, they were given ice cream and cake.

The reason for getting up so early this morning is that I awoke at about 3:30 and could not sleep. I took a walk before six o'clock and did considerable on the Book of Mormon before breakfast.

Monday, 1 July 1907, Tokyo

Clear—Hot Up at 6:10. Spent the forenoon arranging the roll of merit in the Sunday School and deciding upon presents to be given to the children who have been faithful in their attendance during the last half year. Taught Elder Roskelley a lesson in Japanese before dinner. After dinner, I taught two of the Sunday School children a lesson in singing. Then I went down town in the interest of the Sunday School. Returned at supper time. After supper, I did some work on the Book of Mormon translation.

Tuesday, 2 July 1907, Tokyo

Clear—Hot—Still Breeze. Up at 5:30. Spent the forenoon teaching Japanese to Elder Roskelley and working with the Book of Mormon. In the afternoon I did a little more on the Book of Mormon. Mr. Shimotsu a Japanese who has been in Utah six years and a student at the Latter-day Saints University for two years, called on us this afternoon with a letter of introduction from Bro. Horace S. Ensign. He had nothing but good things to say about Salt Lake City, Ogden, and the Latter-day Saints. Today a card was received from Mr. Kinza Hirai relative to the criticism of my Book of Mormon translation. He writes in an undecided manner—half inclined to undertake the work and half inclined to refuse it. This uncertain attitude is very unsatisfactory still it leaves room for further negotiation and the exercise of hope that he will yet undertake the work under a satisfactory agreement.

Thursday, 4 July 1907, Tokyo

Clear—Calm & Hot Up at 6:00. Spent most of the day working on the Book of Mormon. We had all the patriotic songs we know and decorated with flags. Some Sunday School children came and with them I indulged in a game of house quoits. Though far from my native land and in a position where noisy celebration would be difficult still I think I have felt as grateful for the liberty of my America as any who love the Stars and Stripes.

Sunday, 7 July 1907, Tokyo

Rain—Cooler Up at 6:00. Today we had special exercises in the Sunday School in celebration of the end of the first half years work and the beginning of the second. Twelve children received prizes for fine attendance. Two had never missed and had always been early. One had never missed but was late once. One had been late twice but present every time. Four had missed once. Two had missed once & been late once. One had missed twice, and one had missed twice and been late five times. The program was carried out well and satisfactorily. After a few minutes past eleven fast meeting commenced. A spirited meeting was held. In the afternoon I read a long address delivered by B. H. Roberts at the Y.M. & Y.L.M.I.A. Conference at Salt Lake City in June in defense of the Church against the Utah Ministerial Association. Ate dinner. The evening meeting was held with a fair-sized audience. The speakers felt a distressing influence.

Monday, 8 July 1907, Tokyo/Omori/Tokyo

Cloudy—Rain Up at 6:00. Spent the forenoon teaching Japanese to Elder Roskelley and doing odd jobs. After dinner I called on the House Department to inquire about the payment of texts by foreigners. **Went from there to Omori and had a conversation with Mr. Kinza Hirai relative to the criticism of the Book of Mormon translation. It was made clear that Mr. Hirai can not do the work if their is any time limit placed. And not feeling that it would be proper to contract for the work without there being some kind of a limit, I concluded to give up the effort to get Mr. H's services. I then asked him if he had any friend whom he could recommend and guarantee. He said he had one who if he had the time, would be just the man for the work. I requested to Mr. Hirai to communicate with that friend and ask him if he can do the work. The friend is in Kōbe. Mr. Hirai promised to write immediately. I returned to headquarters.** Ate supper and talked with Mr. Uehara about the gospel.

Friday, 12 July 1907, Tokyo/Omori/Tokyo

Clear—Hot Up at 6:00. Spent the forenoon working on the Book of Mormon. After dinner I did a little more of the same work then taught Elder Roskelley a lesson in Japanese. Received a letter from Mr. Hirai telling me he had received an answer from his friend Mr. Noguchi to whom he wrote regarding the criticism of my translation of the Book of Mormon. I went to Mr. Hirai's to learn the particulars and decide on the next move. As Mr. Hirai, in his first letter, did not give any particulars about the nature of the work, but just inquired about the possibility of the man doing such a work, the answer simply limited that in case it was a work that he had ability to do he could perhaps find some hours to devote to it. I had Mr. Hirai describe the nature of the book and the translation, and explain fully who it is that is requesting the work to be done. In the same letter I had him ask how many hours a day the man would be able to devote to the work if he decided to accept it. On the way home I posted the letter. A well attended Bible Class was held this evening.

Monday, 15 July 1907, Tokyo

Clear—Hot. Up at 6:15. Spent the forenoon teaching Japanese to Elder Roskelley, talking to Elder Anderson and reading some of the copy of my Book of Mormon translation which had been written by Mr. Hachiro Mori and others. In the afternoon I wrote a letter to the Elders and then worked on the Book of Mormon till after 5:00 p.m. Took an hours exercise. After supper we held the first session of the Missionaries Bible Class. I will take charge assisted by Elder Stoker. We will study the New Testament considering the four Gospels at once according to the outline given in the Bible helps. We voted to appoint a lesson and have everyone ready and prepared to discuss it if called upon. Retired.

Wednesday, 17 July 1907, Tokyo

Cool breeze—Fair. Up at 6:30. Spent the day at headquarters working hard on the Book of Mormon translation revision. Today I got over more ground than I have ever covered in one day since I started the revision. I looked over the translation of twelve pages of the English. Besides the work on the Book of Mormon, I taught Elder Roskelley a lesson in Japanese and at noon joined with my brethren in special prayer circle.

Thursday, 18 July 1907, Tokyo/On the Train

Cloudy—Hot. Up at 6:00. During a part of the forenoon I worked on the Book of Mormon translation. A postal card from Mr. Hirai came telling that his friend Mr. Noguchi had written him from Kōbe telling him that he can devote more than an average of three hours to the Book of Mormon translation if he sees his way clear to do the work. He desires to see the original and the translation before deciding the matter. I decided to take the books to Kōbe myself so will be able to take talk the matter over fully. Thinking it proper to call on Mr. Hirai before going I went to Omori. He was not home. I returned to Tokyo and attempted to secure a ticket to Kōbe for the 6:30 express but was told that on account of the heavy rains, the track was damaged between Shimada and Kanaya and that distance would have to be covered by jinrikisha and boat. I decided to take the 11:00 p.m. train so as to reach Shimada after daylight and cross the river (Oigawa) in the day instead of the night. Went the headquarters, ate supper, read a little and then left for my train. I went to bed immediately.

The translation of the Book of Mormon has occupied the major part of my time during the last three years and through the blessings of the Lord, I have been able to translate the entire book and then revise my translation. This revision is drawing to a close but I realize that while this is a representation of my very best efforts there are still many places that cannot be considered idiomatic Japanese and I hope that my conference with Mr. Noguchi will result favorably and he will soon begin the labor of criticizing my work.

Friday, 19 July 1907, On the Train

Heavy Rain. Up at 5:15. Got up and made my toilet. Arrived at Shimada about 6:00 a.m. Left the train and took a rikisha to a resting place. The reason for this stop was that the report had come from the Oigawa that the sailors' would not row the boats unless a higher price was paid. I stayed in the house for about 45 minutes, but I felt nervous and felt as though I should go to the ferry. I did so and after wading through mud and water up to my knees I got into a boat and was nearly drenched with rain. This boat landed on a drift in the middle of the river. I walked across the drift through sand and water to another boat which finally landed me safely on the shore. I took a rikisha to the station in Kanaya and fortunately caught the train about to leave. Being just in time for the train I realized the reason for my nervousness at the waiting place. I changed socks and dried my feet but had to endure my wet pants & underware. Arrived at Hamamatsu at 10:00, and waited till 1:5 p.m. for the departure of the through express train for Kōbe. I stayed at the Hanaya hotel till the train left. Left Hamamatsu at 2:00 p.m. and went direct to Kōbe where I arrived at 9:25. On the way there was nothing of particular interest unless it was the way a mother and father struggled to keep their two children from falling into the spittoons, walking on the floor and sticking their peach stained hands all over everything and everybody. Upon the arrival at Kōbe I took a rikisha to the Nishimura hotel. It was full. The man drew me around from hotel to hotel till at last, by accident, when on the way to a foreign hotel we passed in front of a Japanese hotel where I got a six mat room at ¥3.00 per day, just ¥1.00 higher than I think it ought to be. The name of the place is "Bingoya" located at Motomachi 1 Chome. I took a bath and retired.

Saturday, 20 July 1907, Kōbe
Clear—Hot—Cloudy later—Slight Rain. Up at 6:30. After breakfast, I went to Mr. Noguchi's home and had a long chat with him regarding the criticism of the Book of Mormon translation. He did not impress me as a duplicate character to Mr. Hirai the difference all being in favor of the latter. However from his remarks I glean that he has been so closely related to Mr. Hirai that the history of one's life is the history of the other's life. I told the gentleman as best I could what importance we placed on the book and how desirous we are to have a true translation and I also told him something about the nature of the criticism I expected him to make (if we agree that he shall do it at all) and the care with which his criticisms will be gone over by me and perhaps others when they are made. I had a two hours consultation with him and left the English Book of Mormon and some of the translation for him to look over and make an estimate on the time he will be able to devote to the work and the time it will take him to complete it. I arranged to call on him again tomorrow morning at 10:00 o'clock and hear what he has to say and discuss the preliminary particulars and questions if I find his reply satisfactory and decide to entrust him with the work. I will take dinner with him.

I went from Mr. Noguchi's place to the Bank of Formosa and met our old friend Katsumi Tokoyo. He seemed most pleased to see me. I arranged to go with him to see some of the sights at 4:00 p.m. Walked along the Bund[16] viewed the ships in the harbor. Wandered around a little then went to the hotel and ate some fruit for lunch. Took a walk and got fagged.[17] Returned to the hotel and took a nap. Met Mr. Tokoyo at the appointed hour. We went to the top of Suwayama where I had a fine view of the city and harbor. Went next to see Nunobiki water-fall. This was a beautiful picture, one of the choicest mountain scenes I have seen in Japan. Went to the Oriental Hotel (foreign style) and talked till supper. Had supper and parted. Returned to the Bungoya and retired.

Sunday, 21 July 1907, Kōbe
Clear—Hot Up at 7:00. After breakfast I called in on the Methodists and heard one of the members who is wise in the things of the world tell the financial sorrows of the church and request the members to increase their subscriptions twenty five percent. I had to leave just as the sermon began in order to keep my promise with Mr. Noguchi. I arrived at his home a few minutes past ten and spent five and a half hours talking with him about several things especially the Book of Mormon translation revision. He estimates that the work can be easy and will finished in a year and asked ¥40.00 per month for his time—from three to four hours a day. I ate dinner with him and tried my best to study him and read his heart and character and my impressions were of such a nature, that I considered it wise to leave the matter of making a contract for some days to give me time for reflection and inquiry. At dinner I was not at all pleased to see him drink a bottle of beer and I was not pleased to see him smoke like he did during my visit.

I left his home and called at the hotel. I then started for the Bank of Formosa where I had promised to meet Mr. Tokoyo at 4:00 p.m. I met him on the street. I called and bought a box of foreign sweet meats and sent them to Mr. & Mrs. Noguchi. Then Mr. Tokoyo and I had a long walk through the Hyogo district of Kōbe which is also know as the old city because it was built long before the other half. Was very tired when I said "good-bye" to Mr. Tokoyo and returned to the hotel. Took a bath, ate supper, and then attended the "St. Mickel's Episcopal Church. I had the good fortune to see a baptismal service as three young men were initated. Of all the hollow, spiritless, preverted ordinances this is certainly a fine example. The beginning was rather interesting but as it wore on it grew absolutely monotinous. Returned to the hotel and wrote my journal, paid my bill, left orders to be awakened at 4:30 a.m. and retired.

Monday, 22 July 1907, Kōbe/on the Train

Clear—Terrible Heat. Up at 4:30. Washed and dressed and left Kōbe in the 5:00 a.m. Train. Arrived in Kyoto at 4:37. Left my things in the cloak room at the station and started out to see Kyoto. The first thing was Higashi Hun Guan Ji,[18] perhaps the largest Buddhist shrine in Japan. I walked till I could hardly stand up. So I boarded the car and went to the end of the line. On the way back I got off and walked past the Imperial Grounds where the Emperor lived when Kyoto was the capitol. I saw the famous Christian school. (The Doshisha) I boarded the car again and went to the "Zoo" and Museum Grounds. From here I went to the station and took the 12:30 train and went to Nara where there is the famous shrine of [blank] and the great image of Buddha.[19] All of these things were of little interest to me but the beauty of the great mountani park where these building and images stayed is charming Here many hundreds of deer run loose as the do in their own wild forests, but they are unmolested so are tame and will eat cake etc. from a person's hand. Deer were first placed in the beautiful spot in the age of [blank] and have been living and dining here ever since After the rest of the train and walk from the depot, it was certainly an excellent rest for the body and joy to the soul to sit in the shade of the beautiful trees watching the flocks of deer graze in the tall grass. I left Nara on the 4:55 p.m. train and returned to Kyoto. I washed and ate supper at the station and boarded the 8:20 express for Tokyo. I tried to sleep but only had a brief snooze occasionally.

Tuesday, 23 July 1907, On the Train/Tokyo

Clear—Opressive heat Was awake all night. The train arrived at Kanoya at 4:00 a.m. I took a rikisha to the ferry and crossed the Oigawa by boat. Then I took rikisha again and reached Shimada just in time to catch the first train out. The ease with which the river was crossed was quite in contrast with the difficulty I had last Friday morning. When the train arrived at Shizuoka the passengers were told that the first and second class cars would be held for two hours but there would be a third class express train leave immediately. Thinking a wait of two hours more unpleasant than a five hours ride in a third class car, I took the third class express and arrived in Tokyo at 11:00 a.m. tired, hot and almost sick as I have been suffering with diarahoea for two days. Upon arriving at headquarters, found all well. A letter from Bro. Geo. Reynolds informs us that two young men saild from Seattle for this mission on July 9th so they will arrive in Yokohama on the 25th This letter also told of six others who will leave in a short time. Such news is more than good to us. I spent the afternoon and evening doing odd jobs and trying to keep awake I telegraphed to Elder Chadwick inquiring about Mr. Suzuki. The answer came that he was in Sendai now so I decided to go to Sendai and discuss about the Book of Mormon translation revision with him as his name has been suggested for the work and his acts and knowledge well spoke on. I took a bath before supper. Retired early

Wednesday, 24 July 1907, Tokyo/Sendai

Cloudy—Much cooler. Up at 7:45. Got up rather late, but considering my fatigue last night I haven't slept any too much. Wrote a little, ate breakfast, and after giving some instructions to the brethren, I left for Sendai taking the 11:45 a.m. train from Ueno Station. Nothing of interest happened on the way as I simply read and looked at the scenery along the road. Arrived at Sendai at 8:40 p.m. I thought the brethren would be the at the depot to meet me, but not seeing them, I went immediately to the mission house and found the brethren absent. The housekeeper said they had gone to the depot to welcome me. I sat down and began to eat dinner. While doing so, the brethren came in. I chatted with them for about an hour and then retired. They had arranged for Mr. Suzuki to come to this place tomorrow morning at 8:30 o'clock.

Thursday, 25 July 1907, Sendai

Clear—Cool. Up at 6:00. Spent the major part of the forenoon talking to Mr./Genta/ Suzuki regarding the criticism of the Book of Mormon translation. I told him what I wanted in connection with the work and all that I expected to critic to do. He took a sample of the translation and the English so that he can estimate the time it will take to do the whole work. I arranged to meet with him at his home tomorrow afternoon and hear his estimate of the time and cost of his work and discuss with him any matters that need discussing. Ate dinner and then went to a shrine located on a hill to the south of the city. It is at this place that Date Massumuna[20] is said to be buried. Returned and spent the rest of the afternoon resting. After supper we went out intending to meet Mr. Yamamoto and inquire a little about Mr. Suzuki but he was absent. Returned to the Mission House and after a chat retired.

Friday, 26 July 1907, Sendai

Clear—Cool Up at 7:00. Spent the forenoon in the house reading. At noon called on Dr. Yamamoto with Elder Woodland. Briefly inquired about Mr. Suzuki both as a writer and as a man. Dr. Yamamoto said "There are better writers but he is a high type of good manhood." Returned to the mission house and just before 4:00 p.m. took Elder Chadwick and called according to yesterday's promise on Mr. Suzuki to hear his estimate on the time it would take him to correct my translation, how much renumeration he would expect and to hear his ideas on how the translation should be made—in gembunichitai or buntai. He estimates that it will take him one year to do the work and could not set any price. He stated that while he was in favor of gembunichitai that there was as yet no standard form of this tai and he said he felt it quite necessary to write a translation of such an important book in buntai. I was disappointed in this remark, for I have always felt that the translation should be in gembunichi. However, I have been deeply impressed with Mr. Suzuki's personality and believe that he is as clean a man, morally speaking, as any I have approached in regard to the Book of Mormon /translation/ revision. I decided to accept his suggestion which is that he translate or rather revise one chapter of my translation and send it to me for my consideration. So I left him an English Book of Mormon and the first part of the manuscript. He will, if he keeps his promise, criticise either the 1st or 12th chapter of I Nephi and sent it to me at Tokyo by Wednesday of next week. I was impressed with his humble manner. I enjoyed the spirit around his home a home which consists of father, mother, and five fair untainted children. Returned to the mission house and ate supper. After supper I walked down town with Elder Chadwick and purchased some trinkets to give to some of my Tokyo friends. After returning I talked a short time with Mr. Ishikawa, a young man in the Tohoku News who has been kind to the Brethren. Retired after devouring 1/4 of a pineapple.

Saturday, 27 July 1907, Sendai/Tokyo

Clear—Cool—Rather hot. Up at 4:45. Took the 6:10 a.m. train for Tokyo. The morning was quite cool and pleasant. As the day wore on and the train neared Tokyo, it became very hot. Arrived at Ueno Station at 3:15 P.M. Went direct to headquarters where I met Elders M.S. Marriott and E. C. Taylor two new missionaries who arrived from Zion yesterday. Bro Taylor is the second son of Moses Taylor the Prest. of Summit County. He is therefore a grandson of Prest. Jns. Taylor the third president of the Church. Bro Marriot is from Ogden, being one of the many sons of a good "Mormon" father whose family includes more than one wife. Cleaned up a little after reaching headquarters Bro. Taylor brought a letter from Bro. Louis A. Kelsch Ate supper, took a bath and retired.

Tuesday, 30 July 1907, Tokyo

Clear—Hot Up at 6:15. Spent the forenoon teaching Japanese to Elder Roskelley and working on the Book of Mormon translation. Today I reviewed the suggestions made by Elder Caine on the fifth book of the translation. The sample which Mr. Genta Suzuki promised to send me was received today. He criticised the 1st chapter of I Nephi and has written it in the buntai. I read it over once but have not carefully considered it. A letter accompanying the manuscript states that Mr. Suzuki would expect thirty sen for one page /of manuscript/ containing twenty lines of twenty characters each. This means that the 1st Chapter of I Nephi would cost for criticism ¥1.00. As the first Chapter covers two pages /of the English/ the criticism of the whole translation would cost ¥311.50. However, Mr. Suzuki would have to use much of his time in consultation with me so it would reach nearly ¥400.00 before the work is finished. I wrote a card acknowledging the receipt of the above manuscript. I sent my first book of translation and a letter to Kōbe to Mr. Noguchi requesting that he criticise and write in gembunichitai the same 1st Chapter of I Nephi so I can have a sample of his work to study before deciding what to do.

Thursday, 1 August 1907, Tokyo

Clear—Hot—Slight Breeze. Up at 6:10. Spent the forenoon and also the afternoon doing work on the Book of Mormon. I taught Elder Roskelley a lesson in Japanese during the forenoon and in the evening we did nothing by talk and go through a few gymnastics. This evening at supper we had ice cream in honor of my twenty fifth birthday.

Saturday, 3 August 1907, Tokyo

Slight Rain—Later, fair—Hot. Up at 7:00. Spent the forenoon working on the Book of Mormon. Today I received a letter from Mr. Zenshiro Noguchi in which he states that the book of manuscript I sent him together with my letter requesting him to criticize the 1st Chapter of I Nephi and send it to me as a sample of his work, had reached him and that he would comply with my request immediately. A letter from Mr. Katsumi Tokoyo gave quite a favorable report of Mr. Noguchi's character as learned from a man who for seven years was associated with Mr. N. in the same firm. I received a card from Mr. Genta Suzuki in which he states that he will attempt the criticism of my translation in gembunitchi. The conditions seem to be growing more favorable each day. I am very thankful for this and hope, through the assistance of the Holy Spirit to choose the right man. Before supper, I swept the yard. After supper I had a long talk with a gentleman who frequently visits us.

Sunday, 4 August 1907, Tokyo/Omori/Tokyo

Changeable—Hot—Showers Up at 6:15. The Sunday School this morning was largely attended. The work in this department of our missionary work is exceedingly encouraging especially when we see such interest at this time of the year when the heat is so intense. At 11:00 a.m. we held fast meeting. After meeting Elder Stoker and I went to Omori and visited for a long time with Mr. Hirai and family. I told him my impressions of Mr. Noguchi and asked him a number of questions in the attempt to understand the character of the man more fully. Enjoyed the visit very much. Returned to Tokyo and had dinner. The evening meeting commenced at 7:30. The attendance was not so large. The subject discussed was "Latter-day Revelation." I simply bore a brief testimony at the end of the meeting.

Monday, 5 August 1907, Tokyo

Showers—Sultry— Up at 6:15. Immediately after breakfast I went to visit Bro. Yasubeiye Chiba who according to reports is not well. He is living in a district on the extreme east of Tokyo so it took me sometime to make the return trip. I found upon arriving at his home that he was at some school in Honjo-Ku receiving special instruction relative to his school work. I wrote a note to be given to him on his return. Reached headquarters at 1:00 p.m. Ate dinner. Spent the afternoon writing, studying and consulting with Elder Stoker about photos to be reproduced in the history. After supper, which was prepared by the elders, Sister Nachie having taken a days rest, our Bible Class for the elders was held.

Tuesday, 6 August 1907, Tokyo

Clear—Hot Up at 5:00. Took a walk and a cold water bath. After breakfast I taught Elder Roskelley a lesson in Japanese. This is the last lesson in Japanese I will give him as he leaves for Hokkaido tomorrow. I had a long talk with Mrs. Fude Tai, Sister Tsune Nachie's sister, in regard to the responsibility and covenants [s] persons take[s] upon them when they receive baptism and confirmation into the Church of Christ. She applied for baptism last Sunday. Today I told her to reflect more deeply and examine her own heart and faith and love for God more thoroughly. I warned her against the inconstancy of the Japanese heart, the seriousness of breaking a covenant made with the Lord, and the danger of growing lukewarm. I questioned her closely to find how much faith she really had and learn if possible if it was independent faith or simply faith dependent upon her sister or a passing emotion. In the afternoon, I did odd jobs. I had Mr. Mori copy the 1st Chapter of I Nephi and I sent it together with a letter to Mr. Suzuki in Sendai, requesting him to criticise it, leaving it in gembunichitai. I desire a sample of Mr. Suzuki's gembunichi, so I can compare it with Mr. Noguchi's work and decide which man to engage. After supper I wrote a letter to the First Presidency informing them of the condition of the work in the mission and requesting an increase of our monthly allowance to defray the expenses which are increasing all the time.

Wednesday, 7 August 1907, Tokyo

Cloudy—Then Fair—Slightly cooler. Up at 6:10. Spent part of the morning working on the Book of Mormon and then I read a little of the translation copy made by Mr. Mori to see that he had made no mistakes. At 10:40 a.m. Elder Taylor and I went with Elders Roskelley and Marriott to Ueno station to see them off to Hokkaidō. On the way back we attended to some business on the Ginza. After returning to headquarters, we held prayer meeting. After the meeting I wrote a letter to Mr. Noguchi asking him to hurry the criticism of the chapter /of the B. of M./ I asked him about. I talked with Maeda for a little while. Ate supper. After supper I had a long-pleasant gospel conversation with Mr. Uehara who has been calling on us very often, inquiring about the gospel.

Thursday, 8 August 1907, Tokyo

Showers & Hot. Up at 6:45. During the forenoon Elder Caine and I read part of the copy of my translation of the Book of Mormon. In the afternoon I worked on the revision of the translation. Some Sunday School children came and I conducted a singing practice for them. Received some mail conveying the good news that all are well at home. Mother is having a long trip through the Northwestern States and Idaho.

Sunday, 11 August 1907, Tokyo

Clear—Hot! Hot!! Up at 6:00 Ate breakfast. Directed the Sunday School. Presided over the Sacrament Meeting. Ate dinner. Consulted with Elders Stoker and Caine about trying to engage the entire time of Mr. Noguchi during a whole year for the criticism of the Book of Mormon translation. Wrote out an agreement and conditions relative to the same and read them to my brethren. They suggest that before such a proposition is made to Mr. Noguchi that I should simply ask him if it is possible for him under ordinary circumstances to give his whole time during a year to us. Ate supper. Presided over the evening meeting which was well attended.

Tuesday, 13 August 1907, Tokyo

Clear—Hot Up at 6:30. Before breakfast received the sample of Mr. Noguchi's criticism of my translation. Quite to my disappointment he had written the chapter corrected in the classical style in spite of my distinct request that he write in gembunichi (conversational style). After breakfast I sent a telegram to him asking why he did this. I also called on Mr. Hirogoro Hirai to see if he could find time to critise my translation as I desire it criticised. He could not make a definate answer, but I left the proposition with him to consider and also requested that he look over some of my translation to see how much work it would take to correct it and as a sample of his criticism to send the 1st chapter of I Nephi in it's criticised form. Returned and ate dinner. Received a letter from Mr. Suzuki in which was a sample of his criticism of my translation in gembunitchi. I now have my Suzuki's work both in bunsho and gembunitchi and also Mr. Noguchi's work in bunsho. I want Mr. Hirai's in bunsho and gembunitchi if I can get it and then I will consider all the samples and have them read by my friends so as to be able to choose the most suitable critic for the important work of criticising the Book of Mormon translation. In the afternoon I worked a little on the B. of M. translation revision and did more of the same work after supper.

Thursday, 15 August 1907, Tokyo

Strong Wind—Heavy Showers—Cooler. Up at 6:30. Spent the forenoon writing letters to Mssrs. Noguchi and Suzuki. I received a letter from Mr. Noguchi giving his reasons for correcting my translation in "Bunsho," classical style. He gave many reasons, but the one that is the strongest, (and this point has already been mentioned to me by Mr. Kinza Hirai) is that based on the difference of dialects as "gembunitchi" uses verbs in their colloquial form, it is very difficult to find a standard spoken style that is used throughout all Japan. The classical, however, is the same in every part of the Empire. But the classical is more difficult than the colloquial therefore it was my hope to avoid it. But inasmuch as there is not standard collquial which is current in every part of Japan, a translation written in the dialect of the northeastern part of the island would be no good in the southwestern part and vice versa. This seems to be a vital objection to the claims of gembunitchi in which I have written the whole translation, little realizing that I was using the Tokyo dialect which is not entirely understood by the less educated in other parts of the land. While I know that the classical language known as "bunshotai" uses difficult verb endings never heard in ordinary talk and is therefore difficult to those who don't read but simply listen, yet in the event of a commonly understood colloquial which is a standard in all parts being impossible, I may after further deliberation and investigation have to decide for my translation to be remodled into "bunshōtai." Some people state that a good carefully chosen "gembunitchitai" can be understood in all parts, but the difficulty that then arises is where is there a many so well aquainted with all the dialects that he may know the words and verb endings that are common to all, and whose time and labor can be engaged for the [~~revision~~] /criticism/ of my translation? Did a little work on my translation today.

Friday, 16 August 1907, Tokyo

Showers—Cooler Up at 6:00. Spent the forenoon and part of the afternoon working on the revision of my Book of Mormon translation. The rest of the afternoon was spent proof reading the copy of the translation being made by Mr. Mori. After supper a Bible class was held. After the class, I had a long and pleasant talk with Mr. Uehara. I know that the Spirit of God accompanied my words bearing testimony of their truth to the heart of Mr. Uehara. The talk was on "How shall a man know which is the true church, when there are so many all claiming to be the Church of Christ and founded upon the scriptures.

Sunday, 18 August 1907, Tokyo

Clear—Hot as blazes. Up at 6:45. Ate breakfast. Conducted Sunday School teaching the Primary Department as usual. Was pleased to see Sister Ota with us. She has been absent from all meetings for a long time. At 11:00 a.m. a meeting for the elders and saints was held and the sacrament administered. At 12:00 n. ate lunch. In the afternoon wrote a letter to Prest. Ralph A. Badger of the South African Mission. I also studied up on the "Kingdom of God on Earth" in order to have my mind prepared to address the evening meeting. During the afternoon while we were studying and singing a sneak thief stepped into the front hall and got away with two umbrellas. I made a short unsuccessful chase. Ate supper. The evening meeting was blessed with a peaceful spirit. I did the speaking.

Monday, 19 August 1907, Tokyo

Clear—Very Hot. Up at 6:40. Ate breakfast. Went to Azabu to see a house. I didn't suit. Returned and started to do a little on the Book of Mormon but the cook dropped a platter of fish down the well and it took sometime for us to let a man down to hunt for it and bring it out. Even after all the trouble we didn't get it out. Spent the rest of the morning reading news from America. In the afternoon I began to make a diagram showing the order of the Priesthood in the Church. Then I spent an hour or two proof reading some of the copy of my translation. Read a little in the Bible preparatory to the lesson this evening. After supper the Elder's Bible Class was held.

Wednesday, 21 August 1907, Tokyo

Clear—Hot—Dusty. Up at 7:00 Spent the forenoon looking over the Book of Mormon translation. At 12:00 n. we held a prayer and council meeting. Discussed the great and important question as to the style of language the Book of Mormon should be written in. The feelings of the brethren seemed to be somewhat unsettled and their minds not entirely made up on the question, but the inclination was in favor of a very simple bunshō style. Without making any decision, I allowed the question to go over for a day or two. After the meeting, I did an odd job or two. Received a letter from Mr. Hirogoro Hirai relative to his criticism of my translation of the Book of Mormon. After supper, I went to Mr. Hirai's to discuss with him the matter mentioned in his letter. He was not home. I left a note asking him to call tomorrow or I would visit him the day following. Returned and did a little on the Book of Mormon before retiring.

Thursday, 22 August 1907, Tokyo

Cloudy—Showers—Cooler Up at 6:15. Spent most of the forenoon at the Shueisha Printing Co. hauling the company's men over the coals for their carelessness in correcting the mistakes in printing. Did a very little on the Book of Mormon translation revision. In the afternoon Mr. Hirogoro Hirai called and we had a very long talk with him about the best style of writing for the Book of Mormon; also discussed the matter of making a contract with him for his entire time and labor for one year. I offered him ¥35.00 for the criticism of each book of the translation manuscript. There are about 27 or 28 of these books. Besides this, I promised to give him ¥625.00 or ¥125.00 per month for five months, making a total for his years work of from ¥1,570.00 to ¥1,605.00 He did not decide to accept the offer but promised to decide on or before the 25th inst. In the evening I dictated to Elder Caine who wrote on the typewriter the Articles of Agreement to be made between Mr. Hirai and the Japan Mission if he decides to accept my offer. I mailed a copy of the Articles to Mr. Hirai. Before retiring corrected two proof sheets of the Brief History.

Friday, 23 August 1907, Tokyo

Strong east Wind—Heavy Showers Up at 7:00. Spent the forenoon working on the Book of Mormon. In the afternoon, I read with Elder Caine part of the copy of the Book of Mormon translation and then discussed a few questions with Mr. Mori. After supper a Japanese Bible Class was held. I attended it.

Sunday, 25 August 1907, Tokyo

Rain—Hot as blazes. Up at 5:45. Ate breakfast. Held Sunday School. After school we had a Sacrament Meeting. **After dinner we held a discussion regarding the style of language to be adopted in correcting the Book of Mormon translation. The feelings of the brethren were more strongly in favor of bunshotai[21] than ever. I decided to try and find out who made the "Zokugo"[22] translation of the "Gospel of Mark" and find his opinion regarding "gunbunitchitai."[23] Took a walk. Called at the shipping agency's office and ordered a box of books sent to Sendai. Called at Mr. Nakagawa's to have a chat with him, but he was not home.** Today a sample bound copy of the Brief History was brought from the printer. I noticed a few points that needed attention so I made a swift run to the printers and had them fixed up. Returned and ate supper. Our meeting was fairly attended, but the character of the audience was not very inspiring. After meeting I talked with Mr. Hayakawa. **A letter from Mr. Hirai relative to the contract for correcting the Book of Mormon translation came. It was not a pleasing letter.**

Monday, 26 August 1907, Tokyo

Rain & Cooler Up at 6:00. **Spent the day in odd work. Just after** breakfast, I called the elders together and we discussed the suggestions and demands in Mr. Hirai's letter relative to the agreement to be made on the work of criticising the Book of Mormon. He suggested some changes in the wording all of which suggestions were accepted. He made a demand for ¥500.00 to be used in securing the suggestions of competent scholars. This demand was denied. He requested that an article be added to the agreement guaranteeing him employment for five months after the expiration of the year agreed upon for the Book of Mormon work. This request was granted.

After this meeting, Elder Caine and I went and visited Mr. Hirai. We talked the matter over. He recognized our right to object to the extra ¥500.00 for the purpose named and withdrew his demand. But he held tenaciously to the demand that a clause be put in stating that we would be bound to treat each other as gentlemen. I tried to show him the folly of such a thrust at our characters for it would asume that we are not gentlemen already. His feelings, however were not without a cause as he is aware that some, most, foreigners who engage Japanese treat them like dogs and he does not desire to receive such treatment. He also wanted some assurance of what reward he would get if we discharged him before the time was up. He wanted an article promising him so much money. I reasoned with him on this point, but he finally decided that he would suspend negotiations and refused to accept the position as critic of my translation, mainly he said because I could not consent to an article declaring that we should treat each other as gentlemen. The conversation lasted over two hours.

Elder Caine and I left Mr. Hirai's and came home. I felt disappointed in the outcome of our interview for I certainly had strong hope that Mr. Hirai would eventually start upon and complete the work. However, I said to myself, "there are others and the Lord will bring me to them soon so I have nothing else to do but begin to look around again." In the afternoon, I had Mr. Mori write a chart or diagram to be used in teaching the saints the order of the Priesthood in the Church. I also had him write an advertizement for the "Brief History of the Church" which will be out and on sale in a day or two. I studied the lesson to be discussed in the elder's Bible class. The class was held in the evening after supper. Elders Stoker and Anderson expected to leave for Kamakura today, but the weather having been so bad lately and there having been such a heavy rainfall the railroad between Tokyo and Yokohama had been suspended, being too dangerous.

Today the whitewashers and painters were working in some of the rooms.

Tuesday, 27 August 1907, Tokyo

Heavy rain all day—Cooler Up at 5:45. **This morning a letter came from Mr. Hirogoro Hirai and apologized for the tenacity of his position yesterday. He said that his wife who at the time of our conversation was in hearing distance, severely reprimanded him for his stand on the questions discussed, and that altho he has closed the negotiations he was ready to have them renewed stating that he will accept the articles of agreement as amended. I read the letter to my brethren and asked their feelings. This evening I answered the letter (see Letter Book B page [blank]).** Elders Anderson and Stoker left and took boat to Yokosuka from which point the expected to go to Kamakura by train. The greater part of the forenoon was spent on business down town. In the afternoon I did a little work with Mr. Mori, taught Elder Taylor a lesson in Japanese and did an odd job or two.

Wednesday, 28 August 1907, Tokyo

Clear—Hot. Up at 6:00. After the long heavy rain which began a week ago, the sunshine today has been very much appreciated even by us, so no doubt the unfortunate thousands who have had either their homes or their fields destroyed by the flood, have welcomed the brightness with more than thankful /hearts/. The papers this morning are simply filled with tales of destruction and loss. The lower parts of this city are submerged in water. The entire district from Ōmori to the other side of Tabata is turned into a sea. The river dikes have given way letting whole rivers out upon the fields of growing rice and utterly destroying thousands of houses. In Saitama-ken the next neighbor to Tokyo-Fu, there are over 13,000 houses washed away and completely submerged. The lower districts of Tokyo (Asakusa, Honjo) are in many parts being traversed by boats instead of Kuruma.[24] While Japan is used to heavy rains and river overflows and the consequent loss of crops etc, such a great loss by floods has not been known for the last 40 years at least. The storm has been quite general all along the Tokaidō[25] reports having come of floods from Kyoto southwest to fifty miles north of Tokyo and from Nagano Ken.

In Hokkaidō the greater part of the largest seaport city in the Island—Hakodate, was destroyed by fire on the 24th & 25th inst. Over 13,000 families were burned out and with one or two fortunate exception, every public office, large commercial firm bank, school, etc., were entirely destroyed. The loss is therefore exceedingly great. The dead are numbered at 300 but facts regarding the real loss in property and life are not yet obtainable. In the extreme south west of the main island and in the northern part of Kyushu the people are trying to stamp out an attack of cholera. Thus at the present time the whole land is in distress. Would that this people could understand the warning voice of floods, fires and pestilence and turn from the paths of sin into the straight and narrow path which leadeth to life eternal. May God give to his servants who duty it is to make clear the warning, power to bear convincing testimony and make clear the divinity of the gospel of our Lord.

This afternoon Mr. Mori came and did some writing which brought him to the close of his work for us. He had dinner with us. He has been faithful and diligent and perfectly honest and always pleasant. His actions prove that he is a young man of superior character and integrity. I hope he will eventually be converted to the gospel and endure to the end in loyalty to his God. He has copied the revised translation up to the last of the 11th book of my manuscript. He has also read over once the proof sheets of the Brief History. He has written signs, charts, advertizements and letters for us. His work has been neat, careful and quick.

Today I have done several jobs. Read the copy of my translation for an hour or so. **Wrote a letter to Mr. Zenshiro Noguchi telling him I have decided to entrust the translation criticism to someone else. Wrote** several cards. Taught Japanese to Elder Taylor. At noon we held prayer meeting. **Late at night, a letter from Mr. Hirogoro Hirai came telling me he was now ready to sign the revised agreement for the criticism of my B. of M. translation. The date set for the signing is Sept. 2nd.** The English Bible class was not held this evening for lack of audience.

Friday, 30 August 1907, Tokyo

Clear—Hot. Up at 6:30. Spent the forenoon working on the Book of Mormon. **While we were eating dinner, five hundred copies of the Brief History of the Church came. This is all of the paper bound copies I ordered. There are five hundred copies bound in cloth yet to be delivered. Elder Taylor and I spent two or three hours wrapping them up in bundles of six so as to get them out of the way of dust and scratches. Elder Caine reported the completion of the book to the Home Department and asked for permission to distribute it. The law is that if the Home Department does not issue an order forbidding the distribution within three days from the time of printing the publisher is free to begin the distribution.**

Taught Elder Taylor a brief lesson in Japanese. **Last night Mr. Gento Suzuki sent a letter to me saying he would be unable to take the work of criticising the B. of M. translation. This morning I acknowledged his refusal and sent ¥5.00 in recognition of the work he did in connection with my proposition and requests for samples.** Attended Bible class at 7:30 p.m. Talked with Mr. Uehara.

Saturday, 31 August 1907, Tokyo

Clear—Hot. Up at 6:30. Spent the forenoon working on the Book of Mormon and making a trip down town. I called in at the Home Department to file a request for a copyright for the Brief History translation. I secured a copy of the forms required in making the request, but being unable to write the requ/e/st suitably I brought it home, doing some business on the way home. In the afternoon I wrote letters to Sendai and Sapporo giving a program of the meetings I desire to hold at these places when I visit them. I swept the garden and took a bath. After supper I walked to Yotsuya and made arrangements for a different groceryman from the one we have had thus far to supply us with groceries from now on.

The remainder of the copies of the Brief History (500 in cloth binding) were delivered. The order of 1000 copies is now complete and I am pleased with the appearance of the books. This is the grand climax of the greatest literary event in the history of the Japan Mission—an event of which we are proud. The next and what will be the supremist of all will be the completion and publication of the Book of Mormon translation.

Sunday, 1 September 1907, Tokyo

Cloudy—Slight rain—Hot. Up at 6:30. Sunday School commenced at 9:00 a.m. I taught the First Intermediate Class in Elder Stoker's place. At 11:00 a.m. sacrament meeting was held. In the afternoon I couldn't keep awake so I took a nap. At about five o'clock we ate supper. After supper, I read a little. The evening meeting was quite well attended. I was one of the speakers. After meeting I talked with Sister Hakii advizing her to leave the place where she is now working as the master of the house is reputed to be exceedingly immoral and ungentlemanly.

Today is the sixth anniversary of the dedication of this land by Apostle Heber J. Grant and his companions. The blessings of that meeting held in the woods were vividly before my mind and today I have felt to rejoice exceedingly over the experiences and progress of the past six years. I rejoice to be still in this land and trust that I shall be permitted to remain here considerably longer.

Monday, 2 September 1907, Tokyo

Clear—Hot as blazes. Up at 6:00. Swept and dusted the down stairs. **At about 9:00 a.m. Mr. Hirogoro Hirai came. He had received a letter from Mr. Noguchi in which a copy of a letter to me was enclosed. The original letter from Noguchi reached me early this morning. It manifested a bitter spirit and showed plainly that Noguchi's character is not suitable to Book of Mormon translation criticism. I am glad Mr. Noguchi's name was dropped in the consideration of men for the criticism of my translation. But his bitterness and unwarranted letter is not pleasant as both Mr. Kinza Hirai's name and Hirogoro Hirai's name are drawn into the matter. Mr. Hirogoro Hirai listened to my explaination of the afair. I showed him my letters to Noguchi and Mr. Hirai altho a close friend of Mr. Noguchi's was not slow to see the Noguchi was greatly at fault in growing angry at me for the investigation I made of his character and my final rejection of his services. Mr. Hirogoro Hirai signed with me the contract for his services for a year during which time he is to devote his whole time to the Book of Mormon translation criticism or any other literary work the mission may demand of him. His wages for the year will be ¥1568.00. In the afternoon I wrapped up some histories to send away.**

Later I went to Omori to see Mr. Kinza Hirai about Mr. Noguchi's anger. Mr. Hirai had already received a copy of Noguchi's letter to me. He was frank in exonerating me and acknowledging Mr. Noguchi's lack of ground for his ire and bitter letter. Owing to poor transportation accommodations, my return was so late that our Bible Class could not be held. On the train a French Catholic preacher mistook me for a Japanese and talked with me in Japanese for quite a while. When I informed him that I am an American, he squared off and looked at me hard and said he had certainly taken me for a native. As he could not speak English and I could not speak French we continued to talk in Japanese. After flattering my language and kindness (He being an old man I insisted on him taking my seat) he asked who I was. I told him and it was quite evident that he thought he had put his foot into it.

Wednesday, 4 September 1907, Tokyo

Clear—Hot—Later Cloudy Up at 6:45. Spent the entire forenoon writing letters and arranging announcements and advertizements. At about 1:00 or 1:30 p.m. we held prayer and council meeting. After meeting, I went out to the post office and then attended a little to the needs of Elder Anderson who is and has been suffering a great deal with his head and stomach. In the evening I walked as far as Aoyama and after supper I expected to teach the English Bible Class, but no one came except Mr. Wakabayashi. I had a long talk with him. Administered to Elder Anderson before going to bed. He is quite sick.

Thursday, 5 September 1907, Tokyo

Cloudy—Showers—Hot. Up at 6:00. Spent the forenoon tending to Elder Anderson and doing several odd jobs. Walked to Aoyama and back. In the afternoon I did little besides helping Elder Anderson and thinking about his condition. In the forenoon Elder Caine went for a doctor to diagnose Elder Anderson's case. The places called at first could not respond at the doctors were out of reach. So Dr. [blank] of the Luke's Hospital[26] in Tsukiji was asked to come. He came between four and five o'clock and after looking at Elder Anderson, said that the symptoms are those of typhoid fever[27] and said he ought to be removed to the hospital. To this I did not consent. The doctor gave three prescriptions which Elder Caine took and had filled immediately. This morning Elder Stoker went to Yokohama to meet the new missionaries if it happened that they are on the Ryojun Maru. He came back in the evening without them. The ship had not arrived.

Friday, 6 September 1907, Tokyo

Clear—Hot. Up at midnight. Retired at 4:00 a.m. Elder Caine taking my place as nurse to Elder Anderson. Until the close of my watch there was not much change in his condition, but a tendancy towards the better. Slept until 10:45 a.m. Spent the day working on the Book of Mormon and tending to Elder Anderson. Retired at 10:00 p.m. Elder Anderson remained about the same today.

Saturday, 7 September 1907—Sunday, 8 September 1907, Tokyo

Cloudy—Hot—Windy Up at 6:30. Spent the forenoon cleaning house. During the afternoon I guarded at the bedside of Elder Anderson. This afternoon he has suffered a great deal. Today we decided to change doctor's. So at about 10:30 p.m. a doctor from the Tanō Hospital came and saw our sick brother. He prescribed for his sickness. Elder Anderson grew much easier after 11:00 p.m. and slept quite well the rest of the night. I continued on watch till 4:15 a.m. then took a bath. I had two hours rest and then prepared for Sunday School. We had a fair school today. Our sacrament meeting was very brief. After dinner I had a short nap. Took a little walk for exercise. Ate supper. The doctor called about 7:00 p.m. At 7:40 p.m. our evening meeting commenced. Not a very large audience. While Elder Stoker made the first speech, I went out and secured a messenger to go to the hospital for medicine. Returned and spoke for about 40 minutes. Retired at 9:30.

Monday, 9 September 1907, Tokyo

Cloudy—Heavy Showers—Cool Up at 6:30. **Spent the forenoon and part of the afternoon at the house of Mr. Hirogoro Hirai attending to the perliminary work in connection with the Book of Mormon translation revision which Mr. Hirai begins today. I am very thankful to my heavenly Father that his long hoped for work has begun and I sincerely hope that the blessings of God will attend the work in great abundance and strengthen both the heart and mind of the critic. I feel the necessity of great wisdom in connection with this labor and pray that I shall be given power and intelligence to do well and quickly my part of the work.**

Today Elder Anderson has been much easier but his fever has continued still high. The doctor came again today. Before supper I walked to Aoyama on business. After supper, till bed time I watched Elder Anderson's condition. He is still a sick man, but fortunately pretty free from pain.

Wednesday, 11 September 1907, Tokyo

Rain—Much cooler Up at 6:45. Swept and dusted the lower rooms in the foreign part of the house. During the forenoon I did several jobs and a little work on the Book of Mormon. At about 12:40 p.m. we held prayer meeting. We administered to Elder Anderson, who is much improved today. I wrote to the Elders in Sendai and also to those in Kōfu. Walked as far as the shipping company's office before supper. After supper, I conducted an English Bible Class. We had prayers and I went on guard or rather watch over Elder Anderson. Was attending to this duty at midnight.

Thursday, 12 September 1907, Tokyo

Cloudy & Very Cool Continued my watch over Elder Anderson, from midnight till 3:45 a.m. Elder Taylor took my place and I retired. I got up at 10:45 a.m. Ate dinner. In the afternoon I went down town and attended to mission business. Among other things, I called at some of the newspapers and left a copy of the Brief History at the Yomiuri one at the Jiji. The Hochi News man was away.

I called at the home of Mr. Saburo Shimada the proprietor and editor of the Mainichi News. This man is one of the most eloquent speakers and ready writers in all Japan. When the mission was first opened, he said a number of things about us which were not true. So this evening I was very glad to meet him face to face and ask him to introduce in his paper the Brief History and give it a write up that will advertize very well. He received me very cordially and seemed delighted to get the book which he promised to read and review in his paper.

From Mr. Shimada's I went to Bro. Saburo Kikuchi's home and talked with him about the performance of his duties as a member of the church. He bought a copy of the history. Returned and retired.

Monday, 16 September 1907, Tokyo

Clear—Colder. Up at 7:30. During the forenoon, I did a few odd jobs and then proof read with Elder Caine some of the copy of my Book of Mormon translation.

After dinner talked a while with Mr. Hirai who called to discuss with me about a point or two in the work of criticism. He brought the title page,[28] testimony of the three & eight witnesses,[29] all of the first chapter of I Nephi and part of the second chapter of the same book as he had corrected the translation. He left it for my review. After he returned, I went out as far as Aoyama to buy some paper & post some magazines and as far as Hanchō to order some newspapers. Read American newspapers and magazines. After supper I directed the English Bible Class for the Elders.

Tuesday, 17 September 1907, Tokyo

Cloudy—Rain. Up at 6:30. **Spent most of the day reviewing the criticisms of Mr. Hirai on the title page and first chapter of the Book of Mormon and the testimonies of the three and eight witnesses. This is the first sample of his criticism of my translation that I have seen and I have truly taken delight in my day's work. I feel satisfied with the kind of criticism he has made for he does not rob me of my individuality as seen in my translation. The decision to change the translation into bunsho having been reached on the 9th instant at which time Mr. Hirai's work began, it is necessary for him to change the form of nearly every verb that appears in the gembunitchi style in which I have written my translation. I handed Mr. Hirai's work to Sister Nachii and had her read it. She says, that it is all very simple indeed, every word being perfectly plain to her.** Today, I have not felt very well, but the pleasure of the work has made me forget myself. Today I spent about two & a half hours talking with Mr. Sakuraba.

Thursday, 19 September 1907, Tokyo

Clear—Warm Up at 5:30. Swept & dusted the downstairs rooms. Last night my nose gave me considerable distress and today it has been running freely. During the forenoon, I worked on the Book of Mormon. In the afternoon, I went to the Imperial University Hospital to see Dr. Okada who is a specialist in nasal diseases. He was not there, but at his own hospital in Kojimachi where I went. There were a great many patients waiting to see him, so I sent in my card and requested an appointment for some certain hour. Appointed Saturday at 9:00 a.m. Went to the Ushigome post office to get the ¥10.00 paid back which I sent to Mr. Noguchi in Kobe and which he returned as "fuketsu no Kane."[30] From Ushigome, I went to Mr. Hirai's home and consulted with him about a point or two in the Book of Mormon criticism. Walked from his house to headquarters. Ate supper. Wrote a letter to Spencer Clawson. Retired

Today Elder Stoker went to Yokohama to meet new missionaries from Zion. They did not come.

Friday, 20 September 1907, Tokyo

Cloudy—Cool Up at 7:00. Spent the day in the house working on the Book of Mormon. Mr. Hachiro Mori came today and informed us that he had left the Azabu Chū Gakko[31] and taken a position with a tobacco company. I fear this change in his avocation will bring a change in his diligence in attending our meetings and studying the Gospel. However this young man has had splendid opportunity to **know** the truth and he will be without excuse if he does not heed the word and obey. In the evening I attended the Japanese Bible Class.

Saturday, 21 September 1907, Tokyo

Cloudy—Rain Up at 6:45. Spent the forenoon at Doctor Okada's and looking for houses. The doctor after looking at my nose said that it was in a bad condition which only an operation would cure. He said that the middle bone was deformed and this was partly the cause of the irritation which makes my nose run so much. If the operation is performed it will be after I return from the north but I am not entirely converted to the operation theory. In the afternoon I worked on the Book of Mormon translation at headquarters. After supper I felt quite unwell as my nose was running and my eyes sore. I took a bath and retired early.

Wednesday, 25 September 1907, Tokyo

Cloudy—Rain—Colder Up at 7:00. Spent the entire day working on the Book of Mormon translation. It has been one of the longest, hardest days I have ever devoted to the work. I have been reading my corrected translation and comparing it carefully with the English. I always, after going over the book of the translation, and correcting as much as I can the Japanese, carefully read over the corrected translation and compare it closely with the English before I consider the revision complete. Today I read over & compared with the English the translation of nearly 20 full pages of the English which is equal to about half a book of my original /character/ manuscript. Just before supper, however, I took a short walk to relieve my mental strain and create a better feeling for food. I gave Elder Stoker charge of the English Bible Class in the evening so I could continue the work on the Book of Mormon as I desire to complete the book I am working on before I leave for Sendai next Friday night.

Friday, 27 September 1907, Tokyo/Train

Clear—Warmer. Up at 6:00. Spent the forenoon working on the Book of Mormon. I reviewed the translation up to the end of the book of Mormon from the 22nd chapter of III Nephi. There is only one and a fourth books of the manuscript which I have not gone over. I sent the 4th book of the /copied/ manuscript to Mr. Hirai as, judging from his speed thus far, he will be able to criticise to the 4th book before I return from my trip to the north. In the afternoon I prepared for my trip and gave a few instructions to Elder Stoker who will have charge of the work at Tokyo during my absence. After supper I took rikisha to the Ueno Station. Mr. Sakuraba was at the station to see me off. The train left at 7:35 p.m. I having secured a berth retired as soon as possible.

Saturday, 28 September 1907, Train/Sendai

Clear—Warm Up at 5:00. At 5:15 the train arrived at Sendai. I took a jinrikisha and went immediately to the mission house where I found the elders just getting up. They seemed well and happy, but Elder Woodland looks like a sick man, having had a severe cold lately which has resulted in a slight bronchitis.[32] Ate breakfast, chatted, studied a little on the subject I was appointed to discuss in the afternoon meeting. Ate dinner.

At 2:00 p.m. the first listener came. By 3:00 p.m. there were about a dozen people present. The meeting began at 3:15. In all there were about 20 in attendance. The meeting lasted over two hours. The audience gave strict attention. I discussed the Book of Mormon under the title "The Bible of Ancient America." Elder Caine discussed "Latter-day Revelations." We ate supper. Elder Caine and I took a walk. The evening meeting began at 7:15 with an audience which grew in size to 32. This meeting also lasted over two hours and the strictest attention was paid. I discussed Mormonism and Elder Caine explained the Kingdom of God on Earth."

Sunday, 29 September 1907, Tokyo

Clear—Calm—Warm. Up at 6:30. Ate breakfast. The Sunday School children came at 8:00 a.m. I enjoyed the visit to this school which has good materials but needs a little careful training. At 9:30 a.m. our first public meeting should have begun, but there were only three present. I engaged in conversation with these especially with one who was afterwards said to be a preacher. The conversation was on God, a personal Being. The preacher offered a criticism to my explanation. This gave me an opportunity to deal with the subject more fully and answer the objections of other religionists to our views on this vital subject. The preacher finding his remarks and objections answered and riddled one by one grew pale and his hands trembled like a leaf in the breeze. He attempted a defense of his position but grew utterly silent when he found himself getting in a tighter corner. There were others came in as the conversation progressed so that there were 8 or 9 listeners. The Lord greatly sustained me in explaining the views of the

Latter-day Saints and defending the truth of our position. The preacher went away somewhat humilated but with something to think about. This conversation grew so interesting that nearly the entire morning was spent in it.

The afternoon meeting could not be held as only two came. The indifference of the people today has been a surprise and disappointment for I certainly felt that if we could make a go of the Saturday meetings that Sunday meetings would be a sure thing. I read during most of the afternoon. Ate supper. At 7:15 our evening meeting commenced with a fair audience which numbered 32, /nearly/ half of them being women. This meeting lasted over two hours and Elder Caine and I discussed the subjects "Man, though he dies yet shall he live" and "Who has authority to initiate me into the Kingdom of God." We retired feeling very grateful for the blessings received during our series of meetings but regretted very much the failure to see much of our literature.

Monday, 30 September 1907, Tokyo

Clear—Warm Up at 7:40. Spent the forenoon in conversation with Mr. Suzuki of the "Kahoku Shimpo" and in writing. In the afternoon we had a horse-shoe throwing contest which proved a very pleasant recreation. At 3:15 we held a priesthood meeting and discussed the condition of the mission work in this city. The elders have labored hard and have been over the available parts of the city with gospel tracts and the resident parts they have visited two or three and sometimes four times, but there has been practically no response from the people and they count only one who, at present, seems to be investigating the gospel with the proper spirit. After meeting we took a pleasant walk over the neighboring hills. Returned and ate supper. I had a long interesting talk with a man who, having heard the sermons last night, had some questions arise in his mind which he desired answered. Packed my valise preparatory to leaving for the north early in the morning. Took a bath and retired.

Tuesday, 1 October 1907, Sendai/Morioka

Clear—Calm—Warm. Up at 4:15. Left Sendai at about 5:45 and arrived at Ichinoseki about 8:15. Walked around the town to see how it is built and what the people look like and what they are doing. We (Elder Caine & I) called at the Town Office to see how many churches and followers there are. We found that both the Roman & Greek Catholics are at work and the Christian Church & the Nihon Kirisuto are in the field. We called on the Nihon Kirisuto Kyokwai's preacher and were received royally, but we left him rather surprised to know that we are "Mormons" and after a swift run to the station we caught the 11:22 a.m. train and went to Morioka. Morioka is the capitol of Iwate Ken.

We went directly from the station to the Takayo Hotel. After washing, we went around the town and called at both the City and Ken Offices and learned about the Christian's missionary work here. The earliest church in Morioka is the Roman Catholic which began in Meiji 8 and has now in the neighborhood of 314 followers. The Greeks began work here the year after the Romans and have now about 245 members. The Baptists have been here since Meiji 13 and have 150 enrolled as members. The Methodists are also in the fight having started their work 10 years ago and report 100 members. The Nihon Kirisuto Kyokwai has been here 20 years, but counts only 65 followers. There are three or four foreign missionaries living here the city has a population of 32,000. The strongest native sect is the Sodoshu of Buddhism, but the people are not in the least hostile to Christianity. The national progress of this part of Japan is much slower than the southern districts and the people are all engaged in agriculture pursuits. Therefore, they are said to be plain and honest. There is a High School each for boys & girls, a Normal school, Agriculture School, Middle School & Primary Schools here. The city is far superior in appearance & spirit than Sendai. In all Elder Caine and I have been impressed with our stay here. After looking the town over we returned to the hotel, ate supper, shaved and retired early as we will be called about midnight to catch the train to Aomori.

Wednesday, 2 October 1907, Morioka/Hakodate

Cloudy—Cold—Slight Wind Up at 12:20 a.m. Spent the hours till 7:00 a.m. on the train between

Morioka and Aomori. It was very cold. Arrived in Aomori about 7:00. Had breakfast at the Kagiya Hotel. Took the "Osumi Maru" for Hakodate. Left at 10:30 a.m. and reached Hakodate at 4:30 p.m. I left Elder Caine at the depot and went in search of a place to stay over night. On account of the terrible fire at Hakodate on the 25th of August all of the hotels except a sort of foreign style place in Hakodate Park have been destroyed. I found poor but expensive lodgings at the latter place, so I sent for Elder Caine. After supper, I took a walk to get warm. Retired.

Thursday, 3 October 1907, Hakodate/Sapporo

Cloudy—Rain—Cold Up at 6:30. Ate breakfast and walked to the station where Elder Caine and I took the train for Sapporo leaving Hakodate at 8:00 a.m. The weather being bad, it was not as pleasant as it would otherwise be still the scenery was enjoyed. At 8:00 p.m. we arrived at Sapporo. Elders Seely and Marriott were at the depot to meet us. Found all well and happy at the mission field home. Had supper and retired happy to have made the trip in safety and to find my brethren well.

Friday, 4 October 1907, Sapporo

Cold—Cloudy—Rain Up at 7:00. During the forenoon I worked on the Book of Mormon. After dinner, I prepared for the night meeting. There being so many of us together and each having so much to say and so many questions to ask, I did not get in many hours of actual work. The evening meeting, the first in the series to be held here began at 7:15. We had an audience of 28 or 29 and about twelve children. Six of the latter sang during the meeting.

After the meeting I talked with Brother Kawanaka and told him that while I am here he may copy the first book of the Book of Mormon translation manuscript as corrected by Mr. Hirai. He consented to do it.

Saturday, 5 October 1907, Sapporo

Cloudy—Cold—A little rain Up at 8:00. Spent the forenoon talking with my brethren, cleaning up and doing odd jobs. Bro. Kawanaka came this morning and began to copy the translation mentioned in my yesterday's journal At 3:30 p.m. we held a meeting which was not as largely attended but we enjoyed abundantly the Spirit of the Lord. After meeting we worked rapidly and got supper ready. After supper we held another meeting which was a little better attended than the afternoon meeting and enjoyed again a rich outpouring of the Holy Spirit. After the meeting I had a long conversation with two gentlemen who for over a year have been earnestly investigating the gospel as taught by the elders. These gentlemen are careful readers of the scriptures and their questions pertained to some of the deepest points of teachings.

Sunday, 6 October 1907, Sapporo

Cloudy—Cold—Heavy rain Up at 7:00. The Sunday School in this field began at 9:00 a.m. There are two departments in this school. Elder Seely having charge of the older students and Elder Roskelley having charge of the young children. Considering the very limited experience of Elder Roskelley, he did very well as a teacher. There were about 76 children present and every one of them was a decoration that couldn't be spared. This body of children is one to be proud of—the best congregation of children that I have seen in a "Mormon" Sunday School in Japan. After school we administered the sacrament.

Then followed a new and interesting experience. Feeling that our preaching meetings should be better attended I decided to announce them on the public highways of the city. Accordingly I took Elders Seely, Roskelley, Cutler and Marriott and went out on the streets. We sang to mandolin accompanyment until a large crowd gathered and then announced our meetings. We did this on eight prominent corners. This is the first time I have participated in any kind of a street demonstration in Japan. I naturally felt rather shaky at first but before were through I became attached to the experience.

Returned in time to get a little rested before the 3:00 p.m. meeting commenced. This meeting was not as well attended as our former meetings but the Spirit was enjoyed in rich abundance. Ate dinner after the meeting. At 9:15 another meeting was held with an audience which at last grew to number 9 adults 7 or 8 of whom slept during the majority of meeting so there was mighty little to talk to and little inspiration from the audience. This ended our series of meetings—we sort of went in at the big and came out at the little end of the horn so far as the audience was concerned, but the meetings did a good deal of good as we had the chance to testify to a few who have manifested quite an interest in our message.

Monday, 7 October 1907, Sapporo/Asahikawa

Cloudy, Cold, Rain Up at 4:30. Ate an early breakfast and with Elder Seely left Sapporo on the 6:10 a.m. train for the north. Stopped for two hours at Iwamizawa. Walked over the entire town to get an idea of the people and style of the place. Called at the town office and inquired about the influence of the two Christian church established here. There are two sects in the field and considering the size of the place and time their mission work has been in operation, they have done exceedingly well in getting numbers at least. Took the next rain and went to Takikawa. On the train met a long time resident of this village. He told me about all I wanted to know about the place, so all we did was to hurridly walk over the place and take the next train. We went to Fukagawa. After seeing the village, we called in at a hotel and had supper. The night train to Asahigawa was two hours and a half late so we did not get to Asahigawa till 11:00 p.m. Went directly to a hotel near the station and retired.

Tuesday, 8 October 1907, Asahikawa/Sapporo

Cloudy—Cold Up at 6:00. Elder Seely and I walked around the town before breakfast. After breakfast we took the train to Nayoro, the most northerly point reached by the railroad. Spent an hour looking over this very little village and to the train at about 12:30 p.m. and arrived in Sapporo at 9:30 p.m. A little south of Asahikawa the train passes through a canyon through which a large beautiful river flows. The autumn leaves in this place are the most famous in Hokkaidō so this strip of scenery is said to be the best this island affords.

I was glad to get back to Sapporo. The trip was nothing more nor less than hard work in bad weather. The object of this trip was to get an idea of the places beyond Sapporo so as to know the most suitable places to settle some elders. The country is all new, the people are poor the towns and villages, except Asahikawa, are all too small to keep an elder at work more than a week or two. I found Christian Preachers in every berg we visited and was greatly surprised to see church buildings in even the farthest and smallest settlements. It speaks much for the push of the missionaries and the liberality of the man in America or elsewhere who holds the purse. I have wondered if the policy of vigorous proselyting in a new country like this is not just the proper thing, for in some villages temples and shrines are very scarce and the people are inclined to forget the traditions they followed before they came to the island. They may be just as easily influenced to the right way as the [—] wrong one if good capable work is performed among them. At any rate the people of Hokkaido are a good class of people and on an average far better educated than those of many parts of the main island. Took a bath and ate supper before retiring.

Wednesday, 9 October 1907, Sapporo

Clear—Warm Up at 8:00. Spent the forenoon cleaning up after the trip. At noon we held a meeting which was a combination of the regular prayer meeting and a special priesthood meeting. In this meeting I gave the elders instructions regarding their work. After the meeting I went to the Agriculture University Museum and from there to Mr. Kintaro Oshima's home. He was not there so I went to the University and met him. Returned to the mission house and had supper and also a long talk with Bro. Aritatsu Kawanaka our only native member in Hokkaido. Packed up preparatory to leaving for Tokyo the next morning.

Thursday, 10 October 1907, Sapporo/Ship

Clear—Warm Up at 5:00. Said good-bye to the brethren and left Sapporo on the 6:10 a.m. train. **We got off the train at Shiraoi were a number of Aino, the natives of Japan live. We spent about an hour in their village. We talked with some of them who can speak Japanese. We bought a few trinkets and saw the bears they are raising for the great bear festival to be held on the old calendar New Years. Originally when this island was not disturbed by the Japanese and the natives had everything** their own way their chief sport was to catch and kill bears which were found in great quantities everywhere. One of the natives today said that his race was dying away rapidly due to the diseases introduced among them by the Japanese, who after polluting the poor natives have done nothing to check the ravages of the disease among them. The fall of the natives of this land is not unlike the fall of the American Indians. The women tattoo their mouths and eyebrows so that at a distance they look like men with whiskers. The men are hairy and wear very long beards and long hair parted in the middle. They are larger than the Japanese and have well shapped heads. I enjoyed our brief visit with them.

Ate lunch at the station and took the 1:18 p.m. train for Muroran. We arrived at Muroran at 2:40 p.m. Left our chattles in the waiting house and took a walk over the town and climbed some hills to get a good view of the city, ocean etc. The sight from the hights ascended was delightful. Ate supper at the waiting house and then went on board the Higo Maru. The steamer sails for Aomori at 3:00 a.m. tomorrow morning. At about 8:00 p.m. I went to·bed.

Friday, 11 October 1907, On board Higo Maru/Odate

Clear—Calm—Warm Up at 7:30. The voyage from Muroran to Aomori was delightful. The sea was calm and the sun warm and the one passanger in the first cabin, besides Elder Caine and I was very congenial altho she was greatly surprised to learn what we are doing here and who we are. The lady is a missionary stationed at Sapporo but is on her way to Tokyo to attend a conference. After dinner and for a few minutes before I had a good talk with her about Mormonism and showed her how mistaken many of her ideas regarding us are. She listened with respect and was perhaps very enlightened. The boat arrived in Aomori at 1:30 p.m. Elder Caine and I took the 2:30 p.m. train and went as far as Hirosaki where we spent two hours looking over the city. It is quite a place. About 35,000 people. A division of the army is located here. The Methodists have a very large church building here. The appearance of the streets is good but the houses as a general rule look dilapidated. Ate supper at a hotel near the station took the evening train and went to Ōdate where we stopped for the night.

Saturday, 12 October 1907, Ōdate/Akita

Cloudy—Colder—Rain Up at 7:00. Ate breakfast at the hotel (Saitō Hotel) and then went around the town of Ōdate. The town is one of the dirtiest unkept places I have seen on this trip and there is little evidence of education among them. There are two churches said to be at work here. The town is perhaps a little over three quarters of a mile from the station. Took the 11:27 train and went to Noshiro. Ate dinner on the way. Noshiro is separated from the railroad about two & a half miles. There are some copper mines and smelters in the vicinity. Two or three saw mills are located here. The town is quite clean and in general appearance very much better than Ōdate. We called at the town office and were told that there used to be a Christian mission in the town, but it was abandoned about six years ago. After looking around the town, Elder Caine and I took the stage back to the railroad station and left on the 4:17 train for Akita the capitol of Akita Ken. We arrived at the Kobayashi Hotel at 7:00 o'clock. Took a bath, ate supper, wrote my journal and retired.

Sunday, 13 October 1907, Akita

Clear—Warm—Calm Up at 6:45. After breakfast, Elder Caine and I called on the kindergarden department of the Christian Church. There were 62 little tots between the ages of 4 & 7 in the class and aside from the noise inside and outside the room the session was very interesting to me. After the school Elder Caine and I walked around part of the town. We got a good view of the city from the park. Akita City Park is the best City park I have seen in my travels around Japan. It is not as large as many I have visited but its design and location is almost ideal. It is very well kept a thing that can't be said of most parks. Returned to the hotel and had dinner. After dinner Elder Caine and I /proof-/read the remaining part of the copy of a small part of the Book of Mormon translation made by Bro. Aritatsu Kawanaka while I was in Hokkaidō.

After this we went out and look around the city again visiting those parts we did not see in the forenoon. This is certainly an attractive city and built in the right style for missionary work; the stores and residences are distinctly separated like in Tokyo and the streets are generally at right angles. The report on the religious nature of the people and their attitude towards Christianity is not good. The people are said to be non religious and generally pronounced against the name of our Savior. Educationally the city is behind Sendai if the number and kind of schools are made the standard of judgment. There is a commercial school, normal school and middle school & High Girls' School. A regiment of soldiers is stationed here. This being the capitol of Akita Ken there are of course a great many local government offices. The people look bright and clean and the streets and houses are a boquet compared to what we have seen since leaving Sapporo. The population is approximately 40,000. After supper at the hotel, Elder Caine and I attended the evening services held at the Christian Church. We heard a preacher who has plenty of words but no spirit or elevating ideas. Returned to the hotel and retired.

Monday, 14 October 1907, Akita/Yamagata

Clear—Warm—Calm Up at 6:00. Left Akita City on the 7:35 a.m. train and went direct to Yamagata City the capitol of Yamagata Ken. We intended to call at Yokote and Shinjō but found that these places are so small and unimportant that it was not worth while stopping in them. Arrived at Yamagata City at a little past 5:00 p.m. We took rikisha to the Gōdō Hotel. We went out immediately and by rapid walking were able to see most of the city before dark. Yamagata City is not quite so populous at Akita and is not such a well built city, but it is not dirty like Sendai and other places I have seen on this trip. This being a capitol city the usual schools are found here and the various Ken & city & county offices & courts. A regiment of soldiers is stationed here. One very attractive feature of one half of the city is the streams of crystal water that flow down the streets on each side of the road way.

Tuesday, 15 October 1907, Yamagata/Fukushima

Fair—Warm Up at 6:00. Took the 7:33 a.m. train and went as far as Yonezawa City. Arrived at that place at about 9:45 a.m. Elder Caine and I walked around the city for two hours or more. We called at the Mayor's Office and learned all we care to know about the Christian Churches established in the city. The city's population is 30,000 and the people must all be old fashioned as their homes are nearly all thached roofs and with one or two exceptions all the buildings are purely Japanese architecture. Christianity must have had a harder time here than in other places for they haven't made many converts considering the length of time they have been at work. The city is not as clean and well laid out as others seen on the trip, but it is far cleaner than some places farther north. We called at a kind of hotel and waiting house located near the station and had dinner.

We took the 1:40 p.m. train and went as far as Fukushima the capitol city of Fukushima Ken. The scenery between Yonezawa and Fukushima is both pretty and grand. The train passes through two canyons in each of which runs a picturesque crystal stream. The train track is far above the river bed and at times passes along rocky precipice that almost makes one dizzy to look down at the sparkling water many feet below. This is the best scenery on our trip and the engineering skill required in building this railroad is of the very best. We arrived in Fukushima on time; 4:04 p.m. We went to the Matsuba Kwan (Fukushima Hotel) and left our valises. We spent two hours looking around the city seeing nearly all there is to see and learning enough about the city before darkness overtook us. Went to the hotel. I took a bath and shaved. Ate supper and retired. Fukushima is about the same as Yamagata.

Wednesday, 16 October 1907, Fukushima/Tokyo

Clear—Quite Warm—Calm Up at 6:05. Ate breakfast and paid the hotel bill. Elder Caine and I walked to a high point on a hill near the city and got a fine view of the entire valley. Went to the station and left for Tokyo on the 9:14 a.m. train. After a rather tedious ride we reached Tokyo at 6:15 p.m. We soon reached headquarters. I was very happy to see at headquarters four new faces. Elder Elbert D. Thomas & wife, Elder Charles W. Hubbard and Elder O. Ellis Harris. Ate a chicken supper. Talked a little while and retired. Tonight headquarters was lit with electric lights for the first time the house having been just wired.

Wednesday, 23 October 1907, Tokyo

Cloudy—Rain—Cold Up at 6:15. Spent a hour sweeping and dusting the downstairs rooms. The rest of the forenoon I spent writing letters and attending to matters connected with the mission work. **At noon we held a prayer meeting. At this meeting, Elder Elbert D. Thomas was made Secretary of the mission, Elder Caine being released so he can devote all of his time to Book of Mormon translation work**. I worked on the Book of Mormon translation in the afternoon. In the evening I attended the English Bible Class.

Wednesday, 30 October 1907, Tokyo

Clear—Warmer Up at 7:00. Washed and went immediately to Mr. Hirai's and continued the discussion of points in the Book of Mormon translation. Returned in time to join the missionaries in prayer meeting at noon. After meeting I worked at the Book of Mormon translation. Ate supper. Attended a part of the English Bible Class.

Had a long talk with Mrs. Fude Tai regarding her feelings about the Church and inquired if she was as anxious as ever to join us and become a member of the Kingdom of God. She stated positively, but humbly, that it was her earnest desire to receive baptism and hoped with the blessings of God together with her own strength to be able to endure faithfully to the end. I told her that she might be baptized and that we would immediately seek a suitable place and time.

Friday, 1 November 1907, Tokyo

Clear—Warm—Afternoon, calm Up at 6:45. Spent the forenoon hunting for a house. Elder Stoker accompanied me.

Ate dinner at headquarters and then in company with all the elders in Tokyo and Sister Hakii and Nachie and the latter's little girl Ei and Mrs. Tai went to Tamagawa to witness and direct a baptismal service, by which Mrs. Tai was added to the fold of Christ. This is our only baptism thus far this year. The weather being ideal, the water clear and the spot quiet and secluded all hearts rejoiced in the privilege of being present. Mrs. Fude Tai is Sister Tsune Nachie's younger sister and has been a believer of the Episcopal Church for a long time; in fact her second husband who died about eighteen months or two years ago was connected with the Episcopal Church as a *preacher in Kawagoe. Returned and ate supper. Attended the Bible Class which was exceptionally good.

*This is a mistake. Her husband never was a preacher but her father-in-law with whom she lived after her husband's death is the preacher at Kawagoe.

Sunday, 3 November 1907, Tokyo

Rain—Cold Up at 6:30. Washed and went with Elder Stoker to see a house advertized for rent. Spent nearly the entire morning in hot pursuit and after seeing a number of places and getting good and wet, we decided on one place to be used temporarily. Returned to headquarters and wrote and read a little. At 2:00 p.m. the fast and sacrament meeting began. In this meeting Sister Fude Tai was confirmed a member of the church by Elder John W. Stoker. All of the speeches were translated from English into Japanese and from Japanese into English so that the words of every speaker were made intelligable to all. The meeting lasted nearly three hours. Ate supper and then held evening meeting. In spite of the heavy rain we had a fair crowd. Today being the emperor's birthday a military review was held on the parade grounds in front of headquarters. Exercises were held in his honor in all the primary schools so we had to suspend Sunday School.

Tuesday, 5 November 1907, Tokyo

Rain—Cold Up at 7:15. Spent the entire day down town buying things for the house which will be occupied by some of the elders. The house in located at #69 Yochōmachi Okubo, Ushigome Ku, Tokyo. Returned in time for supper and then read a little before retiring.

Wednesday, 6 November 1907, Tokyo

Cloudy—Cold Up at 6:45. Went to Yotsuya to order bedding for the brethren in the new house at Yochōmachi. Spent the rest of the day at headquarters, writing letters, attending to various questions connected with the mission work and in the evening I did a little on the Book of Mormon. At noon today we held our prayer meeting.

Sunday, 10 November 1907, Tokyo

Clear—Calm—Colder Up at 7:00. Ate breakfast. Had a very pleasant time in Sunday School. After school a Mr. Kuroda came inquiring about a bad insulting letter that a student had sent to Sister Nachie's daughter. The gentleman represented the school attended by the student, and stated that any member of the school found guilty of such an act, would be suspended or expelled. A fine rule—worthy of strict enforcement. Ate lunch.

At 2:00 p.m. we held sacrament meeting. After meeting Bro. Yasubeiye Chiba called. He has not visited us or attended to his duties as a saint for a long time. He acknowledged his neglect and promised to do better. Ate supper. Had a good spirited evening meeting but not so large as we would like to have seen it.

Saturday, 16 November 1907, Tokyo

Clear—Later cloudy—Rain Up at 6:00. Spent the forenoon cleaning house. In the afternoon I worked on the Book of Mormon translation and in the evening after supper until bed time I discussed translation questions with Mr. Mori. Took a bath and retired.

Sunday, 17 November 1907, Tokyo

Cloudy—Cold Up at 7:00. Ate breakfast. Held an interesting Sunday School. After school I talked a little with Mr. Okada. Ate dinner. Held sacrament meeting. Elder Harris and I took a walk. We called on the Katagiri family. Returned to headquarters and ate supper. The evening meeting was exceedingly well attended—the largest meeting of the year, 32 being present. I held the meeting and did all the preaching. Elder Woodland prayed and assisted in the singing and ushering. This evening the first preaching meeting in the new mission field house in Yochōmachi, Tokyo was held by Elders Stoker and Caine. The meeting was held with success. Eighteen were present and good attention was paid. Today I have had talks with Sister Hakii and Miss Ishikawa the latter being one of Sister Nachie's intimate friends. The day has been an exceedingly delightful one to me.

Tuesday, 19 November 1907, Tokyo

Clear—Later cloudy & Rain—Cold Up at 7:30. Spent the forenoon writing letters. In the afternoon I did odd jobs and spent the evening discussing Book of Mormon translation questions with Mr. Mori. Also had quite a long chat with Mr. Sakuraba, who said that he had been convinced that "Mormonism" is the only true Christianity, but he is having a struggle to break loose from his old mooring in the Methodist Church, because he is a student in the Methodist College where he hoped to finish his education.

Saturday, 23 November 1907, Tokyo

Rain—Cold Up at 7:00. Spent nearly the entire day trying to compose a song but failed. Did some work on the Book of Mormon. This evening just at supper time a messenger came with a letter from Mr. Hachiro Mori in which he confessed his faith in the gospel and asked for baptism. Considering the fact that Mr. Mori has seldom missed one of our Sunday Night preaching meetings and Sunday Schools and Bible Classes during the past year and a half and during that time he has copied fully 2/3 of the Book of Mormon translation and done many jobs for us; never once doing or saying anything that has not favorably impressed us, this request for baptism was received by all of us with great joy.

Sunday, 24 November 1907, Tokyo

Fair—Very Warm—Calm—A ideal day. Up at 6:45. Ate breakfast. Held Sunday School. After school talked with Mr. Mori and told him that if he was ready and willing to take upon him the covenants and responsibilities of a Latter-day Saint that were were ready and pleased to baptise him to the fold. After lunch, we held Sacrament Meeting. After this meeting, I went to the Yochōmachi preaching station and after eating supper with Elders Harris and Hubbard, I held a meeting. There was quite a number of people came out to hear but they didn't seem to have courage to come inside. There were only ten people inside but twice the number outside so it was sort of a street meeting with the preacher on the inside. Spent the night at Yochomachi.

Monday, 25 November 1907, Tokyo

Cloudy—Clear—Calm. Up at 6:45. Ate breakfast at Yochōmachi. Went to headquarters and found Mr. Mori there ready to go to the river with us and receive baptism. We went to the Tamagawa River and at the same place we baptized Sister Tai on the 1st we baptized Mr. Mori. It was about 11:15 a.m. when the ordinance was performed. I officiated. All the missionaries now in Tokyo were present on the river bank. This is the second baptism I have performed in Japan, my first being when Bro. Yasubeiye Chiba joined the Church over a year ago.

Returned to headquarters and wrote letters to the elders in the out of Tokyo fields also sent a draft to Mr. Hirai in payment of the work he has done on the Book of Mormon translation during the last month. At 3:30 p.m. we ate dinner and supper both. At 4:00 p.m. Elder Stoker and I tested some of the Sunday School children's voices, so as to know who to select to sing our Christmas songs. In the evening we held an elders Bible Class.

Sunday, 1 December 1907, Tokyo

Clear—Cold Up at 7:00. Taught in Sunday School. After School did several things about Christmas. At 2:00 p.m. we held our fast and sacrament meeting. At this meeting Elder Fred A. Caine confirmed Bro. Hachiro Mori a member of the Church and gave him the Holy Ghost. A good spirit prevailed in the meeting which lasted two hours. After this meeting I went with some of the brethren to the Yochomachi branch where Elder Stoker and I conducted the evening meeting. There was only a very small audience. After meeting returned to headquarters and went to bed feeling very well pleased with the work and spirit of the day.

Friday, 6 December 1907, Tokyo

Clear—Calm—A little warm Up at 7:15. Spent the entire day working on the Book of Mormon translation and at 8:35 p.m. I finished my own criticism of my own translation up to the end of book. This is one of the great mile posts in the work and I feel like a big, heavy load had rolled off from my shoulders and there swells in my bosom an unspeakable joy for the blessings of the Lord upon the work which I feel has in every way been successful and well done. My conscience is free and my mind at rest for I have done my work to the best of my ability and in humility relying upon the help of God.

This criticism began May 14th 1906 and has been almost a complete new translation hence the many days of long hours work devoted to it. I have gone through the translation many times in making this criticism. First I read the translation to improve the Japanese and then I read it again carefully comparing it with the English to see that nothing had been ommitted and that the meaning, so far as I am able to interpret it, had not been mistaken or weakened or in any way exaggerated. The Lord has given me good health and mental vitality together with a sufficient supply of determination and stick-to-it-iveness. My criticised translation is being gone over by Elder Fred A. Caine who offers suggestions on the translation, interpretation of the English, and carefully compares it with the translation to make it doubly sure that nothing has been ommitted or carelessly rendered. His review of the translation is about two thirds completed and the final criticism by Mr. Hirogoro Hirai is well under way.

My next great work in the translation is the review of Mr. Hirai's criticisms and final preparation for the printer's copy. But before the criticism is considered complete and the manuscript ready for the printer I expect to have it read by at least three people—one a scholar, one an ordinary person, and one an uneducated person—and get and consider their suggestions so as to have it clear, simple, forceful and as near as possible grammatically correct. Thus while today is a red letter day, a great day for me, there is still much more work to be performed, many long hard hours of study and thought and discussion to be spent before the Japanese Book of Mormon appears in the world of literature & scripture. The blessings of the Lord are still essential; diligence, toil, endurance, care, wisdom and humility must characterize the great work to the end.

This evening a successful Japanese Bible Class was held by Elder Caine.

Thursday, 19 December 1907, Tokyo

Clear—Cold. Up at 7:20. Spent the forenoon at home working on the Book of Mormon translation. Ate an early dinner and then went to Mr. Hirai's where I spent the afternoon discussing translation questions with him. Walked home. In trying to find a shorter way home, I fell a victim to Tokyo's crooked streets and lost myself. However, I got home with the help of the street car in about the same time it would have taken to walk the well known way. Spent part of the evening translating a prayer to be used in blessing a bottle of oil, which oil I blessed at evening prayer time. *This is perhaps the first time the oil has been blessed in Japanese. It was Sister Nachie's oil, blessed for her. I am glad to see the saints manifesting their faith in the use of oil and the administration of the same in the household of faith.

*This I learned later was the second time the first being on the day Bro. Yasubeiye Chiba was confirmed.

Sunday, 22 December 1907, Tokyo

Clear—Warmer Up at 7:15. This morning we had quite a large Sunday School. The final instructions and business in connection with this year's Christmas Party were given. After dinner we held a brief sacrament meeting. I went to Yōchomachi and held a meeting there. The meeting was exceedingly small. Returned to headquarters and retired. Today I have endeavored to keep my mind upon Jesus, the Savior, and Joseph Smith the Prophet and in all my talking, praying and singing I have made the birth and life of these two children of God my principal theme.

Monday, 23 December 1907, Tokyo

Cold wind—Dusty—Clear Up at 6:30. Spent the day working for the Christmas Party. I have been doing carpenter's work most of the time.

Tuesday, 24 December 1907, Tokyo

Clear—Cold Up at 7:00. The day before Christmas is a busy day at headquarters. House decorating in preparation for Christmas Day is in order and all hands were at work. But today I have spent most of the time writing a dialogue for Santa Claus and the master of ceremonies at the Christmas Party. I was suprised to see when I got through that I had about twelve pages of closely written matter and nearly all for Santa Claus to say, but this could make no difference to anyone but me as I had been chosen to play Santa Claus. Helped the decoration work and learned my part on the program. Retired tired and sore— Sore from the exercise of the day before.

Wednesday, 25 December 1907, Tokyo

Clear—Warm—Calm—Ideal Day. Up at 6:30. Did a few finishing touches on the house decoration work and the arrangement of seats etc. Among other things I scattered two wagon loads of gravel which had been dumped in our front yard by the landlord. This had the result of leaving me stiff and sore as soon as the heat of the job passed off. Cleaned up and walked to Aoyama to buy some things necessary in Santa Claus make up. Rehearsed my part on the program twice.

At about 5:30 p.m. the guests began to arrive. All was on the move again till 7:50 o'clock when Elder John W. Stoker announced that the Christmas party would begin. There was a "jammed house," and a better audience has never assembled in our home. The Sunday School children, dressed in their very best and with happy faces beaming with expectancy and joy gave an aspect to the assemblage which was truly inspiring to our hearts. God's blessings had been earnestly asked for this occasion and the children and grown people on the program had come together with faithful and trusting hearts in the assistance of God. Under these conditions conditions anything other than a grand success could hardly be expected. My most earnest hopes in connection with the party were more than realized. Everyone on the program did well and while clapping on these occasions is not allowed at a number of places where brilliant climaxes were reached by the children the hands of the people seemed naturally impelled to break the rule. The opening and closing prayers the songs—solos, duets and congregational—the speeches, dialogues, and instrumental selections we well given and well received.

Santa Claus dropped in quite unexpectedly—or rather unannounced—He took the children and grown people by storm and keep all eyes and ears open wide during his stay and the hearty laughs that followed his actions and sayings gratified his heart and in all it may be safe to say that it will be a long time before he is forgotten by those he met here. All the children were given suitable presents and cane candy, cakes etc. The visitors also were remembered with a picture each of the life of Christ, or rather illustrating some part of his life. The hearty "Thank yous," Good-nights" etc given by the people at the went out; the cheerful voices of the children prattling together and saying "God-bye teacher" all bore witness that with the help of the Lord our efforts to do good and praise our Savior on this Christmas day had not been in vain. To God be all the praise and honor forevermore.

Master Shinichi Hada a nephew to Bro. Hachiro Mori received the best present because of his faithful attendance at Sunday School during the year. Up to Christmas he had not missed a day. The second places was claimed by two Master Hitoshi Saitō and Miss Fuyu Tojō both of whom had only missed once. The third place was also claimed by two who had missed two Sundays. Their names are /Miss/ Hisa Takahashi and Miss /Shika/ Sakazaki. The Hada boy and two last named girls are members of the First Intermediate Department. The Saitō boy and Tojō girl are members of the Primary class.

The day has been one of intense joy and satisfaction. Retired at midnight with a heart so full of gratitude that I could not go to sleep for a long time.

Thursday, 26 December 1907, Tokyo

Clear—Warm Up at 7:00. Did part of the cleaning up after the festivities of yesterday. Ate a late breakfast. Walked to Aoyama. Started out for Mr. Hirai's but met him at Shinjuku Station where I handed him a Christmas present for himself and wife. I also gave him another book of the translation manuscript to work on and paid him for his work during the past month. Returned to headquarters and presided over a turkey dinner nicely prepared by Sisters Thomas and Nachie. After dinner I exercised a little and then wrote my journal. In the evening we danced, played games, and ate Christmas Cake and cracked nuts and jokes. Before separating we lit the Christmas tree. We sang a song. I talked, first in Japanese, then in English. We had prayer and retired. I felt a little conscience smitten for some of the foolish statements I made in jokes during the evening and felt that wisdom in play is as essential as wisdom in work.

Sunday, 29 December 1907, Tokyo

Clear—Cold Up at 7:00. Ate breakfast. Held a good Sunday School. After school had quite a long conversation with Mr. Okada. Ate lunch. Held sacrament meeting. Had a long talk with Sister Nachie's daughter Miss Ei about the obligations that come upon those who join the church. This little girl desires to be baptized. Ate supper. The evening meeting was not very large, but a good class of people were present. We enjoyed a fair spirit. After meeting I talked a little with Sister Hakii who is cooking in the home of a sectarian minister where she meets considerable criticism.

Tuesday, 31 December 1907, Tokyo

Clear—Cold. Up at 7:15. Spent the day at headquarters doing several jobs connected with the end of the year. From now on I shall have to give considerable of my time to report making. This evening we all went to Yochōmachi where we were entertained by the elders living there. We had a number of games which lasted till about 12:30. Before parting we wished each other a Happy New Year and had prayers. After getting to headquarters, I took an internal bath.

During the year 1907 I have been greatly favored of the Lord physically, mentally and spiritually. I have enjoyed my work in the field and give to my Father in Heaven all the praise for any good that I may have been able to accomplish. I have tried to use the precious hours properly and feel that so far as my duty to the work is concerned I have nothing to mourn over. My conscience has no case against me for neglect of duty. One thing also which has given me joy is the blessings of God upon my relatives at home. The totals for my year's work so far as they can be shown in figures are as follows. . . .

Notes

1. Sōdō-shuu. "Branch of the Zen-shuu sect, brought from China in 1228 by the bonze Dōgen. Its principal temple was the Eihei-ji temple." Papinot, *Historical and Geographical Dictionary of Japan*, 2:597.

2. *Mura*. A small village.

3. *Gunyakusho*. District government office.

4. *Guncho*. District government official.

5. *Nihon Kirisuto Kyōkwai* (The Japan Church of Christ). In 1872, Reverend James C. Ballagh of the Reformed Church organized "The Church of Christ" in Japan.

6. *Kotatsu*. A foot warmer with a quilt over it.

7. *Aichi Kencho*. Aichi prefecture office.

8. Nagoya Castle. The Nagoya castle is located in the city of Nagoya. It was originally built in 1610–14 by Tokugawa Ieyasu, on the site of an abandoned castle formerly occupied by Oda Nobunaga. It was strategically located to protect the *Tōkai* region in central Japan. "Nagoya," *Japan: An Illustrated Encyclopedia*, 1:1035.

9. *Jōdo-shinshuu*. Also called Ikkō-shuu, or Monto-shuu, is a Buddhist sect found by Shinran-shōnin in 1224. It teaches that man cannot be saved by his works or prayers, but only by the mercy of Amida. It is the Buddhist Protestantism of Japan. Papinot, *Historical and Geographical Dictionary of Japan*, 1:233.

10. Tokugawa. Tokugawa Ieyasu.

11. Meiji. The boy Emperor, Mutsuhito (1852–1912), later know as the Meiji Emperor. Pyle, *The Making of Modern Japan*, 71.

12. *Zen-shū*. "Buddhist sect, which when first introduced from China in the 7th century had no success in Japan. Later on, the bonze Eisai after having made two voyages to the Continent, returned to Japan in 1192, built the Shōfuku-ji temple at Hakata and began to preach the doctrines of the sect. 10 years later, the Shōgun Yoriie having founded the Kennin-ji at Kyōto chose Eisai to be its first superior, and from that time, the sect spread rapidly. This sect which may be called the "sect of contemplation" is based upon the principal that every one may arrive at the knowledge of the law and nature of Buddha by meditating upon one's self and this without being influenced by other dissenting doctrines on this matter." Papinot, *Historical and Geographical Dictionary of Japan*, 2:764.

13. *The North American Review* (Boston: O. Everett), 4 June 1907.

14. During this time, apostle Reed Smoot's legal team and the LDS Church were fighting to have Smoot seated in the U.S. Senate. For various reasons (including charges of polygamy), many U.S. citizens and Senate members were opposed to Smoot's seating. See Harvard S. Heath, *Reed Smoot: The First Mormon* (Master's Thesis, Brigham Young University, 1990), 84–197.

15. On 20 February 1907, apostle Reed Smoot was seated in the U.S. Senate as a senator from the state of Utah.

16. Bund. An embankment used to control the flow of water.

17. Fagged. Tired.

18. *Higashi-Hongwan-ji*. "The Higashi-Hongwan-ji temple in Kyōto, built in 1602, was destroyed by fire four times since its foundation, the last time in 1874. It has been rebuilt from 1879 to 1895, and is now the largest temple in Japan: it measures 63 met. In length, 57 in breadth, and 38 in height." Papinot, *Historical and Geographical Dictionary of Japan*, 1:153.

19. *Tō-dai-ji*. "Buddhist temple erected at Nara in 728 by the bonze Ryōben. It is the headquarters of the Kegon-shuu sect. In 746, a large statue of Buddha (Daibutsu), was erected. This statue which represents him, as is customary, seated on a lotus flower, measures 15.9m. height." Papinot, *Historical and Geographical Dictionary of Japan*, 2:655.

20. Date Massumuna (Date Masamune, 1567–1636). A famous warrior of the Azuchi-Momoyama and early Edo periods. Fought for Toyotomi Hideyoshi and Tokugawa Ieyasu and was awarded the Sendai domain for his efforts at the Battle of Sekigahara. Built up Sendai as a castle town. "Date Musamune," *Japan: An Illustrated Encyclopedia*, 1:274.

21. *Bunshotai*. Classical mode or style of Japanese literary language.

22. *Zokugo*. Colloquial language; slang.

23. *Gunbuintchitai* (Gembunitchi). Modern colloquial Japanese written language started in 1880s.

24. *Kuruma*. A wheeled vehicle; a conveyance; a carriage.

25. *Tōkaidō*. Literally the "Eastern Sea Road" or 303 mile road that connected Edo (Tōkyō) and Kyōto.

26. Luke's Hospital. St. Luke's Hospital was the medical center for the foreign settlement of Tsukiji.

27. Typhoid Fever. "Acute infectious disease caused by the typhoid bacillus *Salmonella typhi*. The bacillus is transmitted by milk, water, or solid food contaminated by feces of typhoid victims or of carriers, that is, healthy persons who harbor typhoid bacilli without presenting symptoms. The incubation period of typhoid fever lasts one to three weeks. The bacteria collect in the

small intestine, from which they enter the bloodstream. This induces the first symptoms, chills followed by high fever and prostration. Victims may also experience headache, cough, vomiting, and diarrhea." "Typhoid Fever," *Microsoft Encarta 98 Encyclopedia.*

28. Title Page From Book of Mormon. "Joseph Smith once wrote, "I wish to mention here that the title-page of the Book of Mormon is a literal translation, taken from the very last leaf, on the left hand side of the collection or book of plates, which contained the record which has been translated . . . and that said title-page is not . . . a modern composition, either of mine or of any other man who has lived or does live in this generation" (*HC* 1:71.). The title page is therefore the translation of an ancient document, at least partially written by Moroni 2, son of Mormon, in the fifth century A.D. It describes the volume as an 'abridgment of the record of the people of Nephi, and also of the Lamanites' and 'an abridgment taken from the Book of Ether also, which is a record of the people of Jared.' According to the title page, the Book of Mormon is addressed to Lamanites, Jews, and gentiles and is designed to inform Lamanites of promises made to their forebears and to convince 'Jew and Gentile that Jesus is the Christ, the Eternal God, manifesting himself unto all nations.'" Eldin Ricks, "Book of Mormon," *Encyclopedia of Mormonism,* 1:144.

29. "Beginning with the first edition of 1830, the Book of Mormon has generally contained two sets of testimonies—the 'Testimony of Three Witnesses' and the 'Testimony of Eight Witnesses.' When Joseph Smith first obtained the gold plates, he was told to show them to no one. As translation progressed, he and those assisting him learned, both in the pages of the Book and by additional revelation, that three special witnesses would know, by the power of God, 'that these things are true' and that several besides himself would see the plates and testify to their existence (Ether 5:2–4; 2 Nephi 27:12–13; D&C 5:11–13). Richard Lloyd Anderson, "Book of Mormon Witnesses," *Encyclopedia of Mormonism,* 1:214.

30. *Fuketsu no kane.* Loosely translated as "dirty money."

31. *Azabu Chū Gakko.* Azabu Middle School.

32. Bronchitis. "Acute or chronic inflammation of any part of the bronchi and bronchial tubes. The bronchi are large delicate tubes in the lungs that are attached to the trachea and carry air to smaller tubes in the lungs. Acute bronchitis is characterized by fever, chest pain, severe coughing, and often the secretion of *sputum* (mucous material coughed up from the respiratory tract)." "Bronchitis," *Microsoft Encarta 98 Encyclopedia.*

Alma O. Taylor (left), Heber J. Grant (center), and others enjoying a traditional Japanese dinner. Courtesy John W. Welch.

Missionaries visit the Nikko Shrine, c. early 1900s. Courtesy John W. Welch.

Chapter 12

Alma O. Taylor Journal, 1908

Wednesday, 1 January 1908, Tokyo

Cloudy, A little snow—Cold Up at 9:00. Swept the downstairs rooms. Spent the day making reports. At 12:00 n. we held our regular council meeting followed by prayer. We discussed our Sunday Schools, Bible Classes, Saints' Meetings, and public preaching meetings. **Decided to call Sister Fude Tai and Brother Hachiro Mori to work in the Sunday School and to appoint Sisters Tsune Nachie and Nami Hakii as missionaries to visit the other sisters** once a month and try to keep them in the line of their duty. After prayer in the evening, I informed Sisters Nachie and Tai of our decisions regarding them.

Friday, 3 January 1908, Tokyo

Clear—Cold Up at 7:30. Spent the day at headquarters doing odd jobs and nursing Elder Woodland who is in bed with a very painful right lung the result of a cold. The doctor called today to examine him. He said their seemed nothing serious to be the matter at present but said he should take good care of himself lest scrofulous deposits[1] of the lungs should result. Before supper, I went to the hospital to get some medicine.

Sunday, 5 January 1908, Tokyo

Clear—Cold—Calm Up at 7:15. Spent the day very pleasantly. Had family prayers. Before the Sunday School the teachers and officers had prayers. After the school the teachers and officers held a meeting to discuss about the School work. Had a hours rest and then Fast Meeting began. After fast meeting I walked a little for exercise. Then I ate supper after which the public preaching meeting began. I had a conversation with an old lady after the meeting. Today I introduced to the Sunday School Bro Hachiro Mori and Sister Fude Tai who will act as teachers of the Primary Class this year. Sister Tsune Nachie and I will retire as teachers. Sister Nachie becoming a student in the Theological Department and I will continue as Superintendent with an oversight of the whole school. Being teacher of the Primary Department I have not been able to visit the classes and note their exercises. Today a weekly report from Hokkaido showed a baptism for the week commencing Dec. 22nd. The particulars have not reached us.

Wednesday, 8 January 1908, Tokyo

Clear—Cold Up at 8:00. Spent the forenoon talking to a man who became so insulting in his questions and remarks that I finally had to ask him to leave. Had I not been a missionary I might have used some muscle on him for he was so stubborn that he didn't desire to go when commanded to. In the afternoon I went down town and purchased a copy of Aston's "Grammar of the Japanese Written Language"[2] by which I hope to get a little better insite into the theory of the written language in which the Book of Mormon translation is being written. Worked in the late afternoon and evening on the yearly reports of the mission.

Thursday, 9 January 1908, Tokyo

Clear—Cold Up at 6:30. Spent the forenoon reading the Book of Mormon translation copy with Elder Caine. Mr. Hirogoro Hirai called. He desired that his agreement with the Japan Mission to give all of his time for one year to the criticism of the Book of Mormon translation be modified so he can spend eight hours a week teaching at the Waseda University,[3] the officers of the latter having been very persistant in their requests for his services. I told Mr. Hirai that time was more valuable than money and as I was just ready to devote my whole attention to Book of Mormon translation work that this request came just at the most unopportune time. I requested that he deny the University's request. In the afternoon, I worked on the yearly reports and talked with Bro. Chiba who payed us a visit and also with a young man named Onae who came with a letter from Mr. K. Tokoyo. In the evening I took a short walk.

Friday, 10 January 1908, Tokyo
     Clear—Cold. Up at 7:00. Spent nearly the entire day working on the yearly reports. After dinner, however, Mr. Watanabe came and stole a precious hour or two talking about matters that interested him but not me. After supper I walked to the hospital to get some medicine for Elder Woodland who is quite recovered, but still using a little medicine. I prepared an outline for the coming months work in the Primary Department of the Sunday School and after the Bible Class I presented it to Bro Mori and Sister Tai the new teachers of the class. I discussed about Sunday School work with them till about 10:00 p.m. Then I talked for thirty minutes with Sister Tai. I then resumed work on the yearly reports and worked till 1:00 a.m. Retired with an accountant's head.

Saturday, 11 January 1908, Tokyo
     Clear—Cold Up at 8:30. Spent the day on the reports. Received a letter from Mr. Kinza Hirai asking me to please consent to a modification of the agreement with his brother so his brother could keep up his friendship with the school. As Mr. Kinza Hirai has been exceedingly kind to us I consider this request as one of great weight and shall no doubt finally conclude to modify the terms of agreement. The day closed and the reports were not finished. I took a bath and retired very sleepy and worn out.

Sunday, 12 January 1908, Tokyo
     Very warm breeze—Like Spring—Clear Up at 7:00. Ate breakfast. Prepared for Sunday School. Took charge of the Primary Class again as the new teachers desired to be broke into the work gradually. We had a large school today and the exercises were all very interesting. Ate dinner. At 2:00 p.m. our Sacrament Meeting was held. I spoke. After meeting I took a walk. Returned and ate supper. The evening meeting was not large, but blessed with a good spirit. We (Elder Caine and I) enjoyed testifying to the divinity of the mission of Joseph Smith. I had a talk with Miss Katsu Ishikawa. This young lady is a dear friend to Sister Nachie and has received several testimonies regarding the Latter-day Work. She always comes here when she has a few hours off. She is a member of the Church of England and when her coming here became known to her church people she was called before one of her former teachers and reprimanded for her acts, but as she says, assisted by an unseen power, she defended herself and the Latter-day Saints and leaving the presence of her old teacher she came direct to visit her friend Sister Nachie who lives with us. I told this young lady tonight that she had been greatly blessed of God and he had manifested his power to show her that He sustained and led the Church of Jesus Christ of Latter-day Saints. During the day I have read the newspapers and magazines a little.

Tuesday, 14 January 1908, Tokyo
     Cloudy—Cold Wind Up at 7:15. Spent the forenoon proof reading one chapter of the Book of Mormon copy classifying last year's bills and writing. After dinner I went to Mr. Hirogoro Hirai's and began with him the discussion of the questions pertaining to Book 3 of the second manuscript. **Just before dinner Elder Caine and I talked over the matter of modifying the agreement with Mr. Hirai so that he can spend eight hours per week in the Waseda University. We decided that it would be better to permit the modification and avoid any bad feelings that might grow out of a refusal. But when I visited Mr. Hirai today, I found that he had written a refusal and sent to the University.** However, if the University officials again renew their request he may find it necessary to renew his request to me for permission to comply with the schools request.* In the evening I gave instructions by letter to the elders in the field regarding their reports during the coming year.

*The school renewed its request and Mr. Hirai, with my permission, began about Jan 29th to spend three hours on Wednesdays & Fridays in the Waseda University.

Thursday, 16 January 1908, Tokyo
    Clear—Cold—Calm Up at 6:50. Spent the forenoon reviewing Mr. Hirai's criticisms and the afternoon was spent at his home discussing questions that arose because of his criticisms. Made fair progress. In the evening I investigated the amount of money used by each elder in this mission during 1907 and found that only one had lived for an average of less that ¥40.00 per month. The average cost for living & working in Japan during the year was ¥46.12. The average should not be more than ¥40.00 and to this end the elders shall be advised for 1908.

Saturday, 18 January 1908, Tokyo
    Clear—Warm comparatively Up at 6:30. Spent the forenoon cleaning house. After dinner I went to Mr. Hirai's and discussed with him about the Book of Mormon translation till nearly five o'clock. I walked home calling in at the barber's on the way. At supper and began a letter to the First Presidency presenting to them various problems in connection with the important translation I am making. In May 1906 I wrote a long letter of questions, but the First Presidency inform me that they do not remember seeing it so this letter is in the main a copy of the former letter.

Sunday, 19 January 1908, Tokyo
    Clear—Warm Up at 7:00. The largest Sunday School for over a year was held today. There were in all 69 present. The children all did well and were full of sunshine. At 2:00 p.m. we held Sacrament meeting. After meeting I worked on the letter spoken of in yesterday's journal. Ate supper. I held the meeting in the evening alone. The subject was "Now is the day of Salvation." The meeting lasted one hour and a half. After meeting I talked with Mr. Okada for about an hour and a half. Elder Hubbard being ill, did not come to headquarters today.

Monday, 20 January 1908, Tokyo
    Cloudy—A mist fell all day—Not cold. Up at 7:00 Spent the day at headquarters doing all kinds of jobs. Proof read a little of the copy of the Book of Mormon translation, looked over Elder Caine's suggestions on one book of the manuscript, noted in red ink any important changes or peculiarities of the English from Alma 50th to the end of Heleman, (I do this so Mr. Hirai will know the reason for some translations which he would otherwise think incorrect.) Translated from Japanese into English an antidote for Mr. Sakuraba who came today and began to copy some of my B. of M. translation, studied the Bible lesson for the missionaries class this evening. Immediately after breakfast this morning I went to Yōchomachi to see Elder Hubbard and take him some medicine. Was pleased to see him better. This evening the Bible Class was held at Yochōmachi so we all (except Elder Woodland) went there for the class.

Thursday, 23 January 1908, Tokyo
    Clear—Less wind— Up at 6:30. Swept the downstairs rooms. Spent the forenoon working on the Book of Mormon. Went to Mr. Hirai's in the afternoon and spent two hours with him. On the way back, I called a Yochōmachi branch and saw Bro. Hubbard who is still in bed. His cold has left him with a fever, a bad headache and sore lungs. We administered to him. I rubbed his chest. In the evening I worked on the Book of Mormon, read a little and talked a little with Mr. Sakuraba. Both Mr. Sakuraba and Bro. Mori have been copying Book of Mormon translation all evening.
    A letter from Hokkaidō says that another convert was baptized at Sapporo January 15th 1908, by Elder Cutler.

Sunday, 26 January 1908, Tokyo

Clear—Warmer—Calm. Up at 7:15. Ate breakfast. Our Sunday School was not so large today but it was still bigger than our ordinary school. I took charge of the Primary Department again today. From next Sunday Bro. Mori and Sister Tai will have full charge. After dinner we held Sacrament Meeting. I walked over to the Yochōmachi branch and was glad to find Elder Hubbard up and better. With a little care, he should be entirely recovered in a day or two. Ate supper. Our evening meeting was held as usual. There were 16 natives present. Elder Caine and I did the preaching.

Monday, 27 January 1908, Tokyo

Clear—Cold Up at 7:25. Spent the entire forenoon and most of the afternoon working on the Book of Mormon translation. At 4:30 I took a walk. Studied the lesson for Bible Class. Ate supper. After supper the missionaries assembled and discussed the scriptures for two hours.

This evening Mr. Sakuraba came and finished copying my Book of Mormon translation. This has been a great work. The copied translation fills twenty six and a half books each containing one hundred and forty-four pages. Inasmuch as some pages in the end of several of the books are blank it is quite conservative to estimate the entire manuscript as containing 3,800 pages. It is this manuscript that Mr. Hirai is reading and criticising. He is now working on the 17th book. I am pleased that the manuscript is finished. Elder Caine is reviewing it before it goes to Mr. Hirai. About another weeks work will finish Elder Caine's review. Three have worked on this manuscript—Hachiro Mori, Yasubeiye Chiba and Takeshiro Sakuraba the first named having written over three fourths of it.

Friday, 31 January, 1908, Tokyo

Cloudy—Rain—Cold Up at 7:10. During the night I was troubled quite badly with my nose. Spent the day in the house working on the Book of Mormon. This evening a Bible class in Japanese was conducted by Elder Caine. **Today Elder Caine finished the review of my translation of the Book of Mormon. He has worked on this review for about a year and a half. This labor has been careful and faithful and his suggestions have been of great value.**

Saturday, 1 February 1908, Tokyo

Clear—Cold—Calm Up at 6:15. Before breakfast I went to Dr. Naichiro Okada expecting to consult with him about having my nose operated upon. (See page 33). The doctor was not up when I arrived at his house which was 7:15 a.m. His hours for today are advertised to be from 7:00 a.m. to 10:00 a.m. Imagine my surprise when his servant told me to call at ten o'clock. I returned to headquarters, read a while and then went again to the doctors. He looked at my nose. I reminded him of what he said last September when I called on him, but he said that my nose was in a fair condition and an operation would not be necessary unless it became very bad again. He said I should come once a week and have medicine put in that will keep me from taking cold and that after three or four applications of the medicine I would no doubt be pronounced cured. Returned and wrote a letter to my brother Samuel. In the afternoon I went to Mr. Hirai's. Called at Yōchomachi on the way home. Elder Hubbard is not well again. Spent the evening working on the Book of Mormon translation.

Sunday, 2 February 1908, Tokyo

Cloudy—Much warmer—Calm. Up at 7:30. We had a very large Sunday School today. Today I took charge of the whole School but the teaching of the Primary Department has been entirely turned over to Bro. Mori and Sister Tai so I was free from the day of teaching in the school for the first time since the first Sunday School was organized in this Mission over four years ago. After Sunday School, the monthly meeting of officers and teachers was held. We discussed plans for the coming month. After this meeting adjurned, Sacrament and Fast Meeting commenced. A good spirit was present. Today Elders Hubbard & Harris were not with us. The former is in bed sick at Yōchomachi and the latter is attending him. I went with Elder Stoker to Yochōmachi. I had supper there and assisted the meeting in the evening. After meeting I had quite a talk with a Mr. Kuga who has been much impressed with our teachings and has attended most of the meetings recently. Arrived at headquarters rather late. Retired immediately.

Tuesday, 4 February 1908, Tokyo

Cloudy—Cold Up at 7:15. Spent the forenoon writing letters and working on the Book of Mormon. After dinner I walked to Yochōmachi to see how Elder Hubbard is. He is much better today. During the rest of the afternoon I worked on the Book of Mormon. After supper we began the reading of the report of last October's General Conference held at Salt Lake City. The sermons delivered on the first day were read. President Lund and Apostle Grant spoke of the Japan Mission and especially of its president. I regret to have my name published in such a way, but I do appreciate the kind feelings the leading brethren have for me and I trust that my life shall be so true and upright and faithful that they cannot cease to love me. The reading of the sermons gives me great joy and nourishment.

Monday, 10 February 1908, Tokyo

Clear—Warmer Up at 7:10. Spent most of the day working on the Book of Mormon reviewing the suggestions made by Elder Caine on that part of the translation contained in the 19th & 20th volumes of the manuscript. Did not quite complete volume 20. Took some exercise and read the Bible a little before supper. This evening the missionaries Bible Class was held at Yochōmachi. Was surprised to find Elder Harris sick almost ready to go to bed with cold & fever. I sent him to headquarters in a rikisha and after reaching headquarters myself, I doctored him up with "Mother's remedies" and sent him to bed for a sweat.

Wednesday, 12 February 1908, Tokyo

Clear—Windy—Warm. Up at 7:15. Spent the entire day at headquarters working on the Book of Mormon translation. In the forenoon Mr. Yoneju Nakamura, one of Bro. Mori's friends called and I arranged with him for some work in copying a part of the criticised Book of Mormon translation He will begin his work tomorrow at 9:00 a.m. Elder Harris has been in bed all day. His fever is high. He has very little pain.

Thursday, 13 February 1908, Tokyo

Clear—Cold wind—Dusty Up at 7:00. Spent the forenoon working on the Book of Mormon at headquarters. We ate early dinner, went to Mr. Hirai's and discussed translation questions with him for over four hours In the evening we read the sermons delivered at two of the meetings held on the last day of the general conference at Salt Lake City October 6th 1907. Elder Harris has greatly improved today. Before going to bed I doctored Elder Harris up and changed his bedding and clothes. Today Mr. Nakamura began his work copying the criticised Book of Mormon translation.

Saturday, 15 February 1908, Tokyo

Clear—Warmer. Up at 6:30. Spent the forenoon, housecleaning, doctoring the sick and having myself doctored. Elder Harris is very much improved today. He sat up during the hour it took to clean and air his room. Today Dr. Okada told me that my nose was well and that I need not use any more of his medicine. After dinner, I went to see the Shugiin (House of Commons) About two years ago I saw the Kizoku In (House of Lords). The House of Commons is much more combative and characterized by much more tumult than the House of Lords. In the House of Commons there are two characters greatly respected and who may be considered leaders or champions in the body. One is Saburo Shimada the owner of the Mainichi and a friend of the common people. The other Mr. Ebara the head of the Azabu Chu Gakko and an educator of considerable ability, who is in the Parliment because of real worth as a capable man intellectually and morally. The appearence of the Upper and Lower Houses is much the same. After listening to the proceedings for a little while attended to some business and returned. After supper Bro. Mori came and said his firm had called him to go to Korea to work in its branch there. Took a bath and retired.

Sunday, 16 February 1908, Tokyo

Clear—In the afternoon a terrible dust storm raged. Up at 7:00 Ate breakfast. The Sunday School was exactly the same size that it was last week—a total attendance of 62. The children all worked in interest. After school, I asked Bro. Mori if he would not accept a position in the mission and work for us until he can find suitable employment in Tokyo this making it possible for him to be with his mother and attend to his duties in the church, neither of which he would be able to do if he goes to Korea. He said he would consider the proposition Ate dinner. At 2:00 p.m. our sacrament meeting was held. There were five saints present. This is the largest attendance of saints for a very long time. Elder Stoker and I did the speaking. After meeting I took a walk. Ate supper Owing to the terrible clouds of dust that covered the parade ground and vicinity, we had a very sliml[p]y attended meeting. There were only three who came from without. These together with the few who had been at headquarters all day composed the audience. I did all the speaking.

A letter received from Sapporo announces that another convert was baptized there on Feb 7th 1908.

Tuesday, 18 February 1908, Tokyo

Clear—Cold—Calm. Up at 7:10. Spent the forenoon at headquarters working on the Book of Mormon. The afternoon was devoted to a discussion of Book of Mormon questions with Mr. Hirai at his home. In the evening Bro. Mori came and wrote a new roll for the children of the Sunday School. He also informed me that he had decided to go to Korea and not accept my proposition to work for us. We read the last of the October Conference sermons. Took a bath and retired.

Friday, 21 February 1908, Tokyo

Clear—Quite warm and spring-like. Up at 7:00. Spent the entire day at headquarters working on the Book of Mormon, nursing the sick and listening to the exercises in the Japanese Bible Class held in the evening. Just before supper I took a thirty minutes walk. Elder Woodland went to bed this evening suffering from a cold that has again settled in his lungs. Elder Harris has only just recovered in time to vacate the sick room for the next patient. We are having quite a seige of troubles lately.

Saturday, 22 February 1908, Tokyo

Cloudy—Rain in afternoon—Warm. Up at 6:30. During the forenoon, I cleaned house and brushed my clothes. Ate an early dinner and went to Mr. Hirai's with whom I discussed Book of Mormon translation questions for two hours. Returned to headquarters. This evening we had all the missionaries in Tokyo to supper which was especially prepared for Bro. Hachiro Mori who leaves for Korea on the 26th next. I gave Bro. Mori instructions regarding his duties while separated from us and warned him of some of the dangers which will no doubt surround him. He returned about 9:30. We had prayers and a bath and retired. I have had a slight sore throat today.

Sunday, 23 February 1908, Tokyo

Cloudy—Colder—Calm Up at 7:00 Ate breakfast. The Sunday School this morning was the largest held in Tokyo for years. There were 79 present. Bro Hachiro Mori gave his farewell speech and Miss Shizu Yoshida (12 years old a member of his class) replied in behalf of the students. The exercises in the different classes were much enjoyed. Ate dinner at 2:00 p.m. held sacrament meeting. Four saints were present a good spirit prevailed. Ate supper. The evening meeting began at 7:00 p.m. There were 15 Japanese present. Elder Caine spoke on the Second Coming of Christ. Sister Fude Tai played the piano. Sister Thomas and I sang a duet in Japanese. This is the first attempt of its kind for Sister Thomas—she did well Bro. Hachiro Mori explained in a twenty or thirty minute talk why he joined the Church of Jesus Christ of Latter-day Saints. He gave us the three reasons for his action (1) That the Church of Jesus Christ of Latter-day Saints was to him the true church of God (2) That repentance of sins and the remission of the same were necessary to salvation and a holy life and that the authority to forgive sin was in the "Mormon" Church (3) That he desired spiritual happiness which he found possible in the church of his choice.

Tuesday, 25 February 1908, Tokyo

Clear—Warm—Calm. Up at 7:00 Spent most of the day working on the Book of Mormon translation. At about 3:00 p.m. I took all of the translation Mr. Hirai has corrected—20 volumes of the manuscript—back to him. He is going to go over his entire work from the beginning and unify the translation and correct, especially in the first part many errors which he himself is conscious of. I told him about the points I had observed as far as I have reviewed his work and told him clearly that I desired his very best efforts on this work which will be the last, so far as Mr. Hirai is concerned, and that time and money should be no consideration in the effort to perfect the translation and make it understandable to the masses. He gladly accepted my suggestions and promised to do his best. I returned to headquarters and ate supper. Afterward I wrote letters to the brethren in Kōfu and Hokkaido. A letter from Morioka states that Elder Anderson has been quite sick as a result of vaccination. Took a bath and retired. Bro. Mori paid us his last visit this morning.

Wednesday, 26 February 1908, Tokyo

Fair—Wind—Cold. Up at 8:00 Spent the forenoon working on the Book of Mormon. After dinner I went down town to attend to some business and bid Bro. Hachiro Mori good-bye. He left for Korea on the 5:30 p.m. train from Shimbashi Station. He was in good spirits. In the evening I had a long talk with Sister Tai regarding the work in the Primary Department of the Sunday School.

Thursday, 27 February 1908, Tokyo

Clear—Calm—Cold Up at 6:30. Swept the downstairs rooms before breakfast. The rest of the day was devoted to Book of Mormon translation work. Just before dinner I called on Mr. Katagiri to inquire of him about the different kinds of swords used in Japan anciently and at the present time; hoping if possible to learn of one having a shape similar to the "cimeter" mentioned in the Book of Mormon.[4] I have been troubled about the translation of this word. After supper I went to Mr. Hirai's on Book of Mormon business. Returned to headquarters at about 10:00 p.m. and retired immediately.

Friday, 28 February 1908, Tokyo

Clear—Warm—Calm Up at 7:10. Spent the major part of the day doing odd jobs around headquarters preparatory to leaving for Kōfu. After dinner I walked to Mr. Hirai's taking him some more books containing the translation of the Book of Mormon. On the way I called in and said good-bye to the brethren at Yōchōmachi. Talked with Mr. Hirai for about an hour. Returned to headquarters and after supper attended the Japanese Bible Class

Saturday, 29 February 1908, Kōfu

Cloudy—Snow—Cold Up at 5:45. Left Tokyo on the 6:57 a.m. train and went to Kōfu where I arrived at 12:35 p.m. Arriving at the Mission Field House at Fujikawamachi, I found the brethren all well and enjoyed the dinner prepared. Talked of the things that elders are used to talk about when meeting after a long absence. Indexed my last journal. Today there should have been two English Bible Classes held but owing to my coming or the coming of one of the Royal Princes or some other cause neither class was held. This called to my mind the absolute failure of our meetings 11 months ago when I visited Kōfu at which time the meetings were very well advertized. In the evening I took a bath and retired.

Sunday, 1 March 1908, Kōfu

Cloudy—Warmer—Calm. Up at 7:15. Fasted today. At 10:00 a.m. a Sunday School was held by Elder Fairbourn. Thirty five children were present. They are very keen bright children. Many of them were exceedingly clever in the way they answered the questions. I enjoyed witnessing the exercises and saying a few words to them. I sang "In Our Lovely Deseret" and in George Goddard style had the children join in the chorus. At 11:30 we held fast meeting. The Sacrament was administered and the elders all bore good testimonies. At about 2:00 p.m. a Japanese Bible Class was held four natives were present. I spoke for about twenty minutes. After this class I talked with Mr. Monoō till the beginning of another Japanese Bible Class held for young ladies. It began a little after four o'clock and continued till 5:45. I spoke for perhaps thirty minutes to this class on the subject of baptism. I suffered with quite a headache during the afternoon so as soon as this latter class closed, I took a short walk with Elder Taylor. Ate supper at about six thirty. Until 8:30 we chatted together and I listened to Elders Stimpson and Taylor perform on the flute and violin. Retired early.

Monday, 2 March 1908, Kōfu

Clear—Warm—Slight Breeze Up at 7:15. The forenoon was spent reading and working on the Book of Mormon translation. After dinner, I took a short walk going up on the neighboring hills from where I had a good view of the city and surrounding country. After returning I talked for a few minutes to Mr. Shirai and then continued to work on the Book of Mormon translation. In the evening, Elder Fairbourn and I called on Mr. Oshima, principal of the Middle School but he was not at home. We took a walk. After prayers we chatted about our last Christmas.

Tuesday, 3 March 1908, Kōfu

Cloudy—Calm—Cold Up at 7:45. Spent the forenoon working on the Book of Mormon and giving the brethren some instructions in Japanese. In the afternoon I walked some for exercise. Looked at some houses for rent. Worked again on the Book of Mormon and after supper, I continued the same work till bed time. But two young ladies who are members of the Bible Class called and I being introduced to them talked with them for a few minutes. Elder Fairbourn informs me that both of them have applied for baptism. Today I received some American mail. The folks at home are reported in good health.

Wednesday, 4 March 1908, Kōfu

Snow & rain all day—Very Cold. Up at 7:30. Spent the entire day at the mission house working on the Book of Mormon translation and talking with my brethren. At noon we held a spirited prayer meeting. I took some exercise in the house and then had an hour's nap.

Thursday, 5 March 1908, Kōfu

Clear—Windy—Warmer

Up at 7:30 Spent the forenoon and part of the afternoon in the house working on the Book of Mormon. /Today I finished looking over Elder Caine's suggestions/ At about 3:00 p.m. Elder Stimpson and I called on Mr. Monoō. Elder Stimpson gave Mr. Monoō his regular Thursday lesson in the Book of Mormon. After the lesson I spoke to him for about an hour. He lives just a step or two from the Mission Field Home. I took a twenty minutes walk. Ate supper. This evening Elder Stimpson conducted a Bible Class which is made up of teachers of English in the various Schools in Kōfu. This class was very interesting. I spoke to them after the lesson was finished.

Friday, 6 March 1908, Kōfu

Cloudy—Cold. Up at 7:10 Spent the forenoon having my hair cut and working on the Book of Mormon. My work today brought me up to the end of Elder Caines suggestions on my translation this completing another of the important considerations in connection with the translation. After dinner, at 2:00 p.m., I called the elders together in Priesthood Meeting. Each of the elders spoke reviewing their work and expressing their feelings. The all were united in faith and hope for the outcome of their labor in Kōfu feeling sure that some fruit will be gathered. I spoke to them giving instructions regarding their labors and then I read & spoke at great length on the power of faith in the hearts of the messengers of the word. After the meeting, Elder Fairbourn and I called at Mr. Oshima's place expecting to have a chat with him, but he was just preparing to leave home to fill an appointment. I gave him a copy of the Brief History. Elder Fairbourn and I then took a walk, visiting the Kōfu Park. After supper, I had a long conversation with

Mr. Furuya a Methodist friend of the elders. I then had an opportunity to again bear my testimony to Mr. Monoō. Retired at 11:30 feeling well satisfied with my days doings.

Saturday, 7 March 1908, Tokyo

Snow—Cold. Up at 4:00 a.m. Left Kōfu on the 5:20 A.M. train and arrived at headquarters in Tokyo at 12:00 n. Found all well and happy. On the way from Kōfu I talked a little with a man who has studied at Yale University, New Haven. The conversation was in Japanese much against his will, but I would not speak in English to give him an opportunity to show off to the other passengers which he evidently desired very much to do. Ate dinner and then cleaned up a little and read letters from America. A letter from the Presiding Bishopric[5] compliments us on the excellent condition of our reports for the year 1907. Went to Mr. Hirai's to get one of the books containing that part of the corrected translation of the Book of Mormon that I am now reviewing. He was not home but I got the book. In the evening read & sang a little before taking a bath

Tuesday, 10 March 1908, Tokyo

Snow—Cold. Up at 7:30. I spent the whole day at headquarters working on the Book of Mormon. In the forenoon a young lady, thinking that our church was one of the sectarian class with the sectarian methods came to know the rules pertaining to membership. I explained to her what the church is and the sacredness of all the ordinances made and covenants entered into by those who come into the church through the proper channel. In the afternoon I talked a short time to Mr Yano regarding the organization of the church.

Thursday, 12 March 1908, Tokyo

Clear—Cold Up at 7:00 Spent the forenoon at headquarters reviewing Mr. Hirai's corrections in the Book of Mormon translation Ate an early dinner and went to Mr. Hirai's home where I discussed translation questions with him for some hours. Returned just in time for supper. After supper I talked for a little while with Miss Honda who came with her little brother to see us. This is the young lady who came Tuesday wanting to know the rules for entering the Church. After she went I talked with Sister Tai about the Sunday School work. Then Sister Nachie's little girl, Ei, had something to say to me so I talked a little with her. She renewed her request for baptism and I promised to have the ordinance performed for her at any time she desired. She requested that it be done during the school holiday which commence about the 26th inst. This little girl has been impressed with the teachings of the church for a long time and about a year ago first spoke of entering the church. He asked for baptism some months ago but I had a long talk with her about the sacredness of the ordinance and the covenants made thereby and also of the obligations that come upon members of the church and asked her to think well upon what I told her and continue to pray earnestly to her heavenly Father for his Spirit to enlighten her mind and confirm her faith. I was glad to hear her request and grant the same this evening.

Tuesday, 17 March 1908, Tokyo

Clear—Warm Up at 6:45. Spent the forenoon working on the Book of Mormon. After dinner, I went to Mr. Hirai's home and was made acquainted with a circumstance that has given me much pain and which I hope to have cleared up one way or the other immediately. Mr. Hirai handed me a copy of the "Bauchō Ho" a prominent and widely read newspaper here in Tokyo. In it was quite a long article in which a serious charge is made against Mr. Hirai. It charges him with being a lover of fast women and a frequent patron of a certain whore house located at Itabashi some two miles distant from his home in the Tokyo Fuka. And the climax of his acts came recently when he went to the house of ill fame and bought (that is paid a certain sum of money to the owner of the place, thereby securing the girls liberty) the whore whom he had so frequently used and took her home to his wife who was sunk in sorrow and disgrace. This act was reported as especially reprehensible because of Hirai's position as teacher in a well respected University. Mr. Hirai's acts before the students were also reported in unfavorable light.

After reading the article, I asked if it were true. Mr. Hirai replied that Messrs Abe and Yoshida of the Waseda University had called on him yesterday to find out about the report. Mr. Hirai to prove that he was not guilty went with Messrs Abe & Yoshida to the Itabashi Police Station and had the police authorities call the chief clerk of the whore house to the station where Mr. Hirai stood before him and the question asked if this was the man who had bought the girl. The chief clerk answered, "no, this is not the man." (All this is what Mr. Hirai himself told me). I left Mr. Hirai's house and went to the police station at Itabashi and inquired about the correctness of Mr. Hirai's story. The police officers said, after making considerable inquiry around among themselves trying to find one who heard what the chief clerk said to Messrs Abe & Yoshida that the "bautō" (chief clerk) stated that Hirai Hirogoro /(Japanese style)/ who stood before him was not the man, and stated and showed that the books containing the account of the transaction gave the name of the man as Hirai Hirogoro (Japanese order given name last). I returned to headquarters feeling very much distressed about the matter for I confess that I do not feel absolutely sure that there is not any truth in the story. Mr. Hirai told me that Messrs. Abe and Yoshida promised to make the Bauchō Ho publish the result of their investigation into the matter and suggested to Mr. Hirai that if he were innocent that he should file suit against the newspaper for the vile thrust at his good name. I stated that I considered it his duty to see that the absolute proof of his innocence was given to the public. If he don't prove his innocence, I shall no doubt have to sever my connections with him.

Wednesday, 18 March 1908, Tokyo

Rain—Warm. Up at 8:00. Spent the major part of the forenoon working on the Book of Mormon translation At 11:00 a.m. our prayer meeting was held I went to Hirai's hoping to find his wife alone so that I could question her about the charges against her husband. No one was at home, the house was locked up. I went to Yochōmachi and continued the work on the Book of Mormon until about 4:00 p.m. when Elder Stoker and I called on a Mr. Okubo who is a graduate of Waseda University now doing postgraduate work there. He at one time received lessons in English from Mr. Hirai and should know pretty well what kind of a reputation Hirai has in the school among the students. At first Mr. Okubo did not desire to speak about his teacher but he finally spoke freely and said in substance. Hirai is generally disliked by the students of the school who have often complained against him, but to their astonishment he is retained as a teacher. He is disliked for three reasons 1st he is quick tempered and unkind, 2nd He is guilty of speaking about improper things in the class room, and 3rd he is not considered by many /as/ qualified mentally for his position. Mr. Okubo stated that the newspaper report about Mr. Hirai was not read by the students with the least bit of surprise, but they rather remarked, "That's nothing for a man like Hirai." "Nothing more than we would expect from Hirai" etc. Mr. Okubo said he would try and learn the exact feelings of the students who are now under Mr. Hirai in English work. I returned to Yochōmachi and had supper with the brethren then walked back to Mr. Hirai's hoping to find the chance to question his wife, but he came home about two minutes after I arrived. Nothing new developed from the conversation. A few questions were asked about the Book of Mormon translation. It was 9:00 p.m. when I got back home. Had the sign announcing Sunday night's meeting written and then had prayers, a chat with my brethren and retired.

Thursday, 19 March 1908, Tokyo

Rain—Colder Up at 7:30. Spent the forenoon reading the newspapers and also went to the Yotsuya Police Station to consult with Mr. Arai about a point in the investigation of Mr. Hirai's police affair. After an early dinner, I went to the Ginza calling at the Kondo Shoten to report that the 20,000 tracts the delivered yesterday are 120 copies short. I bought a newspaper containing the charge against Mr. Hirai I then took the car to Shinjuku Station from where I went to Itabashi. I went direct to the police station and had the "bauto" of the whore house called before me. I asked him all the questions considered necessary about the man who had frequented the house lately and secured a description of him and the dates when he was there, etc. I had to wait at the police station for such a long time that it was 5:25 p.m. when

I left Itabashi Station . I had intented to call at Hirai's but it being so late I went directly home. Read a little in the Brief History of the Church.

Friday, 20 March 1908, Tokyo

Rain—Warmer Up at 7:30. Spent the forenoon continuing the investigation of Mr. Hirai's case. I called a Hirai's home and found that he had gone to the University at the request of Mr. Abe who expected to show Mr. Hirai's innocence to the students. I took advantage /of the opportunity/ to have a private talk with Mrs. Hirai about the affair. I sort of obtained an upper hand on her from the beginning of the talk and believe that she answered truthfully all the questions. To her knowledge Hirai has not been away from home at the time he is reported to have been at the house of ill fame. His actions have not led his wife to be suspicious of him or believe in the least the report against him. And as for the story of the whore was brought to her home she said positively that it was false. I left Hirai's with the clouds of darkness concerning him considerably removed. I walked a little ways then took a rikisha to the Elders home in Yochōmachi. On the way I called in at Mr. Okubo's to ask him to make some inquiries at the school regarding Abe's speech. Mr. Okubo was not home. I walked from Yochōmachi to headquarters. Spent the afternoon rather idly so far as profitable work is concerned. I tried to write a sign in Japanese, and sing some of Elder Woodland's songs. After supper I went to Yochōmachi and listened with interest to the exercises conducted in the Japanese Bible Class. I met Mr. Okubo and made the aforementioned request to him. He promised to get the address of some of the students studying English under Mr. Hirai and who heard Mr. Abe's defense, so that I can hear direct from them what was said for Mr. Hirai etc. He promises to have these addresses by Monday night. Returned to headquarters and retired feeling pretty well worn out after my much walking through the mud.

Today I wrote a letter to Mr. Kinza Hirai regarding his brother.

Sunday, 22 March 1908, Tokyo

Clear—Warm Up at 7:00. Ate breakfast. Prepared for Sunday School which was well attended and interestingly carried on. After school I ate dinner. At 2:00 p.m. our sacrament meeting began. Was pleased to see Sister Kawabe and felt her humble genial spirit. After meeting, I went with faith to the home of Sister Ota hoping to be able to stir her up to diligence in her duties to God. The opportunity was good and the Lord sustained me in the words I uttered. Mr. Ota was there and heard it all. I trust the Spirit will sancitfy my words to the good of both especially Sister Ota. Returned to headquarters and ate supper. The evening meeting began at 7:00 p.m. There were only 7 natives present but a peaceful spirit was with us.

Tuesday, 24 March 1908, Tokyo

Clear—Quite Warm Up at 6:30. After breakfast, Elders Caine & Thomas, Sister Thomas and I went to the Ōjima Primary School which is situated on the extreme east border of Tokyo Fu. Brother Chiba is a teacher in this school and it was at his invitation that we visited the school today to see the graduating exercises. This is the first time I ever saw such exercises and I thoroughly enjoyed them. A Primary school is divided into two courses; a higher & lower each requiring four years to complete. There were 158 graduates in the lower course and 26 graduates from the higher course. All of these received graduating certificates and those worthy of special merit received letters attesting the same. Ordinarily a girl who completes the higher course is considered sufficiently educated to leave school work and begin work in the home. However the higher education movement for girls is becoming very strong and the few higher girls schools that are established are pretty well filled. The boys, of course, are generally able to continue their schooling into manhood. However the schooling obtained in the Primary Schools is all the law requires. The bestowal of certificates was attended with special ettiqutte which executed by the Japanese was very commendable and well done. It was 2:00 p.m. or later when I got to headquarters. I worked on the Book of Mormon translation and in the evening talked with Sister Tai about Sunday School work and Miss Nachie Ei who will be baptized day after tomorrow.

Thursday, 26 March 1908, Tokyo

Cloudy—Slight Rain—Cooler Up at 7:00. Ate breakfast and went immediately to Mr. Hirai's where I consulted with him for two or three hours about the Book of Mormon translation. Returned to headquarters in time for dinner. Then, in company with three of my brethren I went to Tamagawa where we met the rest of our brethren and some of our sisters We repaired to the usual spot on the river bank and sang a song. I offered a short prayer then Elder Daniel P. Woodland led Sister Ei Nachie down into the stream and baptized her. We sang again and had a closing prayer before leaving the river. Got back to headquarters about 4:30. I prepared for supper. After supper I worked on the Book of Mormon till bed time.

Saturday, 28 March 1908, Tokyo

Cloudy—Cold Up at 7:00. Spent the forenoon working on the Book of Mormon translation. After dinner I went to Mr. Hirai's. On the way I hunted up two of the Waseda University students who are said to be in Mr. Hirai's class. However, one young man, Mr. Moriyama, is not a student of Mr. Hirai's this year but was under him last year. His experience with Mr. Hirai has not had any unpleasant features and to his knowledge Mr. Hirai has not been and is not guilty of improper remarks before the students and the recent charges in the paper against him are generally disbelieved. This report of Mr. Hirai in school is quite in contrast with what Mr. Okubo said to me the other day. (See page 28.) The other student whose residence I found was not at home. I got to Mr. Hirai's rather late and spent only an hour with him. It was seven o'clock when I got to headquarters. I ate supper worked an hour on the translation and retired. Today, on the way from headquarters to Mr. Hirai's I read an article on faith written by Elder Stoker.

Today's American mail brought a letter from the First Presidency in which my questions on the Book of Mormon are answered. The letter is copied in my Letter Book B. page 436

Sunday, 29 March 1908, Tokyo

Cloudy—Colder Up at 7:00. Today we have had a fine Sabbath. At Sunday School there were 73 in attendance. The sacrament meeting was particularly happy because we were able to confirm a new member in the Church. Sister Ei Nachie (15 years old) who was baptized last Thursday was confirmed by Elder John W. Stoker. After the sacrament meeting I visited for an hour with Bro. Saburo Kikuchi at his home. I was received kindly and had one of the most successful talks with him that I have ever had since he has become so negligent of his duties. In the evening we held a meeting which was a little better attended than our night meetings have been lately. Elder Caine and I did the speaking. After the meeting I talked and sang for an hour. Retired very tired.

Monday, 30 March 1908, Tokyo

Clear—Warm Up at 7:15. Spent the day at headquarters working on the Book of Mormon translation and preparing for the Missionaries Bible Class which was held in the evening. Today I read in the Miyako Shimbun of the 27th an article written in defense of Mr. Hirai. While the article proves fairly well that Mr. Hirogoro Hirai is not the man who visited the whore house still it states that Mr. Hirai had never severed his connections with the Waseda University but was away from the school on account of sickness. Mr. Hirai when making the contract with me for the criticism of the Book of Mormon stated that he did leave the school and that it was at great sacrifice for him to do it. As the position was one assured as long as his deportment is good, it would leave him without a good position if he gave up his school work for the Book of Mormon. Therefore in the agreement I made allowances for his sacrifice and assured him a good salary for 17 months. But the report in the papers which I am quite inclined to believe, that he did not sever his connections with the school but only played sick, places him in the position of a liar and deceiver. I shall visit the school tomorrow and learn about the matter thoroughly. It makes me sick at heart to have these unpleasant things come up which affect the translation work.

Tuesday, 31 March 1908, Tokyo

Clear—Warm. Up at 6:45. Spent the major part of the day hunting for Prof. Abe of the Waseda

University I went in the forenoon to the University and inquired first for President Takada but he is sick and does not attend the school. Mr. Abe was not at school, it being the holiday period. I returned to headquarters and did two hours work on the Book of Mormon. After dinner, I again went to the University to meet Prof. Abe but he had not yet come. I inquired where he lived and went to his home but he had just gone to school. So back to school I went and after considerable inquiry found him with the atheletes on the tennis court. I asked him about what he had learned in investigating the charge of immorality against Mr. Hirai. I showed him the Miyako Shimbun and then listened to his statements which contained nothing particularly new. But in speaking in Mr. Hirai's defense he stated that Hirai was a poor man who only received ¥40.00 per month from the school and while he was sick he only received ¥20.00 per month. Then I asked Mr. Abe if Mr. Hirai did not resign his position and leave the school entirely. Mr. Abe said, "No, that is not the case." Then I asked if, when Mr. Hirai returned to school in the latter part of January, the officers of the school did not go to Mr. Hirai and solicit his return to the school. Mr. Abe said, "No, Mr. Hirai simply returned to his post after his recovery from the illness." I repeated my statement that I had been informed that Hirai did resign and leave the school absolutely, but Mr. Abe assured me again that such was not true and sighted the paying of the money to Hirai as witness of the fact. I returned to headquarters much grieved and perplexed.

Mr. Hirai at the time of the contract last September told me that he would sever all connections with the school and be absolutely free from all relations with it and fearing that this great sacrifice for the Book of Mormon translation would leave him at the end of the year he was to work with us without a suitable position. I contracted to employ him for five months if he didn't find a suitable position after the expiration of the year of agreement. Later Mr. Hirai said it would be quite difficult to leave the school suddenly so he requested the privilege of continuing the school work till the end of September. This request was granted by a supplement in the agreement.

Then in January of this year Mr. Hirai came stating that the officers by personal visit and letter had requested him to return to the school. So urgent had been their requests that he found it difficult to refuse them without rupturing the friendly feelings between himself and school. He earnestly requested me to allow him to do a little teaching in the school. I consented as the second supplement to the conditions of the agreement shows. But according to the testimony given by Mr. Abe today. It appears, first, that Hirai's statement to me that he was getting ¥80.00 per month from Waseda was a falsehood, told to get a large amount of money for his work on the Book of Mormon; Next, that his statement that he was absolutely disconnected with the school was made to make it appear that he was making a big sacrifice for us and help us to decide on more money for his work, and lastly that his statement that the school officers came to him last January desiring his return to school was a falsehood told to avoid being detected in his pretended ill health, which made it impossible to attend school for the school had discovered that he was not so sick and wondered why he did not return to his post which he had never resigned.

I presented the matter to Elder Caine. We discussed it pro & con and I decided to bring the points of my investigation before Hirai and if he confessed and desired to make reparation for his sins that I would have him sign a new agreement for the rest of the original year of contract and give him only ¥60.00 per month for all of his time. In the event that he confesses not I determined to sever all connection with him. So feeling I retired, sick & sad.

Wednesday, 1 April 1908, Tokyo

Cloudy—Warm. Up at 7:20. After breakfast, I went with Elder Caine and called on Mr. Hirai. I told him what Mr. Abe told me and the light it put Mr. Hirai in. Instead of acknowledging his faults, he tried to blame the mistakes onto a misunderstanding of his statements to the school. I asked him to go with me and meet Mr. Abe. At first he said he would go, but then refused and the result was the signing of a paper which dissolved the contract between us. I took all of the manuscripts and books he had which belonged to me and returned with them. Thus, then, is the ending of Mr. Hirai's work on the Book of Mormon. Sad indeed am I over this outcome of recent affairs for I realize that the translation work will be somewhat belated. But thank God no sacred work need be destroyed because of the wrongs of men. The Lord is able to accomplish his labor in spite of the default of men and insomuch as the translation of this sacred volume is God's work if will, by his blessings, prosper and speedily be accomplished. At noon we held prayer meeting. In the afternoon I taught some of the Sunday School children some songs for our meeting next Sunday night. Did a little on the Book of Mormon. Retired.

Saturday, 4 April 1908, Tokyo

Rain—Colder. Up at 7:00. Spent the forenoon at Mr. Kumura's a gentleman who teaches in the Imperial Agriculture College. The purpose of my visit, was to inquire about the translation of some words in the Book of Mormon which are names of certain species of animals & plants. Called at Sister Ota's on the way home and invited her to meeting. Then stopped into the barber shop and got a hair cut. When I returned to headquarters, I found Elders Seely, Chadwick, and Anderson there. They were well and hearty. In the afternoon Elders Fairbourn, Stimpson, and Taylor arrived from Kōfu. They also were looking and feeling fine. Elders Seely, Chadwick, and Fairbourn will make their home at headquarters while the other three will stop at Yochōmachi with the elders there. Couldn't do much with so many around, some playing the piano, others playing the fiddle or acordian. I managed however to write about my recent investigation /of Mr. Hirai/ for the Mission Journal including the causes leading up to the dissolving of the contract with him relating to Book of Mormon translation. Took a bath in the afternoon.

Sunday, 5 April 1908, Tokyo

Rain—Cold wind. Up at 7:00. Today has been one of continual joy and satisfaction. The Sunday School was a grand success from every standpoint. After school I practiced the children in the songs they are going to sing for us tonight. Then we held a Sunday School teacher & officers meeting to discuss the work for the ensuing month. At 2:00 p.m. we held fast meeting a good spirit was present. After meeting, I rested a little while. Ate supper. The meeting in the evening began at 7:30 p.m. 18 were present besides the three little Sunday School girls who were on the program. This was an entirely satisfactory number considering the location and bad weather. This program of the meeting was interesting all the talks being short. Musical numbers, instrumental and vocal gave spice to the meeting. After the meeting some of our earnest enquirers remained to chat with the elders. I, feeling anxious to have the little ones home safe sent one of the elders with one girl, one girls father came for her and I went home with the little one who lives nearly a mile and a half from headquarters. There was no rikisha in the neighborhood so we trudged through the mud and rain each step increasing my love for the faithful little Sunday School girl who had come so far in such bad weather to answer the request of her teacher for a song. It was 10:30 when we reached her home. God bless this little one. Woe indeed to him /who/ offendeth such! Returned and had family prayer then retired grateful to my Father for his blessings.

Monday, 6 April 1908, Tokyo

Cloudy & Later, Clear & Warm. Up at 5:45. Swept the room before breakfast. At 9:30 a.m. the first session of the Missionaries Conference convened. I opened with a speech of about 45 minutes telling of the recent happenings in connection with the Book of Mormon translation Elders Fairbourn, Chadwick, Stimpson, Anderson and Taylor followed reporting their work and the work in their fields of labor. After dinner, we held another meeting in which the rest of the fourteen elders spoke presenting the conditions of the work in Hokkaido and the two fields in Tokyo. I took a walk after meeting with Elder Seely and chatted with him about future prospects in Hokkaido. Ate supper. Sang a little. Thought a little and then retired.

Tuesday, 7 April 1908, Tokyo

Clear—Warm Up at 7:05. After breakfast, at 9:30, the first session of the second day of conference was opened. A good spirit prevailed. After dinner the next meeting convened. Although the meeting was long, all the business could not be finished so another meeting was appointed for Wednesday morning. In the evening, I pumped the bath water, or rather helped to do it. After supper I sang a little, took a bath and retired.

Wednesday, 8 April 1908, Tokyo

Cloudy—Rain—Colder. Up at 7:30. Spent the entire day at headquarters. At 9:30 we held the last session of our Conference. At 2:00 p.m. we held prayer meeting. At 5:00 we had a delicious spread as a final big supper for all the elders before the parting. After supper, we had a program which consisted of songs, recitations, games and instrumental music. At about 10:00 p.m. we had family prayer and those who are living at Yochōmachi returned while those that were at headquarters retired. The minutes of the Conference are in Letter Book B.

Thursday, 9 April 1908, Tokyo

Heavy Snow Storm. Up at 7:30. Was greatly surprised to see about 9 or 10 inches of snow when I got up. The storms continued for more than half the day nearly every telegraph and telephone wire in the city was broken down. The cars couldn't run and the railroads were all interfered with. Elder Seely desired to leave for his field on the 11:45 train, but after a hard walk thru the snow to Ueno Station he found that the train would not go. He and those who accompanied him returned to headquarters tired and wet. I wrote a little and talked with some callers. I also shoveled snow and made ditches for the water. I spent the evening talking to the brethren.

Tuesday, 14 April 1908, Tokyo

Clear—Warmer. Up at 7:10. Spent the day working on the Book of Mormon. Made fine progress. Mr. Nakamura called this morning and I engaged him to come and work with me on the Book of Mormon promising him ¥25.00 per month and his noon meal. He will begin work by the 21st or 22nd of the present month. He will give from 7 to 8 hours every day except Sunday. He will also be handy in writing letters, signs etc. for the mission. I took a walk at noon for exercise. In the evening I pumped the bath water. Our little sister Ei Nachie is quite sick today, being unable to leave her bed.

Wednesday, 15 April 1908, Tokyo

Cloudy—Warmer Up at 7:15. Spent the day at headquarters. Worked on the Book of Mormon during the forenoon and for a little while in the afternoon. At 12:00 n. whe held prayer meeting. After meeting Elders Stoker, Caine, Woodland and I discussed a tract Elder Stoker has written in English on the subject of Faith. With the suggestions offered the tract was accepted and Elder Stoker will begin its translation immediately. Elder Caine and I administered to Sister Ei Nachie. I began a special fast in behalf of this Sister yesterday morning and in our prayer meeting today she was especially remembered before our Father. She is naturally weak in body, but of late she has been particularly ill and knowing the goodness and power of God, He has been sought after in her behalf. In the late afternoon I wrote to the First Presidency and to my father. After supper I took a walk. Talked with Sister Hakii

Tuesday, 21 April 1908, Tokyo

Clear—Hot & Terrible Dust. Up at 6:45. Spent the forenoon with Mr. Nakamura discussing questions about the Book of Mormon translation. Mr. Nakamura begins his work with me today. [‡] He will copy the received translation and be on hand to answer all my questions and render an opinion on any point I may bring up. After dinner I went to the optician's and got a new lens put in my glasses. I then went to Dr. Whitney's and had the lens examined. I did some shopping. Returned to headquarters and worked a number of hours on the translation. Took a bath and retired.

Tuesday, 28 April 1908, Tokyo

Cloudy—Rain—Cool Up at 6:40. Spent the entire day in the house working on the Book of Mormon. Made good progress and felt satisfied when I retired, with the work done. Received a very fine spirited letter from Bro. Hachiro Mori who is now in Corea.

Thursday, 30 April 1908, Tokyo

Clear—Warmer Up at 6:00. Spent the day working at headquarters. The forenoon was devoted to work in the office cleaning up and also killing a rat that somehow got in and played havoc during the night. The scene of Elder Woodland and I after the rat was about as funny as any story that has ever been written on such events. We had to disarrange everything in the room before capturing him. In the afternoon I finished discussing with Elder Caine the questions which his first view of my translation brought out. This entirely completes such questions and the only ones remaining are those in connection with the final review. Played baseball for an hour before supper. After supper discussed Sunday School work with Sister Tai

Wednesday, 6 May 1908, Tokyo

Clear—Hot Up at 7:15. Spent the day & evening working on the Book of Mormon. At noon I went to Yochōmachi and joined the elders there in prayer meeting. I appointed Elders Harris and Hubbard to begin tracting next Monday. Received a letter from Prest. Ralph Badger of the South African Mission telling of his release and the rapid growth of the work.

Wednesday, 13 May 1908, Tokyo

Clear—Still quite cool Up at 7:10. Spent the day at headquarters working on the Book of Mormon. Received a letter from mother and one from father. The letter from father contained considerable about the condition of his business and the ability and disposition of his son Samuel to take charge of it. Sad to say Samuel had not manifested a filial or grateful or industrious spirit hence father cannot think of giving the business into his hands, and, being too old and feeble to bear the burden much longer himself, he is having serious thoughts about selling out entirely. He asks me to write my feelings in regard to the matter. After supper, I went to Hongo and visited for an hour or more with Mr. Kawabe, husband of Sister Kawabe. Today at noon we held a prayer meeting. Elder Stoker's tract on faith was today given into the hands of the printer.

Thursday, 14 May 1908, Tokyo

Clear—Warm Up at 7:00. Spent the entire day preparing an answer to the letter received yesterday from father and attending to other correspondence. This mornings Asahi News had a two and a quarter column article giving an account of the visit of a party of Japanese tourists in Salt Lake City. The article is a fine advertizement for Utah and her people and will surely do us good.

Thursday, 21 May 1908, Tokyo

Cloudy—Quite warm Up at 6:30. Spent the entire day at headquarters working mostly on the Book of Mormon. During the forenoon, however, I spent considerable time solving a problem about one of the accounts in the missions books. This evening we entertained the members of the Theological Class in Sunday School, members of the English Bible Class, and members of the Japanese Bible Class. We gave them a cold spread to begin with. We then indulged in games that took with all the guests very well. At about 10:15 the entertainment closed having been a very pleasing success. After the entertainment Mr. Eisaburo Kuga remained for about thirty or forty minutes and I talked with him about entering the church, it being his desire to enter. After family prayers we retired feeling grateful for the experiences and pleasures of the day.

Sunday, 24 May 1908, Tokyo

Clear—Very warm Up at 6:10. Ate breakfast. Our Sunday School was quite small today, but it was a huge success from the standpoint of the exercises. After school I talked a little with Mr. Shimamura. Then I wrote a letter releasing Elder John W. Stoker from his labors in this mission, he having filled nearly six years with excellent work in this vineyard. Discussed Book of Mormon questions with Bro. Chiba for about an hour. Presided over the sacrament meeting. Took a short walk. Ate supper Presided over and preached in night meeting. After meeting I talked with Sister Tai.

Friday, 29 May 1908, Tokyo
     Rain in forenoon—Cloudy all day Up at 7:10. Spent the major part of the day working on the Book of Mormon. A soldier, Mr. Imani, called I talked with him for a while about the establishment of the church and the events leading up to it. At about 4:00 p.m. I packed my trunk and returned to headquarters. The home had been entirely renovated and the new matting gave it the smell of a hay field while the white wash stinks like a glue pot. Elder Stoker left Yochōmachi this forenoon expecting to take Sister Thomas to Yokohama and do some purchasing preparatory to leaving for home, but he took sick at headquarters. He was feeling better when I arrived so I sent him to Yochōmachi in a rikisha. Thinking that he would perhaps be unable to conduct the Bible Class I went after supper to Yochōmachi to take his place, but he succeeded in conducting the class all right. Returned and retired.

Saturday, 30 May 1908, Tokyo
     Cloudy—Cool Up at 6:45. Spent the forenoon cleaning the garden and myself. After dinner, went with my brethren and sisters to Tamagawa where I witnessed and directed the baptism of Bro. Eisaburo Kuga who received the ordinance from Elder John W. Stoker. This man has left the Baptist Church to gain the true fold. Before the baptism I spoke regarding the ordinance and read the account of Alma at the waters of Mormon from the Japanese translation of the Book of Mormon. We were especially blessed, for the Lord who held off the /threatening/ rain till we all got home from the river. Ate supper, read a little, took a bath and retired.

Sunday, 31 May 1908, Tokyo
     Forenoon Stormy—Afternoon Clear—Hot. Up at 6:30. There were only fifty at Sunday School today. Elder Stoker made his farewell speech. Owing to his return, I will have to take his place in the First Intermediate department leaving Sister Tai in full charge of the Primary Department. After school I talked for a while with a young man from Sapporo. Ate dinner. After dinner discussed Book of Mormon translation questions with Bro. Chiba till time for meeting. At our sacrament meeting Bro. Kuga was confirmed a member of the church by Elder Daniel P. Woodland. Elder Stoker made his farewell remarks to the saints. I spoke at this meeting. Read a little after meeting. Ate supper. Our evening meeting commenced with four present. Four more came in and then a young boy arrived so we had just 7 ½ people as an audience. Had prayers and retired.

Monday, 1 June 1908, Tokyo
     Clear—Warm Up at 6:30. Spent the forenoon tending to mission business in the office. In the afternoon, worked on the Book of Mormon finishing to the end of volume 13 of the criticised manuscript which is the end of Alma 29th chapter. Took a long walk for exercise before supper. Supper this evening was especially elaborate in honor of Elder Stoker who had his farewell evening with all his companions at Tokyo. We presented him with a sort of semi-dressing case as a token of our love and esteem. The evenings doings ended at 11:30 p.m.

Tuesday, 2 June 1908, Tokyo
     Clear—Hot Up at 7:30. Spent the forenoon and a majority of the afternoon working on the Book of Mormon In the evening, I went out in search for some poor families to be assisted in the fast offerings of the saints. Found two families. In the evening I talked with a number of friends who called to say goodbye to Elder Stoker.

Wednesday, 3 June 1908, Tokyo
     Clear—Warm Up at 6:40. This morning I did a little work on the Book of Mormon, then prepared

to go to Yokohama to bid farewell to Elder Stoker. From Shimbashi station we all rode together to Yokohama and then visited the spot where the first elders to Japan assembled and Prest. Grant dedicated this land for the proclamation of the Gospel. We sang hymns and I offered a prayer. Some ate a little lunch. Walked to the steamship pier and took a launch out to the S.S. "Mongolia." This is the largest steamer I have ever been on. Elder Stoker had a very nice room and a few hundred fellow passengers. After bidding him good bye, I returned by launch to shore and then did a little work for the mission. On the way to Tokyo, I stopped at Omori and had a chat with Mr. Kinza Hirai. He and some others have recently joined a society for the study of Psychical Phenomena and seemed anxious to know about the present position of our church regarding miricals, visions, dreams, revelations, prophecies etc. After reaching home, I ate supper and then did some work for the Sunday School.

Monday, 8 June 1908, Tokyo

Cloudy—Hail and Rain Up at 7:20. Spent the forenoon and afternoon working on the Book of Mormon translation. In the afternoon we had a hailstorm. The hail stones were nearly all 3/4 of an inch in diameter and some were as large and larger than hens eggs. They fell with great force. Some of the windows were struck by the stones and broken. In order to prevent a complete destruction of the windows exposed we put amado[6] up outside. This is quite a remarkable storm so far as my experience goes. In the evening we held missionaries Bible Class at headquarters; the brethren from Yochōmachi being in attendance.

Wednesday, 10 June 1908, Tokyo

Clear—Still cool. Up at 6:30. Spent the entire day working on the Book of Mormon translation. After supper, I called on Mr. Kawai to ask about Dr. Tsubouchi and Prof. Koda men whom I have in mind for work on the Book of Mormon translation criticism. Mr. Kawai gave both men a good reputation he having at one time been a student under Dr. Tsubouchi. Mr. Kawai mentioned a Mr. Natsuma who writes for the Asahi News as a capable writer and critic in Japanese. From Mr. Kawai's I went to the house of the Awaya family I talked for a moment or two with the son who comes to Sunday School occasionally. Returned to headquarters read a little and retired.

Monday, 15 June 1908, Tokyo

Cloudy—Hot Up at 6:15. Spent the forenoon discussing Book of Mormon translation questions with Mr. Nakamura. In the afternoon I went to Mr. Iwano's to see him and learn from him what he knows of Mr. Tsubouchi, Mr. Koda and Mr. Natsumi whom I have in mind for the final criticism of the Book of Mormon translation. Mr. Iwano gave me a letter of introduction to Mr. Tsubouchi. Prepared the lesson for the Elders Bible Class which was held at Yochōmachi

Wednesday, 17 June 1908, Tokyo

Clear—Warm Up at 6:30. Spent the day at headquarters working on the Book of Mormon translation. After supper, I went to Yuzo Tsubouchi's home and met the gentleman but he was not in a position to comply with my request regarding the final review of the Book of Mormon translation. I went to the home of Mr. Kinnosuke Natsume but could not meet him as he refuses all visitors except on Thursdays. Called at one of the Sunday School childrens' houses on the way back and had a pleasant chat. The home was that of Hide Nishimura whose parents were both home and received me quite pleasantly.

Thursday, 18 June 1908, Tokyo

Cloudy—Rain—Hot Up at 6:45. Spent the forenoon hunting for a man to review the Book of Mormon translation. I called on Mr. Natsuma Kintaro a famous writer. He was unable to do the work and suggested the name of Koji Ikuta whom he said was entirely capable to do the work and no doubt had plenty of time to do it. After dinner I called at Mr. Ikuta's home, but he was not in. Today I did some work on the Book of Mormon translation. After supper, I talked a little while with Sister Tai about Sunday School work and then listened to some of the sermons delivered at the 78th annual conference of the Church.

Friday, 19 June 1908, Tokyo

Up at 6:40. Mr. Koji Ikuta called this morning I talked to him about the criticism of the Book of Mormon translation. He said, if I considered him competent, he would undertake the work. Not knowing anything of his ability except the Mr. Natsuma recommended him, I let him take the first book of the manuscript as criticised by Mr. Hirai and requested him to review it as a sample of his work. Spent the rest of the day on the Book of Mormon criticised translation. In the evening I ate supper early and went to Yochōmachi where I presided over the Japanese Bible Class. After class returned to headquarters.

Thursday, 25 June 1908, Tokyo

Clear—Hot—Calm Up at 6:30. Spent the entire forenoon and afternoon working on the Book of Mormon translation made fine progress. In the evening, listened to the reading of the sermons delivered in the closing two sessions of General Conference held at Salt Lake last April. Took two short walks in the neighborhood and turned the ice cream freezer for exercise

Friday, 26 June 1908, Tokyo

Rain—Sultry Up at 6:45. Spent the greater part of the day working on the Book of Mormon translation. In the forenoon, Mr. Ikuta came with the 1st book of the manuscript with his suggestions written in lead pencil. There are quite a number of changes, but they do not appear to be of great importance except from the standpoint of euphony. I shall look over his corrections and then have three or four Japanese read the manuscript as Mr. Hirai wrote it and then as Ikuta has corrected it so as to find out if Ikuta's ideas improve the translation or not. After this investigation I shall decide whether or not to employ Mr. Ikuta. In the evening I went to Yochōmachi expecting to hold a Bible Class. Only two came. They have not been to the class since I have been teaching, so I engaged them in conversation. Today we received a letter from Elder Stoker. His voyage as far as Hawaii was pleasant and safe.

Saturday, 27 June 1908, Tokyo

Cloudy—Slight rain—Cool Up at 6:15. Spent nearly all the forenoon cleaning house and cleaning myself. The rest of the day was spent working on the Book of Mormon translation After supper, I called on Mr. Ikuta and requested him to make suggestions on the 20th book of the translation manuscript just as he has already made them on Alma's instructions to his son Corianton and the account of a great war between the Nephites and Lamanites.[7] This book is there quite different in the nature of its expressions to the 1st book and is one of the most difficult deep parts of the sacred record. In order to judge fairly the ability of Mr. Ikuta to pass criticism upon the whole I desire to test him on the difficult as well as the simple verses and also give him an opportunity at all the various styles in the Book. Returned and studied the Sunday School lesson Took a bath and retired. Today I received a letter from Bro. James E. Talmage containing an article entitled, "Lord of All" which he submits in answer to a request to write about the providences of God in mortal calamities.

Sunday, 28 June 1908, Tokyo

Cloudy—Quite Cool Up at 6:30. Ate breakfast. We had a large successful Sabbath School. My class was unusually well attended. Sang a little with Sister Thomas. Ate dinner. Talked with Bro. Chiba about the Book of Mormon translation Presided over the Sacrament Meeting and did the speaking. Talked with Miss Katsu Ishikawa. Took a long walk. Ate supper. Presided over the evening meeting. Also spoke at this meeting. The attendance was the largest for four or five months and the nature of it was better than we have had for a long time. Today the Lord has heard my prayers. Every meeting has been a success and the good Spirit has been give to us all in rich abundance. The praise is the Lord's forever.

Friday, 3 July 1908, Tokyo

Rain—Cloudy—Cool Up at 7:15. Spent the day working on the Book of Mormon translation. Made good progress. In the evening I went to Yochōmachi and held a Bible Class After the class, I walked home with Bro. Kuga instructing him that is was not right under any circumstances to attempt to borrow money from the church and the elders—he having desired a small loan.

Saturday, 4 July 1908, Tokyo

Cloudy—Little rain—Cold Up at 7:00. Spent the forenoon working on the Book of Mormon translation. After dinner I sang some patriotic songs in remembrance of the day so dear to the hearts of all true Americans. Fussed around with some men who have been trying to mend the bath /fire pot/ for a whole week. Read a little in the newspapers and magazines from America. In the evening, we had a good 4th of July supper.

Tuesday, 7 July 1908, Tokyo

Just a little sunshine—Warmer Up at 6:15. Spent the major part of the day reviewing the quarterly financial and statistical reports of the mission. Signed and sent them off to America in fine shape, trusting that when they come back to us audited they will not be covered with red ink corrections. Took two walks and played ball a little for exercise.

Wednesday, 8 July 1908, Tokyo

Clear—Cool Up at 7:00 Spent the forenoon reviewing and changing Dr. Talmage's essay on "Lord of All" preparatory to sending it to Elder Anderson who will translate it into Japanese with the view of publishing it a a tract for use in this mission. In the afternoon, I wrote to the elders in the outlying fields. Took a walk and a nap before supper. After supper sang a little then worked a little on the Book of Mormon translation. At noon we held a prayer meeting. Mr. Nakamura finished his work on the Book of Mormon translation today at noon. He has copied nearly the entire translation down to the end of Heleman chapter one. He has been quite careful and neat writing in a very clear legible hand. He retires from the work to make room for Bro. Eisaburo Kuga who has been engaged to make the copy of the remaining two books of the corrected part of the translation. Bro. Kuga has had some little misfortunes lately and I am giving him this work to help him.

Sunday, 12 July 1908, Tokyo

Clear—Evening cool with heavy shower Up 6:00. Ate breakfast. Directed Sunday School teaching the 1st Intermediate Department. At 11:00 A.M. we held sacrament meeting over which I presided. In the afternoon I read a little. I wrote a letter to Elder Seely. He asked me to explain Daniel 8:14; 9:25 and Rev. 11:3.[8] The first two I could not explain satisfactorily; the last I explained only by a reference to Voice of Warning pages 58–62.[9] Took a short walk calling on Mr. Ikuta to hurry him up with my translation of a portion of the Book of Mormon he is looking over. Ate supper. Just before meeting we had a heavy shower. There were 11 in attendance. After the meeting I chatted a little with Mr. Sato who has been coming a great deal of late to our meetings

Wednesday, 15 July 1908, Tokyo

Clear—Hot—Later Cloudy Up at 6:30. Spent an hour or two in the forenoon working on the review of Mr. Hirai's criticisms of the Book of Mormon translation. I finished this review at a few minutes to ten. There are a few questions to ask Bro. Kuga before he copies the last book and then so far as Hirai's criticisms go, I am through with them. This is another important period in the work and I feel as though another load ha[d]s rolled off my shoulder. This review has been a much more arduous labor than was anticipated. However, the Lord has blessed me in it and all honor a praise for the progress made is given to Him. The next important step is the selection of a Japanese to review that that I have just finished reviewing and change from gembuchitchitsi to buntai the part untouched by Mr. Hirai. I hope to have perfect success in this selection. Today we went to Yochōmachi for prayer meeting. I talked to the elders. In the afternoon I did several odd jobs. After supper I visited the Kataoka family living at Uraubamcho Yotsuya Ku.

Friday, 17 July 1908, Tokyo

Clear—Hot Up at 6:45. Spent most of the forenoon talking with Mr. Chiko Ikuta who returned the part of the Book of Mormon /translation/ manuscript he has been reviewing. After dinner, I went over Mr. Ikuta's suggestions which were made right in the manuscript with lead pencil. After going over them myself, I took this part of the manuscript and the first book of the manuscript which also Mr. Ikuta has reviewed and called on Mr. Yuzo Tsubouchi, a famous writer and professor in the Waseda University I asked Mr. Tsubouchi to read the two books and answer these questions: First, If the translation simple being clear to a hearer as well as a reader? Second, Is it easy, smooth and well toned? Third, Is it dignified and forceful? Fourth, Is it well unified? Apart from these questions I had one which I intended to ask after Mr. Tsubouchi went over the books, but which he answered immediately. It was Has Mr. Ikuta's suggestions improved the translation? Mr. Tsubouchi did not manifest much of a desire to comply with my desire, but took the books one at a time in his hand and read a number of passages here and there. He said "This translation is good. No matter where I read there is no sentence which is peculiar or obscure. You are quite safe with such a translation. I bear the responsibility of assuring you that. In the passages noted, Mr. Ikuta's corrections are good. He is quite a capable man so you may feel safe with his suggestions." Mr. Tsubouchi said that he had read an essay written by Mr. Ikuta and said it was very well prepared. He also said that there was no necessity for him to read the books all through as he can tell as well by reading a passage here and there. Consequently I had to leave him without getting the desire of my heart entirely satisfied for I hoped to have him read the two books and then answer my questions. He said one book (containing from title page to I Nephi 8:19) was simpler than the other in style (the other containing from 40th to 45th chapters of Alma). He said there was perhaps too much dignity in the latter book as compared with the former; but the difference in the subject handled perhaps justified a deeper tone. His only suggestion about any change was a little more simplicity in the latter book if possible. However, he said the words and sentences were themselves quite clear—clear to anyone who reads and also to the majority of hearers.

I ate supper at Yochōmachi and then explained some principles of the gospel to four listeners who did not come in time or manner for a regular Bible Class. Walked to headquarters and retired.

Thursday, 23 July 1908, Tokyo

Cloudy—Very Sultry. Up at 6:00. During the forenoon worked on the Book of Mormon, beginning the translation of the contents. After dinner, I went to Mr. Iwano's and listened to his opinion of the Book of Mormon translation. He said, "In general it is good and in point of simplicity need not be improved." However, so far as tone and dignity is concerned it can be improved by paying more attention to the conjunctions and also avoiding the arbitrary use of words that are not euphonic in the positions they occupy. The style is sufficiently solemn for scriptures. After hearing these opinions I asked him if he knew Mr. Ikuta? He said he did and testified that he was a clever writer but not much of a thinker. He added that he was a coming critic of literature. So much for Iwano's opinions. Iwano himself claims to be among the literate of the present school, but he would be a more impressive personage if there were less self in his manner. In general, I consider his criticism as favorable to the translation and his testimony for Mr. Ikuta is like Mr. Tsubouchi's. I took the part of the translation already reviewed by Mr. Iwano to Mr. Kawai and asked him to read it and pass judgment upon its merits or demerits. He promised to report his opinion by the night of the 27th inst. In the evening I discussed translation questions with Bro. Kuga

Friday, 24 July 1908, Tokyo

Cloudy—Hot as blazes Up at 6:00 Spent the forenoon translating the table of contents of the Book of Mormon. After dinner I went to Yokohama to inquire into the method followed by the Bible Society in printing the Bible in Japanese. I found that the translation is stereotyped from the ordinary paper moulds. The printers told me that if the paper moulds are carefully made, that ten different stereotypes can be made and one stereotype will print 60,000 times hence with proper care the Book of Mormon translation if preserved in paper mould will /produce in/ good form 600,000 copies before a resetting of type is necessary. An electroplate, according to the printer is quite unnecessary and uneconomical, costing 04 1/2 sen per square sun. Returned to Tokyo, ate supper went to Yochōmachi and held a Bible Class. Eight Japanese were present. Walked home and retired.

Monday, 27 July 1908, Tokyo

Hot—Calm— Up at 6:00 Spent the forenoon working on the Book of Mormon translation. After dinner I went to the Hakubun Kwan Printing establishment to get a bid on 5,000 copies of the Book of Mormon in Japanese. They promised to send the bid by mail. Then went to the Toyo Printing Company and secured a bid which was ¥2,163.00. Then took the train to Omori where I had a long talk with Mr. Kinza Hirai relative to the words "Mitama," & "Seirei" which are used in the Japanese Bible for "Holy Ghost" etc. Returned to Tokyo and went directly to the home of Mr. Kawai. He had read the two volumes of the translation left at his home last Thursday. His criticism was in brief this: The translation is not a brilliant classic but it is simple, easy to read, honest and says things straight to the point without ornament. I reached headquarters at 9:15 p.m. tired and hungry. Ate supper, reported the days doings to my companions and retired.

Tuesday, 28 July 1908, Tokyo

Hot—Clear—Calm Up at 6:40. Spent most of the forenoon at Mr. Ikuta's home. Having had Mr. Tsubouchi's, Iwano's & Kawai's criticisms of the Book of Mormon translation or rather that part received by Mr. Ikuta, and they all having testified that Ikuta's corrections were good and stated that Ikuta had ability and was known as a very brilliant young literary critic, I decided that I would be safe in committing the last and deciding criticism of the translation to him. We talked over the terms of contract. In the afternoon I wrote the agreement and also a letter to the First Presidency telling of my doing and asking for money to publish the first edition of the translation. In the evening I took a walk.

Wednesday, 29 July 1908, Tokyo

Still hot, but a pleasant breeze Up at 6:00. In the forenoon Mr. Ikuta called and after reading over the agreement, he and I signed it. It allows him to work in his own home but requires five hours every day except Sunday. For his labor the mission promises to pay ¥100.00 month. The labor is calculated to be great enough to last for six or seven months. Bro. Kuga called today to do some copying. He announces the birth of a fine girl in his home. In the afternoon I went out and did some shopping. Packed up in preparation to leave for the north on a two weeks trip. At noon today we held prayer meeting. Bro. Harris came in the late afternoon and announced that he was on the way to the hospital. He had been suffering from a slight hemorrhage from the kidneys or bladder and the doctor had suggested his entering the hospital. After questioning him, it appeared that the doctor's convenience was the only thing demanding retirement to the hospital. I refused to let him go but told him to use my bed a headquarters and keep quiet.

Thursday, 30 July 1908, Tokyo

Clear—Hot as blazes

Up at 5:00. Ate breakfast. Went to Ueno Station and took the 7:25 a.m. train for Morioka. After a long hot ride without anything interesting to break the monotony, arrived at my destination at about 10:30 p.m. Elders Anderson and Chadwick were at the station to meet me. They were in good health. Went immediately to the elders home and after a brief chat retired.

Friday, 31 July 1908, Morioka

Cloudy—Hot Up at 7:00. Spent the forenoon and afternoon at the mission house working on the Book of Mormon translation. After supper Elder Chadwick and I took a walk visiting the city park. This park is the remains of the castle of the old shogun of this district called Nambu. As a park both pretty and quaint it is better than any I have seen in Japan, not excepting the one in Akita City which is beautiful indeed, but not quaint like the one here. The elders home is a house built on the edge of the city and with the marks of the antiquity claimed for it. It is the home of a samurai named Kikuchi. The front is decorated with a row of tall cryptomeria trees while the garden is large and full of moss grown stones. The house itself has about 11 rooms a monstrous kitchen and bathroom and there are 78 mats. The rent is ¥15.00 per month and is altogether too high according to the people's opinion. The district is as calm as a grotto, the cry of the crow, hum of insects, croaking of frogs, and twitter of birds are the only noises that pierce the stillness.

Saturday, 1 August 1908, Morioka

Cloudy—sprinkling of rain—Hot Up at 6:50. During the forenoon swept part of the garden which is nearly as large as a field. After dinner we went to the top of the highest mountain in the immediate vacinity of the city. From this point we had a very fine view of the entire valley and we could see the smaller rolling hills for many miles around. After returning I did a little work on the Book of Mormon and in the evening continued this labor. Took an early bath and retired. Today I passed the 26th milestone of my life.

Sunday, 2 August 1908, Morioka

Clear—Hot—Calm Up at 6:45. Sunday School commenced at 9:00 a.m. There were 10 children and one adult present. This is the average sized school for this place. Dividing this small number into two classes makes each department very small. Elder Chadwick presided over the Primary class and Elder Anderson over the First Intermediate Department. I talked to a gentleman for a little while after school. At eleven o'clock we held sacrament and testimony meeting. After this meeting I took a nap and wrote a letter to mother. Read considerable in the several magazines received in this field. Ate supper. The evening meeting began about five minutes late. Only three were present to begin with but before it was out we had seven. The man with whom I talked in the forenoon asked some questions After a conversation with him, I talked with Mrs. Kikuchi till 11:15 p.m. Retired.

Monday, 3 August 1908, Morioka

Clear—Very Hot Up at 7:00 After breakfast, we took a walk down to the river front—A cool pleasant spot. I did some work on the Book of Mormon translation. Slept and rested the rest of the day. After supper, we held a Priesthood Meeting in which I gave the elders some instructions and also listened to their remarks about their work in this district. At nine o'clock we went to the depot. I expected to take the 9:59 train to Aomori and make connections with the morning boat but I found that the morning boat from Aomori to Hakodate was undergoing repairs and the evening boat was the only one in running order, so I concluded to stay over another night in Morioka. Walked back to the house and went to bed.

Tuesday, 4 August 1908, Morioka

Clear—Cooler and farther north—Calm. Up at 7:00. Ate breakfast, wrote my journal and walked to the station expecting to take the train for Aomori at 10:27 a.m., but the train was an hour later. Bid the brethren good-bye and had quite a pleasant ride. The scenery from Morioka to Aomori was entirely new to me. I have been over the road three time before, but it was always at night. This is exceptionally well adapted to stock raising as it is hilly and abundant in grass that is very nourishing. One or two flocks of horses were seen along the way. One thing of the greatest interest was a field of haymakers who were using hayrakes, pitchforks and other implements like are seen on American farms. I met a representative of the Tokyo Plant Seed and Implement Co. who is on his way to Hokkaido in the interest of American farming implements. Mr. Watase whom Prest. Grant met about six years ago is the president of the Company. After arriving at Aomori, I purchased first class passage on the Tamura Maru for Hakodate. Waited in the station waiting room for 30 minutes then went to the steamer. This steamer is a new one built in England for the Imperial Railway Company's service between Aomori and Hakodate. It is a new style ship and a beauty but the fare does not include food or any special accomodations. First class ordinary passengers have two rooms one for gentlemen the other for ladies. Each passenger has a seat large enough to lie down. I washed and sat on the deck till supper was ready. At supper I had a short, interesting talk with my table companions. Enjoyed the rest of the evening, in fact till we arrived at Hakodate, looking at the stars and fishing crafts. Now is the season for ika fishing.[10] About two or three thousand little crafts, each holding from six to ten men in a line six or seven deep entirely across the mouth of the harbor. Each craft had a lantern burning for the purpose of decoying the fish into their nets. The sight was the only one of the kind I have thus far in my life seen. We arrived at Hakodate at about 10:45 p.m. but owing to some trouble were unable to get into position for nearly an hour. Went to the Katsu[y]ta /Hotel/ and took lodgings for the night. Retired at midnight.

Wednesday, 5 August 1908, Hakodate

Cloudy, Cooler—Slight breeze. Up at 8:15 Spent the forenoon in the hotel reading and writing. Ate some fruit for dinner. Started out to find Brother Sakura to meet and talk with whom I stopped over in Hakodate . To my surprise and disappointment, I found after a search that lasted all afternoon and part of the evening that he had gone to a village about 20 or 30 ri from Hakodate. After supper I took a stroll around the main streets of the town and witnessed a lively throng out to buy and see the sights. Considering the fact that Hakodate was nearly destroyed by fire a year ago, it is now in a wonderfully revived condition. The new buildings will be an improvement over the old ones. Took a two hours sleep. Paid my bill and left for the station were I was waiting the departure of the train for Sapporo when the midnight hour tolled.

Thursday, 6 August 1908, Hakodate

Hot—Clear The train left Hakodate at 12:20 a.m. I tried to sleep, but failed, so at daylight I got up and washed and amused myself looking at the scenery till about 7:30 when I had sour bread and badly canned hard, green peaches for breakfast. As the day wore on it became very hot. Arrived at Sapporo on schedule time (12:37 p.m.) and reached the elders home at 1:15 p.m. Elder Roskelley Culter and Marriott were just finishing dinner. I washed and had lunch. Spent the afternoon brushing and cleaning up. Also talked a good deal with the elders. Bro. Seely came back from Teinei village looking very much like a farmer with his kaki suit and big straw hat. He had been to prepare a place to preach and arrange for the first meetings. After supper I went with the brethren to the hall in Toyohira village where the elders expected to hold a meeting. At the hour appointed, only one Japanese was present. I had Elder Seely preside and speak so as to give someone a chance to come in. Two more came. I talked for about forty-five minutes. On the way home, we passed through the park where the evening festivities of the "shokonsai" were on in full swing.[11] The crowd was too great to be pleasant so we did not linger. Had prayer early and retired. I was quite ready for a rest.

Friday, 7 August 1908, Sapporo

Cloudy—Slight Rain—Hot. Up at 7:30. Spent all the forenoon and part of the afternoon in the house writing, reading, and talking. In the evening, after supper, I took a walk. Returned and had a pleasant hour or more talking and singing with the brethren.

Saturday, 8 August 1908, Sapporo

Rain—Wind—Cool. Up at 8:00. Spent the greater part of the forenoon conversing with Miss. Watanabe an investigator. After dinner, I talked with some children. I wrote a letter to father than took a walk. In the evening, I talked with Brother Kawanaka

Sunday, 9 August 1908, Sapporo

Clear—Hot Up at 7:00. At 9:00 a.m. we held Sunday School. I enjoyed witnessing the exercises. There is a fine school here. It is divided into four departments. At 11:00 a.m. a sacrament meeting was held. I spoke. Ate dinner At 2:00 o'clock a Bible Class was held by Elder Roskelley I attended this class and spoke. After the class I engaged a young man in conversation. Took a walk. Ate supper and then attended and addressed the evening meeting. After meeting I talked till about 11:30 p.m. to Mr.

Tominaga. Today Elder Seely opened a Sunday School in Tenei Village about 4 or 5 miles from Sapporo. Elders Cutler and Marriott held a meeting in Toyohira Village. I retired very much in the humor for a good rest.

Monday, 10 August 1908, Sapporo

Clear—Hot as blazes. Up at 7:30. After breakfast, all the elders accompanied me on a long walk to the top of a mountain near the city.[12] It took nearly two hours to reach the top. From the top we could see the whole valley and far over many of the lower mountains. We decided to decend on the opposite side of the mountain and walk home by the river. The descent was a hard one as their was no path most of the way. When we reached the river two of us watched the other three swim We then walked to the government live stock experiment farm at Makomanai village. We were conducted through the whole farm and saw all of their horses, cows, pigs and chickens. One of their finest stallions, imported from America is named "Mormon." There are four coults from this sire all fine animals knows as Mormon II, III etc. Elder Roskelley was overcome by the heat & long walk so he sat in the office of the farm while we went over it. This was a happy hour for me for it was the first time I had been close to horses, cows, chickens etc. since I left America. We walked home arriving there at about 6:00 p.m. Mr. Okafuji was waiting to see me. We c/h/atted for about thirty minutes. He returned. I ate supper, then went to Bro. Kawanaka's home and spent the evening conversing with him.

Tuesday, 11 August 1908, Sapporo

Clear—Calm—Very Hot. Up at 7:00. Spent the early hours of the forenoon holding a priesthood meeting with the elders. In this meeting I gave that advice, reproof and encouragement that I considered to be for the good of the work. I then went out and did some purchasing. Ate dinner. About 2:00 p.m. I went with Elder Seely and their housekeeper and a Miss Itsu Watanabe to the river. Here Elder Seely baptized Miss Watanabe. Returned to the mission house and a brief service was held in which Sister Watanabe was confirmed, Elder Cutler and I officiating—I was mouth. This was an unexpected pleasure for me today: the more so because Sister Watanabe is the first female convert in Hokkaido. She is not yet 20 years old. She is a teacher in a Primary School. Her parents are both alive and although they are staunch Methodists, they gladly gave their consent to the baptism of their daughter, thinking it no right of parents to trample upon the religious freedom of those of their children who are old enough to think and judge for themselves. In the evening we had, an especially good meal. I packed my goods preparatory to an early start next morning.

Wednesday, 12 August 1908, Sapporo

Clear—Hot. Up at 7:00. Bade the elders good bye and took the 8:40 a.m. train for Muroran. Elder Seely & Sister Watanabe went with me to the first station out of Sapporo. Bro. Kawanaka, Miss Tominaga and Mr. Okafuji were at the station to see me off. The elders of course were all there. Arrived at Muroran at 2:50 p.m. Took passage on the Ishikari Maru for Aomori. Sailed at 4:40 p.m. Tried to sleep but didn't have much success. Arrived in Aomori at 3:15 a.m. next day.

Thursday, 13 August 1908, Ship

Cloudy—Cooler Up at 3:00. As soon as I got up I prepared to leave the ship. Went to the station waiting rooms. Took the 6:05 a.m. train and went to Morioka. Arrived at the latter place at 12:25 p.m. Took rikisha to the elders' home. They were surprised to see me. Nothing of particular note had happened since I left them some 9 or 10 days before. Rested at their home till time to leave for the night train to Tokyo. Ate a fine supper. The elders walked with me to the depot. Left Morioka at 7:48 p.m. Had one little nap before midnight.

Friday, 14 August 1908, Train

Cloudy—Cool Had another slight snooze before daylight. Washed my face about 6:30 a.m. at Mito station. Ate a Japanese lunch for breakfast. The train arrived at Ueno Station Tokyo at 9:25 a.m. I took the car home. All were in good health at headquarters, but Elder Harris is resting most of the time till his kidneys recover. He has been under the doctor's care ever since I have been away. Spent the afternoon resting, cleaning up, putting my clothes in order, and writing. After supper, I went to Yochōmachi and taught a Bible class. Reached headquarters at 10:15 p.m. very tired. Went directly to bed.

Monday, 17 August 1908, Tokyo

Clear—Hot Up at 7:15. Spent all day working on the Book of Mormon. In the evening Mr. Ikuta called bringing the first two volumes of the corrected manuscript I talked with him a little relative to some translation questions. After supper, I presided over the missionaries Bible Class.

Tuesday, 18 August 1908, Tokyo

Clear—Hot—Calm. Up at 7:10. Spent most of the day working on the Book of Mormon translation and enjoyed the labor very much as it was the beginning of my review of Mr. Ikuta's work There are so few changes that the labor of review is very easy compared with what I have had heretofore. It looks good to see the translation in its completed garb and the feelings that pass through my heart when I look upon this translation feeling satisfied that it is well done, are undiscribable. The joy is just a taste of what I hope it will be when the whole labor is finished. In the evening I pumped some water for the bath, Ate supper and read papers from America.

For about 2 hours in the forenoon I was looking up houses advertized for rent. None suited. The house in which we are now living is to be torn down to make a broad street for the Fair to be held in 1912.

Wednesday, 19 August 1908, Tokyo

Clear—Hot—Calm Up at 6:20. Spent the forenoon and a majority of the afternoon working on the Book of Mormon translation. At noon we held prayer meeting. After supper, I went to visit the family of Mr. Hirai a soldier who lives on Aisumi Street; Yotsuya District. They were not home so I went on to Yochōmachi and attended the English Bible class held by Elder Hubbard. Returned, read a few letters from America and retired. One letter from father says he expects to turn the business over to Samuel taking a royalty on the transactions. He hints at a trip around the world with mother, picking me up en route.

Thursday, 20 August 1908, Tokyo

Clear—Very Hot. Up at 7:10. Spent the greater part of the day working on the Book of Mormon translation. Wrote a letter to President's Office relative to Elders Marriott and Stimpson, Elder David O. McKay having inquired about the progress of Elder Marriott in his missionary work. In the evening, I walked to the hospital to get some medicine for Elder Harris. Then I read till bedtime.

Sunday, 23 August 1908, Tokyo

Clear—Very Hot. Up at 6:45. Ate breakfast. Presided over the Sunday School. If any other church in Japan had a more delightful Sunday School than we had this morning, it must have been absolutely idea, for our session was nearly so. At 11:00 a.m. the saints and missionaries met and partook of the sacrament. After lunch I went and visited Bro. Kuga. Found him rather down in the dumps because of sickness in his family. On the way home from Bro. Kuga's, I called on Sister Kawabe. She is well and received me gladly. Sprinkled some water on the street. Ate supper and presided over the evening meeting which was very small. Sang a little and retired.

Wednesday, 26 August 1908, Tokyo

Clear—Hot—Calm Up at 7:30. Spent most of the forenoon talking to Mr. Taue and Mr. Mori; the latter made application for baptism. He has recently come to Tokyo from Sapporo for the purpose of attending school. He has been acquainted with the brethren in Sapporo and has been quite a diligent attendant at their meetings for some time. I talked to him about the responsibilities that come to those who enter the church and the sacredness of the covenants they make in the waters of baptism. I suggested that he consider well all that I said to him and ask himself once more, if he is prepared to make the step with determination to meet all the consequences of his act and endure to the end. In the afternoon, I did work on the Book of Mormon translation. At noon we held prayer meeting. After supper, I visited a member of the Bible Class held at Yochōmachi. Had a long talk and returned to headquarters just in time for prayer.

Thursday, 27 August 1908, Tokyo
Clear—Hot Up at 6:30. After breakfast I went to Mr. Ikuta's and had a long discussion with him about the Book of Mormon translation. There is all the difference in the world between Mr. Ikuta and Hirai in the matter of questions about translation. Hirai was quick tempered, angered often, said nasty things and often made our discussions very unpleasant. Mr. Ikuta is a gentleman. He is quick and frank in acknowledging his errors. He gives respectful ear to my side of the questions discussed and thus we get along well and rapidly. Today, I paid him ¥100.00 for his first month's work. He has completed the review of four books of the manuscript. I have read over and discussed three with him. Returned to headquarters just in time for dinner. In the afternoon I worked on the translation. In the evening, I went out to distribute the fast offerings. After supper again worked on translation

Saturday, 29 August 1908, Tokyo
Sunshine and heat. Up at 7:15. Spent the forenoon cleaning the garden and brushing up myself. In the afternoon, I worked on the Book of Mormon and visited Sister Ota. After supper I studied the Bible lesson for Sunday School and talked with Mr. Koizumi. This young man has been attending our meetings for nearly a year. At one time he applied for baptism but we did not feel disposed to administer the ordinance till he had studied more. This evening he said he had come to inform us that he has decided to continue his studies at another church, for he cannot see how God should every give a commandment to his people to practice plural marriage. All the other things he has learned here, he believes as true and only in this one point has he felt to doubt the divinity of Joseph Smith's call to be a prophet of God. At first, on the question of plural marriage, he was satisfied to look upon it as a dead issue, but because of the persuasions of some of his friends he has come to regard it as a vital question when considering the claims of Joseph Smith to the title of Prophet, Seer and Revelator. Mr. Koizumi is too well bred to leave us without expressing his thanks for our care in teaching him and speaking clearly and boldly his reasons for seeking satisfaction elsewhere. He manifested such a good honest spirit in his manner and words that I felt that a brief experience studying at another church would do him more good than harm and cause him to come back to the true fold with a faith stronger than any he has know before in the divinity of "Mormonism".

Tuesday, 1 September 1908, Tokyo
Rain—a little chilly Up at 6:45. Spent the entire day in the house working on the Book of Mormon. I have worked hard and only been able to get the references on one book of the manuscript. I taught the Thomas family another lesson in Japanese. Seven years ago today, Apostle Heber J. Grant together with his three missionaries repaired to a wood near Yokohama and held a prayer and council meeting at which the land of Japan was dedicated for the proclamation of the gospel. Having, been in this mission continually since that day, I have seen every movement in our work, known all our joys and felt all our sorrow. In reflecting over the seven year past, I recognize the hand of God in the work which has progressed from day to day against gigantic obstacles and is now in a very healthy condition. The growth has been like the oak and I believe it is as enduring in its nature and that while there are only 17 native saints in the church here still the labor and progress that is not estimated in figures has been remarkably great when all conditions are taken into consideration. Therefore, on this the 7th birthday of the Japan Mission my heart is full of gratitude for the protecting helping hand of God in the past, and our present good condition and my faith and hope in the future is doubly strong.

Thursday, 3 September 1908, Tokyo

Rain all day. Up at 6:15. Spent the greater part of the forenoon downtown seeing about passage to America for Elders Chadwick and Woodland. In the afternoon I wrote Elder Chadwick's release and also wrote a long letter to Elder Anderson. In the evening I worked on the Book of Mormon.

Friday, 4 September 1908, Tokyo

Rain—Cool Up at 7:00 Spent the forenoon down town and teaching Elder & Sister Thomas Japanese. In the afternoon I worked on the Book of Mormon and later went to Yochōmachi taking Elder Woodland's release. I had supper there and then presided over the Bible Class. Talked with two young men for a little while and returned to headquarters. /Today Elder Caine returned from Kōfu with the good news of another baptism there./

Saturday, 5 September 1908, Tokyo

Cloudy—Cold Up at 6:50. Before breakfast I went to Shinjuku and ordered some wood. Ate breakfast and left for Yokohama where I went to try for a better cabin for the elders. Returned to Tokyo and did some work on the Book of Mormon. In the evening, I worked on the Sunday School plan for September.

Friday, 11 September 1908, Tokyo

Clear—Warmer. Up at 6:15. Spent all the forenoon and part of the afternoon looking over the critisims of Mr. Ikuta and part of the translation. Went down town to get some medicine for my nerves. In the evening, I went to Yochōmachi and held a Bible Class, the last to be held there before the contemplated discontinuance of that house. I expected to remain all night but Elder Woodland returned from Nikko, bringing Elder Chadwick with him, so I went back to headquarters.

Saturday, 12 September 1908, Tokyo

Cloudy—Warmer—Later Rain Up at 6:30. Spent the greater part of the forenoon housecleaning. Just before dinner I went to the offices of the Nippon Yusen Kwaisha to complete arrangements for Elders Woodland & Chadwick's cabin. After dinner, I worked on the Book of Mormon translation and wrote a letter to Elder Anderson. In the evening I prepared for Sunday School and other meetings.

Sunday, 13 September 1908, Tokyo

Cloudy—Rain nearly all day—Warm Up at 6:30. Ate breakfast. Sunday School was very small. Held sacrament meeting with only three saints and the missionaries Ate dinner. Consulted with Bro. Chiba about the Book of Mormon translation and then related to him three interesting testimonies that appeared in the Millennial Star of recent arrival. This talk and discussion took the entire afternoon. Ate supper and then presided over the evening meeting. This being Elders Woodland and Chadwick's last Sunday in Japan the were given most of the time in both the saints meeting and the evening preaching meeting.

Monday, 14 September 1908, Tokyo

Clear—Warm Up at 7:00. Spent most of the day working on the Book of Mormon translation. In the evening we had a special supper for Elders Woodland and Chadwick who leave for America on Wednesday next.

Tuesday, 15 September 1908, Tokyo

Clear—Warm Up at 6:30. After breakfast, I went to Mr. Ikuta's and held with him a long discussion about the Book of Mormon translation. Returned to headquarters and worked till supper time on the Book of Mormon. After supper talked with two young men who came to say good-bye to the brethren who leave tomorrow.

Wednesday, 16 September 1908, Tokyo

Clear—Warm—Later rain. Up at 6:30. Swept the downstairs rooms. Ate breakfast. Then went out to tend to some business. Arriving at Shimbashi station in time to accompany my companions to Yokohama. But Elder Woodland's baggage did not arrive in time. I waited and took it on the next train. It got to the depot just in time to catch the fatal train by a hair's breadth. Had it been thirty seconds later Elder Woodland would have left Japan without his baggage. The brethren were comfortably located in a well located cabin and the steamer, "Iyo Maru," left just at 2:00 p.m. I returned to headquarters attending to a little business on the way.

Friday, 18 September 1908, Tokyo

Cloudy—Hot Up at 6:30. Spent the forenoon working on the Book of Mormon. In the afternoon my nose gave me so much trouble that I could not work. I walked to two of the saints homes to inform them of the change in hour for the sacrament meeting. I thought the walk would help me out, but it didn't. I retired early feeling quite out of sorts more pained in feelings than in reality because my running nose had caused me to lose half a days work.

Saturday, 19 September 1908, Tokyo

Cloudy—Warmer. Up at 7:00. Spent the forenoon at Dr. Okada's having my nose examined and at headquarters discussing translation questions with Mr. Ikuta In the afternoon I worked on the translation The evening also was taken up in the same labor.

Sunday, 20 September 1908, Tokyo

Clear—Warm Up at 6:30. Ate breakfast. Presided over the Sunday School which was smaller than normal. Ate dinner and studied a little. At 2:00 p.m. I presided over the sacrament meeting. Only the missionaries and saints at headquarters were present. The lack of diligence in some of the members is very, very distressing. Took a walk. Ate supper. Presided over and preached in the night meeting.

Tuesday, 22 September 1908, Tokyo

Cloudy—Some Rain & Mild. Up at 6:25. Spent the day at headquarters working on the Book of Mormon translation. In the afternoon, however, some time was spent at the home of Sister Rin Ota, who had written a letter requesting to be forgotten among the saints. After my talk, she manifested a spirit of repentence. She was left to reflect seriously upon her condition.

Thursday, 24 September 1908, Tokyo

Rain—Cooler Up at 7:00. Spent all the forenoon on the Book of Mormon translation work. Afternoon I went to Dr. Okada's and had a small operation performed on one of my nostrils. The purpose of this operation was to keep me from suffering with nasal catarrah and colds in the head. After returning from the doctor's, I worked on the Book of Mormon again. Today Elder Caine finished his review of the translation as corrected by Mr. Hirai as far as Mr. Hirai went.

Saturday, 26 September 1908, Tokyo

Clear—Warmer Up at 6:30. Spent part of the forenoon at the doctors in the interest of my nose. The rest of the forenoon I spent reading the newspapers and magazines from America. In the Deseret News of September [blank] I noticed the following article regarding my father's retirement from the undertaker's profession. . . .

This is the most delightful piece of news I have had for a long time as it has been one of my strong standing desires that father retire from the labor of so streneous a life as he has led. Now that the desire has been realized the difficulty of fully realizing that it is a fact presses upon me. The attempt to picture him in any other position than the director of funerals and caretaker of the dead is quit an impossible task. The news seems too good to be true. But may the rest that this retirement will afford prolong his years on the earth. My brother Samuel having become head of the large farm I wish him great success that the good reputation and standing of the business built by my father may be perpetuated. The question as to who the "& Co." part of the new regime is, is still unknown to me.

In the afternoon I did some work on the Book of Mormon and in the evening I prepared for Sunday.

Thursday, 1 October 1908, Tokyo

Clear—Warm Up at 6:30. Spent the forenoon working on the Book of Mormon translation. The early hours of the afternoon were spent at Dr. Okada's. He performed a slight operation on my right nostril similiar to the one performed a week ago today on the left nostril. During the rest of the day I worked on the Book of Mormon and in the evening I discussed Sunday School work with Sister Tai.

Monday, 5 October 1908, Tokyo

Clear—Warm. Up at 6:20. Spent the forenoon and the afternoon in the interest of the Book of Mormon translation The early hours of the forenoon however, were devoted to giving my head a good scrubbing. Recently I have been troubled a little with pimples on my scalp. In the evening the regular Missionaries Bible Class was held.

Tuesday, 6 October 1908, Tokyo

Clear—Hot. Up at 6:30. Spent a hour and a half in the early morning getting some medicine put in my nose. Worked with my scalp a little while. Went to the American Embassy to find out if permission to board one or more of the American war ships while they are in Yokohama is to be obtained through the Embassy or otherwise. I was directed to the home of the Naval Attache but he not being at home, I had to return without finding out anything. Spent all of the afternoon and evening working on the Book of Mormon translation.

Thursday, 8 October 1908, Tokyo

Clear—Hot—Later Cloudy. Up at 7:30. Spent the forenoon trying to find out when permission to board the american warships while they are in Yokohama is to be obtained. Learned that such permission is given by the officers of each vessel. In the afternoon and evening I worked on the Book of Mormon. Took a walk before retiring.

Friday, 9 October 1908, Tokyo

Clear—Warm. Up at 6:30. Ate an early breakfast and went to Dr. Okada's. From there I went to the Hakubun Kwan Printing Co. to get them to make another bid on the printing of the Book of Mormon. Returned and began working on the translation. This work lasted till bedtime. Received word of a baptism in Sapporo.

Tuesday, 13 October 1908, Tokyo

Clear—Cool—Calm Up at 7:00. Spent the forenoon and most of the afternoon working on the Book of Mormon. Went to the home of Mr. Ijichi to see if he would rent his old home making some changes as we suggested a week ago. I was told that he had almost concluded to sell the house instead of rent it. After supper, I went to Bro. Kuga's and had a talk with him.

Wednesday, 14 October 1908, Tokyo

Clear—Cold. Up at 7:00. Spent the entire forenoon at headquarters working on the Book of Mormon and reading the American newspapers. Most of the afternoon was spent down town inquiring for a house suitable for Mission headquarters, consulting the printers about the printing of the Book of Mormon, buying a hat etc. In the evening, I worked again on the translation.

Friday, 16 October 1908, Tokyo

Cloudy—Cold. Up at 7:15. Spent the majority of the day working on the Book of Mormon translation. In the evening I took a walk calling on the Kataoka family to inquire about the health of their little girl, Kotomi, who was reported sick. She is now recovered. In the evening, after supper, I attended the Bible Class conducted by Elder Caine. Today Bro. & Sister Thomas went to Yokohama where they will stay for a day or two viewing the American Fleet which is due to arrive on the 17th and stay in Yokohama for one week. However, a "goywai"[13] this evening announced that the fleet will be a day late.

Monday, 19 October 1908, Tokyo

Clear—Warm Up at 7:00 Spent the forenoon discussing Book of Mormon questions with Mr. Ikuta at headquarters. In the afternoon, I did a little on the translation work. Cleaned and pressed some of my clothes. Talked with the elders from Kōfu and enjoyed very much their recital of the blessings of the Lord upon them in their work. Their happiness gives happiness to me and I praise the Father for his manifold blessings.

Tuesday, 20 October 1908, Tokyo

Cloudy—Warmer Up at 6:15. Ate breakfast. With the elders went to Yokohama and tried to meet Lieut. Commander H. A. Pearson but he was directing the coaling of his vessel and could not meet us. We were permitted to go on board the US.S. Nebraska by Ensign R. R. Smith who is a Utah boy having received his appointment from Senator Smoot. A sailor was called to conduct us over the fleet. I enjoyed what we were permitted to see and got my first real knowledge of a war ship. The steam launch belonging to the steamer took us out and also landed us. The sixteen white vessels forming the fleet are certainly very beautiful to look at and it makes one proud of the nation they represent. The Japanese reception fleet consisting of sixteen vessels also presented a formidable appearances, but they being painted in their war color were not as attractive to the eye. The elaborate decorations, the free drinks, rides shows, presents and entertainments extended to the offices and men of the fleet are perhaps the greatest demonstration of their kind every shown to a foreign guest. Especially is this cordial and elaborate reception significant when one remembers the wild rumors of war between the U.S. and Japan which filled American and European papers only a few months ago. The American vessals are not the black omens of war. They are the white messengers of peace. Returned to Tokyo in time for 6 o'clock supper and after an early bath retired. By letter Lieut. Pearson invited us all to visit him on Thursday afternoon By letter I accepted the invitation.

Thursday, 22 October 1908, Tokyo

Cloudy—Warm. Up at 6:30. Ate breakfast and read a little. With five of my brethren went to Yokohama. Went out to the battleship "Illinois" and met Lieutenat Commander H. A. Pearson from Draper Utah. He received us cordially and took great pains to explain all the machinery of the ships to us. Especially did he make the inspection of the 13 inch gun terrets minute and interesting. At his direction, I opened the breach of a 13 inch gun and sighted it getting a dead aim on one of the Japanese battle ships lying off in the distance. It would be useless for me to attempt a repition of what we saw and heard. The wonders connected with these big guns are very numerous. We were shown everything about them except the actual firing. We were taken into the shell and powder store rooms, the engine and boiler rooms, the storing rooms all around the gun deck, and then through the officers apartments. The only things we didn't see on the "Illinois" we had seen two days before on the "Nebraska." He treated us to mineral water. I gave him "The Mikado's Empire" in two volumes.[14] We were taken to the ship from the shore and from the ship to the shore in the steam launch belonging to the battleship. I took the first train for Tokyo reaching headquarters in good time for supper. Did a little on the Book of Mormon.

Friday, 30 October 1908, Tokyo

Cloudy—Cold—Calm. Up at 7:00. Spent the day at work on the Book of Mormon translation. Took a good walk for exercise before going to bed.

Saturday, 31 October 1908, Tokyo

Cold—Rain all day. Up at 6:00. Spent the forenoon cleaning house and searching for a new headquarters. After dinner I read the Bible and prepared the outline for work in the First Intermediate Department during the coming month. Called on Sister Ota to influence her if possible to repent of her neglect of duty. In the evening talked a little and exercised.

Sunday, 1 November 1908, Tokyo

Clear—Cold—Calm. Up at 7:00. Presided over the Sunday School and also over the teachers and officers meeting. At 2:00 p.m. our fast meeting was held. The absence of over half the members who live in Tokyo was a matter of disappointment. Had a short discussion with Bro. Chiba about the Book of Mormon translation. Talked with our landlord, learning that he is going to make such extensive changes around us and even in our house, that we cannot stand to live here while the work is going on and do not care to live here after his changes are made. This makes the old question of moving one of great importance. They say the Mormon never move till they have to. We are now in a position where we have to move. After supper, the evening meeting was held but the attendance was very small. I engaged Mr. Suzuki in conversation.

Tuesday, 3 November 1908, Tokyo

Cloudy—Cold. Up at 7:00. Today being the Emperor's birthday there was held on the parade grounds in front of headquarters the annual fall military review by his Majesty. The forenoon I spent working on the Book of Mormon translation and the afternoon I spent hunting a house for the headquarters. Didn't find anything that was at all suitable. In the evening I worked again on the translation.

Thursday, 5 November 1908, Tokyo

Clear—Warmer Up at 7:15. Spent the day at headquarters working on the Book of Mormon. After dinner I called on Mr. Taniuchi to see if I could not rent his two houses just below us. He called in the evening and said we could not. When I got back from Mr. Taniuchi's there was a man at headquarters to see if he could not arrange to make two houses into one large one for us. Knowing the place I answered "no." At about 4:30 I left for Oshima Machi where I spent a pleasant evening with Bro. Chiba and the family with whom he is living. The entire family gathered around the hibachi and for at least an hour and a half sit and listened attentively to a talk on the work of Jesus. In fact, it was at the request of the family that I talked to them as I had only intended to visit with Bro. Chiba and ask him some questions relative to the Book of Mormon translation. I reached headquarters at 10:20 p.m. Retired with a heart filled with gratitude for the blessing of the day.

Friday, 6 November 1908, Tokyo

Clear—Warm. Up at 7:00. Spent part of the forenoon looking at a house in Haramachi Ushigome Ku. Was delighted with it in every particular, and prayed earnestly in my heart that the Lord would touch the heart of the owner and incline his heart so towards us that he would make the rent within the limit we can afford to pay. The owner not being at home, I arranged to meet him tomorrow at which time he is to tell me how much the rent will be. In the afternoon I worked on the translation of the Book of Mormon.

Monday, 9 November 1908, Tokyo

Clear—Cold wind Up at 7:00 Spent the forenoon hunting for a house Also in the afternoon I went down town to see if the company I asked to get one for us had been at all successful in its searches. It had not. Returned and did a little on the translation. After supper, we all discussed the question of moving and decided between one of Koyama's houses and the one I saw in Sendagaya yesterday morning. The decision was in favor of the Sendagaya house. This discussion took all the evening and therefore the Bible Class was postponed.

Tuesday, 10 November 1908, Tokyo

Clear—Cold. Up at 7:15. Spent the greater part of the day working on the Book of Mormon translation. Immediately after breakfast, I went to the Sendagaya house and had a talk about building the kitchen over so it will be convenient to our use of opening holes in two of the walls for stove pipes; of making the rent cheaper etc. the person with whom I talked could not decide the questions. The decision was therefore deferred for a day. Before dinner I called at Mr. Togo's home in Koyama and told them we had decided not to rent their house. Before supper I walked for an hour. After supper investigated Book of Mormon references. Took exercise, and a bath before retiring.

Wednesday, 11 November 1908, Tokyo

Cloudy—Very Cold Up at 7:00. Swept the down stairs rooms. Devoted a majority of the day to work on the Book of Mormon reference review. The investigation of the correctness of the references is quite a job and I find that this careful investigation is necessary for there are many mistakes and references that would rather confuse than help the Japanese. In the evening, before supper, Elder Caine and I went to see a house for rent. The house was a beauty but it was located "out of civilization," hence no good for us. At noon today we held our prayer meeting and asked the Lord to help us out of the distress we are in over the moving question. After supper I discussed Book of Mormon translation questions with Bro. Chiba.

Thursday, 12 November 1908, Tokyo

Clear but cold Up at 7:10. Spent the forenoon at headquarters working on the Book of Mormon and reading papers from America. After dinner, I went to the sendagaya house to see afbout changing the kitchen to suit our purposes, if we move to this house. In the evening before supper I worked again on the Book of Mormon investigating the references. After supper I called on Mr. Matsuno a man I met first when I was laboring in Chiba City four years or more ago. He is now a judge and has his family with him here in Tokyo.

Friday, 13 November 1908, Tokyo

Clear—Cold Up at 6:50. Spent the forenoon visiting the Shueisha in the interest of the Book of Mormon publication I asked them for a bid which they promised to have at headquarters by tomorrow night. The last time I called there and asked for a bid they promised one but not being able to begin such a job this year they answered that they desired the bid to be made next year when the work could begin at which time the price of material might be higher or lower. This is a hard part of the year to get printing done. In the afternoon I worked on the Book of Mormon references and gave the contract for remodeling the kitchen in the Sendagaya house to a carpenter whom I took to see the house early this morning. In the evening, I went to Koishikawa and solicited the services of Mr. Iwano a man who is closely connected with the owner of the the Ushigome house we want to rent, asking him to see if he can't persuade the owner to rent it. He agreed and will give the result of his efforts by 11 o'clock Sunday so we can know what to announce to the Sunday School. After returning had Mr. Taue write the sign for sunday night meeting and four names for the Sunday School roll.

Saturday, 14 November 1908, Tokyo

Clear—Cold. Up at 7:00. Made out some advertizements of our removal. Did a little figuring in connection with the printing of the Book of Mormon. Estimated that there will not be over [a] 1000 pages in the book and that a 5,000 edition will not cost much over ¥2,000.00 This estimate is made on the basis of a new bid from the Toyo Printing Co and one from the Shueisha Printing Co. Did several odd jobs in connection with our contemplated move next week. In the evening Mr Ikuta called. He did a little job on the Mission Records.

Wednesday, 18 November 1908, Tokyo

Clear—Warmer Up at 6:30. Spent most of the day trotting here and there getting the last touches of the removal preparations finished. At noon we held the last prayer meeting at Kasumigaokamachi. In the evening an English Bible Class was held by Elder Thomas.

Thursday, 19 November 1908, Tokyo

Clear—Warm—Calm. Up at 6:00. Today Mission Headquarters was moved to its new home #870 Sendagayamachi Tokyo Fu This has therefore been a very, very busy day for all of us. I received the goods at the new place and by dark was exceedingly tired with the long hard lift of the day. Quite unexpectedly, we found the new quarters in quite a filthy condition and therefore I was pretty well in the dirt all day and made a record for high climbs and deep digging. We employed eight rigs to haul our chattels and keep the eight men and two horses on the jump from 7:30 a.m. to 4:30 p.m. when the last load was dropped at its destination. This is the first house moving that I have ever taken part in and I find that it is quit a job especially when the thing to be moved is a mission headquarters and the time limit one day. No accidents happened, nothing was lost and there were no scratches on the precious things. There were plenty on the other things. The new home is a strictly Japanese house with 1 ten mat room 1 six mat room, 5 eight mat rooms, 2 four and a half mat rooms, and 2 three mat rooms. The kitchen is three times as large as the one in the old home and it has a fine store room of about 12 mats, but the mats are not in In their place is a good floor which also has a large dry space underneath. The garden is a beauty with grass and pretty walk, a summer house and flower bushes. A vegetable garden is attached. We have a fine bath, a pretty good well, a large coal and wood house, /and/ an outdoor store house. There are two enterances, one private and the other public. Electric light and gas for heating purposes. Three closets and in general every convenience The heating however is quite a question as gas is quite high and the house so built that we can't put up stoves very well except in the kitchen. The neighborhood at present is not particularly good for missionary work but it is no worse than where we have been. Leaving the old home where the "Mormons" have lived for over seven years was not without considerable feelings a regret at the parting, but with the feeling also that the move was the proper thing. Retired very much fatigued.

Friday, 20 November 1908, Tokyo

Clear—Warm Up at 6:30. Did not sleep well last night. It has been found in our experience that generally the first visitor after a move is a "night visitor" so I besides being too tired to rest well was listening for the stealthy footsteps of the burglar. A rat was the only intruder. Spent the day attending to business all over the city. Among other things, I called at our old landlord's home and made my formal farewell speech and fixed up all money matters between him and me. There is a custom in Japan which says a new comer shall take a small present (always something to eat) to his nearest neighbors and ask for their good will. So this evening, after supper I started out on the tour of our neighbors but most of their gates were locked and I had to postpone the etiquette for another day. Retired, more worn out than yesterday.

Saturday, 21 November 1908, Tokyo

Clear—Warm Up at 6:30. Went to Yotsuya to make some purchases, returned and worked around the house laying matting, mending locks, studying how to use the bath tub (I have never seen such a tub before), directing the carpenter, etc. In speaking of the house I have failed thus far to mention that it is situated outside of the city limits in what is known as Tokyo Fu. A Fu is a district which includes a city and its suberbs. Only the four largest places in Japan have reached the rank of Fu. Took a bath and retired quite ready for a good rest. Today's work has put nearly everything in good order, so that we are ready for the Sabbath with its duties and its rest.

Monday, 23 November 1908, Tokyo

Clear—Warm Up at 6:30. Today I dusted swept and scrubbed. Was nearly exhausted by bed time. However, today we had a fine surprise. Elders Jay C. Jensen and Wm S. Ellis dropped in on us as a living message from Zion. In the forenoon I received a letter from the Presidency's Office stating that they had been set apart, but we did not expect them so soon. The brought good news and packages for many of the elders. Elder Jensen had two visits with my folks before he left and brought the good news that they are in health and seem happy. He comes from Heber City where one of my sisters is living. From her he brought a letter and a box of silk handkerchiefs.

Sunday, 29 November 1908, Tokyo

Clear—Cold—Windy Up at 6:30. Today we had a fine Sunday School. There were 63 present. The first announcement of Christmas was made and those who will take part on the program were chosen and their parts assigned. The enthusiasm with which the children consented to the call to take part was indeed gratifying and an inspiration. There is a lesson taught in their willingness to do the best they can. Some of our elders could profit by this lesson. After the Sacrament meeting, I had a long talk with Brother Chiba about the priesthood and the duties accompanying it. The evening meeting was not largely attended but we had a peaceful spirit. Tracting in this district has only been carried on for one day so we are not yet advertized.

Saturday, 5 December 1908, Tokyo

Clear—Colder than usual Up at 7:00 Spent the entire day at headquarters writing. A letter from the First Presidency showed that they had not received my letter of Aug. 15, asking important questions about the mean/ing/ of some expressions in the Book of Mormon. I have been postponing [the] the work on the printing till their answer comes. There letter today which I thought would surely contain the answer so earnestly looked for made it clear that they had not received my letter so I am greatly disappointed. I restated the questions in another letter and /will/ send it tomorrow. Waiting till I can get an answer will throw the printing at least one and a half months late.

Tuesday, 8 December 1908, Tokyo

Clear—Cold—Wind Up at 6:15. Worked on the Book of Mormon for sometime in the forenoon and then consulted with Mr. Ikuta about translation questions. In the afternoon, I continued work on the translation. After supper listened to a reading of part of the last October General Conference Report. The sermons read were certainly full of the very finest advice and the Spirit of the Lord impressed them upon the walls of my heart.

Wednesday, 9 December 1908, Tokyo

Clear—Very Cold and windy. Up at 7:00. Spent the entire day working on the translation made fine progress. At noon we held prayer meeting. After supper, I went to Bro. Kuga's and had a talk with him about his condition. He is in hard circumstances temporally and has been neglecting his duty to such an extent that he is not receiving the blessings of God. I talked very plainly to him and told him how important it is for one in his condition to rely upon the Lord. He manifested a humble spirit.

Saturday, 19 December 1908, Tokyo

Clear—Warmer Up at 7:10. During the forenoon and part of the afternoon I worked on the Book of Mormon translation and then taught Japanese to Elders Jensen & Ellis In the evening, listened to the reading of a part of the 49th annual conference of the church held in Salt Lake City 1880, it being the 50th anniversary of the church's organization.

Sunday, 20 December 1908, Tokyo

Clear—Cold. Up at 7:00. Presided over the Sunday School, taught the First Intermediate Department, listened to some of the children practice their parts on the Christmas program. Ate dinner. Presided over the sacrament meeting, and taught the saints. Talked with Bro. Chiba. Ate supper Directed the evening meeting and did all the preaching.

Monday, 21 December 1908, Tokyo

Clear—Cold Wind. Up at 7:15. Spent the entire day writing Santa Claus' speech for Christmas and teaching Japanese to the two new brethren. Didn't go out of the house all day.

Tuesday, 22 December 1908, Tokyo

Clear—Cold—Wind. Up at 7:00. Finished Santa Claus' speech today and taught Japanese to Elders Ellis and Jensen. Did two or three odd jobs.

Wednesday, 23 December 1908, Tokyo

Clear—Mild Up at 7:30. Went down town to do some shopping both for myself and for the Christmas Party Returned and had prayers with the brethren. The rest of the day was spent doing odd jobs.

Thursday, 24 December 1908, Tokyo

Fair—Cold Up at 7:30. Today I studied Santa's speech. Did several odd jobs. Among the rest fussed with the Christmas Tree. In the evening went out and bought a few things. Today the news of three baptisms at Sapporo reached us.

Friday, 25 December 1908, Tokyo

Beautiful, warm, sunshiny Christmas Day. Up at 7:00. Spent the forenoon studing Santa's part and getting ready for the evening party. After dinner went to Aoyama and rented 120 zabuton[15] for our guests. Ate bread & milk at 4:00 p.m. In the evening we held a very entertaining, instructive, and inspirational Christmas Party under the auspices of the Sunday School. These parties are the great events of our yearly work. Our home being arranged so that we could entertain more people than at the old place we issued over 180 invitations, but only a little over 120 responded. The children who furnished nearly all the numbers on the program were blessed in the rendition of their parts and the audience was very well pleased. The program consisted of songs, speeches, dialogues, magic lantern pictures all about Christ and then an hour with Santa Claus who was liberal with his gifts to the children I played Santa's part much to my own delight as well as the mirth of all present. The program lasted 3 ¾ hours. It was voted a big success and I hope the object for which we worked—the glory of God and the testimony of his truth—was attained. Retired with a thankful heart. Received a nice sofa-pillow from Mrs. Kiyo Umeda and two or three other presents.

Sunday, 27 December 1908, Tokyo

Rain all day—Cold. Up at 7:00. Prepared for Sunday School, which on account of the bad day was quite small. After school discussed a question relative to the personal appearance of the members of the Sunday School. Decided to take steps to clean the hands, feet, faces, heads and noses of some of our students. Talked to the saints and elders who assembled in Sacrament meeting. Addressed the night meeting. Talked with Mr. Tanimura

Monday, 28 December 1908, Tokyo

Clear—Cold. Up at 7:15. Spent the forenoon working on the Book of Mormon translation. Also wrote a long circular letter to the elders in the fields. Today at about 3:20 p.m. we sat down and enjoyed a fine turkey dinner prepared by Sisters Thomas and Nachie. In the evening we assembled in the large room and enjoyed a social time. We had songs and jokes, candy, nuts and cakes the latter and parts of the candy having come from America. We read two Christmas stories, lit the Christmas tree and enjoyed ourselves till nearly midnight.

Wednesday, 30 December 1908, Tokyo

Changeable—Warmer Up at 8:30. Woke up this morning with a severe pain in my abdomen. Went to bed. Got up at noon long enough to have prayer with my brethren and sister at noon. From about 3:00

p.m. till 1:00 a.m. the pain was quite severe. At five o'clock the elders administered to me. This pain may be the result of a Christmas dinner and it may also be the result of a slight cold settling in my abdomen. Later the pain went into my pelvic cavity where it was most severe.

Thursday, 31 December 1908, Tokyo

Clear—Warmer Up at 8:40. Spent the day working on the Book of Mormon and teaching the elders Japanese. Received letters from Kōfu and Sapporo giving an interesting account of their Christmas exercises. The pain of yesterday and last night has not been felt today, but my abdomen is very sore.

Notes

1. Scrofulous deposits. Relating to tuberculosis of lymph nodes.

2. William George Aston, *A Grammar of the Japanese Written Language*, 2d ed. (Yokohama: Lane, Crawford & Co., 1877).

3. Waseda University. A private university located in Shinjuku Ward, Tōkyō. Established in 1882 by Ōkuma Shigenobu as the Tōkyō Semmon Gaddō. Renamed Waseda in 1902. "Waseda," *Japan: An Illustrated Encyclopedia*, 2:1688.

4. Cimeter. See Book of Mormon references: Enos 1:20; Mosiah 9:16, 10:8; Alma 2:12, 27:29, 43:18, 20, 37, 44:8, 60:2; Helaman 1:14.

5. Presiding Bishopric. "The Presiding Bishopric consists of three men, the Presiding Bishop and his two counselors, who comprise one of the presiding councils of The Church of Jesus Christ of Latter-day Saints. These General Authorities, who each hold the office of bishop, serve in their positions under the direct supervision of the First Presidency. Since its formation, the Presiding Bishopric has been responsible for many of the temporal affairs of the Church. These have included involvement in receiving, distributing, and accounting for member tithes, offerings, and contributions; administration of programs to assist the poor and needy; design, construction, and maintenance of places of worship; and auditing and transferring records of membership." H. David Burton and Wm. Gibb Dyer, Jr., "Presiding Bishopric," *Encyclopedia of Mormonism*, 3:1128.

6. *Amado*. Rain shutter.

7. See Book of Mormon, Alma 40–45.

8. Prophecies regarding the last days and the Second Coming of Jesus Christ.

9. Parley P. Pratt, *A Voice of Warning and Instruction to All People, or, An Introduction to the Faith and Doctrine of the Church of Jesus Christ of Latter-day Saints* (Liverpool: F. D. Richards, 1854).

10. *Ika*. Squid.

11. *Shokonsai*. A festival held to honor the spirits of the war dead.

12. Moiwa Mountain.

13. *Goywai*. Unable to discern meaning.

14. A later edition of William Elliot Griffis, *The Mikado's Empire* (New York: Harper, 1883).

15. *Zabuton*. Pillow used for sitting on the floor.

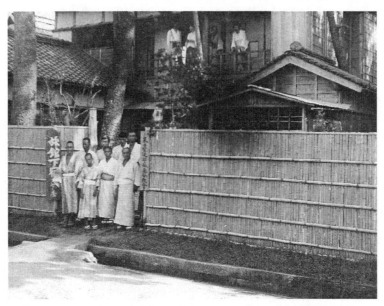

Japanese members and investigators standing outside an early church meeting house. Courtesy John W. Welch.

Alma O. Taylor (center) and Louis A. Kelsch (right), in kimonos, meet with a friend. Courtesy John W. Welch.

Chapter 13

Alma O. Taylor Journal, 1909–10

Friday, 1 January 1909, Tokyo

Clear—Windy—Cold Up at 7:30. Spent the day at home working on reports. I felt quite well today, although my abdomen was still somewhat sore. There were a few New Year's callers

Saturday, 2 January 1909, Tokyo

Clear—Warm—Calm Up at 7:15. Visited Bro. Mori's mother in the forenoon Bought some New Year's cards and sent them off to friends and acquaintences. Spent the rest of the day with Bro. Chiba and friends at headquarters.

Tuesday, 5 January 1909, Tokyo.

Fair—Mild. Up at 7:20. Spent most of the day writing to Bro. Hachiro Mori. Yesterday a letter came from him. He requested to have his name taken off the Church records. The reason for such a request is that he has been studying various things in connection with the Bible since he went to Corea last Spring and not having a guide to keep him from getting wrong impressions and making wrong interpretations of the scriptures he has fallen into error on doctrine getting the strange thought that no one can be a Christian and still be loyal to Japan. His letter revealing this condition of his mind came as a thunder bolt from a clear sky for all during the past year Bro. Mori has written very fine spirited letters and paid his tithes regularly and honestly. May the Lord help us to properly lead him and bring him back to a proper understanding of the gospel. After dinner, I taught the new elders Japanese. After supper I started to write the letter to Bro. Mori in the characters.

Sunday, 10 January 1909, Tokyo

Cloudy—Cold Up at 7:00 Last night a fine snow storm waged making a beautiful landscape for us to see on getting up. Due to the bad streets we had a very small Sunday School. The saints meeting was very small and the preaching meeting at night was only just big enough to hold. I wrote a letter to the folks today also one to the First Presidency.

Wednesday, 13 January 1909, Tokyo

Cold—Snow. Up at 7:00. Mr. Ikuta came today and discussed with me about some translation questions. Today he returned the last of the part of the translation which was criticized by Mr. Hirai. This is to the end of III Nephi 3 chapter. He now begins to do the work which Mr. Hirai was not permitted to finish—the changing of my translation from gembuchitai to buntai from III Nephi 4 chapter to the end. May he enjoy the blessings of the Lord in his work and bring it to a successful and speedy close. After dinner I went to the Shueisha Printing Co. to get a bid on the second edition of our Hymn Book. Also called at Yotsuya and attended to a little business there. Read in the evening.

Thursday, 14 January 1909, Tokyo

Rain—Snow—Warmer Up at 7:00. Spent the forenoon doing business down town. The afternoon was devoted to teaching Japanese and letter writing. Received word from Sapporo, that two young ladies were baptized there on the 7th inst. After supper listened to a very interesting talk on the culture of bees by Elder Ellis. Then worked a little on the Book of Mormon translation.

Sunday, 17 January 1909, Tokyo

Clear—Warmer—Calm Up at 7:00. Spent the day pleasantly at headquarters. Presided over the three meetings held at our home. Taught the First Intermediate Department in Sunday School. Spoke to the saints in sacrament meeting and also addressed the evening meeting. In sacrament meeting Bro. Yasubeiye Chiba was ordained to the office of a Priest I being mouth in the ordination. This is the first ordination to the priesthood every made in the Japanese language so far as this mission is concerned and I doubt if the Japanese language has ever been used in ordaining anyone in any other land. Bro Chiba is the first one to receive the priesthood in the last six years. At present there is only one native member in the mission who besides Bro. Chiba, holds the priesthood. That is Bro. Saburo Kikuchi who is an elder. Hajime Nakazawa was ordained an elder and Yoshiro Oyama was ordained a priest but both of these have apostatized. Bro. Kikuchi altho ordained seven years ago has never magnified his calling. The failure of those who had already received the priesthood to honor it, and other reasons which are too numerous to mention here has made me feel very very delicate about giving the priesthood to the male native members. But Bro. Chiba has manifested a good spirit for a long time. His humility and willingness to receive and obey counsel have made me decide to give him the priesthood which I have done with the sincere desire that God will bless him with all the power and privileges which his priesthood entitles him to.

Tuesday, 19 January 1909, Tokyo

Rain—Cold—Later a warm south wind. Up at 6:45. Spent the day on the Book of Mormon translation. Taught Japanese to Elder Jensen and Ellis. After supper Elder Jensen and I called on Bro. Kuga and Sister Kawabe. At supper time a letter was received from Bro. Mori acknowledging receipt of my long letter to him answering his request that his name be taken off from the Church records. The letter received today repeated his request and the main point of his argument this time is that if a person does right in the present that is all that is necessary and such future hopes as Christ's second coming etc. should not occupy the minds of men. He also insists upon being opposed to any and everything that threatens to rise about the empire of Japan in power. Infering that he wants no supreme rule of Christ above his country.

Wednesday, 27 January 1909, Tokyo

Clear—Warm Up at 7:15. Spent the forenoon investigating the references in the Book of Mormon. At noon had prayer meeting and then taught Elders Ellis and Jensen Japanese. While doing this a letter from the First Presidency containing answers to two important questions relative to the Book of Mormon was received. (See Letter Book B page 414 for my letter and same book, page 407 for a copy of the Presidency's letter). This being the letter for which I have been looking for a long time I was greatly delighted. In harmony with the instructions contained in it, I made some changes in the first part of the translation and prepared the first two books of the manuscript to go to the printer's. This preparation kept me busy till about 10:00 p.m. The joy coming from the thought that the printing cont/ra/ct could now be made made me so happy that I had to take some exercises to quiet my nerves before retiring

Thursday 28 January 1909, Tokyo

Up at 7:00 Spent most of the forenoon making the contract with the Shueisha Printing Company for the printing of 5,000 copies of the Japanese Book of Mormon This company made a bid on the job some time ago. Today a new bid was made on the estimate that there will be 1,000 pages in the book and that it have a good cloth binding. The amount of the bid is ¥2,150. I accepted this bid and left the first book of the manuscript in the printer's hands he giving the promise that work will begin on the type-setting in three or four days. The book should appear in its completed form in less than six months but in not less than four months. In the afternoon, I taught Japanese to two of the elders and then worked on the Book of Mormon references. In the evening, Sister Thomas and I called on Sister Ota.

Friday, 29 January 1909, Tokyo

Clear—Windy—Bitter Cold. Up at 7:00. After breakfast went to Mr. Ikuta's in the interest of the

Book of Mormon translation. In the afternoon, I taught Japanese to Elders Ellis and Jensen and worked on the Book of Mormon references. I succeeded in completing the investigation of the references as they are given in the English. I have found that there are a number of mistakes, typographical and otherwise. I have also found that there are some comments made which are unnecessary in the Japanese translation and also find some that I have taken the liberty to change because I have considered the change necessary in presenting the same ideas to the Japanese readers. The time spent in this review has born its fruit. I feel that my care to be sure that each reference is correct before translating it, has been approved of God and entirely profitable. I have already translated and inserted into the Japanese translation all the references down to the end of page 400. This evening, I went with Elder Harris and had supper at Mr. Kuniharu Yashiro's home. Also spent a pleasant evening with him.

Sunday, 31 January 1909, Tokyo

Clear—Calm—Much warmer than yesterday Up at 7:00 Taught the First Intermediate Department of the Sunday School and presided over the general exercises of the whole School. Wrote a little and studied the scriptures for an hour on the subject of marriage which subject I discussed in the sacrament meeting held in the afternoon at 2:00 o'clock. Had a brief discussion with Bro Chiba relative to some points in the Book of Mormon translation and then gave him some advice relative to some relations he has formed as a forerunner to marriage. The customs of Japan which control the relation of the sexes before marriage are a great barrier to the fostering of true affection and deep love between those who marry. The marriage contract being in most cases made by a middle man, the real parties seldom know anything of what they ought to know about each other before they become man and wife. Thus marriage in Japan is in very many cases a great disaster to both parties—Divorce is exceedingly common. The customs regarding this most sacred covenant are so bad that its sacredness is nearly all lost and its obligation is not always truly felt. This to me is a very regretable condition and I hope to persuade all the young saints to firm belief and knowledge that marriage is one of the most weighty sacraments in the great plan of God and must be performed as nearly as possible with his holy laws regarding it. Ate supper and then presided over the evening meeting. Also spoke briefly.

Tuesday, 2 February 1909, Tokyo

Cloudy—Warmer. Up at 7:00. Sent a telegram to Kōfu instructing the elders to pay the taxes demanded. Commenced to review that part of the Book of Mormon translation that Mr. Ikuta is changing from gembunitchitai to bunsho. This review is the most important of all and requires much time and close application of thought. Taught Japanese to Elders Ellis and Jensen. Washed the bath and bath room. Did more on the translation in the late afternoon and evening. Mrs. Baba spent considerable time at headquarters today. I met and talked with her just a little.

Just on going to bed this evening a letter came from Bro. Hachiro Mori. He has not been affected by my second letter and states that his determination to leave the church has not changed in the least. He refuses to receive further communications on the question. This is truly a sad message. But apostacy cannot hurt God's work even if the apostate be one who has been looked upon as a support and model saint. There must be something, still unknown to us, in Bro. Mori's life that has caused him to so suddenly sever all connections with the Church. May God be merciful to him.

Wednesday, 3 February 1909, Tokyo

Clear—Warm—Later rain. Up at 8:00. Spent the forenoon working on the Book of Mormon translation. At 12:00 we held prayer meeting. At this meeting, I reviewed the correspondence between Bro. Hachiro Mori and myself in relation to his withdrawal from the Church. The purpose for making this review was that my brethren could understand the situation and if called upon to sit in council be able to speak and act properly. I went to the printers after teaching Japanese to Elders Ellis and Jensen. Mr. Iida said the sample proofs of the typesetting for Book of Mormon had just been mailed. Returned and did some more work on translation and after supper attended the English Bible Class.

Friday, 5 February 1909, Tokyo

Clear—Warmer Up at 7:15. Went to Mr. Ikuta's expecting to consult Book of Mormon translation questions with him but he had gone to Yokohama to attend the funeral of a relative. I returned to headquarters then went down town. I had two teeth filled. Attended to other business and got back just in time for dinner. In the afternoon I taught Japanese to two of the elders and then wrote to Elder Seely. After supper I went to Mr. Yashiro's and asked if he could recommend someone to help the rest of the work on the Book of Mormon such as copying corrected translation and reading proof sheets. He mentioned one man whom he promised to send around to consult with me. I called on Sister Kawabe on the way home and had a long talk with her.

Sunday, 7 February 1909, Tokyo

Fair—Warm Up at 7:00. Directed the Sunday School, taught the first Intermediate Department and wrote a letter. Presided over the Fast Meeting. In the meeting Bro. Yasubeiye Chiba took part in administering the Sacrament. He blessed the water. This is the first time any Japanese has taken part in the ordinance in the native language. Ate supper. Presided over and addressed the evening meeting.

Thursday, 11 February 1909, Tokyo

Cloudy—Warm south wind Up at 7:00. Today Mr. Hiroyuki Namekawa, the man suggested by Mr. Yashiro last Friday night as suitable for our work during the publication of the Book of Mormon, came and began to work in the Mission's service as, proofreader, translation copier, sub-critic, letter writer etc. I worked all day on the translation, with the exception of an hour or two in the afternoon which was used in going down town.

Saturday, 13 February 1909, Tokyo

Clear—Warm Up at 6:45. Spent the day working on the Book of Mormon. Today the first 16 pages of the Book of Mormon in type were received for proof-reading. This therefore marks the beginning of the actual work of printing. I looked over these 16 pages once along. Then Mr. Namekawa read them aloud while Elder Caine and I followed the printer's manuscript and the corrected manuscript from which the printer's manuscript was taken. I returned these proof sheets in the evening by mail. Studied lesson for Sunday School. Took a bath and retired. In the late afternoon, I taught Japanese to Elders Jensen and Ellis.

Wednesday, 17 February 1909, Tokyo

Clear—Colder—Windy Up at 6:45. Spent most of the day on the Book of Mormon translation. Was discussing translation questions with Mr. Ikuta all afternoon. In the evening taught Japanese to Elders Jensen and Ellis and wrote to the elders in the out fields. In our prayer and council meeting held at noon, on the motion of Elder Fred A. Caine seconded by Elder Elbert D. Thomas, Hachiro Mori was excommunicated by an unanimous vote of all the elders present. The charge being apostacy.

Monday, 22 February 1909, Tokyo

Fair—Warmer. Up at 6:00 Scrubbed the veranda. Spent the greater part of the day and evening reviewing Elder Caine's article prepared as an introduction to the Book of Mormon and also as an evidence for its divinity and a weapon for its defense. In the forenoon I visited the printers in the interest of the Book of Mormon publication.

Tuesday, 23 February 1909, Tokyo

Fair—Warm Up at 7:00 Worked on the article which Elder Caine has written in explanation, defense & introduction of the Book of Mormon. Finished reading and making suggestions on the same. This article is a very able one indeed. The Lord has greatly assisted its preparation and I hope he will continue his blessings upon its translation and publication. In the afternoon, I worked on Translation work. Wrote to Elder Anderson calling him to Tokyo to review and publish his translation of Dr. Talmage's essay, "Lord of All." Took a walk before going to bed.

Wednesday, 24 February 1909, Tokyo

Fair—Cold wind. Up at 7:00. Spent the day working on the Book of Mormon translation and proof sheet reading. At noon our regular Wednesday fast and prayer meeting was held. In the evening I took a walk inviting some of the members of my class in the Sunday School to attend a party to be given for the class at headquarters next Saturday.

Today Mr. Ikuta came reporting his findings on a grammatical question which Mr. Namekawa brought up and which if as Mr. Namekawa explained would greatly affect the Book of Mormon translation. The answer of Mr. Ikuta was based on the opinions and statements of such men as Tsubouchi, Natsume and other famous novelist & poets and vindicated the use of certain verb endings appearing in the translation. This question when first raised caused me no little concern but I am satisfied that Mr. Ikuta's remarks are correct & the translation above criticism on the point attacked by Mr. Namekawa.

Tuesday, 16 March 1909, Tokyo

Cloudy—Cold Up at 7:20. Spent the day at headquarters working on proof-sheets. After supper, I called on Bro. Kuga. He has just met with more trouble. On the 3rd of March a letter reached him from his younger sister stating that she was going to kill herself and requested him to look after her baby. Since the reception of the letter diligent search has been made for her body but has not yet been found. Bro. Kuga has the child at his home. He looks upon this disaster as a fulfillment of my words to him last year when I told him if he did not return to God with full purpose of heart and obey his laws as he covenanted to do by baptism, that greater distress would overtake him than that he was then experiencing. He manifested a desire to return to the Lord this evening. I pray that his actions will accord with his desire and he will from now on be a brother in very deed.

Wednesday, 24 March 1909, Tokyo

Cloudy—Cold. Up at 7:15. Worked on the Book of Mormon during the early forenoon. Later I went to Mrs. Saito's to see what she had done about putting electric lights in the [new] house /we expect to rent from her/ and to see what she had decided about the agreement I wrote and presented to her. She suggested a few additions & one change to which I consented. I took the papers to headquarters to have them rewritten. Went to the house in Ushigome and met the contractor who is building and making changes there. Returned to headquarters in time to hold prayers before supper. Worked on the Book of Mormon in the evening.

Friday, 26 March 1909, Tokyo

Clear—Warm—Windy Up at 7:00 Went to Mrs. Saitō's and signed the agreement of lease between her and me for her house & lot located at 81 Yakuojimae Machi Ushigome Ku. Spent the rest of the day working on the Book of Mormon translation.

Saturday, 27 March 1909, Tokyo

Clear—Warmer Up at 6:45. Went to Ushigome to meet with Mrs. Saito and the electrician and decide on the lights. Called at the printers and got a copy of the first 64 pages of the Japanese Book of Mormon as they have been printed to go in the book. It is indeed a gratifying sight to look at these pages—a foretaste of the intense joy I expect to experience when the finished book comes to hand. It was late when I got home. I did some work on the translation and then taught two of the elders Japanese.

Thursday, 1 April 1909, Tokyo

Cloudy—Cold Up at 7:15. Spent the forenoon working on the Book of Mormon translation. After an early dinner I went to the Shueisha to talk about the Book of Mormon printing. Went from there to

Dr. Komoto's with Elder Ellis who is having his eyes treated. Then went to Dr. Obata's to have my teeth repaired. Then went to the tailor's and tried on some new clothes. From there I went to the Seibundo[1] to see about the printing of two blank record books to be used in the Mission. Bought an umbrella and returned to headquarters getting there about 7:30 p.m. Ate supper and did an odd job or two before retiring.

Sunday, 4 April 1909, Tokyo

Cloudy—Quite Warm Up at 7:00 Directed the Sunday School and taught the First Intermediate Department. Presided in the Fast Meeting, which was a very fine one, and then read good news from the First Presidency. Their letter in answer to one I wrote on Feb 9th states that after my release, which they hint will be as soon as the Book of Mormon is published, that I may go to China and Korea for the purpose of looking over the field in the interest of missionary work and they advise taking Elder Fred A. Caine with me. They also grant a liberal amount of money for the advertizing of the Book of Mormon. In the evening I presided over the evening meeting which was the largest held in our Sendagaya house. Elder Caine spoke instructively and entertainingly on the subject, "What Kind of a Being Is God." Wrote my journal and retired.

Monday, 5 April 1909, Tokyo

Cloudy—Showers—Warm Up at 7:00. Spent the forenoon with my translation manuscripts. Ate an early breakfast and then went with Elder Ellis to the doctor's to have his eyes treated again and find out if he needed glasses. He said that he did not need glasses. We went directly from the doctor's to Tama River and witnessed the baptism of Tokujiro Taue a young man who has been studying the Gospel for a long time. Returned to headquarters where Bro. Taue was confirmed by Elder Elbert D. Thomas. The baptism was performed by Elder Fred A. Caine who has been very faithful in teaching Bro. Taue for over a year. In the evening I taught Japanese to Elders Ellis and Jensen.

Thursday, 8 April 1909, Tokyo

Clear—Wind Up at 6:30 Spent all the forenoon and a big part of the afternoon working on the Book of Mormon translation. After supper Elder Ellis and I left for Hokkaido. Went to bed on the train about 9:30.

Friday, 9 April 1909, Train

Clear—Warm Up at 7:00. Last night I did not sleep extra well but it was much better than a sitting position would have given. During the day on the train I did a little on the Book of Mormon translation work. We passed over a place where a recent wind and rain storm had destroyed many fields and a number of houses. We also saw the remains of the train which was blown off from the track just as it was nearing Aomori. We had a one hours wait at Aomori. Took passage on the "Ishikari Maru" for Muroran which sailed at 6:00 p.m. After supper I wrote a letter. Took some vigorous exercise before retiring.

Saturday, 10 April 1909, Ship

Cloudy—Rain—Colder Up at 5:30. The steamer entered Muroran harbor and cast anchor about 6:00 a.m. Elder Ellis and I landed, ate breakfast at the waiting rooms and took the 7:00 a.m. train for Sapporo where we arrived at about 1:45 p.m. When reaching the elders home received a hearty welcome and was glad to find them all in health. Chatted with them for some hours. Ate supper and then took a walk with Elder Marriott to inquire about his views regarding the work in Sapporo and vacinity.

Sunday, 11 April 1909, Sapporo

Cloudy—Cold—A little snow. Up at 7:00. Ate a toothsome breakfast. Attended the Sapporo Sunday School. Spoke briefly to the students. Ate dinner. Went with Elders Marriott and Cutler to the Toyohira Sunday School and Bible Class held in the afternoon. Spoke to the Bible Class students. Returned to Sapporo and ate supper. Attended the evening meeting and after listening to remarks by Elders Cutler,

Marriott, and Roskelley, I addressed the meeting for about thirty minutes. Took a walk with Elder Cutler having a private talk with him about the mission work. Retired about 10:45 p.m.

Monday, 12 April 1909, Sapporo

Clear—Warmer Up at 6:15. Took a walk with Elder [Seely] before breakfast. Also had a talk with Bro. Seely. After breakfast we held a brief meeting in which I investigated the actions of two of the elders in taking a trip in company with one of the young female saints. Gave some advice to the elders. After this meeting, I visited Bro. Kawanaka's family. Then held another meeting in which I released Elder Seely to return home and appointed Elder Marriott to preside in Sapporo. After this meeting I ate dinner and then started to the depot. On the way, I called at the Fukido Book store to see if they would be inclined to handle the Book of Mormon. They appeared favorable to the proposition but wanted to know more particulars than I was able to give. Took the 2:20 p.m. train and was on my way to Hakodate when sleep overtook me. On this trip, I met for the first time Sisters Tamano Kumagai, Chiyo Tanifuji and Ei Ogawa and Brother Takahashi.

Tuesday, 13 April 1909, Train

Clear—Strong wind—Cold Up at 3:15. Arrived at Hakodate about 3:45 a.m. Waited at the station till about 6:15 when I boarded the "Hirafu Maru" for Aomori. The sea was rough. Arrived at Aomori just in time to catch the train for Tokyo. At 7:15 p.m. reached Morioka. Met Bro. James Anderson at the station and had a chat with him for about fifteen minutes. Went to bed on the train at about 8:30.

Wednesday, 14 April 1909, Train

Clear—Warm Up at 7:00. Being fast day did not eat breakfast. Changed cars at Nippori about 9:30 and arrived at Shinjuku Station at about 10:20 a.m. Was soon at home. I cleaned up, read messages from home and did several odd jobs. Did some writing.

Thursday, 15 April 1909, Tokyo

Rain—Cooler Up at 7:00. Spent the forenoon on the Book of Mormon work. Devoted the afternoon to correspondence. Sister Chizo Koji called today for the first time since coming to Tokyo. This young lady is a convert of the elders laboring in Hokkaido and recently came to Tokyo to attend school

Sunday, 18 April 1909, Tokyo

Clear—Warm Up at 7:00. The Sunday School was very small today. Good weather and beautiful flowers are more attractive to most people than the word of God. Was pleased to see eight saints to sacrament meeting. Bro. Toshichi Sato who, with his class of schoolmates, is touring the main island called and participated in the meeting. Sister Chizo Koji from Sapporo was recommended by Elder Seely to the Tokyo Branch. She was received today by unanimous vote. Talked with Bro. Sato and then took a walk with Elder Caine In the evening I addressed the congregation which assembled to hear the advertized discourse on prayer.

Saturday, 24 April 1909, Tokyo

Clear—Warm Up at 7:00. Spent the forenoon [a] /and/ part of the afternoon working on the Book of Mormon translation The Sunday School Primary Class was here in the afternoon having a good time both in and out of the house Realizing that our home in Yakuojumaemachi will be too far away from this district to expect many of the little tots to come to Sunday School this party was given as a sort of farewell to them. Bro. Justus B. Seely arrived from Hokkaido today.

Sunday, 25 April 1909, Tokyo

Clear—Cool Up at 7:00 Spent the day pleasantly. Presided over the Sunday School and taught the First Intermediate Class. Ate dinner. Presided in Sacrament Meeting and addressed the saints. Went to the Ushigome house to see its condition. Call on Bro. Kuga and Sister Kawabe on the way home. Presided over the evening meeting and addressed the audience. This is our farewell Sunday in this quarter.

Monday, 26 April 1909, Tokyo

Clear—Hot Up at 7:00 Worked all forenoon in the interest of the move we contemplate on the 29th In the afternoon had a very important discussion with Mr. Ikuta regarding the translation. Worked on the translation in the evening.

Tuesday, 27 April 1909, Tokyo

Clear—Hot Up at 6:30. Spent the day at headquarters trying to finish the review of Mr. Ikuta's criticisms to the end of the Book of Mormon translation. Just as I was finishing the 9th Chapter of Moroni, he came and I spent the afternoon discussing points in the translation. Ate a late long supper. Spent a few minutes with Elder Seely.

Wednesday, 28 April 1909, Tokyo

Clear—Warm Up at 7:00. Spent the forenoon attending to business about the new house. Went to Shinjuku Station to see Elder Seely off. He sailed today at 2:00 p.m. on the S.S. "Tanyo Maru." Went to the Ushigome house again and laid matting all afternoon. The evening was spent packing my trunk and getting after laborers.

Thursday, 29 April 1909, Tokyo

Cloudy—Warm Up at 7:00. Spent the entire day working at the Ushigome house getting it ready to move in. The condition yesterday clearly showed that the house could not be made ready to move on the 29th Elder Jensen and I slept at the new home.

Friday, 30 April 1909, Tokyo

Up at 6:00 a.m. The day was bad a drizzling rain fell almost constantly so we couldn't move today. All hands therefore turned out to try and finish up the cleaning. We were quite successful Elder Jensen and I again stayed as watch-dogs.

Saturday, 1 May 1909, Tokyo

Clear—Ideal moving weather. Up at 5:30. Did some nasty jobs by way of finishing up the cleaning of the home before the furniture arrived By dark we were all moved and everything inside the house with a great deal in its place. This has been a strenuous week for all the missionaries and our servants. Everyone had obeyed orders and done our full share so this evening we are all sore and very tired. We trust the Lord will acknowledge our labors and be willing to acknowledge the house prepared as suitable and fit for the Mission headquarters and the presence of his Spirit. The address of the new home is 81 Yakuojimae Machi, Ichigaya, Ushigome Ku, Tokyo.

Monday, 3 May 1909, Tokyo

Clear—Warm Up at 7:15. Spent the forenoon helping to arrange the furniture etc. in the house. In the afternoon I tried to do something on the Book of Mormon translation but there were so many interferences that I didn't make any headway. After all the rest had retired, I was able to do a little. I finished the review of Mr. Ikuta's first criticism of the translation down to the end of Moroni. I have yet to compare it with the English and discuss a few questions with Mr. Ikuta before Mr. Namekawa can copy it. My next duty will be to review Mr. Ikuta's second criticism which begins at the 4th chapter of III Nephi. Then I shall have someone else read the translation and offer suggestions. After those suggestions, I shall translate and attach the references before sending to the printer.

Sunday, 9 May 1909, Tokyo

Clear—Warm—Calm. Up at 6:30. Prepared for Sunday School. This being the first Sunday School in the new place we had practically an entirely new school so far as the Primary Class is concerned. In all 63 were present. The prospects are good for a large and interesting school in this place. Ate dinner. Presided over and addressed the saints meeting. Presided over the Sunday School officers meeting At this meeting Sister Fude Tai resigned as teacher of the Primary Department and Bro. Yasubeiye Chiba was appointed to lead the class with Sister Edna H. Thomas as assistant. Sister Tai is going into the country to live. After supper I prepared for evening meeting. I presided over this meeting and addressed it. There were 13 in attendance. Today I paid Sister Tai for making me a complete outfit of Japanese clothes her bill was ¥4.40. The goods cost in all ¥74.92 ½.

Tuesday, 11 May 1909, Tokyo

Clear—Cooler—Later, cloudy. Up at 7:00. Ate breakfast and then taught Japanese to Elder Jensen. Worked on the Book of Mormon translation during the forenoon and evening. In the afternoon, I helped read proof-sheets. Today Mr. Ikuta came and finished his final criticism of the translation It is this final criticism that I am now reviewing. By referring to my journal of July 29, 1908, the account of the contract with Mr. Ikuta may be learned. It was on that date that he began his work on the translation so he has been connected with it for nearly ten months. He has been very patient with me in all my questions and has been pleasant in his manner—a remarkable contrast to Mr. Hirogoro Hirai who was very impatient and irratable in many of our discussions. However, at times, I have felt that Mr. Ikuta has not devoted the hours to the work that he promised and therefore has unnecessarily lengthened out the work for about 3 months. But had he worked more rapidly, I should have been under the necessity of giving him three months holiday as my part of the work has kept me working as hard as I can from morning till night.

Friday, 14 May 1909, Tokyo

Rain—Warmer Up at 6:00. Taught Japanese to Elder Jensen before breakfast. Spent all the forenoon at Mr. Ikuta's discussing translation questions. In the afternoon, I worked on the translation. Bro. F. J. Hewlett of Salt Lake City, called in and spent a few hours with us. He has just been with his wife to China and the Philippine Islands. After supper, I went to Bro Kuga's home and spent an hour with him.

Tuesday, 18 May 1909, Tokyo

Clear—Warm Up at 6:00. Taught Japanese to Elder Jensen. Ate breakfast. Spent the majority of the day on the Book of Mormon translation. Bro. and Sister Frank J. Hewlett called in the late afternoon and spent the evening with us. I talked and visited with them.

Wednesday, 19 May 1909, Tokyo

Clear—Warm Up at 6:15. Taught Elder Jensen a lesson in Japanese Spent the early forenoon repairing a broken glass door. Then started the days work on the Book of Mormon translation. This work occupied the rest of the day with the exception of an hour or so spent in prayer meeting with my brethren. After supper, I called on Bro. Eisaburo Kuga. The purpose of my call was this: Last night a letter came to me from England just as I was going to bed. This morning I read the letter. It was from Wm Greenwood of Mufield, Yorkshire, England. He is a member of the church. In his letter was a "Quarterly Letter" of the Police Missionary Union. This letter is devoted principally to a report of the Union's work in Japan in charge of some man named Taylor. A letter from Taylor to the writer of the above mentioned "Quarterly Letter" contained the English translation of a letter written by Bro. Kuga to Taylor in Nov. of last year. This letter of Bro. Kuga's contained statements which, if true, make him a liar and a hypocrite. It was to ascertain the correctness or incorrectness of this letter that I went to his home this evening. He confessed to the writing of the letter and revealed things that indicates an apostacy at heart from the church. I talked to him clearly about his condition and told him he would now have to chose between the church and the world.

Friday, 21 May 1909, Tokyo

Clear—Hot Up at 6:45 Spent the forenoon at Mr. Ikuta's discussing translation questions. This discussion brought us up to the end of the book. In the afternoon I did some work on the translation. After supper, I went to the home of a Mr. Ishii, a friend of Mr. Ikuta's, whom I asked to design the cover for the Book of Mormon. Mr. Ishii is an artist.

Friday, 28 May 1909, Tokyo

Clear—Hot Up at 6:00. Worked on a newspaper article in answer to the twaddle of a Japanese traveler who misrepresents us in an article in the Asahi News. Spent the rest of the forenoon and most of the afternoon working on the translation of Book of Mormon references. Took the newspaper article to the Asahi office. The editor took the article but will not allow it just as it is Parts of it may come out. In the evening a good Bible Class was held by Elder Caine. Some rowdy boys and young men gathered at the gate and made considerable disturbance. We gave no heed to their actions till one of them threw a stone through the upstair window. I quietly slipped out the back door and through the neighbor's yard to the police box and reported the rowdism, but evidently frightened at their own act in breaking the window, the actual offender escaped while some who evidently enjoyed the disturbance were severely reprimanded by the officer of the law who took two of them to his box and continued to chastize them for a long time.

Monday, 31 May 1909, Tokyo

Clear—Hot Up at 6:00 Taught Japanese to Elder Jensen for an hour before breakfast. After breakfast, I did an odd job or two, then wrote a letter to Bro. Wm Greenwood of Mufield, Yorkshire, England, relative to Bro. Eisaburo Kuga's unfaithfulness and his reported conversion to another church (See Journal of May 19th). In the afternoon I attempted an article for the Improvement Era about the Japan Mission. In the evening, I presided over the Missionaries' Bible Class.

Sunday, 6 June 1909, Tokyo

Rain—Hot. Up at 7:00. Spent the day in streneous work. Presided over the Sunday School and taught the First Intermediate Department. Presided over the fast meeting. Presided over the Sunday School teacher's meeting. In this meeting Elder Warren E. Harris was appointed to the Office of Assistant Superintendent of the school with the view of training him to take the position of Superintendent in the near future. I will have sooner or later, to give up the position of Superintendent which I have held ever since the school was organized, so it is quite necessary that someone should be put in training for the position. After this teacher's meeting, I talked with Sister Tai for a few minutes and then discussed Book of Mormon translation questions with Bro. Chiba for about an hour and a half. Then ate supper. After supper, I got ready for evening meeting which at the proper hour was very unpromising, but which finally grew in attendance till we had 21 natives and 6 missionaries present.

Thursday, 10 June 1909, Tokyo

Clear—Hot Up at 6:10. Taught Elder Jensen his regular morning lesson in Japanese before breakfast. Then worked on the translation of the Book of Mormon references till 12:30 p.m. when I completed this labor. This is the final of the Book of Mormon translation an arduous labor that has lasted for over five years. On the evening of Jan. 18, 1904 at the Makinoya Hotel in Chiba City, Chiba Ku I made the very first effort at translation. In the meeting held Saturday, July 16, 1904 I was appointed to devote the major part of my time to the translation. The next day Prest. Horace S. Ensign set me apart by the laying on of hands for this labor. This really marks the real, earnest beginning of the work for since the first effort made Jan 18th I had so much else to do in tracting, visiting, etc. that I had only been able to do a very little by July 16th when I was appointed to devote most of my time to this labor. Hence, since the earnest, real beginning of the work not quite five years have elapsed. This labor has received my best efforts and the great majority of my time as my journal from that date shows. Hence, today the finishing of the translation which includes all the references makes this day of great importance and one long to be remembered as the day looked forward to and striven hard for mid toils, prayers and fasting for almost five years. God has blessed me abundantly and sustained me, physically, mentally and spiritually so that I was able to lay down the pen of translation today in health and strength of body and mind and with a grateful heart for the countless blessings of heaven bestowed upon me and the work. Of course there still remains a question or two regarding some parts of the latest translations which will have to be decided before this part can go into the printer's hands but such things as dotting i s and crossing t s will not cease till the last proof sheet is approved. The faithful assistance given by Elder Caine to the work since he was first called to take part July 30, 1905 is fully appreciated by me and for his care and devotion to this translation I have and do now again commend him to the Lord as one who has done his duty well. His suggestions have been of great value and his untiring work has not been inferior to my own. After the publication of the translation I expect to write a history of the work from the beginning to the end.

After dinner I went to the printers and then called on Miss Yuki Fujita's parents. They live in Yotsuya. I was kindly received. Returned and spent the evening talking to Mr. Jiro Fukuyama on the gospel and reading my old journal referring to the early work on the Book of Mormon.

Saturday, 12 June 1909, Tokyo

Clear—Hot Up at 6:10 Spent the forenoon reading proof sheets. Did some of this work also in the afternoon. Then walked to Aoyama Street for exercise getting a shave on the way. In the evening, I prepared the lesson to be taught to the Sunday School class tomorrow. Two young ladies came asking for lessons in English. I turned them over to Sister Thomas. Took a bath and retired.

Friday, 18 June 1909, Tokyo

Clear—Hot Up at 7:00 Spent the day proof reading. After supper I went Mr. Tsukakoshi's home to get him to pass an opinion on the title of the Book of Mormon as written by several Japanese. He was not home. Returned and went to bed with a slight pain in my intestines.

Saturday, 19 June 1909, Tokyo

Rain—Cooler Up at 4:00 P.M. Spent most of the day in bed nursing a very painful abdomen. Since last night my intestines have been failing to do their work giving me great distress. About noon the most severe pain passed away and towards evening I felt well enough to get up, but not well enough to work so I read some of the recent papers from America. Had a light supper. Took a bath before retiring.

Sunday, 20 June 1909, Tokyo

Cloudy—Cool Up at 6:30. Our meetings today were not quite so large as last Sunday, but still they were very good. Elder Warren E. Harris had charge of the Sunday School today. This is the first time I have been present in the Tokyo Sunday School without having charge of it since its organization. In our last officers meeting Elder Harris was appointed Assistant Superintendent to prepare him to take full charge of the school when I have to leave it. I taught the First Intermediate Department. After School I presided over and addressed the saints' meeting. After dinner I discussed Book of Mormon translation questions with Bro Chiba for about two hours. I then wrote to mother. Presided over the evening preaching meeting. Also spoke.

Tuesday, 22 June 1909, Tokyo

Cloudy—Hot Up at 6:15. This morning Elder Elliott C. Taylor left for Shizuoka the capitol of Shizuoka Ku. He will look the city over in the interest of missionary work. I spent the day working on proof sheets and the evening visiting. I called first at the home of Sister Ota and later on the Katagiri family both in Aoyama.

Saturday, 26 June 1909, Tokyo

Rain—Sultry Up at 7:00 Spent two hours in the forenoon working on proof sheets. Then prepared for and started on a journey to Kōfu in company with Elder Taylor who was returning to his field. After an uninteresting ride of seven hours arrived safely at Kōfu finding Elders Fairbourn and Stimpson in good health. Talked with the brethren all evening and then took a bath before retiring.

Sunday, 27 June 1909, Kōfu

Rain—Hot Up at 6:15. After breakfast attended the Sacrament meeting held in Kōfu. All of the Kōfu saints but one were present. I addressed the meeting. From this meeting till the beginning of Sunday School I talked with Bros. Yoneyama and Shirai. After hearing and seeing the exercises in the various classes, I addressed the school. I then ate dinner after which I read and rested till about 3:00 p.m. when I attended the regular Sunday Japanese Bible Class. After the class, I talked with two young lady investigators for a few minutes Later ate supper and then attended the evening meeting I addressed the meeting for about forty minutes on "Faith." After meeting I met Sister Yoneyama who was unable to be present at the morning sacrament meeting. I talked a little to Sister Iso. Then I had a chat with Elder Stimpson He is a man of noble faith and has one of the most perfect spirits of self-sacrifice I have ever seen. His two sisters at home who are his main financial supports are also jewels of whom our Heavenly Father even may well be proud. After prayer retired.

Monday, 28 June 1909, Kōfu

Clear—Hot Up at 6:30. Left Kōfu on the 8:17 a.m. train. After a seven hour ride without interest, arrived safely at Tokyo. Went directly to headquarters and prepared the outline of the work in the First Intermediate Department for the coming month. Also prepared for the evening Missionaries' Bible Class which I presided over after supper. Prepared to retire. Was about to get into bed when three new missionaries arrived. I welcomed them in my night attire saw that places to sleep were prepared and something to eat brought out then retired. The new elders names are Melvin F. Barton and Robert H. Barton cousins of Kaysville Davis Co. Utah and Walter W. Steed Jr. of Syracuse Davis Co. Utah.

Tuesday, 29 June 1909, Tokyo

Rain—Hot Up at 6:45. Spent the entire forenoon talking to the new elders and appointed them as follows: Melvin F. Barton to Kōfu; Robert H. Barton to Hokkaido; Walter W. Steed to Shizuoka. In the afternoon I attempted an hours nap but got a two hour's sleep. Did a little on the proofs of the Book of Mormon. Devoted the evening to writing letters.

Wednesday, 30 June 1909, Tokyo

Clear—Hot Up at 7:00 Spent the greater part of the day working on the proof sheets of the Book of Mormon At noon we held prayer meeting. In the forenoon Elder Melvin F. Barton left for Kōfu which will be his field of labor. In the evening I accompanied Elder Robert Barton to Ueno Station where he took the 11:00 p.m. train for Hokkaido. Got back home and to bed about midnight.

Saturday, 3 July 1909, Tokyo

Clear—Hot Up at 6:20. Spent the day working on proof sheets and talking to Sister Mary Hooper Jennings who is visiting Japan on her way home from the Phillipine Islands. Not being in good health and having had many sorrows recently, she was feeling very nervous and unhappy. At her request, we blessed her.

Sunday, 4 July 1909, Tokyo

Cloudy—Cool—Almost Cold Up at 7:15. Presided over a fine Sunday School and taught the First Intermediate Department. Sacrament Meeting was held at 11:00 a.m. After this meeting the teachers and officers of the Sunday School met to discuss the work for the coming month. For about three hours there was a period of rest during which period I read a little and prepared my mind for the evening meeting

which I addressed. At 5:00 p.m. I gave some instructions to the missionaries about them leaving their work and fields without permission

Monday, 5 July 1909, Tokyo

Rain—Cooler Up at 7:10. Spent the entire forenoon on proof sheets In the late afternoon Bro and Sister Frank Hewlett of Salt Lake came to spent the evening with us. We had arranged for a little party for them and in celebration of America's independence. Before supper, we enjoyed a pleasant chat. Supper was especially delicious. After supper we had music and recitations and the reading of part of the Declaration of Independence. The party closed about 10:40 p.m. Bro & Sister Hewlett returned to Yokohama. This will be our farewell to the Hewletts who sail for home on the 11th inst.

Tuesday, 13 July 1909, Tokyo

Cloudy—Hot Up at 7:10. Spent the day working on proof sheets. In the evening went to Bro. Kikuchi's home. He was absent so I returned and read a little about Korea written by Frank G. Carpenter.

Wednesday, 14 July 1909, Tokyo

Cloudy—Calm—Hot—Sultry. Up at 8:00 Spent the day on proof sheets. At the noon prayer and council meeting Eisaburo Kuga was excommunicated for hypocrisy, lying and apostacy. In the evening I spent several hours at Mr. Yashiro's home discussing translation questions.

Tokyo, Sunday, July 18, 1909

Clear—Exceedingly Hot Up at 6:35 Spent the day happily working in our several meetings which were very fine spirited. I wrote a few communications to the elders in the field and walked to the post office Just after getting into bed Elder Harris handed me a letter from Morioka containing news worse a hundred times over than news of death it was the news of an elders moral downfall. This news necessitated sending a telegram which I did at midnight. Returned and after prayer retired. Slept a little

Monday, 19 July 1909, Tokyo—Tuesday, 20 July 1909, Morioka

Clear—Very hot Up at 6:00. Wrote some letters. Ate breakfast and went to the American Embassy for identification papers needed in signing the new contract for the lease of our house with the true owner, Mr. Sensuke Saitō. After calling at the Embassy I went to the native notary public who is going to prepare the contract papers I then went back to the Embassy and got my identification papers. It was too late to call Mr. Saitō and go with him before the Notary as I had arranged to go to Morioka with Elder Caine on the 12:40 o'clock train. Ate an early lunch and left for the depot where Elder Caine was waiting. The train left on time. We arrived in Morioka at a little before 4:00 oclock a.m. next morning Went to the elders house and found them still in bed. After washing, cleaning and chatting for a while ate breakfast. After breakfast a meeting was held in which Elder [~~Charles H. Hubbard~~] was tried, found guilty upon his own confession in detail, and excommunicated for having immoral intercourse with a neighbor's daughter. He manifested a true spirit of repentance and accepted humbly and obediently the advice given regarding his homegoing and future. In fact his repentance was so beautiful as to be a great comfort to all of us who witnessed it (Elders James Anderson and I sitting in the trial). To have to excommunicate him was a hard trial to me but I have learned that God's word and laws cannot be improved by man so I voted for the excommunication and I believe if our brother (for I feel to call him this still) will retain the same control over himself that he has by the assistance of God obtained, will regain his standing in the Church and have the priesthood restored to him. To this end I shall ever pray. After this meeting, I walked down town on business. Returned and ate dinner. After dinner had a little nap. Then I had a long talk with the lady who is keeping house for the missionaries in Morioka. I had another sleep. After supper, I went with Bro. Hubbard and Elder Caine for a walk to the top of a hill where we had a fine view of the city and surrounding country. After returning I attended the English Bible Class which was a struggle

for both teacher and students but quite entertaining to the onlooker. I then had a nap till train time. Left Morioka with Elder Caine and Hubbard at 12:33 a.m. and began our journey to Tokyo.

Wednesday, 21 July 1909, Morioka

Cloudy—Slight breeze—Later, Fair and Hot. As stated left Morioka at 12:33 a.m. for Tokyo. After a ride of little interest reached Tokyo at 3:15. Went directly to headquarters where I attended to some correspondence. Before retiring I appointed Elder Elbert D. Thomas and wife to go to Morioka to continue their missionary work, and appointed Elder Warren E. Harris to go to Shizuoka to take the place of Elder Steed who has been appointed to go as a companion to [~~Bro. Hubbard~~] home. I also walked as far as the Ushigome Post Office and sent a telegram to Elder Taylor telling him that he would be joined by Elder Harris tomorrow.

Thursday, 22 July 1909, Tokyo

Clear—Hot Up at 7:00. Washed and went to Mr. Totsuka's to see if I could not get him to write a letter to his parents requesting them to assist the elders in Shizuoka to find a suitable house-keeper. He said he was going to Shizuoka in a day or two and would look up a suitable person himself. On the way back I called at the Ushigome Kuyakusho and found out for sure that Sensuke Saitō is the owner of the place we occupy. I then called on Mr. Saito and appointed the afternoon at 2:00 o'clock as the hour to meet him at the notary public's office to sign the rental agreement. I returned ate breakfast, bid Elder Harris good bye. He left on the 11:00 a.m. train for Shizuoka. I wrote two letters concerning the case of [~~Charles H. Hubbard~~]; one to the First Presidency and one to the bishop of the Bench Ward Bannock Co. to which [~~Bro. Hubbard~~] belonged. After dinner, according to appointment, I went to the notary public's office and signed the agreement between Mr. Saitō and myself regarding the house in which we are living The agreement assures us pretty well for five years unless there is a sale. Attended to other business before returning Among other things, I have today made Elder Jay C. Jensen Secretary of the mission in place of Elder Thomas who leaves tomorrow night for Morioka.

Friday, 23 July 1909, Tokyo

Cloudy—Cool breeze Up at 6:30. Wrote a long letter to the elders out in the field telling of [~~Bro. Hubbard~~] case and giving them the warning that the devil is after them also so they must beware and attend to counsel. I attended to other correspondence. I gave Bro. and Sister Thomas some instructions about their work in Morioka They left on the 11:00 p.m. train for Morioka. While most of the people were gone to the depot I talked to Elder Jensen.

Saturday, 24 July 1909, Tokyo

Clear—Hot. Up at 7:00 Spent most of the day working on correspondence I wrote an important letter to the elders giving instructions about their writing letters to the native females and receiving female investigators etc. In the late afternoon, I put the last corrections in the last books of the Book of Mormon translation preparing them for the printer. This finishes the preparation of the manuscript for the printer up to the end. Took a bath and retired.

Monday, 26 July 1909, Tokyo

Clear—Very hot Up at 7:00. Did an odd job or two and then went to the bank where I drew enough money to pay the return fares of Elder Steed and [~~Charles H. Hubbard~~]. I went from the bank to Yokohama. I secured the tickets and then went to the steamer "Monteagle" where I waited for the brethren. They all arrived in time. We stayed on board as long as possible, but the time was short. After our farewell wishes we went ashore and directly to headquarters at Tokyo. Washed and ate supper. After supper did a little reading then retired.

Sunday, 1 August 1909, Tokyo

Shower—Cooler Up at 7:00 Tradition has it that 27 years ago today I was born. Fortunately it is fast day so there is no temptation to overeat in celebration of the day. The Sunday School Fast Meeting and Preaching Meeting held today were all very much blessed by the Good Spirit. I presided over them all and directed the monthly meeting of the Sunday School officers and teachers. In the afternoon I walked as far as Mr. Saitō's and paid the rent for headquarters for the months of August, September, and October.

Tuesday, 10 August 1909, Tokyo

Clear—Very hot Up at 7:00. Spent the forenoon hunting up the aut[—]o[-]y factory that makes the small trays sold at the Bureau of Information Salt Lake City. I was successful in my hunt. After dinner I wrote to Bro. Benjamin Goddard in regard to the making of the trays and what they cost at the factory. Spent the rest of the day on the Book of Mormon and the evening on the part of the mission journal that is missing—from Nov 4, 1901 to July 17 1902. I am doing the best I can to compile from my own personal journal a record of all important events during this period. I have tried for a long time to get Bro. Grant's journal to assist in this work, but my effort has failed. Being the only remaining witness to the events of those days I feel it a duty to leave as good a record as possible of many important things that transpired and I regret that the secretary of the mission did not keep a faithful account of those days as they were important to our history. I began the work of taking notes from my journal last night and finished the note taking this evening.

Thursday, 12 August 1909, Tokyo

Clear—Hot Up at 6:45. It is eight years ago this morning since the pioneer missionaries to Japan arrived at Yokohama. In the eight years that have past the Lord has been good to me in body and spirit. He has given me the victory in all temptations and been my support in the hour of severe trial. He has enabled me to do some little for the salvation of my fellows and especially has he assisted me in my Book of Mormon translation work and in the duties resting upon me as president of the mission. If, therefore, anything great has been achieved by my labor the praise and glory of that achievement is the Lord's forever. I thank him for his blessings to me, to my companions, to the saints here, to my loved ones at home and /to/ all the interests of this mission.

Today I worked on the Book of Mormon proof-sheets. Bro. Chiba called in the evening. I finished writing what record is possible from my own personal journal for the period from Nov. 4 1901 to July 16, 1902 which record was not keep by him whose duty it was to write the mission journal at that time. It was an important period and in making up the record, I hoped to have other references besides my own journal, but in spite of the fact that I have asked for the loan of my companions' journals for that time, I have not been able to borrow them and the time of my sojourn in Japan is getting short, so I have done the best I could in making this Mission's record complete, by consulting my own writings.

Monday, 23 August 1909, Tokyo

Cloudy—Cool Up at 6:30. During the forenoon I was down town in the interest of the Book of Mormon and I also purchased ¥46.70 worth of books on Japan, Korea and China. Spent the afternoon reading proof sheets. In the evening I taught Elder Jensen a lesson in Japanese.

Wednesday, 1 September 1909, Tokyo

Bright—Windy—Dust. Up at 5:30 Prepared to go to Yokohama. Left in company with Elders Jensen and Caine on the 8:20 train. At Yokohama we went directly to the spot in the woods where eight years ago the first elders to Japan held the prayer service in which the land was dedicated by Apostle Grant for the proclamation of the gospel. Feeling that this would no doubt be the last opportunity for me to celebrate the day in this land I wanted to open my heart to my Heavenly Father on that spot where eight years ago I experienced one of the greatest outpourings of the Holy Spirit I have ever had. We sang the hymn "Earth with her ten thousand flowers," Elder Caine prayed. We then sang again after I had made a few remarks about the spot and its importance to the history of the mission. Elder Caine spoke of the interest he had in this place because of the outpouring of the Spirit he had witnessed here. He like me was full of gratitude for the blessings of the Lord to him since being in Japan. /Elder Jensen made a few remarks./ We sang again and then Elders Caine and Jensen prayed. We sang once more and then I prayed. The burden of my prayer was that God would recognize the work done on the Book of Mormon translation and send the Holy Spirit to be its companion wherever it may go in this land. I asked God to bless the efforts to advertize and sell the book so that its mission in this land could be well accomplished. We sang again and Elder Jensen offered the benediction. We returned to Tokyo directly I called at a number of places on the Ginza to attend to odd jobs. After reaching headquarters I helped get the house read for the party arranged for in commemoration of the eighth anniversary of the dedication /of the land/ and commencement of the Japan Mission. Our guests 19 in number were all here and began supper at about 7:00 p.m. After supper we held a meeting. Opening song "Love at Home" Prayer by Bro. Yasubeie Chiba, Piano selection by Bro. Jensen. I then delivered a long talk about the Japan Mission referring especially to the events of eight years ago. Elder Jensen then played another selection on the piano. The pictures taken of the prayer ground near Yokahama eight years ago were shown to those present Sister Chiyo Koji then read a congratulatory speech directed to me and the elders, prepared in behalf of Sister /Tsune/ Nachie. We then sang, "See the mighty angel flying and I offered the closing prayer. It was past 11:00 p.m. The saints and investigators who were our guests returned. I retired about midnight very tired.

Saturday, 4 September 1909, Tokyo

Cloudy—Cooler Up at 7:00 Spent the day on proof sheets and letters to the book stores soliciting orders for the Book of Mormon Went to the printer's once. Posted 47 letters to the book stores Each letter was accompanied by an illustrated statement concerning the book and a page of the final print and two order blanks. This is the beginning of my efforts to sell the books. I hope most earnestly for a favorable reply from the stores.

Thursday, 9 September 1909, Tokyo

Clear—Hot Up at 6:45. Spent the day on proof sheets and letters to book stores. Today the first order from /a/ book store was received. It is for 20 Books of Mormon and 10 "What Is The Book of Mormon." The store placing the order is Mizogoshi Shoten of Yokosuka, Kanegawa Ken. Today Sister Tanifuji from Hokkaido called at headquarters. She is in Tokyo expecting to enter the Shokugyo Gakko.[2]

Monday, 13 September 1909, Tokyo

Rain—Very Cool Up at 7:10. Spent the forenoon at Mr. Ikuta's having him criticise an article I expect to use in the advertizement of the Book of Mormon. In the afternoon I took all of the list of contents of the Book of Mormon except six pages to the printer. I also took a manuscript consisting of three pages which is an explanation of the use of the references and various marks in the Book of Mormon. In the evening the proof sheets up to the last were delivered The hombun (book without title page, contents, etc) covers 942 pages. It was a great delight to see the end in type.

Wednesday, 15 September 1909, Tokyo

Cloudy—Cool—Later, Fair Up at 6:45 Spent the day on proof sheets. Mr. Iida brought the design for the cover /of the Book of Mormon/ intended for the Emperor, Empress, Crown Prince & Crown Princess. It was a very fine thing. Today, Elder Caine's eyes feasted on the proof sheets of his article introducing the Book of Mormon. Took a walk in the evening.

Monday, 20 September 1909, Tokyo

Cloudy—Rain—Warmer Up at 6:30. Took a little exercise before breakfast. Read a proof sheet or two. Went to the printer's. Went to Mr. Ikuta's and got the manuscripts for advertizements in the Taiyō and Chuōkōron Magazines. I took them to the advertizing agency. Returned to headquarters and mailed the last of the letters to the book stores relative to the sale of the Book of Mormon. These letters announce 30% off to book dealers. For orders of 50 or more copies we allow the book store giving the order to place their name and address in /any one of/ the newspaper advertizements twice. For orders of 100 or more we offer besides the above discount and advertizing an equal number of Elder Caine's pamphlet, "What Is The Book of Mormon" free. For orders of over 200 copies we offer besides all the above an additional discount of 10%. 373 letters have gone to stores outside of Tokyo. Two of this number have been returned undelivered. Those that I mailed today are all for stores in Tokyo. There were 132 of these.

Tuesday, 21 September 1909, Tokyo

Clear—Warm Up at 7:00 Spent the day working on proof sheets and taking exercise etc. In the evening I prepared the outline of lessons in my Sunday School Class for October. Read about Korea. Took a bath and retired.

Friday, 24 September 1909, Tokyo

Rain—Cold Up at 6:30. Spent the day reading proof sheets In the evening I attended the Bible Class. Then I read till quite late in the Americana, an historical magazine published in New York. This magazine in the July number containing the first of a promised series of articles on "History of the Mormon Church" by Elder B. H. Roberts.[3]

Sunday, 26 September 1909, Tokyo

Clear—Warmer Up at 6:45. Ate breakfast read over the lesson to be given in my Sunday School class. Presided over the Sunday School and taught the First Intermediate Department Presided over and taught the saints in sacrament meeting. Then presided over the Sunday School teachers monthly meeting. After this meeting Sister Koji told me of some evil rumors that had reached her affecting the virtues of one of our native sisters. I read American newspapers, magazines and a chapter in a book on Korea. Ate supper and prepared for evening meeting

Thursday, 30 September 1909, Tokyo

Heavy Rain—Cold Up at 7:30 After breakfast I began work on the last few unfinished proof sheets of the Book of Mormon and about 11:15 I wrote the finished sign on the last form and laid down my last pen in connection with this great labor of love The rest of the work before the finished book arrives is all the printer's and book binders. I simply await the book's arrival. This then, so far as my work is concerned, is the grand finale. My feelings of joy, my gratitude, my satisfaction at being permitted to attain this day and see the successful close of this colossal labor cannot be described. It is a day I have hoped, prayed and walked hard for, and I must acknowledge that the work has been so arduous, and confining, requiring the consentration of all my physical and mental power for such long stretches at a time, that in taking a retrospective view of the last 5 years and 9 months, I consider my physical and mental endurance almost a miracle—at any rate a direct answer to fervant appeals to God for strength to hold out to the end. And if the Lord sees fit to recognize the fruit of this labor performed in weakness as worthy of his benediction, and commissions the Holy Spirit to companion the Japanese Book of Mormon in its travels in Japan or wherever it goes, then will my most earnest and ultimate hope in regard to the work be realized, and all my toils and anxiety become my ever-joyful memories. I praise the Lord with all my might mind and strength. I thank him forever for the faithful, untireing, and most valuable aid he has given to the work through Elder Fred A. Caine. Elder Caine is a Latter-day Saint after my own heart and his associations with me in the work of translation—he has acted mostly as critic, scribe and councelor—has endeared him to me with a bond of the closest affection. The Lord also has raised up in time of need sufficient Japanese help thus making it possible to eliminate most if not all the grammatical and rethorical blunders in my manuscript I expect to write an outline of the work from the beginning so will leave further facts and thoughts till then.

In the afternoon, I worked on the arrangement of the newspaper advertizements.

Monday, 4 October 1909, Tokyo

Cloudy—Sprinkling rain—Chilly Up at 7:00. Every Monday morning we have the job of packing away benches used on Sunday and have to rearrange for the weeks work three of the rooms. This was my job this morning before breakfast. The rest of the day was devoted to work on the Financial and Statistical Reports of the Japan Mission for the third quarter Elder Caine completed his proof reading today.

Wednesday, 6 October 1909, Tokyo

Cloudy—Warmer Up at 7:30. Spent most of the day preparing advertizements for publication in Christian magazine's and papers. At noon, I joined my brethren in special prayer. In the evening I went to give in one of the ads, but the man in charge of the paper was not at home. In the evening I visited Elder Jensen's Bible Class. Word of the first baptism in Asahikawa was received. Mr. Genkichi Shiraishi, a young man 19 years old being the new member.

This forenoon two completed, bound copies of the Japanese Book of Mormon were brought to headquarters by Mr. Iida and the head of the binding department. These are for filing in the Home Department in obedience to the law regarding all publications. It was a source of more great joy to see and handle the completed volume. A few suggestions were made in relation to the binding of the other books which will improve the appearance somewhat.

Thursday, 7 October 1909, Tokyo

Cloudy—Cool Up at 7:15 Spent part of the day filing the Book of Mormon and its Introduction in the Home Department. I attended to other business down town, principally in connection with the advertizing of the Book of Mormon.

Yesterday the Kokumin Newspaper had an article about us and our work in this place. It described in a rather insulting manner our services last Sunday evening saying somethings which the writer surmized about us entirely false and with the evident object to do us harm. My picture was reproduced from the Brief History.

This morning's "Nippon" newspaper had the first of a series of efforts on Mormonism as a result of a reporter's visit here last Sunday. We are being discussed as "good and evil.' Agigation of the Mormon name will sell the Book of Mormon, but we are never pleased with slander of the truth.

Friday, 8 October 1909, Tokyo

Windy—Cold—Clear Up at 7:15. Spent the forenoon down town. I made application at the Home Department for the Book of Mormon copyright. In the afternoon I prepared two full page advertizements for the Christian World published at Osaka. In the evening, I attended a session of the semicentennial of Protestantism in Japan. Mr. Shimada was the main speaker. His subject was the question "Influence of Christianity upon People's Rights and Liberty." He claimed, and evidently upon sound authority, that the rights and liberty now enjoyed by the people of Japan were not due **directly** to any Christian influences, but to the statesmanship and patriotism of the nation's leaders. In so far as the good laws and customs adopted by Japan from other countries were influenced in those countries by Christianity so far could Japanese rights and liberty be said to be **indirectly** influenced by Christianity. He also showed the great contrast between the methods of the early Catholic missionaries we worked with political backing and the methods of the early Protestant missionaries who used Christian love as their support. The removal of the national prejudice of the Japanese against Christianity and making it possible to see that Christianity was not an enemy to the Japanese nation was practically accomplished by the deeds of kindness and humble attitude of the early Protestant missionaries. The very fact that these missionaries did not attempt as the Catholic's had done to have a direct influence upon the forming of the people's rights and civil liberty was the one thing of all others that Christians and non-Christians in Japan should be thankful for, for it made the clause in the constitution of Japan granting religious liberty possible. Therefore Christianity's influence being great, in an **indirect** was a cause for great rejoicing and no tears should be shed for her not having played any direct part as the fact that she did not is what gave the nation confidence in her.

Sunday, 10 October 1909, Tokyo

Cold—Rain Up at 7:00. Today in spite of the bad weather we have had good services both from the standpoint of the audience and spirit. I taught the First Intermediate Department and presided over the Sunday School. Presided over and addressed the sacrament meeting. In the afternoon I read about Korea and wrote a letter to the Kokumin Newspaper relative to their insulting article which appeared on the 6th inst. Presided over and addressed the evening meeting. /Today first Book of Mormon newspaper ad came out in Jiji/

Monday, 11 October 1909, Tokyo

Rain—Cold Up at 7:00. Spent the forenoon doing odd jobs. About noon the first installment of the Book of Mormon (1000 copies) was delivered. The afternoon was spent in filling orders and making shipments. After supper, I went out and delivered 10 copies to book dealers. 349 copies were sent off this afternoon and evening. Second advertizement appeared in this morning's Jiji.

Tuesday, 12 October 1909, Tokyo

Cloudy—Later Rain—Warmer Up at 7:00. Devoted the day to wrapping and sending off complimentary copies of the Book of Mormon and writing letters. Had two interviews with newspaper men— one about advertizements and one about the Church. A card from the Y.M.C.A. informed me that they had concluded not to allow the Book of Mormon advertizement appear in their magazine "The Pioneer" and that they had mailed the manuscripts back by parcel post.

Sunday, 17 October 1909, Tokyo

Clear—Cold Up at 6:45. Spent the entire day at headquarters The Sunday School this morning was rather small. My class only had two in attendance so I allowed them to visit the Theological Department and I witnessed the exercises in the Primary Department. I presided over the sacrament meeting. In the afternoon I had a long talk with Sister Tanifuji (now Ishigaki) about her marriage, it having been rumored that her marriage was irregular and therefore a sin. But the conversation today did not bring out anything that indicated any irregularity and all Sister Tanifuji says is corroborated by the statements made by her mother and reported to me in a letter from Elder Marriott. Today several men with secular business have been here taking some of my time. In the late afternoon, I took a nap. The third installment of 1000 Books of Mormon were delivered today. In the evening I presided over the preaching meeting and delivered an address. In the audience this evening was a vice count. But Elder Caine insists that his manners discredit his title. But, of course, in Japan good breeding is not an essential qualification for a title so even if he did go to sleep, yawn, and in other ways prove ungentlemanly, he is nevertheless titled and no doubt my dry, uninteresting remarks are sufficient excuse for his drowsiness.

Tuesday, 19 October 1909, Tokyo

Cold—Rain Up at 7:30 Spent the forenoon at headquarters talking with Mr. Kano one of our earliest Japanese friends. By referring to my Journal for Jan. 2 & 3 1902 the kind hospitality of this young man and his family can be learned. Though much changed and now a man of affairs with wife and children, he is the same pleasant dispositioned friend of seven years ago. After dinner we were favored with a call from Mr. Akimoto a Japanese who has been engaged in beet raising in Idaho for a long time He is now in Japan both for pleasure and business. He has letters from Idaho Mormons. He brought a letter from Manager Thomas R. Cutler of the Utah Idaho Sugar Beet Co to the government officals requesting that they select and send some Japanese families to Idaho to engage in sugar beet raising. The government's policy however will not permit such a move. Mr. Akimoto says he has delivered two lectures on the Mormon people doing all in his power to disabuse the evil opinions of our people. Among the many things he said was this. A friend of his who is /a/ high official in the government told him that when Apostle Grant and his companions came to Japan, Marquis (now Prince) Ito proposed welcoming officially, by public reception, the Mormon missionaries. All Buddhist & Shinto sects approved the suggestion but the Christians (?) were unanamus in their opposition and said they could not accept an invitation to such a reception. This manifestation of ill-will caused the Marquis to withdraw his proposal. If true, this is a point of great value to our history for it shows that the Japanese have from the first been liberal in their attitude towards us. Mr. Akimoto could not say too much in praise of the kindness and hospitality of the Latter-day Saints and he said he was trying to enlist the strength of some of the newspapers in praising to the public the Latter-day Saints. He bought copies of our literature and left saying he would come again before going back to America.

In the late afternoon I went and visited Sister Ota who with her husband is in very distressed circumstances I made arrangements to render what assistance we can give. The day has been quite stormy and very cold. Many country newspapers with Book of Mormon advertizements have come to hand.

Thursday, 21 October 1909, Tokyo

Clear—Cold Up at 7:30 Spent the day at headquarters selling books and teaching songs to the Sunday School children. Today has been the second red letter day in sales. 77 Books of Mormon sold at headquarters. One book store took 50 copies.

This evening the editors of the New Woman's World (Shinjōkai see Oct 18th) returned the advertized manuscript sent in for that journal. The same editor accepted the manuscript for the Shinjin magazine. They say they are afraid that the feelings of the women will be wrought up against them if the word "Mormon" is published in large type in their magazine, but they are not afraid of hurting the feelings of the men hence the rejection of one manuscript and the acceptance of the other. The silly asses!

Friday, 22 October 1909, Tokyo

Clear—Cold Up at 7:00. This forenoon I went down town and secured space in the Fujiu Gahv for a Book of Mormon /advertizement/ The rest of the day I spent at headquarters selling books, writing etc. Was glad to see a full page advertizement of the Book of Mormon in the Christian World—the largest native Christian paper in Japan.

Tuesday, 26 October 1909, Tokyo

Cloudy—Little Rain—Warm Up at 7:00 Spent part of the day at headquarters and part of the day down town attending to mission business. Today has been the biggest day in Book of Mormon sales so far. Mr. Iida came and I paid him for all the books delivered. Some bound in leather are yet undelivered hence unpaid for. I asked the manager of the Methodist Publishing Houses to buy and sell the Book of Mormon in his store. He declined. I asked the privilege of leaving some hand bills for the book to be given to the store's guests. He said he would have to think about the matter. He said he had seen the place where the Book of Mormon "was first made" and the press on which it was first printed. In the evening I attended the Bible Class held by Elder Caine.

Wednesday, 27 October 1909, Tokyo

Cloudy—Warmer Up at 7:00 Spent the forenoon and nearly all of the afternoon at headquarters doing odd jobs and writing. This morning's papers announce the assassination of Prince Ito the greatest statesman modern Japan has had. He has almost made modern Japan and if there has been any power behind the throne it has been Prince (until recently Marquis) Ito. His death has thrown the whole nation into mourning. He was assassinated at Harbin, Manchuria by a young Corean on Oct 26th between 9 &

10 o'clock. Today the largest single order for Books of Mormon was received. The Tokyo Dō of Kanda took 70 copies This store bought 30 copies yesterday. Elder Jensen not doing well today, I took his place in the English Bible Class.

Monday, 1 November 1909, Tokyo

Clear—Warmer Up at 7:00. Spent the day at headquarters writing. I finished preparing the history of the translation and publication of the Book of Mormon in Japanese. /See Letter Book C 55/ After supper I took a long walk for exercise

Wednesday, 3 November 1909, Tokyo

Clear—Cool Up at 7:00. For the celebration of the 58th birthday of the Emperor, this has been an ideal day. I spent the day mostly at headquarters. In the forenoon I went to the barbers. I devoted my time to preparation for conference and to work on the Christmas program. This afternoon Elders Harris and Taylor arrived from Shizuoka. In the evening Elders Fairbourn Stimpson and Barton arrived from Kōfu bringing the good news of a baptism performed this morning at Kōfu at 5:00 a.m. After the last arrivals had eaten their supper, I directed them to the Izumi Kwan a small hotel in Yotsuya where five of the brethren will lodge during conference. The brethren who arrived today are all looking well and they express themselves as feeling very well.

Thursday, 4 November 1909, Tokyo

Clear—Later cloudy & rain Up at 6:30. I spent a majority of the day at headquarters preparing my mind for conference and chatting with my brethren. This forenoon the national funeral for Prince Ito was held. From reports given it has been very elaborate and grand.

Friday, 5 November 1909, Tokyo

Clear—Cool Up at 6:30 Spent the day at headquarters. This morning at 9:30 the elder's conference began. The demonstration of the Spirit's presence was remarkable. My report of the general condition of the mission and the relation of the history of the Japanese translation of the Book of Mormon occupied most of the time of the first session. The afternoon session began at 2:00 p.m. This meeting also enjoyed abundantly the blessings of the Holy Ghost. In the evening, I took a walk then looked over some questions and suggestions which the elders had written and handed in. I decided on the proceedure for the next day.

Saturday, 6 November 1909, Tokyo

Clear—Cold Up at 6:30. In the forenoon, we held the third session of Conference. In the afternoon, the final session was held. The same good Spirit present with us yesterday was with us again today. I took a walk in the evening. Some of the Books of Mormon bound in leather were delivered today. In the evening I had a talk with Elder Fairbourn.

Sunday, 7 November 1909, Tokyo

Cloudy—Later Clear—Cold Up at 6:30. Helped prepare the rooms for Sunday Services. We had a fair Sunday School this morning especially was the number of older students unusually large. At 11:00 a.m. fast meeting began. A usual good time was had. In the afternoon, I chatted for a while with a young lady who has recently come to Tokyo from Sapporo and who learning that the Sapporo elders are in Tokyo called to see them. Took a walk later. After supper, a successful meeting was held. We had four special musical numbers. The audience seemed pleased with the services. A little before meeting started, Mr. Nasa came and told us that Mormonism was the topic advertized to be discussed in the Uniterian Church tonight. Elders Fairbourn and Roskelley were sent to hear the speech. The preacher was talking when they entered and before they had reached their seats he "Said there is Mr. Caine (mistaking Elder Roskelley for Elder Caine who a day or two ago had a conversation with Elder Caine at our headquarters) now. If you want to know about the Mormons talk to him." This beckoned all eyes to the brethren. After the meeting Elder Fairbourn distributed Book of Mormon advertizements while Elder Roskelley shook hands with the preacher and met Mr. T. Hiroi my old teacher in Japanese. The speech was very liberal and quite accurate. This made the people take from Elder Fairbourn the advertizements with much enthusiasm. On the 1st of this month the official organ of the Uniterian Church contained a full page ad of the Book of Mormon Every little helps. We are glad we have received this helping advertizement.

Monday, 8 November 1909, Tokyo

Rain—Warmer Up at 6:45. Spent the day at the house. There were so many people around that I couldn't do much of anything but keep out of the way. In the evening, we had a special supper to which all the saints were invited but to which only six came. After supper, we had a musical program etc. The Japanese suit which I had made last winter was taken out of the trunk and worn by me this evening for the first time. This is the first time I have had on a complete set of Japanese clothes.

Wednesday, 10 November 1909, Tokyo

Clear—Cold Up at 7:15. Walked to Shinjuku Station where I said good-bye to the elders who left for Kōfu and Shizuoka. At noon today we held a prayer meeting. Ate dinner. In the afternoon, I reviewed Sister Koji's efforts for our coming Christmas. I also chatted with the elders. On the 11:00 p.m. train from Ueno Station Elders Marriott, Roskelley and Cutler left for Hokkaido. I went to see them off. Had only returned and got into bed when the fire bells woke me up. Went to sleep again and was again aroused by the fire bells. Seeing the blaze was in Yotsuya, I dressed and went to see if any of our friends were in danger. Found that one of our best Sunday School children lived next to the burning building. Their home was saved.

Thursday, 11 November 1909, Tokyo

Clear—Cold wind Up at 7:45 Spent most of the day at headquarters. Among other various jobs I started writing a dialogue for Christmas In the afternoon I took a walk. After supper, I went to the home of Mr. & Mrs. Nabeshima to see if they are willing to allow their daughter to join the church. Their consent was not given neither was it denied. They were left to reflect more on the matter. Returned to headquarters and then went to Ueno Station to say good-bye to Elders Anderson and Thomas and Sister Thomas, who left on the 11:00 p.m. train for Morioka. This leaves only Elders Caine and Jensen and I at headquarters.

Friday, 12 November 1909, Tokyo

Clear—Cold Up at 9:30. Spent the day at headquarters preparing for Christmas. I am having a terrible time getting the speeches and dialogues into shape. I got a little exercise today by walking. /This evening Miss Nabeshima called and said her father had refused to let her be baptized/

Tuesday, 16 November 1909, Tokyo

Clear—Calm—Cold Up at 7:15. Spent most of the day at headquarters preparing for Christmas. In the evening Miss Nabeshima called bringing from her parents a written permission for her to join the church. This is a quick answer to our prayers in her behalf. I had a long talk with her regarding the duties and responsibilities of Latter-day Saints. She joined in our family prayers. Today I took the printer's manuscript of the Japanese Book of Mormon to the Shueisha to be bound.

Wednesday, 17 November 1909, Tokyo

Clear—Milder—Calm Up at 7:45. Spent the forenoon finishing the last speech I have to prepare for the children to render on Christmas. At noon we had prayer meeting. In the afternoon, I took a long walk. In the evening, I went to the Saitō Drug Store to inquire about doctor's who have specialized in Kidney diseases. Elder W. E. Harris being troubled with his kidneys wrote me today about his condition.

Friday, 19 November 1909, Tokyo

Windy—Clear—Cold Up at 7:00 Spent the day at headquarters doing several things. I read over and completed the history of the Book of Mormon translation which I wrote before our recent conference. Elder Jensen will write this history on the typewriter and insert a copy in the Mission Journal. I will have one copy, Elder Caine will be presented with one copy and one copy with the printer's manuscript etc will be given to the Historian's Office, Salt Lake City. In the evening, I attended the Bible Class. I then had a chat with Miss. Kuma Nabeshima. Permission was given for her to enter the church. The ordinance of baptism will no doubt be performed sometime next week.

Monday, 22 November 1909, Tokyo

Clear—Warmer Up at 7:45. In the forenoon I went to the American Embassey and met Ambassador O'Brien. The purpose of the visit was to learn how to proceed in getting the Book of Mormon before the Imperial House and the heads of the various departments of the government. I was directed to the Minister of Foreign Affairs. Mr. O'Brien said no letter or card from him would be necessary in seeking an interview I walked to the Ginza and then took the car home. The afternoon was devoted to an attempt to find Sister Ishigaki's house but failed. I then wrote in a preservable form, the typographical errors already noted in the Japanese Book of Mormon. In the evening, I read a little about Korea and China.

Tuesday, 23 November 1909, Tokyo

Clear—Mild—Calm Up at 7:50. Spent the day at headquarters doing several jobs principally comparing the last or "O.K." proofs of the Book of Mormon with the printed book. This work I am doing to detect any ommitted corrections or mistakes to be considered at the time of the publication of the second edition. Today, I with my brethren, have been observing a fast in behalf of Elder Warren E. Harris who has been afflicted slightly for almost a year. In the evening, I attended the Old Testament class. Bro. Taue was here most of the afternoon.

Wednesday, 24 November 1909, Tokyo

Cloudy—Rain—Warm Up at 6:25. Took the 8:30 a.m. train for Shizuoka. Elder Jay C. Jensen accompanied me. Arrived safely at the mission field house at about 1:00 p.m. At 2:00 p.m. we held a meeting in which Elder Harris was anointed and administered to for his health. After the meeting we broke our fast which had been observed since Monday night. After a pleasant chat with the elders, I retired.

Thursday, 25 November 1909, Shizuoka

Clear—Warm Up at 6:30 Left Shizuoka on the 9:06 a.m. train and arrived with my companion, Elder Jensen, safely at Tokyo about 2:00 p.m. Went to headquarters. Nothing particularly had happened in the day of absence. Spent the rest of the afternoon and evening doing several jobs. Among other things I finished comparing the very last proof sheets of the Book of Mormon with the completed volume, and have placed on file one copy of the book containing all the corrections that should be made before the second edition is printed. I find that aside from a few mistaken "kana" (the most trivial of typographical errors) there are only 7 mistaken characters in the whole volume. This is all at least that have so far been discovered and I am free to express the opinion that there is no book of the same size in Japan with less mistakes in its first edition than this book. It is a proof that the Lord has helped us wonderfully in our proof-reading.

Friday, 26 November 1909, Tokyo

Clear—Colder Up at 7:30. Spent the forenoon at headquarters. This morning the very last of the Books of Mormon came from the printer's. The especially bound copies for the Imperial Family also arrived. They are very beautiful indeed. I carefully examined them before enclosing them in their final wrapping preparatory to presentation. In the afternoon I went to visit Mr. Ikuta. He was not home having gone to the hospital to have perhaps a slight operation performed. On the way home, I went around by the Ginza and did some purchasing. In the evening, I attended the Bible Class conducted by Elder Caine. Today a letter from Kōfu contained the good news of two more baptisms in that field.

Saturday, 27 November 1909, Tokyo

Clear—Calm—Mild Up at 7:30. Spent the forenoon at headquarters doing several odd jobs. After dinner, we went to Tama River and witnessed the baptism of Sister Kuma Nabeshima Elder Jensen officiated. In the evening I prepared for Sunday's duties. Took a bath and retired.

Monday, 29 November 1909, Tokyo

Clear—Windy—Warm Up at 7:30. Spent the forenoon and most of the afternoon trying to see Count Jūtarō Komura Minister of Foreign Affairs, but was unsuccessful. I met his Private Secretary Mr. Yoshida. The purpose in seeking an interview was to present Count Komura with a copy of the Book of Mormon and to get, if possible, the hope of presenting in person copies of the same scripture to the Emperor and Empress. The Private Secretary didn't have anything encouraging to say. In the evening I wrote Christmas Cards and letters.

I should state that the Book of Mormon for Count Komura was handed to Mr. Yoshida who promised to hand it to the Count at the very first opportunity.

Tuesday, 30 November 1909, Tokyo

Clear—Cooler Up at 8:15 In the forenoon I went to the Office of the Privy Council but the man I wanted to meet was out. I went again in the afternoon and found my man still absent so I secured an audience with one of the secretaries who hearing my desires said I should come the following day at 1:30 P.M. and meet the General Secretary Mr. Kawamura who would tell me all about presenting copies of the Book of Mormon to the members of the Council. Some of the Sunday School children who are on the Christmas program came and practiced their parts. In the evening, I read about Korea. Today I sent Christmas letters and greetings to America.

Wednesday, 1 December 1909, Tokyo

Clear—Calm—Mild Up at 7:30. Spent most of the day in the interest of the distribution of copies of the Book of Mormon among the high government officials. This afternoon I met Mr. Kingoro Kawamura the head secretary of the Privy Council and secured his services as transmitter of the books to the 30 titled men who are members of the council. Their names are as follows: Prince Aritomo Yamagata, President. Count Tsūsen Higashikuze, Vice President. Marquis Masayoshi Matsakata, Count Shiki Kabayama, Viscount K[—]t[-] Fukuoka, Marquis Takoyuki Sasaki, Baron Junjiro Hosokawa, Viscount Michitaka Kawase, Viscount Kuranosake Nakamuda, Baron Kusuke Ōtori, Baron Ryuichi Kuki, Baron Seifu Takasaki, Viscount Magoshichiro Sugi, Marquis Mosho Hachisuka, Viscount Tomonosuki Takashima Viscount Miyoji Itō, Viscount Kiyotsuna Kuroda, Baron Takujiro Nishi, Viscount Atushi Saisho Viscount Kentarō Kaneko, Viscount Kencho Su[-]matsu, Viscount Keigo Kujoura, Baron Kameō Nambu, Baron Hiroyuki Katō, Viscount Shuzo Aoki, Baron Keiroku Tsuzuki, Count Keizo Kagawa, Viscount Watanabe, Count Go Okyu /and/ Baron Shuiken Makino.

The evening I spent with sister Ota and her husband at her home in Aoyama.

Thursday, 2 December 1909, Tokyo

Clear—Calm—Cold Up at 7:15 Spent the forenoon at headquarters doing odd jobs. In the afternoon I took the Books of Mormon to the Privy Council's office and delivered them to Mr. Kawamura. I also presented him with a copy. I also left as many "Introductions to the Book of Mormon" to be distributed to the members of the council at the same time. I secured introductions to Mr. Shibata the Chief Secretary to the Cabinet and to Mr. Kurihara Secretary in the Imperial Household Department. I called at Mr. Shibata's residence but he was ill and couldn't see me. I went to the Imperial Household Department and after some delay at the outer gate, a boy came with a written permit to pass in. I was conducted to one of the waiting rooms in the Department and then had a talk with Mr. Kurihara about presenting the Book of Mormon to the Their Majesties, Their Highnesses and to Prince Iwakura, Minister of the Imperial Household Affairs. They said there would be no objections to making the presentation to the Imperial Family, but according to custom the books must come through the American Ambassador and the Foreign Office. I then learned that Prince Iwakura would be glad to receive a copy of the book and that while it would be difficult to meet him I could take the book to his home and Mr. Kurihara would telephone the family to receive it and he would speak to the Prince himself about the presentation. In going out I had to surrender my pass ticket. This is the closest I have been to the Imperial spirit and no doubt it will be as close as I will get. The opportunity of presenting the book in person to his majesty seems to be less hopeful each hour. I returned to headquarters and after tending to a job or two, ate supper. I called on Sister Chiyo Tanifuji Ishigaki but her husband not being home I did not go in. I should state that besides the odd jobs performed this morning, I called on the American Ambassador Mr. O'Brien in the hope of getting a letter or card of introduction to Prince Iwakura but Mr. O'Brien was not prepared to introduce me.

Friday, 3 December 1909, Tokyo

Clear—Cold Up at 7:20. In the forenoon I went to the home of Prince Iwakura, and left a copy of the Book of Mormon and an "Introduction to the Book of Mormon," for him. Mr. Kurihara whom I met yesterday at the Imperial Household Department had by telephone informed Prince Iwakura's family of my expected visit so they gladly received the book. I returned to headquarters and spent most of the afternoon reading American news. After supper I went to Mr. Kawai's and had him dress up a letter I had written to accompany the copies of the Book of Mormon that are going to the Imperial Family.

Monday, 6 December 1909, Tokyo

Clear—Cold Up at 7:45. After breakfast, I wrapped up the copies of the Book of Mormon prepared for the Imperial Family and started to deliver them. I also took along the copies for eight of the Members of the Cabinet. I called first at the home of Mr. Shibata Chief Secretary of the Cabinet but learned that he was sick in the hospital and was directed to see Mr. Sakata one of the under secretaries. I went from Mr. Shibata's to the American Embassy and met Ambassador O'Brien. He took the copies of the book for the Imperial Family and promised to forward them that day to the Foreign Office from where they would be sent to the Imperial Household Department I also presented Mr. O'Brien with a copy of the English text which he received gladly. From the Embassy I went to the Cabinet which is quartered inside the Imperial compound wall. After waiting sometime at the gate for permission to enter from the officials, I was ushered into a reception room where I met Mr. Sakata and upon his approval of my request to present the members of the Cabinet copies of the Book of Mormon I left eight copies in his care each being directed to the person for whom it was intended. He promised to hand the books to their owners at the first opportunity. Having already presented Count Jutarō Komura, Minister of Foreign Affairs with a copy, the eight copies left with Mr. Sakata are for Marquis Tarō Katsura, Prime Minister and Minster of Finance, Vise Count Seiki Terauchi, Minister of War, Baron Minoru Saitō, Minister of the Navy, Baron Tosuki Hirata, Minster of Home Affairs, Baron Ka[-]etaki Ōura Minister of Commerce & Agriculture, Baron Shimpei Gotō Minister of Communications, Eitarō Komatsubara, Minister of Education, Vise Count Chōshoku Okabe Minister of Justice. In the afternoon I began the writing of a reply to an article /by a Rev. Ochiri on Mormonism & Polygamy/ in the December number of the Y.M.C.A.'s magazine "The Pioneer." This article is a terrible mixture of truth and falsehood which to fair minded people of thought would appeal as absurd, but to the ordinary reader as a "terrible" exposition of "Mormonism." This is the magazine which after receiving the Book of Mormon advertizement manuscripts sent them back saying it would be impossible to allow them to appear in their organ.

Wednesday, 8 December 1909, Tokyo

Clear—Cold Up at 8:15 Spent the forenoon reading, teaching one of the Christmas songs to a little

S.S. girl—Mrs. Makino's little tot—and doing an odd job or two. After dinner I read my writing, finished yesterday, to Mr. Nasa who wrote it in characters and started to criticise it. Some of the Sunday School /children/ came to practice their parts on the Christmas program. After supper received a letter from Elder Elliot C. Taylor stating that his companion, Elder Warren E. Harris was not improved. I sent a telegram calling Elder Harris to Tokyo and sent a letter to Kōfu instructing Elder Melvin F. Barton to go to Shizuoka to take Elder Harris' place in that field. Walked to the Yotsuya post office & back.

Thursday, 9 December 1909, Tokyo

Clear—Calm—Cold Up at 7:00. Spent the forenoon hunting up a doctor for Elder Harris. In the afternoon, I read about China, investigated some songs for translation, did a little work outside etc. Elder Harris arrived about bed time.

Friday, 10 December 1909, Tokyo

Clear—Cold—Windy Up at 7:00 After breakfast, went with Elder Warren E. Harris to Dr Dohi's. This doctor will take our brother under his wing and I believe with the help of our Father he will soon be enjoying perfect health and strength. Returned to headquarters and spent a majority of the remaining time of the day working on yearly reports they having been called for one month ahead of time.

Saturday, 11 December 1909, Tokyo

Clear—Cold—Calm. Up at 7:00 Accompanied Elder Harris to Dr. Okada's. Elder Harris will also be treated by this doctor for a little while for catarrah of the throat. The rest of the day I devoted to personal cleaning up at the barber's and to report mading, as well as directing some practices on parts in the Christmas program.

Tuesday, 14 December 1909, Tokyo

Clear—Cold Up at 6:30. Went to Dr. Aoyama and had him prescribe for my nerves which are not as strong as they should be and which cause me considerable restless sleep. I reviewed all the annual reports and the quarterly reports today. Elder Barton arrived from Kōfu. He is on his way to Shizuoka. In the afternoon and evening I did some running around in connection with the Christmas Party. One boy has failed to come up to the mark in his part and so I shall have to entrust it to someone else. This is the first failure we have ever had among our Sunday School students who have been asked to assist the Christmas program. I had a long talk with Elder Barton and then doctored up for a cold and retired.

Friday, 17 December 1909, Tokyo

Clear—Warmer. Up at 7:00. Spent most of the forenoon at headquarters attending to Sunday School affairs. In the afternoon I went down town to try and get some information regarding travel by rail in Corea and China. I was not successful in learning the particulars. Returned and had a talk with Mr. Nasa about the church. Mr. Nasa's older brother sent a letter to me giving his permission for his younger brother to join the Church. After supper, I attended the Japanese Bible Class.

Saturday, 18 December 1909, Tokyo

Clear—Cold Up at 7:00 Spent the early forenoon trying to get some information about the railroads in China. I called at the Chinese Legation, but they didn't know much about what I desired to learn. They advised me to write to the Consulate at Yokohama. I did this after returning to headquarters. The majority of the afternoon was occupied working with the children who have parts on the Christmas Program. I later had a long chat with Mr. Nasa.

This forenoon, I received a letter from the First Presidency containing my release to return home. The same letter also released Elder Fred A. Caine. A draft for ¥2000 was enclosed to enable Elder Caine and I to tour Korea and China before turning our faces homeward. I wrote a brief letter to Elder Caine repeating his release and expressing my satisfaction in his labors as a missionary.

Having learned through letters from father than my release had been decided upon and that the duty of calling someone of my companions to act as president was entrusted to me, I have been thinking upon the condition and had decided that Elder Elbert D. Thomas' appointment would be best for the mission. Therefore in obedience to the instructions given by the First Presidency in the letter received today I wrote to all the elders in the fields submitting to their vote Elder Thomas' name. The Presidency directs that the elder I appoint shall only act as president of the mission till my successor is selected and arrives at his post.

Sunday, 19 December 1909, Tokyo

Clear—Cold Up at 6:45. Ate breakfast. Directed the Sunday School and taught the First Intermediate Department. After school a long practice of parts on the Christmas program was held. We then held a saint's gathering and administered the sacrament. After this I talked with Bros. Taue and Chiba and Mr. Nasa for sometime. Ate supper and prepared for night meeting at which time I spoke for three quarters of an hour on "The way to know the good or evil of Christianity." Today we decided to baptize Mr. Katsuzō Nasa who has been a faithful investigator for about a year or longer.

Monday, 20 December 1909, Tokyo

Cloudy—Very Cold. Up at 6:00. Ate an early breakfast and then in company with Elders Caine and Jensen and Mr. Katsuzō Nasa I went to the Tama River and witnessed the baptism of Mr. Nasa. Elder Caine officiated. We returned to headquarters and held a brief meeting for the purpose of confirming our new brother. I was mouth in the confirmation. In the afternoon, I spent most of the time helping some of the children in their parts on the Christmas program. In the evening I walked to the penman's home and hired him to write a few membership certificates.

Wednesday, 22 December 1909, Tokyo

Clear—Cold Up at 7:00. Went down town to do some buying for Christmas. After returning to headquarters I presented Elder Thomas to my companions as my successor in the presidency of the Japan Mission. He was sustained by the elders at Tokyo. This is the first announcement of my release to my companions at Tokyo. Of course, Elder Caine was privileged to see the letter of release as soon as it came as it also released him. In the afternoon, I helped the Sunday School children practice their parts on the Christmas program.

Thursday, 23 December 1909, Tokyo

Clear—Cold—Calm Up at 7:00 Spent the forenoon down town buying for Christmas. In the afternoon, I worked till late with the children who are on the Christmas program. Walked to Sister Ishigaki's to give her some tickets to the Christmas entertainment. She was not home.

Friday, 24 December 1909, Tokyo

Clear—Milder Up at 7:00. Worked all day in connection with Christmas preparations. Went to Sister Ishigaki's and to Aoyama. Mailed some presents.

Saturday, 25 December 1909, Tokyo

Cloudy—Clear later—Cold Up at 7:00. Walked to Sister Nabeshima's home to deliver a message regarding our Christmas program. Spent the rest of the day preparing for the party held this evening. The children were all out in rich attire and bright expectant faces that thrilled my heart and made me feel glad that I was alive and permitted to associate with these dear children in Japan. I remarked to my companions that I believed these children were the sweetest in the world. At any rate, not having had such close association with little ones at home as I have had with little ones in Japan I can't help the feeling that these Japanese children (or some of them) are the sweetest children I know At 6:40 p.m. we started the entertainment with all present but one or two who were unavoidably belated. The program lasted till nearly

10:30 and everything went off quite satisfactorily. Having the program in charge there were a few parts I thought that could have been rendered more skillfully if the children had been a little more brave in facing so many people. The program was all on our Savior; His birth and babyhood was thoroughly talked and sung about and His Messiahship was discoursed upon so that any honest soul present who was capable of hearing and understanding must surely have been impressed. A count of the tickets and the number of admissions without tickets showed that besides the four elders 113 were present. Santa Claus, represented by Elder Fred A. Caine gave all the children of the Sunday School a present and candy canes and okoshi (Japanese pop-corn) were freely distributed among all the children present and each adult guest was presented with souvenir pictures of Bible places, events and persons.

After the entertainment, I read letters from Sapporo and Asahikawa in which all the brethren in these fields sustain Elder Thomas as temporary president of the mission. The approval from the other fields having already been received I announced to the saints who remained to chat, the release of Elder Caine and I and appointment of Elder Thomas to preside. After a few minutes pleasant conversation, we had prayers and retired. Today I received a present or two from friends and saints.

Sunday, 26 December 1909, Tokyo

Clear—Cold Up at 6:00 Sent a telegram to Elder Thomas informing him of his call to preside. Returned and ate breakfast. Presided over the Sunday School and taught the First Intermediate Department. Presided over and addressed the saint's meeting. In the afternoon we held a /S.S./ teachers meeting. I then did a little reading. After supper we held a fairly well attended preaching meeting. I spoke for a few minutes. After this meeting the saints and a few friends lingered and we had an instructive and pleasant conversation

Monday, 27 December 1909, Tokyo

Clear—Very Cold Up at 7:00. Today the elders have been having their Christmas celebration and at noon enjoyed a good turkey dinner. In the forenoon I wrote up the record of the Sunday School party held Christmas night and left this record together with copies of the speeches etc on file for future reference. In the afternoon I took a long walk. After supper, I spent some time talking to Bro. Taue. Today I wrote to the First Presidency telling of the appointment of Elder Thomas to preside. I also dropped a card to mother. Besides this I wrote to the elders informing them of Elder Thomas' appointment and giving them permission to make all matters regarding this change in presidency public.

Tuesday, 28 December 1909, Tokyo

Cloudy—Severe cold Up at 7:30. Spent the forenoon down town attending to personal business. In the afternoon I made up the annual report of the Tokyo Sunday School. Miss Saigv (her given name is Masayuki) called and expressed the desire to enter the church. I had a long talk with her about the matter. Later Mr. Watanabe came and I spent about an hour with him answering his wandering questions. After supper I entered into conversation with Sister Nabeshima who called to pay her tithing. This conversation lasted till after 9:00 o'clock.

Wednesday, 29 December 1909, Tokyo

Cloudy—Cold Up at 7:00 Spent the forenoon arranging papers etc. At noon we had prayer meeting. In the afternoon I called on the landlord to see about getting ¥65.20 half the price of a new closet build on to our house. He promised to send the money tomorrow. Bro. and Sister Thomas arrived from Morioka in time for supper. They were well. Reported a fine Christmas at Morioka. After supper I had a conference with Elder Thomas regarding the changes necessary and decided to call Elder Anderson from Morioka to Tokyo, send Elder Fairbourn from Kōfu to Morioka and Elder Roskelley from Sapporo to Morioka, and Elder Jensen from Tokyo to Kōfu. All of these changes are to take place so that Elder Caine and I can get away by Jan 10th as contemplated.

This forenoon I spent about two hours talking with Miss. Masayuki Saigō.

Thursday, 30 December 1909, Tokyo

Clear—Warmer Up at 7:00 Spent the major part of the day at headquarters. In the afternoon I wrote a farewell letter to the missionaries dating it Jan 1, 1910. Walked as far as Yotsuya in the evening and then went to visit Bro. Kikuchi. He was not at home. Elder Thomas accompanied me.

Friday, 31 December 1909, Tokyo

Cloudy—Still milder Up at 7:15. Spent nearly most of the day at headquarters assorting and filing away letters received during the year. The totals for work done during the Year are as follows. . . .

During the year I have had many experiences some the most pleasant in life and some the most bitter that humans are called upon to experience. The completion of the Book of Mormon and its publication has been perhaps the most important triumph of the year so far as great deeds are concerned. My release to return home having been withheld till this great effort was completed is a cause for much rejoicing. I now feel that my homegoing is not a disaster to me or anything else. Great is the debt of gratitude I owe to the Lord for His many blessings.

Saturday, 1 January 1910, Tokyo

Rain—Warmer Up at 7:00 Spent the greater part of the day writing a farewell address to all the native saints in Japan. In the evening, I turned the Mission Business over to Elder Elbert D. Thomas. . . .

Sunday, 2 January 1910, Tokyo

Cloudy—Colder Up at 6:45. Prepared for Sunday School which was reorganized today, but Elder Caine and I will continue to discharge our duties in the school till we leave Tokyo. Having presided over the Tokyo Sunday School ever since it was organized in the days of Prest. Ensign I regret very much the parting with this work for it more than anything else has given me the chance to interpret the children and youth of Japan. I have learned to love the children deeply for I know they are worthy of the love of any right-hearted man. I also presided over the fast meeting. After this meeting I took a walk to Yotsuya I presided over and addressed the evening meeting which considering the New Years festivities was very well attended.

Monday, 3 January 1910, Tokyo

Clear—Cold Up at 7:00 Today I rewrote my final address to the saints. Miss Masayuki Saigō came and said that after considering deeply and carefully what she had heard about the sacredness and importance of the covenants one enters into when joining the Church, she felt it her duty to make these covenants with a sincere heart and strong determination to keep them faithfully to the end. It was arranged that she be baptized next Saturday.

This forenoon I went and had my picture taken at Kobayashi's studio.

Tuesday, 4 January 1910, Tokyo

Clear—Cold Up at 6:45. Ate breakfast and went to Yokohama on mission business and to get as much information about traveling in Corea and China as possible. Returned to Tokyo about mid-day. The afternoon I spent dictating to Bro. Nasa my farewell address to the saints. In the evening I talked with Elder Thomas giving him advice about Mission Affairs.

Wednesday, 5 January 1910, Tokyo

Rain—Cold. Up at 7:00 Spent the forenoon clearing up unfinished business. At noon, in our meeting, I said my farewell to the elders at headquarters. In the afternoon some guests were entertained. Elder Fairbourn arrived from Kōfu on his way to Morioka. This gave me a chance to say good-bye to him.

Thursday, 6 January 1910, Tokyo

Clear—Cold Up at 7:45. Went to Shinjuku Station to see Elder Jensen off. Then went down town and had my account with the bank transferred to Elder Thomas I attended to a personal job or two and after returning entertained guests who came to say farewell and also closed up some of my business with the mission. Spent the evening pleasantly at Mr. Yashiro's

Friday, 7 January 1910, Tokyo

Clear—Warmer Up at 7:00 Spent part of the forenoon writing and the rest of the forenoon and part of the afternoon down town on business. The rest of the afternoon was devoted to friends who called. In the evening I bid good-bye to Elder Fairbourn and then said a few words as a parting to the Japanese Bible Class which has been held for so long a time under the able direction of Elder Caine.

Saturday, 8 January 1910, Tokyo

Cloudy—Cold Up at 6:30. After an early breakfast I went to Tama River with my companions and some of the saints and witnessed the baptism of Sister Masayuki Saigō a young woman of great promise. Returned and made some final preparations for my journey to Corea and China. Had a lesson in the Corean language. After supper I went to Bro. Kikuchi's to investigate his condition. He is far far away from the gospel and the Lord. Elder Thomas accompanied me.

Sunday, 9 January 1910, Tokyo

Pleasant—Not extremely cold Up at 7:00. Ate breakfast. In Sunday School I turned over the gavel to Prest. Thomas who will be Superintendent in my place. I taught the First Intermediate Department for the last time. Elder Harris will succeed me as instructor in this department. Before the school closed I made a few farewell remarks. In the sacrament meeting held at 11:30 a.m. I presided, confirmed Sister Saigō and delivered my farewell speech to the saints. After this meeting which was attended by all but two of the saints living in Tokyo and vicinity, I blessed Sister Ota's baby. After eating dinner I did several jobs which finished my business in the mission. In the evening meeting over which I presided, I delivered a final testimony. After this I said a special farewell to my young Sister in the gospel Ei Nachie, who has lived at headquarters with her mother for several years. During the past year I have been paying her way at school and have taken great pains to have her grow up as the Lord would have her do. As a token of my interest in her and my love for her and as a reminder of the instructions given to her I gave her a small pearl ring and had Sister Thomas who was present when I gave this present and my final instructions fit it on her finger. I have loved this little girl as a sister and regret more the farewell to her than I did the farewell to my own blood sisters when I left America. In fact this is the first time in my life that I have had a sister in the same home with me. I also had a little farewell talk with Sister Nachie the little girl's mother who has been such a faithful servant at headquarters and been a great help to all the female saints. Some of my photos were brought from the photographer's today and given to some of the saints. Some farewell presents were received.

Monday, 10 January 1910, Tokyo

Cloudy—Rain—Later clear and cold Up at 6:30 Ate a light breakfast and left headquarters and went to Shimbashi Station where, in company with Elder Caine, I took train and started on the Korea China trip. A number of saints and friends were at the depot to see us off. Mr. Sakuraba introduced us to one of his friends, a Mr. Tanaka who was going to Osaka. This gentleman proved a very pleasant traveling companion. At Shizuoka, Elders Taylor and Barton met us at the station where we had the chance to say good-bye to them. The night was spent at Kobe at the Chūōkwan just across the street from the depot.

Notes

1. *Seibundo.* Famous publishing house in Tokyo.
2. *Shokugyo Gakko.* Trade school.
3. B. H. Roberts, "History of the 'Mormon' Church," *Americana Illustrated* 4–10 (July 1909–June 1915). This series formed the basis for Roberts's later *Comprehensive History of the Church.*

Chapter 14

Epilogue

After two weeks at sea aboard the *Empress of India*, Alma and his companions steamed into Tokyo Bay on 12 August 1901. They rode a dingy to Japanese soil and were suddenly bombarded with a visceral barrage of new sights, sounds, smells, and experiences. Alma recorded, "I indeed felt like 'a stranger in a strange land.'"[1]

For the next eight and a half years, Alma dedicated himself to the Japan Mission with incredible fervor and religiosity. He drew deeply on his upbringing—the best that Mormonism could offer. His devout parents, who had earlier blessed him with education and position, now supported him emotionally through constant letters and prayers. Members of the thirteenth ward and neighborhood also corresponded regularly with Alma and buoyed his spirits from a distance. But ultimately it was Alma's own character, natural intelligence, work ethic, and abiding faith that sustained his mission. He demonstrated his own mettle and proved that the confidence placed in him by Elder Grant was well deserved.

His accomplishments included learning both the spoken and written Japanese word; assisting in the translation of missionary tracts and Church hymns; organizing Sunday School classes; serving as president of the Japan Mission from his early to late twenties; performing gospel ordinances; opening new proselyting areas throughout Japan;[603] finding, teaching, converting, and strengthening many of the early Japanese Saints; and leading other missionaries to do the same. Alma considered his Japanese translation of the Book of Mormon his crowning work.

Finally on 18 December 1909, Alma received his release from the Japan Mission, signed by all three members of the First Presidency—Joseph F. Smith, John R. Winder, and Anthon H. Lund. "Whenever the question of your release has been referred to in our Councils," the letter began, "we have had in our minds associated with it the accomplishment of the important work undertaken by you, namely, the translation and publication of the Book of Mormon in Japanese; and now since success has so signally crowned your labors . . . we have great pleasure indeed in tendering to you the release which we feel you so well deserve." It continued, "In thus releasing you, after having spent so long a time on a foreign mission, we feel to say that your labors as a missionary and presiding officer have met with our hearty approval and entire satisfaction."[2]

The First Presidency concluded the release by raising an important issue very much on Alma's mind, and one which I posed in the introduction of this thesis: can a missionary "successfully" fulfill his "duty" while failing to "succeed." In the case of[604] Alma's long tenure in Japan (August 1901–January 1910), only thirty-five Japanese were baptized, but even many of them left the Church.[3] Was Alma successful?

Echoing the earlier words of President Lorenzo Snow, the First Presidency emphasized to Alma that while the Lord desires proselyting success, he seemingly expects missionaries only to fulfill their duty. "Whether or not the Japanese as a nation or as individuals to any great extent, shall be found sufficiently honest in their hearts to accept the Book of Mormon as a divine record, and to yield obedience to the requirements of the Gospel so plainly taught in it, the future alone must determine," they concluded. "But however this may be, the fact nevertheless remains, that through your diligence and patience and indomitable perseverance, under the blessings of the Lord, and in keeping with His providences and the desires of their forefathers, that people have now within their reach, and in their own tongue, the book of all books best calculated to bless and interest them."[4] Thus, Alma was successful.

Farewell to Japan

After receiving his release, Alma busied himself with the transfer of mission records and affairs to Elbert D. Thomas, participated in the baptism and confirmation of Nasa Katsuzō in the nearby Tama River, and finalized Christmas preparations. On 25 December, they held a Christmas party at the mission home, and Alma was reminded of his love for the Japanese people, especially the children. "The children were all out in rich attire and bright expectant faces that thrilled my heart and made me feel glad that I was alive and permitted to associate with these dear children in Japan. I remarked to my[605] companions that I believed these children were the sweetest in the world."[5] Besides the elders, 113 Japanese friends were present.

On the last day of 1909, Alma recorded his feelings regarding his last year in Japan.

> During the year I have had many experiences some the most pleasant in life and some the most bitter that humans are called upon to experience," he began. "The completion of the Book of Mormon and its publication has been perhaps the most important triumph of the year so far as great deeds are concerned. My release to return home having been withheld till this great effort was completed is a cause for much rejoicing. I now feel that my homegoing is not a disaster to me or anything else. Great is the debt of gratitude I owe to the Lord for His many blessings.[6]

Finally, on the morning of 10 January 1910, Alma and his longtime missionary companion Fred Caine ate a light breakfast and headed to Shimbashi Station, Tokyo, where they began their fact-finding mission to Korea and China. Over the next nine and a half weeks, Alma and Fred toured Korea and China for the First Presidency. Relying on their own senses and a variety of other sources, Alma later concluded that conditions in China did not then favor the preaching of the restored gospel.[7]

The two men returned to Tokyo on 19 March 1910 and were welcomed by the Japanese Saints and missionaries. That evening Alma recorded: "It was a happy meeting. I was happy beyond words. . . . Everything and everybody at headquarters was in fine shape." He then opened a letter from home that reported his mother sick, his brother[606] Edward Theodore dead, and his brother Samuel's little girl dead and little boy sick. Of this news he wrote, "Calamities always come together and often as an aftermath of joys."[8] He was comforted the following day as he attended his church meetings. "The priviledge to attend the sacrament /meeting/ and worship with the saints was one which came as a drink to /a/ man dying of thirst in the desert," he wrote. "In the public preaching meeting held in the evening, I was called upon to speak. I felt quite out of practice." Already Alma was fading from missionary to member.[9]

The following Thursday, the Japanese Saints threw a farewell party for Alma and Fred. "All the saints in Tokyo except Bro. Kikuchi were present," noted Alma of his earlier convert's absence. "This expression of love was thoroughly appreciated and I thank God for the satisfaction of knowing that my labors in Japan have /not/ been in vain."[10] Finally on 30 March 1910, Alma and Fred said their final goodbyes and departed for America.

Home at Last

On 26 April 1910, Alma arrived in Salt Lake City after an absence of eight years and eight months. Reunited with his father, mother, sisters, and brothers, he naturally felt disoriented. "It was a strange home into which I was received," he wrote, "one that has been built since I went to Japan. . . . Dear old father has aged and weakened considerably. . . . I felt glad and then sad. I felt homesick for Japan, but rejoiced in being at my aged parents' side. I felt almost like being in an unknown world."[11] The evening of[607] his arrival, Alma and Fred reported on their missions to the First Presidency and received President Joseph F. Smith's "blessing." That evening Alma slept in a Western-style bed.[12] He was home at last.

The following morning, Alma and Fred met again with the First Presidency. The two elders reported on their lengthy service in Japan and on their fact-finding mission to Korea and China. They continued presenting their report that Friday and the following Monday. Excited to have Alma and Fred home, family, friends, and fellow Saints held a number of welcome-home celebrations. Home just a few days, Alma and Fred attended a reception hosted by the Salt Lake Second Ward. Present were Alma's original companions, Heber J. Grant, Horace S. Ensign, and Louis A. Kelsch, "making the first reunion of the original pioneers of the Japan mission since the summer of 1902."[13] During his first several weeks back in Utah, Alma was often called on to speak during church meetings on his Japan mission.

Amidst the excitement and homecomings, Alma struggled to readjust to non-missionary life. Bereft of his missionary calling and mantle, Alma made plans for his professional future while becoming reacquainted with his former life. It was apparent that his father's mortuary business was in trouble. "I have been looking into conditions around home and I find that everything pertaining to father's affairs is in a distressing condition and I don't see how I can help much," he noted with sadness.[14] The following day he recorded: "Have been trying to decide on a job by which to make my bread. Have looked into the proposition of accepting a position with the Beneficial Life Insurance Co.[608] as head of the corps of agents for Salt Lake and vicinity."[15] In early June he determined to break into the insurance business as a soliciting agent. However, during his first day of work, his elderly father had an attack of lumbago, which forced Alma to spend a considerable amount of time around his parent's home.

By the end of his first month with the Beneficial Life Insurance Co., Alma felt tremendous pressure from his father and brother Samuel to return to the family undertaking business. "So I decided to go back to the family calling and serve the dead," he conceded. That July he and Samuel bought out nearly all of their father's undertaking supplies for about $4,400 "in the hope of relieving him of work in this line it being clearly evident that he could not take care of any sales without making himself nervous and without suffering resultant physical pain." Before resuming the irregular and strenuous life of a funeral director and mortician, Alma decided to head to the mountains "in the hope of reviving a full supply of physical and nervous strength."[16]

Alma departed Salt Lake City in late July 1910 and traveled north to the Teton Basin, where many of his relatives were then living. He moved into the home of his aunt and uncle Martha and George Little for the next month. "Here I was welcomed and given all of the comforts their home would allow," he recorded. "I had horses saddles and buggies at my disposal so

that I could visit far and near, hunt or fish just as I pleased." This much needed vacation provided Alma with plenty of exercise, recreation, amusement, along with healthy food and clean air to help settle his nerves, which had been bothering him from the latter part of his mission in Japan. That August he traveled with a group of[609] friends to Jackson Hole, Wyoming "and spent there a delightful, healthful two weeks of camping and fishing." Alma remembered it as a "jolly time."[17]

He returned to Salt Lake City seemingly rejuvenated and eager to work with his brother Samuel. However, he quickly discovered that his "nerves were not yet strong enough and the recreation [he] had while good had not been long enough." He spent the next two weeks vacationing in the Cache, Wasatch, and Sanpete valleys with family and friends and then returned to Teton Basin, Idaho, for another two months of relaxation. "While in Jackson Hole and the Basin I tried to serve the Lord and do all the good I could so spiritually I had a good time," he recorded.

Properly rested Alma returned again to Salt Lake City on the night of 16 November 1910 and the following morning resumed his undertaking career, this time working for the undertaking firm of "Samuel M. Taylor and Company," earning a salary of $125.00 per month. "It only took a day or two to get back into the harness of the old business of my boyhood days," noted Alma. "I took to it as naturally as a duck takes to water."[18] Shortly thereafter, Alma and his brothers Samuel and Joseph united their business interests with S. George of the Colorado Casket Company and K. Howe to incorporate the Salt Lake Casket Company. Their corporation issued five hundred shares of stock valued at $100 each, of which Alma held twenty-five shares. Only other undertakers involved in the retail business were admitted as stockholders. Alma was named treasurer of the new company.[19] [610]

Alma retained his strong interest in the Japan Mission and the Church. During this first year back he noted, "I have done considerable speaking about Japan both in and out of the city and have been appointed once on the home mission of the Ensign Stake. Several interesting communications have come from my old mission field and the news of continual growth in Japan is very gratifying to my soul."[20] That first November, Alma was set apart as a member of the Ensign Stake Board of Sunday Schools. Nineteen months later he was set apart as Brother William Atkin's second councilor in the Sunday School Board, a calling which he fulfilled until he was released in September 1921.[21] In January 1911, Alma was also set apart by Elder J. Golden Kimball as one of the presidents of the eighth quorum of Seventy and was further invited to become a member of the First Council of the Seventy's weekly temple prayer circle, until he was ordained a high priest years later. The prayer circle was a "pleasant association with inspired men—a much appreciated opportunity—a profitable experience" in Alma's mind.[22] President Joseph F. Smith also gave Alma the "splendid privilege" to participate in the monthly fast and testimony meetings held in the Salt Lake Temple.[23]

The Salt Lake Casket Company prospered despite the death of Alma's father on 17 February 1913. Alma "devoted [his] time and effort exclusively to the wholesale funeral supply business." He was eventually made manager of the company, a position he[611] held until March 1919, when the sale of his father's estate forced him to sell his equity to other stockholders and leave the business.[24]

Secure in his profession, Alma turned his attention to marriage. Already considered a mature bachelor in Utah, he began courting Angeline Holbrook. Born on 30 March 1881, in Fillmore, Utah, to Lafayette and Emily Angelina Hinckley Holbrook, she was the granddaughter of the famous Mormon pioneer Ira Nathaniel Hinckley. An intelligent and proper woman, Angeline had taught for a time on the Brigham Young College and University of Utah faculties as an English teacher. Alma, age 33, and Angeline, age 34, were married on 26 October 1915, in the Salt Lake Temple. They made Salt Lake City their home.

In June 1919, Alma helped organize The Intermountain Casket Company (two thousand shares at $100 per share), a new wholesale funeral supply company. His father-in-law, Lafayette Holbrook, was the largest shareholder, as well as president and director. The company immediately acquired property on the northeast corner of 200 West at 100 South and erected a three story concrete building for their new business. Once

the building was completed, they moved into it on 2 January 1920. They started as wholesale distributors and sellers of the complete line of caskets and all types of funeral supplies, so they solicited funeral directors and cemeteries of the intermountain area.

After eight years of marriage and no children, Alma and Angeline hoped to adopt. Finally in early February 1923, they were able to adopt a newborn boy who had just been delivered by Angeline's brother-in-law Dr. Albert Hansen. They named him Richard.[612] Alma, now age 41, and Angeline, now age 42, were finally parents. He would be their only child.

While acting as a father and working in the undertaking industry, Alma was a sought-after public speaker. He was invited numerous times to speak to large congregations in the Salt Lake Tabernacle and Assembly Hall (located on Temple Square) and over the Church's radio station, KSL. His sermon topics included the "judgment of man," "Christ the great example," "America: a land of liberty," "how to comprehend God," "the spirit of thanksgiving," and "the Book of Mormon and America."[25]

Alma served as the manager of the Intermountain Casket Company from its organization until April 1939, when he was named its president and director. By this time Alma, his wife, and his brother-in-law Paul L. Holbrook, had repurchased most of the issued stock. The company continued to prosper. Alma recalled, "In spite of the appearance of local competitors and the activity of outside competitors, we held the commanding position in the field." Ironically, it was only after Alma's beloved Japan forced the United States to enter World War II that his undertaking business began to decline. Classified by the U.S. government as a "non-essential" wartime industry, Alma's casket manufacturing company soon faltered for the lack of materials. Fearing bankruptcy, Alma, Angeline, and Paul decided to voluntarily liquidate their company and[613] dissolve their corporation in August 1943. And so Alma retired and became a "man without a job," a condition he "enjoyed very much."[26]

Four years after retiring, Alma died suddenly of a heart attack while fishing with life-long friend George A. Taylor in Ashton, Idaho, on 19 June 1947. He had lived 64 years, 10 months, and 19 days. At the time of his death, he, Angeline, and Richard were living at 245 East South Temple Street, Salt Lake City.[27] Judging Alma a "prominent Salt Lake businessman," Alma's obituary noted that he had died a "very active member of the South Eighteenth Ward."[28]

Alma's life had come full circle, as his body was again cradled in a morgue and laid in a casket. Bishop Rulon S. Howells conducted his funeral service on 23 June 1947.[29] Alma was interned in the Salt Lake City Cemetery in a plot overlooking the broad Salt Lake Valley, which Mormon pioneers had entered a hundred years previously.[30] Alma, too, was a Mormon pioneer in his own life. As Japanese missionary extraordinaire, he had been a "stranger in a strange land."[614]

Notes

1. Alma O. Taylor, Journal, 12 August 1901.

2. Letter from Joseph F. Smith, John R. Winder, and Anthon H. Lund to Alma O. Taylor, 23 November 1909. Alma wrote in his journal: "This forenoon, I received a letter from the First Presidency containing my release to return home. The same letter also released Elder Fred A. Caine. A draft for ¥2000 was enclosed to enable Elder Caine and I to tour Korea and China before turning our faces homeward. I wrote a brief letter to Elder Caine repeating his release and expressing my satisfaction in his labors as a missionary.

"Having learned through letters from father than my release had been decided upon and that the duty of calling someone of my companions to act as president was entrusted to me, I have been thinking upon the condition and had decided that Elder Elbert D. Thomas' appointment would be best for the mission. Therefore in obedience to the instructions given by the First Presidency in the letter received today I wrote to all the elders in the fields submitting to their vote Elder Thomas' name. The Presidency directs that the elder I appoint shall only act as president of the mission till my successor is selected and arrives at his post." Alma O. Taylor, Journal, 18 December 1910.

3. Nichols, *History of the Japan Mission*, 133.

4. Letter from Joseph F. Smith, John R. Winder, and Anthon H. Lund to Alma O. Taylor, 23 November 1909, Alma O. Taylor Collection, Perry Special Collections.

5. Alma O. Taylor, Journal, 25 December 1909.

6. Alma O. Taylor, Journal, 31 December 1909.

7. See Reid L. Neilson, "Alma O. Taylor's Fact-Finding Mission to China," *BYU Studies* 40, no. 1 (2000): 176–203.

8. Alma O. Taylor, Journal, 19 March 1910.

9. Alma O. Taylor, Journal, 20 March 1910.

10. Alma O. Taylor, Journal, 24 March 1910.

11. Alma O. Taylor, Journal, 26 April 1910.

12. Alma O. Taylor, Journal, 26 April 1910.

13. Alma O. Taylor, Journal, 27 April 1910.

14. Alma O. Taylor, Journal, 24 May 1910.

15. Alma O. Taylor, Journal, 25 May 1910.

16. Alma O. Taylor, Journal, 17 June 1910–12 February 1911.

17. Alma O. Taylor, Journal, 17 June 1910–12 February 1911.

18. Alma O. Taylor, Journal, 17 June 1910–12 February 1911.

19. Alma O. Taylor, Journal, 17 June 1910–12 February 1911; and Harry W. Nelson, "The Casket Industry in Utah," *The Utah Payroll Builder* 13 (January 1925): 6.

20. Alma O. Taylor, Journal, Book M, no date.

21. Alma O. Taylor, Journal, Book M, no date.

22. Alma O. Taylor, Journal, Book M, no date.

23. Alma O. Taylor, Journal, Book M, no date.

24. Alma O. Taylor, Journal, 4 September 1946.

25. Several of Alma's speeches were published in the Church's *Deseret News*. "Men Will Be Judged For What They Are, And Not What They Seem To Be," 18 March 1916; "Life Of Christ The Great Example To Mankind; His Work A Living Model For Today; True Liberty And Peril Of Disregard For Law," 25 February 1922; "America Is A Land Of Promise And Destiny To Those Who Will But Keep The Commandments That Have Been Laid Down," 12 December 1925; "The Messiah As Life's Master Model," 3 January 1926; "Speaker Affirms God Is Not Discoverable—He Is Revealed; Vision of the Prophet Joseph Smith Is True About Deity," 3 December 1927; "Lest The Spirit Of Thanksgiving Shall Fail Of It's Purpose," 28 November 1928; "The Book Of Mormon's Emphasis On America," 3 March 1934.

26. Alma O. Taylor, Journal, 4 September 1946.

27. "Final Rites Set for S.L. Businessman," *Deseret News*, 20 June 1947.

28. "Final Rites Set for S.L. Businessman," *Deseret News*, 20 June 1947.

29. "Final Rites Set for S.L. Businessman," *Deseret News*, 20 June 1947.

30. Salt Lake City Cemetery, Plot X-1-139-1-W. It is bordered by 1150 East, 355 North, 1200 East, and 325 North, Salt Lake City.

Biographical Register

This register provides biographical information on every person Alma mentions in his Japanese missionary journals reproduced in this volume. I have begun each entry with the individual's surname as Alma recorded it. In some cases, Alma spelled a name both correctly and incorrectly. As such, I have listed both names, with the incorrect spelling in parentheses. If he used two equally possible spellings, I have noted both in capital letters, connected by *or*. All Asian names have been listed first by surname and then by given name with no comma to retain the nomenclature style prevalent in Asia. Although I've attempted to note birth and death dates together with other biographical information for each individual, in many cases I've only been able to provide information that highlights the role of each individual in Alma's journals. For the benefit of historians studying the early years of the Japan Mission I have also included entries for each of the early Latter-day Saint converts during Alma's mission. Please see the bibliography following this register for full citations of sources abbreviated in brackets at the end of each entry. Refer to the index to locate the relevant page numbers for each individual.

ABE, Mr., was a member of the Waseda University faculty who investigated Hirai Hirogoro's moral character in March and April 1908.

ADAMS, Mr., was a fellow Japan-bound passenger of Alma's onboard the *Empress of India* in July and August 1901.

AGUMA FAMILY, was a family whose children attended the LDS Sunday School in Tokyo. Alma visited their home on 3 April 1907.

AKASU Hiroshi, was a preacher of the Nihon Kirisuto Kyōkwai (Japan Church of Christ). Alma met him on 13 January 1907.

AKIMOTO, Mr., moved to Idaho to raise sugar beets. Visited the Japan Mission home on 19 October 1909.

ALLCOT, George A., was an older gentleman who met with Alma and his companions on 31 August 1901 by introduction of Mrs. Parker.

ALVIN V. *See* Taylor, Alvin V.

ANDERSON, Edw. H., is Edward H. Anderson (1858–1928), born on 8 October 1858, in Billeberga, Sweden, to Nils and Pehrailla Pehrsdotter Andersson. Emigrated to America in 1864. Baptized on 1 July 1869, and ordained an elder in 1880. Married Jane Susannah Ballantyne on 29 June 1882, in Salt Lake City. Helped edit and manage the *Contributor* magazine. Presided over the Scandinavian Mission from 1890–1892. Wrote *A Brief History of the Church* and *A Life of Brigham Young.* Served as clerk of the Weber Stake, superintendent of the Y.M.M.I.A., and associated editor of the *Improvement Era.* Died on 1 February 1928, in Salt Lake City. [*AF, BE* 1:715.]

ANDERSON, James (1883–1963), was born 3 August 1883, in Elsinore, Utah, to Jens Christian and Johannah Sorsen Anderson. Baptized at eight and set apart for the Japan Mission on 7 June 1905, by J. Golden Kimball. Served in Tokyo and Sapporo Conferences and the city of Morioka. Married Lydia Bean on 18 June 1913, in Salt Lake City. Died on 21 October 1963, in Thousand Oaks, California. [*AF, JMMH.*]

AOKI, Rev., was a German Mission preacher living in Chiba. Well versed in Biblical scripture and the English language. He and Alma became friends while Alma was living in Yokohama.

AOYAMA, Dr., practiced medicine in Tokyo. Alma visited him on 14 December 1909, to have his nervous condition diagnosed.

APOSTLE LYMAN. *See* Lyman, Francis M.

APOSTLE MERRILL. *See* Merrill, Marriner W.

ARAI, Mr., was a member of the Yotsuya Police Station. Alma visited him during the Hirai Hirogoro affair on 19 March 1908.

ASHTON, Elias (1880–1919), was born on 16 February 1880, in Salt Lake City, to Edward Treharne and Effie Walker Morris Ashton. Grew up with Alma. Was apparently called to the Japan Mission in summer 1902 but for some reason did not come. Married Rosabel Hall on 23 September 1908, in Salt Lake City. Died on 14 October 1919, in Salt Lake City. [*AF.*]

AUNT CLARA. *See* Taylor, Clara Ann Sudbury.

AUNT ELIZA. *See* Smith, Eliza M.

AUNT HATTIE. Was a member of Alma's large extended family in Utah.

AUNT JANE. Was a member of Alma's large extended family in Utah.

AUNT LUCY. Was a member of Alma's large extended family in Utah.

AUNT MARGARET. *See* Goodman, Margaret.

AUNT MARTHA. Was a member of Alma's large extended family in Idaho.

AUNTIE DALE. Was a member of Alma's large extended family in Utah.

AVERALL, Mr., was an expatriate living in Tokyo. Met Alma on 13 August 1901, and shared information regarding life in Japan.

AWAYA FAMILY, had two sons who attended the LDS Sunday School in Tokyo. Alma visited the family on 10 June 1908.

AZUMA, Mr., was a poor man whose children attended the LDS Sunday School in Tokyo. Assisted in the Japanese translation of the missionary tract, "In the Lineage of the Gods."

BABA, Mrs., visited the Japan Mission home on 2 February 1909.

BADGER, Bessie (b. 1883), was likely born in about 1883, in Fort Hall, Idaho. Was one of Alma's close friends from Salt Lake City. Married John J. Jones. [*AF.*]

BADGER, Ralph A. (1880–1963), was born on 8 April 1880, in Salt Lake City, to Rodney C. and Louisa Noble Ashby Badger. Baptized on 6 August 1888. Set apart for the South African Mission on 10 March 1905, and returned 10 July 1908. Served as president of the South African Mission, 1906–1908. Died on 6 October 1963, in Murray, Utah. [*AF, BE* 4:378.]

BAGGERLY, Miss. *See* Baggerley, Maud.

BAGGERLEY or BAGGERLY, Maud (1879–1918), was born on 20 September 1879, in Windsor, Missouri, to Charles Milton and George Ann Munday Baggerley. Friends with Grace Frost and corresponded with Alma for part of his mission as a friend. Married Theadore McKean in 1907, in Salt Lake City. Died on 29 November 1918, in Toppenish, Washington. [*AF, IGI.*]

BAGNELL or BAGHELL, Mrs., was an expatriate woman living with her daughter (who traveled to Japan onboard the *Empress of India* with Alma and his companions), in Yokohama. Alma and his companions attended a Christmas Eve party at her home in 1902.

BARTON, Melvin F. (b. 1887), was born on 25 November 1887, in Kaysville, Utah, to Frank and Rachel Mansell Barton. Baptized on 1 July 1899, and set apart for the Japan Mission on 3 June 1909, by Seymour B. Young. Served in the Kōfu Conference and the city of Shizuoka. Released early due to ill health. [*IGI, JMMH.*]

BARTON, Robert H. (1888–1958), was born on 2 February 1888, in Kaysville, Utah, to Peter and Mary Elizabeth Beesley Barton. Baptized on 1 October 1896, and set apart for the Japan Mission on 3 June 1909, by Seymour B. Young. Labored in the Sapporo Conference, the city of Asahikawa, the city of Sapporo, and lastly the Tokyo Conference as Conference President. Released early due to sickness of his father. Married Jenness Elizabeth Wiggill on 29 November 1916, in Salt Lake City. Died on 10 February 1958, in Ogden, Utah. [*AF, JMMH.*]

BATT, Emma, was friends with Alma in Salt Lake City.

BECKER or BRECKER, Mr., was the manager of the Brandenstein Tea Company's branch house and a friend of Mr. Averall in Tokyo. Alma met him on 2 October 1901.

BERGSTROM, Mr., was the longtime minister of the Swedish church in Chiba, Japan. Alma heard him preach on 20 September 1903.

BERRY, Dr., was an expatriate living in Shanghai, China who had traveled to Yokohama, Japan to meet his new bride. Alma met him in fall 1901.

BEVAN, Heber (1860–1902), was born on 31 March 1860, in Tooele, Utah, to James and Mary Shields Bevan. Married Alma's cousin, Maria Little, on 9 April 1890, in Logan, Utah. Died on 1 March 1902, in Hayden, Idaho. [*AF.*]

BEVINS, Mrs. Heber is Maria Little Bevan (1870–1951), was born on 18 September 1870, in West Jordan, Utah, to George Edwin and Martha Taylor Little. Was Alma's first cousin. Married Heber James Bevan on 9 April 1890, in Logan, Utah. Died on 30 July 1951, in Pocatello, Idaho. [*AF.*]

BIRKELUND, J. R., was the author of several derogatory article published in the *Japan Mail* against the Latter-day Saints in fall 1901.

BOOTH, General, was a member of the Japan Salvation Army. Alma attended one of his sermons on 23 April 1907 in Tokyo.

BOWMAN, Mr., was an Englishman who boarded with Alma and his companions at the Metropole Hotel, Tokyo. Friendly to the Latter-day Saints.

BRINK, Miss., was a Christian missionary serving in the Far East. She boarded with Alma and his companions at the Metropole Hotel, Tokyo. Friendly to the Latter-day Saints.

BRINKLEY, Captain is Captain F. Brinkley, the editor of the *Japan Mail,* an English newspaper based in Yokohama. He was a former member of the British Royal Artillery and vehemently anti-Mormon in his writing.

BROTHER or BROTHER SAM. *See* Taylor, Samuel M.

BUTTER, Malcolm, was friends with Alma in Salt Lake City.

CABLE, Mr. and his wife boarded at the Metropole Hotel, Tokyo with Alma and his companions. Very friendly to the Latter-day Saints.

CABLE, Mrs. and her husband boarded at the Metropole Hotel, Tokyo with Alma and his companions. Very friendly to the Latter-day Saints. She regularly accompanied singer Horace S. Ensign on the piano.

CAINE, Fred. *See* Caine, Frederick A.

CAINE, Frederick A. (1884–1929), was born on 24 March 1884, in Coalville, Utah, to Alfred Henry and Margaret Ann Mitchell Caine. Baptized on 22 March 1892 and set apart for the Japan Mission on 26 June 1902, by Heber J. Grant. Helped Alma translate the *Book of Mormon* into Japanese and served in Japan for over seven and a half years—second longest missionary service in the history of the Japan Mission. Likely Alma's closest friend in the mission. Labored in Nagano. Toured Korea and China with Alma for the First Presidency in 1910. Married Esther Hazel Howe on 4 June 1912, in Salt Lake City. Died on 14 August 1929, in Idaho Falls, Idaho. [*AF, JMMH.*]

CANNON, Angus M. (1834–1915), was born on 17 May 1834, in Liverpool, England, to George and Ann Quayle Cannon. Emigrated with family to America in 1842. Served a mission in the eastern United States, 1854–58. Married two sisters, Ann Amanda and Sarah Maria Mousley, in 1858. Called to help settle St. George, Utah. Married four more wives in the 1870s and 1880s. Served as president of the Salt Lake Stake, 1876–1904. Died on 7 June 1915, in Salt Lake City. [*BE* 1:292–95.]

CANNON, Geo. J., friends with Alma in Salt Lake City.

CANO, Mr. *See* Kano Mr.

CAPENER, Helen, was a member of Alma's large extended family in Utah.

CAPENER, Sister, was a member of Alma's large extended family in Utah.

CAPENER, Ellen, was a member of Alma's large extended family in Utah.

CAREW, Mr., was a New Zealand expatriate clerking for the Pollock Trading House in Japan. Boarded with Alma and his companions at the Bluff Hotel, Yokohama in fall 1901.

CARRIER, Miss., was a woman from New York touring the world. Boarded with Alma and his companions at the Bluff Hotel, Yokohama in fall 1901.

CHADWICK, John L. (1886–1960), was born on 3 August 1886, in North Ogden, Utah, to John Samuel and Charlotte Emily Godfrey Chadwick. Baptized on 5 September 1894, and set apart for the Japan Mission on 11 May 1905, by Hyrum M. Smith. Labored on the island of Hokkaidō. Married Pearl Triess Woodland on 24 June 1909, in Salt Lake City and Anna May Hunter on 25 September 1937, in Manti, Utah. Died on 16 April 1960, in Warden, Washington. [*AF, JMMH.*]

CHAFFEE, Gen., was introduced to Alma and his companions on 13 August 1901, in Yokohama, by William R. Clarke.

CHIBA Yasubei or Yasubeie (b. 1882), was born on 5 June 1882, in Kogata Mura, Miyagi-Ken, to Chiba Sukesaburo and Ogata Haru. Was baptized on 29 August 1906, by Alma O. Taylor and confirmed on 2 September 1906, by Fredrick A. Caine. Married Ikuyo Daikoku in August 1911. [*REJM.*]

CLARK, W. T., was an elder serving in Portland, Oregon, that Alma met on 26 July 1901.

CLARKE, Wm R. is actually William Rockwell Nelson (1841–1915), was born in Fort Wayne, Indiana and became famous for his involvement with the *Kansas City Star* newspaper in Kansas City, MO.

CLAWSON, Apostle or Bro. *See* Clawson, Rudger.

CLAWSON, Rudger (1857–1943), was born on 12 March 1857, in Salt Lake City, to Hiram B. and Margaret Gay Judd Clawson. Called on a mission to the Southern States in 1879. While in Georgia, his companion Elder Joseph Standing was murdered by an anti-Mormon mob. Returned to Utah and entered into plural marriage. Married Lydia Elizabeth Spence on 29 March 1883, in Salt Lake City and Dorothy Ann Dinwoody on 1 August 1882. Was arrested for unlawful cohabitation and sentenced to prison from 1884–87. Upon release was called as president of the Box Elder Stake. Called as an apostle in October 1898. Died on 21 June 1943, in Salt Lake City. [*AF, BE* 1:174–78.]

CLAWSON, Spencer, was friends with Alma in Salt Lake City.

CLEGG, Brigham, was friends with Alma in Salt Lake City.

COWDERY, Oliver (1806–50), was born on Oct. 3, 1806, in Wells, Vermont. Became Joseph Smith's scribe for the Book of Mormon translation in April 1829. Received the Aaronic and Melchizedek Priesthoods with Joseph Smith and became one of the Three Witnesses of the Book of Mormon and one of the first members of the Church. Married Elizabeth Ann Whitmer in 1832. Was excommunicated for apostasy in 1838, but rebaptized by Orson Hyde in 1848. Before traveling to Utah, died in Richmond, Missouri, in 1850. [*JWM*, 429.]

COWLEY, Matthias F. (1858–1940), was born on 25 August 1858, in Salt Lake City, to Matthias and Sarah Elizabeth Foss Cowley. Baptized on 1 November 1866, and ordained an elder on 28 December 1874 when he received his temple endowments. Served two missions to the Southern States between 1878 and 1882. Married Abbie Hyde on 21 May 1884, in Logan, Utah. Served ten years in the Oneida Stake (Idaho) until being called as an apostle in 1897. Died on 15 June 1940, in Salt Lake City. [*BE* 1:168–72, *ELDSH*, 263–64.]

CRESSWELL, Mrs., and her daughter, Mrs. Kochi, visited the Japan Mission home on 4 July 1904, as the guests of President and Sister Ensign.

CUNNINGHAM, Mabel, was friends with Alma in Salt Lake City.

CUTLER, Joseph P. (1885–1940), was born on 1 July 1885, in Salt Lake City, to Joseph Gregory and Mary Alice Felt Cutler. Was baptized on 7 August 1893, and set apart for the Japan Mission on 23 November 1906, by Rudger Clawson. Served in the Sapporo, Kōfu, and Tokyo Conferences and in the city of Asahikawa. Married Elizabeth Albrecht on 16 August 1916. [*AF, JMMH.*]

CUTLER, Thomas R. Acted as general manager of the Utah-Idaho Sugar Company and its predecessors, 1891–1917.

DEGUCHI Kato Tsuta (b.1884), was born on 21 March 1884, in Shinjuku Kitamachi, Tokyo, to Deguchi Tajuu and Odak Nobu. Baptized on 8 May 1904, by Horace S. Ensign and confirmed the same day by Alma O. Taylor. [*REJM.*]

DEGUCHI Tomi, was a friend of the Mormon missionaries and attended the 1904 mission Christmas Party.

DOHI, Dr., was a Tokyo physician who treated Elder Harris in December 1909.

DONE, Willard (1865–1931), was born on 10 December 1865, in Moroni, Utah, to John and Sarah Barker Done. Graduated from the Brigham Young Academy in 1883 and was called in November 1886 to manage the new Salt Lake Stake Academy (Latter-day Saints' University) where he remained until 1899 and served as Alma's principal. Married Amada Forbes on 23 December 1885. Served as a member of the general board of the Y.M.M.I.A. Died on 10 January 1865, in Salt Lake City. [*AF, BE* 1: 716.]

DUBOIS, Senator is Fred T. Dubois (1851–1930), was born on 29 May 1851, in Crawford City, Illinois. Graduated from Yale in 1872. Made Idaho his home. Served in the U.S. Senate for several terms. Helped Idaho gain statehood. Helped the federal government persecute the Mormons for their practice of plural marriage. Died in 1930.

DYRE, Miss, was an expatriate living in Yokohama who accompanied Maria S. Featherstone and her newborn son to America onboard the *Tremont* in June 1904.

EATON, John, was the president of Sheldon Jackson College, Salt Lake City and served as the U.S. Commissioner of Education. Published anti-Mormon literature.

EBARA, Mr., was the head of the Azabu Chu Gakko (Azabu Middle School) and a leader in the Japanese House of Commons.

ED or EDWARD. *See* Taylor, Edward.

EGAWA, Mr., was a friend of the Latter-day Saints in Tokyo. Met with the Latter-day Saints to discuss Mormonism during the summer of 1904.

EGLI, Emil (1879–1953), was born on 8 March 1879, in Salt Lake City, to Emil and Mary Blair Egli. Friends with Alma in Salt Lake City. Married Etta Cannon Lambert on 12 October 1906, in Salt Lake City. Died on 13 June 1953, in Salt Lake City. [*AF.*]

ELLIS, Lulu, was friends with Alma in Utah.

ELLIS, William S. (1886–1966), was born on 6 January 1886, in North Ogden, Utah, to Frederick M. and Sarah Jane Barker Ellis. Was baptized on 31 January 1894, and set apart for the Japan Mission on 30 October 1908, by J. Golden Kimball. Labored in the Sapporo Conference. Married Rose Catherine Vaughn Parry on 3 February 1915, in Salt Lake City and Mary Elizabeth Ward. [*AF, JMMH.*]

EMMA. *See* Batt, Emma.

EMPEY, Bp. N. A. is Nelson A. Empey (1837–1904), was born on 7 May 1837, in Preston, Canada, to William and Mary Ann Morgan Empey. Served as bishop of the Salt Lake Thirteenth Ward, 1891–1904. Was Alma's bishop. Died on 4 September 1904, in Salt Lake City. [*BE* 4:464, *EHC*, 749, *IGI.*]

EMPEY, Sister. Was the wife of Nelson A. Empey.

ENBERGER, Mr., was from New York and working as a sales agent for the Singer Sewing Machine Company in Japan. Boarded with Alma and his companions in the Bluff Hotel, Yokohama.

ENSIGN, Bro. *See* Ensign, Horace S.

ENSIGN, Horace S. (1871–1924), was born on 10 November 1871, in Salt Lake City, to Horace Sobeski and Martha Triplet Ensign. Baptized on 18 November 1879. Famous soloist in the Mormon Tabernacle Choir. Married Mary Linda Whitney on 21 June 1894, in Salt Lake City. Served in the Colorado Mission for two and a half years. Set apart for the Japan Mission on 18 July 1901, by George Teasdale. One of the original four Latter-day Saints called to the Japan Mission. Labored in Tokyo, Nagano, and Boshu. Served as president of the Japan Mission, 1903–05. Married Ara Elizabeth Hunsaker on 24 January 1918, in Salt Lake City. Died on 29 August 1924, in Salt Lake City. [*AF, JMMH.*]

ENSIGN, Sister. *See* Ensign, Mary W.

ENSIGN, Mary W. (1872–1916), was born on 17 August 1872, in Salt Lake City, to Horace K. and Mary Cravath Whitney. Baptized at eight. Married Horace S. Ensign on 21 June 1894, in Salt Lake City. Set apart to join her husband Horace in the Japan Mission by George Teasdale. Labored in the Japan Mission as her husband's missionary companion and mission president's wife. Died on 27 April 1916. [*AF, JMMH.*]

EPPINGER, Mr., was an expatriate living in Yokohama at the Grand Hotel. After meeting the Latter-day Saints in Yokohama, he traveled to America with letters of introduction from Heber J. Grant.

EREKSON, Isabelle B. (1852–1914), was born on 28 August 1852, in South Cottonwood, Utah, to John and Rosetta Wright Benbow. Married Jonas Hendriksen on 30 October 1852, in Salt Lake City. Died on 3 May 1914, in Murray, Utah. [*AF.*]

EREKSON, Will. *See* Erekson, William B.

EREKSON, William B., (1879–1947), was born on 17 January 1879, to Jonas and Isabella M. Benbow Erekson. Friends with Alma in Salt Lake. Served a mission to New Zealand. Married Esther Marie Young on 27 January 1904, in Salt Lake City. Ordained a high priest and bishop of the South Cottonwood Ward on 21 February 1904 where he served until 1914. Died on 12 January 1947, in Salt Lake City. [*AF, BE* 4:444.]

EVANS, Jno., is John A. Evans (1865–1906), born on 23 March 1885, in Cedar City, Utah, to David W. and Elizabeth Alldridge Evans. Ordained an Elder on 23 March 1879, by Erastus Snow and served many years as president of the Eight Quorum of Elders. Employed by the Deseret News. In 1906 he was ordained a High Priest and acted as a first counselor to Bishop Clawson until his death. Died on 2 June 1906, in Salt Lake City. [*AF, BE* 2:499.]

FAIRBOURN, William R. (1887–1967), was born on 10 April 1887, in Draper, Utah to William and Hannah Marie Rynearson Fairbourn. Baptized on 4 August 1895, and set apart for the Japan Mission on 11 May 1905, by Rudger Clawson. Labored in the Sendai, Kōfu and Tokyo Conferences. Married Violet Veneda Jensen on 10 April 1913, in Salt Lake City. Died on 23 October 1967, in Salt Lake City. [*AF, JMMH.*]

FATHER. *See* Taylor, Joseph E.

FEATHERSTONE, Brother. *See* Featherstone, Joseph F.

FEATHERSTONE, Horace Zentaro (1904–1927), was born on 6 April 1904, in Tokyo, Japan, to Joseph F. and Marie S. Featherstone. Died on 30 November 1927. [*AF.*]

FEATHERSTONE, Joseph F. (1881–1955), was born on 26 June 1881, in American Fork, Utah, to Thomas and Martha Richards Featherstone. Baptized on 13 July 1889. Married Annie Marie Snow on 18 June 1902, in Salt Lake City. Set apart for the Japan Mission on 26 June 1902, by George Teasdale. Labored in Boshu and the Tokyo Conference. Died on 16 January 1955, in Salt Lake City. [*AF, JMMH.*]

FEATHERSTONE, Marie S. (1883–1982), was born on 15 August 1883, in American Fork, Utah, to John L. and Annie G. Eastmond Snow. Baptized in 1893. Married Joseph F. Featherstone on 18 June 1902, in Salt Lake City. Set apart for the Japan Mission on 26 June 1902, by John W. Taylor. Labored in Boshu and the Tokyo Conference as her husband's missionary companion. Died on 30 January 1982. [*AF, JMMH.*]

FEATHERSTONE, Sister. *See* Featherstone, Marie S.

FELL, Mr., was an American expatriate selling rice-cleaning machines in Japan. Boarded with Alma and his companions at the Bluff Hotel, Yokohama.

FELT, Joseph H. (1840–1907), was born on 9 May 1840, in Salem, MA, to Nathaniel H. and Eliza Ann Preston Felt. Married Sarah Louise Bouton on 24 December 1866; Alma Elizabeth Mineer on 23 August 1875; Elizabeth Liddell on 29 March 1881. Died on 19 June 1907, in Salt Lake City. [*AF.*]

FJELDSTED, Christian D. (1829–1905), was born on 20 February 1829, in Copenhagen, Denmark, to Henry Ludvig and Ane Katherine Henriksen Fjeldsted. Baptized on 20 February 1852. Served as a traveling elder in the Copenhagen Conference, Denmark. Married Karen Olsen on 12 April 1849, in Copenhagen, Denmark. Emigrated to Utah in 1858. Married Johanne Maria Christensen on 3 July 1859, in Salt Lake City; Catrina Marie Christensen on 13 May 1865, in Salt Lake City; Josephine Margarethe Larsen on 4 September 1871, in Salt Lake City. Returned to Scandinavia several times as a missionary and mission president. Ordained as one of the First Seven Presidents of the Seventies in 1884. Died on 23 December 1905, in Salt Lake City. [*AF, BE* 1:203–4.]

FLORENCE. *See* Grant, Florence.

FRAWLEY, Daniel, was a famous actor that performed the play "Secret Service" on 20 September 1902, in Yokohama.

FROST, Grace (b. 1874), was born on 24 September 1874, in Salt Lake City, to John F. and Elizabeth Grace Mackintosh Frost. Was friends with Alma in Salt Lake City. Received treatment in Coe's Nervous Sanitarium, Portland, Oregon, for mental health problems. Friends with Maud Baggerley. [*AF.*]

FUJISHIMA, Mr., was a friend of Katō Kanzo. Katō used Mr. Fujishima's home to hide some stolen money on 19 October 1904.

FUJITA Yuki, was a member of the LDS Sunday School in Tokyo. Alma visited her parents on 10 June 1909.

FUJIU K., was a Japanese Christian minister. Met with Alma on 10 March 1902 to discuss religion.

FUKUYAMA, Mr., met with Alma on 10 June 1909 to discuss the Mormonism.

FURUUCHI, Mrs., was the mother of one of the children in LDS Sunday School in Tokyo. Was visited by Alma on 27 February 1905.

FURUYA, Mr., was Methodist living in Kōfu who was kind to the Latter-day Saints. Met with Alma on 6 March 1908.

GODDARD, Benjamin (1851–1930), was born on 27 July 1851, in Kuddersfield, England, to Joshua and Mary Ruth Williamson Goddard. Emigrated to Utah in 1879 and was baptized that same year. Served two missions to New Zealand, even serving as its president for a time. Head of the Bureau of Information, Salt Lake City, for twenty-seven years. Died on 5 December 1903. [*BE* 4:239.]

GODDARD, Heber S. (1863–1904), was born on 25 September 1863, in Salt Lake City, to George and Mary Sutton Goddard. Became a noted Utah baritone singer. Married Harriet Lucinda Kearnes on 7 November 1888. Member of the Old Folks Central Committee from 1901 to 1914. Died on 15 December 1904, in Salt Lake City. [*AF, BE* 4:726.]

GILES, Mrs., was friends with Alma in Salt Lake City.

GODSEY, Mr., was an employee of the American Tobacco Trust Company. Boarded with Alma and his companions at the Metropole Hotel, Tokyo.

GODSEY, Mrs., was perhaps an employee of the American Tobacco Trust Company with her husband. Boarded with Alma and his companions at the Metropole Hotel, Tokyo.

GOODCELL, Mr. was a Protestant missionary who had previously lived in Shanghai, China. Boarded with Alma and his companions at the Bluff Hotel, Yokohama.

GOODMAN, Margaret, was a member of Alma's large extended family in Arizona.

GOODMAN, Lizzie, was a member of Alma's large extended family in Arizona.

GRANT, Augusta W. (b. 1856), was born on 7 July 1856, in Pleasant Grove, Utah, to Oscar and Mary Ann Stearns Winters. Baptized at age ten. Studied at the Brigham Young Academy. Married Heber J. Grant in 1884. Served as member of the General Board of the YWMIA. Set apart to join her husband Heber J. Grant in the Japan Mission on 26 June 1902. She labored as a missionary in Japan until her husband was released in 1903. [*BE* 4:260–61, *JMMH.*]

GRANT, Apostle or Bro. *See* Grant, Heber J.

GRANT, B. F. is Brigham F. Grant (1856–1936), was born on 17 October 1856, in Salt Lake City, to Jedediah M. and Maryette Kesler Grant. Married Johannah Schluter on 21 November 1878, in Salt Lake City. Died on 30 August 1936, in Los Angeles, California. [*AF.*]

GRANT, Florence (1883–1977), was born on 7 February 1883, in Salt Lake City, to Heber J. and Lucy Stringham Grant. Friends with Alma in Salt Lake City. Married Willard R. Smith on 3 February 1910, in Salt Lake City. Died on 6 March 1977, in Salt Lake City. [*AF.*]

GRANT, Heber J. (1856–1945), was born on 22 November 1856, in Salt Lake City, to Jedediah M. and Rachel B. Ivins Grant. Baptized on 3 June 1864. Ordained an apostle 16 October 1882, by George Q. Cannon. Married Lucy Stringham on 1 November 1877. Was sealed to August Winters and Emily Wells as plural wives in 1884. Called to preside over the newly created Japan Mission in February 1901 by President Lorenzo Snow. Served as president until 1903. Called to preside over the European Mission, 1904–06. Served as church president, 1918–1945. [*ELDSH*, 437–40, *JMMH*.]

GRANT, Lutie (1880–1966), was born on 22 October 1880, in Salt Lake City, to Heber J. and Lucy Stringham Grant. Friends with Alma in Salt Lake City. Married George J. Cannon on 26 June 1902, in Salt Lake City. Died on 27 May 1966, in Salt Lake City. [*AF.*]

GRANT, Mary (b. 1889), was born on 6 February 1889, in Provo, Utah, to Heber J. and Augusta Winters Grant. Baptized at eight. Set apart to accompany her parents to the Japan Mission on 26 June 1902, by J. Golden Kimball. Labored in Japan as a missionary. Married Robert L. Judd on 22 September 1914. [*AF, JMMH.*]

GRANT, Sister. *See* Grant, Augusta W.

GRANT FAMILY. *See* Grant, Heber J., Augusta W., and Mary.

HADA Shinichi, was Mori Hachiro's nephew. Attended the LDS Sunday School in Tokyo. Recorded best Sunday School attendance in 1907.

HAKII Nami (Staru?) (b. 1881), was born on 25 March 1881, in Sakurada Fushimi-cho, Shiba ku, to Watanabe Nobudaka and Hakii Tama. Baptized on 20 December 1903, by John W. Stoker and confirmed the same day by Alma O. Taylor. Married Suzuki Morisaburo on 6 February 1905. [*REJM.*]

HARA Sentara, was a resident of Kusori (Chiba) who rented his home to the Latter-day Saints for a cottage meeting in April 1904.

HARA Toyozo, was a resident of Yahagi (Chiba) who rented his home to the Latter-day Saints for a cottage meeting in April 1904.

HAROLD. See Taylor, Harold.

HARRIS, O. Ellis. *See* Harris, Warren E.

HARRIS, Warren E. (1888–1957), was born on 23 November 1888, in Glendale, Utah, to Warren and Beulah Ann Webb Harris. Baptized in 1896. Set apart for the Japan Mission on 3 September 1907, by Heber J. Grant. Labored in Okubo and Shizuoka, but released early due to poor health. Married Claramay Aston on 20 September 1916. Died on 30 March 1957. [*AF, JMMH.*]

HARRISON, Mr., was editor of the *Japan Herald.* Visited the Latter-day Saints on 2 February 1902, in Tokyo.

HART, Charles H. (1866–1934), was born on 5 July 1866, in Bloomington, Idaho, to James H. and Subina Scheib Hart. Graduated from the University of Utah with valedictorian honors and from the University of Michigan Law

School. Married Mary Lalene Hendricks on 23 June 1915, in Salt Lake City and Adelia Greenhalgh on 25 September 1889, in Logan, Utah. Served as member of the General Sunday School Board and Y.M.M.I.A. Called as one of the Seven Presidents of the Seventy in 1906. Died on 29 September 1934, in Salt Lake City. [*AF, BE* 3:478–50.]

HAYAKAWA, Mr., investigated the gospel in 1907.

HAYASAKI, Mrs., was a resident of Sendai with whom the Latter-day Saints stayed for a short time. Alma visited her on 7 April 1906.

HAYASHI, Miss., attended the LDS Sunday School in Tokyo. Participated in the 1906 Sunday School Christmas program.

HEDGES, Mr. is William S. Hedges (1859–1914), born on 29 May 1859, in Terre Haute, Indiana, to George E. and Rachel Catherine Lovell Hedges. Married Clara Ellen Hedges on 23 October 1882, in Salt Lake City. Died on 24 February 1914, in Salt Lake City.

HEDGES, Mrs. is Clara Ellen Wells Hedges (1862–1946), born on 23 October 1862, in Salt Lake City, to Daniel H. and Louisa Free Wells. Married William S. Hedges on 23 October 1882, in Salt Lake City. Died on 30 April 1946, in Salt Lake City.

HEDGES, Sister. See Hedges, Mrs.

HEDGES, Sandford (1884–1954), was born on 21 August 1884, in Salt Lake City, to William H. and Clara Ellen Wells Hedges. Baptized at eight. Set apart for the Japan Mission on 26 June 1902, by Rulon S. Wells. Labored in Boshu, Nagano, and the Tokyo and Sendai Conferences. Excommunicated for fornication with a Japanese woman. Returned to America, was rebaptized and married Sarah Coulam on 9 May 1907. Died on 15 March 1954. [*AF, JMMH.*]

HENNEFER, Mrs. William, was friends with Alma in Salt Lake City.

HEWLETT, Frank J. (b. 1875), was born in 1875, in Croyden, England, to George and Fanny Hewlett. Emigrated to Utah and later worked for his father's wholesale firm. Visited Japan to represent the Hewlett Bros. Firm in April 1907. While in Tokyo, met often with the Latter-day Saints in Tokyo and spent time at the mission headquarters. Served as president of the South African Mission, 1912–14. [*AF.*]

HEWLETT, Sister Frank, was the wife of Frank J. Hewlett.

HEPBURN, assisted in the translation of the Bible into Japanese.

HIATT, Elijah (1878–1980), was born on 13 August 1878, in Payson, Utah, to Samuel M. and Mary Eleanor Taylor Hiatt. Married Sarah Llene Clark on 15 December 1903. Died on 3 February 1980, in Milton, Oregon. [*AF.*]

HIJIKATA, Miss., was a student in the LDS Sunday School in Tokyo.

HIRAI, Mr., was a soldier who Alma tried to meet on 19 August 1908.

HIRAI Hirogoro, was the brother of Hirai Kinza and an English teacher at Waseda University. Alma met him in March 1907, and he began helping the Latter-day Saints with their Japanese translations until it was discovered that he had lied on a number of occasions.

HIRAI Kinza, was the brother of Hirai Hirogoro. Alma met him in July 1903 and they became good friends. He often donated his labor to helping translate Japanese texts for the Latter-day Saints.

HIRAI, Mrs., was the wife of Hirai Hirogoro. Alma questioned her about her husband's moral conduct on 20 March 1908.

HIRATA K., was the assistant to Nakai Shochin of Kawagoe. Alma met him on 8 January 1907.

HIROI T., was a teacher and former German Evangelical Church preacher. He served as a early Japanese language tutor, translator, and interpreter for the Latter-day Saints in Japan.

HIRON, Miss., boarded with Alma and his companions at the Bluff Hotel, Yokohama.

HIROSE, Mrs., was the head of the Kawagoe girls high school. Alma tried to visit her on 8 January 1907.

HOMMA, Mr., was a friend of the missionaries. Alma visited him on 26 June 1905.

HONDA, Miss., visited the Japan Mission home on 12 March 1908.

HOOPES, George A. (1886–1949), was born on 14 January 1886, in Weston, Idaho, to Daniel L. and Catherine Heaver Clarke Hoopes. Was called in 1905 to the Japan Mission but for some reason never came. Married Edna Baker on 18 June 1914, in Salt Lake City. Died on 2 July 1949. [*AF.*]

HORACE. *See* Ensign, Horace S.

HORIGUCHI, Mr., was a man studying Christianity. Alma visited him on 12 January 1907.

HORIKAWA Katsuzo (b. 1887), was born on 3 December 1887, in Tatsuoka Mura, Yamanashi-Ken, to Horikawa Katsuuemon and Shimizu Mura. Baptized on 22 November 1887, by William R. Fairbourn and confirmed on 23 November 1909, by Joseph H. Stimpson. [*REJM.*]

HOSHI, visited the Latter-day Saints on 23 January 1902, to discuss religion.

HOSHIISHI, Mr., was the recipient of a letter written by Alma on 3 July 1905.

HOUSTON, H. C., was a Baptist preacher from Ohio who met Alma in a Salt Lake City LDS Sunday School meeting.

HOWARD, Allan, was friends with Alma in Salt Lake City.

HUBBARD, Charles W. (1888–1980), was born on 25 May 1888, in Willard, Utah, to James W. and Emma Pettingille Hubbard. Baptized at eight. Set apart for the Japan Mission on 3 September 1907, by Heber J. Grant. Labored in Okubo. Excommunicated and sent home early for fornication with a Japanese woman. Returned to America and was rebaptized. Married Elsie Jane Dalton on 6 June 1912, in Salt Lake City. Died on 3 October 1980, in Soda Springs, Idaho. [*AF, JMMH.*]

HUME or HUMES, Mr., was an English gentleman who visited the Latter-day Saints on 31 December 1901.

HYDE, Orson (1805–78), was born on 8 January 1805, in Oxford, Connecticut, to Nathan Hyde and Sarah (Sally) Thorpe. Active as a Campbellite minister with Sidney Rigdon until he learned of Mormonism and was baptized on 2 October 1831. Later that month ordained a high priest. Married Marinda (Nancy) Johnson in 1834. Faithful member of Zion's Camp in 1834 and was ordained an apostle in 1835. Served a mission to the British Isles, 1837–38. Sent by Joseph Smith to dedicate Palestine for the prophesied gathering of the Jews. After moving West with the Saints, died on 28 November 1878, in Sanpete County, Utah. [*JWM, 443.*]

ICHIKAWA, Mr., was the father of Ichikawa Sue, a student in the LDS Sunday School in Tokyo. Alma visited the family in 1905.

ICHIKAWA, Mrs., was the mother of Ichikawa Sue, a student in the LDS Sunday School in Tokyo. Alma visited the family in 1905.

ICHIKAWA Sue, was a member of the LDS Sunday School in Tokyo. Participated in the 1904 Sunday School Christmas program.

ICHIKAWA GIRL. *See* Ichikawa Sue.

ICHIKI S., was a prominent leader in the Japanese Meiji Restoration. Visited with Alma and his companions on 13 February 1902 to discuss Mormonism.

IEDA, Mr., helped Alma with the Japanese translation questions on 3 February 1901.

IGUCHI, Mr., was an editor of the *Chiba Daily News* and a member of a Tokyo Protestant church. He met with the Latter-day Saints several times and wrote a number of even-handed articles on Mormonism.

IJICHI, Mr., was a Tokyo landlord Alma tried to rent a home from in October 1908.

IKEDA, visited Alma on 5 October 1905, to discuss Mormonism.

IKEDA, Mr., ate Christmas dinner with Alma in 1904.

IKUTA or IKUDA Koji or Chiko, was a famous author suggested by Natsuma Kintaro to Alma to help with the Book of Mormon translation. Alma visited with him on 19 June 1908, and Ikuta agreed to help with the translation for the next several months.

IMAI, Mr., visited Alma on 23 November and 10 December 1905. Tried to rent a room with the Latter-day Saints.

INOYE, Mr., was a friend of Erastus L. Jarvis who met Alma on 13 May 1904.

ISHIGAKI, Sister. *See* Tanifuji Chiyo.

ISHII, Mr., was an artistic friend of Mr. Ikuta's who Alma hired to design the cover of the Japanese *Book of Mormon* in May 1909.

ISHIKAWA Katsu, was Nachie Tsune's friend. Although a member of the Church of England, she received numerous testimonies of Mormonism and even defended its teachings against her former preachers. She met with Alma on 12 January and 28 June 1908.

ISHIKAWA, Mr., was an employee of the *Tohoku News* and a friend of the Latter-day Saints. Alma visited him on 26 July 1907.

ISHIKAWA Sai (b. 1891), was born on 7 September 1891, in Oaza Shinorohei Mura, Hokkaido, to Chikahisa Shuntaro and Ishikawa Zen. Baptized on 18 December 1908, by Justus B. Seeley and confirmed on 20 December 1908, by Moroni S. Marriott. [*REJM.*]

ISO Yasue (b. 1892), was born on 15 January 1892, in Kōfu, Yamanashi-Ken, to Iso Gumpoo and Muramatsu Haru. Baptized on 25 December 1908, by William R. Fairbourn and confirmed on 27 December 1908, by Elliot C. Taylor. [*REJM.*]

IMANI, Mr., was a soldier who visited Alma on 29 May 1908, to discuss Mormonism.

ITŌ Hirobumi, was "Ito Hirobumi, Marquis (1841–1909), Japanese statesman, born near Shimonoseki, and educated in Japan and Great Britain. Itō served as prime minister four times between 1885 and 1901. During his career he made several visits to the U.S. and Europe; he was instrumental in introducing Western political ideas and economic reforms to Japan. Together with the Japanese statesman Saionji Kimmochi, he drafted a constitution for Japan, patterned on European models, that was in effect from 1890 to 1945. Following the Sino-Japanese War of 1894–95, Itō negotiated the Treaty of Shimonoseki (1895), which ended the war and made Korea an independent nation. He negotiated an alliance between Japan and Great Britain, signed in 1902. After conducting negotiations that led to a Japanese protectorate over Korea, Itō served as resident-general of Korea from 1905 until his assassination at Harbin, Manchuria." [*Microsoft Encarta.*]

ITŌ, Mr., was a distant relative of Itō Hirobumi. Visited Alma on 9 March 1902.

IWAI, Mr., was visited by Alma on 30 July 1905.

IWANO, Mr., was a friend of the owner of a home located in Ushigome that Alma attempted to rent in November 1908 for the new Japan Mission home.

IWANO Y., helped translate the LDS psalmody in 1904. Alma considered him to help with the final literary criticism of the *Book of Mormon* and met with him on 15 June 1908.

IWATO Shinsaburo, was a Yokohama doctor who visited the Japan Mission home on 9 March 1902.

JARVIS, Erastus L. (1882–1971), was born on 14 November 1882, in St. George, Utah, to Brigham Y. and Mary Forsyth Jarvis. Baptized at age eight. Set apart for the Japan Mission on 26 June 1902, by John W. Taylor. Labored in Naoyetsu, Boshu, and Nakano. Was released early due to poor mental health. Married Genevieve Hilton on 6 November 1907, in St. George, Utah. Died on 12 March 1971, in Salt Lake City. [*AF, JMMH.*]

JARVIS, George. *See* Jarvis, Erastus L.

JENNIE is Jennie E. Taylor (1871–1951), was born on 3 January 1871, in Salt Lake City, to Joseph E. and Louisa Rebeckah Capener. Married James E. Synder. Died on 21 February 1951. [*AF.*]

JENNINGS, Mary H., is likely Mary Hooper Jennings (1858–1913), was born on 18 September 1858, in Salt Lake City, to William H. and Mary Ann Knowlton Hooper. Married Thomas W. Jennings on 1 November 1875, in Salt Lake City. Died on 12 June 1913, in Salt Lake City. [*AF.*]

JENSEN, Jay C. (1888–1943), was born on 1 September 1888, in Ogden, Utah, to James C. and Joannah E. Jennings Jensen. Baptized on 1 September 1896. Set apart for the Japan Mission on 30 October 1908, by Seymour B. Young. Labored as secretary of Japan Mission, president of Tokyo Conference, and president of Osaka Conference. Married Eva Margaret Bonner on 10 June 1914, in Salt Lake City. Died on 1 February 1943, in Salt Lake City. [*AF, JMMH.*]

JIHEI Takai, was a resident of Chiba who rented his home to Alma for a cottage meeting in February 1904.

JOHNSON, Bro. See Johnson, Charles A.

JOHNSON, Chas. A. is Charles A. Johnson. Was friends with Alma in Salt Lake City.

KAMIYAMA, Mr., was the father of Kamiyama Rin. Investigated the gospel but was never baptized.

KAMIYAMA, Mrs., was the mother of Kamiyama Rin. Investigated the gospel but was never baptized.

KAMIYAMA Rin (b. 1886), was born on 26 November 1886, in Yamagata, Yamagata ken, to Kamiyama Ikari and Tsuchiya Tsuna. Baptized on 8 May 1904, by Horace S. Ensign and confirmed on the same day by Frederick A. Caine. Married a Mr. Ota on 13 April 1905, and was known thereafter as Sister Ota. [*REJM.*]

KANABE Sister. *See* Deguchi Kato Tsuta.

KANO, Mr., was an English-speaking Japanese man who invited Alma to his family village, Kameari, over the 1902 New Year's holiday. Remained friends throughout Alma's mission.

KATAGIRI CHILDREN. *See* Katagiri Fuyu, Massa, and Miki.

KATAGIRI FAMILY. *See* Katagiri Mr., Mrs., Fuyu, Massa, and Miki.

KATAGIRI GIRL. See Katagiri Fuyu.

KATAGIRI Fuyu, attended the LDS Sunday School in Tokyo with her sisters.

KATAGIRI Massa, attended the LDS Sunday School in Tokyo with her sisters.

KATAGIRI Miki, attended the LDS Sunday School in Tokyo with her sisters.

KATAGIRI, Mr., was the father of Fuyu, Massa, and Miki.

KATAGIRI, Mrs., was the mother of Fuyu, Massa, and Miki.

KATAOKA Kotomi, was a young daughter in the Kataoka family. Alma visited her on 16 October 1908.

KATAOKA FAMILY, was a family living in Yotsuya. Alma visited them on 15 July 1908.

KATO, was a young man who lived with General Kawamura in Harajuku. He visited the Japan Mission home on 5 April 1907, to learn about English conversation classes.

KATO Hisa, investigated the gospel. Was already a member of the Church of England and married to Kato Shintaro. A friend of Nachie Tsune, she began attending LDS meetings and in March 1906 requested baptism. No record of her ever being baptized.

KATŌ Kenzo (b. 1883), was born on 8 January 1883, in Tokyo. Studied the law. Baptized on 11 October 1903, by Joseph F. Featherstone and confirmed on the same day by Horace S. Ensign. Married Katō Tsuta. Excommunicated on 19 October 1904 for hypocrisy and theft. [*REJM.*]

KATO Shintaro, was the husband of Kato Hisa.

KATŌ Tsuta, was the wife of Katō Kenzo.

KATŌ FAMILY. *See* Katō Kenzo and Tsuta.

KATOGI, Mr., was the nephew of Katsunuma Tomizo. He had spent time in Utah and even lived in the Beehive House. He called on the Latter-day Saints on 19 August 1901,

KATSUNUMA Tomizo or Thomaz or Thomas (1863–1950), was born on 6 October 1863, in Miharu, Japan, to Katogi Naochika and Yo Hanazawa. He immigrated to America in 1889 and spent time in California, Idaho, and Utah. He studied veterinary medicine at Brigham Young College in Logan, Utah. Baptized by Guy W. Thatcher on 8 August 1895. Very likely the first Japanese member of the Church. Moved to Hawaii where he became a well-known community leader. Died on 11 September 1924. [Takagi, 73–84.]

KAWABE, Mr., was the husband of Sister Kawabe. Alma visited him on 13 May 1908.

KAWAI Kosaburo, was a respected literary critic and former student of Dr. Tsubouchi. Alma relied upon him to help determine who should work on the *Book of Mormon* final translation in 1980.

KAWAMURA, General was a resident of Harajuku whose guest, Katō, learned English from the Latter-day Saints.

KAWANAKA Aritatsu (b. 1873), was born on 6 March 1873, in Ushigome, Tokyo, to Kawanaka Arikuni and Takada Nao. Baptized on 3 August 1906, by Justus B. Seeley and confirmed on 5 August 1906, by John W. Stoker. [*REJM.*]

KAWANAKA, Mrs., was the wife of Kawanaka Aritatsu. Was not baptized with her husband.

KAWASAKI, Mr., was a Presbyterian preacher living in Chiba who would not rent his meeting hall to Alma for a cottage meeting in October 1903.

KELSCH, Elder. *See* Kelsch, Louis A.

KELSCH, Louis A. (1856–1917), was born on 28 November 1856, in Vinningen, Bavaria (Germany), to Louis and Sarapine Kelsch. Baptized on 25 October 1876. Served a mission to the Northern States Mission, acting as president from 1896 to 1901. Set apart for the Japan Mission on 18 July 1901, by Joseph F. Smith. Was among the first group of Latter-day Saints sent to Japan. Served on the General Board of the Y.M.M.I.A. from 1905 to 1909. Died in 1917. [*BE* 4:241, *JMMH.*]

KICHIRO Adachi, rented his second home to the Latter-day Saints to hold a cottage meeting in March 1904.

KIKUCHI Saburo (b. 1861), was born on 2 April 1861, in Yamato Mura, Fukuoka-Ken, to Kikuchi Nobukazu and Adachi Kino. Before meeting the Latter-day Saints, held open-air revival religious meetings in Uyeno Park. Baptized on 10 March 1902, by Heber J. Grant and confirmed on the same day by Louis A. Kelsch. [*JMMH.*]

KIKUCHI, Mrs., likely the wife of Kikuchi Saburo. Alma visited her on 2 August 1908.

KIMBALL, Prest., is Andrew Kimball (1858–1924), was born on 6 September 1858, in Salt Lake City, to Heber C. and Ann A. Ghenn Kimball. Married Olive Woolley on 2 February 1882, in Salt Lake City. Served a mission to the Indian Territory, 1885–87.Called as president of the St. Joseph Stake in 1898. Father of future church president Spencer W. Kimball. Died on 6 September 1924, in Thatcher, Arizona. [*AF, BE* 1:364–66.]

KING, was a student at the University of Michigan Law School with James H. Moyle.

KITADA (1), visited the Japan Mission home with his brother on 17 January 1902.

KITADA (2), visited the Japan Mission home with his brother on 17 January 1902.

KITAHARA, Miss, visited the Japan Mission home on 26 June 1905.

KNAPP, Arthur M., was a Unitarian missionary and editor of the *Japan Advertiser,* 1899–1902.

KOCHI, Mrs., was the daughter of Mrs. Creswell. Visited the Japan Mission home on 4 July 1904.

KOGU Take, was a friend of the Latter-day Saints. Gave Alma a bookmark for Christmas 1904.

KODA, Prof., was a professor Alma considered hiring for the *Book of Mormon* translation criticism.

KOIZUMI, Mr., investigated Mormonism for one year and even desired baptism until he learned of plural marriage. Quit studying Mormonism on 29 August 1908.

KOJI Chiyo (b. 1892), was born on 14 February 1892, in Oaze, Sawamoshiri machi, Esashi machi, Hiyagun, Hokkaido, to Hamano Kichisaburo and Koji Tami. Baptized on 7 January 1909, by Justus B. Seeley and confirmed on 10 January 1909, by Moroni S. Marriott. Married Sadachi Shiogi. Moved to Portland, Oregon on 12 April 1912. [*REJM.*]

KOJUNA, Mr., met with Alma on November 1903, to discuss his colloquial translation of the Bible into Japanese. Claimed to be an officer of the Imperial Educational Society of Tokyo.

KOMAROFFSKY, Georges, was a Russian general Alma met on 13 August 1901.

KOMATSU, Mr., was the father of one of the children attending the LDS Sunday School in Tokyo. Alma visited him on 31 January 1905.

KOMORITA, attended the LDS Sunday School in Tokyo and sent improper notes to a fellow female student named Nomura.

KOMOTO, Dr., was a Tokyo eye doctor who treated the Latter-day Saints' eyes, April 1909.

KOMURA, Baron, is Komura Jūtarō, a leading Japanese delegate sent to Washington, D.C., following Japan's victory in the Russo-Japan War.

KOSHIISHI, Mr., was an editor of the *Tokyo Shimbun* newspaper. He visited Alma and his companions on 9 March 1902.

KOYAMA, Mr., was a laborer who visited Alma and his companions in August 1901. He translated some Japanese materials into English and tutored the Latter-day Saints for a time.

KOZA, Mr., was the father of one of the LDS Sunday School in Tokyo boys. Alma visited him on 22 February 1905.

KUGA Eisaburo (b. 1873), was born on 17 September 1873, in Katsuura machi, Chiba Ken, to Kuga Saburouemon and Yashiro Hana. Former member of the Baptist church. Baptized on 30 May 1908, by John W. Stoker and confirmed on 31 May 1908, by Daniel P. Woodland. Helped with the Japanese translation of the *Book of Mormon*. Excommunicated on 14 July 1909, for hypocrisy, lying, and neglect of duty. [*REJM.*]

KUMAGAI Tamano (b. 1892), was born on 1 January 1892, in Sendai, Japan, Chokuon Kumagai and Kiku Nakamura. Baptized on 16 December 1908, by Justus B. Seeley and confirmed on 20 December 1908, by John H. Roskelley. [*REJM.*]

KUMURA, Mr., was a teacher at the Tokyo Imperial Agriculture College. Alma visited him on 4 April 1908, to discuss how to translate certain flora and fauna words from the *Book of Mormon* into Japanese.

KURIBARA Genji, was a friend of Mr. Clarke who visited the Latter-day Saints on 27 August 1901, and discussed Mormonism.

KURODA, Mr., apologized to Ei Nachie and Alma for her having received an insulting letter on 10 November 1907 at his school.

KUWANA, Mr., lived next door to the Japan Mission home with Mr. Yokoyama's family. Visited with Alma on 10 August 1905.

KUWANA FAMILY. *See* Kuwana Mr.

LANGE, Rudolf, was a professor of Japanese living in Germany who wrote *A Text Book of Colloquial Japanese*. Alma bought a copy of the book on 10 October 1903.

LISADORE or LISS. *See* Taylor, Lisadore A.

LITTLE, Perry, was a member of Alma's large extended family in Utah.

LITTLE, Bp. Ed., was a member of Alma's large extended family in Utah.

LITTLE, Geo., was a member of Alma's large extended family in Utah.

LOOMIS, H., was the manager of the American Bible House in Japan. He visited Alma on 5 January 1904, to learn about Mormonism.

LUCILE. *See* Taylor, Lucile.

LUND, Anthon H. (1844–1921), was born on 15 May 1844, in Aalborg, Denmark, to Henrik and Anne Kirstine Anderson Lund. Raise by his grandmother, Lund joined the Church at age nine. Emigrated to the United States at age eighteen. Married Sarah Ann Preston in 1870. Served two missions to Scandinavia, the second as president. Called as an apostle in 1889. Called as president of the European Mission in 1893. Served in First Presidency, 1901–21. Died on 2 March 1921, in Salt Lake City. [*AF, ELDSH*, 684–85.]

LUND, Prest. *See* Lund, Anthon H.

LUNDQUIST, A. H., was a missionary from Logan, Utah, Alma met while in Portland, Oregon.

LURS, Mrs., was the aunt of Mable K. Richardson.

LUTIE. *See* Grant, Lutie.

LYMAN, Prest. *See* Lyman, Francis M.

LYMAN, Francis M. (1840–1916), was born on 12 January 1840, in Good Hope, Illinois, to Amasa M. and Maria Louisa Tanner Lyman. Crossed the plains at eight years old. Called to serve a mission in England in 1860. Called to preside over the Tooele Stake in 1877. Called as an apostle on 27 October 1880 and president of that quorum on 6 October 1903. Died on 18 November 1916 [*ELDSH*, 687.]

MABEL. *See* Snow, Mable.

MACBARA, Mr., was the principal of the Kawagoe Middle School. Alma met him on 8 January 1907, to discuss the religiosity of the local Japanese.

MAESER, Karl G. (1828–1901), was born on 16 January 1828, in Saxony, Germany, to Johann G. and Johanna Christina Frederica Zocher Maeser. Married Anna Meith in 1854. Baptized in 1855. Emigrated with his family to America in 1856. Served missions in the British Isles, Southern States, Germany, and Switzerland. Married Emilie Damke in 1875. Sent to Provo as the principal of the Brigham Young Academy in 1875. Died on 15 February 1901, in Salt Lake City. [*ELDSH*, 692–93.]

MAGGIE. *See* Taylor, Elizabeth Margaret.

MAGLEBY, John E. (1862–1939), was born on 27 November 1862, in Salt Lake City, to Hans O. and Marie Christensen Magleby. Baptized at eight. Married Jane A. Warnock on 12 June 1885, in Logan, Utah. Served a mission to New Zealand 1885–9. Served as mission president in New Zealand 1900–3 and 1928–30. President of the Sevier Stake from 1921 to 1928. Died on 30 September 1939, in Monroe, Utah. [*AF, BE* 4:361.]

MAGLEBY, President. *See* Magleby, John E.

MAHONRI. *See* Taylor, Mahonri M.

MAKIMURA, Baron, was visiting Hirai Kinza when Alma called on Hirai on 29 September 1906, in Tokyo.

MAKINO, Mrs., was the mother of one of the children attending the LDS Sunday School in Tokyo.

MANO, Mr., visited Alma on 9 July 1906.

MARGARET. *See* Taylor, Elizabeth M.

MARQUARDT, Herr, performed a concert in the Yokohama Public Hall on 1 October 1901, which Alma and his companions attended on the invitation of Mrs. Warton.

MARQUARDT, Madame, performed a concert in the Yokohama Public Hall on 1 October 1901, which Alma and his companions attended on the invitation of Mrs. Warton.

MARRIOTT, Moroni S. (1885–1966), was born on 6 December 1885, in Marriott, Utah, to Moroni S. and Rose Winnifred Parry Marriott. Baptized on 1 November 1894. Set apart for the Japan Mission on 2 July 1907, by Seymour B. Young. Labored in the Sapporo and Morioka Conferences. Married Laura May Mickelson on 5 July 1930, in Idaho Falls, Idaho and later married Margaret Crawford. Died on 31 January 1966 in Ogden, Utah. [*AF, JMMH.*]

MARSHALL, O. P., was captain of the *Empress of India*, which Alma and his companions traveled onboard to Japan. He and Alma had a gospel discussion on 31 August 1901.

MASHIMO, Miss, was a friend of the Latter-day Saints in Tokyo.

MASHIMO, Mr., was a friend of the Latter-day Saints in Tokyo. Elders Stoker and Jarvis lived in his home for a short time in 1902.

MASHIMO, Nobu, was a friend of the Latter-day Saints in Tokyo.

MATUSDA T., was a student at a Tokyo Semmon Gakko (specialty trade school) and member of the Church of England. He visited Alma on 20 May 1902.

MATSUDAWA or MATSUDAIRA, Mrs., visited the Japan Mission home on 1 January 1904, with her two daughters.

MATSUDORI, Mrs., received a letter sent by Alma on 9 August 1906.

MATSUI, Mr., was hired by Alma to create maps for Elder Stoker's translation of "The Brief History of the Church" in 1907.

MATSUNO, Mr., was a man Alma met while laboring in Chiba in 1904 and then again in 1908.

MATSUOKA, Mr., was a wealthy gentleman who offered Alma and his companions free lodging in Tokyo if they would move from Yokohama in August 1901.

MATSUSHITA, Mr., was a friend of the Latter-day Saints in Tokyo.

MCCALEB, Rev., was a Protestant preacher who invited Alma and Louis A. Kelsch to his home to discuss Mormonism in June 1902.

MCCULLA, Mr., was an employee of the *Japan Times*. Alma and his companions entertained him on 27 October 1901.

MCDONALD, Dr., was an expatriate physician practicing in Tokyo. Alma visited him on 1 August 1903, to have a boil examined.

MCKAY, David O. (1873–1970), was born on 8 September 1873, in Huntsville, Utah, to David and Jeanette Evans McKay. Graduated from Weber Stake Academy and the University of Utah. Served a mission to Great Britain, 1897–99. Married Emma Ray Riggs on 2 January 1901. Ordained an apostle on 9 April 1906. Served as general superintendent of the Deseret Sunday School Union and Church commissioner of education. Served as president of the European Mission. Became President of the Church in 1951. Died on 18 January 1970, in Salt Lake City. [*ELDSH*, 724–27.]

MCMURRIN, James (1864–1902), was born on 26 March 1864, in Salt Lake City, to Joseph and Margaret L. McMurrin. Married Mary Jacobson on 16 March 1887 and later Edith Mary Turpin. Was a prominent missionary in the Church having served many years in the European Mission presidency. Died on 7 August 1902, in Salt Lake City. [*AF*.]

MCQUARRIE, Pres., is John G. McQuarrie (b. 1869), born on 10 October 1869, to Hector and Agnes Gray McQuarrie. Baptized on 5 April 1868. Set apart for the Eastern States Mission in 1900. Served as mission president, 1901–08. [*ELDSH*, 331.]

MCRAE, Joseph. A. (1865–1958), was born on 19 March 1865, in Salt Lake City, to Joseph and Maria Taylor McRae. Baptized in 1873. Married Alma's cousin Eunice Higbee on 31 December 1891, in Salt Lake City. Set apart for the Colorado Mission on 19 March 1899. Served as president of the Colorado Mission from 1901–07. Died on 13 September 1958, in Salt Lake City. [*AF*, *BE* 4: 325.]

MCRAE, Alexander. *See* McRae, Joseph A.

MERRINER, W. Merrill (1832–1906), was born on 25 September 1832, in Sackville, Canada. Converted to Mormonism in 1852 and immigrated to Utah thereafter. Married Sarah Atkinson in November 1853. Helped settle Cache Valley, Utah and served as preisent of the Logan Temple. Called as an apostle in 1889. Died on 6 February 1906, in Richmond, Utah. [*ELDSH*, 737.]

MIGANOHARA, H., had spent time in Salt Lake City. Visited the Latter-day Saints in Japan on 22 July 1902.

MISUMI, Mr., wrote a book in Japan entitled *Colonization among the Mormons*. Visited the Japan Mission home on 3 April 1907.

MITCHELL, Robert, was friends with Alma in Salt Lake City.

MIYAZAKI or MIYAZUKI or MIAZAKI, was an insane man who visited the Japan Mission home on several occasions to discuss his delusional religious claims.

MIYASAKI, Mr., was a famous historical figure in Japan. Visited Alma and his companions on 13 February 1902, to discuss Mormonism.

MIZUGUCHI, was a Christian preacher living in Funabashi, Tokyo. Alma visited him on 14 November 1903.

MIZUKAWA, Mr., was a passenger agent working at the head office of the Nippon Yusen Kaisha (NYK). Met Alma on 4 July 1905 and made subsequent travel arrangements for him on the NYK.

MIZUNO Miyo, was a member of the LDS Sunday School in Tokyo. Had the best attendance record in 1906 and participated in the 1906 Christmas program.

MOCHIZUKI, Mr., visited the Japan Mission home to investigate Mormonism on 1 June 1904.

MONOŌ, Mr., was a resident of Kōfu, Japan. Alma visited him several times in 1907 and 1908.

MORI, Hachiro (b. 1885), was born on 1 December 1885, in Suizawa Mura, Mie-Ken, to Hada Yosobei and Nakagawa Mitsu. Baptized on 25 November 1907, by Alma O. Taylor and confirmed on 1 December 1907, by Frederick A. Caine. Excommunicated on 17 February 1909, for apostasy. [*REJM*.]

MORI, Mr., was the private secretary of the Minister of Finance and a friend of Mr. Tokoyo's who wanted to practice his English with the Latter-day Saints. By October 1906, Mori was helping copy Alma's *Book of Mormon* translation.

MORI, Mr., was a former resident of Sapporo. He moved to Tokyo after meeting with the Latter-day Saints in Sapporo to attend school. He approached Alma about baptism on 26 August 1908.

MORIYAMA, Mr., was a former student of Hirai Hirogoro at Waseda University. Alma visited him regarding Hirai's moral character on 28 March 1908.

MOSS, Mr. boarded with Alma and his companions at the Bluff Hotel, Yokohama. He discussed the gospel with the Latter-day Saints on 5 October 1901. Was an employee of the Pollock Trading Company in Japan.

MOTHER. *See* Taylor, Lisadore W.

MOYLE, J. H., is James H. Moyle (1858–1946), was born on 17 September 1858, in Salt Lake City, to James H. and Elizabeth Wood Moyle. Served a mission to the Southern States, 1879–81. Studied at the University of Utah and graduated from the University of Michigan Law School in 1885. Married Alice Dinwoodey on 17 November 1887, in Logan, Utah. Father of future apostle Henry D. Moyle. Died on 19 February 1946, in Salt Lake City. [*AF, BE* 1:783.]

MYERS, Miss, was a Protestant missionary who had previously lived in China. Boarded with Alma and his companions at the Bluff Hotel, Yokohama.

NABESHIMA, Kuma (b. 1886), was born on 16 December 1886, in Matsubara-machi, Saga-shi, Saga-ken, to Nabeshima Atsushi and Tanaka Tsuru. Baptized on 27 November 1909, by Jay C. Jensen and confirmed on 28 November 1909, by Frederick A. Caine. Married Midorikawa Fumioo on 19 September 1916. [*REJM.*]

NABESHIMA, Mr., was the father of Nabeshima Kuma. Alma visited him on 11 November 1909, for permission to baptize his daughter.

NABESHIMA, Mrs., was the mother of Nabeshima Kuma. Alma visited her on 11 November 1909, for permission to baptize her daughter.

NACHIE Ei (b. 1892), was born on 31 October 1892, in Komasawa Mura, Ibara gun, Tokyo, to Iwata Akakichi and Ishida Fude. Later adopted by Nachie Tsune and lived in the Japan Mission home. Baptized on 26 March 1908, by Daniel P. Woodland and confirmed on 29 March 1908, by John W. Stoker. Married Nagao Yoshio on 29 December 1920. [*REJM.*]

NACHIE Tsune (b. 1856), was born on 12 May 1856, in Aza Shimmachi, Komosawa Mura, Ibara Gun, Tokyo, to Ando Tokizo and Ishida Cho. Baptized on 26 September 1905, by Frederick A. Caine and confirmed on 1 October 1905, by Alma O. Taylor. Adopted Nachie Ei and lived in the Japan Mission headquarters as a cook for many years. Eventually moved to Hawaii where she worked in the Latter-day Saint temple. [*REJM.*]

NAGASHIMA, Mr., was a resident of Chiba who rented his home to Alma for a cottage meeting in 2 March 1904.

NAKACHI Kin (Sumiya) (1855–1913), was born on 13 April 1855, in Yonezawa, Yamagata Ken, to Furuahata Shuji and Sumiya Hase. Baptized on 28 September 1908, by Justus B. Seeley and confirmed on 4 October 1908, by Joseph P. Cutler. Died on 3 April 1913, in Sapporo, Japan of stomach cancer. [*REJM.*]

NAKAGAWA, Mr., was a friend of the Latter-day Saints in Tokyo. Met with Alma in June 1904.

NAKAI Shochin, was the mayor of Kawagoe. Alma tried to visit him on 8 January 1907, but instead met with his assistant Hirata K.

NAKAKUKI, S., was the editor of the *Shakwai Shimpo* newspaper in Tokyo. Met with Alma on 25 August 1901.

NAKAMURA, Mr., visited Alma and his companions on 20 August 1901.

NAKAMURA, Mr., visited Alma on 26 September 1902 to learn about the gospel.

NAKAMURA Kikujiro, was a resident of Chiba who rented his home to Alma for a cottage meeting in February 1904, despite the protests of a local Buddhist priest.

NAKAMURA Yoneju, was Hachiro Mori's friend. He helped Alma with the *Book of Mormon* translation through-out summer 1908.

NAKAZAWA, Elder. *See* Nakazawa Hajime.

NAKAZAWA Hajime (b. 1858), was born on 8 April 1858, in Oomachi, Mizuuchi Gori, Shinnano, to Nakazawa Shimesu and Fujisawa Miyo. Was a Shinto priest. Baptized and confirmed on 8 March 1902, by Heber J. Grant. Became the first Latter-day Saint convert in Japan. Excommunicated on 7 December 1903, for lying and house-breaking. [*REJM*.]

NAKAZAWA, Mrs., was the wife of Nakazawa Hajime. Had dinner with the Latter-day Saints on 20 July 1902.

NAMEKAWA Hiroyuki, was suggested by Mr. Yashiro to help with the publication of the Book of Mormon. Began his publication work on 11 February 1909.

NASA Katsuzō (b. 1887), was born on 3 February 1887, in Ushigome, Tokyo, to Nasa Katsubumi and Ikushima Shizu. Baptized on 20 December 1909, by Frederick A. Caine and confirmed on the same day by Alma O. Taylor. Excommunicated on 14 May 1914, for apostasy. [*REJM*.]

NATSUMA Kintaro, was a famous Japanese author who Alma asked to help with the translation of the *Book of Mormon* on 18 June 1908. Too busy, he suggested the name of Ikuta Koji.

NATSUME Kinnosuke. *See* Natsuma Kintaro.

NIRAYAMA, Mr., invited Elders Caine and Hedges to live with him in fall 1902.

NISHIJIMA Kakuryo, was the reverend of the Buddhist Mission in America stationed in Sacramento, California. In 1899, Reverend Kakuryo Nishijima and Dr. Shuei Sonada, head of the Academy of Literature of the Hompa Hongwanji of Kyōto, arrived in San Francisco and created the Buddhist Mission of North America. Together they taught classes on Buddhism and introduced traditional Jodo Shishu rites and practices to interested Americans and Japanese living in the Bay area. [Fields, *How the Swans Came*, 143–45 and Tuck, *Buddhist Churches of America*, 2–3.]

NISHIMURA Hide, attended the Latter-day Saint Sunday School in Tokyo. Alma visited his family on 17 June 1908.

NISHIMURA Shigeaki, was a Buddhist linen merchant who offered to help Alma and his companions find a home in Tokyo in September 1901.

NOGUCHI, Mrs., was the wife of Noguchi Zenshiro.

NOGUCHI Zenshiro, a resident of Kōbe, was recommend to help with the *Book of Mormon* translation. Alma traveled to Kōbe to meet with him about the project on 20 July 1907. He decided not to hire Noguchi.

NOMOTO, Mr., was a drunken young man who visited Alma on 20 January 1902.

NOMURA, Miss, was a young girl who attended the LDS Sunday School in Tokyo. She was given an improper note from a young man named Komorita. Alma was present on 19 February 1905, when Komorita apologized to Nomura.

NORDA, Mr., was a miner who had discovered a sulfur and gold mine. He attempted to borrow money from the Japan Mission on 29 November 1906.

NORMON or NORMAN, Mr., was an English gentleman acquainted with Mr. Aoki in Chiba. Alma visited with him about Biblical history and the gospel on 8 November 1901.

NOSO, Christopher, was the translator of Rudolf Lange's *A Text Book of Colloquial Japanese* from German into English. Was a professor of Ethics & Apologetics in the North Japan College located in Sendai.

NUNN, Brother, was friends with Alma in Salt Lake City.

NUNN, Sister, was friends with Alma in Salt Lake City.

NUTTING, Mr., is Rev. John T. Nutting, a Protestant minister who had once lived in Utah. He gave a famous lecture entitled, "The Menace of Mormonism" in Providence, Rhode Island.

OBATA, Dr., was the dentist Alma visited in July 1906.

O'BRIAN, Ambassador, was the U.S. ambassador to Japan. Alma met with him on 22 November 1909 to discuss the distribution of *Book of Mormon* copies to members of the Japanese government.

ODA, Mr., was the owner of the *Shawkwai Shimpo* newspaper. He offered to introduce the Latter-day Saints to the Japanese people in Tokyo in August 1901.

ODAN Harue, participated in the 1905 LDS Sunday School Christmas program in Tokyo.

ODAN, Mr., was the father of Odan Harue. Alma visited the Odan family on 29 March 1905.

ODAN, Mrs., was the mother of Odan Harue. Alma visited the Odan family on 29 March 1905.

OGAWA Ie. *See* Ogawa Sue.

OGAWA Sue (b. 1891), was born on 24 August 1891, in Fukuyamamachi, Matsumae Gun, Ojima Koku, Hokkaido, to Ogawa Koju and Hamatani Kiku. Baptized on 7 January 1909, by Justus B. Seeley and confirmed on 10 January 1909, by Moroni S. Marriott. Married Takahashi Ryugo on 11 June 1910. [*REJM.*]

OI, Mr., was the owner of the house Alma and Horace S. Ensign lived in during fall 1901, in Tokyo. Talked with Alma about Mormonism on 5 December 1901.

OKAFUJI, S., was a teacher in the Normal School at Sapporo who helped correct John W. Stoker's translation of the "Brief History of the Church" tract. Alma visited with him on several occasion when in Sapporo.

OKONOGI, T., visited Alma on 2 September 1906.

OKUBO, Mr., was a postgraduate student at Waseda University. Alma visited him on 18 March 1908, to discuss the moral character of Hiroi Hirogoro, his former teacher.

OKUMA, Count, owned the famous gardens Alma and other Latter-day Saints visited on 19 September 1906.

ONAE, visited Alma on 9 January 1908, with a letter from K. Tokoyo.

OSHIMA, Mr., was the principal of a Kōfu middle school. Alma visited him on 2 March 1908.

OSHIMA or OJIMA Kintaro, was a professor in the Agricultural College at Sapporo. Studied at the same school in Germany as John A. Widtsoe. Fluent in English, Oshima and Alma talked on 10 April 1906, about Utah and Mormonism. On 13 April 1906, Alma introduced Oshima to the Latter-day Saints living in Sapporo.

OSTLER, Joe, was friends with Alma in Salt Lake City.

OKADA Naichiro, was a physician specializing in nasal diseases at the Imperial University Hospital, Tokyo. Alma called on him for his nose problem on 19 September 1907. Visited again on 21 September 1907 and 1 February 1908.

OKADA, Mr., visited the Japan Mission home on 26 June 1905. Continued to visit the Latter-day Saints during 1906 and eventually asked for money. Attended LDS church meetings during 1908.

OKADA Kataro, was the Yokohama Bluff Police Station head inspector who delivered a message from the Yokohama chief of police to the Latter-day Saints living in Yokohama on 7 September 1901.

OKAMOTO or OKOMOTO, Mr., was a photographer who befriended the Latter-day Saints in Tokyo. Took many pictures for the Latter-day Saints.

OKAYOTO, Mr., was one of Alma's old acquaintances from Tokyo. He and Alma met in Sendai on 9 April 1906.

OKUNO, Mr., helped Dr. Hepburn translated the Bible into Japanese. He was an advocate of the Independent Japanese Christian Church movement. Alma visited him on 24 September 1906, to discover how he translated the Bible. Alma visited him again on 17 April 1907, to ask further questions about translation and possible literary critics.

OSAKI Yoshiei (b. 1888), was born on 5 July 1888, in Takamuku Mura, Fukui ken, to Osaki Sannoei and Matsuzaki Tano. Baptized on 7 February 1908, by John H. Roskelley and confirmed on 9 February 1908, by Justus B. Seeley. [*REJM.*]

OSHIMA, Mr., was a resident of Kōfu and a principal of the Middle School that Alma visited on 9 January 1907. Friend of Uchimura Kanzo the famous Independent Christian in Tokyo and Oshima Kintaro of Sapporo.

ŌTA, Mr., was a criminal advocate in the Chiba Court House. Alma visited him on 21 November 1903.

OTA, Sister. *See* Kamiyama Rin.

OUOZAWA Motoi, attended the LDS Sunday School in Tokyo. Received the third place best attendance award for 1905. Participated in the 1905 Sunday School Christmas program in Tokyo.

OURDAN, Mr., and his wife, originally from Washington, D.C., were in Tokyo selling samples of his invention, the hydographic engraving machine. The boarded with Alma and his companions in the Metropole Hotel, Tokyo. Friendly to the Latter-day Saints.

OURDAN, Mrs., and her husband, originally from Washington, D.C., were in Tokyo selling samples of her husband's invention, the hydographic engraving machine. The boarded with Alma and his companions in the Metropole Hotel, Tokyo. Friendly to the Latter-day Saints.

OWADA, Mr. (Takeki), was a noted poet living in Tokyo. Alma hired him to translate some of the Mormon hymns into Japanese on 2 November 1903.

OYAMA Yoshirō (b. 1878), was born on 11 November 1878, in Tokyo, to Sakayuki Funawo and Tachibana Sen. Baptized on 8 October 1902, by Heber J. Grant and confirmed on the same day by Alma O. Taylor. Apostatized on 27 March 1907. [*REJM.*]

PALLISTER, Mr., was an Englishman who became good friends with the Latter-day Saints in Tokyo. Spent time with the Latter-day Saints on 7 May 1902.

PALLISTER, Mrs., an Englishwoman who became good friends with the Latter-day Saints in Tokyo. Spent time with the Latter-day Saints on 7 May 1902.

PALLISTER, Mrs., was the sister of Mrs. Pallister. Spent time with the Latter-day Saints on 7 May 1902.

PARKER. *See* Parker, Mrs.

PARKER, Mrs., was the boarding house lady in Yokohama who let the Latter-day Saints stay with her after the "Staniland" incident in summer 1901. Friends with Mrs. Warton.

PATRICK, Maud, was friends with Alma and William R. Clarke in Salt Lake City.

PATTEN, Clarance, was friends with Alma in Salt Lake City.

PAUL, Mrs. Ted, was a member of Alma's large extended family in Utah.

PEARSON, H. A., was from Draper, Utah. Commander of the battleship *U.S.S Illinois*, which visited Japan in October 1908, with some other U.S. Navy ships. Alma met with Pearson on 22 October 1908, and was given a tour of the ship.

PEDERSON, Chas. R., was friends with Alma in Salt Lake City.

PENROSE, Charles W. (1832–1925), was born on 4 February 1832, in London, England, to Richard and Matilda Penrose. Immigrated to America. Served missions in England. Became editor of the Deseret News and the Salt Lake Herald. Elected to the territorial legislature. Called as an apostle in 1904. Served as president of the European Mission. Served as second counselor in the First Presidency, 1911–25. Died on 15 May 1925, in Salt Lake City. [*AF*, *ELDSH* 903–4.]

PETT, Imer (1875–1935), was born on 4 July 1875, in Brigham City, Utah, to James and Elizabeth Jane Brandon Pett. Was friends with Alma in Salt Lake City. Married Josephine Arnold on 27 September 1899, in Salt Lake City. Died on 25 February 1935, in Salt Lake City. [*AF.*]

PIEPER, Christian, was friends with Alma in Salt Lake City.

PIERCE, Mr., visited Alma and his companions on 30 August 1901.

PONSEFORTE, Mr., previously lived in Salt Lake City and was a member of the Church. Was an actor in Salt Lake City. Apostatized and moved to Japan during the late 1870s or early 1880s and married a Japanese woman. Operated a boarding house known as the Shakespeare Race Track in Yokohama. Passed away in the late 1890s leaving his wife and two children in Yokohama.

PONSEFORTE, Mrs., was the wife of Mr. Ponseforte. Alma and Horace S. Ensign her on 14 August 1901, looking for a cheap lodgings.

REYNOLDS, George (1842–1909), was born on 1 January 1842, in London, England, to George and Julia Ann Reynolds. Baptized in 1856 and emigrated to Utah in 1865. Served a mission in Great Britain, 1871–72. Polygamist. Acted as test case for plural marriage in the late 1870s. Sentenced to prison for his religious beliefs. Sustained as on of the First Seven Presidents of Seventies, 1890. Died on 12 August, 1909, in Salt Lake City. [*AF*, *BE* 1:206–10.]

RICHARDS, George F. (1861–1950), was born on 23 February 1861, to Franklin D. and Nanny Longstroth Richards, in Farmington, Utah. Married Alice Robinson on 9 March 1882, in Salt Lake City. Practiced polygamy. Died on 8 August 1950, in Salt Lake City. [*AF.*]

RICHARDSON, Mabel K., was an eighteen-year-old member of the Church from Hawaii. Came from a wealthy, large family of thirteen children. Came to Japan in 1905 to be treated for leprosy. Alma and the other Latter-day Saints met with her occasionally to give her blessings and comfort.

ROBERTS, Brother, is B. H. Roberts (1857–1933), was born on 13 March 1857, in Warrington, England. Emigrated to America as a child. Named valedictorian of the University of Deseret. Served a mission to the Northern States Mission. Called to First Council of Seventy. President of the Eastern States Mission, 1923–27. Completed A Comprehensive History of The Church of Jesus Christ of Latter-day Saints in 1930. Died on 27 September 1933, in Salt Lake City. [*ELDSH*, 1034–35.]

ROOSE or RUSE, Mr., visited the Japan Mission home on 4 July 1904.

ROSKELLEY, John H. (1886–1972), was born on 30 October 1886, in Smithfield, Utah, to Samuel and Mary Jane Rigby Roskelley. Baptized on 30 October 1894. Set apart for the Japan Mission on 2 August 1906, by Seymour B. Young. Labored in the Tokyo and Morioka Conferences. Married Hannah Favell Buck on 20 September 1911, in Logan, Utah. Died on 17 January 1972, in Nampa, Idaho. [*AF, JMMH.*]

RUCKERT, Leonard, was friends with Alma in Salt Lake City.

RUTH. *See* Taylor, Ruth E.

SAIGO, Admiral, was a national military hero in Japan. Alma and his companions attended his state funeral on 22 July 1902.

SAIGŌ Masayuki (b. 1884), was born on 7 February 1884, in Kajiyazawa, Okuchi-mura, Miyage-ken, to Saigo Masayuki and Ōta Kyo. Baptized on 8 January 1910, by Elbert D. Thomas and confirmed on 9 January 1910, by Alma O. Taylor. [*REJM.*]

SAITO Hisa, attended the LDS Sunday School in Tokyo. Participated in the 1904 Sunday School Christmas party.

SAITŌ Hitoshi, attended the LDS Sunday School in Tokyo. Recorded second best Sunday School attendance in 1907.

SAITŌ Sensuke, was the owner of the Japan Mission home located in Ushigome in 1909.

SAITŌ, Mrs., was the wife of Saitō Sensuke.

SAKAZAKI Shika, attended the LDS Sunday School in Tokyo. Participated in the 1906 Sunday School Christmas party. Recorded third best Sunday School attendance in 1907.

SAKUMA Mitsuwo (b. 1883), was born on 18 January 1883, in Azabu, Tokyo, to Sakuma Kunitoshi and Kobayashi Iku. Baptized on 23 December 1907, by Justus B. Seeley and confirmed on 5 January 1908, by John H. Roskelley. [*REJM.*]

SAKURABA Takeshiro (b. 1887), was born on 15 December 1887, in Kanaoka-mura, Yamamoto-kori, Akita-ken, to Sakuraba Takeji and Nakada Sumi. Baptized on 24 February 1910, by James A. Anderson and confirmed on 27 February 1910, by Elbert D. Thomas. Married Takahashi Ai on 17 November 1910. Helped with the Japanese translation of the *Book of Mormon*. [*REJM.*]

SAM or SAMUEL. *See* Taylor, Samuel M.

SANFORD, Mr., was the acting manager of the Bluff Hotel, Yokohama, where the Latter-day Saints were staying. Invited Horace S. Ensign to sing for the hotel guests on 13 August 1901.
SARA. Likely a member of Alma's large extended family in Utah.

SATO Frajuo Mogi, visited Alma on 9 September 1901. Had graduated from the University of Michigan law school in 1890, where he had become acquainted with James H. Moyle.

SATO Toshichi (b. 1889), was born on 3 April 1889, in Kurazo Mura, Higashi Murayama gun, Yamagata ken, to

Sato Genshichi and Uematsu Kie. Baptized on 15 January 1908, by Joseph P. Cutler and confirmed on 19 January 1908, by Justus B. Seeley. [*REJM.*]

SCHULTHESS, Brother, is Arnold H. Schulthess (1865–1924), born on 9 June 1865, in Neukirch, Switzerland, to Arnold R. and Marie Moor Schulthess. Immigrated to Utah in 1879 and was baptized on 3 January 1882. Served in the European Mission 1884–86. After returning to Salt Lake City, presided over the German Church meetings for eleven years. Married Rachel B. Theurer on 14 December 1887, in Logan Utah; Louise Billeter on 13 March 1891 in Logan Utah; Barbara Billeter on 25 November 1895. Presided over the German Mission, 1898–1901. Served as first counselor to President Bryant S. Hinckley of the Salt Lake Liberty Stake, 1904–1919. Died on 7 July 1924, in Salt Lake City. [*AF, BE* 1:598.]

SCHULTHESS, Jacob (1872–1934), born on 8 February 1872, in Neukirch, Switzerland, to Arnold R. and Marie Moor Schulthess. Married Margaretha Steudler on 3 June 1896, in Salt Lake City. Worked for the Bureau of Justice of the Philippine Islands. Died on 25 November 1934, in Los Angeles, California. [*AF.*]

SEBENSTEIN or SEIBENSHINE or SIEBENSHEINE, Mr., was originally from Vienna, Austria and was working in Yokohama as a traveling salesman. Boarded with Alma and his companions in Yokohama. A friend of the Latter-day Saints in Japan.

SEELEY, Justus B. (1882–1943), was born on 14 April 1882, in Indianola, Utah, to William H. and Charlotte L. Reynolds Seeley. Baptized on 24 August 1890. Set apart for the Japan Mission on 11 May 1905, by Rudger Clawson. Labored in Hokkaidō. Married Mable Marie Larsen on 14 October 1903. Died on 16 November 1943. [*AF, JMMH.*]

SEELEY, Sister Justus B., is Mable Marie Larsen Seeley (1885–1945), born on 6 February 1885, in Ephraim, Utah, to Ingvort and Karen Marie Pedersen Bach Larsen. Married Justus B. Seeley on 14 October 1903. Died on 15 March 1945, in Ephraim, Utah. [*AF.*]

SEIDENFADEN, Berenice, was friends with Alma in Salt Lake City.

SEIDENFADEN, Mrs., was friends with Alma in Salt Lake City.

SEIDENFADEN, Wm, is William Seidenfaden, was friends with Alma in Salt Lake City.

SENATOR SMOOT. *See* Smoot, Reed.

SHIBATA Keiichiro, worked in the Kōfu governor's office. Alma visited him on 9 January 1907.

SHIMADA Saburo, was the proprietor and editor of the *Mainichi News.* A leader in the Japanese House of Commons. Was very critical of the Latter-day Saints initially but met with Alma on 12 September 1907, and agreed to review John W. Stoker's "Brief History of the Church" tract in his newspaper.

SHIMAMURU, Mr., visited Alma on 24 May 1908.

SHIMOTSU, Mr., had lived in Utah for six years; two of the years as a student at the Latter-day Saints University. Visited the Japan Mission home on 2 July 1907.

SHIOIRI Ioe (b. 1891), was born on 26 November 1891, in Miyamoto-mura, Yamanashi-ken, to Ishihara Toshize and Shioiri Urage. Baptized on 23 November 1909, by Joseph H. Stimpson and confirmed on the same day by William R. Fairbourn. [*REJM.*]

SHIRAI Jooji (b. 1877), was born on 28 February 1877, in Kōfu, Yamanashi ken, to Shirai Koozoo and Tonegawa Take. Baptized on 1 September 1908, by Joseph H. Stimpson and confirmed on the same day by William R. Fairbourn. [*REJM.*]

SHIRAISHI Genkichi. Investigated Mormonism in Asahikawa.

SIMS, Brother, was an elder serving in Portland, Oregon that Alma met on 26 July 1901.

SMITH, Eliza M., was a member of Alma's large extended family in Utah.

SMITH, R. R., was a member of the U.S. Navy who gave permission to Alma and the other Latter-day Saints to board the *U.S.S. Nebraska* while it was docked in Yokohama on 20 October 1908.

SMITH, John H. (1848–1911), born on 18 September 1848 in Kanesville, Iowa, to George A. Smith. Married Sarah Farr on 20 October 1866. Later married Josephine Groesbeck in 1877. Serve a mission to Europe, 1874–75. Ordained an apostle 27 October 1880. Served as president of the British Mission, 1882–85. Sustained as second counselor to President Joseph F. Smith on 7 April 1910. Died on 13 October 1911, in Salt Lake City. [*ELDSH*, 1122.]

SMITH, Patriarch John (1832–1911), was born on 22 September 1832, in Kirtland, Ohio, to Hyrum and Jerusha Barden Smith. Became patriarch to the Church on 18 February 1855 after moving to Utah. Served a mission to Scandinavia. Was patriarch for 56 years and gave nearly 20,000 blessings. Died on 6 November 1911, in Salt Lake City. [*ELDSH*, 1121.]

SMITH, Joseph (1805–44), was born on 23 December 1805, in Sharon, Vermont, to Joseph Smith and Lucy Mack. Received the First Vision in 1820. Was called as the Restorations first prophet. Married Emma Hale on 18 January 1827. Received and translated the Gold Plates into the Book of Mormon. Received the Aaronic Priesthood with Oliver Cowdery from John the Baptist on 15 May 1829. Later received the Melchizedek Priesthood from Peter, James, and John. Published his translation of the *Book of Mormon* in 1830 and reorganized The Church of Jesus Christ on 6 April 1830. Restored essential gospel ordinances. Martyred by a mob in Carthage, Illinois, on 27 June 1844. [*JWM*, 461.]

SMITH, Joseph F. (1838–1918), was born on 13 November 1838 at Far West, Missouri, to Hyrum and Mary Fielding Smith. At the age of ten, drove his mother's covered wagon across the plains to Utah. Ordained and elder and sent on a mission to Hawaii at age fifteen. Married Levira A. Smith in 1859. Became a polygamist. Served a three year mission to Great Britain. Worked in Church historian's office. Ordained an apostle in 1866. Served as a counselor to President Lorenzo Snow before succeeding him as president of the Church in 1901. Issued the Second Manifesto forbidding plural marriage. Died on 19 November 1918, in Salt Lake City. [*ELDSH*, 1129–31.]

SMITH, Prest. *See* Smith, Joseph F.

SMOOT, Reed (1862–1941), was born on 10 January 1862, in Salt Lake City, to Abraham and Anne Smoot. Graduated from Brigham Young Academy at age 17. Called as member of Utah Stake Presidency in 1895. Ordained an apostle in 1900. Elected Republican senator for in 1902 but had great difficulty being seated officially. Was defeated by Elbert D. Thomas in the election of 1932. Died on 9 February 1941 in St. Petersburg, Florida. [*ELDSH*, 1145.]

SNELGROVE, Charles (1887–1977), was born on 30 June 1887, in Salt Lake City, to Charles R. and Emily Brooksbank Snelgrove. Was friends with Alma in Salt Lake City. Married Fidella Flint Laird on 24 November 1909, in Salt Lake City. Died on 30 December 1977, in Salt Lake City. [*AF.*]

SNELGROVE, Mrs. Geo., is Elva Grace Gray Snelgrove (b. 1893) was born in about 1893, in Salt Lake City. Was friends with Alma in Salt Lake City. Married George Brooksbank Snelgrove on 18 June 1913. [*AF.*]

SNODGRASS, Rev., was a member of the "Church of the Living God" and an associate of Mr. McCaleb. Discussed religion with Alma and Louis A. Kelsch on 4 June 1902.

SNOW, Pres. L. *See* Snow, Lorenzo.

SNOW, Lorenzo (1814–1901), was born on 30 April 1814 in Mantua, Ohio, to Oliver and Rosetta Pettibone

Snow. Studied at Oberlin College. Baptized in 1836. Served short missions to Ohio, Missouri, Illinois, and Kentucky. Served mission to Great Britain. Married nine wives and eventually had 41 children. Called to the apostleship in 1849. Served mission to Italy and other parts of Europe, 1849–52. Built up the united order in Brigham City, Utah. Served as president of the Salt Lake Temple. Called to succeed Wilford Woodruff as president of the Church. Strong advocate of tithing. Died on 10 October 1901, in Salt Lake City. [*ELDSH*, 1151–53.]

SNOW, (Minnie) Mable (1879–1962), was born on 23 May 1879, in Brigham City, Utah, to Lorenzo and Sarah Minnie Ephramina Jensen Snow. Was friends with Alma in Salt Lake City. Married Alfred Laurender Cole on 10 February 1904. Died on 3 December 1962. [*AF.*]

SOGA, Mr., was the father of one of the children attending the LDS Sunday School in Tokyo. Alma visited him on 15 April 1905.

SOGA, Mrs. was the mother of one of the children attending the LDS Sunday School in Tokyo. Alma visited her on 15 April 1905.

SPENCE, W. C., was a member of the Church in Salt Lake City involved in the shipping business.

STANILAND, Rev., was a former Protestant missionary and boardinghouse landlord, refused to board Alma and his companions in August 1901. This incident became known as the "Staniland Incident."

STEED, Walter W. (1886–1969), was born on 30 October 1886, in Farmington, Utah, to Walter W. and Julia Wilcox Steed. Baptized on 30 June 1895. Set apart for the Japan Mission on 3 June 1909, by Seymour B. Young. Labored faithfully in Shizuoka but was released early from Japan to accompany Charles W. Hubbard, who had been excommunicated for fornication, back to the United States. After seeing Hubbard home, Steed was transferred to the California Mission in November 1909. He finished his California mission on 1 June 1911. Married Elma Cook on 19 June 1912. Died on 30 July 1969. [*JMMH, PRF.*]

STIMPSON, Joseph H. (1885–1964), was born on 12 June 1885, in Riverdale, Utah, to William Jr. and Ann Mary Christensen Stimpson. Baptized on 12 June 1893. Set apart for the Japan Mission on 12 November 1906, by Rudger Clawson. Labored in the K_fu Conference. Married Mary Emeline Allen on 21 October 1914, in Salt Lake City. Died on 22 April 1964, in Salt Lake City. [*AF, JMMH.*]

STOKER, John W. (1883–1973), was born on 5 June 1883, in Doncaster, England, to John and Clara Swaby Stoker. Baptized at nine and then emigrated to Utah. Set apart for the Japan Mission on 26 June 1902, by J. Golden Kimball. Labored in Naoyetsu. Married Ruby Davis on 20 January 1909. Died on 6 August 1973. [*JMMH.*]

STONE, Mr., is Walter S. Stone, an American merchant who was living in Japan when the Latter-day Saints arrived.

STRONG, Mrs. Charles, was friends with Alma in Salt Lake City.

SUDA Suketomo (b. 1887), was born on 19 September 1887, in Isawa-machi, Yashiro-gori, Yamanashi-ken, to Suda Shirouemon and Tsuchiya Seki. Baptized on 3 November 1909, by William R. Fairbourn and confirmed on the same day by Joseph H. Stimpson. [*REJM.*]

SUGA, Mr., met with Alma in December 1906.

SUGAHARA, Mr., investigated the Church for six months and decided to be baptized in March 1907. However, he withdrew his petition after learning of the tithing requirement.

SUGIYAMA, visited with Alma on 7 November 1906.

SUKAKOSHI or SUKUKOSHI, Mr. *See* Tsukakoshi Mr.

SUYENAGA, Mr., was an editor of one of the major Tokyo newspapers. Met with Alma on 13 February 1902.

SUZUKI, Mr., investigated Mormonism and applied for baptism in 1904.

SUZUKI Genta, was an employee of the *Kahoku Shimpo* newspaper and a resident of Sendai. Alma approached him to assist in the translation of the *Book of Mormon*. Suzuki declined the invitation on 29 August 1907. Visited with Alma on 30 September 1907 and 1 November 1908.

TAI Fude (b. 1872), was born on 17 May 1872, in Aza Shimmachi, Komosawa Mura, Tokyo, to Ando Tokizo and Ishida Cho. Was the sister of Nachie Tsune. Baptized on 1 November 1907, by Fred Caine and confirmed on 3 November 1907, by John W. Stoker [*REJM.*]

TAGUCHI, Mr., was visited by Alma on 25 May 1905.

TAKADA, Mr., was a military officer who attended an LDS church meeting on 18 November 1906.

TAKADA, President, was the president of Waseda University in 1908. Alma tried to visit him on 31 March 1908 to question Hirai Hirogoro's moral character.

TAKAGI CHILDREN. *See* Takagi Ai and Ei.

TAKAGI SISTERS. *See* Takagi Ai and Ei.

TAKAGI Ai, attended the LDS Sunday School in Tokyo. Participated in the 1904 Sunday School Christmas party.

TAKAGI Ei, attended the LDS Sunday School in Tokyo. Participated in the 1904 Sunday School Christmas party.

TAKAGI, Grandma, was the grandmother of Takagi Ai and Ei.

TAKAGI, was a young man who attended some LDS meetings in 1906.

TAKAHASHI Goro, was a teacher and well known Japanese scholar and literary critic who helped with the Japanese translation of the Bible. He defended the Latter-day Saints in Japan early on and won their trust and friendship. He spoke fluent English and met with the missionaries often to learn about Mormonism and teach them about Japan. He agreed to write a book about the Church for Japanese readers. *Morumonkyo to Morumon Kyoto* (Mormonism and Mormons) was published in August 1902 but experienced poor sales. His relationship with the Latter-day Saints deteriorated in 1903, following the excommunication of Nakazawa Hajime.

TAKAHASHI Hisa, attended the LDS Sunday School in Tokyo. Received the second-best attendance record in 1906 and third best in 1907. Participated in the 1906 Sunday School Christmas party.

TAKAHASHI Nikichi (b. 1892), was born on 25 March 1892, in Kutsukata Mura, Rishiri gun, Kitami Koku, Hokkaido, to Minato Sokichi and Takahashi Hanayo. Baptized on 5 September 1908, by Moroni S. Marriott and confirmed on 6 September 1908, by Justus B. Seeley. Eventually moved to Tokyo. [*REJM.*]

TAKAYA, Mr., visited the Japan Mission home on 7 October 1903.

TAKEDA, Mr., visited Alma on 9 November 1903.

TAKEYAMA, Mr., was the official English/Japanese interpreter for Chiba Ken who investigated Mormonism on behalf of the Japanese government. While initially prejudiced by anti-Mormon literature, he read Takahashi Goro's *Mormons & Mormonism* and became friendly. Visited Alma on 8 April 1904.

TALMAGE, James E. (1862–1933), was born on 21 September 1862, in Hungerford, England, to James Joyce and Susannah Talmage. After joining the Church, his family emigrated to Utah in 1876. Studied under Karl G. Maeser at the Brigham Young Academy. Married May Booth in 1888. Served as president of the University of Utah. Called to the apostleship in 1911. Presided over the European Mission from 1924–28. Wrote *Articles of Faith* and *Jesus the Christ.* Died on 27 July 1933, in Salt Lake City. [*ELDSH*, 1217–18.]

TAMANO Sokichi, allowed Erastus L. Jarvis to live at his farmhouse in Nakano. Alma visited the Tamano home on 1 July 1904 and again in August 1906.

TAMANO FAMILY. *See* Tamano Sokichi.

TAMANO, Messrs. *See* Tamano Families.

TAMURA, Mr., was visited by Alma on 4 October 1906.

TAMARU, Mr., visited Alma to investigate Mormonism in March 1904.

TANAKA, Mr., was a middle school student living in Chiba who read Takahashi Goro's *Mormons & Mormonism.* Visited Alma on 8 November 1903.

TANAKA, Mr., visited Alma on 12 February 1902.

TANAKA, Mr., was a friend of Mr. Sakuraba who traveled on the same train with Alma and Frederick A. Taylor in January 1910.

TANAKA, Mrs., was a friend of Miss Kogu and Miss Umeda who let Alma visit her home on 6 March 1905, to see her display of the girl's festival of dolls.

TANIFUJI (ISHIGAKI), Chiyo (1890–1918), was born on 17 October 1890, in Sapporo, Hokkaido, to Tanifuji Zempachi and Kitano Sei. Baptized on 19 December 1908, by Justus B. Seeley and confirmed on 20 December 1908, by Joseph P. Cutler. Married Ishigaki Inokichi in August 1909. Died of influenza on 12 December 1918. [*REJM*.]

TANIMURA, Mr., met with Alma on 27 December 1908.

TANIUCHI, Mr., owned two homes that Alma tried to rent for the new Japan Mission home in November 1908.

TAUE Tokujiro (b. 1888), was born on 3 November 1888, in Nechi-mura, NishiKubiki-gun, Niigata ken, to Taue Genhyoe and Inomata Take. Baptized on 5 April 1909, by Frederick A. Caine and confirmed on the same day by Elbert D. Thomas. [*REJM*.]

TAYLOR, Clara Ann Sudbury (1858–1939), was born on 28 April 1858, in Salt Lake City, to Samuel J. and Emma Lovina Crossland Sudbury. Married Joseph E. Taylor on 1 April 1884, in Salt Lake City. Died on 3 January 1939, in Salt Lake City. [*AF*.]

TAYLOR, Edward (1858–1910), was born on 31 December 1858, in Salt Lake City, to Joseph E. and Louisa Rebeckah Capener. Married Fanny Mulholland on 29 September 1879, in Salt Lake City. Died on 13 January 1910, in Salt Lake City. [*AF*.]

TAYLOR, Elizabeth M. (1867–1950), was born on 10 April 1867, in Salt Lake City, to Joseph E. and Louisa Rebeckah Capener. Married Benjamin J. Beer. Died on 2 April 1950, in Salt Lake City. [*AF*.]

TAYLOR, Elliot C. (b. 1888), was born on 12 July 1888, in Salt Lake City, to Moses W. and Dorah Campell Taylor. Baptized on 12 July 1896. Set apart for the Japan Mission on 2 July 1907, by Rulon S. Wells. Labored in the K_fu Conference and in the city of Shizuoka. Released early after losing the spirit of his mission. Married Mary Marian Walker on 21 February 1912. [*JMMH*.]

TAYLOR, Florence, was a member of Alma's large extended family in Utah.

TAYLOR, Geo., was a member of Alma's large extended family in Utah.

TAYLOR, Harriet A.W., was a member of Alma's large extended family in Utah.

TAYLOR, Harold (1904–1959), was born on 18 January 1904, in Salt Lake City, to Samuel M. and Sophia Lucile Badger Taylor. Died on 17 August 1859, in Salt Lake City. [*AF.*]

TAYLOR, John (1808–1887), was born on 1 November 1808, in Milnthorpe, England, to James and Agnes Taylor. Emigrated to America and then moved to Canada. Married Leonora Cannon on 28 Janaury 1833. They joined the Church from the preaching of Parley P. Pratt in 1836. Moved to Kirtland, Ohio and then to Missouri. Ordained an apostle in 1838. Served a mission to Great Britain. Editor of the *Times and Seasons* newspaper in Nauvoo. Served mission to Europe in 1850s. Moved west to Utah and succeed Brigham Young as president of the Church in 1880. Forced to live "underground" due to plural marriage persecutions. Died on 25 July 1887, in Kaysville, Utah. [*ELDSH*, 1223–26.]

TAYLOR, John W. (1858–1916), was born on 15 May 1858 in Provo, Utah, to President John Taylor. He served missions throughout the United States, Canada, and Mexico. He was called to the apostleship but resigned over the discontinuation of plural marriage in 1905. He was excommunicated from the Church in 1911. He died on 10 October 1916 in Salt Lake City. [ELDSH, 1226.]

TAYLOR, Joseph W. (1855–1931), was born on 16 January 1855, in Salt Lake City, to Joseph E. and Louisa Rebeckah Capener. Married Margaret Littlefair on 15 April 1880. Died on 11 January 1931. [*AF.*]

TAYLOR, Joseph E., Alma's father.

TAYLOR, Lisadore A. (1886–1971), was born on 21 August 1886, in Centerville, Utah, to Joseph E. and Clara Ann Sudbury Taylor. Married William D. Campbell on 24 April 1907, in Salt Lake City. Died on 29 September 1971, in Murray, Utah. [*AF.*]

TAYLOR, Lisadore W., Alma's mother.

TAYLOR, Lucile (1881–1952), was born on 6 July 1881, in Salt Lake City, to Rodney C. and Harriet Ann Whitaker, Badger. Married Samuel M. Taylor on 15 April 1903, in Salt Lake City. Died on 14 September 1952, in Los Angeles, California. [*AF.*]

TAYLOR, Mahonri M. (1890–1971), was born on 25 January 1890, in Salt Lake City, to Joseph E. and Clara Ann Sudbury Taylor. Married Cora Platt on 26 October 1911. Died on 21 March 1971. [*AF.*]

TAYLOR, Moses (1862–1922), was born on 9 March 1862, in Salt Lake City, to President John and Sophia Whittaker Taylor. Baptized on 2 August 1877. Served a mission to the Southern States, 1890–93. Married Sarah Stewart Campbell on 11 November 1885. Served as president of the Summit Stake, 1901–21. Died on 13 January 1922, in Salt Lake City. [*BE* 4:73.]

TAYLOR, Ruth E. (1885–1965), was born on 16 January 1885, in Salt Lake City, to Joseph E. and Clara Ann Sudbury Taylor. Married August Carl Thomstorff on 20 June 1910. Died on 4 December 1965. [*AF.*]

TAYLOR, Samuel M. (1880–1954), was born on 11 March 1880, in Salt Lake City, to Joseph E. and Lisadore Williams Taylor. Alma's only full-blooded sibling. Married Sophia Lucile Badger on 15 April 1903, in Salt Lake City. Died on 7 July 1954, in Salt Lake City. [*AF.*]

TAYLOR, Theadore, was a member of Alma's large extended family in Utah.

TEASDALE, George (1831–1907), was born on 8 December 1831, in London, England. Attended the University of London. Joined the Church and emigrated to Utah. Served as president of the European Mission and helped the Church colonize Mexico. Served for 24 years as an apostle. Died on 9 June 1907, in Salt Lake City. [*ELDSH*, 1228–29.]

TESTUKA Y., visited Alma and his companions on 17 September 1901, to investigate Mormonism. Purchased the first *Book of Mormon* (English edition) sold in Japan on 18 September 1901.

THOMAS, Elbert D. (1883–1953), was born on 17 June 1883, to Richard K. and Caroline Stockdale Thomas. Baptized on 30 June 1891. Married Edna Harker on 25 June 1907, in Salt Lake City. Set apart for the Japan Mission on 3 September 1907, by George Albert Smith. Served as mission secretary for two years and then three years as mission president, 1910–12. In 1932 elected as a senator from Utah after defeating Reed Smoot to the U.S. Congress. Married Ethel Evans on 6 November 1946, in Salt Lake City. Died on 11 February 1953, in Honolulu, Hawaii. [*AF, JMMH.*]

THOMAS, Sister. *See* Thomas, Edna H.

THOMAS, Edna H. (1883–1942), was born on 11 April 1881, in Taylorsville, Utah, to Benjamin and Hattie Bennion Harker. Baptized at eight. Married Elder D. Thomas on 25 June 1907, in Salt Lake City. Set apart for the Japan Mission with her husband, Elbert D. Thomas, on 3 September 1907, by Heber J. Grant. Served with her husband. Died on 29 April 1942, in Washington, D.C. [*JMMH.*]

THOMAS, C. J., was friends with Alma in Salt Lake City.

THOMAS, Joseph H., of Manasaw, Colorado, was called to the Japan Mission in 1906 and expected to depart that May. Alma received a letter from him announcing his call on 14 February 1906. Never did come to Japan.

THOMAS, Lizzie or Lizie, was friends with Alma in Salt Lake City.

THURMAN, was a classmate of Sato Frajuo Mogi at the University of Michigan Law School.

TILSON, Mr., was a citizen of Utah who traveled to the Philippines during the Spanish-American War. Following the war, he visited Japan. He met with Alma and his companions several times in January 1902.

TOIHURA, Mr., broke his appointment to meet with Alma on 23 October 1903, because he was drunk.

TOGO, Mr., rented a home to Alma in November 1908.

TOJŌ Fuyu, attended the LDS Sunday School in Tokyo. Recorded the second best Sunday School attendance for 1907.

TOKADA, Mr., visited Alma on 10 June 1906.

TOKOYO Katsumi, was a long-time friend of the Latter-day Saints in Japan. Moved from Tokyo to Kōbe with the Bank of Formosa. Alma visited him in Kōbe on 20 July 1907.

TOMINAGA, Miss, was the wife of Mr. Tominaga.

TOMINAGA, Mr., was a resident of Sapporo. He met Alma on 9 August 1908.

TOTSUKA, Mr., invited Alma to come live with his family in Tokyo on 30 June 1905, so Alma could improve his Japanese. Eventually, Daniel P. Woodland lived with his family for a short time.

TOTSUKA, Mrs., was the wife of Mr. Totsuka.

TOWELL, Mr., boarded with Alma and his companions at the Metropole Hotel, Tokyo.

TOWELL, Mrs., boarded with Alma and his companions at the Metropole Hotel, Tokyo.

TOYO, Mr., offered to rent the Latter-day Saints one of his homes in Koyama in November 1908.

TSUBOUCHI Yuzo, was a famous author and a professor at Waseda University. Alma visited him on 17 June 1908, to ask if he would help with the final review of the translation of the *Book of Mormon*. Alma visited him again on 17 July 1908, to assess Mr. Ikuta's translation ability.

TSUKAKOSHI, Mr., assisted Frederick A. Caine in translating a missionary tract into Japanese. Visited the Latter-day Saints often and was helpful in their work.

TSUNEDA, Mr., visited with Alma on 27 September 1902.

TSUOKA, Mr., visited the Japan Mission home on 29 November 1904.

TSUTSUI, Mr., visited Alma many times during May and June 1904. Occasionally helped with translation questions.

TUNG Ho Pei., was a Chinese teacher. He lived with several other Chinese and Japanese men and invited Alma and Horace S. Ensign to live with them cheap. Alma visited him on 14 and 16 December 1901.

UCHIDA, Mr. *See* Ushida Mr.

UCHIMURA Kanzo, was one of Japan's best known writers. Alma visited him on 13 September 1905.

UEHARA, Mr., investigated Mormonism during summer 1907.

UESUGI Yae, attended the LDS Sunday School in Tokyo. Participated in the 1904 Sunday School Christmas party.

UMEDA Kiyo, gave Alma a Christmas present in 1904.

UMEHARA, Mr., was the pastor of the Fujimichō Christian Church. Referred to Alma to help with the *Book of Mormon* translation by Mr. Okuno on 17 April 1907.

UNO Yasutaro, met Alma onboard the *Higo Maru* in route to Hakodate on 10 April 1906.

USHIDA, Mr., was a simple laborer who painted ships for a living. He claimed to have attended the LDS College in Salt Lake City for four months on a scholarship from the LDS Church in the mid–1890s, where he became well acquainted with Thomas Katsunuma. Visited Alma and his companions on 19 August 1901. Gave his first language lesson to the Latter-day Saints on 30 August 1901. Several days later they decided to hire a new teacher.

VANBUSKIRK, Mr., was a Protestant minister traveling with his wife to the Philippines onboard the *Empress of India* with Alma in summer 1901.

VANBUSKIRK, Mrs., was the wife of a Protestant minister and an accomplished musician who was traveling with her husband to the Philippines onboard the *Empress of India* with Alma in summer 1901.

WADA, H., was a Christian minister who met with Alma on 10 March 1902, to discuss religion.

WAKABAYASHI, Mr., attended Alma's English Bible class on 4 September 1907.

WALLACE, Mrs. Howard, was a member of Alma's large extended family in Utah.

WARTON, Mrs., became good friends with the Latter-day Saints in Yokohama. A devote Christian, she invited them to a number of entertainment events as her guests.

WATANABE Yoshijiro, was a member of the Methodist Episcopal Church. He visited the Japan Mission home several times during 1904. Called on Alma again on 14 February 1907, before traveling to London, England.

WATANABE, Mr., visited the Japan Mission home on 10 January 1908.

WATANABE Itsu (b. 1889), was born on 23 January 1889, in Shukunami Mura, Hyogo Ken, to Watanabe Takeji and Katsuyama Tsune. Baptized on 11 August 1908, by Justus B. Seeley and confirmed on the same day by Alma O. Taylor. First female convert in Hokkaido. Parents belonged to Methodist church. [*REJM.*]

WATASE, Mr., was president of the Tokyo Plant Seed and Implement Co.

WELLS, Rulon S. (1854–1941), was born on 7 July 1854, in Salt Lake City, to Daniel H. and Louisa Free Wells. Served a mission to Europe. Married Josephine Eliza Beatie in 1883. Sustained to the presidency of Seventy in 1893. Served as president of the British Mission, 1896–98. Died on 7 May 1941, in Salt Lake City. [*EDLSH,* 1327.]

WHITNEY, Orson F. (1855–1931), was born on 1 July 1855, in Salt Lake City, to Horace Kimball and Helen Mar Kimball Whitney. Served a mission in the eastern United States. Acted as bishop of the Salt Lake Eighteenth Ward. Called to the apostleship. Beloved writer and thinker. Died on 16 May 1931, in Salt Lake City. [*ELDSH,* 1341.]

WHITNEY, Dr., was a Tokyo eye doctor. He took care of the elder's eyes and made glasses for several individuals. Alma asked him about Miss Richardson's leprosy on 17 February 1906.

WHITNEY, J. P., was a Protestant minister who met Alma while riding an electric car in Tokyo on 14 July 1906. Very condescending to the Latter-day Saints.

WILL. *See* Erekson, William B.

WITSOE (Widtsoe), John A. (1872–1952), was born on 31 January 1872, in Norway, to John A. and Anna Karine Daarden Widtsoe. Emigrated with his mother at the age of eleven. Called as an apostle in 1921. Serve as president of the European Mission for six years. Editor of the *Improvement Era* periodical. Married Leah Dunford. Died on 29 November 1952, in Salt Lake City. [*ELDSH,* 1343–44.]

WINDER, John R. (1821–1910), was born on 11 December 1821, in Biddenham, England. Joined the Church and emigrated to Utah. Called to serve as member of presiding bishopric in 1887. Served as a member of the First Presidency. Died on 27 March 1910, in Salt Lake City. [*ELDSH,* 1348.]

WOODRUFF, Abraham O. (1872–1904), was born on 23 November 1872, in Salt Lake City to Wilford and Emma Smith Woodruff. Called to Swiss-German Mission in 1893. Called to the apostleship in 1897. Helped settle the Big Horn Basin of Wyoming. Died on 20 June 1904. [*ELDSH,* 1360–61.]

WOODLAND, Daniel P. (1882–1954), was born on 17 February 1882, in Oneida, Idaho, to William W. and Laura Peters Woodland. Baptized on 9 April 1892. Served in the Malad Stake Presidency, 1898–1900 and 1928–30+. Set apart for the Japan Mission on 7 June 1905, by Francis M. Lyman. Labored in the Sendai Conference. Was asked to accompany recently excommunicated Sandford Hedges home to Utah. Faithfully returned to Japan and resumed mission but was released in 1908 due to physical sickness. Married Ruth Blanche Hatch on 24 June 1909, in Salt Lake City. Died on 12 February 1954, in Logan, Utah. [*AF, BE* 4:523, *JMMH.*]

WOOLEY (Woolley), Fanny (1864–1946), was born on 2 February 1864, to Edwin D. and Mary Ann Olpin Woolley. Baptized on 2 July 1874. Called as first Primary president of the Salt Lake Thirteenth Ward and eventually served as a member of the General Primary Board. Was called to the Colorado Mission in 1901 with Lutie Grant. Married George C. Parkinson on 17 January 1902, in Salt Lake City. Died on 29 July 1946, in Salt Lake City. [*BE* 4:293.]

WOOLLEY, Geo. E., was friends with Alma in Salt Lake City.

WOOLLEY, Brother, was friends with Alma in Salt Lake City.

WOOLLEY, Hyrum, was the owner of the Woolley Furnace Company in which Heber J. Grant owned shares.

WOOLLEY, Samuel E. (b. 1859), was born on 20 October 1859, in Salt Lake City to Samuel and Maria Angell Woolley. Baptized in 1868 and served mission to Sandwich Islands, 1880–84. Presided over the Hawaiian Mission, 1895–1919. Oversaw the construction of the Hawaii Temple. Died in Salt Lake City. [Harvey, "The Development of the Church in Hawaii," 137.]

WUNSCH, Dr., was a doctor in Tokyo gave Alma a medical exam on 26 January 1907.

YAMAMOTO, Dr., met with Alma on 26 July 1907, to discuss Genta Suzuki's literary abilities.

YAMASAKI, Mr., was a long-time Christian. Visited the Latter-day Saints often and applied for baptism in November 1903.

YAMASAKI T., was the editor of the *Skakwai Shimpo* newspaper. Visited Alma and his companions on 25 August 1901.

YAMASAKI U., was a member of the Japanese Bible Society studying to become a Baptist preacher. He visited Alma and his companions on 30 August 1901, to discuss Mormonism. They invited the missionaries to one of their meetings, which they did on 8 September 1901.

YANO, Mr., visited Alma on 10 March 1908.

YOKOYAMA FAMILY. *See* Yokoyama Mr.

YOKOYAMA, Mr., lived next door to the Japan Mission home. A member of the lower house of the Japanese Parliament.

YONEYAMA Muraji (b. 1876), was born on 10 August 1876, in Minobu Mura, Minami Koma-Gun, Yamanashi-ken, to Yoneyama Ryohyoe and Ichikawa Ai. Baptized on 29 July 1908, by William R. Fairbourn and confirmed on 2 August 1908, by William R. Fairbourn. Married Ichikawa Hana. [*REJM.*]

YONEYAMA Hana Ichikawa (b. 1875), was born on 29 October 1875, in Yawate-mura, Higashi-Yamanashi-gun, Yamanashi-ken, to Ichikawa Ichiemon and Tsuruta Shō. Baptized on 29 July 1908, by William R. Fairbourn and confirmed on 2 August 1908, by Joseph H. Stimpson. Married Yoneyama Muraji. [*REJM.*]

YONEYAMA Morizo (b. 1902), was born on 2 March 1902, in Shinaonuma-cho, Kōfu, Yamanashi ken, to Yoneyama Muraji and Ichikawa Hana (both became members). Baptized on 10 March 1910, by Joseph H. Stimpson and confirmed on 20 March 1910, by Jay C. Jensen. [*REJM.*]

YOSHIDA, Mr., was a friend of the missionaries and helped with some minor Japanese translation during 1903.

YOSHIDA, Mr., was the secretary of Count Komura Jūtarō. Alma met him on 29 November 1909.

YOSHIDA, Mr., was the member of the Waseda University faculty who investigated Hirai Hirogoro's case in March and April 1908.

YOSHIDA Shizu, attended the LDS Sunday School in Tokyo.

YOSHIDA, Mrs., was a resident of Sendai who Alma visited on 7 April 1906. She was the mother of Mr. Yoshida who helped the Latter-day Saints in 1903.

YOSHIKAWA, Mr., visited Alma and his companions on 22 July 1902, to discuss Mormonism.

YASHIRO Kuniharu, invited Alma to his home for dinner on 29 January 1909.

YOSHIMURA, Mrs., visited with the Latter-day Saints on 12 November 1906.

YOUNG, was friends with Alma in Salt Lake City.

YOUNG, Dean, was a member of Alma's large extended family in Utah.

ZEMBA, Mr., was a resident of Sapporo who was introduced to the Latter-day Saints by Mr. Tokoyo. Alma met him on 13 April 1906.

Biographical Register Bibliography

AF. LDS Ancestral File.

BE. Jenson, Andrew. *Latter-day Saint Biographical Encyclopedia,* 4 vols. Salt Lake City: Deseret News, 1901–1936.

ELDSH. Arnold K. Garr, Donald Q. Cannon, Richard O. Cowan. eds. *Encyclopedia of Latter-day Saint History.* Salt Lake City: Desert Book Company, 2000.

EHC. Andrew Jenson. *Encyclopedic History of The Church of Jesus Christ of Latter-day Saints.* Salt Lake City: Deseret News, 1941.

Fields, Rick. *How the Swans Came to the Lake: A Narrative History of Buddhism in America* (Boston & London: Shambhala, 1986).

Harvey, Richard C. "The Development of the Church of Jesus Christ of Latter-day Saints in Hawaii." Master's Thesis. Brigham Young University, 1974.

IGI. International Genealogical Index.

JMMH. Japan Mission Manuscript History. Archives Division, Historical Department, The Church of Jesus Christ of Latter-day Saints, Salt Lake City.

JWM. Jan Shipps and John W. Welch. eds. *The Journals of William E. McLellin.* Provo, UT and Urbana, IL: BYU Studies and University of Illinois Press, 1994.

Mircrosoft Encarta 98 Encylopedia, CD-ROM. Redmond, WA: Microsoft, 1998.

PRF. Pedigree Resource File.

REJM. Record of Early Japanese Members. Archives Division, Historical Department, The Church of Jesus Christ of Latter-day Saints, Salt Lake City.

Takagi, Shinji. "Tomizo and Tokujiro: The First Japanese Mormons." *BYU Studies* 39, no. 2 (2000): 73–84.

Tuck, Donald R. *Buddhist Churches of America: Jodo Shinshu* (Lewiston/Queenston: The Edwin Mellon Press, 1987).

Bibiography

Manuscripts

"Alma Owen Taylor," typescript, copy in possession of the author.

Brigham Young Office Journals—Excerpts, 1853–62. New Mormon Studies CD-ROM. Smith Research Associates, 1998.

Cannon, Abraham H. Abraham H. Cannon Collection. L. Tom Perry Special Collections, Harold B. Lee Library, Brigham Young University, Provo, Utah.

Diary Excerpts of Heber J. Grant, 1887–1899. New Mormon Studies CD-ROM. Smith Research Associates, 1998.

Diary Excepts of Thomas A. Clawson, 1895–1904. New Mormon Studies CD-ROM. Smith Research Associates, 1998.

Journal History of the Church. Library Division, Historical Department, The Church of Jesus Christ of Latter-day Saints, Salt Lake City.

Judd, Mary Grant. Journals. Archives Division, Historical Department, The Church of Jesus Christ of Latter-day Saints, Salt Lake City.

Salt Lake City Thirteenth Ward Manuscript History. Archives Division, Historical Department, The Church of Jesus Christ of Latter-day Saints, Salt Lake City.

Taylor, Alma O. Journals, 1901–1946. L. Tom Perry Special Collections, Harold B. Lee Library, Brigham Young University, Provo, Utah.

Taylor, Lisadore Williams. Journal. Archives Division, Historical Department, The Church of Jesus Christ of Latter-day Saints, Salt Lake City.

Books

Adler, Jacob and Robert M. Kamins. *The Fantastic Life of Walter Murray Gibson: Hawaii's Minister of Everything.* Honolulu: University of Hawaii Press, 1986.

An English Dictionary of Japanese Culture. eds. Honna Nobuyuki and Bates Hoffer. Tokyo: Yuhikaku Pub. Co., 1986.

Arrington, Leonard J. *Great Basin Kingdom: An Economic History of the Latter-day Saints, 1830–1900.* Salt Lake City: University of Utah Press and Tanner Trust Fund, 1993.

———. *History of the Utah-Idaho Sugar Beet Company.* Logan: Utah State University Press, 1973.

Bitton, Davis. *George Q. Cannon: A Biography.* Salt Lake City: Deseret Book Company, 1999.

Britsch, R. Lanier. *From the East: The History of the Latter-day Saints in Asia, 1851–1996.* Salt Lake City: Deseret

Book, 1998.

———. *Moramona: The Mormons in Hawaii.* Laie, HI: Institute for Polynesian Studies, 1989.

———. *Nothing More Heroic: The Compelling Story of the First Latter-day Saint Missionaries in India.* Salt Lake City: Deseret Book, 1999.

Campbell, Eugene E. *Establishing Zion: The Mormon Church in the American West, 1847–1869.* Salt Lake City: Signature Books, 1988.

Clawson, Rudger. *A Ministry of Meetings: The Apostolic Diaries of Rudger Clawson.* ed. Stan Larson. Salt Lake City: Signature Books, 1993.

Collinwood, Dean W. Ryoichi Yamamoto, Kazue Matsui-Haag. *Samurais in Salt Lake: Diary of the First Diplomatic Japanese Delegation to Visit Utah,* 1872. Salt Lake City: US-Japan Center, 1996.

Cowan, Richard O. *The Church in the Twentieth Century.* Salt Lake City: Bookcraft, 1985.

Drumm, Mark. *Drumm's Manual of Utah, and Souvenir of the First State Legislature, 1896.* Salt Lake City: Mark Drumm, 1896.

Encyclopedia of Mormonism. ed. Daniel H. Ludlow. 4 vols. New York: Macmillan, 1992.

Fields, Rick. *How the Swans Came to the Lake: A Narrative History of Buddhism in America.* Boston & London: Shambhala, 1986.

Gibbons, Francis M. *Lorenzo Snow: Spiritual Giant, Prophet of God.* Salt Lake City: Deseret Book Company, 1982.

Grant, Heber J. *A Japanese Journal.* comp. Gordon A. Madsen. n.p.: the compiler, 1970.

Hayasaka, Jiro. *An Outline of the Japanese Press.* Japan: Kenkyusha Press, 1938.

Heart Throbs of the West. comp. Kate B. Carter. Salt Lake City: Daughters of Utah Pioneers, 1945.

History of Oregon, Volume II. Chicago–Portland: The Pioneer Historical Publishing Company, 1922.

Japan: An Illustrated Encyclopedia. 2 vols. Tokyo: Kodansha, 1993.

Jenson, Andrew. *Encyclopedic History of The Church of Jesus Christ of Latter-day Saints.* Salt Lake City: Deseret News Publishing Company, 1941.

———. *Latter-day Saint Biographical Encyclopedia: A Compilation of Biographical Sketches of Prominent Men and Women in The Church of Jesus Christ of Latter-day Saints.* 4 vols. Salt Lake City: Andrew Jenson History Co. and Andrew Jenson Memorial Association, 1901–1936.
———. *The Historical Record.* Salt Lake City: Andrew Jenson, 1887.

Kitagawa, Joseph M. *Religion in Japanese History.* New York: Columbia University Press, 1990.

Malone, Michael P. *James J. Hill: Empire Builder of the Northwest.* Norman, Oklahoma: University of Oklahoma Press, 1996.

Martin, Albro. *James J. Hill and the Opening of the Northwest.* New York: Oxford University Press, 1976.

Men of Affairs in the State of Utah: A Newspaper Reference Work. Salt Lake City: The Press Club of Salt Lake, 1914.

Microsoft Encarta 98 Encyclopedia. Redmond, WA: Microsoft, 1998.

LDS Conference Report. The Church of Jesus Christ of Latter-day Saints. April 1901.

LDS Conference Report. The Church of Jesus Christ of Latter-day Saints. October 1901.

Our Heritage: A Brief History of The Church of Jesus Christ of Latter-day Saints. Salt Lake City: The Church of Jesus Christ of Latter-day Saints, 1996.

Our Pioneer Heritage. comp. Kate B. Carter. Salt Lake City: Daughters of Utah Pioneers, 1970.

Papinot, Edmund. *Historical and Geographical Dictionary of Japan.* Tokyo: Librarie Sansaisha, 1910.

Pioneers and Prominent Men of Utah Comprising Photographs, Genealogies, Biographies. ed. Frank Esshom. Salt Lake City: Utah Pioneers Book Publishing Company, 1913.

Pyle, Kenneth B. *The Making of Modern Japan.* Lexington, MA: D. C. Heath and Company, 1996.

Roberts, B. H. *A Comprehensive History of The Church of Jesus Christ of Latter-day Saints, Century One.* 6 vols. Provo, Utah: Corporation of the President, The Church of Jesus Christ of Latter-day Saints, 1965.

Seidensticker, Edward. *Low City, High City: Tokyo from Edo to the Earthquake.* New York: Alfred A. Knopf, 1983.

Tate, Mowbray. *Transpacific Steam: The Story of Steam Navigation from the Pacific Coast of North America to the Far East and the Antipodes, 1867–1941.* New York: Cornwall Books, 1986.

The Book of Mormon: Another Testament of Christ. Salt Lake City: The Church of Jesus Christ of Latter-day Saints, 1981.

The Holy Bible. Salt Lake City: The Church of Jesus Christ of Latter-day Saints, 1979.

The Diaries of Walter Murray Gibson, 1886, 1887. ed. Jacob Adler and Gwynn Barrett. eds. Honolulu: The University Press of Hawaii, 1973.

The Life of William Willes: From His Own Personal Journals and Writings. ed. Charleen Cutler. Provo, UT: Family Footprints, 2000.

The Story of Salt Lake Stake, The Church of Jesus Christ of Latter-day Saints: 150 Years of History, 1847– 1997. Salt Lake City: Salt Lake Stake, n.d.

Tuck, Donald R. *Buddhist Churches of America: Jodo Shinshu.* Lewiston/Queenston: The Edwin Mellon Press, 1987.

Utah: Her Cities, Towns, and Resources. Chicago: Manly & Litteral, 1891–92.

Utah History Encyclopedia, ed. Alan Kent Powell. Salt Lake City: University of Utah Press, 1994.

Utah Since Statehood: Historical and Biographical. Chicago-Salt Lake: The S. J. Clarke Publishing Company, 1919.

Whitney, Orson F. *History of Utah.* Salt Lake City: George Q. Cannon & Sons, 1892–1904.

Wilgus, William J. *The Railway Interrelations of the United States and Canada.* New Haven: Yale University Press, 1937.

Woodruff, Wilford. *Wilford Woodruff's Journals.* ed. Scott G. Kenney. 9 vols. Midvale, UT: Signature Books, 1985.

Newspapers

"Alma O. Taylor Going to Japan: Young Man Called to Accompany Apostle Heber J. Grant and Elders Louis A. Kelsch and Horace S. Ensign to the Orient." *Deseret News.* 11 May 1901.

"American and Japanese Flags." *Deseret News.* 19 June 1901.

"Opening of a Mission in Japan." *Deseret News.* 6 April 1901.

"Some People of the Far East." *Deseret News.* 29 November 1897.

"The Japanese Mission Benefit." *Deseret News.* 30 May 1901.

"The Japanese Troupe." *Deseret News.* 25 April 1870.

Early Church Periodicals

"A Commercial City of Japan." *Juvenile Instructor* 30 (15 January 1895): 41–42.

"A Country Scene in Japan." *Juvenile Instructor* 8 (25 October 1873): 169–70.

"A Japanese Execution." *Juvenile Instructor* 19 (15 April 1884): 126–27.

"A Japanese Idol." *Juvenile Instructor* 8 (10 May 1872): 73–74.

"A Japanese Meal." *Juvenile Instructor* 19 (15 March 1884): 81–82.

"A Japan Shoe Store." *Juvenile Instructor* 13 (15 June 1878): 133–34.

"A Japanese Tea-House." *Juvenile Instructor* 18 (15 March 1883): 81–82.

"A Japanese Traveling Equipage." *Juvenile Instructor* 23 (15 April 1888): 113.

Cannon, Abraham H. "A Future Mission Field." *The Contributor* 16 (October 1895): 764–65.

Cannon, George Q. "Editorial Thoughts." *Juvenile Instructor* 8 (17 February 1872): 28.

———. "Editorial Thoughts." *Juvenile Instructor* 18 (15 January 1883): 24.

———. "Editorial Thoughts." *Juvenile Instructor* 18 (1 June 1883): 168.

Editor. "Japanese Progress." *Juvenile Instructor* 32 (1 June 1897): 354–55.

———. "Strength in Unity, Not in Numbers." *Juvenile Instructor* 30 (1 June 1895): 341–43.

"Festival of the Idol Tengou in Japan." *Juvenile Instructor* 9 (28 February 1874): 49.

"In the Land of the Mikado." *Juvenile Instructor* 33 (15 December 1898): 809–11.

"Japan." *Juvenile Instructor* 31 (1 January 1896): 9–12.

"Japanese Amusements." *Juvenile Instructor* 10 (21 August 1875): 193–94.

"Japanese Children." *Juvenile Instructor* 13 (1 November 1878): 245.

"Japanese Customs." *Juvenile Instructor* 11 (15 January 1876): 18–20.

"Japanese Peasant in Winter Costume." *Juvenile Instructor* 9 (23 March 1874): 81.

"Japanese Soldiers." *Juvenile Instructor* 17 (1 May 1882): 138–39.

"Japanese Temple." *Juvenile Instructor* 11 (1 June 1876): 127–28.

"Opening of Japan." *Millennial Star* 16 (2 September 1854): 552.

Smith, Joseph F. "The Last Days of President Snow." *Juvenile Instructor* 36 (15 November 1901): 689–90.

Talmage, James E. "The Philosophy of Mormonism (cont)." *Improvement Era* 4 (May 1901): 497–506.

———. "The Story of "Mormonism." *Improvement Era* 4 (April 1901): 459–68.

Taylor, Alma O. "Life in the Orient." *Improvement Era* (February 1902): 288–90.

———. "Some Features of Japanese Life." *Improvement Era* (April 1902): 449–55.

———. "Some Features of Japanese Life (cont)." *Improvement Era* (May 1902): 523–29.

———. "Speakers' Contest—The Oration Which Won the First Place and the Silver Cup—'My Spirit Shall not Always Strive with Man.'" *Improvement Era* 9 (July 1901): 676–82.
———. "The First Vision: An Address Delivered at the Speakers' Contest, Y.M.M.I.A., Salt Lake Stake of Zion." *Improvement Era* 3 (July 1900): 682–86.

———. "The Holy Spirit Bears Witness." *Millennial Star* 67 (21 December 1905): 815–16.

"The City of Yokohama, Japan." *Juvenile Instructor* 20 (15 June 1885): 177–78.

"The Metropolis of Japan." *Juvenile Instructor* 22 (15 November 1887): 337–38.

"The Parliament of Religions." *Juvenile Instructor* 28 (1 October 1893): 605–8.

"Varieties: A Word for the Japanese." *Juvenile Instructor* 19 (15 May 1884): 149.

Vidi. "A Progressive People." *Juvenile Instructor* 28 (1 October 1893): 595–97.

Willis, William. "Tidings from Japan and China." *Juvenile Instructor* 19 (1 October 1884): 291–92.

Articles and Book Chapters

Arrington, Leonard J. "Historical Development of International Mormonism." *Religious Studies and Theology* 7 (January 1987): 9–22.

———. "Utah's Ambiguous Reception: The Relocated Japanese Americans." As found in *Japanese Americans: From Relocation to Redress*. Roger Daniels, Sandra C. Taylor, and Harry H. L. Kitano. eds. Salt Lake City: University of Utah Press, 1986.

Brady, Frederick R. "Two Meiji Scholars Introduce the Mormons to Japan." *BYU Studies* 23 (Spring 1983): 167–78.

Butler, Wendy. "The Iwakura Mission and Its Stay in Salt Lake City." *Utah Historical Quarterly* 66 (Winter 1998): 26–47.

Cannon, Donald Q. "Angus M. Cannon: Pioneer, President, Patriarch." As found in *Supporting Saints: Life Stories of Nineteenth-Century Mormons.* Donald Q. Cannon and David J. Whittaker. eds. Provo, UT: Religious Studies Center, Brigham Young University, 1985.

Corcoran, Brian D. "'My Father's Business': Thomas Taylor and Mormon Frontier Economic Enterprise." *Dialogue* 28 (Spring 1995): 105–41.

Hartley, William G. "Adventures of a Young British Seaman, 1852–1862." *New Era* 10 (March 1980): 38–47.

———. "From Men to Boys: LDS Aaronic Priesthood Offices, 1829–1996." *Journal of Mormon History* 22 (Spring 1996): 109–10.

———. "Latter-day Saints and the San Francisco Earthquake." *Ensign* 28 (October 1998): 22–29.

Gordon Irving. "Numerical Strength and Geographical Distribution of the LDS Missionary Force, 1830–1974." *Task Papers in LDS History.* no. 1. Salt Lake City: Historical Department of the Church of Jesus Christ of Latter-day Saints, 1975.

Lyman, Edward Leo. "From the City of Angeles to the City of Saints: The Struggle to Build a Railroad from Los Angeles to Salt Lake City." *California History* (Spring 1991): 76–93.

Nelson, Harry W. "The Casket Industry in Utah." *The Utah Payroll Builder* 13 (January 1925: 6–7.

Smith, Dwight L. "Robert B. Stanton's Plan for the Far Southwest." *Arizona and the West* 4 (Winter 1962): 369–72.

Smith, Dwight L. "The Engineer and the Canyon." *Utah Historical Quarterly* 28 (July 1960): 262–73.

Takagi, Shinji. "Mormons in the Press: Reactions to the 1901 Opening of the Japan Mission." *BYU Studies* 40, no. 1 (2000): 141–75.

Walker, Ronald W. "'Going to Meeting' in Salt Lake City's Thirteenth Ward, 1849–1881: A Microanalysis." As found in *New Views of Mormon History: A Collection of Essays in Honor of Leonard J. Arrington.* eds. Davis Bitton and Maureen Ursenbach Beecher. Salt Lake City: University of Utah Press, 1987.

———. "Heber J. Grant's European Mission, 1903–1906." *Journal of Mormon History* 14 (1988): 16–33.

———. "Strangers in a Strange Land: Heber J. Grant and the Opening of the Japanese Mission." *Journal of Mormon History* 13 (1986/1987): 20–43.

Dissertations and Thesis

Brady, Frederick R. "The Japanese Reaction to Mormonism and the Translation of Mormon Scripture into Japanese." Master's Thesis, Sophia University, Tokyo, Japan, 1979.

Heath, Harvard S. "Reed Smoot: The First Mormon." Master's Thesis, Brigham Young University, 1990.

Hughes, William E. "A Profile of the Missionaries of the Church of Jesus Christ of Latter-day Saints, 1849–1900." Masters Thesis, Brigham Young University, 1986.

Nichols, Murray L. "History of the Japan Mission of the Church of Jesus Christ of Latter-day Saints, 1901–1924." Masters Thesis, Brigham Young University, 1957.

Other Sources

LDS Ancestral File

Abstract

A thesis submitted to the Department of History, Brigham Young University,
In partial fulfillment of the requirements for the degree of Masters of Arts

On 14 February 1901, the First Presidency of The Church of Jesus Christ of Latter-day Saints announced the opening of the Japan Mission and the selection of Elder Heber J. Grant as its first president. The idea of sending Mormon missionaries to Japan had earlier been entertained by President Brigham Young and several other Church leaders and lay members.

Until 1854, Japan was closed to Western nations and their religious influences. Finally, Commodore Perry forced the Japanese to open their borders and minds to the economic and political entreaties of the United States. In time, other Western nations and their Christian theology were admitted into Japan. Aware of their technological inferiority when compared to the West, the Japanese government set out to Westernize their nation. During the second half of the nineteenth century, Mormons and the Japanese made a series of positive contacts. On two occasions, plans were made at the highest Church levels to send missionaries to Japan. Both ended in failure.

Finally, in 1901, the Church again committed its resources and one of its finest leaders, Elder Grant, to open the Japan Mission. After accepting his own calling, Elder Grant began the selection process of his own companions. He chose Horace S. Ensign, Louis A. Kelsch, and a young man from his home ward, Alma O. Taylor. Eighteen-year-old Alma was raised with the best Mormonism had to offer. His parents blessed him with education and position. He was also blessed with a sharp mind and a determined soul.

Alma served in Japan for over eight and half years. During this time he kept detailed journal entries of his experiences and impressions. The body of this thesis is devoted to making his writings available to other scholars and Church members interested in the foundational events of the Church in Japan.

Committee Approval:

Ronald W. Walker, Chair
R. Lanier Britsch, Committee Member
John W. Welch, Committee Member
Frank W. Fox, Department Chair